Theory of World Security

What is real? What can we know? How might we act? This book sets out to answer these fundamental philosophical questions in a radical and original theory of security for our times. Arguing that the concept of security in world politics has long been imprisoned by conservative thinking, Ken Booth explores security as a precious instrumental value which gives individuals and groups the opportunity to pursue the invention of humanity rather than live determined and diminished lives. Booth suggests that human society globally is facing a set of converging historical crises. He looks to critical social theory and radical international theory to develop a comprehensive framework for understanding the historical challenges facing global business-as-usual and for planning to reconstruct a more cosmopolitan future. *Theory of World Security* is a challenge both to well-established ways of thinking about security and alternative approaches within critical security studies.

KEN BOOTH is E. H. Carr Professor in the Department of International Politics at the University of Wales, Aberystwyth. He is a Fellow of the British Academy and the current editor of *International Relations*.

Theory of World Security

Series list continued after index

Theory of World Security

Ken Booth

CAMBRIDGE
UNIVERSITY PRESS

CAMBRIDGE UNIVERSITY PRESS
Cambridge, New York, Melbourne, Madrid, Cape Town, Singapore, São Paulo

Cambridge University Press
The Edinburgh Building, Cambridge CB2 8RU, UK

Published in the United States of America by Cambridge University Press,
New York

www.cambridge.org
Information on this title: www.cambridge.org/9780521543170

First published 2007

Printed in the United Kingdom at the University Press, Cambridge

A catalogue record for this publication is available from the British Library

ISBN 978-0-521-83552-7 hardback
ISBN 978-0-521-54317-0 paperback

This book is dedicated to
the memory of my grandfather
ALAN BOOTH
(1892–1971)
As an Able Seaman in the Royal Navy in the Great War
he sailed around the world twice,
and to his dying day
never knew
why

Contents

Preface

This book is a work of analysis, argument, and advocacy. Its purpose is to explain and advance the case for a particular theoretical framework with which to explore and engage with the security of real people in real places. The overall approach is an attempt to construct a *critical theory of security*, and at its heart is *emancipatory realism*. Focusing on the primordial search for security, the book grapples with some of the biggest questions faced by human society. What is real? What can we know? How might we act? As such, it seeks to offer a theory for our times, a small bugle-call in an era of world-historical crisis.

Theory of World Security addresses various (overlapping) audiences: students of security within universities, people everywhere who are angry at the world they have inherited and disappointed at the complacency of the most powerful, and readers who already share the general conclusions of the book but who need more light to be shed on them. It would be encouraging if the book were to be read with an open mind by officials and politicians, or managers in control of the most powerful corporations: but I do not expect it. Nor do I expect much sympathy from the self-referential international relations orthodoxy in the United States and elsewhere – 'realists' of one sort or another – because the theorising represented here will be regarded as alien (even where it is allowed to be regarded as theory). Plenty of colleagues in the non-orthodoxy will also be unsympathetic. Be that as it may, the overlapping audiences who will be amenable to the arguments below are growing: they are people who know that world politics do not work for most of the planet's inhabitants, who believe that the future is ever threatening even for the privileged minority world, and who are certain that business-as-usual on a global scale is not the answer to the looming threats (among others) of spreading nuclear dangers, coming environmental chaos, and global population overload.

The book will have failed if those readers who manage to stay with it to the end do not put it down with a promise (at least to themselves) to do something different – however little, however fallibly – in the interests of promoting world security. This promise could be anything from undergraduate students deciding to write more thoughtful essays in a security studies class, to research students changing their thesis to a topic more relevant and challenging, to people deciding to donate time or money to organisations (political parties even) promoting social justice, locally or globally. However often it is used, Gandhi's aphorism in this regard is always mint fresh: 'We must be the change we wish to see in the world.'

Acknowledgements

This book is dedicated to my grandfather, who was a miner, sailor, socialist, local politician, and person who struggled through his life to improve the prospects for succeeding generations; without people like him, people like me would never have received a free and lengthy education, and the benefits of the NHS. My biggest thanks for completing this book go to Eurwen, Rob, and Tom, who have changed my mind on many things, and from whom I have learned most about life; they will find in these pages more reflections of their own ideas than they will expect.

As this work represents the longest elaboration so far of what I understand to be a critical theory of security, it is a pleasure to record some old intellectual debts. In particular, on engaging with the great issues of peace and war, the people who have been most important over the years have been Bernard Brodie, Kenneth Boulding, Richard Falk, Michael Howard, and Michael MccGwire. In different ways, they lit the way for the critical security theory the book will analyse, argue, and advocate. Influential in a different way, I must also acknowledge the robust realism of John Garnett and Colin Gray, whose ideas have been a source of productive challenge for many years.

In the long process of discovering the inadequacies of much of what I learnt as a student of international politics, exchanges with Nicholas Wheeler and Richard Wyn Jones have been decisive. Between the anvil of the former's English school expositions, and the latter's Anglesey school hammer, there emerged what I long ago started calling – in provocation – the Welsh school of critical security studies (CSS). It was Nick who showed me how international relations theory could challenge the rolled-up-sleeves approach to practice (the common sense of so-called practitioners) and the potential for developing a more reflexive, theory-guided approach to who gets what in the world. The experience of co-authorship with Nick has been one of the pleasures of my career, not least the twenty years' crisis of writing *The Security Dilemma* together. Others no doubt will have a different version to mine of the intellectual history of CSS to date. My own claims that it was in the Department of International Politics at the University of Wales, Aberystwyth, that actually existing CSS was born and nourished. One catalyst for this was the prolonged gestation of the doctoral thesis of Richard Wyn Jones, which began at the end of the 1980s and was published at the end of the 1990s as *Security, Strategy, and Critical Theory*. The discussions I was involved with during this period, as Richard's PhD supervisor and then colleague, were central to the development of a particular critical theory of security, bringing together long-established international relations concerns about security and strategy with the discipline's growing interest in critical political and social theory. Without the influence of Nick and Richard, it is unlikely that the theory of world security advanced in this book would have taken the shape it has.

It was in Aberystwyth that the first course explicitly organised as Critical Security Studies was taught. Many students have now taken it at Master's level, and some have gone on to do PhDs. They have taught me, as much as they have been taught and supervised, and it gives me pleasure to acknowledge the promising work of the first generation: the theses of Pinar Bilgin, Simon Davies, Eric Herring, Thomas Jaye, Tungay Kardas, Patricia Owens, and Paul Williams combined theoretical exposition with empirical case studies, and vastly improved my knowledge of the Middle East, Turkey, South America, the Indian subcontinent, various parts of Africa, and the United States – not to mention the Frankfurt school, nuclear strategy, conflict resolution, regional organisations, Hannah Arendt, the role of intellectuals, and international relations theory. There are many other PhD students I could mention, though I did not work closely with them, but all contributed to the incomparably stimulating graduate school that grew in Aberystwyth during the 1990s, and which continues to the present. But for my efforts in helping to build this vibrant community of young scholars, together (in particular) with Tim Dunne, Len Scott, Steve Smith, and Nick Wheeler, this book might have been written many years ago, but I know for sure that I was right in judging which project should have priority.

I have benefited enormously from the writings of a number of far-flung friends, although in some cases they were not self-consciously writing about security. I want to recognise the work of Hayward Alker, Philip Allott, Chris Brown, Hedley Bull, Cynthia Enloe, Tony Giddens,

Fred Halliday, John Herz, James E. King, John Mearsheimer, Bhikhu Parekh, James N. Rosenau, Ann Tickner, Peter Vale, Rob Walker, and Kenneth Waltz. Barry Buzan deserves particular mention. Not only has his work on the concept of security been so influential, but when he was chair of the British International Studies Association he invited me to give the plenary lecture at the organisation's 1990 annual conference. For reasons to do more with curiosity than vision, I entitled it 'Security and Emancipation', and I have subsequently followed where that moment of curiosity pointed. Barry, like other realists mentioned earlier, shares more responsibility for actually existing critical security theorising than he probably realises.

At an important stage in the development of the Welsh school, following the emancipatory bugle-call, a conference was held in 1994 at York University in Toronto, organised by Keith Krause and Michael C. Williams. The conference was an attempt to think through what it meant to be studying security in the final years of the twentieth century. I want again to thank them for one of the most stimulating conferences I have attended. Their own account of CSS, and the papers from the conference, were published in *Critical Security Studies: Concepts and Cases* (1997). Mike Williams, I am pleased to record, now works in the Department at Aberystwyth, within the embrace but not (yet) control of the Welsh school.

While I wait for the phone to ring from Whitehall, I record thanks to several organisations over the last few years which have helped me try out and spread some of the ideas in this book, as well as learn about different perspectives: the Armed Forces Defence Academy in Canberra, the Diplomatic Academy in Lima, the Center for Eurasian Studies in Ankara, the Instituto da Defesa Nacional in Lisbon, Just Defence in the UK (regrettably wound up in 2005), the Oxford Research Group, and the World Council of Churches in Geneva. Peripheries of the world unite!

Had I put in a proposal to a funding body with such a preposterously ambitious title as *Theory of World Security*, immediate rejection would have been predictable. Special thanks for coming to a different conclusion are therefore due to Cambridge University Press, its Social Science editor John Haslam, and the Board of the BISA/CUP Series. I want to thank John for his patience, support, and advice and Mike Leach for preparing a first-class index. An anonymous reader gave me more encouragement from his/her remarks than could have been imagined.

For commenting on parts of the manuscript I want to thank Caroline Kennedy-Pipe and Doug Stokes, while Paul Williams deserves very special thanks for reading it all, and sending me material. My apologies go to all three for not always following their advice, but I did always engage with their points. Emilia Faria and Vitorina Augusta Becker Córte provided me with gracious hospitality which helped me to break the back of the writing, allowing me to work with the sun streaming through the balcony doors, and the sound of the sea outside: *muito obrigado*.

Colleagues (past and present) in the Department at Aber have been especially significant, and I want to record my appreciation of William Bain (for his intellectual rigour and the use of his bookshelves), Ian Clark (for showing how to embed theory in history), Mick Cox (for his intellectual brio and breadth), Tim Dunne (for being such an energiser and enthusiast for the subject), Toni Erskine (for reviving normative theory), Andrew Linklater (for his immense knowledge of the subject, and for making critical theory relevant to the discipline), Colin McInnes (for casually suggesting over coffee that I should write this book, and offering the view that it might not be too difficult), Steve Smith (for leading the way on so much), Colin Wight (for his ability to see the flaw in all arguments at one hundred paces), and Howard Williams (for leading me through the work of Kant). I could not have contemplated the book without the Department's great support staff. They are now too numerous to list for praise, but they know they are the skilful unsung in British higher education who help make academic life still possible when so many in higher places conspire to undermine it. When I was Head of Department, Caroline Haste was an outstanding co-worker, and Elaine Lowe and Joan Williams continue to be. Colleagues such as these make the Department at Aberystwyth, the world's first International Politics Department, a place of collegiality, as well as a home for cutting-edge pluralistic research and teaching. As the Department's centenary approaches, it continues to go from strength to strength, and is now housed in a magnificent new building. For so generously backing the Department in this material form, following years of my nagging, I owe enormous thanks to the former and present Vice-Chancellors of the university, Professor Derek Llwyd Morgan and Professor Noel Lloyd respectively.

In 1975 I came out of a panel at the ISA Annual Convention in Toronto having presented a paper entitled 'Strategy and Ethnocentrism'. It was a very long paper in a very small panel. The other presenter did not show, nor did the chair. The audience was three strong. As I was leaving, the peace researcher Charles Chatfield said: 'You have given yourself

Acknowledgements

a thirty-year project to work on.' In the course of writing this book, I have come to realise that the attempt in this book to construct a critical theory of world security is indeed a culmination of that concern long ago with the perils of allowing world politics and military strategy to be dominated by the views of those people who are convinced that the beliefs they inherited from their own people in their own patch of earth are truer, better, and more important than those of people from other places. Charles, I am amazed by your prediction, and – wherever you are – thank you for filling out the audience that day and giving me encouragement. I hope this latest version of that ancient paper meets with your approval.

Introduction

The evidence is all around that the world has entered one of the most decisive phases of its history since the first recognisable humans (*Homo erectus*) moved around on two legs. Never before in this span of one and a half million years (with the contested exception of the danger of 'nuclear winter' during the Cold War) have we, *the collective of global human society*, been able to inflict as much decisive damage on each other and on the natural world on which we utterly depend; and never before have we, *individually and in small groups*, been as capable of transporting and visiting as much politically targeted destruction against those whose minds and actions we want to change. These realities alone would be enough to mark out our times as demanding a reconceptualisation of world security; but the threats to our safety are proliferating and growing in destructiveness. They include the multidimensional predicaments of globalisation, inflamed religious and cultural sensibilities, militant nationalism, growing disparities in life chances between the haves and the have-nots, the inexorable rise of the world's population (which will create future challenges that almost everybody today prefers to ignore), and on and on. The sheer *quantity* of issues threatening political turmoil, as Lenin might have said, has a *quality* all of its own. And yet this period of unprecedented historical change goes hand in hand with the persistence of traditionalist attitudes about world politics. The heads of the powers-that-be are stuck in the past, as we speed into an increasingly threatening future. Something must be done: sparks are already flying, and politically combustible material continues to be piled up. Running through this book is the idea that human society globally is living in a *New Twenty Years' Crisis*.[1] It began, symbolically, on 11 September 2001,

[1] The idea of a New Twenty Years' Crisis owes an obvious debt to E. H. Carr's seminal work, *The Twenty Years' Crisis 1919–1939. An Introduction to the Study of International Relations* (London: Macmillan, 1939; 2nd edn, 1946).

and is part of a more general crisis facing the world in the first half of the twenty-first century; I call this *The Great Reckoning*. If a series of key decisions about world security are not made in the first two decades of the century, and are not made sensibly, then by mid-century human society faces the prospect of a concatenation of global turmoil unlike anything in the past.

In the face of such a prospect, the challenge addressed in this book is to reconsider how we – *the global we* – conceive and practise security, and how we – *students of the subject* – theorise security studies.[2] This book seeks to contribute to these goals, recognising that each of us cannot individually do much to change things, but believing that collectively we can do anything.

The Iron Curtain that symbolised world politics during the Cold War not only imprisoned people in the Soviet empire to the east, it also imprisoned the rest of us to varying degrees, politically, strategically, culturally, and psychologically. That particular physical barrier was pulled down in the aftermath of the great events of 11/9 (1989) but its disappearance left plenty of other structures that divide and imprison. Indeed, some of them are much more powerful than the Iron Curtain: so powerful, in fact, that they do not need barbed wire, bricks, and rifles to exert their discipline. Poverty, class, gender, and religion come immediately to mind. Following the terror attacks on the United States on 9/11 (2001) and the conflicts in Afghanistan and Iraq, further twists have been added to the tangled knots of global politics, as different worlds have come into spectacular and not-so-spectacular collision. Trying to make sense of the more complex realities of security these days is one of the two main tasks of the theory of world security to be elaborated in this book; the other is to contribute to reconceptualising world security away from its nationalist and statist orthodoxies – which promote the idea of security *against* others – to an approach that conceives security as an instrumental value concerned to promote security *reciprocally*, as part of the invention of a more inclusive humanity. In other words, a critical theory of security seeks to be both realistic and emancipatory.

The *global we* desperately need a theory of security for our times. We have seen what was practised in the past and know it does not work for much of human society. The price for continuing global

---

[2] The word 'we' will be used frequently in this book. It will usually be obvious whether I am referring to the global (species) we, or the specific (academic) we who specialise in international politics/security studies. I will only add an adjective to 'we' when I think the referent is not clear.

business-as-usual is unacceptably high, when measured daily in the unnecessary ill-health and poverty of millions, premature deaths, and unspeakable oppression. The framework of the theory to be elaborated derives from a body of ideas I call *critical global theorising*. These ideas, in turn, mostly derive from key themes of the eighteenth-century Enlightenment. The inspirations and themes of the Enlightenment – the object of so much misbegotten criticism over recent decades – have never been needed so urgently as today; and world politics represents the Enlightenment's most significant unfinished business.

The approach to theorising developed through the book is pragmatic, holistic, and personal, following where three great thinkers have led: first, Hannah Arendt's pragmatic approach, which she described as *Perlenfischerei* or pearl-fishing (that is, looking for wisdom not through the study of the history of ideas, genealogies, or categories of thinkers, but through plundering ideas that have survived and seem rich in possibility for one's purposes);[3] second, Mary Midgley's rejection of the 'austerity' of reductive as opposed to holistic thinking (favouring instead 'Many Maps, Many Windows');[4] and finally Nadine Gordimer's recognition that insight comes from experience more than literature ('books are not made out of other books, but out of life', she once wrote) and because of this there will be occasional references below to personal experience.[5] These approaches inform the spirit of the book's theoretical framework, which is based on Philip Allott's typology of 'practical', 'transcendental', and 'pure' theory.[6] The aim is to explore, comprehensively, key themes relating to being, knowing, and doing in relation to world security. The outcome, as will become apparent, is a framework at the very opposite end of the theoretical spectrum from Kenneth Waltz's 'parsimonious' neorealism that hit the discipline of international relations in the late 1970s.[7]

I have tried to make this book accessible. Though some parts discuss complex issues of philosophy and theory, I trust that every reader will

[3] Elisabeth Young-Bruehl, *Hannah Arendt. For Love of the World* (New Haven, Conn.: Yale University Press, 1982), pp. 94–5. This is a superb intellectual biography.
[4] To be particularly recommended is Mary Midgley, *Wisdom, Information and Wonder. What Is Knowledge For?* (London: Routledge, 1989); see also *The Myths We Live By* (London: Routledge, 2003), pp. 26–8, 29–35.
[5] Nadine Gordimer, *Between Hope and History. Notes from our Century* (London: Bloomsbury, 1999), p. 41.
[6] Philip Allott, *The Health of Nations. Society and Law Beyond the State* (Cambridge: Cambridge University Press, 2002), pp. 70–96.
[7] This was the aim of the structural theory elaborated in Kenneth Waltz, *Theory of International Politics* (New York: Random House, 1979).

understand – if not actually agree with – every sentence. The security of human society is worth speaking about in plain language (accepting the need to use the odd technical term here and there). Like the writers of the Enlightenment, and such notable figures in international relations theory as Hedley Bull, I have no time for those who parade their claim to understand important things by using language that even knowledgeable people struggle to understand.

Before outlining the organisation of the book, the phrase *world security* needs explanation. While always recognising the importance of 'the international' (relations between states), the challenge we face in world politics in the decades to come – whether as students or citizens – must be thought of more holistically. In this sense, international politics is but one (though certainly one of the most significant) of the worlds of world politics. The phrase *world politics*, as opposed to *international politics*, was first popularised by Robert Keohane and Joseph Nye in the burgeoning era of interdependence in the early 1970s,[8] but it has extra purchase in today's global age. By using the term *world politics* I am not implying that the *international* is dead. Far from it. Borders are critical, and sometimes a matter of life and death. The frequent-flyer elites of London, New York, Paris, Tokyo, and other world cities can be heard talking about the 'borderless world', the growing 'irrelevance of space' and so on; but every moment of every day, somewhere in the world, people are desperately trying to ensure they live their life on *this* rather than *that* side of a particular boundary. We live in what James Rosenau has called a 'post-international world' only in the sense of needing to recognise that there is more to politics on a global scale than relations between those entities called states.[9]

The concept of *world security* is more encompassing than the notion of international security. It includes a more extensive range of referents, above and below the state level, and a wider range of possible threats and risks: *world security refers to the structures and processes within human society, locally and globally, that work towards the reduction of the threats and risks that determine individual and group lives. The greater the level of security enjoyed, the more individuals and groups (including human society as a whole) can have an existence beyond the instinctual animal struggle merely to survive. The idea of world security is synonymous with the freedom of individuals and*

---

[8] Robert O. Keohane and Joseph S. Nye (eds.), *Transnational Relations and World Politics* (Cambridge, Mass.: Harvard University Press, 1972).
[9] This is a major theme of James N. Rosenau, *Turbulence in World Politics* (Princeton, N.J.: Princeton University Press, 1990).

groups compatible with the reasonable freedom of others, and universal moral equality compatible with justifiable pragmatic inequalities.

The definition just presented contains strong echoes of Hedley Bull's notion of 'world order'. In his modern classic, *The Anarchical Society*, Bull defined world order as 'those patterns or dispositions of human activity that sustain the elementary or primary goals of social life among mankind as a whole . . . Underlying the questions we raise about order among states there are deeper questions, of more enduring importance, about order in the great society of all mankind.'[10] He went on: 'Order among mankind as a whole is something wider than order among states; something more fundamental and primordial than it; and also, I should argue, something morally prior to it.' What he was getting at here is something close to the idea of world security in this book, but I want to distance myself from Bull in several crucial ways: his emphasis on *order* to sustain essential social life is too negative and implicitly statist (this argument could have been used to legitimise Stalinist Russia); his conception of the causal relationship between order and justice is too conservative ('order first' has been the persuasive cry of military dictators over the years, asking for additional time before implementing human rights – something they had no serious intention of implementing in the first place); his concern only with 'elementary or primary goals' is too unambitious in a world where more is available; and his normative commitment to 'international society' was one I find unconvincing, especially if he really believed in world society having moral primacy (at least as 'unconvincing' as Bull himself found all alternatives to his preferred states system).[11]

Theory of World Security is a long book. A short overview will help readers see where they are being taken:

> **Part I: Context** establishes the empirical and theoretical starting-points of the argument. Chapter 1 offers a sketch of the contemporary global situation, a world that does not work for most of its inhabitants. It introduces the idea that we are in a *New Twenty Years' Crisis*, in which 'morbid symptoms' have been proliferating, demanding urgent and radical decisions to be made if

[10] Hedley Bull, *The Anarchical Society. A Study of Order in World Politics* (London: Macmillan, 1977), p. 20.
[11] Bull, *Anarchical Society*, esp. pp. 20–2, 318–20. Also to be challenged is Bull's rejection of conclusions that can be presented as 'solutions' or 'practical advice' (on the grounds that they represent a 'corrupting element' in the study of world politics); this is a bizarre opinion, and will be discussed more fully in chapter 4.

the Great Reckoning challenging the whole of human society in the first half of the century is to be characterised by tolerable stresses and strains rather than catastrophic turmoil. Chapter 2 identifies the most productive site of ideas from which the theoretical framework of the book (to help us understand and react to the Great Reckoning) will be constructed. Within the tradition of thought I call *critical global theorising* two main areas have been plundered for ideas: *critical social theory* and *radical international theory*.

Part II: Theory describes and explains the elements making up the book's *critical theory of world security*. Chapter 3 defines and discusses three central concepts: *security, emancipation,* and *community*. Chapter 4 focuses explicitly on security, and explains in particular what it means to *deepen* and *broaden* the concept, and then *critique* and *reconstruct* ideas into a coherent theory of world security. Chapter 5 reframes the discussion of the previous two chapters in relation to basic philosophical questions that must be addressed by any theory of world security: *What is real? What can we know? How might we act?* Chapter 6, necessarily the longest in the book, is a systematic account of the themes that together make up the overall framework of the critical theory of world security being advanced. It rests on three pillars: a 'pure' theory (*human sociality*), a 'transcendental' theory (*critical global theorising*), and a 'practical' theory (*emancipatory realism*).

Part III: Dimensions moves from the relatively abstract theoretical section of the book to the more empirical part. Its two chapters show what a critical theory of security does when it engages with some of the major issues in the contemporary world. Chapter 7 is a *critique* of US power, contemporary political violence, human security, and the state of nature. The insecurities produced by global business-as-usual are exposed, and the case for radical change underlined. Chapter 8 moves beyond critique to look at the political values of *emancipatory realism*, whose realisation would bring about world security. The chapter examines major issues involved in humanising power, promoting social justice, and embedding human rights. Both chapters raise questions for critical theory about the relationship between reality and representation. Chapter 7 discusses the contested nature of reality, and chapter 8 the contested representation of reality.

Part IV: Futures pulls together the arguments about the terrible consequences for world security if human society does not attend urgently and radically to the concatenation of threats that are converging on the present era. Chapter 9 describes the contours of the New Twenty Years' Crisis, pointing to six priority areas where decisions must be taken in order to reorient world security, and warning of the consequences of failure. This *decisional crisis* is embedded in simultaneous *epochal* and *structural crises*; together they make up *the Great Reckoning* confronting human society globally in the first half of the twenty-first century. Facing the challenge of a *long hot century* ahead, chapter 10 discusses some of the modalities of cosmopolitan politics, including *non-dualism* in means/ends, the negotiation of tolerant *norms* between people (separated from their metaphysical *beliefs*), and the pursuit of values that will invent and embed a more inclusive humanity, free from regressive and divisive ideas of the past such as 'the human condition' and 'evil'. Only if human society, collectively, learns and practises cosmopolitan norms, animated by the goal of inventing an egalitarian humanity, can we have rational hope of coping in civilised ways with the geopolitical, environmental, and ideological challenges of the Great Reckoning.

Late in her life Hannah Arendt, the engine herself of so many ideas, told a friend that 'we all have only one real thought in our lives, and everything we then do are [sic] elaborations or variations of one theme'.[12] I was struck by this when I first read it, and not a little perturbed, for one thought a lifetime does not fit an academic's self-image. If Arendt was right, what has mine been? The answer crystallised almost instantly, which makes me think she was correct. The 'one real thought' is the challenge to human societies of creating the material and social conditions of life whereby people can live in reasonable equality, and so have the possibility of conducting their intimate and collective lives in dignity, freedom, and hope. These are not quite the words my grandfather would have used to express the same thought, but they do represent the vision on which he acted for many years. His life was shaped by growing up in absolute poverty, including forced migration after his father had been sacked and blacklisted in the Yorkshire coalfields for joining the newly formed Labour Party. He, too, then had little choice but to become

[12] Quoted by Young-Bruehl, *Arendt*, p. 327.

a coal miner, before joining the Royal Navy when the Great War broke out. After seeing some of the world, he returned, disappointed, not to 'a home fit for heroes' but to a country lurching towards the General Strike and the Great Depression. These were things I knew long before I discovered international relations theory, as I grew up in a coal-mining village in West Yorkshire in the immediate aftermath of yet another World War. The desirability of a universal human community, committed to egalitarian principles, is the one real thought running through this *Theory of World Security*.

Part I
Context

1   Present imperfect: future tense

We are as we are because we got that way.

Kenneth Boulding[1]

Si monumentum requiris, circumspice was originally the epitaph for the architect of a great cathedral. After the Second World War the phrase was revived by the historian Alan Bullock as the epitaph for the architect of a world calamity. Bullock was contrasting the tyrannical ambitions of Adolf Hitler with the utter devastation of the fatherland in 1945: 'If you seek a monument, look around.'[2] The same epitaph might be chiselled, though with a sense of paradox rather than irony, on a monument to the powerful ideas (and ideas full of power) that made us (global human society) what we are today.

Together, and in order of appearance historically, patriarchy, proselytising religions, capitalism, sovereign statism/nationalism, race, and consumerist democracy conspired to construct a particular sociology of global human society; a world resulted that does not work for the majority, and in time will not work even for the privileged minority. Other powerful ideas have also played a part in this development, especially scientific and technological development,[3] and, in the primordial search for security between political units, the theory of realism. Together, these world-constructing ideas have created an imperfect present and a future

[1] Quoted by Anatol Rapoport in a Rapoport–Boulding double act at the University of London, 1989. It is not standard practice to give references to epigraphs, but I will do so because, as in this case, I do not think the source can be checked against any written account, and in all other cases I hope readers will go where the epigraphs lead.

[2] These are the last words in Alan Bullock, *Hitler. A Study in Tyranny* (London: Odhams Press, 1960), p. 738; the epitaph was originally an inscription in St Paul's Cathedral, London, and it is attributed to the son of the architect Christopher Wren.

[3] See William McNeill, *The Pursuit of Power* (Chicago: University of Chicago Press, 1982), and Geoffrey Blainey, *A Very Short History of the World* (London: Allen Lane, 2004).

tense with danger. Poverty, oppression, war, misery, death, and disease are the everyday realities of life across swathes of humanity; then add fear, and stir. Debilitating and determining insecurity seem to be in permanent season, and *you and I, him and her, and us and them* will never be what we might become as long as human society, globally, is imprisoned by the regressive ideas that sustain world insecurity. As you read this book, look forward in anger, but keep thinking.

Seeing but not seeing

I shall weep, but tell my story through my tears.

Count Ugolino in Inferno[4]

This chapter introduces six themes that carry through the book: a world that is not working for most of its inhabitants; a body of regressive ideas that continue to dominate politics, economics, and society globally; a growing world crisis that is not being attended to by the globally powerful; a particular set of challenges resulting from the convergence of traditional ideas and new material conditions created by environmental despoliation and population expansion; a regressive realist hegemony in the way policymakers and academics think about security; and the need to reconceptualise world security in the light of a self-consciously critical perspective with an emancipatory orientation.

Let me begin with some facts which reveal a contagion of 'morbid symptoms'[5] across human society. For the most part these pass fleetingly through the consciousness of many who inhabit what J. K. Galbraith in the early 1990s brilliantly termed 'the culture of contentment':[6] the

---

[4] Dante, *Inferno*, canto XXXIII, quoted by Nancy L. Rosenblum in 'Memory, Law, and Repair', in Martha Minow (ed.), *Breaking the Cycles of Hatred* (Princeton, N.J.: Princeton University Press, 2002), p. 1.

[5] Quoted from Antonio Gramsci's *Prison Notebooks* by Ken Booth, 'Introduction. The Interregnum: World Politics in Transition', in Ken Booth (ed.), *New Thinking about Strategy and International Security* (London: HarperCollins Academic, 1991), p. 1. The idea of an 'interregnum', characterised by 'morbid symptoms' and the clash of old and new, was used as the theme for a panel at a BISA conference in early 1989 (the collection of chapters in Booth, *New Thinking*, was one result). Gramsci's image was still appropriate, ten years later, when it was used as the title for a retrospective on the 1990s: see Michael Cox, Ken Booth, and Tim Dunne (eds.), *The Interregnum. Controversies in World Politics 1989–1999* (Cambridge: Cambridge University Press, 1999). Michael C. Williams is not the only person to interpret the usage of the term as implying a period when 'power and its imperatives' took a back seat. The opposite was the case: an interregnum is not a power vacuum, but a period of struggle between the power of the old and the new, materially and ideationally, but there is an impasse; see Michael C. Williams, *Culture and Security. Symbolic Power and the Politics of International Security* (London: Routledge, 2007), p. 2.

[6] J. K. Galbraith, *The Culture of Contentment* (London: Sinclair-Stevenson, 1992).

comfortable world that enjoys the riches of consumerist democracy. An authoritative place to start is the annual reports of the United Nations Development Programme (UNDP), which regularly draw attention to the deep poverty of much of the world's population, the huge gap between the haves and the have-nots, and the widespread lack of food, decent sanitation, clean water, healthcare and education.[7] Since Caroline Thomas led the way in bringing these reports to the academic international relations literature, it is not as unusual as it once was for students of international relations to be confronted by UNDP statistics. In the late 1990s, Thomas used UNDP figures to expose global priorities. It was recorded that the estimated annual cost of achieving basic education for all it was $6bn; for water and sanitation $9bn; reproductive health for all women $12bn; and for basic health and nutrition $13bn. In comparison, the figures for annual spending on cosmetics in the United States were $8bn, ice cream in Europe $11bn, and military spending globally $780bn.[8] While many enjoy the lifestyles even nobility in the past could not dream of, the daily life of most people across the world is desperate. This is evident from such diverse sources as Christian Aid, the International Rescue Committee, Jubilee 2000, *Nature*, Reuters, the United Nations, the World Health Organisation, and the World Bank.

In this world that is not working children perform a similar function for human society that canaries once carried out in coal mines: their lives are monitors of the health of the environment. By this test, international society is sick.[9] One-third of children, globally, are undernourished. One hundred million children live or work in the streets. Children are used as soldiers in over twenty states. Starving Afghans sell girls as brides, some as young as eight. Child prostitution is common in certain global cities. More than 30,000 children die, daily, from easily preventable diseases. Youth gangs pass for society in some countries, such as El Salvador. Child abuse comes in many forms, and it is global. Some people, well-meaning, express pity for 'the world's children', but this formulation is

[7] UNDP, *Human Development Report 1998* (Oxford: Oxford University Press, 1998), p. 2.
[8] Caroline Thomas, 'Where Is the Third World Now?' in Cox *et al.*, *Interregnum*, p. 244.
[9] Among the sources for the examples following are: Human Rights Watch: Child Soldiers (http://hrw.org/campaigns/crp/index.htm); Peter Beaumont, 'Starving Afghans Sell Girls of Eight as Brides', *The Observer*, 7 January 2007; Sonja Wolf, 'Political Participation in Post-War El Salvador: An Analysis of NGO Responses to the Youth Gangs' (University of Wales, Aberystwyth, PhD thesis, in process); Thomas G. Weiss, Tatiana Carayannis, Louis Emmerij, and Richard Jolly, *UN Voices. The Struggle for Development and Social Justice* (Bloomington: Indiana University Press, 2005).

flawed. The children who are hungry, homeless, and helpless are not *the world's* children. They are the children of the very poor; and they are not hungry, homeless, and helpless because it is their fault, or because it is natural: they are as they are because *they are made to be* hungry, homeless, and helpless. Global poverty is not an existential condition; it is the outcome of world politics – of human choices made in specific conditions.

Children's lives are just one of the monitors of a world that is not working. Others include what the World Wildlife Fund rightly insists on calling 'climate chaos' (as opposed to the neutral term 'climate change'[10]); the global depletion of fish stocks; the disparities between men and women; the debt burden on the poor which means that the 'less-developed world' repays the West far more than it receives in aid; the continuing growth of population, which places increasing pressure on resources and societies; and on and on the list goes of negative indicators. There is system overload building up almost wherever one looks. Before 2030, unless unprecedented urban growth is controlled, one person in three globally will live in a slum (already 940 million people, about one-sixth of humanity, live in 'squalid, unhealthy areas, mostly without water, sanitation, public services or legal security').[11] Anybody who thinks that such dynamics do not have the potential to provoke rage and turmoil on a vast scale, as the global population rises and sustainable resources decline, is living in a dreamworld. But this, for many, is to be preferred over uncomfortable reality.[12]

In addition to so much system overload across the world, and the threat of worse to come as a result of expanding numbers of people with expanding expectations, traditional interstate and intrastate conflicts persist. The much vaunted boundary-free world of globalisation has not eliminated the most basic foot-slogging struggles over the possession of land. The violence in Israel/Palestine has shown this every day for many years. Boundaries matter profoundly. While the risk of major wars might have declined since 1945,[13] the prospect of a new era of resource

---

[10] Johan Harri, 'Don't Call it Climate Change – it's Chaos', *The Independent*, 15 November 2005.

[11] John Vidal, 'Every Third Person Will Be a Slum Dweller within 30 Years, UN Agency Warns', *The Guardian*, 4 October 2003.

[12] See Susan Buck-Morss, *Dreamworld and Catastrophe. The Passing of Mass Utopia in East and West* (Cambridge, Mass.: MIT Press, 2000). The dreamworld described is of mass utopia, first of capitalism, then of the socialist imaginary.

[13] This is debated in Raimo Väyrynen (ed.), *The Waning of Major War. Theories and Debates* (London: Routledge, 2006).

wars grows, and security dilemma dynamics throw up the prospect of a Cold War spiral between the United States and China.[14] The threat and use of violence represents normal politics in many parts of the world. The death-toll from the War on Terror (or whatever label is spun for the fight against international terrorism orchestrated by the world's most powerful state) has risen inexorably since 9/11, with a growing number of victims of terrorist actions, steadily rising death-tolls in the wars unleashed in Afghanistan and Iraq, and an unknown number of killings resulting from the dirty campaigns the anti-terrorist backlash has legitimated. One estimate in 2003 put the annual worldwide death-toll from war between 1998 and 2003 at 310,000, with three million being the number of people thought to have died in the Congo's civil war ('Africa's Great War').[15] Since the First World War, since 1945, since Vietnam, since . . . and since . . . leaders have repeated the mantra 'Never Again' (and perhaps some of them even believed it). But war goes on. So does genocide.[16]

Before security can be improved globally, the truth of the world must be revealed, systematically and accessibly – if with contention. Nevertheless, most media in all countries give world news a low priority.[17] The interested public (everywhere) have invariably to rely upon nation alised and nationalist statistics, concerned to advance state/government interests,[18] or on 'dodgy dossiers' of one sort or another, concerned to manipulate minds rather than advance knowledge.[19] For students of world security, committed to knowing, there is much to be gained from shifting attention away from the corporate media and governmental sources (and those who do their bidding through conviction or

---

[14] Ken Booth and Nicholas J. Wheeler, *The Security Dilemma: Fear, Cooperation, and Trust* (Houndmills: Palgrave, 2008), Conclusion.

[15] *Time*, 26 May 2003, p. 25.

[16] For a powerful indictment of US policy, see Samantha Power, *A Problem From Hell: America and the Age of Genocide* (London: Flamingo, 2002).

[17] Compare the work of some of the great investigative journalists since the mid-twentieth century excerpted in John Pilger (ed.), *Tell Me No Lies. Investigative Journalism and its Triumphs* (London: Jonathan Cape, 2004).

[18] A lack of statistics can speak more loudly than any figures. This was the case with the failure of the British and US governments to count the bodies of Iraqi civilian deaths in and after the war of 2003. Civil society provided the information: see, for example, *Iraq Body Count, A Dossier of Civilian Casualties in Iraq, 2003–2005* (Iraq Body Count and Oxford Research Group, 2005): http://reports.iraqbodycount.org/a dossier of civilian casualties 2003–2005.pdf.

[19] Among the growing number of sources on the inglorious and ultimately counter-productive attempt to parade politicised intelligence as truth, see Dilip Hiro, *Secrets and Lies. The True Story of the Iraq War* (London: Politico's, 2005).

self-censorship[20]), to the information disseminated by the many non-governmental bodies engaged in world politics. Some British-based examples (as I know them best) include the publications of Amnesty International, the Campaign Against the Arms Trade, Greenpeace, the *Index on Censorship*, the Medical Council for the Victims of Torture, the *New Internationalist*, Oxfam, the Refugee Council, Survival International, and the World Development Movement. A week spent solidly reading their newsletters, reports, and other publications would inspire some cheer about the human spirit, just as it would cast much gloom about the state of the world. This is not to claim that every statistic presented in the literature of a progressive NGO is correct, or that every case they make is water-tight, or that they are free of bias, or even that the organisations that produce them are necessarily well (democratically) run; but it is to say that the picture of the world they paint is important, authentic, relevant, necessary, and less tainted than that produced by governments, whose every communication is calculated to promote their power.[21]

We in the rich world see, but do not see, until perhaps there is a human face in front of the numbers. Statistics never speak for themselves, and they often lie when spoken by governments, for truth is not their game. None understood this better than the Soviet tyrant, Joseph Stalin. He knew how to manipulate statistics, and also appreciated the psychological gulf between a set of cold figures and the reality of a warm human: 'One death is a tragedy', he is supposed to have said, 'a million deaths is a statistic.'[22] He understood that an anonymous tragedy is an oxymoron.

Naturally, we in the West most clearly see a disaster if the warm human involved is a fellow national. The holiday-makers caught up in the tsunami on the day after Christmas 2004 gave a human and familiar face to death in faraway places, not least because of the record left

---

[20] A study of the reporting on the Iraq War, during its Clausewitzian military phase, showed that dissenting views made up only 2 per cent of the BBC's coverage: John Pilger, *New Statesman*, 28 April 2003, p. 11. The figure for ABC in the United States was a healthier 7 per cent, yet the BBC has a worldwide reputation for its relative independence, and only weeks earlier the biggest ever public political demonstration in British history had taken place in opposition to the war.

[21] NGOs are certainly not without their problems. Some, almost all in the rich world, 'have gone global and grown so vast as to acquire an identity all of their own: "bingos"': the *New Internationalist*, 'BINGO! The Big Charity Bonanza', no. 383, October 2005, and particularly David Ransom, 'The Big Charity Bonanza', pp. 2–5. A bingo is a big international non-governmental organisation.

[22] Every book on world politics must include a reference to the phenomenon that was Stalin; a detailed account, revealing his conception of power all the way down, is Simon Sebag Montefiore, *Stalin: The Court of the Red Tsar* (London: Weidenfeld and Nicolson, 2003).

by so many tourists' video-cameras. The same visibility did not occur where the tsunami had crashed into remote coastal villages, where the locals could not afford cameras. Nor did the terrible earthquake in Pakistan in the following year crash into our consciousnesses to the same degree. This is why NGOs and others concerned to spread understanding about the extent of daily distress in the world attempt to turn cold statistics into real humans. A familiar way to stimulate compassion is to show children in distress – preferably children who are starving, dying, naked, or all three.[23] It still usually needs a Westerner there, to make such pictures news. One fascinating image from the US humanitarian intervention in Somalia in 1992 shows a media circus of photographers pointing their cameras at a starving boy, who stands a few feet away (is he unaware of what is happening, or is he posing to solicit rewards?), while a US Marine stands guard with his finger on his gun (is he guarding the photographers or the child, or simply playing his role in the drama?).[24] There are statistics, damned statistics, and photographs.[25] The opposite of manipulating what is visible is creating invisibility. Following the war against Iraq in 2003 the British and US governments did not count or name the Iraqi civilians killed as a result of their invasion; this represented a major propaganda blunder, but above all it was a human failure.[26]

These points are not related out of ethno-guilt on my part. Many people in the rich world are brilliantly responsive to the radically disadvantaged across the world, and not only at times of crisis. (Indeed, they often seem to be more compassionate than some of the richer governments of the non-Western world.) Donations are given to charities in large amounts, and considerable work is done to show transnational human solidarity. In moments of disaster, donations surge, pop concerts are attended, heads are shaken, and promises are made. But global life goes on once the disaster is forgotten: a world that is not working. Charity can help, so every penny counts (or should), but only radical structural shifts in attitudes and relations between haves and have-nots (between and within countries and regions) can turn compassion into

[23] In 2006 Granta commissioned an ironic and powerful advert for its *The View from Africa* issue: 'How to Write About Africa in Five Easy Steps' by Binyavanga Wainaina. All who are interested in Africa, about to visit Africa, and especially about to write about Africa should read it. It was published in *Prospect*, February 2006, p. 45.
[24] The photograph is by Paul Lowe, in Ransom, 'Charity Bonanza', pp. 2–3.
[25] See Susan Sontag, *Regarding the Pain of Others* (London: Hamish Hamilton, 2003). These questions are discussed further in chapter 8.
[26] See *Iraq Body Count*.

a situation Richard Sennett has called an ethics of autonomy, whereby the unfortunate in the world are treated as ends and never as means, as subjects not objects, and with the goal of strengthening *their* autonomy rather than exercising *our* sense of pity. This is the meaning of non-demeaning help.[27]

Morbid symptoms are all around, yet their pervasiveness and culminating danger are rejected by powerful and influential opinion. Panglossian periodicals such as *The Economist*, feel-good airport books for globalisers such as Thomas L. Friedman's *The World Is Flat*, and optimistic surveys of the environment (such as Bjørn Lomberg's *The Skeptical Environmentalist* and Julian Simon's celebration of population growth) argue that while of course everything is not perfect, problems can be fixed, and this is the best of all possible worlds.[28] The argument here, to the contrary, is that morbid symptoms are proliferating, and those most able to do something about them are in a state of denial. This mindset conforms with what the sociologist Stanley Cohen, after studying reactions to torture victims, called 'seeing but not seeing'.[29] This, I think, is the mental state, today, of the world's most powerful states and leaders in the face of the growing threat of world-historical turmoil – humanity's Great Reckoning. The comforting idea that 'all is for the best in this the best of all possible worlds' – the foolishly optimistic adage of Candide's pedantic tutor, Dr Pangloss – looks set to remain strong for some time to come. Cognitive dissonance is at play, evident in the

---

[27] This formulation is based on the approach advocated in Richard Sennett, *Respect. The Formation of Character in an Age of Inequality* (London: Allen Lane, 2003), pp. 101–26, 247–63.

[28] In the editor's introduction to *The World in 2006* (p. 11) Daniel Franklin looked back on the previous nineteen editions of *The Economist*'s annual survey, and admitted that a 'lot' had been wrong. He then added that not all the predictions in the current survey would be 'entirely accurate'. Even so, he confidently asserted that many of the 'essentials' had been right, 'including an abiding confidence in the march of globalisation and progress'. Despite the gathering risks ahead in 2006, he predicted that the 'march will surely go on'. Thomas L. Friedman's book is *The World Is Flat. The Globalized World in the Twenty-First Century* (London: Penguin, 2006). This updated and expanded edition of the book has a sticker on it announcing that it is the 'Best-Selling Non-Fiction Book in the World'. Bjørn Lomberg's much criticised book is *The Skeptical Environmentalist: Measuring the Real State of the World* (Cambridge: Cambridge University Press, 2001). Julian Simon, Professor of Business Administration, made his case in Norman Myers and Julian L. Simon, *Scarcity or Abundance? A Debate on the Environment* (New York: W. W. Norton, 1994), arguing that indicators of human welfare would show improvement year on year, and that population (and therefore more of us) represents 'the ultimate resource' (which of course in one sense it is for humans, but we should be able to understand that we can have too much of a good thing).

[29] Quoted by Sennett, *Respect*, p. 147.

tactics of denial we tend to employ when we know bad news will disturb us. International history records many policymakers in the past who ignored discrepant information or assimilated it into pre-existing beliefs, thereby perpetuating false images and buttressing unwise policies.[30] A favourite illustration – because it is all too human – occurred in the mid-1930s, when the British Prime Minister, Stanley Baldwin, was shown a report on German rearmament. The latter was causing increasing anxiety on the part of the victors of the First World War, who above all hoped to avoid a repeat of the Western Front. Baldwin did not want to accept what in his heart of hearts he knew to be the case – that the air threat from Nazi Germany was growing – so he responded brusquely to the request to look at the report: 'Oh, for God's sake, take that stuff away. If I read it I shan't sleep.'[31]

It is not difficult to imagine a replay of that scene from the mid-1930s in 2003, when another British Prime Minister, Tony Blair, was also in denial. When asked to consider *the lack of evidence* about Iraqi 'weapons of mass destruction' (an unhelpful and obfuscating term), in the aftermath of an unnecessary, unwise, illegal, and unpopular war fought ostensibly because such weapons represented a clear and present ('45-minute') danger, Blair firstly kept insisting that they did exist. He then claimed that their absence proved they must have existed (and were hidden); following that was the argument that 'programmes' existed if weapons did not; and finally, retrospectively, he altered his rationale for the war in order to change the subject. And then, because he had convinced himself he was right, he presumably slept soundly.

Denial – seeing but not seeing – is clearly more serious at the level of state leaders than it is at the level of ordinary citizens. With power comes responsibility. Unfortunately, the present era is not being well served by its political leaders. It is difficult to disagree with Russell Baker, writing in the *New York Review of Books*, that since the end of the Cold War government in Washington 'has seemed to be mostly about raising money to get elected, and then reelected repeatedly in order to service those who put up the money. There is no moral urgency in it, no philosophical imperative at work.' It is an 'insider's game', he wrote.[32] This picture of the world's most powerful state is familiar across the

---

[30] See Robert Jervis's path-breaking *Perception and Misperception in International Politics* (Princeton, N. J.: Princeton University Press, 1976); on 'Cognitive Consistency' see pp. 119–202, esp. pp. 172–81.
[31] *Ibid.*, pp. 172–3.
[32] Russell Baker, 'In Bush's Washington', *New York Review of Books*, 13 May 2004.

whole democratic world, and undoubtedly plays a part in the low voter turnout in elections. World security is not in safe hands. There are many committed individuals in global civil society who work hard to bring about progressive change, but there is largely complacency at the level of states, where the most decisive action could be taken. Governments spin a good talk, of course, but check the action, and especially watch the money. Leaders continue to shed crocodile tears about the state of parts of the world, but it is the challenge of hanging onto power that gives them sleepless nights.

At some level the human species is as collectively mad as it is brilliantly innovative. We are able to imagine the infinite, but sometimes cannot see what is in front of our eyes. It is always worth recalling that for most of history the greatest brains of the day were convinced that the earth was flat. Today, human society is *still just as trapped* in old ideas. Given the usage rate of the world's non-renewable resources, the growing pressures on renewables, and the continuing failure of governments to cooperate effectively and alleviate the risks, what will future historians think of the continuing global desire to consume more, to produce more babies, to teach everyone to be perfect capitalists, and to honour statism? Globally, we hope that things work out. They may do. We cannot rule out that the scientists predicting global warning have got it wrong, or the possibility that we will be rescued by fabulous inventions and discoveries (will the 'hydrogen economy's' day finally dawn?). But in the meantime the only rational way to behave is prudently, frugally, and globally. New Orleans in 2005 serves as a warning to any latter-day Pangloss. Over a few days, when nature did what nature does, comfortable assumptions about the future collapsed; human systems failed; and the world's most powerful government was found badly wanting.

The rich world lives in collective denial, believing itself to be too sensible, too rich, too intelligent, too privileged for life not to go on as hoped. In the 1980s nuclear disarmers used a joke to unmask the illogic of the pro-deterrence argument that because there had been no nuclear war for the previous forty years, we could assume it would continue for the rest of history. The image was of a man falling from a skyscraper. Those half-way up the building heard him shout as he passed their window, 'So far so good.' In this age of terror, we have seen people choose to throw themselves from skyscrapers. 'So far so good' is not a recipe for world security. The worst is possible. We see it, but yet we do not.

Sanity without sense

Talking to her, he realised how easy it was to present an appearance of orthodoxy while having no grasp whatever of what orthodoxy meant . . . [People] could be made to accept the most flagrant violations of reality, because they never fully grasped the enormity of what was demanded of them, and were not sufficiently interested in public events to notice what was happening. By lack of understanding they remained sane.   Winston Smith in *Nineteen Eighty-Four*[33]

To try to explain how we, *the global we*, got to be as we are at this point in history would require multiple volumes. We are as we are (as individuals) for many reasons – the genetic inheritance from our parents, the life opportunities thrown up by the roll of the cosmic dice, and so on – but at the broadest structural level, the shape of our lives comes from the interplay in specific historical circumstances of the forces of patriarchy, proselytising religion, capitalism, sovereign statism/nationalism, race, and consumerist democracy. These shape the cultures and identities into which people are born or which they choose. Luck plays its part, including bad luck. As it happens, 'we are as we are' in part because of a great historical paradox: the global playing-out of the law of unintended consequences. Human society, dysfunctional in so many ways, is partly the result of the interplay of sets of ideas that for much of history seemed to be the answers to life's ultimate questions.

Humans may be made of what Kant called 'crooked timber',[34] but who can doubt that the grain would have been different if the broad structural patterns of our lives globally had been shaped according to sets of different ideas. Rather than those just mentioned, what if the structural drivers had been feminism, humanism, and cosmopolitanism for example? But we have to work with the grain we inherited, and that means dealing with the following:[35]

---

[33] George Orwell, *Nineteen Eighty-Four* (London: Penguin Books, 1989; first published 1949), p. 163.
[34] The leading liberal theorist, Isaiah Berlin, used this phrase of Kant's as the title of his book arguing the case for pluralism: *The Crooked Grain of Humanity* (London: Fontana, 1991). See n. 180, p. 83.
[35] These ideas were first presented in a lecture: 'Where Are We Now? Between Helplessness and Hope' (Millennium Lecture Series, University of Wales, Aberystwyth, 2000). Thanks are due to all those who have carried on the discussion. Part of the lecture was written up in 'Two Terrors, One Problem', in Ersel Aydinli and James N. Rosenau (eds.), *Globalization, Security, and the Nation State. Paradigms in Transition* (Albany, N.Y.: SUNY Press, 2005), pp. 27–32. There is an encouraging trend towards big-picture analyses of

(i) *Patriarchy*. Over the past 4,000 years or so patriarchy has been justified as representing a biological truth about the superiority of the male sex. Men have been deemed to be stronger and more rational than women; this has profoundly shaped both the public and private spheres of human society, and has manifested itself in the oppression of women. According to Kaufmann McCall, 'the oppression of woman is not a contingent historical fact . . . Woman has always been subordinate to man', and they 'have internalized the alien point of view that man is the essential, woman the inessential'.[36] Ideas about women being both different and inferior have played out over time in men having protective roles and superior rights, evident in everything from political and military decision-making to inheritance advantages, and from unequal pay to honour killings.[37]

(ii) *Proselytising religion*. Between roughly 1,000 and 2,500 years ago, a number of proselytising religions developed in the Middle East and Asia, committed to spreading their own versions of the one true word. The word (whatever version) was powerful, but its spread depended more on the contingencies of the military power of its supporters than on the court of ultimate truth.[38] Local sects became world religions because at some point they had behind them the most powerful army around. Nonetheless, belief gave answers to the meaning of life, and curiosity about the sacred was more or less satisfied. Successful (powerful) religions became primary markers of identity, as well as advocates of ultimate truth, and they contributed to a global sociology in which people learned to accept answers from authority rather than inventing or discovering them through reason. Proselytising religions by their nature have been uncomfortable with pluralism, and alongside their good works they

world history – long and short. The shortest is Chris Brazier, *The No-Nonsense Guide to World History* (London: New Internationalist/Verso, 2001).

[36] Dorothy Kaufmann McCall, 'Simone de Beauvoir, *The Second Sex*, and Jean-Paul Sartre', *Signs*, vol. 5(2), 1979, p. 210.

[37] The classic statement of this position is Simone de Beauvoir, *The Second Sex* (New York: Vintage Books, 1974); note the first three chapters in particular, 'The Data of Biology', 'The Psychoanalytic Point of View', and 'The Point of View of Historical Materialism'.

[38] Introductions to religion and politics are William A. Lessa and Evon Z. Vogt (eds.), *Reader in Comparative Religion. An Anthropological Approach* (New York: HarperCollins, 1979), and Steve Bruce, *Politics and Religion* (Cambridge: Polity, 2003).

have promoted intolerance, bigotry, war, guilt, and division. And they still do.[39]

(iii) *Capitalism*. About 500 years ago capitalism began to gather momentum, and by the end of the twentieth century had achieved global dominance, in both the breadth and depth of its impact on life. Driven by the desire to expand wealth and to avoid being tamed by anything but the market, capitalism became a global culture, *the* global culture – indeed for some *The End of History*.[40] Capitalism has proved to be history's most powerful economic idea, showing a genius for increasing production and legitimising selfishness, and at the same time manifesting an adaptability that (so far) has enabled it to overcome all its challengers. The public and private consequences of capitalism's predatory nature have often been disastrous, evident in the destroyed lives of people who have been no more than cogs in its machines, the blatant evidence of institutional greed, the record of commerce profiting from human rights abuses, and the inflicting of massive environmental despoliation.[41]

(iv) *Statism/nationalism*. Modern statism – the idea that not only should the sovereign state be the pinnacle of decision-making, but also the highest focus of loyalty for people – is associated with the system that emerged out of the treaties of Westphalia in 1648. This settlement, which ended the Thirty Years War, seemed to offer a political solution to the religious rivalry whose wars over previous centuries had torn European society apart.[42] The principles of territorial sovereignty, independence, and non-intervention were instituted. One consequence of such statism was the legitimation of homogeneity, first of religion and later through the inexorable power of nationalism. The 'nation-state' (invariably a euphemism for one-nation imperialism within Westphalian boundaries) became the

---

[39] The case for the regressive influence of religion as we know it is made by Richard Norman, *On Humanism* (London: Routledge, 2004), and Sam Harris, *The End of Faith. Religion, Terror, and the Future of Reason* (London: The Free Press, 2004).

[40] Francis Fukuyama, *The End of History and the Last Man* (London: Hamish Hamilton, 1992).

[41] The key work in conceiving the capitalist world economy as part of a world-system perspective is Immanuel Wallerstein, *The Modern World System*, 3 vols. (New York: Academic Press, 1974–89).

[42] A different interpretation of the pivotal significance of Westphalia in the development of modern international relations is Benno Teschke, *The Myth of 1648. Class, Geopolitics, and the Making of Modern International Relations* (London: Verso, 2003).

dominant political global form.[43] The states system that emerged, even in the sometimes civilised guise of 'international society', enabled governments to behave badly at home while seeking to maximise their power in the structure of mistrust and competition that had been constructed between them.[44] Westphalia proved to be another of the West's failures.[45]

(v) *Race.* 'All is race. There is no other truth', wrote Benjamin Disraeli, British Prime Minister in the late Victorian era.[46] In the Europeanised world by that time, according to Kenan Malik, 'Race explained the character of individuals, the structure of social communities and the fate of human societies.'[47] But this had not always been the case; ancient cultures and medieval Europe lacked any idea of race in the modern sense.[48] There was prejudice, but it was prejudice against the unknown, not the different as such. According to Stephen Eric Bronner, concern with race began in fifteenth-century Spain, with 'purity of blood' statutes directed against Jews who had converted to Christianity. The actual term 'race' seems to have been first used in 1684 as a way of categorising peoples on the basis of physical attributes.[49] Paradoxically, it took the Enlightenment to turn prejudice into politics. In Malik's view, racial difference and ideas of superiority/inferiority could 'only have meaning in a world which has accepted the possibility of social equality and a common humanity'; and this, of course, was one of the Enlightenment's chief contributions to universal moral progress.[50] In other words, it is the ideal of equality that turns 'colour prejudice' into 'racism'. The outcome of this change in

---

[43] Adam Watson, *The Evolution of International Society* (London: Routledge, 1992).

[44] Booth and Wheeler, *Security Dilemma*.

[45] Ken Booth, 'Human Wrongs and International Relations', *International Affairs*, vol. 71(1), 1995, p. 123. This idea was later expanded by Susan Strange into a critique of the Westphalian system to cope effectively with the problems created by globalisation: 'The Westfailure System', *Review of International Studies*, vol. 25(3), 1999, pp. 345–54.

[46] Quoted by Kenan Malik, *The Meaning of Race. Race, History and Culture in Western Society* (Houndmills: Macmillan, 1996), p. 1.

[47] *Ibid.*

[48] Philip Yale Nicholson, *Who Do We Think We Are? Race and Nation in the Modern World* (Armonk: M. E. Sharpe, 1999), pp. 14–38; Malik, *The Meaning of Race*, p. 43.

[49] Stephen Eric Bronner, *Reclaiming the Enlightenment. Toward a Politics of Radical Engagement* (New York: Columbia University Press, 2004), p. 89.

[50] On the Enlightenment and race, see *ibid.*, pp. 81–94, and Jonathan Israel, *Enlightenment Contested. Philosophy, Modernity, and the Emancipation of Man 1670–1752* (Oxford: Oxford University Press, 2006), pp. 593–6, 598–600.

consciousness, Malik thought, separated the modern discourse of race from pre-Enlightenment understandings of differences between peoples.[51] The Enlightenment's commitment to equality also of course explains why believers in racial superiority/inferiority opposed its universalist principles.[52] The first political programme based on 'purity of race' was proposed by German romantic nationalists in the nineteenth century,[53] and from then on – if not before – racism became deeply complicit with nationalism, and especially expansionist nationalism.[54] Race went global. Ideas of racial superiority played a part in the growth of the white empires in the nineteenth century, but ideas of racial equality also helped embed the global human rights culture in the aftermath of the Holocaust in the mid-twentieth. Today, for many people, ostensible biological differences between people generate violence, inform official policies, and shape social behaviour (including 'confiscatory and exploitative practices beyond the scope of existing national laws').[55] For many other people, however, combating racial intolerance is a spur to global civil society activism.

(vi) *Consumerist democracy*. From the end of the nineteenth century consumerist democracy has spread and promoted consumption, resource depletion, globalisation, and a 'culture industry'. Modern democracy arose to counter non-accountable government, but as the scale of modern societies expanded far beyond that conceivable by the first democrats in ancient Greece, so its forms and processes evolved and became unrecognisable.[56] Democracy came to be seen across the world as the only form of legitimate authority, and it became a cliché in some circles that democracies did not fight each other as a result of externalising practices of negotiation and non-violence. But all was not well. The most powerful democracies became associated with Galbraith's 'culture of contentment', in which protecting the well-off (now the majority in their societies) became the essential business of elections, the economy, and foreign and defence

---

[51] Malik, *The Meaning of Race*, p. 42. [52] Bronner, *Reclaiming*, p. 89.
[53] *Ibid.* [54] Nicholson, *Who Do We Think We Are?* chs. 4, 5, 6.
[55] *Ibid.*, p. 6; Mark Cocker, *Rivers of Blood, Rivers of Gold. Europe's Conflict with Tribal Peoples* (London: Jonathan Cape, 1998), is a compelling read on these matters.
[56] David Held (ed.), *Prospects for Democracy: North, South, East, West* (Cambridge: Polity, 1993).

policy.[57] No longer did these societies have to interact as much with the poor at home or abroad, while threatening to put up taxes (which might help social justice through redistribution) became the kiss of death electorally. The rich world, living in their culture of contentment, looked increasingly like the smug occupiers of a lifeboat, while all around thrashed about for survival, or sank, with screams unheard.

Each of these world-constructing ideas, separately, offered answers to the great riddles of life; in so doing, they helped make today's very particular and peculiar global sociology. By their excesses and successes, the structures produced by these ideas created patterns of power that have tended to corrupt, replicate, and oppress. They have promoted mistrustful identity groups that degrade efforts to bring people willingly together, and they have contributed to the destruction of nature. Through the great ideas that made us, *the global we* face the Great Reckoning.

The picture is bleak, but not without hope. There are also powerful positive forces for world security, but it is a race against time. There are new opportunities and resources for the promotion of security, emancipation and community, as a result of developing global networks, the growing questioning of some old thinking and practices, and an urgent sense in some quarters that something has to be done about surviving on an ever-smaller planet. As individuals we can only do a very limited amount to win the race against time in our collectively self-induced crisis. This is why political activity is so important; only collective action can have radical effects. For those of us who are students of international politics – however recent, however ancient – one of the main challenges is to reconceptualise security studies, replacing regressive ideas with radical alternatives – alternatives that are, at the same time, both more realistic about the state we are in and more rational about the practices that offer real hope. Our times demand radical change, but the discipline of international politics has rarely been a place to look for progressive thinking. Unrealistic realism has ruled (a theory of the powerful, by the powerful, for the powerful[58]). This hegemonic realism has been interested in power, not truth, and in dividing humanity, not pulling it together. In such pivotal times, academic subjects need to

---

[57] Galbraith, *Culture of Contentment*.
[58] Ken Booth, 'Critical Explorations', in Ken Booth (ed.), *Critical Security Studies and World Politics* (Boulder, Colo.: Lynne Rienner Publishers, 2005), pp. 4–10.

be reborn. 'No crisis, no academic discipline' is Fred Halliday's law.[59] The sub-discipline of security studies, realist-dominated, was born of the crisis of the Cold War; the discipline of international politics, state-centric, had been born of the crisis of 1914–18. Neither, to use contemporary bureaucratic jargon, is fit for purpose as the coming crisis of the Great Reckoning speeds towards us.

Ceaseless exploration

> given the mounting problems of the dominant problem of the state . . .
> fringe groups do not look as insane as they once did . . . In the mean-
> time, the dissenters can perhaps, as a consolation, remind themselves
> that no system becomes morally acceptable merely because human
> imagination has failed to produce an alternative to it at a given point
> in time.   Ashis Nandy[60]

The spirit of the critical project in this book was brilliantly expressed by T. S. Eliot, in a poem written in the early 1940s entitled 'Little Gidding'.[61] An odd copyright ruling forbids the reprinting of key lines on the grounds they may be read out of context. More prosaically than the original, therefore, the poem speaks about 'ceaseless exploration', with the end (meaning both *purpose* and *destination*) being to return to 'where we started' and to 'know it' for the first time. This describes (almost) perfectly what is required in reconceptualising security from a critical perspective.

The critical project has two stages.[62] The first, which is well underway, is the development of critical security studies as *a body of critical knowledge about security*. As such it encourages the *ceaseless exploration* of security, a field that has been central to the evolution of academic international relations. This is *where we started* just after the First World War, 1914–18. In the years that followed, the hope was widespread – though certainly not universal (remember the militant revisionist states) – that there would never again be war, and those involved in the academic development

---

[59] Fred Halliday, 'The Future of International Relations: Fears and Hopes', in Steve Smith, Ken Booth, and Marysia Zalewski (eds.), *International Theory: Positivism and Beyond* (Cambridge: Cambridge University Press, 1996), p. 318.
[60] Ashis Nandy, 'State', in Wolfgang Sachs (ed.), The *Development Dictionary. A Guide to Knowledge as Power* (London: Zed Books, 1992), p. 272.
[61] The lines are from T. S. Eliot, *Collected Poems 1909–1962* (London: Faber and Faber, 1963), p. 222.
[62] I first made this argument in print in Booth, *Critical Security Studies and World Politics* (Boulder, Colo.: Lynne Rienner, 2005), pp. 12–17, 259–78.

of the subject attempted to play their part through the dissemination of ideas and knowledge about the world.[63] But security on a global scale remained elusive, and still does. The armistice was followed by what E. H. Carr famously called *The Twenty Years' Crisis*,[64] after which erupted the most globally violent conflict in history, culminating in the dropping of the first atomic bombs. The Second World War, 1939–45, had not ended before a Cold War gripped the United States and its allies on one side, and the Soviet Union (and soon after, its new allies) on the other. This rivalry structured international politics for nearly half a century, and in its nuclear dimension became literally MAD,[65] threatening the future of civilised life on earth. After the Berlin Wall was knocked down after 1989 (it did not 'fall'), the conditions seemed to present themselves for the proclaiming of a 'new world order' (for the third time in the century). Like the other 'new starts', this one quickly went missing in inaction, in the complacent 1990s. The 'post-Cold War' era came to a shocking end with the terror attacks on the United States on 11 September 2001. A few years earlier, the Cold War had seemed to be a quasi-war without end;[66] now the world faced the War on Terror, a new global quasi-war apparently without end. But this too will pass, when events throw up their next big surprise.

From the beginning of the academic study of international politics, the concept of security has focused on sovereign states, military power, and the preservation of international order. Security studies therefore derived from a combination of Anglo-American, statist, militarised, masculinised, 'top-down', methodologically positivist and philosophically realist thinking, all shaped by the experiences and memories of the interwar years and the Second World War, and the perceived necessities

---

[63] Origins are important. The world's first chair and first department in the subject was endowed by David Davies, then a Liberal MP, in memory of those students of the University College of Wales, Aberystwyth, who had fought and died in the Great War. For some perspectives on what the discipline has achieved, see Tim Dunne, Michael Cox, and Ken Booth (eds.), *The Eighty Years' Crisis. International Relations 1919–1999* (Cambridge: Cambridge University Press, 1998).

[64] E. H. Carr, *The Twenty Years' Crisis: An Introduction to the Study of International Relations* (London: Macmillan, 1939; 2nd edn, 1946).

[65] MAD – mutual assured destruction – was the name given to the condition that developed between the superpowers in the 1960s whereby each had the nuclear capability to destroy the other whatever damage it may have suffered itself in a surprise attack, thereby supposedly creating a situation of stable mutual deterrence. See Ken Booth, 'Cold Wars of the Mind', in Ken Booth (ed.), *Statecraft and Security: The Cold War and Beyond* (Cambridge: Cambridge University Press, 1998), p. 29.

[66] One thought-provoking interpretation was Mary Kaldor, *The Imaginary War* (Oxford: Blackwell, 1990).

of the Cold War. Critical security studies, as it developed through the 1990s, sought to investigate what security might mean in theory and practice from perspectives on global and local politics that start from very different political, methodological, and philosophical standpoints. CSS is a body of knowledge about security in world politics; it is not a *theory* of security as such, telling us (like realism) who are the key actors, and what are the most rational strategies. This is where the second stage of the ceaseless exploration comes in: the construction of a specific *critical theory of security* from within this developing body of knowledge. The critical theory of security advanced below challenges the pre-defined answers of orthodox international politics in relation to three fundamental questions: what is real in security studies? what is reliable knowledge? and how might we act? The answers of traditional security studies are confined to the trinity of statism, strategy, and the status quo; this book replaces that trinity with reconceputalised notions of security, emancipation, and community.

Although there is a place in academic work for tracing the way ideas develop, readers will not be subjected here to yet another conducted tour through the different schools of thought about security, and be asked to choose a favourite (usually the one set up to be chosen by the author). Edward Kolodziej's *Security and International Relations* (2005), for example, while purporting to provide readers with 'the critical conceptual tools to develop their expertise', managed to ignore most of what is interesting in the discipline, especially the work of those delivering critical conceptual tools; the book reinforces, deliberately or otherwise, the view that only a narrow selection of mainstream approaches is available.[67] Where is feminism? Third Worldist approaches? the realist-oriented work of Buzan? and the critical work of the sort discussed in this book?[68] Be that as it may, the aim of this book is very different: it is not to open up yet another schools-of-thought supermarket (even one with fuller shelves) but rather to provide analysis, argument, and advocacy on behalf of one specific theory.

So far, I have talked about 'critical security studies' and a 'critical theory of security' as if they were unproblematic terms, likely to be widely

[67] Edward A. Kolodziej, *Security and International Relations* (Cambridge: Cambridge University Press, 2005). The quotation is from the back-page blurb.
[68] One curious attempt to do this – revealing all the problems of writing by committee – is the CASE Collective, 'Critical Approaches to Security in Europe: A Networked Manifesto', *Security Dialogue*, vol. 37(4), 2006, pp. 443–87; unfortunately, this 'Manifesto' will confuse more than it will act as a call to critical scholarship.

recognised and understood. This is not so. They are controversial, contested, and frequently misunderstood (when not actually ignored). The fiercest critics have been realists theoretically, and positivists methodologically. Realists argue that any critical perspective threatens disciplinary chaos in security studies and the end of international order in practice, while positivist social science berates critical approaches for undermining hopes for a true science in the study of human affairs.[69] But there has also been civil war within the critical project. Those drawn to poststructuralism and postcolonialism, for example, assert that anything close to Frankfurt school critical theory is too wedded to the Enlightenment 'story', and what they consider flawed 'Eurocentric' concepts such as emancipation, progress, and common humanity. I will argue the opposite, but first some definitions.[70]

Stage I: critical security studies. Critical security studies is a sub-field within the academic discipline of international politics concerned with the pursuit of critical knowledge about security. Critical knowledge implies understandings that attempt to stand outside prevailing structures, processes, ideologies, and orthodoxies while recognising that all conceptualisations of security derive from particular political/ theoretical/historical perspectives. Critical theorising does not make a claim to objectivity but rather seeks to provide deeper understandings of oppressive attitudes and behaviour with a view to developing promising ideas by which human society might overcome structural and contingent human wrongs. Security is conceived comprehensively, embracing theories and practices relating to multiple referents, multiple types of threat, and multiple levels of analysis.

Stage II: a critical theory of security. Critical security theory is both a theoretical commitment and a political orientation concerned with the construction of world security. As a theoretical commitment it is a framework of ideas deriving from a tradition of critical global theorising made up of two main strands: critical social theory and radical international relations theory. This body of ideas provides a framework for reconceptualising the ontology, epistemology, and praxis of security. As a political orientation it is informed by the aim of enhancing world security through emancipatory politics and networks of community at all

---

[69] The debate about international relations and its sub-fields as a 'science' goes back at least to the 1930s and has been repeated by each generation; see the overview by Colin Wight, 'Philosophy', in Walter Carlsnaes, Thomas Risse, and Beth A. Simmons (eds.), *Handbook of International Relations* (London: Sage, 2002), pp. 23–51.

[70] The definitions that follow are variations of Booth, 'Critical Explorations' and 'Beyond Critical Security Studies', in Booth, *Critical Security Studies*, pp. 15 and 268.

levels, including the potential community of all communities – common humanity. By broadening and deepening the concept of security, a critical theory of security engages more comprehensively with questions of reality, knowledge-production, and practice, and in so doing begins to unite theories of politics with security.

These definitions require much unpacking, and this task takes up the rest of the book. For the moment, I want to make two general claims about the approach. First, the theoretical commitment and political orientation of critical security theory offers a much richer understanding of security than that provided by mainstream approaches.[71] In particular, it looks towards an ontology embracing a more extensive set of referents for security (from individuals to the whole of humanity); an epistemology which is post-naturalist (always being willing to engage with the real in world politics, but rejecting approaches to knowledge that assume we can scientifically access the social world in the same way as we do the natural world); and an orientation towards praxis (the unity of theory and practice in politics) which is explicitly emancipatory (culturally sensitive and pragmatic, but also universalistic). Second, broadening the security agenda in the manner proposed below is not intended to turn every political problem into a security issue (what is sometimes unhelpfully called a 'securitising' move, tying the concept of security inexorably with the military dimension);[72] on the contrary, the aim of this book is to turn every security issue into a question of political theory. In other words, the book seeks to politicise security, not securitise politics. By so doing, it hopes to develop a theoretical commitment and political orientation towards a conception of world security in the collective human interest, under the shadow of a past that was imperfect and a future that will be tense.

The prisms and prison of realism

our view of possible alternatives to the states system should take into account the limitations of our own imagination and our own inability to transcend past experience.   Hedley Bull in *The Anarchical Society*[73]

---

[71] Elaborated in Booth, 'Critical Explorations', pp. 10–17.
[72] The notion of 'securitisation' will be discussed at length in chapter 4.
[73] Hedley Bull, *The Anarchical Society. A Study of Order in World Politics* (London: Macmillan, 1977), p. 256.

The growth of critical thinking about security was necessary, and I believe should be celebrated, because the academic sub-discipline of security studies as it developed after the Second World War had many shortcomings. Its serious deficiency as a theory of world security is evident in the tension that exists in the work of sophisticated realists – none better than Bull – who accepted the moral primacy of world society, but looked for progress in that direction through what Stephen Krasner called the 'organised hypocrisy' of the Westphalian system.[74] Realism has been both a theory and ideology of statism, the main target of this book, and this is why it is given prominence.

The discussion of the strengths and (especially) weaknesses of the theory of realism that has dominated academic international politics/ security studies can be relatively brief at this point, because it is a theme developed throughout the book. My starting-point is similar to that of Jack Donnelly in his comprehensive survey of realism; he said that any sound international theory 'must come to terms with, but refuse to be limited to, realism. Realism should be studied, but not allowed to determine the study and practice of international relations, as it has for so much of the past half-century.'[75]

The arguments for and against realism have been much debated over the years, and there is an extensive literature on both sides.[76] Students of security need to know this material because it provides the prevailing ideas in the discipline; it has constituted what has largely been taken, taught, and replicated as the legitimate knowledge of the subject. Students also need to know much more, not least the alternative voices (classical political theorists such as Kant and non-mainstream approaches such as peace research, for example) which have largely been silenced by the discipline. Realism has been powerful in its ability to silence, and also in every other sense. It has been congenial to those in power and it has been plausible to those seeking to understand power. It is seductive and can be passed off as timeless. Everybody interested in world security must therefore engage with realism, not because it is true

[74] Stephen D. Krasner, *Sovereignty. Organized Hypocrisy* (Princeton, N.J.: Princeton University Press, 1999), pp. 46–8. For Bull's critique of 'alternative paths' see *Anarchical Society*, pp. 233–56.

[75] Jack Donnelly, *Realism and International Relations* (Cambridge: Cambridge University Press, 2000), p. 5.

[76] Donnelly's *Realism* is a critical yet sympathetic analysis. He describes himself as 'undeniably non-realist', but drawn to a 'sophisticated, heavily hedged form of realism' – but only as part of a 'pluralistic discipline of international studies'. In contrast with this form of sympathetic engagement, it is sometimes difficult to recognise the 'realism' attacked by writers from poststructural perspectives.

but because it is influential; and not because it is obsolete but because it is not. Realism is one of the ideas that (academically) made us, and so all serious students of CSS must be serious students of realism.

Realism is best considered as a family of ideas, because while families share similarities, they have differences.[77] The main family quarrel within realism has focused on the primary causal factor in state behaviour: between those believing that what determines selfish state competition is flawed human nature (political realists), and those who believe the driver is the condition of international anarchy (neorealists). But there are also differences over the permissible degree of theoretical parsimony, between the purists (structural realists) and those who want to bring in unit-level explanations ('fine grain realism' and 'neoclassical realism'[78]); between those who think a significant degree of security is available in anarchy (defensive realists) and those who believe it is a jungle where power must always be maximised (offensive realists); and between those who think policy choices are mechanistically determined (materially minded realists) or the result of voluntaristic behaviour (ideationally inclined realists). As realism has become more criticised, so its exponents have sought to update, refine, and bypass some of the weaknesses that were exposed. After 9/11 realism has often been said to be coming back, with the terror attacks being followed by wars in Afghanistan and Iraq, all of which confirmed for many the image of international politics as a domain of conflict, necessity, and violence. But realism never really went away. Some mistook the power politics of the Bush/Blair push for war against Iraq for a revival of realism, though the fact is that leading academic realists in the United States opposed the war. Good realists do not allow themselves to become embroiled in unnecessary, unwise, illegal, and unpopular wars. The commitment of good realists to the prudent use of state military power is by no means always contrary to the political orientation of critical security thinking. However, whereas the latter seeks to work towards creating the conditions whereby such situations do not recur, realism replicates practices that ensure they will.

---

[77] I have discussed these matters at more length in Booth, 'Dare Not to Know: International Relations Theory Versus the Future', in Ken Booth and Steve Smith (eds.), *International Relations Theory Today* (Cambridge: Polity, 1995), pp. 328–50, and 'Critical Explorations', pp. 1–18.
[78] The first term is Stephen Van Evera's, in *Causes of War: Power and the Roots of Conflict* (Ithaca, N.Y.: Cornell University Press, 1999), pp 1–13; the second is Gideon Rose's, in 'Neoclassical Realism and Theories of Foreign Policy', *World Politics*, vol. 51(1), 1998, pp. 144–72.

Although any set of generalisations about the realist family will be open to the criticism of oversimplifying a complex tradition, the themes identified below represent the family's main genetic inheritance in relation to the three philosophical themes running through the book:

> *Being*. For realists, the categorical referent is the sovereign state; it is the ultimate actor in international politics and the main defender of the security of people(s). There should be no higher political loyalty than the state, and no higher power of decision-making (these goals constitute what is meant by 'statism'). For classical realists 'human nature' drives state behaviour, while neorealists have emphasised the causal power of the structure of the international system. State-centrism has been associated with a refusal to countenance the possibility of fundamental change or learning in human society, except in the technological realm. Its unspoken or less vocalised assumptions have been as significant as the stated theoretical core of realist-derived security studies: these include the neglect of subjects of insecurity other than the state, notably class and gender; the distinction between 'high' politics (such as military security) and 'low politics' (such as human rights); and the prioritisation of the victims of politics over the victims of economics.
>
> *Knowing*. A key claim of realists is to describe the world 'as it is'. The dominating method has been positivism (understood as empirical verification and falsification). Practice creates theory, as politics creates ethics. The role of the academic should therefore be to explain the world in the manner of a social scientist rather than 'preach' how it 'ought to be' in the manner of a political activist. Security studies (often under the label of 'strategic studies' or 'national security studies') has been overwhelmingly US–British in its agenda, priorities, and practicalities. The discipline deriving from this geopolitical/cultural core has been both ethnocentric and dominated by masculinist values. This has affected prevailing ideas about what constitutes security, the type(s) of threats to be studied, and the manner in which issues have been conceived and communicated through the language employed.
>
> *Doing*. For realists, the anarchical world of states creates a competitive environment which in turn defines the necessities of policy demanded by the imperative of survival. The driver of

action is the interests of states (the controversial and misleading concept of 'the national interest'). Regardless of family quarrels over other issues, realism has a strong consensus about appropriate strategic behaviour. In an arena of never-ending conflict and competition, law and morality have always to bend before the interests of the powerful; power is the key to survival, and successful military strategy is the bedrock of security. Mistrust rather than morality must shape state policy. Ethics are only considered relevant within sovereign states (where there is supposedly 'order' and 'choice'); beyond is the domain of 'anarchy' and 'necessity'. The test of policy is success in the contention for power between states, and in that contention military strength is the ultimate form of power.[79]

This snapshot of the main ideas of realism provides the basis for understanding the framework within which traditional security studies developed in the main centres in which the subject has been studied in the Anglo-American world, and in those regions whose politics seem to have been scripted by realism (notably the Middle East and most of Asia). Although realism dominates the academies, and its expertise is frequently a passport into the offices of power, its key ideas have attracted considerable criticism.[80] These can be summarised as follows: realism is not realistic (it does not provide an accurate picture of the world); it is a misnomer (it is an ideology masquerading as a theory of knowledge); it is a static theory (without a theory of change); it is reductive (it leaves out much of the picture); its methodology is unsophisticated (it sacrifices richness for efficiency of explanation); it fails the test of practice (it does not offer a reliable recipe book); its unspoken assumptions are regressive (it leaves no space for gender or class); its agenda is narrow (it over-concentrates on the military dimension to the exclusion of other threats); its ethics are hostile to the human

---

[79] 'Classical realism' has begun to reassert itself after two decades dominated by the rational egoism of the neorealist branch of the family. Richard Ned Lebow has argued that classical realism saw a close link between interests and ethics; see his *The Tragic Vision of Politics. Ethics, Interests and Orders* (Cambridge: Cambridge University Press, 2003), esp. pp. 257–309. In addition, Michael C. Williams has argued that the realist tradition represents a politics with ethics at its core; see his *The Realist Tradition and the Limits of International Relations* (Cambridge: Cambridge University Press, 2005), esp. pp. 11 and 171. The problem is not that the realist tradition has lacked ethics – for there can be no ethic-free zones in world politics – but the shortcomings of the values realism has replicated.
[80] These are summarised in Booth, 'Critical Explorations', pp. 1–18.

interest (by placing the 'cold monster' of the state at the centre); and it is intellectually rigid (its proponents have marginalised or silenced other approaches).

If these criticisms are valid, then the hold of the family of realism on world politics must be lessened in an era of growing complexity, confusion, and crisis. Many certainties have been under challenge since the winding down of the Cold War; philosophical confidence in the West has been shaky for even longer; the academic study of international relations has been rent by divisions over theory, agenda, and method since the 1980s; and globalisation is one of several processes that have undermined further the case for regarding 'the international' as an autonomous realm of politics. At such a time it is foolhardy to attempt to shoehorn a unique and still-changing period of history into a traditional and flawed theoretical category. The comprehensive 'symbolic order' that realism represents, to use Lacan's concept, continues to be accepted though it is out of sync with reality. It is a case of trying to maintain a sort of sanity at the expense of sense.

Realism is not calculated to deal with the challenges faced by human society, globally, in this period of world-historical danger (about which I will say much more in later chapters). Like the ideas that sustained feudalism towards the end of the middle ages, or the divine right of kings by the late eighteenth century, realism is rationally out of time. But politically it is not, for it is interested in power, and power is interested in it. The world it helped build is being challenged, but its symbolic order could hang on for the foreseeable future; it is not foretold, moreover, that it will be followed by a more rational alternative. Like the other ideas that made us, realism has been pregnant with its opposite. It is supposed to produce security, but it generates insecurity externally and combines with statism to legitimise insecurity internally. Global business-as-usual, in which realism is king, is a recipe for predictable global turmoil. 'All that is solid melts into air', observed Marx.[81] Today, the problem is that the glaciers are melting too quickly, and the ideas that constructed world politics not quickly enough.

[81] Karl Marx and Frederick Engels, *Selected Works* (London: Lawrence and Wishart, 1991); the quotation is from the 'Manifesto of the Communist Party', p. 38.

2   Thinking theory critically

> Oh, this 'sublime silence of eternity' in which so many screams have faded away unheard. It rings within me so strongly that I have no special corner of my heart reserved for the ghetto: I am at home wherever in the world there are clouds, birds and human tears.
>
> Rosa Luxemburg, at the end of her life[1]

The previous chapter identified where a critical theory of security should start: a global political context in which 'so many screams have faded away unheard'. A radically different world politics is conceivable, though its complete achievement may ultimately elude humankind. International politics must become the art of the impossible, for the alternative is almost too unpleasant to contemplate. With this in mind, the present chapter begins to sketch a map of sites of ideas to help create the political conditions for a more secure future. These ideas are not to be found in the national ghettos of realism, but in the cosmopolitan spirit of the unfinished work of the Enlightenment.[2]

---

[1] In a letter, at the end of her life, to Mathilde Wurm: Stephen Eric Bronner, *Rosa Luxemburg. A Revolutionary for our Times* (University Park, Pa.: Pennsylvania State University Press, 1997), p. 112, n. 1.

[2] When the writing of this book was already well advanced, I found Stephen Eric Bronner's *Reclaiming the Enlightenment. Towards a Politics of Radical Engagement* (New York: Columbia University Press, 2004). It is a superb defence of Enlightenment values, and *Theory of World Security* might be regarded as an attempt to try to reclaim those values in relation to world politics. In a different field, but also sharing the same spirit, is Terry Eagleton's sparky *After Theory* (London: Penguin Books, 2004).

Critical global theorising

> His attitude toward the world was neither positive nor negative, but radically critical.　　　　　　　　Hannah Arendt on Gotthold Lessing[3]

The theoretical framework developed in this book derives from a body of thought I call *critical global theorising*. These ideas, for the most part, were inspired by the Enlightenment, a profoundly significant episode in world history that took place primarily *in* Europe in the eighteenth century, though its key ideas were not exclusive *to* Europe at that time in origin or relevance. The search for enlightenment, then and now, has been cosmopolitan in its sensibility. In the course of the following discussion I will show that the Enlightenment has been subjected to much stereotyping and ignorance, and I will argue that this must be countered, even as we turn its own critical spirit in on itself.

Critical global theorising, as conceived here, shares six overlapping characteristics. It is:

- *Universalist.* Based on the historical and anthropological evidence that good ideas travel, and are not exclusive to particular cultures, critical global theorising is *for* all human society; it is not 'reserved for the ghetto'.
- *Inclusive.* Some ideas can be universalist without being inclusive (faiths that claim to be the one true religion, for example). The cosmopolitan spirit attempts to embrace all, including those whose screams have faded away, or are fading away unheard, in the 'sublime silence of eternity'.
- *Normative.* This body of ideas assumes that the answers to the fundamental questions about politics are not to be discovered by science, but by ethical reasoning conducted through dialogue. Equality is the foundational idea of this way of thinking.
- *Emancipatory.* Critical global theorising seeks to construct a world politics that is not shackled by the chains of oppressive ideas and practices. It seeks to promote freedom.
- *Progressive.* Critical theory attempts to bring theory and practice together in the interests of humankind in general and of the suffering in particular. It assumes that progressive change is possible in morality and politics, not just technology.

---

[3] Her biographer says that such was also her attitude: Elisabeth Young-Bruehl, *Hannah Arendt. For Love of the World* (London: Yale University Press, 1984), p. 261.

- *Critical.* The method of critical theorising is to stand outside the status quo, identify the oppressions within existing structures and processes, and then develop the resources for change. This method consists of both a theoretical commitment and a political orientation.

Three further prefatory points are necessary about the character of critical global theorising:

- Several of the schools of thought to be discussed have relatively little to say explicitly about international relations. Nonetheless, they do all have something to contribute to thinking about the world.
- I deliberately use the term 'theorising' rather than 'theory', because this body of thought does not offer a homogeneous theory, only family resemblances.
- Finally, critical global theorising asks us to think about the very purposes of life at the same moment as we think about the structures and processes of international politics. A critical theory of security must go beyond concern with the techniques of state survival, and instead situate global political arrangements in ideas about the purposes of that survival. Security implies *survival plus*, and for a species with a highly developed consciousness, this means creating space for human self-invention beyond merely existing. Thomas Hobbes understood the instrumental value of security, and thus its role in life beyond simply surviving. He fully grasped that safety is the necessary condition for well-being; the aim is 'not mere survival in any condition, but a happy life so far as that is possible'.[4]

The approach I adopt towards critical global theorising – and indeed theory in general – is pragmatic. Hannah Arendt talked about *Perlenfischerei* (pearl-fishing), meaning an 'informal' approach rather than a dogmatic identification with one system of thought. The source of her pearls was the history of ideas, but she was not concerned with the history of ideas as such. Academic purists might think this not quite respectable, and

---

[4] This is discussed further in chapter 3. See Thomas Hobbes, *On the Citizen*, ed. and trans. Richard Tuck and Michael Silverthorne (Cambridge: Cambridge University Press, 1998), p. 143; I thank William Bain for drawing this to my attention: see his 'Introduction', p. 1, and Robert Jackson, '"The safety of the people is the supreme law" Beyond Hobbes but not as far as Kant', pp. 15–23, in William Bain (ed.), *The Empire of Security and the Safety of the People* (London: Routledge, 2006).

indeed Arendt was sometimes criticised for her approach. Be that as it may, she searched, in the words of one of her interpreters, 'beneath the historical surface' for ideas that were 'sea-changed, rich, and strange'.[5] The two large sections that follow adopt the same approach, diving into, first, the critical tradition in social theory, and then the radical tradition in international relations theory. The goal is to find pearls of ideas that might be strung together to make a theory of world security for our time.

Perlenfischerei I: critical theory

De omnibus dubitandum.   Karl Marx[6]

The term *critical theory* has been a source of some confusion and not a little controversy since it became commonplace in the academic study of international relations in the late 1980s. It has been used in a broad sense to refer to a range of theories that take a 'critical' stance towards traditional ideas about knowledge and society. This understanding refers to the range of approaches to knowledge that have challenged the orthodoxies in Western thought. In particular, these critical theories are 'antifoundational', arguing that claims about what is true in the social world cannot be finally determined against any objective or ultimate standard. More specifically, Critical Theory (often capitalised) is used to refer to the particular tradition of the Frankfurt school.[7]

Before the confusion grows, it has to be admitted that there is an identity problem with respect to critical approaches to security: which school or individual is in or out of CSS? Students often talk of CSS as an 'it', but in reality there are enormous (and unbridgeable) gulfs between some of the approaches which are deemed to be 'in'. This identity crisis was evident early on, in the edited collection of Keith Krause and Michael C. Williams, *Critical Security Studies. Concepts and Cases* (1997). Their version of CSS offers a promiscuous range of viewpoints, including so-called subaltern realism, poststructuralism, contributions 'that

[5] So described in a letter written in 1960: Young-Bruehl, *Arendt*, p. 95.
[6] 'Everything should be doubted' (said to be Marx's favourite motto): Francis Wheen, *Karl Marx* (London: Fourth Estate, 1999), p. 388.
[7] Chris Brown, '"Turtles All the Way Down": Antifoundationalism, Critical Theory, and International Relations', *Millennium*, vol. 23(2), 1994, pp. 213–36. I will not follow the habit of capitalising Frankfurt school critical theory to distinguish it from other antifoundational approaches; it will be clear from the context whether the discussion is referring to the general or the specific.

lean on' Wittgenstein, and several others. Some of their contributions are not 'critical' at all in the usual sense of the term, while the influence of the Frankfurt school was only minimally represented.[8] In their defence, Krause and Williams attempted to offer a set of approaches standing outside the core of mainstream security studies, rather than defining a distinctive *critical* approach (even on their own part). They deliberately chose not to define a precise meaning of the term *critical* (or even *security*) for fear of invoking 'a new orthodoxy'.[9] This is definitely not the approach adopted in this book. In the worlds of world politics, being an orthodoxy is less of a worry than being irrelevant, while intellectual promiscuity is no basis from which to launch research strategies and still less political projects. What follows is therefore more focused, and it begins with the pearl-bed of the critical theory tradition proper. Four main sites of ideas are plundered to assist the development of a theory of world security: the Frankfurt school, the Gramscian tradition, the legacy of Marx, and critical international relations theory. An outline of each follows, with some brief contextualising, and a summary of key ideas.

The Frankfurt school

Michel Foucault once lamented that he would have 'saved useful time' and 'avoided certain errors' had he encountered the work of the Frankfurt School earlier.   Richard Wyn Jones in 'On Emancipation'[10]

I share with Richard Wyn Jones the view that not all critical theories are equally useful when thinking about security, and that the work of the Frankfurt school is particularly significant.[11] That said, I do not want to make the Frankfurt school something that it was not, is not, nor can be. Change and controversy have characterised workers within the Frankfurt tradition, and the approach I adopt towards it is as pragmatic as towards theory in general. For present purposes, it is the earlier work of the Frankfurt school that is especially useful.

---

[8] On their conception of 'critical', see Keith Krause and Michael C. Williams (eds.), *Critical Security Studies. Concepts and Cases* (Minneapolis: University of Minnesota Press, 1997), pp. x–xiii.
[9] *Ibid.*, p. viii.
[10] Richard Wyn Jones, 'On Emancipation', in Ken Booth (ed.), *Critical Security Studies and World Politics* (Boulder, Colo.: Lynne Rienner, 2005), p. 233.
[11] Richard Wyn Jones, *Security, Strategy, and Critical Theory* (Boulder, Colo.: Lynne Rienner, 1999), p. ix and *passim*.

The Frankfurt school is the label given to the philosophical and sociological movement associated with the work of the Institut für Sozialforschung (Institute for Social Research or IfS) established at Frankfurt University (Frankfurt am Main) in 1922.[12] It promised a new way of theorising society. From its early days the IfS was characterised as 'post-Marxian', meaning that it was Marxist-inspired but that its leading figures had become disenchanted with Marxism. They challenged the central tenets of what then passed as its orthodoxy, particularly that strain emanating from the power of the Kremlin rather than the workings of reason, as the former rapidly become authoritarian and ahistorical after 1917.[13] As a result, the IfS became an important voice in the defection of some Western Marxists from the orthodoxies of the USSR and its acolyte parties. As it ceased to be identifiably 'Marxist'[14] in its explorations of modern society, the concerns and perspectives of the IfS broadened. Questions relating to the 'culture industry', ideology, aesthetics, and psychoanalysis attracted interest, replacing earlier concerns with historical materialism.

Following the rise to power of the Nazis in Germany, major figures in the early IfS (many of whom were Jewish) moved to New York in 1934. After the Second World War, some (but not all) of these individuals returned to Germany. The key thinkers in the first generation of the IfS were Max Horkheimer and Theodor Adorno. After 1945, the influence grew of Herbert Marcuse (who stayed in the United States) while in the new Federal Republic of Germany, Jürgen Habermas became the

---

[12] There are many excellent accounts of the Frankfurt school and critical theory; see David Held, *Introduction to Critical Theory: Horkheimer to Habermas* (London: Hutchinson, 1980); Stephen Eric Bronner, *Of Critical Theory and its Theorists* (Oxford: Blackwell, 1994); J. M. Bernstein, *Recovering Ethical Life. Jürgen Habermas and the Future of Critical Theory* (London: Routledge, 1995); Peter M. R. Stirk, *Critical Theory, Politics and Society. An Introduction* (London: Pinter, 2000); and Fred Rush (ed.), *The Cambridge Companion to Critical Theory* (Cambridge: Cambridge University Press, 2004). Some aficionados claim that the best introduction was the first one in the field, Martin Jay, *The Dialectical Imagination: A History of the Frankfurt School and the Institute of Social Research, 1923–1950* (Boston, Mass.: Little, Brown and Co, 1973). Useful collections of key work include (the invaluable) Max Horkheimer, *Critical Theory. Selected Essays*, trans. Matthew J. O'Connell and others (New York: Continuum, 1992), A. Arato and E. Gebhardt, *The Esssential Frankfurt School Reader* (Oxford: Oxford University Press, 1978), and Stephen Bronner and Douglas Kellner (eds.), *Critical Theory and Society: A Reader* (London: Routledge, 1989).
[13] Andrew Linklater, 'The Changing Contours of Critical International Relations Theory', in Richard Wyn Jones, *Critical Theory and World Politics* (Boulder, Colo.: Lynne Rienner, 2001), pp. 23–59.
[14] See Meghnad Desai, *Marx's Revenge. The Resurgence of Capitalism and the Death of Statist Socialism* (London: Verso, 2002), p. 39.

major theorist. The list of alumni of the IfS is a roll-call of the twentieth century's leading German leftist intellectuals.

The theoretical standpoint of the IfS became synonymous with critical theory after 1937 when Horkheimer, its then director, published an article in the Institute's journal (*Zeitschrift für Sozialforschung*[15]) entitled 'Traditional and Critical Theory'.[16] The word 'seminal' is a cliché in today's academic grade-inflation, but Horkheimer's essay fully deserves the accolade. It was original and significant, a reference point for later thinkers. Horkheimer set out an agenda for critical theory, based on the idea of the relationship between reflective, self-knowing theorists, shaped by the circumstances in which they found themselves, and theorising that sought to struggle against the injustices of the world.

The first task of critical theory was analytical. According to Stanley Aronowitz, Horkheimer believed that critical theory sought 'to penetrate the world of things to show the underlying relations between persons'; in Horkeimer's own words, it was to see 'the human bottom of nonhuman things'. Such an understanding of 'what is prevalent' was primarily historical in Horkheimer's mind, because the 'facts which our senses present to us' are 'socially preformed' in two ways: 'through the historical character of the object perceived and through the historical character of the perceiving organ. Both are not simply natural, they are shaped by human activity.'[17] As it developed from these beginnings, Frankfurt school critical theory became concerned with revealing the non-theoretical interests at work in social and political enquiry, and to this end proponents attempted to be self-conscious and self-critical about what they were doing. This was the base for a second task, seeking to discover, through 'immanent critique', the resources for an emancipatory project – the politics of a free and self-determining society. Through their political orientation and theoretical commitment they hoped to show how human agents could stand outside existing structures of power and truth, and establish critical leverage on that status quo, in ways that promised the politics of a freer and more self-determining society.

The IfS tradition expanded into an eclectic body of thought about society, yet it does not offer a coherent theory of international relations, and

---

[15] An essential collection of long-out-of-print essays from the journal is Horkheimer, *Critical Theory* (1972); this volume contains a brief preface by Horkheimer, who died in the year following publication, and an introduction by Stanley Aronowitz.
[16] *Ibid.*, pp. 188–243.   [17] *Ibid.*, p. xiii and 200–1.

still less a recipe for world security. Whereas the disputatious family of realism gives a coherent picture of the key referents in world politics, and specific strategies, the Frankfurt tradition is radically open. It does not have an international theory, but rather offers an approach to social theory, explaining how enquiring minds might understand human social conditions. For these reasons, and because the work of some of its key figures has been both peripheral and not always easy to understand, its impact on academic international relations has been limited.[18] It should also be said that its Marxian and German origins probably did not help its influence to spread in the generally anti-Marxist academic communities in which international relations developed in the years following a second war against Germany within a generation.

Radical thinkers are notoriously contrarian, and this was demonstrated most powerfully when Adorno and Horkheimer, against the backdrop of the Nazi era, total war, and the Holocaust, published *Dialectic of Enlightenment*, which some regard at the 'keystone' of the Frankfurt school. It addressed the question that hovered like a dark cloud over Enlightenment-derived thought in the Nazi era: 'why [is] mankind, instead of entering into a truly human condition . . . sinking into a new kind of barbarism'?[19] Aspects of the assault of the *Dialectic* on the reputation of the Enlightenment will be discussed and challenged in chapter 3, but even this assault can be celebrated as an expression of critical reflexivity, and a robust answer to those who suggest that critical theorists and theories are always likely to sink into orthodoxies.

'Frankfurt' is best understood as an inspiration to critique, rather than a narrow or particularly coherent system of thought. Over the years, the school has lacked an agreed methodology, and its voices have varied greatly. Those associated with the IfS have changed their minds and shifted interests. Individuals have disagreed about the drivers of historical change, the sources of injustice, emancipation, and political practice. What has been shared has been an inspiration to theorise reflexively beyond current orthodoxies, and to develop a politics of opposition to those structures that produce, perpetuate, and naturalise human wrongs.

While the IfS has not generated a specific political programme, it has offered a distinctive political orientation, concerned with issues of social

---

[18] Noted in 1987 by Fred Halliday, 'Vigilantism in International Relations', *Review of International Studies*, vol. 13(3), 1987, pp. 165–6.
[19] Theodor W. Adorno and Max Horkheimer, *Dialectic of Enlightenment*, trans. John Cumming (London: Verso, 1997; first published 1944), p. xi.

and other forms of domination, seeking to stand against the injustices of existing society. Although ideas about emancipation have been a source of disagreement, 'emancipatory intent' has been the spirit animating theorising.[20]

Key ideas

All knowledge is historical knowledge, produced in and under particular social conditions; the assumptions of 'traditional' theory (such as the separation of subject and object, fact and value) should be rejected; reflexivity is central to 'critical' theory; the scientific method has spread uncritically and powerfully across all fields; the ideal of 'scientific' objectivity is a chimera in the social world; reductionism should be replaced by holism; the political realm is inseparable from the ethical realm; politics is the arena of emancipation, and therefore of potential freedom; theory is not be separate from practice, but an integral part of it ('praxis'); praxis contributes to emancipation as goal-setter and critical device; there is no sounder basis for practice than immanent critique.

The Gramscian tradition

We must prevent this brain from functioning for twenty years.
Public prosecutor on the imprisonment of Gramsci[21]

In 1928 Antonio Gramsci, then General Secretary of the Italian Communist Party, was imprisoned by Mussolini's regime. He remained in jail until shortly before his death in 1937. During his trial in a Fascist court, the public prosecutor issued a violent tirade against Gramsci and his accused comrades, and hoped to shut him up. The *Prison Notebooks* that emerged out of the years of imprisonment triumphantly show that the Fascist jail did not stop Gramsci's brain functioning, and fifty years later he was reborn for students of world politics. His ideas are alive, whereas nobody remembers the name of the public prosecutor.

J. M. Bernstein has described critical theory as portending 'a different sense of what human knowing is and does'.[22] At the centre of this idea is 'the reflective self-understanding of the theorist'.[23] Theorists do not stand on neutral ('objective') ground, separated from the world they

---

[20] Bronner, *Of Critical Theory*, p. 3.
[21] Giuseppe Fiori, *Antonio Gramsci. Life of a Revolutionary*, trans. Tom Nairn (London: Verso, 1990), p. 230. I thank Richard Wyn Jones for not only drawing this book to my attention, but giving me a copy.
[22] Bernstein, *Recovering Ethical Life*, p. 10.   [23] *Ibid.*, p. 12.

study; they are part of the social processes making that world. Nowhere is this insight about the historically situated theorist better illustrated than in the heroic life and brilliantly reflective theorising of Gramsci.[24] Giuseppe Fiori's biography interweaves Gramsci's personal and political life, and puts a human face to one of the most important theorists in the Western tradition of thinking about Marx. Fiori helps readers understand the experiences that shaped Gramsci's ideas, though he cannot explain the genius that enabled Gramsci to see things with a clarity others did not possess.

Gramsci wrote a great deal but did not produce an integrated body of work. The prison conditions meant he was only able to write fragments, ranging from political theorising to literary criticism. The *Notebooks*, published after his death, helped establish his reputation, and his influence has gradually grown.[25] Gramsci is regarded now as the leading early twentieth-century Marxist emphasising the reflective human subject.[26] Rejecting the absolute materialism of the authorised Marxism of his generation, he gave a role to human consciousness and the reflective human subject. In so doing, he challenged the Marxist interpretation of the relationship between the base and the superstructure. Against the view that the economic base (the modes of production) determined the characteristics of the superstructure, Gramsci argued that the characteristics of the superstructure were themselves of decisive importance in the evolution of society, the revolution, and history.

One characteristic of the superstructure was the tendency to 'hegemony', a central concept in his theorising.[27] Normally associated with the idea of wielding material power, hegemony for Gramsci also depended on the spread of particular sets of ideas and culture. While control of production established dominance for a ruling group, its consolidation and reproduction required civil society (identified primarily as the churches, schools, and the media) to become sources of an ideological hegemony. Here, ideas could infiltrate, become solidified, legitimised, and naturalised as the 'common sense' of society. To overthrow a hegemonic group or class, Gramsci argued that it was necessary for a

---

[24] This is brought out, with sympathy, in Fiori's engrossing biography, *Gramsci*.

[25] Antonio Gramsci, *Selections from the Prison Notebooks*, trans. Quintin Hoare and Geoffrey Nowell Smith (London: Lawrence and Wishart, 1971).

[26] Fiori, *Gramsci*, pp. 238–9 discusses his originality as a Marxist.

[27] David Gorgacs (ed.), *A Gramsci Reader. Selected Writings, 1916–1935* (London: Lawrence and Wishart, 1988), pp. 195, 301–11, 323–6, 422–4.

revolutionary party to undermine their sources of power in civil society, including the political common sense their power had embedded. This concern with the struggle against ideological hegemony meant that intellectuals played a significant role in his thought. For Gramsci 'all men are intellectuals', though not all have the position of intellectuals in society. He identified two types: 'traditional' intellectuals who see themselves as being independent thinkers but are not (in effect they help embed the prevailing hegemony with its particular patterns of power and domination) and 'organic' intellectuals who clarify, theorise, and articulate the ideas of a particular social class.[28]

Gramsci has not been a central figure in academic international relations, but he is not an unimportant one. He himself would not have worried, because he recognised that the 'war of position' for a progressive world order needed time. The *Prison Notebooks* are not directly concerned with international relations, but they offer insights. He rejected the reductionism of both those who argued that everything important was reducible to economic relations and those who claimed that politics made the world go round. For Gramsci it was the interrelationship between the two that mattered; together they created the hegemony-producing 'historic bloc' that in turn characterised particular state or world orders. Over time, his key ideas led to the growth of a 'neo-Gramscian' bloc in the study of international relations. Its pioneer was Robert W. Cox, who did more than anybody in the early 1980s to bring critical thinking (Gramscian rather than Frankfurtian) to the academic study of international relations.[29] Cox's two vital contributions to critical theorising for present purposes are his distinction between 'problem-solving' and 'critical theory', and his account of the 'interests of knowledge'.

---

[28] Gramsci, *Prison Notebooks*, pp. 3–24, 323–77. Bronner questions the usefulness of the typology: *Reclaiming*, pp. 75–7.
[29] Robert W. Cox, 'Gramsci, Hegemony and International Relations', *Millennium*, vol. 12(2), 1983, pp. 162–75; Robert W. Cox with Timothy J. Sinclair, *Approaches to World Order* (Cambridge: Cambridge University Press, 1996); and Robert W. Cox (ed.), *The New Realism: Perspectives on Multilateralism and World Order* (New York: St Martin's Press, 1997). See also Randall Germain and Michael Kenny, 'Engaging Gramsci: International Relations Theory and the New Gramscians', *Review of International Studies*, vol. 24(1), 1998, pp. 3–21, and Stephen Gill (ed.), *Gramsci, Historical Materialism and International Relations* (Cambridge: Cambridge University Press, 1993). In the work in which Cox introduced critical theory he did not cite the work of the Frankfurt school, nor did he later indicate that it had been an influence on shaping his ideas: see Wyn Jones, *Security*, p. 3, and Cox and Sinclair, *Approaches*, pp. 19–31.

These ideas will be discussed later in the book; for the moment it is necessary to keep two distinctions in mind. First, the difference between *problem-solving* and *critical theory* is between what might be called *insider* and *outsider* theorising. In other words, the urgent task for students of world politics is to construct a security studies that goes beyond problem-solving *within* the status quo, and instead seeks to help engage through critical theory with the problem *of* the status quo.[30] Second, Cox echoed Habermas in seeking to reveal the 'interests of knowledge'. This idea was expressed to an international relations audience with influential simplicity. In one of the most quotable and paraphrasable lines in the discipline, Cox wrote that 'theory is always *for* someone and *for* some purpose'.[31] Cox was emphasising that knowledge is socially and historically produced, with knowledge-producers being inseparable from contexts, identities, and interests. The challenge was being thrown down to traditional (problem-solving) theorists to defend their cherished commitment to the social scientific ideal about objective, value-free, timeless, and neutral knowledge about human society. The knowledge-interest of critical theory has been identified as emancipation, as will be elaborated in part II.

Key ideas

Knowledge has interests beyond itself; problem-solving theory replicates society, whereas the analytical and political orientation of critical theory is rooted in change; hegemony is ideological as well as material; common sense is political (either progressive or traditional); power is to be understood as a structure of relationships, requiring both coercion and consent; accounts of human society should not be reduced to the economic or the political – what counts is their interaction; human consciousness is a factor in social development, and so the role of the intersubjective must be recognised in the development of social structures; everybody in society is an intellectual, because all are transmitters of ideas, but those with the functions of intellectuals can serve in either 'traditional' or 'organic' modes; civil society is a decisive level in the struggle for political power; the world capitalist system contains contradictions that can be exploited to promote emancipatory goals, but success cannot be guaranteed.

[30] Ken Booth, 'Critical Explorations', in Ken Booth (ed.), *Critical Security Studies and World Politics* (Boulder, Colo.: Lynne Rienner, 2005), p. 10.
[31] Robert W. Cox, 'Social Forces, States, and World Orders: Beyond International Relations Theory', *Millennium*, vol. 10(2), 1981, p. 128.

The legacy of Marx

Tout que je sais je ne suis pas marxiste.

Karl Marx, on being asked 'What is a Marxist?'[32]

To claim Karl Marx as a resource for a theory of world security is bound to raise eyebrows. At best such a claim might be seen as provocative at worst irrelevant. But it was not an accident, as he might have said, that British radio listeners in 2005 voted him the greatest philosopher ever.[33] His ideas and intellectual significance will survive because the conditions that led his words to be so influential during the past two centuries have not disappeared in this.

Marx's reputation will remain forever tarnished, for many, by the charge that he was responsible for the terrible deeds committed in the name of communism, and especially by the Soviet Union of Stalin, whose symbol is the Gulag.[34] But this is too simple. According to Francis Wheen, writer of a sympathetic biography of Marx, 'Only a fool could hold Marx responsible for the Gulag.'[35] He identified one such person, Leopold Schwarzchild, who claimed to see with complete certainty a line running from Marx's writings in the mid-nineteenth century to the camp system run by the Soviets a century later. '[T]he tree is known by its fruit', Schwarzchild wrote, to which Wheen smartly parried, 'like so many proverbs', this one is 'rather less axiomatic than it sounds'. Questioning the assumption that philosophers should be blamed for 'any and every subsequent mutilation of their ideas', he asked: 'If Herr Schwarzchild found wasp-eaten windfalls in his orchard – or, perhaps, was served an overcooked apple pie for lunch – did he reach for his axe and administer summary justice to the guilty tree?'[36] Marx himself was aware of the danger that his ideas might solidify into an 'ism' (an anxiety later shared by Gandhi about *his* own ideas[37]). This was, of course, the road history did take.

Gramsci argued that the validity of Marxism lay not in the assertion of its scientific truths, but in the success of its related social practices. By these standards, if the Soviet Union was the test, Marxism fails. But

[32] Quoted in Desai, *Marx's Revenge*, p. 39.
[33] Francis Wheen, 'Why Marx is the Man of the Moment', *The Observer*, 17 July 2005.
[34] The camp system – through which eighteen million people passed in the Soviet period – had its origins under the tsars, but reached its terrifying maximum extent under Stalin: Anne Applebaum, *Gulag. A History of the Soviet Camps* (London: BCA, 2003).
[35] Wheen, *Marx*, p. 2.   [36] *Ibid.*, p. 3.
[37] Bhikhu Parekh, *Gandhi's Political Philosophy. A Critical Examination* (Houndmills: Palgrave Macmillan, 1991), pp. 224–5.

Wheen is one who has argued that there are good reasons for not using this particular test. Separating Marx's ideas from some of the practices carried out in his name is critical.[38]

One place to begin thinking about this separation is Marx's own humanity rather than the darkest corners of the Soviet past. 'The father of communism' was the most human of revolutionaries according to Wheen: an émigré and a middle-class English gentleman; an agitator and a theorist; a convivial host and an argumentative individual; a devoted family man 'who impregnated his housemaid'; a scholar and someone who loved drink, cigars, and jokes; and a philosopher who admitted to his daughter that his favourite maxim was *Nihil humani a me alienum puto*.[39]

Beyond the ideologised stereotype, Marx above all was a truly brilliant social theorist. His place as a thinker about human social evolution can be likened to Darwin's discovery of animal evolution in the biological world.[40] Frederick Engels, Marx's collaborator, described his greatest insight as follows, in his graveside oration for Marx, in 1883:

> the simple fact, hitherto concealed by an overgrowth of ideology, that mankind must first of all eat and drink, have shelter and clothing, before it can pursue politics, science, art, religion, etc.; that therefore the production of the immediate material means of life and consequently the degree of economic development . . . form the foundation upon which the state institutions, the legal conceptions, art, and even the ideas on religion, of the people concerned have been evolved, and in the light of which they must, therefore, be explained, instead of *vice versa* as had hitherto been the case.[41]

It is not necessary to believe all of this, or all the implications that Marx and others drew from it, to appreciate that it was one of those rare insights that change how humans understand themselves.

A re-evaluation of Marx's work has been underway since the end of the Cold War, and not before time. Even so, the main body of his ideas

---

[38] Chris Brown, '"Our Side"? Critical Theory and International Relations', in Richard Wyn Jones (ed.), *Critical Theory and World Politics* (Boulder, Colo.: Lynne Rienner, 2001), pp. 193–6.
[39] This description is based on Wheen, *Marx*, pp. 1–2. The maxim 'Nothing human is alien to me' is what Marx put down as his favourite maxim in a game of Confessions with his daughters: p. 388.
[40] The comparison is made by Paul Foot, 'Karl Marx and Rosa Luxemburg', in his *Words as Weapons. Selected Writing 1980–1990* (London: Verso, 1990), p. 274.
[41] Frederick Engels, 'From Karl Marx's Funeral', speech at the graveside, 17 March 1883, in *Karl Marx and Frederick Engels. Selected Works in One Volume* (London: Lawrence and Wishart, 1991), pp. 411–12.

remains a blur to many. This is regrettable, given that a checklist of the areas of his theorising reads like the key concepts for a syllabus for PolSci 101. He wrote brilliantly about reality (historical materialism, capitalism, globalisation, base/superstructure, class, etc.), knowledge (ideology, false consciousness, alienation, etc.) and political action (exploitation, revolution, emancipation, democracy, etc.). He was an outstanding student of capitalism, and had worked out the dynamics of globalisation nearly a century and a half before it became widely understood. According to Gareth Stedman Jones, who wrote the introduction to a 2002 new edition of *The Communist Manifesto* (first published 1848), 'the *Manifesto* sketches a vision of reality that, at the start of the new millennium and against a background of endless chatter about globalization and deregulation, looks as powerful and contemporary a picture of our own world as it might have appeared to those reading it in 1848'.[42] Some of this is now being acknowledged by prominent advocates of global capitalism such as Thomas Friedman.[43] The reassessment of Marx will continue and further temper Cold War stereotyping. For example, Marx was not known for praising the bourgeoisie, but he did; or for respecting the environment, but his views are not as simple as his detractors have claimed;[44] or for being democratically inclined, but it was this that led him to 'communism'.[45]

Such plaudits obviously do not mean that Marx was always right, or that he always included everything he might have in his system of ideas, or that he was successful as a political prophet. He predicted that the state would wither away, and that communism would triumph, resulting in people contributing to society according to their abilities and taking according to their needs. In the event, communism was one of the twentieth century's most unsuccessful utopias.[46] His flawed reasoning led to other errors. His focus on production as the driver of change

---

[42] Karl Marx and Friedrich Engels, *The Communist Manifesto*, introduction and notes by Gareth Stedman Jones (London: Penguin Books, 2002), p. 5. See also Wheen, *Marx*, pp. 4–5, 115; and Desai, *Marx's Revenge*, pp. 4–5, 38–9 and *passim*.

[43] Friedman, *The World Is Flat. The Globalized World in the Twenty-First Century* (London: Penguin Books, 2006), pp. 234–7. John Gray saw more of Marx (as a technological determinist) in Friedman's thinking than the cheerleader of neoliberalism would have recognised: see his 'The World is Round', *New York Review of Books*, 11 August 2005.

[44] Alex Callinicos, *An Anti-Capitalist Manifesto* (Cambridge: Polity, 2003), pp. 46–50; Wheen, *Marx*, pp. 120–1.

[45] Foot, 'Karl Marx and Rosa Luxemburg', p. 278.

[46] It remains to be seen whether and how twentieth-century capitalism also disappears. On the twin utopias of industrial modernisation, see Susan Buck-Morss, *Dreamworld and Catastrophe. The Passing of Mass Utopia in East and West* (Cambridge, Mass.: MIT Press, 2000).

led him to neglect the superstructure and the possibility of human consciousness developing separately; his concern with class encouraged the neglect of nationalism; his teleology (a problematic idea in itself) meant ethical concerns tended to go out the window; his desire to control nature meant he did not work through the implications of this with the brilliance of his projections of the logic of capitalism; and although he wrote about revolution, he did not say much about war. He was, in some of these views, simply a man of his time; this was also evident in his ignoring of gender and race.

Marx also ignored international relations. The games of diplomats, for Marx, belonged to the category of capitalism's epiphenomena, and they would wither away, along with the states that sustained them. In turn, many scholars writing about international relations have ignored Marx.[47] Martin Wight, the most English of the English school, thought he knew why. He told his readers in the 1960s: 'The absence of Marxist international theory has a wider importance than making it difficult to recommend reading to an undergraduate who wants to study the principles of Communist foreign policy in the original sources. It creates the obscurity, so fruitful to the Communists themselves, about what these principles actually are.'[48] The English school ebbs and flows, and will continue to be a small and elitist club as long as its members fail to embrace basic aspects of Marx's agenda: political economy and social change.[49]

The marginalising of Marx has not been universal, of course. In the 1960s/70s, a disparate body of 'Marxist' and 'neo-Marxist' writers developed some of his key themes, notably the relationship between capitalism and imperialism, imperialism and war, dominance and dependence, and injustice and change. *Dependencia* theorists were particularly significant in that period in seeking to explain the apparent paradox between political independence and economic dependence in what was then

---

[47] Hazel Smith, 'Marxism and International Relations Theory', in A. J. R. Groom and Margot Light (eds.), *Contemporary International Relations: A Guide to Theory* (London: Pinter, 1994), pp. 142–55, contains a survey up to that point, and an excellent bibliography.
[48] Martin Wight, 'Why is there no International Theory?' in Herbert Butterfield and Martin Wight (eds.), *Diplomatic Investigations. Essays in the Theory of International Politics* (London: George Allen and Unwin, 1966), p. 25. For a more insightful, brief assessment, see Andrew Linklater, 'Marxism', in Scott Burchill *et al.*, *Theories of International Relations* (Houndmills: Palgrave, 2001; 2nd edn), pp. 129–54.
[49] Evidence of one of its periodical revivals, and weaknesses, can be found in the Special Issue of *International Relations*, vol. 17(4), 2003; see also Andrew Linklater and Hidemi Suganami, *The English School. A Contemporary Reassessment* (Cambridge: Cambridge University Press, 2006).

known as 'the Third World'.[50] These ideas resonated with Johan Galtung's notion of 'structural violence' (to be discussed later), in which he conceptualised inequality as violence, and explained the functional-structural linkages between imperialism and underdevelopment, and domination and dependency.[51] While the workings of the global economy, poverty, and inequality – key issues in Marxian theorising – never extended far into traditional security studies, they did impact on peace research and contemporary thinking about 'human security', as will be discussed later.[52]

Key ideas

Structural interpretations of human society are paramount; material factors determine life and historical change; the dynamics of history are difficult but not impossible to control; ideology is potentially both false consciousness or a factor in revolutionary change; this era is dominated by the global dynamism and power of capitalism, which contains weaknesses and contradictions, and will eventually collapse; class is the primary referent for political and economic activity; world politics is characterised by the pervasiveness of relations between domination and exploitation; imperialism is a ubiquitous feature of global life; taking a global perspective on human society and history is imperative; freedom and equality can be achieved through universal struggles and political solidarity; pursuing emancipation from ignorance and superstition, and promoting democracy, are critical to progress; the cultivation of cosmopolitan solidarities is a key to emancipation; the politics of hope must remember that 'All that is solid melts into air'; human nature changes as humans change nature and the societies in which they live; 'Men make their own history, but they do not make it just as they please; they do not make it under circumstances chosen by themselves';[53] 'philosophers

---

[50] An important work on dependency theory – almost entirely ignored by British and US textbooks on international relations – was Fernando Henrique Cardosa and Enzo Faletto, *Dependency and Development in Latin America*, trans. Marjory Mattingly Urquidi (Berkeley: California University Press, 1979). Richard A. Falk and Samuel S. Kim (eds.), *The War System: An Interdisciplinary Approach* (Boulder, Colo.: Westview Press, 1980), discussed *dependencia* as one of their five theories of imperialism; see 'Socioeconomic Inquiries. Introduction', pp. 371–6.

[51] Falk and Kim's *War System* remains an indispensable reader; see part 5, 'Sociological Inquiries', including the editors' introductory remarks, pp. 371–6.

[52] Note, for example, Caroline Thomas, *Global Governance, Development and Human Security. The Challenge of Poverty and Inequality* (London: Pluto, 2000).

[53] Karl Marx, 'The Eighteenth Brumaire of Louis Bonaparte', in Karl Marx and Frederick Engels, *Selected Works* (London: Lawrence and Wishart, 1991), p. 92.

have only <u>interpreted</u> the world in various ways; the point, however, is to change it'.[54]

Critical international relations theory

The normative realm refers to the nonarbitrary principles that can be used to criticize existing social practices and to imagine improved forms of life; the sociological realm refers to the analysis of the historical development of these principles in past intersocietal systems and in the contemporary society of states; the praxeological realm considers the moral capital that has accumulated in the modern era and that can be exploited to create new forms of political community.

Andrew Linklater's agenda for critical international relations theory[55]

The first three strands of critical theory just outlined had relatively little to say directly about international relations. This final approach makes amends. The point of critical international relations theory (CIRT) is not simply to interpret the Marxian legacy, but to change international relations.[56]

Since the late 1980s, CIRT has been a distinct project, but its proponents have been relatively few and its impact has been limited. Part of the explanation for the latter has been the tension between the varieties of critical thinking comprising CIRT; as in CSS, there has been an unproductive stand-off between those drawn to the legacy of Marx and the Frankfurt school and those drawn to poststructuralist theory and 'continental philosophy'. The foremost theorist of CIRT, Andrew Linklater, has explicitly identified his own approach with a post-Marxist sensibility, though he has sought to build bridges between the various critical strands.[57] Others, such as Hayward Alker and Richard Wyn Jones, have also pointed to the scope for a more productive set of dialogues.[58] The danger of an all-inclusive conception of CIRT (in other words, a project reduced to its lowest common denominator) is that it

[54] Karl Marx, 'Theses on Feuerbach', in *ibid.*, p. 30 (emphasis in original).
[55] Linklater, 'Changing Contours', p. 25.
[56] The key works are Andrew Linklater, *Men and Citizens in the Theory of International Relations* (London: Macmillan, 1982), *Beyond Marxism and Realism: Critical Theory and International Relations* (London: Macmillan, 1990), and *The Transformation of Political Community: Ethical Foundations of the Post-Westphalian Era* (Cambridge: Polity, 1998).
[57] Linklater, 'Changing Contours', p. 23.
[58] Hayward Alker, 'Emancipation in the Critical Security Studies Project', and Richard Wyn Jones, 'On Emancipation: Necessity, Capacity, and Concrete Utopias', both in Booth, *Critical Security Studies*, pp. 189–213 and 215–35.

would become no more than a rag-bag, without a coherent theoretical commitment or political orientation.

The dynamism of CIRT has come from its more explicitly Marxian legacy. It was kick-started by the publication of Richard Ashley's work introducing Habermas, Cox's introducing Gramsci, and then Mark Hoffman's introduction of Horkheimer into academic international relations.[59] The pace gathered. In the 1990s other major contributors to CIRT included Andrew Linklater (who developed late-Frankfurt themes relating to discourse ethics and community), and David Held and his colleagues (who explored the implications of more sophisticated understandings of globalisation and the idea of cosmopolitan democracy).[60] What unified this body of thought, in addition to its post-Marxist sensibility, is democracy. Craig Murphy got it exactly right when he saw this emerging critical theory project being 'today's manifestation of a long-standing democratic impulse in the academic study of international affairs'. In other words, it was academe's contribution to 'egalitarian practice'.[61]

CIRT has attracted criticism: is emancipation, for example, a crucial element in the project, or a distraction?[62] The main point for present purposes, however, is that sophisticated theorising has been taking place in the critical theory tradition in which several classic Marxist concerns (class and production) have been set aside in favour of other Marxian notions, notably changing the world and promoting equality. The agenda for CIRT which Linklater set out in the early 1990s envisaged its 'next stage' as having normative, sociological, and praxeological aims.[63] Linklater's own project at that time was to build on classical Marxism

[59] Richard K. Ashley, 'Political Realism and Human Interests', *International Studies Quarterly*, vol. 25(2), 1981, pp. 204–36, and Mark Hoffman, 'Critical Theory and the Inter-Paradigm Debate', *Millennium*, vol. 16(2), 1987, pp. 231–49.

[60] Linklater, *Men and Citizens*; and David Held, *Democracy and the Global Order: From the Modern State to Cosmopolitan Governance* (Cambridge: Polity, 1995), David Held, Daniele Archibugi, and Martin Köhler (eds.), *Re-imagining Political Community. Studies in Cosmopolitan Democracy* (Cambridge: Polity, 1998), David Held, David Goldblatt, and J. Perraton, *Global Transformations: Politics, Economics and Culture* (Cambridge: Polity, 1999), and David Held and Anthony McGrew, *Globalization/Anti-Globalization* (Cambridge: Polity, 2002).

[61] Craig N. Murphy, 'Critical Theory and the Democratic Impulse: Understanding a Century-Old Tradition', in Wyn Jones, *Critical Theory and World Politics*, pp. 61–76.

[62] Richard Wyn Jones, 'Introduction: Locating Critical International Relations Theory', in *ibid.*, pp. 1–19.

[63] Andrew Linklater, 'The Question of the Next Stage in International Relations Theory: A Critical Theoretical Point of View', *Millennium*, vol. 21(1), 1992, pp. 92–4; see also, Linklater, *Transformation of Political Community*, 'Introduction', esp. p. 11.

'without perpetuating its theoretical fallacies or generating its political consequences'.[64]

CIRT has developed along seven axes. First: *community*. Here issues of inclusion and exclusion are central, together with the relationship between bounded and cosmopolitan citizenship.[65] The idea of political community is central to the security of individuals and groups, and will be discussed at length in subsequent chapters. Two: *ethics*. For Linklater, with Habermas at his shoulder, the project above all involves moving critical theory beyond its origins in materialist theories of history to a commitment to 'dialogic communities that are deeply sensitive about all forms of inclusion and exclusion – domestic, transnational, and international'.[66] Exploring the idea of what it means to be cosmopolitan (that is, regarding all humans as in principle equal, with inherited boundaries such as gender, race, nationality, and so on being regarded as morally insignificant) is central to the ethics of CIRT.[67] Three: *democracy*. The key, and controversial, focus for discussion has been the concept of 'cosmopolitan democracy' – the idea that if democracy anywhere is to flourish, it must be implemented at all levels, including that of states, regional organisations, global functional organisations, and the United Nations.[68] Four: *globalisation*. David Held has been prominent in explaining the processes transforming the spatial organisation of social relations and transactions across the globe at a new stage in history, when the context for international relations is being radically changed in density and momentum.[69] Five: *force*. The emergence of CIRT coincided with the growth in the 1990s of the contested issue of 'humanitarian intervention'. For some its aim was 'solidarist' within the society of

---

[64] Linklater, 'Changing Contours', p. 25.

[65] The issue of citizenship, bounded and cosmopolitan, is debated in Kimberly Hutchings and R. Dannreuther (eds.), *Cosmopolitan Citizenship* (London: Macmillan, 1999).

[66] Andrew Linklater, 'Political Community and Human Security', in Booth, *Critical Security Studies*, pp. 113–31.

[67] Joshua Cohen's edited collection is an outstanding introduction to the debate: *For Love of Country: Debating the Limits of Patriotism* (Boston: Beacon Books, 1996). Useful contributions on the side of cosmopolitanism are Derek Heater, *World Citizenship and Government. Cosmopolitan Ideas in the History of Western Thought* (Houndmills: Macmillan, 1996), and *World Citizenship. Cosmopolitan Thinking and its Opponents* (London: Continuum, 2002); see also Nigel Dower, *An Introduction to Global Citizenship* (Edinburgh: Edinburgh University Press, 2003).

[68] Key works are Held, *Democracy and the Global Order* and Archibugi, Held, and Köhler, *Re-imagining Political Community*. The counter-case is made by David Miller, 'Bounded Citizenship', in Hutchings and Dannreuther, *Cosmopolitan Citizenship*.

[69] See, in particular, Held *et al.*, *Global Transformations* and Jan Aart Scholte, *Globalization: A Critical Introduction* (Basingstoke: Palgrave, 2000).

states,[70] but others saw this as liberal imperialism. The use of force is a particularly troubling issue for those with cosmopolitan sensibilities, for it throws into sharp relief the tension between the aim of delegitimising political violence and the desire to stop massive human rights abuses in conditions where there seems to be no alternative to military intervention.[71] Six: *economics*. The aim here is to challenge orthodox international political economy's claim that economics can be analysed as a purely rational activity to which purely technical solutions are possible. This false separation of economics and politics must be ended by the reconceiving of economics as political economy, especially in global perspective,[72] together with the overcoming of the false separation of ethics and economics.[73] Economic questions are basically questions of human security.[74] Finally, *environment*. This is probably the least-developed area of CIRT, but without doubt a central battlefield for the theory and practice of world politics over the decades to come. Andrew Dobson's view is that a 'thick' cosmopolitanism is required to meet the harms caused by globalisation, based on norms of justice rather than the weaker idea of compassion to all humanity.[75]

While some theorising along these axes is highly abstract – anything involving Habermas, for example[76] – a common feature is a wish to engage with the real world of lived lives and state practice. In Linklater's words: 'Normative arguments . . . are incomplete without a parallel sociological account of how they can be realised in practice . . . and normative and sociological advances are incomplete without some reflection on practical possibilities.'[77] This is theorising *for* common humanity, and as such is basic to any theory of world security.

[70] The major solidarist contribution is Nicholas J. Wheeler, *Saving Strangers: Humanitarian Intervention in International Society* (Oxford: Oxford University Press, 2000).
[71] See Richard Falk, *The Great Terror War* (New York: Olive Branch Press, 2003).
[72] For an explicit linking of CSS and critical IPE, see Roger Tooze, 'The Missing Link: Security, Critical International Political Economy, and Community', in Booth, *Critical Security Studies*, pp. 133–58.
[73] Thomas Pogge, *Realizing Rawls* (Ithaca, N.Y.: Cornell University Press, 1989), presaged an important body of such work.
[74] See Caroline Thomas, *Global Governance, Development and Human Security. The Challenge of Poverty and Inequality* (London: Pluto, 2000).
[75] Andrew Dobson, 'Globalisation, Cosmopolitanism and the Environment', *International Relations*, vol. 19(3), 2005, pp. 259–73.
[76] Some assistance is Michael Pusey, *Jürgen Habermas* (Chichester: Ellis Horwood, 1987), and Stephen K. White (ed.), *The Cambridge Companion to Habermas* (Cambridge: Cambridge University Press, 1995).
[77] Linklater, *Political Community*, p. 10.

Key ideas

Theory and practice can and should go hand-in-hand; all claims to legitimate knowledge should be questioned; political community is a necessary condition for security and emancipation; discourse ethics are a key feature of emancipatory politics, both as process and goal; democracy is an aim and condition of progress, but a diverse process in practice; the key to community is the character of exclusion; community, security, democracy, and emancipation cannot be separated from concerns about the global economy and increasingly the environment; holistic thinking at this point in history means grappling with the implications of globalisation as the new context for all politics, whether between states, classes, genders, races, or animal species; all boundaries are historical, and world politics should be informed by a cosmopolitan sensibility.

Perlenfischerei II: radical international theory

> an affiliation to that polity that exists only in my political imagination as a preferred future, and a commitment to honour its present claims by accepting the obligations to work toward its creation.
>
> Richard Falk, on his academic journey[78]

'Our side' was a phrase used by William Morris, the nineteenth-century socialist, internationalist, agitator, novelist, poet, and visual artist. He had no doubt *who* was on *which* side. His own was 'the side of the people, the wretched of the earth, the dispossessed, the proletariat, the "workers by hand and brain"'; the other was the side of the oppressors, whether imperialists, autocrats, or capitalists.[79] The strand of critical global theorising to be discussed below belongs to *our side*, as understood by Morris. Unlike the approaches discussed earlier, those that follow are generally more explicitly focused on international politics, more explicitly value-oriented, and do not necessarily have an overtly 'critical' epistemology. Having said that, much is shared: if Marx largely directed the light behind the strands of critical global theorising just discussed, Kant (who after all turned on the light) is the critical figure in the strands below.

[78] Richard A. Falk, 'Manifesting World Order: A Scholarly Manifesto', in Joseph Kruzel and James N. Rosenau (eds.), *Journeys through World Politics* (Lexington, Mass.: Lexington Books, 1989), p. 155; see also his *A Study of Future Worlds* (New York: Free Press, 1975), *The Promise of World Order. Essays in Normative International Relations* (Brighton: Wheatsheaf Books, 1987), and *Human Rights Horizons. The Pursuit of Justice in a Globalizing World* (New York: Routledge, 2000).
[79] I owe this reference to Chris Brown, whose sceptical understanding of critical theorising is hard to beat: see '"Our Side"?' pp. 191–203 (quotation at p. 192).

If Horkheimer was correct in claiming that there is no neutral historical knowledge (in other words, no objective truth), and if Cox was correct in claiming that theory is always *for* somebody or *for* some thing, then who or what is international theory *for*? The radical approaches to the discipline explored below (the World Order school, feminist theorising, historical sociology, peace research, and social idealism) have no doubts, as we shall see. Whether or not you are interested in theory, theory is interested in you, and the radical international theorising in these approaches is *for* 'our side'. This is evident in its targets: inequality, patriarchy, statism, war, and regressive traditional ideas. I believe that *radical* is a better term to describe these strands of international relations theory than *normative*, though the mainstream discipline often prefers the latter. Normative is unsatisfactory for two reasons: first, all international theory has normative implications, either in a weak or strong form; and second, to call some theorising normative just because it is explicit about its values plays into the hands of those who want to claim that somewhere there is a class of international relations theory that is neutral.

The World Order school

The road leading to destruction is easy because it is familiar. The road toward achieving peace, economic well-being, justice, and ecological balance is difficult and unfamiliar but promises some hope. Travelling down that road . . . depends upon a popular movement fuelled by our own imagination and willingness to act.

Robert C. Johansen in *The National Interest and the Human Interest*[80]

The World Order school has been best known through it organisational manifestation, the World Order Models Project (WOMP). Its proponents have explicitly embraced a combination of concerns: analytical, empirical, and normative within a world perspective.

Richard Falk, the foremost international relations scholar associated with WOMP, once observed that he had been struck by his own 'marginality' when compared with other colleagues. He was right. Unaware of Falk's work at the time, only his name, I recall one (British) professor telling me that I ought not to waste my time on it. Things have not changed much. There remains a striking absence of the World Order approach in both introductory teaching texts and volumes for graduates. Given that inequality across world society has been a primary concern of World Order theorists, its marginalisation by Anglo-American

[80] Robert C. Johansen, *The National Interest and the Human Interest. An Analysis of U.S. Foreign Policy* (Princeton, N.J.: Princeton University Press, 1980), p. 407.

professors speaks volumes. As a distinct project, therefore, the World Order approach cannot be judged a great success, and not least because the dissemination of its ideas and knowledge was one of its original aims. That said, it has been illuminating for many individuals. I include myself in this, as I learned to unlearn some of the things I had been taught as a student. Even some critics have been admirers. Hedley Bull paid Falk a generous tribute in *The Anarchical Society*, and it is worth noting that some of Bull's own work subsequently became more explicitly progressive.[81]

In the early 1960s Falk and his associate Saul Mendlowitz were concerned with a theory of social change that reasoned that most individuals on the globe (and especially political leaders) were encapsulated in a view of the world in which they believed that war, while perhaps unfortunate, was a necessary and permanent ingredient in human society. They began to distribute educational materials to dispel such widely held views, and in 1968 formally established the World Order Models Project (WOMP). The concern to abolish war was the driver in the institutionalising of the approach, and the perspective promoted was explicitly universalist, to counter what Julius Stone called the 'nationalisation of truth'.[82] This resulted in the exploration of ideas about common humanity, peace plans, non-violence, democracy, and justice. Importantly, the World Order approach sought to show that these issues had not only been explored from within the Western tradition.[83]

The attempt to broaden the focus of scholarly interest beyond the Anglo-American mainstream served at least three major purposes. First, it was a guard against the pitfalls of ethnocentrism. These have been pervasive in the discipline, including the study of strategy as security.[84] Second, it guards against theorising that is too abstract. When thinking about security is divorced from area studies, it is largely thinking in a void. Finally, a better sense of thoughtways beyond one's own reveals important dimensions of the universal. It can reveal the extent to which ideas travel, and also the fact that what matters politically is how they resonate across peoples, not what their origin may have been.

---

[81] Hedley, Bull, *The Anarchical Society. A Study of Order in World Politics* (London: Macmillan, 1977), esp. pp. ix, 148–50, 293–5, 302–5; Bull's (explicitly) normative work was best expressed in *Justice in International Relations. The Hagey Lectures* (Waterloo, Ontario: University of Waterloo, 1984).
[82] Quoted by Falk, 'Manifesto', p. 157.
[83] The ideas of Gandhi were given prominence in Falk and Kim's reader; see Margaret W. Fisher, 'Contrasting Approaches to Conflict', in Falk and Kim, *The War System*, pp. 58–73.
[84] This is the theme of Ken Booth, *Strategy and Ethnocentrism* (London: Croom Helm, 1979).

A particularly helpful contribution confronting all these problems (and with the additional advantage of focusing on India, a remarkably neglected state in mainstream international relations) is Amartya Sen's *The Argumentative Indian*.[85] The book is rich in illustration of themes challenging both regressive ethnocentric attitudes and those of proponents of incommensurability between cultures. Three illustrations will suffice. First, Sen tells us that it was 'a Buddhist emperor of India, Ashoka, who, in the third century BCE, not only outlined the need for toleration and the richness of heterodoxy, but also laid down what are perhaps the oldest rules for conducting debates and disputations, with the opponents being "duly honoured in every way on all occasions"'.[86] Second, it was a Muslim Indian emperor, Akbar, who powerfully defended toleration and 'the need for the state to be equidistant from different religions' at a time when the Inquisition 'was in full swing in Europe'.[87] Third, Rabindranath Tagore, the major figure in the literature of Bengal, which goes back over a thousand years, would confound believers in the 'clash of civilisation' thesis, for his work flourished in the context of growing up in a Bengali family he described as 'a confluence of three cultures, Hindu, Mohammedan and British'. He opposed cultural separatism and encouraged open debate on all issues; according to Sen 'It is in the sovereignty of reasoning – fearless reasoning in freedom – that we can find Rabindranath Tagore's lasting voice.'[88]

As defined by Mendlowitz in its early days, WOMP was a global association of scholars and political activists engaged in promoting a 'just world order' through research, education, dialogue, and action.[89] These scholars understood the world to be facing a set of interrelated threats – war, poverty, social injustice, ecological instability, and alienation – requiring an analytical/ethical scheme looking towards solutions based around certain 'world order values'. The latter have been described by WOMP proponents in various ways over the years, but they always coalesce around non-violence, economic justice, humane governance, ecological sustainability, and human rights.[90] What the pursuit of such values means in concrete settings is always open to debate, but the spirit

---

[85] Amartya Sen, *The Argumentative Indian. Writings on Indian Culture, History and Identity* (London: Penguin Books, 2006).

[86] *Ibid.*, pp. xii–xiii; see also pp. 15–18, 284–9.   [87] *Ibid.*, pp. xiii, 39–42, 287–93.

[88] *Ibid.*, pp. 90, 118–20.

[89] Saul H. Mendlowitz, *On the Creation of a Just World Order* (New York: The Free Press, 1975).

[90] Richard Falk, *Explorations at the Edge of Time. The Prospects for World Order* (Temple, Pa.: Philadelphia University Press, 1992), pp. 56–103.

of the approach demands that contradictions be avoided: violence is not the way to eradicate violence, as will be discussed later. The grounds on which they base their world order values vary between scholars. Some point to shared religious values, others to reason; what counts, ultimately, is not the metaphysical foundation for action, but the practices of a just world order.

WOMPers have been criticised for being a group of idealists ignoring power, but this is unfair: trying to reorganise power in the human interest has been a consistent aim.[91] Falk described his approach to power as involving

> studying the extent to which a given past, present and future arrangement of power and authority is able to realize a set of human goals that are affirmed as beneficial for all people and apply to the whole world, and achieve some objectivity by a connection with a conception of basic human needs, as required for the healthy development of the human person.[92]

Traditional patterns of power, and especially the ongoing states system, are challenged as neither natural nor defensible. Power therefore needed to be reorganised, with the aim of promoting humane networks of governance both above and below the state. Rejecting the excessive centralisation of power at the state level, Falk wrote (long before such views were common) that 'the state is . . . both inhumanly large in its bureaucratic dimension, and inhumanly small in its territorial and exclusionary dimensions'. Global reform along these lines therefore required a diffusion of power, upwards to further global functionalism and downwards to decentralise power at the level of state governments.[93]

Identifying World Order values is only the starting-point; the biggest challenge is to put them into practice in a multicultural, interstate, gendered world of multiple ethnicities, and find (or support) influential agents to advance them. In Gramscian terms, this means overthrowing global common sense in the interest of humanity, and supporting organic intellectuals. World Order proponents have attempted to provide students (defined widely) with better intellectual resources,

---

[91] See Johansen, *National Interest*, for a good example.
[92] Falk, *Peace and World Order Studies*, p. 6.
[93] Richard A. Falk, 'Anarchism and World Order', in Falk and Kim, *War System*, pp. 37–57; this article, first published in 1978, ranks among the most thought-provoking (and short) articles in the field, yet never appears in standard collections.

such as transnational perspectives on major issues.[94] A less familiar dimension of the World Order approach has been the aim of promoting what in later chapters will be called 'non-dualistic behaviour'. In contrast to the utopian, 'who tends to dichotomize present and future, regarding one mode as suitable given present practicalities and another as desirable given future wishes', Falk suggested that the best path is to integrate present behaviour and future hopes, because 'the future is the eventual culmination of the present and . . . liberty is an existential condition enabling degrees of immediate realization'.[95] Such an integration of the present and the future is an essential feature of a critical theory of security.

The World Order approach has frequently been criticised, when it has not actually been marginalised by the international relations orthodoxy. It has been variously attacked for being ideological, vague, prescriptive, elitist, and utopian.[96] Some specific work is guilty-as-charged, but most criticisms are misplaced or easily countered. Against the charge of being prescriptive, for example, WOMP began at a time when the world faced the threat of catastrophic nuclear war. WOMPers felt justified in asking whether traditional 'disinterested' scholarship was a luxury in such a situation. Professing explicit values (rather than disguising insider-theorising underneath a cloak of disinterestedness) and believing in the empirical relevance of theory (rather than seeing theory as separate from practice) have been defended by WOMPers as not only epistemologically sophisticated and professionally honest, but also perfectly consistent with a commitment to the scholarly virtues of respect for evidence, care for language, and an appreciation of logic.

Key ideas

In academic work, values should be brought out into the open; the species must be the primary referent for theorising rather than historically constructed divisions of humans delineated by sovereign

---

[94] In addition to Falk, see the work notably of Johan Galtung, *The True Worlds: A Transnational Perspective* (New York: The Free Press, 1980); see also his *There Are Alternatives: Four Roads to Peace and Security* (Nottingham: Spokesman, 1984), and *Peace by Peaceful Means: Peace and Conflict, Development and Civilisation* (London: Sage, with the International Peace Research Institute, 1996). Peter Lawler, *A Question of Values. Johan Galtung's Peace Research* (Boulder, Colo.: Lynne Rienner, 1995) is an essential analysis, and contains an extensive bibliography of Galtung's work up to the mid-1990s.
[95] Falk, 'Anarchism', p. 42.
[96] Mark Neufeld, 'Pitfalls of Emancipation and Discourses of Security: Reflections on Canada's "Security With a Human Face"', *International Relations* vol. 18(1), 2003, pp. 109–23.

states and other contingent institutions; human suffering should be prioritised in world order theorising; individuals do not exist in an atomised fashion but have a mutually constitutive relationship with societies and communities; the plurality of actors and agents in world politics should be emphasised; statism is a problem rather than the solution in overcoming major global issues; the orthodox emphasis on 'national interests' (the maximisation of state prosperity and security) should be readdressed in favour of emphasising human needs; the power-political emphasis on conflictual interactions should be readdressed in favour of emphasising all significant interactions, including networks of cooperation; the promotion of world order values requires agency beyond states, and looks to progressive social movements to construct new agendas, and be the agents of change; social-scientific claims to knowledge should be treated sceptically; power should not simply be reduced to material factors, but understood in relation to ideas, ideologies, images, religious preferences, and so on; centralised and concentrated power should be distrusted; humans live in a multicultural world and our study of it should reflect this, rather than succumbing to ethnocentrism; harmony with a sense of common destiny is the goal; human survival is problematic unless the future is given priority; key world order values, which promote a common destiny and sense of community are non-violence, care for the environment, good governance, economic justice, and human rights.

Peace studies/peace research

In time we can predict that every piece of fashionable nonsense will disappear by itself, provided only that people are firm in their opposition to it. In the case of Peace Studies, however, firm opposition has yet to exist, and until it exists the political manipulation of children will continue unhindered.

Caroline Cox and Roger Scruton in *Peace Studies.*
A Critical Survey (1984)

the charge entered against peace studies by Dr Robert [sic] Scruton is that it is "intellectually vapid" and not a proper discipline . . . The argument is a reds-under-the-bed herring.

Editorial, *Times Higher Educational Supplement*[97]

---

[97] Caroline Cox and Roger Scruton, *Peace Studies. A Critical Survey* (London: Alliance Publishers Ltd for the Institute for European Defence and Strategic Studies, 1984); and *THES*, 21 September 1984.

According to one text, 'Peace studies is a transformative project which seeks to construct alternative accounts of social and political realities and therefore takes place simultaneously in the domains of theory, research, practice, and activism.'[98] Peace studies/peace research (I will use the terms interchangeably) began with the aim of seeking to understand war in order to eliminate it, and then, over time, broadened it to seek to understand the manifold expressions of conflict, in order to eradicate them. In time, the two strands of thought converged into the formula that the best way to eliminate war/conflict is to construct a stable peace.

From the start, peace studies was explicitly multidisciplinary,[99] and this has been one obstacle to its development as a separately organised discipline or sub-discipline (like chemistry or English literature). Another has been its reputation for being 'political'. During the Cold War, peace researchers were often seen in establishment circles as being the advanced guard of the left, and warned that they were doing the work of the Kremlin. In Britain, for example, the intellectual stormtroopers of the Iron Lady were unleashed.[100] As it happened, the Reagan administration and the Thatcher government strongly rebuffed ideas that were being explored and advocated by the peace studies community (notably common defence, non-provocative defence, and détente) though these ideas found ready listeners in eastern European civil society and in Gorbachev's inner circle.[101] Contrary to right-wing propaganda, the ideas of the Western peace movement took over the Kremlin, not vice versa. And contrary to expectations, Reagan became a convert to nuclear disarmament.[102]

Peace studies grew into a broad church, and it would be a mistake to think of it as simply a sub-field of academic international

---

[98] Martin Griffiths and Terry O'Callaghan, *International Relations. The Key Concepts* (London: Routledge: 2002), p. 241.

[99] The multidisciplinarity is evident, for example, in Leslie E. Sponsel and Thomas Gregor (eds.), *The Anthropology of Peace and Nonviolence* (Boulder, Colo.: Lynne Rienner, 1994).

[100] This outburst of anti-peace studies hysteria deserves fuller study while most participants are still alive. In addition to contemporary newspaper letter pages and editorials, the following, by key players, should be studied: Cox and Scruton, *Peace Studies*; and James O'Connell and Adam Curle, *Peace with Work to Do* (Leamington Spa: Berg, 1985). Brief overviews of the issues are: Colin Gordon, 'Problems of "Peace Studies"', *The Council for Arms Control Bulletin*, no. 10, September 1983, and Elizabeth Richards, 'The Debate about Peace Education', *Background Paper* no. 10 (Canadian Institute for International Peace and Security, December 1986).

[101] Ken Booth and Nicholas J. Wheeler, *The Security Dilemma: Fear, Cooperation, and Trust in World Politics* (Houndmills: Palgrave, 2008), ch. 6.

[102] *Ibid.*

relations.[103] In addition to welcoming international relations scholars, of course, peace studies has built upon the work of sociologists, psychologists, development studies specialists, and anthropologists.[104] One feature of peace studies teaching has been a deliberate engagement with 'the real world', attempting to get students involved with local community work or broader global issues, as part of 'learning by doing'.[105]

Terry Terriff and his colleagues have identified five phases in the development of peace studies.[106] The first was that of interwar idealism associated with the League of Nations, disarmament, and Wilsonian optimism. International institutions were a particular focus of interest. The second phase coincided with the early Cold War, when the dangers of a nuclear catastrophe provoked interest in developing ideas about conflict resolution, arms control, and disarmament. The 1950s was also the time of the behavioural revolution in the social sciences, and of 'scientism' and interdisciplinary projects in peace studies (evident in the interest in game theory, for example). In the 1960s and 1970s, the third phase, the focus of peace studies widened, from East/West to North/South issues. Interest grew in problems of global inequality, political economy, social justice, and the manifestations of all forms of conflict and violence. Methodologically, a challenge began to the presumed objectivity of social science. Peace studies in the 1980s, the fourth phase, returned to superpower concerns, with the Second Cold War reviving fears about nuclear war. Spurred on by the growth of peace movements in society generally, Western peace researchers concentrated their work on arms racing and crises, nuclear strategy and multilevel disarmament,

---

[103] For a flavour of early post-Cold War peace studies, see the interesting collection of essays by Robert Elias and Jennifer Turpin (eds.), *Rethinking Peace* (Boulder, Colo.: Lynne Rienner, 1994).

[104] The tone of the growing field was well illustrated by two early figures in the University of Bradford School of Peace Studies: Adam Curle, 'Peace Studies', in *The Yearbook of World Affairs 1976* (London: Brassey's, 1977), pp. 5–13, and Nigel Young, 'Educating the Peace Educators', *Bulletin of Peace Proposals*, no. 2, 1981, pp. 123–35.

[105] Michael T. Klare (ed.), *Peace and World Security Studies. A Curriculum Guide* (Boulder, Colo.: Lynne Rienner from the 5th edn, and earlier the Transnational Academic Program, New York) have provided students and teachers with excellent study guides from 1972 onwards.

[106] This overview is based on Terry Terriff and his colleagues, 'Peace Studies', in Terry Terriff, Stuart Croft, Lucy James, and Patrick M. Morgan, *Security Studies Today* (Cambridge: Polity, 1999), pp. 65–81; a longer and more detailed survey by an insider, though less chronological in approach, is David J. Dunn, *The First Fifty Years of Peace Research. A Survey and Interpretation* (Aldershot: Ashgate, 2005); a shorter, thematic overview by two other insiders is Paul Rogers and Oliver Ramsbotham, 'Then and Now: Peace Research – Past and Future', *Political Studies*, vol. 47, 1999, pp. 740–54 (n. 5, p. 741 gives a helpful list of reviews of the history of peace research).

'alternative defence' and common security. Finally, the period since the end of the Cold War has seen the development of a broader agenda and the spread of diverse methodologies. New concerns have included gender issues, non-state actors, environmental security, food and welfare issues, and the global South generally. Methodologically, there has been some engagement with the critical turn that took place in the social sciences more broadly.[107]

The proponents of peace studies have shared a commitment to peace as a value, a topic normally ignored by scholars in strategic studies. The latter, like the cynic Ambrose Bierce, have tended to dismiss peace as 'a period of cheating between two periods of fighting', rather than a complex, multilevel, and multifaceted condition.[108] The journey of peace research has gone from 'negative' to 'positive' peace; from concern with interstate relations to matters affecting empires, nations, classes, genders, ethnicities; from stopping war to 'transcending and transforming' comprehensively; and from statist referents downwards to individuals and upwards to Gaia. Overcoming violence, however, has been constant, though the understanding of violence has also broadened.[109] A major milestone in this regard was Johan Galtung's invention of the notion of 'structural violence' in the mid-1960s.[110] Its focus on oppression, and implicitly on the need for emancipation, shifted the perspective from the causes of war to creating the conditions of peace. In this simple move, Galtung reoriented peace research. War ceased to be approached narrowly, but came to be seen as a comprehensive socio-economic process needing a comparably broad response.[111] In short, the elimination of war was not primarily to be achieved through strengthening international

---

[107] For a notable example, see Heikki Pattomäki, 'The Challenge of Critical Theories: Peace Research at the Start of the New Century', *Journal of Peace Research*, vol. 38(6), 2001, pp. 723–37.

[108] Ambrose Bierce, *The Devil's Dictionary* (Toronto: Coles, 1978), p. 98. The two approaches are compared in David J. Dunn, 'Peace Research Versus Strategic Studies', in Ken Booth (ed.), *New Thinking about Strategy and International Security* (London: HarperCollins Academic, 1991), pp. 56–72.

[109] Christopher Mitchell, 'Conflict Research', in A. J. R. Groom and Margot Light (eds.), *Contemporary International Relations: A Guide to Theory* (London: Pinter, 1994), pp. 128–41; Emanuel Adler, 'Condition(s) of Peace', *Review of International Studies*, vol. 24(4), 1998, pp. 165–91; Pattomäki, 'The Challenge of Critical Theories'.

[110] Galtung's seminal contribution was 'A Structural Theory of Imperialism', *Journal of Peace Research*, vol. 8(1), 1971 (reprinted in Falk and Kim, *The War System*, pp. 402–55); see also his 'A Structural Theory of Imperialism – Ten Years Later', *Millennium*, vol. 9(3), 1980, pp. 183–96, Kenneth Boulding, 'Twelve Friendly Quarrels with Johan Galtung', *Journal of Peace Research*, vol. 14(1), 1977, pp. 75–86, and Lawler, *Question of Values*, pp. 72–3.

[111] *The War System* explicitly adopts such an approach; see Falk and Kim, 'General Introduction', pp. 1–12.

institutions (a particular concern in the 1920s) but through the building up of a comprehensive structure of social justice.

Politics is overt in peace studies, in a way it has never been in strategic/national security studies (where it is invisible to its practitioners behind a claim of objectivity). One effect of the broadening of the agenda of peace research since the end of the Cold War, according to Lucy James, has been that it came to embrace 'the left's goal of equality with the right's goal of freedom and personal growth'.[112] Human rights became more central, with the idea of the liberation of individuals from '*all* dynamics of violence . . . and all impediments to self-realisation'. For many, this meant a shift to the individual as the key unit of analysis, rather than the state or ethnic group or class. In addition to the established concerns with life in the majority world (development, neocolonialism, imperialism, racism) peace research fed and was fed by the increasingly prominent 'human security' agenda in the 1990s (discussed in chapter 7). To some extent these developments have led to the attenuation of the traditional concern with non-violence, as value and tactic, though it is still there.[113]

Peace studies have survived many challenges, and have a secure place in a number of countries. The subject continues to be seen as idealistic, even as it seems to converge in its agenda and approaches with the study of international relations. For those interested in developing a critical theory of world security it remains an important resource for ideas. In particular, the intellectual giants of the tradition – Kenneth Boulding, Anatol Rapoport, Johan Galtung and others – are a sadly neglected group of thinkers for all students of contemporary international relations.

Key ideas

Peace is a positive as well as a negative concept; violence should be understood as a structural phenomenon and not simply the use of brute force; normative concerns are implicit in scholarship, so be explicit; multidisciplinarity is a rational approach to a war system that is a complex phenomenon; while the focus on weapons and strategy of traditional security studies must remain on the agenda, the preoccupations (insecurities) of people(s) outside the rich core nations

---

[112] Terriff *et al.*, *Security Studies*, p. 74.

[113] April Carter, 'Nonviolence as a Strategy for Change', in Paul Smoker, Ruth Davies, and Barbara Munske (eds.), *Reader in Peace Studies* (Oxford: Pergamon Press, 1995).

must be given full recognition; conflict prevention and resolution are neglected but promising areas for research and policy; fieldwork of a traditional nature is important, as is 'learning by doing'; power needs to be understand comprehensively; mainstream notions of development, the role of the state, the neoliberal world economy and other conventional wisdom should be challenged; empirical work is critical, and in this social science methods can sometimes play a useful role; peace is a wider concept than traditionally conceived in international relations.

Feminist theorising

We'll Kill You If You Cry
Title of Human Rights Watch report describing rape by UN
peacekeepers[114]

During the prologue, course, and aftermath of the US/British war in Iraq in 2003, my wife kept asking the question Cynthia Enloe taught us all: 'Where are the women?'[115] Women in Iraq were invisible in the run-up to the war, and after the victorious invasion by the most powerful military machine in the world against one of the most eroded; there were no women rushing up to tanks throwing flowers and kisses at the liberators as happened in north-western Europe in 1944. Iraqi women became somewhat more visible after the war, as Western TV screens showed them fanning wounded children in hospitals in which there was little air and few drugs; we then saw them wailing after disasters, holding children in columns of refugees and asking for water. No women were evident in the parades celebrating the overthrow of Saddam; nor did they join the looters. They were not evident in the burgeoning protests against the Americans, and certainly did not appear to be fighting alongside 'the insurgents' and others spreading violence through that benighted country. As terrorism and counter-terrorism escalated, women again became visible as victims, sometimes vocally. On the Western side, in the run-up and course of the war there were a few shrewd female regional experts on TV, a number of wannabe Lee Millers out in the field, and several female defence analysts strategising with the guys. We did not see shots

[114] Quoted by Julia Stuart, 'Dark Side of Peacekeeping', *The Independent Review*, 10 July 2003.
[115] Cynthia Enloe, *Bananas, Beaches, and Bases: Making Feminist Sense of International Politics* (Berkeley: University of California Press, 2000; 1st edn 1989), p. 7.

of female soldiers in the US military actually fighting, but we knew they were there. The Pentagon, when the opportunity arose, re-emphasised Hollywood stereotypes, with the image of brave (male) US soldiers saving pretty Private Lynch (though we did not know at the time that it had been staged).[116] When it could not avoid the bad publicity, the Pentagon had to accept that some of its female soldiers had been complicit in the sexualised torture of prisoners. By enquiring where the women are, and what they are doing, it is possible to learn a great deal about the way the world works. Dictators come and go, but the tyranny of patriarchy still reigns, ok?

Patriarchy (literally the 'rule of the father') is central to feminist theorising. It describes 'the totality of oppressive and exploitative relations which affect women';[117] in other words, it is a 'system of male authority which oppresses women through its social, political and economic institutions.' Feminist theorising invariably sees male domination as a cultural phenomenon, crossing space and time, though within that generality different feminist themes offer different interpretations of the nature of women's subordination. Socialist and Marxist feminists locate patriarchy in a materialist context, for example.[118] Other feminist approaches include (in alphabetical order) existentialist, liberal, postmodern, poststructuralist, psychoanalytic, radical, standpoint, and Third World theorising. What unites them is their concern with the category of gender, as they stand outside the clichéd 'malestream'.[119] Radical feminism is the most essentialist approach, identifying men's 'physiology' at the root of politics and society. Its essential voice, Catharine MacKinnon, conducted a triple attack on the political, religious, and sexual centrality of male power, arguing that men's 'inability to get along with each other . . . defines history, their image defines god, and their genitals define sex'.[120] Whatever the strand of feminist theorising, men are understood to be the defining, normal, dominant gender, the

---

[116] She herself said later: 'I don't think it happened quite like that' and 'They used me as a way to symbolize this stuff.' Quoted in Eliot Weinberger, *What Happened Here. Bush Chronicles* (London: Verso, 2006), p. 154.

[117] Maggie Humm, *The Dictionary of Feminist Theory* (Hemel Hempstead: Harvester Wheatsheaf, 1989), p. 159.

[118] For a critique of the Marxist feminist perspective from a socialist feminist, see Alison M. Jaggar, *Feminist Politics and Human Nature* (Totowa, N.J.: Rowman and Allanheld, 1983).

[119] A good survey of the variety and richness of feminist theorising (though sadly with little about international relations) is Rosemarie Tong, *Feminist Thought. A Comprehensive Introduction* (London: Routledge, 1992).

[120] Catharine A. MacKinnon, *Feminism Unmodified* (Cambridge, Mass.: Harvard University Press, 1987), p. 36.

epitome of the species. The struggle for feminists, as Simone de Beauvoir famously discussed it, is for women to overcome being *The Second Sex*, man's transcultural, transhistorical Other.[121]

Gender is the idea that what shapes these top/subordinate social and other attitudes and behaviour is culture not biology.[122] As Ann Tickner has put it in the context of international relations: 'Unless we recognise gender as a category of analysis, we cannot understand how gender relations of inequality act to exclude women from the business of foreign policymaking and ensure that they are located disproportionately at the bottom of the socioeconomic scale in all societies.'[123] Having recognised the problem, the challenge is then to 'recover women's experiences'. Security has been one area where feminist empirical work was minimal for a long time, and is still in short supply,[124] though women and peace has always been a focus of concern, especially for radical feminists.[125] Those feminists working in security studies have sought to de-naturalise the dominant framework of patriarchal assumptions, explanations, understandings, and prescriptions; the latter have all been attacked as gendered, and so much so that most people have been unaware of it.[126]

Feminist theorising offers empirical, historical, and theoretical richness to the study of politics and society, and as such might have been welcomed by those interested in international relations, but the orthodoxy (especially traditional security studies) has been notoriously unfriendly to women. Few today would be as blatantly sexist as Donald Regan, President Reagan's National Security Adviser, who proclaimed in 1985: 'Women are not going to understand missile throw-weights or what

---

[121] Simone de Beauvoir, *The Second Sex* (New York: Vintage Books, 1974; first published 1953).

[122] For a radical statement on the way gender structures live, see Shulamith Firestone, *The Dialectic of Sex: The Case for Feminist Revolution* (New York: William Morrow, 1970).

[123] J. Ann Tickner, 'Searching for the Princess? Feminist Perspectives in International Relations', *Harvard International Review*, Vol. 21(4), 1999, p. 48.

[124] A major contribution, therefore, was J. Ann Tickner's *Gender in International Relations: Feminist Perspectives on Achieving Global Security* (New York: Columbia University Press, 1992); see also her 'You Just Don't Understand: Troubled Engagements Between Feminists and IR Theorists', *International Studies Quarterly*, vol. 41(4), 1997, pp. 611–32, and *Gendering World Politics* (New York: Columbia University Press, 2001).

[125] Radical feminists have figured prominently here. See Betty Reardon, *Sexism and the War System* (New York: Teachers College Press, 1985), Birgit Brock-Utne, *Educating for Peace: A Feminist Perspective* (Oxford: Pergamon Press, 1985), and Sara Ruddick, *Maternal Thinking: Towards a Politics of Peace* (Boston: Beacon Press, 1989).

[126] For a brief summary see Steve Smith, 'The Contested Concept of Security', in Booth, *Critical Security Studies*, pp. 46–8.

is happening in Afghanistan . . . most women would rather read the human interest stuff.'[127] He gave the phrase 'human interest' a particular meaning, of course, far removed from its conceptualisation by critical theorists. His ability completely to separate issues relating to missile throw-weights and human interest was even more breathtaking than his sexism. Few these days would be as crass as Regan on these matters, but President Bush's Secretary of Defense Donald Rumsfeld tried his best. In April 2006, he made several patronising comments about the opinions expressed on the Iraq War by Condoleezza Rice, his President's choice for Secretary of State.[128]

A priority in feminist theorising has been to uncover what has not been seen, and to 'know it for the first time'. In this regard, I recall a senior (male) figure in the discipline remarking how Enloe's landmark book, *Bananas, Beaches and Bases* had hit him between the eyes on first reading it, and how it had changed fundamentally how he thought about studying the world. Many of us (including many women) have had the same experience: we have discovered that what we thought was natural as we were growing up was cultural, expressing the traditional power of patriarchy.[129] Revealing the complex way in which power works remains one of the tasks of feminist theorising, and Enloe, for one, has criticised orthodox academic international relations for prioritising efficiency of explanation over engaging with life's true complexity. In her words: 'Underestimating the amounts and kinds of power operating in the world is the hallmark of *non*feminist analysis.'[130] These more complex (feminist) analyses of power have developed the idea, for example, that 'the personal is international' and *'the international is personal'*.[131] Following through this insight, Tickner has written that feminist definitions of security come out of 'different literatures and . . . definitions based on different ontologies as well as different normative goals' to mainstream international relations.[132] While Tickner was correct to emphasise the different ontologies and normative goals deriving from

[127] Quoted by Tickner, 'Searching for the Princess?' p. 45.
[128] Julian Borger, 'Rumsfeld and Rice Fall Out over War Tactics', *The Guardian*, 8 April 2006. When Rumsfeld told a radio audience he did not know what Rice was talking about when she spoke of 'tactical errors' in the war, he certainly meant (and almost certainly meant it in a similar way to Regan) that *she* did not know what she was talking about.
[129] Note Enloe's own experience: 'Becoming a Feminist: Cynthia Enloe in Conversation with Three British International Relations Scholars', in Cynthia Enloe, *The Curious Feminist. Searching for Women in a New Age of Empire* (Berkeley: University of California Press, 2004), pp. 155–89; also, Booth, 'Security and Self', pp. 100–1.
[130] Enloe, *Bananas*, p. xiv.   [131] *Ibid.*, pp. 195–6.
[132] Tickner, 'You Just Don't Understand', p. 625.

gendered mindsets, Jean Elshtain has warned against any essentialising of the difference between males and females on the basic ontological level, casting the one sex as corrupt and violent and the other sex as innocent and nurturing.[133] In the same spirit, Brooke A. Ackerly envisioned 'feminism as *humanism*'.[134]

An important role of feminist thinkers has been to make more visible the work done by those women who have written about security-related issues. Of particular significance here was the way Carol Cohn showed how ideas about nuclear strategy and defence in general are genderised by language (and dehumanised).[135] Enloe, as mentioned earlier, has been at the forefront of making women's work visible. Initially, she showed its significance in the functioning of the international military system (such as sex-workers around bases), the diplomatic system (diplomatic wives), and the international political economy (cheap labour);[136] she then uncovered the manifold manifestations of militarisation, which affect not only the obvious people (executives of companies making fighter aircraft) but women in many parts of the economy.[137] Not surprisingly, feminist work has examined matters of closest concern to women. The long-suppressed wrong of rape in war has been particularly prominent.[138] One by product of this was new insight into military practices as a result of clarifying the work done by masculinity.[139] Historical work also revealed masculinity's frailties. One victim of rape following Germany's military collapse in 1945 recorded:

---

[133] Susan Brownmiller, *Against Our Will: Men, Women and Rape* (New York: Simon and Schuster, 1975), pp. 14 15, and Jean Bethke Elshtain, *Public Man, Private Woman* (Princeton, N.J.: Princeton University Press, 1981), p. 228.
[134] Brooke A. Ackerly, *Political Theory and Feminist Social Criticism* (Cambridge: Cambridge University Press, 2000).
[135] Carol Cohn, 'Sex and Death in the Rational World of Defense Intellectuals', *Signs: Journal of Women in Culture and Society*, vol. 12(4), 1987, pp. 687–718; and 'War, Wimps, and Women: Talking Gender and Thinking War', in M. Cooke and A. Wollacott (eds.), *Gendering War Talk* (Princeton, N.J.: Princeton University Press, 1993), pp. 227–46.
[136] Enloe, *Bananas*.
[137] Cynthia Enloe, *Maneuvers. The International Politics of Militarizing Women's Lives* (Berkeley: University of California Press, 2000), and *Curious Feminist*, parts two and three.
[138] Brownmiller, *Against Our Will*, is the standard reference; for a survey of the decisive experience of the 1990s, see Caroline Kennedy-Pipe and Penny Stanley, 'Rape in War: Lessons of the Balkan Conflicts in the 1990s', in Ken Booth (ed.), *The Kosovo Tragedy. The Human Rights Dimensions* (London: Frank Cass, 2001), pp. 67–84.
[139] This is even the case in 'peacekeeping': see Sandra Whitworth, *Men, Militarism, and UN Peacekeeping: A Gendered Analysis* (Boulder, Colo.: Lynne Rienner, 2004) and 'Militarized Masculinities and the Politics of Peacekeeping', in Booth, *Critical Security Studies*, pp. 89–106.

'Among the many defeats at the end of this war is the defeat of the male sex.'[140]

Just as feminist empirical work has sought to strip the veils away from the face of traditional ('naturalised') structures of power, feminist theoretical work has revealed the masculinist mindset behind normalised theory.[141] Tickner importantly reconceived Hans J. Morgenthau's famous 'six principles of realism'.[142] Carol Pateman reconceptualised Rousseau's famous declaration 'Man is born free, but everywhere he is in chains' – a sentence that can only be read with irony by any feminist.[143] Similar reworking has been done on more contemporary political theorists by Susan Okin, among others.[144] Nancy Fraser and Brooke Ackerly have pointed to the gender 'blindspots' of the Frankfurt school giant, Habermas.[145] Of particular interest to students of security, Rebecca Grant produced an original re-reading of the security dilemma from a feminist perspective.[146]

Feminist theorists remain a somewhat beleaguered group within international relations. They are criticised from many sides: for not understanding 'the real world'; for their middle-class bias; for generalising from a distinctively 'Western' position;[147] for overgeneralising; for overlooking other referents (notably men); for dwelling on victimhood; for not 'doing' theory properly; and for a reductive concern with gender.

---

[140] Anonymous, *A Woman in Berlin. Diary 20 April 1945 to 22 June 1945,* introduction by Antony Beevor, afterword by Hans Magnus Enzensberger, trans. Philip Boehm (London: Virago, 2005).

[141] Mary Lyndon Shanley and Carole Pateman (eds.), *Feminist Interpretations and Political Theory* (Cambridge: Polity, 1991), is essential.

[142] Ann Tickner, 'Hans Morgenthau's Principles of Political Realism: A Feminist Reformulation', *Millennium,* vol. 17(3), pp. 429–40, and *Gender in International Relations.*

[143] Carol Pateman, *The Sexual Contract* (Stanford, Calif.: Stanford University Press, 1988).

[144] Susan M. Okin, *Justice, Gender and the Family* (New York: Basic Books, 1989).

[145] Nancy Fraser, 'What's Critical about Critical Theory? The Case of Habermas and Gender', in Shanley and Pateman, *Feminist Interpretations,* pp. 253–76, and Ackerly, *Political Theory and Feminist Social Criticism,* pp. 25–6, 185–90.

[146] Rebecca Grant, 'The Sources of Gender Bias in International Relations Theory', in Rebecca Grant and Kathleen Newland (eds.), *Gender and International Relations* (Milton Keynes: Open University Press, 1991), pp. 14–17; this is discussed in Booth and Wheeler, *Security Dilemma,* chs. 8 and 9.

[147] For some writers giving credit to the particularity of non-Western women's experiences has been a vital but not always recognised task in the feminist project: see Margery Wolf, *A Thrice-Told Tale: Feminism, Postmodernism and Ethnographic Responsibility* (Stanford Ca.: Stanford University Press, 1992). Against those who assume women in the West were always at the fore in securing rights and influence, Sen, in *The Argumentative Indian,* offers counter-evidence from Indian history, of the participation and leadership of women in argumentation, in emancipation and critical agency, in property ownership, and in political leadership: pp. 6–10, 220–2, 234–47, 290–1.

Such charges have been countered vigorously, but the marginalisation persists. Nonetheless, many of the concerns at the heart of feminist scholarship converge directly with those central to a critical theory of world security.

Key ideas

Power is complex and it is a priority to uncover how it works; states, governments, and organisations are not neutral institutions; patriarchy and ideas about masculinity do a great deal of work in making the (social, political, and economic) world go round; what is natural is invariably cultural; what is hidden is often essential; the theorist is embedded and embodied; individual experience is revealing and theory can be grounded in experience; language is constitutive of the world as well as a means of communication, and it is gendered; theoretical blinders mean we can only see what we believe is there; 'The personal is global; the global is gendered';[148] theorising security is not an objective activity, and it will fall far short of aspirations of being realistic if it lacks the empirical and theoretical enrichment that feminist theorising can bring; efficient/elegant theory is not necessarily good theory; there is still a great deal to learn about the world, and so understand the role gender plays (and particularly where it seems least obvious).

Historical sociology

The state? What is that? . . .
 The state is the coldest of all cold monsters. Coldly it lies, too; and this lie creeps from its mouth: 'I, the state, am the people.'
 . . . the state lies in all languages of good and evil; and whatever it says, it lies – and whatever it has, it has stolen.
 Everything about it is false; it bites with stolen teeth.
Friedrich Nietzsche in Thus Spoke Zarathustra[149]

The academic study of international relations is infused by one assumption: the domination of what I call the-definite-article-sovereign-polity, *the state*. Grammar has achieved what history could not. It has produced a universal type out of historical entities that have come in all shapes and sizes (strong/failed, social democratic/monarchic, modern/medieval, and so on). The ideal model of this universal type is the textbook Western state.

[148] Enloe, *Bananas*, p. xi.
[149] Friedrich Nietzsche, *Thus Spoke Zarathustra*, trans. with an introduction by R. J. Hollingdale (London: Penguin Books, 1969), pp. 75–6.

Students of international politics cannot avoid talking about states, but the-definite-article-state does not exist universally, except through grammar. The need to recognise the variety rather than the universality of state formations is why historical sociology is an important resource of critical global theorising. It gives us a more accurate picture of the units that make up the system than realism, and especially in its influential rational choice variant. However, historical sociology is a subject area and an approach rather than a theory of international relations as such, but it has potentially radical theoretical implications. Not only does it counter the unhelpful grammatical reification of a complex political form, but it does not let us forget that sovereign states are the result of ideas not nature, and therefore need to be understood as historical phenomena. State formations in different parts of the world have come into being at different times and in different ways.[150]

Historical sociology is significant for the development of a critical theory of security because, in the words of one of its prominent exponents, it 'necessarily entails a rejection of the mainstream project, which unwittingly seeks to impose a totalising logic of continuity and regularity upon a temporally protean past and present international relations'.[151] At the same time, it rejects the view that the political realm is autonomous, rejects the way the discipline has become separated from others that study human society, and rejects the dominance of the 'domestic'/'international' division (indeed it is this focus above all that has characterised the approach since the 1990s).[152] It also has a normative dimension, which has been put with great clarity by Fred Halliday: 'Historical sociology is, above all, a part of the attempt by human beings to take mastery of their own surroundings, their past and their present, the better to emancipate themselves from it and determine, within the

---

[150] See Theda Skocpol (ed.), *Vision and Method in Historical Sociology* (Cambridge: Cambridge University Press, 1984), Fred Halliday, 'State and Society in International Relations: A Second Agenda', *Millennium*, vol. 16(2), 1987, pp. 215–29, Dennis Smith, *The Rise of Historical Sociology* (Cambridge: Polity, 1991), Stephen Hobden, *International Relations and Historical Sociology. Breaking Down Boundaries* (London: Routledge, 1998), Stephen Hobden and John M. Hobson (eds.), *Historical Sociology of International Relations* (Cambridge: Cambridge University Press, 2002), Walter C. Opello and Stephen J. Rosow, *The Nation-State and Global Order. A Historical Introduction to Contemporary Politics* (Boulder, Colo.: Lynne Rienner, 2004).

[151] John M. Hobson, 'What's at Stake in "Bringing Historical Sociology *Back* into International Relations"? Transcending "Chronofetishism" and "Tempocentrism" in International Relations', in Hobden and Hobson, *Historical Sociology*, p. 20.

[152] Stephen Hobden, 'Historical Sociology: Back to the Future of International Relations?', in *ibid.*, p. 43.

constraints of structure of course, their future.'[153] To date, however, historical sociology has had limited impact on a state-infatuated discipline. Given the tendency in the discipline of international relations to bolster endemic ethnocentrism with temporal short-sightedness – the flaws of parochialism and recentism – the assumption of stateness takes on papal infallibility, and historical sociology therefore sounds like heresy.

What welds the elements of historical sociology together is *time*. According to Stephen Hobden, 'Social relations do not stand apart from time. All social interactions are affected by what has gone before, and in the understanding of the present the past cannot be avoided.'[154] This simple point has been obscured by realism, with its ahistorical assumptions about states. The result has been that neorealists in particular, in the words of Hobden and Hobson, embrace the 'naturalness of their totalised picture' of the state, which they associate with the recurring patterns, struggles, and textures of international politics.[155] A standard criticism made by historical sociologists of mainstream realist theorists is that they have derived their ideas about international relations from a snapshot of the modern states system: 'Waltz (mis)takes the Westphalian moment for the ontology of the international system' is how Hendrick Spruyt put it. Key features were extracted 'without regard to its specific historic settings'. And from this mistake, the elements of the international realm were extracted to derive a 'scientific' theory.[156] For historical sociologists such as John Hobson, the Westphalian 'moment' is not synonymous with international history; indeed, they describe it as 'the temporal exception'. Empires, for example, have characterised world politics more than the sovereign states system.[157]

Sovereign states did not arrive miraculously in history, as if by virgin birth;[158] they evolved into becoming the categorical structures of international politics as a result of the interaction of complex social processes,

[153] On the normative agenda, see Fred Halliday, 'For an International Sociology', in *ibid.*, pp. 259–64 (quotation at p. 264).
[154] Hobden, *International Relations*, p. 24.
[155] Hobson, 'What's at Stake?' pp. 12–13.
[156] Ibid., pp. 19–20; see Benno Teschke, *The Myth of 1648. Class, Geopolitics, and the Making of Modern International Relations* (London: Verso, 2003), in this regard.
[157] See the selection of essays in Michael Cox, Tim Dunne, and Ken Booth (eds.), *Empires, Systems and States. Great Transformations in International Politics* (Cambridge: Cambridge University Press, 2001).
[158] This image is taken from the discussion of 'cultures' in Michael Carrithers, *Why Humans Have Cultures: Explaining Anthropology and Social Diversity* (Oxford: Oxford University Press, 1992), p. 9. See also p. 196 below.

of which war and economics have been paramount[159] (though gender cannot be ignored[160]). The work of Charles Tilly has been especially significant in explaining the rise of national states in Europe through the centuries of struggle for power, prestige, primacy, and security among the continent's political units. To Linklater, the combining of monopoly powers into the modern Westphalian state was a 'totalising project'.[161] It can also be easily read as a Darwinian struggle of the emergence of the fittest, with war as the evolutionary selector. In the well-known formulation of Charles Tilly, 'states made war but war made the state' (and in the process also helped make governing classes and urban elites, who dominated both coercive power and capital).[162] But military and economic power are only part of the story. Michael Mann identified 'the entwinings of four logics, four "sources of social power": ideological, economic, military and political' in the history of states and societies.[163] Another attempt at a synthetic overview was Cox's work on social forces, states, and world orders. He saw states as playing an 'intermediate though autonomous role' between social forces constructed primarily through production and world orders constructed through the states system and the world economy.[164] As these few examples show, historical sociology engages boldly with the biggest questions and across the broadest canvases.

Lacking a proper sense of history insofar as it impacts on the formation of states, historical sociologists argue that scientific theories of international politics extrapolate the present backwards. As a result, for Hobson, they thereby impose 'an historically sanitised and totalised character to past and present international relations . . . obscuring the

---

[159] The major contributions include: Charles Tilly, *The Formation of National States in Western Europe* (Princeton, N.J.: Princeton University Press, 1975), and *Coercion, Capital and European States, AD 990–1990* (Oxford: Blackwell, 1990); Immanuel Wallerstein, *The Capitalist World-Economy* (Cambridge: Cambridge University Press, 1979); Anthony Giddens, *The Nation-State and Violence* (Berkeley: University of California Press, 1985); and Michael Mann, *States, War, and Capitalism: Studies in Political Sociology* (New York: Blackwell, 1988).
[160] For example, V. Spike Peterson (ed.), *Gendered States: Feminist (Re)Visions of International Relations Theory* (Boulder, Colo.: Lynne Rienner, 1992).
[161] Linklater, *Political Community*, p. 29.   [162] Tilly, *Coercion, Capital*, p. 51.
[163] Michael Mann, *The Sources of Social Power*, 2 vols. (Cambridge: Cambridge University Press, 1986 and 1993). See vol. I, pp. 6–10, and 'Authoritarian and Liberal Militarism: A Contribution from Comparative and Historical Sociology', in Steve Smith, Ken Booth, and Marysia Zalewski, *International Theory: Positivism and Beyond* (Cambridge: Cambridge University Press, 1996), p. 222.
[164] Robert W. Cox, 'Social Forces, States, and World Orders: Beyond International Relations Theory', *Millennium*, vol. 10(2), 1981, pp. 137–41; see also his 'Thinking about Civilizations', in Ken Booth, Tim Dunne, and Michael Cox (eds.), *How Might We Live?* (Cambridge: Cambridge University Press, 2001), pp. 217–34.

significant differences and discontinuities between historical systems'.[165] To counter this, he argued that the historical sociological insight sought to achieve three objectives: to tell us new things about international systems historically; to force international relations theorists to look outside their parochial perspectives on time and space, and thereby 'problematise the most basic institutional, moral and spatial forms that constitute modern international relations'; and finally, to offer new and richer ways of theorising and explaining the contemporary international system.

Like the other approaches discussed in this chapter, the study of the historical sociology of the state contains within it a variety of strands: they extend from realist to Weberian.[166] Some see this as a sign of life,[167] but others characterise it as evidence of an 'identity crisis'.[168] Hobden and Hobson described their book *International Relations and Historical Sociology* as 'a kind of *historical sociology manifesto*', with the explicit aim of showing why international relations theorists should engage with the field.[169] There is no quarrel here; but the book strangely ignores security, the central problematic of international relations. Nonetheless, a critical theory of world security will find that historical sociology generates important insights, particularly in this era of globalisation, when the differential 'domestic' capabilities of different state forms reveal different patterns of power in face of the penetration of the global economy. Whether particular countries prosper, or others prosper upon their backs, will be related to the political and economic significance of sovereignty and independence in specific contexts, whatever the juridical norms of the so-called international system.

Key ideas

The study of human society should be interdisciplinary in order to develop better understandings of the units that make up the international system; the definite-article-state is to be challenged on historical, empirical, definitional, theoretical, and normative grounds; history is an open process; de-naturalising states is a step towards de-naturalising 'international politics'; the historical sociology of states

[165] Hobson, 'What's at Stake?', especially pp. 3–5.
[166] John M. Hobson, *The State and International Relations* (Cambridge: Cambridge University Press, 2000), identifies five main theories of the state.
[167] Hobden and Hobson, 'Preface and Acknowledgements', p. ix, and Halliday, 'For an International Sociology', pp. 244–5, in Hobden and Hobson, *Historical Sociology*.
[168] Steve Smith, 'Historical Sociology and International Relations Theory', in *ibid.*, p. 223.
[169] Hobson, 'What's at Stake?', p. 4.

challenges parsimonious/reductionist theories that posit the international as an autonomous realm; political relations between states are embedded in social processes, and so their understanding must be embedded in a multilevel and multifaceted sociology, to find connections and meanings; power is a complex phenomenon; state formations have changed in the past and are currently undergoing transformation under globalisation; temporal parochialism about the 'recent' and the 'present' obscures the changeability of history, and its radical nature.

Social idealism

> Even if . . . [the perfect state] should never come about, the idea which sets up this maximum as an archetype, in order to bring the legal constitution of mankind nearer and nearer to its greatest possible perfection, still remains correct. For no-one can or ought to decide what the highest degree may be at which mankind may have to stop progressing, and hence show how wide a gap may still of necessity remain between the idea and its execution. For this will depend on freedom, which can transcend any limit we care to impose.
>
> Immanuel Kant in *Critique of Pure Reason*[170]

The mind linking the global theorising of the critical theory tradition and the radical tradition in international relations is that of Kant, 'the greatest of all theorists of international relations' according to Chris Brown.[171] Over two centuries after his death, Kant continues to have an enormous influence on philosophy, and has had more visibility in the academic study of international relations (not to mention political rhetoric) since the end of the Cold War than at any time previously. The world may finally be catching up with him. Kant wrote that 'a violation of rights in one place is felt throughout the world', and that 'the idea of a law of world citizenship is no high-flown or exaggerated notion'. While cynics over the past two centuries would no doubt point to the many exceptions to these two statements, the infinitely larger body of

---

[170] 'Appendix from "The Critique of Pure Reason"', in Hans Reiss, *Kant's Political Writings*, trans. H. B. Nisbet (Cambridge: Cambridge University Press, 1977), p. 191.
[171] Chris Brown, *International Relations Theory: New Normative Approaches* (Hemel Hempstead: Harvester Wheatsheaf, 1992), p. 95. Unless stated otherwise, the arguments and quotations below are based on Howard Williams and Ken Booth, 'Kant: Theorist Beyond Limits', in Ian Clark and Iver B. Neumann (eds.), *Classical Theories of International Relations* (Houndmills: Macmillan, 1996), pp. 71–98. We are working on a book-length study of Kant and world politics.

victims of world politics would ask us to celebrate organisations such as Amnesty International or Médecins sans Frontières – practitioners of the Kantian spirit. Global citizens increasingly perform some of his cosmopolitan ideas, while Kant's own reputation in the discipline began to change towards the end of the twentieth century, particularly as a result of the growth of interest in liberal ideas, the democratic peace thesis, the critical challenges to realism, and the revival of normative theory.[172] His work has been influential on a number of writers, though mostly they have worked on the margins of the trade-union definition of international relations theory. These include Onora O'Neill's work on distributive justice, Philip Allott's on ideals actualised through law, and John Rawls's theory of justice.[173] In this brief section, however, I will concentrate only on Kant's own thought.

Kant was the first political philosopher of significance to emphasise the primacy of the international in understanding politics. The breadth of his interests and knowledge was stunning, especially for one who famously did not leave his home city.[174] Kant wrote about issues that became intrinsic to the agenda of academic international relations: war and peace, the relationship between the domestic and the international, international government, and justice. His philosophical ideas transcend the limits of traditional international theory, and his political hopes transcend those of the traditionalist school of diplomacy. Such ambition was evident, above all, in his long essay, *Perpetual Peace* (1795).[175] His project, even his 'guarantee' of the outcome, was not wildly utopian; it did not require the abolition of the states system, but rather its reconstruction. Unlike neorealists, for whom the structure of the system is dominant, Kant believed the units were the prime movers. He argued that if humans had certain ideas, and acted consistently, other

---

[172] In encouraging new interest by international relations scholars, the following were important: Michael Doyle, 'Kant, Liberal Legacies and Foreign Affairs' (parts I and II), *Philosophy and Public Affairs*, vol. 12(3/4), 1983, pp. 205–35, 323–53; and Andrew Hurrell, 'Kant and the Kantian Paradigm in International Relations', *Review of International Studies*, vol. 16(3), 1990, pp. 183–206.

[173] See, in particular, John Rawls, *A Theory of Justice* (Oxford: Oxford University Press, 1978), Onora O'Neill, *Constructions of Reason: Explorations of Kant's Political Philosophy* (Cambridge: Cambridge University Press, 1989), Philip Allott, *The Health of Nations. Society and Law Beyond the State* (Cambridge: Cambridge University Press, 2002).

[174] A standard biography is Ernst Cassirer, *Kant's Life and Thought*, trans. James Haden (New Haven, Conn.: Yale University Press, 1981), a relatively accessible guide is Paul Guyer (ed.), *The Cambridge Companion to Kant* (Cambridge: Cambridge University Press, 1992).

[175] Reiss, *Kant's Political Writings*, pp. 93–130.

things would follow; this was because humans are conscious agents, and ideas shape structures. He was not an unreflexive dreamer.

Kant dealt with fundamental questions of knowledge in *Critique of Pure Reason*. His lasting insight (to simplify the complex) was to distinguish between our knowledge of things perceived through our senses (phenomena or appearances) and knowledge of things as they might exist independently of our faculties (noumena or transcendental experience). Kant believed that we could not know things independently of our perception of them, and that we should be aware of the limits of reason in our understanding of the empirically observed world, because it would be wrong to assume the world is arranged according to the categories of our reason ('the order and regularity in the appearances, which we entitle *nature*, we ourselves introduce'[176]). This epistemology has implications for the use made of empirical knowledge and the role of normative theory in international relations. The Kantian approach to knowledge in politics is not without problems, especially the tension arising over the authority of a critique that begins with the questioning of the authority of authority.[177]

Realism favours empirical enquiry; it has been axiomatic that 'describing the world as it is' should dominate 'speculation about the world as it ought to be'.[178] Kant rejected this way of looking at things. While accepting that empirical studies can have value, he placed normative theory to the fore; here, in the moral sphere, reason is not empirically constrained. Within this normative realm (including international relations) humans are capable of ordering their lives in accordance with rational principles, and aiming for the highest good. This is a central assumption of a critical theory of security.

Mainstream international relations scholarship has traditionally distinguished between the domestic/international, good life/survival and order/anarchy. Kant rejected these binaries, and argued that the search for the good life and order must be universal, for it cannot be successful domestically unless it is successful internationally. This, logically, meant that for Kant international theory had priority over political theory

---

[176] Immanuel Kant, *Critique of Pure Reason*, trans. N. Kemp Smith (Houndmills: Palgrave Macmillian, 2003; first published 1929), with a new introduction by Howard Caygill, p. 147, A125.
[177] Kimberly Hutchings is helpful: *Kant, Critique and Politics* (London: Routledge, 1995), pp. 11–57, 186–91.
[178] For a brilliant exposé of the intoxication with 'istopia', the realist love of the word 'is', see Allott, *Health of Nations*, pp. 3–8.

(traditionally theorising within states). His thinking about the social contract illustrated this.[179] Unlike orthodox social contract theorists up to that point, Kant did not believe that sovereign states were the end-point, creating within them a series of unique communities; rather, they were staging-posts in the construction of a peaceful world society. It must be emphasised here that Kant was not an advocate of world government; he thought such a structure would be too big to be manageable, and so he advocated a federation of free states, infused by the idea of 'universal hospitality'. The world he envisaged would not be an international society without competition, but one in which competition took place in a legalised context ('self-regulated lawful freedom'). Nor did he minimise the obstacles to be overcome, or the time span needed to achieve it, or the difficulty of achieving agreement. After all, Kant was responsible for the famous judgement that 'Out of timber so crooked as that from which man is made nothing entirely straight can be built.'[180]

The 'crooked timber' he described is dualistic. His conception of human nature consists of the intellectual realm in which reason dominates, and the animal realm where instinct prevails. Reason shapes human behaviour, but does not determine it. Humans have the potential to be rational, and it is the exercise of reason that allows us to realise our freedom, including, potentially, in the arena of international relations. By transcending traditional ideas and practices about relations between states, Kant believed it would be possible to move towards fulfilling the potential of human nature; neither the states system nor human nature were immovable constraints. Thus he considered the experience of international relations to be a reality perceived as an idea in the mind, and performed through well-established practices; its future is the result of choices, for individuals and groups, including governments. Its institutions and processes are one manifestation of human-made reality, not a thing-in-itself that is not serving humankind well. This was true in Kant's time and, as chapter 1 showed, it is also the case today.

The relationship between our intellectual and animal sides meant for Kant that humans are both determined and autonomous. It is an

---

[179] Kant, 'Idea for a Universal History from a Cosmopolitan Point of View', in Reiss, *Kant's Political Writings*, pp. 41–53.

[180] Kant's description of humanity provided the title and theme of the famous collection of essays by Isaiah Berlin, *The Crooked Timber of Humanity*, ed. Henry Hardy (London: Fontana, 1991), in which Berlin argued that 'the great goods' of human aspiration can never be coherent. Liberty and equality, for example, are invariably in tension; and so pluralism is the answer and should be the political goal.

unstable relationship, and in the interplay between instinct and reason there is the potentiality for good and evil. Unlike the Christian pessimism of early theologians such as Augustine, Kant emphasised the voluntary nature of human moral failure (or its achievement). Humans can choose 'the good', with emancipation from the power of evil being the 'highest prize'.[181] For Kant, therefore, human nature has the potential for self-liberation through the exercise of reason. However, his understanding of history, anthropology, and politics led him to believe that it would be a long time before human society transcended its 'self-incurred immaturity'.[182]

Peace was therefore possible for Kant, but only with considerable difficulty and conditional upon the achievement of the operational goal of creating, universally, states with republican constitutions operating according to his ideas in *Perpetual Peace* (the nearest he offered to a blueprint for world politics).[183] Perpetual peace depended upon the premises of Kant's logic. If we accept that humans live in a self-constituted world, together with his interpretation of the correct political conditions for peace, then his 'guarantee' is solid as long as humans choose the right path. He thought they would: 'Out of a community of fate will emerge an ethical community, and from that a world society of perpetual peace.' This outcome was guaranteed primarily by political work in three areas: countries adopting (or seeking to adopt) republican constitutions at home (he saw a close relationship between bad governments and leaders at home and aggression externally); the creation of a federated pacific union in their relations with each other; and the growth of relationships based on the principle of universal hospitality (he was cautious here, not expecting people to embrace benevolence, but rather to reject hostility). Kant believed it was rational to hope for a better world, though he knew it would not come quickly or easily; he had confidence in reason and in 'Nature's secret path', which included the role of war in forcing societies to examine their interrelationships. History, to a degree, subsequently bore out his syllogism. It took 'The Great War for Civilisation' (the inscription on one of my grandfather's medals) to bring about the creation of the world's first multipurpose international

[181] Immanuel Kant, *Religion Within the Limits of Reason Alone* (New York: Harper, 1960), pp. 39, 85.
[182] Kant, 'An Answer to the Question "What is Enlightenment?"', in Reiss, *Kant's Political Writings*, p. 54.
[183] Williams and Booth, 'Kant', pp. 86–95; see also the collection in James Bohman and Matthias Lutz-Bachmann (ed.), *Perpetual Peace. Essays on Kant's Cosmopolitan Ideal* (Cambridge, Mass.: MIT Press, 1997).

organisation (the League of Nations) and provoke the invention of international politics as an academic pursuit, initially devoted to the study of war and its prevention. No Great War, no great discipline.[184]

Kant hated war, but was not a pacifist. He accepted that wars would take place, given the existing universal condition of 'immaturity', but he believed that people have choices, including the possibility of morality, even in the cockpit of war. For war itself is a conscious choice, and in deciding to fight, people must elaborate reasons to justify their actions. War will sometimes seem necessary, but it should never be regarded as inevitable, and no war is morally justifiable. Believing the latter, Kant rejected traditional 'just war' doctrine: particular wars may be excusable, but they are never right. In other words, a war might be thought politically necessary, but it cannot be legitimised in theory. His ideas about war should be seen in relation to his belief that the actions and policies taken at any particular time should have the aim of creating in the future a worldwide legal condition. He considered certain acts to be wrong in themselves (for example, assassinations[185]), but what mattered most was not the quality of the victory, but the character of the subsequent peace. In short, choices within today's war system should be calculated to construct a future law system. Consequently, war can be prevented by common reason working its way through the vicissitudes of history. His advice was not designed for 'angels'. He did not assume inevitable progress, and his 'guarantee' did not come with a deadline. Instead, he talked of the human capacity to learn by trial and error, exploring living and trading together, exercising reason, and conducting moral politics. Through dialectical processes, rational cooperation should evolve, and an ethical world community should be created, regulated by law.

The harmony of morality and politics was central to Kant's thinking. Understood 'objectively', he wrote, morality 'is itself practical' because 'there can be no conflict of politics (as a practical doctrine of right) with ethics (as a theoretical doctrine of right)'.[186] He distinguished between the 'political moralist' and the 'moral politician', with the former using morality to conform to a state or leader's advantage, while the latter

---

[184] When in 1919 David Davies, then Liberal MP for Montgomeryshire, endowed the world's first chair in International Politics at the University College of Wales, Aberystwyth, he did it as a memorial to the students of the college who had fought and died in the Great War.

[185] This is Kant's Preliminary Article Six in *Perpetual Peace*; see Reiss, *Kant's Political Writings*, pp. 96–7.

[186] L. W. Beck (ed.), *Kant Selections* (New York: Macmillan, 1988), p. 446.

chose political principles consistent with morality.[187] Kant proposed that there is no more vital interest than acting in good faith and that the principle of 'publicity' is the mechanism to encourage leaders to choose policies that arise out of respect for morality. The moral politician, he believed, did not just wish for perpetual peace as a material good, but as a condition issuing from the acknowledgement of duty. Perpetual peace would not come from pragmatism, but only from rational moral behaviour.

There was therefore no clash of conceptualisations for Kant between order and justice. Law and right were unified; in his *Rechtslehre* (doctrine of right) legality and morality were seamless. Law was the embodiment of right, and self-regulated lawful freedom expressed his idea of peace in a positive sense. Peace was not a mere armistice, but a condition in which people lived in justice and harmony. Order was only possible on a permanent basis through justice. Justice played a central role in Kant's political philosophy, both in the sense of respecting established law and of respecting moral rules that set standards for civilised life. Justice should be universal, encompassing international as well as individual right.

Kant's theory of justice was closely related to his doctrine of virtue, or theory of goodness, and together they helped to create his theory of the good as a whole – in other words, his ethics. This theory of justice was cosmopolitan, based on universal reason. By 'cosmopolitan' he meant the perspective of a gradually emerging world citizenship. His cosmopolitan notion of justice distinguished between human beings as individuals and human beings as citizens of states, but justice is an interconnected whole, with a right being violated in one place being felt everywhere.[188] Even in his own day, Kant criticised the 'civilised and especially the commercial states' of Europe for their ill-treatment of other parts of the world. They assumed superiority and exploited the world's resources and people, he argued; these nations 'drink injustice like water' and 'regard themselves as the elect in point of orthodoxy'.[189] Kant was not the first philosopher to believe in the idea of the universality of rights and justice,[190] but none to that point had expressed it in such a modern fashion.

---

[187] *Ibid.*, p. 448.   [188] *Ibid.*, p. 440.   [189] *Ibid.*, p. 439.
[190] See Williams and Booth, 'Kant', pp. 84–6, for a comparison of Kant with Aquinas and Grotius.

Key ideas

Human knowledge is not of things-in-themselves but of how we perceive them, and so our understanding is limited by the limited categories of our understanding; the future is open to our minds, but its actual outcomes are not guaranteed; it is necessary to transcend the traditional boundaries of political theory, with its state-centrism and emphasis on the constraints of human nature, and instead think universally and with a sense of the potential openness of human capability; human society, including international relations, is self-constituted, and law is one mechanism by which ethics can be actualised; international relations is a realm in which there is scope for the application of morality, but its theory and practice should not ignore the factual and historical studies which add to our understanding of the concrete world in which we try to put our principles into action; political theorists, like philosophers in general, should be free from government interference, but governments should listen to them; human nature is open; normative theories of international relations can attempt to govern the attitudes and behaviour of policymakers and civil society; humans should think beyond conventional limits, dare to know, dare to challenge, dare to hope, and dare to use their own understanding – 'Sapere aude!' (Dare to be wise).[191]

Emancipatory realism

'The best constitution is that in which the power rests with laws instead of with men.' For what can be more metaphysically sublime than this idea . . . If we try instead [of revolution] to give it reality by means of gradual reforms carried out in accordance with definite principles, we shall see that it is the only means of continually approaching the supreme political good – perpetual peace.

Immanuel Kant in *The Metaphysics of Morals*[192]

As a large group of people from Aberystwyth were waiting near Lambeth Bridge to filter into the million and a half people moving towards Hyde Park on 15 February 2003, to register a uniquely powerful protest at what appeared to be the increasingly likely war against Iraq, my eye was caught by the back of one placard a few yards ahead. The crush

---

[191] These final injunctions are taken from, or are in the spirit of, the first paragraph of 'What is Enlightenment?', in Reiss, *Kant's Political Writings*, p. 54.
[192] *Ibid.*, pp. 174–5.

was so great I never got to see the front of the placard, or the carrier. To my surprise, in the middle of the largest political demonstration ever in Britain (and one that was replicated across the world[193]) was the roughly written advice: 'I advise you to read Philip Allott's *The Health of Nations*. Cambridge University Press, 2003. ISBN 0-521-01680-0. Price £19.99'. This was a highly unusual message to project on such an occasion, when blunt political advice or satirical humour are the norms. But here, captured in this moment, was the coming together at a time of international crisis of philosophical critique in the spirit of Kant, and civil society asserting its democratic duty.[194] Books such as *The Health of Nations* cannot stop governments in their tracks once the engines of the military machine have been started by stubborn leaders hungry for war and glory, but the ideas such a book expresses can help shape human consciousness, which over time can transform societies and how they interact, and so help approach 'the supreme political good' identified by Kant. The march did not prevent the outbreak of a disastrous war, but it did not thereby fail. Many of the marchers discovered solidarity, and the demonstration made it unlikely – at least for a very long time to come – that any future British Prime Minister would make the same mistake again.

In such episodes, the theoretical commitment and political orientation of a *critical theory of security* come together in the practical exercise of *emancipatory realism*. These terms need explaining before the body of ideas comprising critical global theorising are translated into a theory of world security.

Why is a critical theory of security necessary?

Chapter 1 described a world that is not working for most of its inhabitants, in order to provide the context for the subsequent discussion. But facts do not speak for themselves; even deadly statistics do not tell us what to do. We need to know why we should respond, and how, and then be able to persuade others to our point of view. In this respect, I disagree with Brian Barry, who, in his excellent book *Why Social Justice Matters*, argues that in the poorest countries 'people do not need a theory to tell them that there is something wrong with a world in which

---

[193] Connie Koch, *2/15: The Day the World Said NO to War*, ed. Barbara Sauermann (Oakland, Ca.: AK Press, 2003).
[194] Philip Allott is a distinguished international lawyer, a former diplomat, and an occasional writer about international politics. *Health of Nations* is a collection of essays; an earlier and more difficult work is *Eunomia. New Order for a New World* (Oxford: Oxford University Press, 1990; 2nd edn 2001).

their children are dying from malnutrition or diseases that could be prevented by relatively inexpensive public health measures'.[195] But they do need a theory, just as much as those people in the richest part of the world who need to be persuaded that they bear some responsibility for such a state of affairs. Without a critical theory of their situation, people in the poorest countries will have traditionalist explanations insidiously forced upon them, which play into fatalism ('it is the will of God', 'the poor will always be with us', 'it is natural') or propaganda ('prosperity will trickle down'). Alternatively, whatever energies they have might be exploited by ambitious elites, with discontent whipped up and targeted against minorities or alien devils of one sort or another. Whether the response is fatalism or violence, the outcome would simply replicate traditional injustices and structures. Without a theory of change, based on a truer reading of how we got to be as we are, history will go around in circles of violence, and politics will continue to be done by the powerful on the powerless.

This point apart, my rationale for a critical theory of world security is similar to Barry's rationale for social justice.[196] Whether the *we* is global or disciplinary, a critical theory of security is needed for three main reasons: to respond to empirical curiosity, to pursue moral politics, and to rise to the challenges of the times.

First, curiosity is a driving force for all students, yet those who study international politics have often been taught only narrow understandings of the world from within the accounts of the family of realism, and these continue to give pre-arranged answers to pre-defined questions. To put it bluntly, we all need the right theory to ask the right questions in order to get the right answers.[197] If I want to know the truth about the world, in as much as it can be revealed, the epistemology (theory of knowledge) offered by critical theory is the most persuasive.

Second, all social, political, and economic theories have ethical implications, and we need a set of answers to what Barry calls 'tricky' questions in order to pursue moral politics. We need to be able to articulate why we think what we think, or feel. In this sense, this book is not offering anything new, but rather reclaiming Enlightenment ideas in the changing international and global context. 'What is Enlightenment?'[198]

---

[195] Brian Barry, *Why Social Justice Matters* (Cambridge: Polity, 2005), p. 3.
[196] *Ibid.*, esp. pp. 4–6.   [197] This was Barry's view, *ibid.*, p. 4.
[198] Kant and Foucault are among those who have written essays with this title; the principles listed below run throughout Bronner, *Reclaiming the Enlightenment*, and Roy Porter, *Enlightenment. Britain and the Creation of the Modern World* (London: Allen Lane, 2000).

is an old and famous question. The answer is complex, but in this book it refers to a philosophical outlook privileging reason (and therefore human self-constitution); a set of principles championing the values of liberty, reciprocity, tolerance, civility (and therefore opposing violence); a perspective on life based on critical reflexivity, scepticism, secularism, universalism, and dissent (and so struggling against dogma, superstition, and prejudice); a politics favouring equality, democracy, emancipation, reformism, accountability, law, social justice, republicanism, and civil liberties (thus seeking to overcome arbitrary abuses of power, and class, gender, and racial privilege); and a sensibility informed by a cosmopolitan spirit (attempting to transcend those thoughtways believing that sectarian loyalties and decision-making should be privileged above all others). These ideas represent the mind-map for creating the conditions of possibility for human equality.

Third, we need a critical theory of world security because business-as-global-usual is not an option. Enlightened social and political values are under threat as a result of the potential unsustainability of the natural world and the other dangers converging on human society which constitute the Great Reckoning (chapter 9). In this first truly global age the answers to the questions about security must begin by being global. The siren calls of the ghetto – whatever form they take – must be resisted. There is time to do something, but it is running out.

Why 'emancipatory realism'?

Since the mid-1980s I have labelled my critical approach to security 'utopian realism'. As it developed, I described it as 'an attitude of mind' rather than a theory proper. Utopian realism sought to couple two 'planes' (utopia and reality) that E. H. Carr said could never meet, and it used a word ('utopia') calculated to provoke.[199] While still believing that it is possible to reconcile the planes, I have become resigned to thinking that the label is unhelpful: 'utopia' is an idea with too much negative baggage, and in any case smacks too much of a static blueprint.

The nudge to label the heart – the practical dimension – of the critical theory of world security being developed in this book *emancipatory realism* was the discussion in *International Studies Quarterly* between Richard Ashley and John Herz in 1981.[200] Herz himself had for many

[199] Ken Booth, 'Security in Anarchy: Utopian Realism in Theory and Practice', *International Affairs*, vol. 67(3), 1991, pp. 527–45 (ref. at p. 533).
[200] Ashley, 'Political Realism and Human Interests', pp. 204–36 (and John Herz, 'Comment', pp. 237–41).

years played around with various labels for his own work ('liberal realism'/'realist liberalism'/'idealist realism') and while Ashley did not actually use the term 'emancipatory realism' in relation to Herz's work, he nearly did. Ashley discussed the work of Habermas, explaining his conception of different knowledge-interests, and identifying Herz's work with the 'emancipatory-constitutive' knowledge-interest. Herz himself (like others subsequently) admitted to finding some of Ashley's theorising baffling. It was the provocation of Carr, who said utopia and reality could not be put together, rather than the positive model of Herz, that led to my effort to synthesise dialectical opposites, but I suspect that my reading of Herz's earlier work, long ago as a student, was doing some work in the subconscious. Other writers have tried to bring together dialectical opposites. In the 1980s, Anthony Giddens also started using the term 'utopian realism', and Radmila Nakarada coined the term 'responsible utopianism'.[201] As a result of re-reading the Ashley–Herz debate, I abandoned the Carr-inspired provocation for the Herz–Ashley signpost. We need a theory as well as an attitude of mind, with a systematic set of ideas about being, knowing, and doing, and *emancipatory realism* is what most of the rest of this book is about.

[201] Radmila Nakarada, 'The Democratic Potential of the New Détente', in Mary Kaldor, Gerald Holden, and Richard Falk (eds.), *The New Détente* (London: Verso, 1989), pp. 391–408, and Anthony Giddens, 'Modernity and Utopia', *New Statesman and Society*, 2 November 1990, pp. 20–2.

Part II
Theory

3　Security, emancipation, community

> the Bulk of Mankind in all Ages, and in all Countries, are violently attached to the Opinions, Customs, and even Habits, which they have been used to . . . Sounds, Shews, Prejudices, vain and idle Terrors, Phantoms, Delusions . . . operate more upon them than true and strong Reasons.
>
> John Trenchard, Enlightenment free-thinker putting down 'folly'[1]

Chapter 1 described the *morbid symptoms* of a world that is not working, and stressed the gathering dangers of global business-as-usual. Chapter 2 plundered a body of ideas – *critical global theorising* – from which a radically different approach to world security can be fashioned. Part II begins to construct the framework of such an approach. The present chapter clarifies the most basic concepts (*security, emancipation, and community*). Chapter 4 explains the critical moves involved in reconceiving security (*deepening, broadening,* and *reconstruction*). Chapter 5 relates these critical moves to fundamental issues in philosophy (*being, knowing,* and *doing*). And then chapter 6 brings all the elements together into a framework of a comprehensive (*transcendental, pure,* and *practical*) critical theory of world security.

Security beyond survival

> I will tell you in what consists of the summum bonum of human life: it consists in reading Tristram Shandy, in blowing a pair of bellows into your shoes in hot weather, and roasting potatoes under the grate in cold.　Archdeacon Paley in *Personal and Literary Memorials* (1829)[2]

[1] Roy Porter, *Enlightenment. Britain and the Creation of the Modern World* (London: Allen Lane, 2000), p. 53.
[2] From H. Digby Beste, *Personal and Literary Memorials* (1829) p. 209, quoted by Porter, *Enlightenment*, p. 258.

If *critical* is the sovereign term in critical security theory, the territory it rules over is *security*. This landscape is by no means as familiar as it should be to students of international relations, despite it being the discipline's mother-country. Over the years students have been led where the 'conventional convictions' of their teachers took them,[3] and this has meant that security became identified as essentially military terrain. The latter is indeed an important part of the landscape (and I do not want to hear of any CSS that deals with it less than seriously), but it is only one part of the complex of world insecurity.

Security has been one of those common-sense, pre-defined terms in international relations orthodoxy that appear to be unproblematic until examined with a critical eye. During the Cold War, the dominating conception of security focused on military power and strategic relationships between states. Since the late 1980s, there has been a swing from theological orthodoxy about security studies to heretical contention, but for the most part proponents of the differing viewpoints have engaged in monologues rather than dialogue. In the aftermath of the 9/11 terror attacks on the United States, the differences between the camps of traditional realism and critical theory grew even more than had previously been the case. The former advocated the strengthening of conventional security instruments and the borders of states, as people and governments felt intensified fears (and the political temptation for governments has been to indulge such fears, if not actually exaggerate them, in order to strengthen domestic control).[4] On the other side, the critics of the way the White House turned the threat of international terrorism into a global war argued that the state of world affairs represented a frightening confirmation of the need for a different world-view, including a radical approach to world security that was more in tune with our times.[5] The modalities and mindsets of the US War on Terror (or whatever label it comes to be given) are part of today's morbid symptoms; they represent the politics of global-business-as-usual and are a sure recipe for ratcheting up world insecurity.

When world security is confronted by multiple and serious dangers, some might question why so much time and effort has been and is being

---

[3] The phrase was a favourite of Charles Manning's (used in a different context, but relevant here); he was Head of Department at LSE for many years.

[4] Corey Robin, *Fear. The History of a Political Idea* (Oxford: Oxford University Press, 2004), discusses the role of fear in US life today; see part 2: 'Fear, American Style'.

[5] Of the many critiques of the Bush administration's conception of a 'War on Terror', Louise Richardson, *What Terrorists Want. Understanding the Terrorist Threat* (London: John Murray, 2006), is outstanding in its clarity.

invested in debating the concept of security. The justification is straight-forward. It is an expression of the scholarly commitment to ask the first-order questions. Bernard Brodie called this commitment the 'single most important idea' in his own field of military strategy, and empha-sised his point by asking the question perennially posed by Marshal Foch, the commander-in-chief of allied forces on the Western Front in the First World War: 'De quoi s'agit-il?' – What is it all about?[6] As worlds collide politically and sometimes militarily, contention arising from ask-ing what security is all about is to be welcomed. It offers some hope that security will be conceptualised as a challenge to innovative political the-ory rather than as insider problem-solving, and as philosophy-in-action rather than as strategy as instrumental technique. A reconceptualisa-tion of security is one of the contributions the academic community can make to shaking up the complacency of the globally powerful in these critical times. The prize, nearly a century after the academic study of international relations began, is that the territory of security can be comprehensively explored and mapped *for the first time*.

Although scholars from within mainstream international relations have written extensively about security, they have sometimes been remarkably coy about the concept they were at the same time arguing was so important. Patrick Morgan, writing in the early 1990s, empha-sised what he thought was the huge difficulty of defining the term secu-rity. He said: 'Security is a condition, like health or status, which defies easy definition and analysis.'[7] In similar vein, a decade earlier, Barry Buzan had concluded in his seminal book *People, States, and Fear*, that 'the nature of security defies pursuit of an agreed definition'.[8] He sug-gested that *because* an agreed definition did not seem possible, it would not be profitable to try to formulate one. He was true to his word, and instead offered a dozen or so of other people's definitions. What is striking about these definitions – ostensibly to show the difficulty of achieving an 'agreed definition' – is actually their distinct resem-blance. The definitions chosen by Buzan were the more or less standard conceptualisations of 'national' or 'international' security from within mainstream Anglo-American Cold War international relations. What is

---

[6] Bernard Brodie, *War and Politics* (London: Collins, 1973), p. 1; discussed in Booth, 'Bernard Brodie', in John Baylis and John Garnett (eds.), *Makers of Nuclear Strategy* (London: Pinter, 1991), p. 44.
[7] Patrick Morgan, 'Safeguarding Security Studies', *Arms Control*, vol. 13(3), 1992, p. 466.
[8] Barry Buzan, *People, States and Fear: An Agenda for International Security Studies in the Post-Cold War Era* (London: Harvester Wheatsheaf, 1991, 2nd edn; 1st edn 1983), p. 16. All references are to the second edition unless stated otherwise.

more, while Buzan drew back from formulating his own definition, his book displayed a distinct set of liberal-realist assumptions. States were the referent objects for security, and although some broadening of the agenda was advocated, it was with statist priorities.[9] Such a mix of definitional timidity infused by orthodox liberal-realist assumptions will always tend to leave things as they are.

Morgan's coyness in face of the challenge of defining security appeared in an article with the give-away title 'Safeguarding Security Studies'. As advertised, the article was a disciplining move against challenges to the orthodoxy, and Morgan used the ostensible difficulty of defining security as a reason for leaving things as they were. He buttressed his defence of the orthodoxy by referring to the difficulty involved in defining other concepts, and he selected health and status. But these are not 'difficult' concepts. Only those who do not have to think about their health or status, because they enjoy both, will think such conditions are not 'easy' to define. Those who lack them, for sure, know what they mean. Just ask people with a serious medical condition (on a cancer ward) what health is. Or those who are homeless (on the winter streets of a wealthy Western city) what it means to have status. These people know with some operational clarity what seems sometimes to evade the best academic minds. The same is true of security. Ask those who have had it taken away from them whether they know what security is – those living in New York City in the immediate aftermath of the 9/11 terror attacks, for example, or in Madrid after 3/11, or in London after 7/7, or in Afghanistan or Iraq after the War on Terror had landed upon them. Of course they know what it is. Like health and status, security is a condition that is not difficult to define; in each case, the starting-point should begin in the experiences, imaginings, analyses, and fears of those living with insecurity, ill-health, or low status.

The urge to define and to clarify is in the DNA of academics. This makes the definitional timidity of scholars such as Morgan and Buzan particularly interesting. The answer may lie in a professional tendency – also displayed by doctors and lawyers in their habit of obfuscation through illegibility and their use of Latin terms – of trying to separate insiders/outsiders, experts/amateurs, and those with professional credentials/those who cannot be expected to understand. The message is clear: please leave security studies alone, and in the safe hands of the

---

[9] An important critique of the assumptions in Buzan's theory of security is Steve Smith, 'Mature Anarchy, Strong States and Security', *Arms Control*, vol. 12(2), 1991, pp. 325–39.

disciplinary gate-keepers. What is more, in my opinion *it does not matter* if a concept is not amenable to precise definition (and leaves important questions open). After all, the very concepts that make people believe life is worth living – love, dignity, and God for example – defy easy and agreed definition (and leave open plenty of important questions). But we must define as well as we can. I have long argued, against Buzan, that if we cannot name security, how can we ever hope to achieve it?[10]

This brings me to a final prefatory point on security, namely Buzan's claim that the word belongs to the category of concepts W. G. Gallie famously called 'essentially contested'.[11] The validity of this view has been forcefully questioned (and correctly so in my opinion) by Bill McSweeney, who has argued that Buzan's work has promoted a 'widespread myth' about the contested character of the concept of security.[12] McSweeney's challenge had two parts. The first was against Buzan's view that the concept of security has actually been a focus of serious disagreement among scholars. McSweeney rejected this, arguing that serious contestation over security only began in the 1990s, not in the period before Buzan's book first appeared. Buzan was not therefore describing an ongoing debate, as he himself seems to have thought; rather, he was one of its opening debaters. The second myth challenged by McSweeney was Buzan's use of the phrase 'contested concept'. According to McSweeney, Buzan was thereby giving security an exceptional position when compared with other key concepts in international relations, such as 'the state'. McSweeney wanted to insist, to the contrary, that these other concepts were equally contestable. For Buzan, however, they seemed to be settled, pre-defined in the discipline's discourse. Unlike Buzan, therefore, McSweeney believed that the concept of security had not for the most part been contested within the discipline, but that it had become so, and that this debate did not make security an exceptional concept, but rather gave it a status similar to other basic concepts necessary for understanding human society, such as 'the state' and 'justice'.

There is a more fundamental question still lurking in this discussion. Is security an *essentially* contested concept, as claimed by Buzan and so many other scholars? When Gallie first coined the term 'essentially

---

[10] This is a theme of Ken Booth, 'Security and Emancipation', *Review of International Studies*, vol. 17(4), 1990, pp. 313–26.
[11] Buzan, *People, States and Fear*, p. 7.
[12] Bill McSweeney, *Security, Identity and Interests. A Sociology of International Relations* (Cambridge: Cambridge University Press, 1999), esp. pp. 83–4.

contested' for a category of concepts whose meaning and usage would always be open to disagreement, the clear implication was that most concepts concerned with ethics, politics, or aesthetics would fall into the category. Terence Ball challenged this in the late 1980s, and described the essential contestability thesis as itself 'contestable and problematic; and if not false, then circular and logically vacuous'.[13] The point Ball was making was that the empirical evidence revealing that any particular concept has been contested – which is often not difficult to show – does not in itself demonstrate that there *must* always be disagreements. His view about the concept of 'power', for example, was that it is 'contingently contested'. Through similar reasoning, we should therefore ask whether security is *essentially* or *contingently* contested. My own guess, for it can be no more, is that security will come to be seen as a contingently and not essentially contested concept. I think we are tempted to see it as essentially contested because of an obsession with the present. After being uncontested for so long in the orthodoxy of the discipline, the interrogating of the concept since the 1980s has encouraged the idea that this contestability is in the nature of security. This, I will show, is misleading: the basic meaning of security is not essentially contested, though its meaning as a practice in world politics may be so (though this is contestable). In other words, my claim is that security as a basic concept consists of core elements that are not essentially contested, but when it comes to world politics this core is then encased in layers of meaning that derive from different political theories, and that *these* are contested (possibly essentially so, possibly contingently so) according to the ebb and flow of political theories, and the rise and fall of international political systemic paradigms.

The *core elements* of security, which I claim are not essentially contested, reveal security to be a simple concept at heart, as Hobbes understood four centuries ago. The standard dictionary definition states that security 'means the absence of threats'.[14] If this formulation is broken into its component parts, three things are implied: the existence of a referent object (someone or some thing is threatened); impending or actual danger; and a desire to escape harmful possibilities. So far so good. But when this template is imposed on world politics, the issues become more complex as the layers of politics are wrapped around it. Which referent

[13] Terence Ball, 'Power', in Robert E. Goodin and Philip Pettit (eds.), *A Companion to Contemporary Political Philosophy* (Oxford: Blackwell, 1993), pp. 553–4; see also Ball's *Transforming Political Discourse* (Oxford: Blackwell, 1988).
[14] Booth, 'Security and Emancipation', p. 319.

object(s) do we wish to consider? (States or individuals?) Which threat to the chosen referent should be prioritised? (Military or economic, short-term or long-term?) How might the referent escape from the threats? (By force or negotiation?) Security, for sure, is a simple concept, not difficult to define, but how it is conceptualised and operationalised in the contingent contexts of world politics is not. For one thing, the answers to the questions above depend heavily on the 'we' being referred to. The problem of security is not in the meaning of the concept, but in the politics of the meaning.

Before elaborating these points, it is necessary to underline the importance of the concept of security.

1. Insecurity is a life-determining condition

It is in the condition of insecurity where the politics of the meaning of security begin. Insecurity involves living in fear, with dangers arising from one or more types of threat.[15] The latter might be direct threats of violence or the more indirect but no less real threats that come from structural oppression such as poverty. The greater the degree of insecurity these threats produce, the more life-determining they will be. An insecure life, for groups or individuals, is a determined life.

People understand what security is by knowing how insecurity feels. The lives of whole societies can be overturned by an assault on their security, such as occurred in the United States after 9/11. As a result of that infamous day, the security landscape in much of the world had to alter. For the first time since the most acute nuclear crises of the Cold War, people in many countries felt that they had become potential victims of the violent intentions (terror or counter-terror) of people in faraway lands. Security became all-consuming. Fear was urgently felt (and manipulated). The anthrax scare in the United States in October 2001 showed the awful power of insecurity; it reminded us that assumptions about the future can change in seconds when an ordinary activity such as opening an envelope is potentially life-threatening.

When a state or nation lives in a condition of war or threatened war, survival – normally taken for granted – then becomes the priority consideration in all dimensions of national life. Second-order political and

---

[15] The literature on fear in international relations is as impoverished as that on international relations in books on fear: Frank Furedi, *Culture of Fear* (London: Continuum, 2005; 1st edn 1997); Robin, *Fear*; and Joanna Bourke, *Fear. A Cultural History* (London: Virago, 2005). The issue is discussed in Ken Booth and Nicholas J. Wheeler, *The Security Dilemma: Fear, Cooperation, and Trust in World Politics* (Houndmills: Palgrave Macmillan, 2008), ch. 2.

social ideals are put on hold, such as public welfare and cultural pursuits. Even some first-order values are subordinated to the demands of survival; the necessities of confronting violence mean that people have to be separated, in the collective interest, from their loved ones. Opportunities of all sorts have to be forgone when survival is at stake, for human and other resources have to be mobilised to prepare for or carry on the fight. In Britain's 'finest hour', when it stood alone against Nazi Germany in 1940, the Prime Minister Winston Churchill was asked about the country's policy. His answer to the House of Commons was blunt and heroic:

> I will say: It is to wage war by sea, land and air, with all our might and with all the strength that God can give us; to wage war against a monstrous tyranny, never surpassed in the dark, lamentable catalogue of human crime. That is our policy. You ask, What is our aim? I can answer in one word: Victory – victory at all costs, victory in spite of all terror; victory, however long and hard the road may be; for without victory there is no survival.[16]

As the war progressed, and the risk of defeat changed into the certainty of victory, people started to dream about creating a land fit for heroes, and resources were committed to the project of postwar reconstruction. But without victory such possibilities would stay a dream. In the meantime, national life had to be determined by the pursuit of victory.

Churchill's speech contained one serious error of logic (though not at that point sufficient to warrant threatening the speech's rhetorical appeal); this was when he equated *victory* and national *survival*. Several nations throughout Europe were not victorious against the 'monstrous tyranny' of Nazi Germany, and were defeated and conquered. Even so, they managed to survive (as national communities, if not for the moment as sovereign political entities). Survival is an existential condition: it means continuing to exist. Survival is not synonymous with living tolerably well, and less still with having the conditions to pursue cherished political and social ambitions. For the latter, security is required, and not just survival. In this sense security is equivalent to *survival-plus* (the plus being some freedom from life-determining threats, and therefore space to make choices). To confuse the existential condition of survival with the political and social instrumentality of security is a category error in security studies, but a common one. Here, critical security theory can

[16] Speech, House of Commons, 13 May 1940, in Alan and Veronica Palmer, *Quotations in History* (Hassocks, Sussex: Harvester Press, 1976), p. 47.

appeal to the authority of Hobbes. Having declared that *'the safety of the people is the supreme law'*, Hobbes wrote: 'By *safety* one should understand not mere survival in any condition, but a happy life so far as that is possible.'[17]

What is true of states and nations is also true of individuals and families. Just as a condition of war determines the behaviour of states, so poverty determines the lives of individuals and families. When the daily round of people is entirely dominated by the search for the basic means to survive, they are deprived of the opportunity to develop more fully as human beings. A mother living in a tenement block in a poor part of Glasgow once wrote: 'The kids ask for some bread. I can only give them a slice each because it is all that is left . . . [My husband] has not got up today . . . The kids go to bed. I want to go for a bath but I have to keep the hot water for Sunday for the kids.'[18] By some standards, such a person had relative security: shelter, some food, and occasional hot water. This is survival-plus, but not *plus* much in relation to contemporary Western standards. The woman speaking next, a worker in a *maquiladora* in Mexico, had less choice: 'I sleep and work. I can do no more.'[19] But even she had a job, and as long as she behaved (and the company she worked for did not make her unemployed) she had the wherewithal for survival. The very worst-off in society are generally silent or, to be more exact, are silenced; theirs are the unnoticed screams that opened chapter 2. A Bengali villager, poor and virtually illiterate, said: 'It is not very hard to silence us, but that is not because we cannot speak.'[20]

Ordinary insecurities determine lives. This is the case for those mostly invisible people who do 'menial' but essential tasks on which society depends. Their work for the most part does not give satisfaction, a sense of dignity, or self-worth. It is work that allows their survival, and in this sense their menial jobs are the moral equivalent of war work, a daily fight for victory in self-defence against a hostile world. There is little security in such work; it is working to survive. Though many who do jobs of the utmost drudgery may be ill-educated, they are not thereby without intelligence, or clear understanding of the meaning of status, security,

[17] Thomas Hobbes, *On the Citizen*, ed. and trans. Richard Tuck and Michael Silverthorne (Cambridge: Cambridge University Press, 1998), pp. 143–4.
[18] Bob Holman *et al.*, *Faith in the Poor* (London: Lion Publishing, 1998), quoted in the *New Internationalist*, vol. 18(3), 1999, p. 24.
[19] The comment was made in 1994: *New Internationalist, Sound Bites* (Oxford: New Internationalist Publications, 1997), p. 100.
[20] As said to Amartya Sen, *The Argumentative Indian. Writings on Indian Culture, History and Identity* (Harmondsworth: Penguin, 2006), p. xiii.

and health. Ordinary insecurity is often what society (the powerful) makes it.

Perhaps the most hideous image of the congruity of insecurity and the determined life in the Western imagination was that of the inmates of the Nazi death-camps. Years after the war, Primo Levi related how, driven by thirst on his first day in Auschwitz, he reached for an icicle. A guard snatched it away. When Levi asked 'Warum?' the guard pushed him away: 'Hier ist kein warum' ('There is no why here').[21] Here was *survival*, for a shorter or longer time, but definitely no *security*, not even the choice of asking 'Why?' The determined life *in extremis* of the death-camp inmate is rare, though not as rare as one would hope. Nonetheless, people can live honourable lives surviving in extreme insecurity. There is some space for human dignity in the death-camp, in the trenches, or grubbing for food on rubbish tips. But there is not much. Such a life is not much different from that of non-human animals existing only to feed and protect their young, driven by some biological imperative to survive. Since the earliest times societies have shared the belief that human being/being human should be more than this.[22] The most basic task for emancipatory politics must therefore be to create conditions in which sentient bodies are never driven into sites of insecurity where the freedom to ask 'Why?' and to live in dignity is never present.

It is important here to distinguish between insecurity that is enforced and life-determining, and danger that is chosen. Insecurity of the sort discussed above and *elective danger* are not synonymous. When people choose risky pastimes or when powerful states choose to take on ambitious foreign interventions, they place themselves in some danger, but they are not facing insecurity in the sense discussed above. Elective danger is synonymous with a sort of freedom. The insecure of the earth have neither the time nor the resources to engage in Formula One car racing, nor in organising expeditions to climb the highest peaks. There is all the difference in the world between those who go into the mountains for recreation and challenge – and have the time and money to do so – and those Kurds who went into the mountains to flee from Saddam Hussein's forces in 1991. Security allows choice, and some choices (the result of security rather than insecurity) may be life-threatening. Elective danger is a privilege of the secure; direct and unavoidable danger is the determining condition of the world's insecure.

---

[21] Primo Levi, *If This Is a Man* and *The Truce* (London: Abacus, 1996), p. 35.
[22] Among many possibilities, see William A. Haviland, *Anthropology* (Forth Worth, Tex.: Harcourt Brace, 1997, 8th edn).

Those whose lives are dominated by the search for scraps of food on a refuse tip on the edges of São Paulo have no choice about what to do. There is no money to buy books, or the opportunity to go across the city to attend the theatre. Such opportunities were also denied the family in Glasgow mentioned earlier, and the woman working in the *maquiladora*. If one lives in an autocratic state, which punishes those who think unacceptable thoughts, it is necessary to self-police those thoughts. Equally, weak states have to defer to mighty and ambitious neighbours. Manipulating insecurity may of course be functional for the powerful (individuals, regimes, and states) by helping to keep the weak 'in their place' through deference and self-policing. But such insecurity obstructs the opportunities for the victims to achieve self-realisation in their lives. A determined life is not one in which humans, in whole or in part, can flourish. Those in such a situation are never even given the opportunity to know 'Why?' because they do not have the power to ask the question in the first place.

2. *Security is an instrumental value*

The idea that security is an instrumental value is at the heart of the political significance of the concept. To understand this, three distinctions are necessary: between absolute and relative security, subjective and non-subjective threats, and (as already suggested) between survival and security.

First, security is always a relative concept. Absolute security is a dream, or perhaps a nightmare, for absolute freedom from (any) fear is synonymous with absolute freedom from imagination, which is no freedom at all. In contrast, it is possible to talk about something like absolute insecurity. This occurs when there is (at least temporary) survival in a physical sense, but also a sense of total fear. Such a condition might be objective (as in the case of the inmates of a death-camp) or subjective (as is the case with sufferers of extreme paranoia).

Second, the last point suggests that it possible to distinguish between what might be called *subjective* and *non-subjective* security ('subjective' is what one feels at the time, 'non-subjective' refers to what hindsight and history reveal, or what a hypothetical omniscient being might know at the time). So, one can *feel* safe (with no sense of imminent danger) without *being* safe, and likewise one can be free of 'real' threats without believing it to be the case. This is true for governments as it is for individuals. The Egyptian leaders at the start of June 1967, for example, did not believe their country was about to be attacked, though we now know from the historical record that their country was highly insecure, with Israel being in the final stages of planning what turned out to be the devastating attack that began the Six Day War. In an opposite illustration, hindsight suggests that many in the United States during the Cold War had a sense of paranoia about the Soviet Union ('Reds under the bed') and that they felt levels of insecurity arising from fears about a Soviet attack that were not justified by Soviet strategic plans.[23] Whether threats are subjective or non-subjective can only be settled by history, or rather, to be more precise, by debates among historians.

The third distinction, already introduced, is between survival and security. Survival was equated with existence – enduring as a physical being – while security was described as survival-plus. The *plus* here is the choice that comes from (relative) freedom from existential threats, and it is this freedom that gives security its instrumental value. Survival does not guarantee security, because it does not eliminate threats. Most blacks in apartheid South Africa survived, but their conditions could not be equated with security.[24] The same can be said today for the countless numbers of refugees in different contexts.[25]

The conflation of survival and security is a serious mistake, but it is not uncommon. The Copenhagen school of security theorists baldly claim: 'In this context ['international security'] security is about survival.'[26] Of course, in one simple sense this statement is true, but it is a trivial point because everything in life at some level is 'about' survival. The distinction between survival and security is significant, and so the blurring of the lines by the Copenhagen school is unhelpful. The proponents of the school's position claim not to be following a 'rigid domestic-international distinction', and recognise that domestic-international connections exist in the concept of security and will become more common.[27] Yet, in effect, by claiming that international security has a 'distinctive agenda' they help to perpetuate the domestic-international distinction, and by defining security in relation to 'existential threats' they

---

[23] Michael K. MccGwire, *Military Objectives in Soviet Foreign Policy* (Washington D.C.: Brookings, 1987).
[24] Ken Booth and Peter Vale, 'Security in Southern Africa: After Apartheid, Beyond Realism', *International Affairs*, vol. 71(2), 1995, pp. 285–304.
[25] See Janie Hampton (ed.), *Internally Displaced People. A Global Survey* (London: Earthscan, 1998), and T. Alexander Aleinikoff and Douglas Klusmeyer (eds.), *From Migrants to Citizens. Membership in a Changing World* (Washington D.C.: Carnegie Endowment for International Peace, 2000).
[26] Barry Buzan, Ole Wæver, and Jaap de Wilde, *Security: A New Framework for Analysis* (Boulder, Colo.: Lynne Rienner, 1998), p. 21; their general approach is critiqued in ch. 4.
[27] *Ibid.*, pp. 21 and 46.

do in effect conceive the terms survival and security to be synonymous. Security for the Copenhagen school is 'when an issue is presented as posing an *existential threat* to a designated referent object' (my italics). They argue that existential threats vary with the character of the object threatened, but their discussion makes it clear that it is survival that informs their outlook.[28] But survival is not synonymous with security; it is the necessary condition.

Security, it must be remembered, is a relative concept. This means that the more an individual's life is determined by insecurity, the more the space for choice, and acting effectively, is closed down. This is why, for example, revolutions and other violent political activities are rarely the result of the actions of the very weakest, the poorest, or the really down-trodden in any society: that is, those whose lives are most determined. Instead, the initiative and the organisation comes from the relatively educated or better-off. What is more, action is taken by those with the most time (invariably men), as opposed to those who have to look after children and prepare food (invariably women). Historically, and across cultures, it has been women who have lived the most determined lives. (Even in the well-off West today, women's domestic chores are generally more determining – food has to be cooked, and children have to be taken to school at regular times – while the stereotypical chores of men – mowing the lawn, putting up a shelf – can be done after the game on TV has finished, or 'tomorrow'.) Terrorism is as gendered and class-based as much of the rest of life. Those who carried out the September 2001 atrocities in the United States, and the earlier bombings in East Africa, were men; they were relatively educated and they also had the freedom that comes from having financial backing from a wealthy sponsor. Their ambitions were not constrained by having to give up their time to the provision of food and shelter, or by the daily and regular need to cook food or carry out the 24/7 duty of childcare.

The corollary of insecurity being determining, therefore, is that security offers choices. It is an instrumental value in that it allows individuals and groups (to a relative degree) to establish the conditions of existence with some expectations of constructing a human life beyond the merely animal. Survival is being alive; security is living. The implication of all this is that security cannot be categorised as an essentially conservative concept. As an instrumental value, security is politically neutral. Security and insecurity are ways of describing the conditions of existence;

[28] *Ibid.*, pp. 21–3.

it is for politics (which can be radical or conservative) to give purposes within those conditions. This being so, the expression 'security for its own sake' is meaningless. Security can never be for its own sake; it is always, to recall Robert Cox, *'for* someone and *for* some purpose'. The challenge, as suggested earlier, is not in defining the concept, but in engaging with the politics of its meaning.

3. Security is a powerful political word

The word security has great power. This is because it refers to something of inestimable value for human societies: relative freedom from life-determining insecurity, and relative enjoyment of the life-enhancing possibilities that arise from this. It is because the word security is related to such positive conditions of living (as opposed to merely surviving) that the very word has come to have so much symbolic importance. (One might draw a parallel with the word 'God', which took on symbolic and actual power because, historically, it referred to an omniscient and omnipotent being.) Here we get into 'speech act' theory, and the writer who has done more to explore this than any in security studies is Ole Wæver.[29]

The idea of a speech act is associated with the philosopher J. L. Austin, who was concerned with words as 'performatives', that is, types of action and not simply statements. Wæver's view, which I share, is that security utterances are a special kind of communicative activity concerned to produce a particular effect on the listener. For Wæver, to name something 'security' is to give what is proposed the particular significance attached to dealing with 'existential threats' and 'extraordinary measures'. Thinking about security in relation to speech act theory is helpful, though chapter 4 will argue that it has been pushed too far in the Copenhagen school's 'theory of securitisation'. Wæver was correct in recognising that to name something 'security' is to give it a particular political significance: 'By saying the words, something is done (like betting, giving a promise, naming a ship).'[30] There is all the difference in the world, for example, in the performative significance of the phrase 'I do' when uttered in response to the question 'Do you enjoy Joni Mitchell's songs?' as opposed to uttering 'I do' in the context of a marriage ceremony. Speech acts are more than verbal communication; they are equivalent to actions.

[29] Ole Wæver, 'Securitization and Desecuritization', in Ronnie D. Lipschutz (ed.), *On Security* (New York: Columbia University Press, 1995), pp. 46–86.
[30] Buzan *et al.*, *Security*, p. 26.

The word security in political discourse signifies priority. If a president of a country announces that 'crime is our biggest national security issue', it means that dealing with crime has been identified as an issue that must be given priority, and hence time, energy, and resources must follow. Once the security label has been attached to an issue, it changes from being a problem to a priority for society. This is why it is important to challenge the discipline's pre-defined conception of security, which in turn leads to a conservative pre-defined agenda. In realist-informed 'national security' theorising in the Cold War, security did indeed appear to be a conservative concept: but it was not *the concept* that was inherently conservative, but rather *the politics behind the conceptualisation.*

4. Security is a derivative concept

The idea that security is a derivative concept is fundamental to a critical theory of security, and the point will be elaborated in the next chapter, in the discussion of the *deepening* move in critical security theorising. For the moment it is enough to say that deepening involves exploring the idea that security outcomes (policies, situations, etc.) *derive* from different underlying understandings of the character and purpose of politics.

In chapter 1 it was argued that traditional security theory derived from statist norms, equating the idea of security with the problem-solving dimension of strategic relations between sovereign states. A conceptualisation of security derived from any different political theory will don a very different mask. A critical theory of security, for example, attempts to open up rather than close down how security is conceived, exploring common humanity rather than national sovereignty, and emancipation rather than power.[31] In seeking to transcend realism's 'false necessities',[32] it is not the meaning of security that is the challenge facing us, but, as was argued earlier, the politics of the meaning.

During the Cold War, a security studies specialist was seen as somebody who knew about nuclear deterrence, the state of the strategic balance, superpower arms control, and so on. Such technicians of strategic power were traditional intellectuals in Gramsci's terminology. Their technical expertise was concerned with manipulating strategic assets

---

[31] Ken Booth, 'Security and Self: Reflections of a Fallen Realist', in Keith Krause and Michael C. Williams (eds.), *Critical Security Studies. Concepts and Cases* (Minneapolis: University of Minnesota Press, 1997), p. 111.
[32] The term is from Roberto Unger, *False Necessities: Anti-Necessarian Social Theory in the Service of Radical Democracy* (Cambridge: Cambridge University Press, 1987).

in the interests of particular states, and was derivative of a particular politics (statist, realist, ethnocentric). This was (and is) pure problem-solving theory in the Coxian sense, and it is this understanding of the remit of security studies (as insider technique) that the critical perspective challenges.

In sum, security is the condition of being and feeling safe. Those who feel safe when they are not (because they do not perceive the threats and risks around them) have a false sense of security; those who feel threatened because they perceive threats and risks that are not present, live with a false sense of insecurity. So far, so good. In the context of world politics, I have argued that security may be a contingently rather than essentially contested concept, but that it has been too little contested within the discipline of international relations. Understanding security begins in conditions of insecurity, which equates with living a determined life (for individuals or groups); it is a category mistake to see security as synonymous with survival; security is always relative, and can be understood subjectively (feeling safe) and non-subjectively (being safe); insecurity that comes from threats to a referent's core values is life determining in a way that lifestyle elective danger is not; security is a word of great political symbolism and is of critical instrumental value; and the politically relevant meaning of security is neither conservative nor neutral but simply derivative of different political theories. What the achievement of a level of security brings to people and groups is some time, energy, and scope to choose to do other things than simply survive as human biological organisms. In this sense, the search for security through emancipatory politics – lifting people as individuals and groups out of structural and contingent oppressions such as war and poverty – is part of the project of inventing humanity.

Emancipation and ideals

The Pursuit of Bread, Knowledge, and Freedom
William Lovett, book title[33]

Emancipation is the heart of a critical theory of world security. It has always been a controversial concept, and will remain so. Ideological critics challenge its implications; friendly critics question its application in specific historical situations; orthodoxies and establishments resist its

---

[33] Discussed by Regina Gagnier, 'Wilde and the Victorians', in Peter Raby (ed.), *The Cambridge Companion to Oscar Wilde* (Cambridge: Cambridge University Press, 1997), pp. 18–33.

threat to their interests; and many others claim they do not know what the term means. In relation to the last point, William Lovett, a Victorian cabinet-maker, radical publisher, and activist gave a brilliantly simple answer. The title of his book pointed to a set of themes that spoke to the idea of emancipation in all places and times: 'the pursuit of bread or material well-being, or freedom from Nature and scarcity; the pursuit of knowledge of Truth, or freedom from ignorance, superstition and lies; and the pursuit of justice, or freedom from political tyranny and economic exploitation'.[34]

Emancipation in theory and practice is concerned with freedom from restraints of one sort or another. In Latin *emancipare* means 'to release from slavery or tutelage'. As the modern conception of emancipation took shape in the Enlightenment, it was inspired by the goal of struggling *against* particular oppressions, notably monarchical despotism, religious intolerance, ignorance, and inequality. In time, a positive side developed, and emancipation became identified with political programmes *for* a better world (characterised by liberty, progress, controlling nature, pursuing equality, and the perfectibility of humanity).[35] Emancipation as an ideal and a rallying cry, in practice, was prominent in many nineteenth-century struggles for independence or for freedom from legal restrictions; notable examples included Jews in Europe, slaves in the United States, blacks in the West Indies, the Irish in the British state, and serfs in Russia.[36]

Emancipation has various definitions.[37] My own conceptualisation follows:[38]

---

[34] As summarised *ibid.*, p. 19.

[35] The literature on the Enlightenment is, of course, immense. A fine and enjoyable study focusing on one country is Porter, *Enlightenment*. For an equally important study, contending that studies of separate national enlightenments are distorting, see: Jonathan I. Israel, *Enlightenment Contested. Philosophy, Modernity, and the Emancipation of Man 1670–1752* (Oxford: Oxford University Press, 2006); see also his earlier *Radical Enlightenment. Philosophy and the Making of Modernity 1650–1750* (Oxford: Oxford University Press, 2001).

[36] For example, Porter, *Enlightenment*, pp. 353ff, 579 (n. 97); Stephen Eric Bronner, *Reclaiming the Enlightenment. Toward a Politics of Radical Engagement* (New York: Columbia University Press, 2004), pp. 86–8, 94; Israel, *Enlightenment Contested*, part III, 'Political Emancipation'; and Jan Nederveen Pieterse, 'Emancipations, Modern and Postmodern', *Development and Change*, vol. 23(3), 1992, p. 8.

[37] For example, the discussion in Pieterse, 'Emancipations', p. 8.

[38] This definition has gone through many refinements, and most are longer than this version. It began with 'A New Security Concept for Europe', pp. 1–7 in Paul Eavis (ed.), *European Security. The New Agenda* (Bristol: Saferworld, 1990); for fuller treatments, see Booth, 'Security and Emancipation', and Booth, 'Three Tyrannies', in Tim Dunne and Nicholas J. Wheeler (eds.), *Human Rights in Global Politics* (Cambridge: Cambridge Uni-

As a discourse of politics, emancipation seeks the securing of people from those oppressions that stop them carrying out what they would freely choose to do, compatible with the freedom of others. It provides a three-fold framework for politics: a philosophical anchorage for knowledge, a theory of progress for society, and a practice of resistance against oppression. Emancipation is the philosophy, theory, and politics of inventing humanity.

The concept's three functions can be briefly described as follows. *As a philosophical anchorage*, emancipation serves as a basis for saying whether something is 'true'; in other words, whether particular claims to knowledge should be taken seriously. An anchorage is not a neutral (objective) foundation, but instead represents the soundest understanding then available on which to frame future political projects. *As a theory of progress*, emancipation offers an account of the actual world of world politics in which projects are possible. Progress is understood, reflexively, as a dynamic and reversible process; it is not therefore an inevitable outcome of politics, nor is it identifiable with one timeless blueprint of social organisation. Finally, *as a practice of resistance* emancipation is a framework for attempting to actualise both nearer-term and longer-term emancipatory goals through strategic and tactical political action based on immanent critique.

Like other key concepts in world politics, emancipation raises as many issues as it settles, and I hope the chief of these will have been addressed by the end of the book. Four are immediately pressing. The first concerns the meaning of freedom. If there is a case for questioning whether security is an 'essentially contested concept', this is not so with 'freedom', one of political theory's most contested concepts. An immediate issue to confront is that of 'false consciousness', the idea that a person or group cannot grasp their true interests because of indoctrination or traditionalist socialisation. Consequently, knowledge – *enlightenment* – is central to freedom, consonant with Kant's motto *Sapere aude!* One cannot have one's own understanding (looking at a matter with some critical distance) under conditions of indoctrination, traditionalist socialisation, and inadequate relevant knowledge. Take the highly controversial and sensitive topic of female genital mutilation, for example. Like many people, I have no doubt at all that this practice is entirely incompatible with freedom, as it is inflicted on girls before they are in any way able to 'freely choose'. What is more, the fact that some compliant older women

versity Press, 1999), pp. 31–70, and 'Emancipation', in Ken Booth (ed.), *Critical Security Studies and World Politics* (Boulder, Colo.: Lynne Rienner, 2005), pp. 181–7.

encourage the practice does not alter this verdict, because there is no reason to suppose they themselves possess the capacity to use their *own* understanding, coming as they do from highly traditionalist cultures (which in this case, as in many others, is a euphemism for patriarchal tyranny).[39] Remembering Kant from chapter 2, we freely choose when our noumenal selves control our phenomenal selves; in other words, when our actions are not the result of error or passion, but are fully voluntary, founded on understanding and reason. Girls who are about to be mutilated do not have the capacity to choose freely in this sense.

Second, I want to distinguish between 'true' and 'false' emancipation. This is not a rhetorical device, but a logical point about the meaning of 'true'. Simply stated, something cannot be true if what exists or is said is its opposite; we understand this point in real life immediately. It cannot be a *fair* division of a picnic hamper if it results in some members of the family being left hungry while others toss buns to ducks. A system cannot be truly *democratic* if there is no way of removing the powerful. And *emancipation* cannot be said to exist if there is oppression (people are deprived of bread, knowledge, and freedom). False emancipation (the opposite of the dynamic philosophical, theoretical, and practical notion of emancipation defined above) is any conception that understands emancipation as timeless or static (whether in relation to ideas, institutions, or situations); undertakes emancipatory politics at the expense of others (making the emancipatory goals of others impossible); or uses emancipation as a cloak for the power of 'the West' or any other entity claiming to have a monopoly of wisdom.[40] False emancipation can come in many guises, and as is the case with any political project there is the danger of mistakes, excesses, 'dark sides', and unpleasant things done in its name. The crucial test lies in concrete historical circumstances.

Three, the invention of humanity needs ideals. The idea of humanity beyond merely being human represents a direct rejection of Rousseau's cry 'Man is born free and is everywhere in chains.' My starting-point is that the species known as 'human' was metaphorically born in chains (like other animal creatures) and, through the evolution of its own consciousness, invented what being free might mean. Being human, in

---

[39] A. Robson, 'Torture not Culture', *AIBS Journal* 63, September–October 1993, pp. 8–9. Although she has been much criticised for her interpretation of Islam, it is difficult not to be moved by the case made by Ayaan Hirsi Ali, *The Caged Virgin. A Muslim Woman's Cry for Reason* (London: The Free Press, 2006), esp. pp. 119–28; the cruelty she is reacting against is graphically described by Nahid Touba, 'Female Genital Mutilation', in Julie Peters and Andrea Wolper, *Women's Rights, Human Rights* (New York: Routledge, 1995), pp. 224–37.
[40] The section below is based on Booth, 'Three Tyrannies', pp. 41–6.

short, is a physiological categorisation, whereas inventing humanity (human being) is a moral choice. One indicator of this categorical difference is suggested by Antonio Damasio's distinction between emotions and feelings: 'Emotions play out in the theater of the body', he has written, 'Feelings play out in the theater of the mind.'[41] By this, he meant that emotions are (usually visible) actions or movements whereas feelings (which are intimately related to emotions) are the mental events that form the 'bedrock of our minds'. Steven Rose puts it like this: 'emotions . . . are physiological phenomena possessed to a degree by all living organisms . . . and feelings, the mental states that are associated with emotions . . . are unique to humans'.[42] In the 'theater of the mind' we can decide whether and how to take the journey from merely being human animals to inventing and reinventing human beings – an ever-becoming humanity. If we decide to take it, the journey needs a road-map of ideals. Allott argued that it is through the 'idea of the ideal' that humans can have hope of self-constituting their future, though they cannot determine it. In the international realm, he said that this creates the opportunity to change 'the scandal of international unsociety' into a new human self-enlightening on a global scale. The 'idea of the ideal' is integral to the idea of emancipation, for it is the road-map and goal-setting denied those still in biological chains, like bulls and budgerigars. Human beings possess *both* innate (Darwin-defined) emotions such as fear, disgust, and happiness *and* evolved (Damasio-defined) feelings essential for inventing humanity, such as trust, love, empathy, and tolerance.

Finally, it is necessary to discuss the relationship between security and emancipation. In my early (now distant) attempts to bring these two concepts together, I described them as 'two sides of the same coin',[43] and came to think of that coin as 'the invention of humanity'. In other words, security would only extend through world society when emancipatory politics made progress in eradicating structural and contingent oppressions. Through this process, people would explore what humanity might become, in terms of peaceful and positive relations, increasingly free of life-determining insecurity: the self-realisation of people(s) would evolve not *against* others, but *with* them.

---

[41] Antonio Damasio, *Searching for Spinoza. Joy, Sorrow and the Feeling Brain* (London: Heinemann, 2003), p. 28; see also pp. 4–7, 28, 70, 184, 277–8.
[42] Steven Rose, *The 21st-Century Brain. Explaining, Mending and Manipulating the Mind* (London: Jonathan Cape, 2005), p. 102; see also pp. 11–56.
[43] Booth, 'Security and Emancipation'.

The image of 'two sides of the same coin' was never as clear as it might have been. A more effective way of explaining the relationship is to conceive security *as the means* and emancipation *and as the end*. This conceptualisation can be done in the manner Gandhi saw the relationship between what he called *ahimsa* (non-violence) and 'Truth', with the former being conceived as the means and the latter as the end. (In one formulation, Gandhi had described the relationship between *ahimsa*/Truth as two sides of a smooth disc such that it was not possible to say 'which is the obverse, and which the reverse'.) The way Gandhi dealt with *ahimsa*/Truth was to say that to practise *ahimsa* is to realise Truth and to realise Truth is to practise *ahimsa*. Ideals should inform means as well as ends, but to be *means* they have to be something we can utilise. In this sense ends and means amount to the same thing, 'since the same moral demands apply to both'. This idea is at the heart of the critical security theory being advanced in this book; it is the idea of non-duality as represented in Gandhi's thinking.[44] This will be elaborated later. For the moment, the non-dualistic relationship between security and emancipation means that to practise security (freeing people from the life-determining conditions of insecurity) is to promote emancipatory space (freedom from oppression, and so some opportunity to explore being human), and to realise emancipation (becoming more fully human) is to practise security (not against others, but with them). Such a conceptualisation fits well with the discussion earlier in the chapter about security being an instrumental concept, and the later definition of emancipation as the political discourse for inventing humanity.

The relationship between security and emancipation proposed here is controversial. Among predictable criticisms is the view that emancipation confuses security studies more than it assists; that emancipation is 'the problem not the solution'; that in real politics (especially in the 'developing' world) the idea of emancipation is worse than confusing, it is dangerous; that emancipation is elitist; and that it is an expression of 'Western'/'Enlightenment' ideas that are not applicable globally. Such criticisms come mainly from realists and their poststructuralist adversary partners. Realists, however, do not necessarily rule out the idea of emancipation in principle; they are only pessimistic about

[44] Glyn Richards, *The Philosophy of Gandhi* (Richmond: Curzon Press, 1995), p. 31. The idea is captured in the title of Johan Galtung's *The Way is the Goal: Gandhi Today* (Ahmedabad: Gujarat Vidyapith Peace Research Centre, 1992); the importance of Gandhi in Galtung's work is evident throughout Peter Lawler, *A Question of Values. Johan Galtung's Peace Research* (Boulder, Colo.: Lynne Rienner, 1995).

its scope, conceiving it as only relevant within an ordered polity, not beyond the latter's boundaries into the anarchy of international relations. Poststructuralists, while critical of the idea of emancipation in principle (naïve, Eurocentric, Enlightenment-derived, imperialist, etc.), nonetheless adopt political stances infused by liberal or other progressivist assumptions.[45] Further criticisms of emancipation will be engaged with later (especially in chapter 6), but one challenge must be addressed immediately, namely hostility among some theorists and historians to the idea of progress. If progress is fundamental to any concept of emancipation, the latter is in serious trouble if the concept of progress cannot be defended.

Enlightenment versus totalitarianism

1789 is abolished.

Nazi victory proclamation in 1933, claiming the demise of the dream of 'Liberty, Equality, and Fraternity' inaugurated by the French Revolution[46]

The Nazis were alien intruders in the 'house of modernity'.[47] They were infused with pre-Enlightenment prejudices and anti-Enlightenment sensibilities. In the aftermath of the industrial-scale mass murder conducted by the Nazis in the name of racial superiority, a body of opinion turned against the Enlightenment, and drew a causal link between it and what happened to Jews in the Nazi era. If a civilised state such as Germany – the land of Kant, Beethoven, and Goethe – could construct factories for gassing people, how could the idea of progress in history have any meaning?

'Enlightenment is totalitarian', wrote Adorno and Horkheimer, central figures of the Frankfurt school, as early as 1944 (that is, before the Nazi era was over, and all its horrific acts exposed).[48] Though the ideas identified with enlightened thinking in Europe through the seventeenth

---

[45] See Hayward Alker, 'Emancipation in the Critical Security Studies Project', and Richard Wyn Jones, 'On Emancipation: Necessity, Capacity, and Concrete Utopias', in Booth, *Critical Security Studies*, pp. 189–213 and 215–35.

[46] Quoted in John Hoffman and Paul Graham, *Introduction to Political Ideologies* (Harlow: Pearson Education, 2006), p. 152.

[47] This quoted phrase is Zygmunt Bauman's in *Modernity and the Holocaust* (Cambridge: Polity, 1989), but the thrust of his argument about Nazi behaviour is just the opposite.

[48] Theodor W. Adorno and Max Horkheimer, *Dialectic of Enlightenment*, trans. John Cumming (London: Verso, 1997; first pub. 1944), p. 6; see Bronner, *Reclaiming*, pp. 95–114, and Wyn Jones, *Security*, pp. 29–52.

and eighteenth centuries had been attacked from the outset by a variety of 'Counter-Enlightenment' voices,[49] their rejection from within its own tradition was particularly striking (though more understandable in view of the backgrounds of Frankfurt's leading exponents). Adorno and Horkheimer argued in their landmark book *Dialectic of Enlightenment* that 'instrumental reason' had led to the bureaucratisation of life, and the reduction of society to the concentration camp.[50] Their exercise in reflexivity argued that far from redeeming the promises of the Enlightenment, Western society had become instrumental reason's monster.[51] Such views were later echoed by postmodern/poststructuralist voices. To Michel Foucault the story of the Enlightenment was not a search for emancipation but a history of control and domination.[52] Other critics found other targets, with the result that it became de rigueur in some circles to stereotype the Enlightenment as the home of totalitarianism.[53] Once the flag had been raised by Adorno and Horkheimer, others followed, and focused on what they saw as the Enlightenment's hubris, errors, and misbegotten faith in progress. And why not? Had not critical theory's leading figures to that point claimed that it was impossible even to write poetry after the Holocaust? Indeed they had, though it has rarely been acknowledged that Adorno later retracted this view, and that several generations of Jewish (and other) poets subsequently rejected it in their lives and work.[54]

Is 'progress' the problem? As ever, a general understanding of the term is necessary before the argument can proceed. According to standard

[49] Bronner, *Reclaiming*, pp. 6–8, 12, 67–9, 88–91.
[50] Adorno and Horkheimer, *Dialectic*, p. 6. See Porter's brusque dismissal of their work as 'historical baloney' in *Enlightenment*, p. xx and n. 15 p. 486, and Wheen's view that their argument is 'so outrageously flawed that polite disagreement is impossible' in *How Mumbo-Jumbo Conquered the World. A Short History of Modern Delusions* (London: Fourth Estate, 2004), pp. 191–2.
[51] Adorno and Horkheimer, *Dialectic*, pp. 3–42. Bronner, *Reclaiming*, was an attempt to 'provide the sequel . . . [they] never wrote in a style they refused to employ'. pp. 1–6 (quotation at p. 5).
[52] Michel Foucault, 'What is Enlightenment?' in Paul Rabinow (ed.), *The Foucault Reader* (New York: Pantheon Books, 1984), pp. 32–50.
[53] For example, John Gray, *Enlightenment's Wake: Politics and Culture at the Close of the Modern Age* (London: Routledge, 1995), and Jonathan Glover, *Humanity: A Moral History of the Twentieth Century* (London: Jonathan Cape, 1999); for further examples, see Porter, *Enlightenment*, pp. xx–xxi.
[54] See Adrienne Rich, 'Legislators of the World', *The Guardian*, 18 November 2006, who argues that in 'dark times we need poetry more than ever'; empirical evidence rejecting Adorno's original verdict is available in Hilda Schiff (ed.), *Holocaust Poetry* (New York: St Martin's Griffin, 1995), a collection of Jewish and non-Jewish poets writing about that for which words ultimately fail.

definitions, progress is *the idea that things (such as technology, the standard of living, society, and even morality) can in some way or another improve over time*. The crux of the debate about the concept obviously focuses on judgements about the empirical evidence for things (technology, morality, etc.) changing, and crucially about what 'improve over time' might mean. Below, I want to argue that improvement in social and political values can indeed be conceived and implemented, though never guaranteed.[55] Under conditions of social justice arising out of the politics of emancipation, not only can basic human needs be met, but also moral progress can be achieved in relation to the human capacity for virtue.[56]

For some, progress has been synonymous with the course of history. History is seen as a teleological process conceived as forward-looking, designed to reach a particular goal, or serve a particular purpose, so that specific events and episodes can be explained in terms of whether or not they contribute to the ultimate goal. Some of the radical conceptions of progress in the nineteenth century, equating history with a story of human perfectibility, belong to such a formulation. Marx's idea of 'historical materialism' was a particularly important expression of teleological thinking, with the evolution of different modes of production shaping peoples' consciousness, which in turn constructed the political, social, and religious contexts and conflicts of the period in question. Out of these conflicts would emerge economic, social, and political progress, with the culmination of history – for Marx – being the triumph of communism; this would be marked by the withering away of the state and other oppressive structures.[57] Another nineteenth-century evolutionary view of progress, arising out of Darwinian thought, portrayed 'mankind' as moving inexorably from a primitive past to future perfectibility. Associated with this was the popular representation of humans literally advancing from apes with floor-brushing knuckles to modern man (the drawings were always of men) standing tall, looking out at the future, and preparing to be the fittest to survive. This image is

---

[55] An eclectic set of readings on the theme of ideal societies – past, present, and future – is Anthony Arblaster and Steven Lukes, *The Good Society. A Book of Readings* (London: Methuen, 1971).

[56] The idea of progress is not the focus but is a key theme in *The Polity Reader in Social Theory*, introduction by Anthony Giddens and others (Cambridge: Polity, 1995).

[57] Karl Marx and Frederick Engels, *Selected Works in One Volume* (Lawrence and Wishart, 1991) is invaluable. A short introduction to Marx's ideas is Peter Singer, *Marx* (Oxford: Oxford University Press, 1985). A longer account, focusing on the man, is Francis Wheen, *Karl Marx* (London: Fourth Estate, 1999), and, focusing on the tradition, is Meghnad Desai, *Marx's Revenge. The Resurgence of Capitalism and the Death of Statist Socialism* (London: Verso, 2002).

less common today than when I went to school, but it remains embedded in many minds.[58]

One criticism of teleological thinking is that it subverts ethics, by generating the belief that the (inevitable) end justifies the means. It is a long-standing criticism of Marx's thought that his theory of history meant that he did not particularly worry about the ethics involved in the means of achieving his goals; his certainty about the outcome largely excused him from this. Partly as a result, it can be argued that the fervour of some of his followers excused their unspeakable means in order to further the triumph of the revolutionary end. The rapid collapse of the ideals evident (among some revolutionaries) in the short gap between the dawn of the Russian Revolution and the callous brutality of Stalinist *Darkness at Noon* stands as a powerful warning to all contemplating revolutionary change.[59] But the danger of instrumental reason is not peculiar to progressive ideologies. Realist thinkers in ancient China, religious zealots during the Inquisition, and Machiavellian leaders in many periods were all practitioners of instrumental reason, separating ends and means, well before the Enlightenment. Teleological thinking tends to subvert ethics, but so can other ways of interpreting history.

It is certainly no part of this book to assume that history is a teleological process. The latter was a common theme among many Enlightenment thinkers, but one that reflexivity demands we eschew. History can no longer be conceived within an overarching vision of progress.[60] Such a perspective for critical theorists was signposted by the use of Boulding's epigraph at the very start of the book. He said that 'We are as we are because we got that way', but any tone of fatalism in his words should not hide his true meaning: human society, globally, could have done very much better. We could also have done much worse. Any progress that has been achieved can be un-achieved. There is nothing stopping the human species, except good luck and an outbreak of good sense, from going further downhill as a collectivity (the gallows philosophy of Yorkshire, where I grew up, begins with sayings such as: 'Things are never so bad that they can't get worse'). Human progress is not

---

[58] 'Social Darwinism' is often taken as extraneous to Darwin's work, but two of his biographers argue that competition, including racial extermination and sexual inequality, were part of 'Darwinism' from the start; see Adrian Desmond and James Moore, *Darwin* (London: Michael Joseph, 1991), p. xxi.

[59] Arthur Koestler, *Darkness at Noon* (Harmondsworth: Penguin, 1971; 1st pub. 1940), is a brilliant account of the logic of violence in dictatorships. The book provokes reflection on ends and means, a central issue in all critical theory.

[60] Porter, *Enlightenment*, p. 230.

guaranteed, whether it be in relation to the growth of global functional institutions, local politics, virtue, standard-setting, and whatever else. My claim is only that progress is possible, and a rational hope.

One of the dangers I want to warn against in this discussion is of flawed reasoning about the past, and its embedding into regressive myths.[61] Giving in to such dangers will obscure the real achievements of human society, and in so doing will contribute to subverting a politics of hope – an essential collective resource.[62] With this in mind, a defence of progress must engage with the myth that elides Enlightenment and totalitarianism. One place to start is the influential attack made on the Enlightenment's ostensible dark side from the sociologist Zygmunt Bauman, who in the late 1980s equated the Holocaust with modernity: '*The Holocaust was born and executed in our modern rational society, at the high stage of our civilization and at the peak of human cultural achievement, and for this reason it is a problem of that society, civilization and culture.*'[63] Bauman went on to interpret the mass slaughter of Jews by Nazi Germany not as a shocking event completely alien to the sensibility of the Enlightenment, but as an integral part of it. His argument was that key features of what he described (vaguely) as 'modernity' were essential to the Holocaust. In Nazi Germany, reason and rationality combined with bureaucratic record-keeping and modern technology to construct the bureaucratisation of mass murder.

History records that politically or racially motivated slaughter, regardless of the perpetrator, is committed with the technology at hand. So it was with the ethnic cleansing of the '500 nations' on the western frontier by the US cavalry and their repeating rifles in the nineteenth century; and so it was, more recently, in the genocidal attacks on the Tutsis in Rwanda in 1994 by the machetes of the *genocidaires*.[64] The Nazis also used what was at hand. At the beginning of the Second World

---

[61] On the latter, Philip Allott, 'The Future of the Human Past', is as brilliant as it is short: in Ken Booth (ed.), *Statecraft and Security. The Cold War and Beyond* (Cambridge: Cambridge University Press, 1998), pp. 323–37.

[62] The agents of progressive change need empowerment; see Pieterse's account of different forms of collective mobilisation: 'Emancipations', pp. 19–22.

[63] Bauman, *Modernity and the Holocaust*, p. x (emphasis in the original).

[64] When Columbus arrived in Hispaniola in 1492, there were around forty million native Americans; by 1890, when the last groups of Sioux were moved onto a reservation following the massacre at Wounded Knee, there were less than 250,000. The struggle of the native Americans for survival, as the United States sought living space across the continent, is told in Alvin M. Josephy, *500 Nations* (London: Hutchinson, 1995). On the genocide in Rwanda, where up to one million people were killed in April 1994 by an estimated 100,000 or more 'foot soldiers of the genocide', see Linda Melvern, *Conspiracy to Murder. The Rwandan Genocide* (London: Verso, 2004) (the cover-photograph is of a single,

War Jews were massacred in pre-industrial ways, as in Kovno at the end of June 1941, where thousands were beaten to death;[65] here and elsewhere, racist killing took place in ways that were neither bureaucratic nor technological.[66] Before 1939 exile had been the chosen way of dealing with 'the Jewish problem', not extermination.[67] Even when the system of death-camps was functioning at the maximum, the murdering of Jews continued by other means. Bureaucratic and industrial slaughter were not necessary features of genocide under what is called 'modernity', though they did become emblematic. Other genocides have not conformed to Nazi industrial modalities, and they are unlikely to. Historical specifics are crucial to such behaviour.[68]

The role of anti-Semitism in German history was central to what happened. Bauman's thesis shifted the blame for the increasingly shameful treatment of the Jews (and other victims of the camps) away from the focus on Nazi racist ideology and the history of anti-Semitism in Germany, to a general criticism of the problems of rational modern society. His book was well received in Germany when it first came out, in contrast to that by Daniel Jonah Goldhagen. *Hitler's Willing Executioners. Ordinary Germans and the Holocaust*[69] was not a title to win friends in Germany, however much the country had changed over the half century since the 1930s/40s. What the *Willing Executioners* did importantly insist upon was the centrality in any account of the Holocaust of giving due weight to historical specifics, particularly the strength of anti-Semitism in Germany and the unfolding momentum of events after 1933. In the interwar years, according to Goldhagen, 'the German people were more dangerously oriented towards Jews than they had been during any other time since the dawn of modernity', and this fed 'eliminationist

mass-murdering machete), and also her *A People Betrayed. The Role of the West in Rwanda's Genocide* (London: Zed Books, 2000).
[65] Daniel Jonah Goldhagen, *Hitler's Willing Executioners. Ordinary Germans and the Holocaust* (London: Abacus, 1996), p. 151; all that was 'modern' about this episode was the camera taking photographs.
[66] On the gathering momentum of genocide, and particularly the methods of the notorious *Einsatzgruppen*, see Goldhagen, *Hitler's Willing Executioners*, ch. 4, 'The Nazis' Assault on the Jews: its Character and Evolution'. With special reference to the development of Auschwitz, see Laurence Rees, *Auschwitz. The Nazis and the 'Final Solution'* (London: BBC Books, 2005), ch. 1, 'Surprising beginnings'.
[67] William D. Rubinstein, *The Myth of Rescue. Why the Democracies Could Not Have Saved More Jews from the Nazis* (London: Routledge, 1997).
[68] As brought out, for example, in Walter Laquer (ed.), *The Holocaust Encyclopedia* (New Haven, Conn.: Yale University Press, 2001).
[69] For Goldhagen's own account of its reception in Germany, see 'Afterword', *Hitler's Willing Executioners*, pp. 463–6.

antisemitism'.[70] If the soil for the brutal treatment of the Jews was fertile, the extent to which eliminationist views were able to grow has to be understood in relation to the momentum of events, and especially the course of the war. Once war had broken out, in 1939, the earlier policies adopted by the Nazis for dealing with their Jewish problem – notably their expulsion from the Reich – were no longer possible. A different solution had to be found, and possibilities opened up after 1941, when total victory over the Soviet Union appeared likely, and created the space to conceive the final solution.[71]

To emphasise historical specificity (in the manner of the historian Goldhagen) rather than sweeping explanations such as 'modernity' (in the manner of the sociologist Bauman) inevitably draws attention to the site of the Holocaust, Nazi Germany. No false conclusions should be drawn from this about 'Germans', however. Primo Levi, with the authority of the victim, made this point, arguing that the historical specificity of the Holocaust should never become an excuse to stereotype all Germans or all German history.[72] It was certainly not the case that all Germans, nor all those from other nations living in Nazi-dominated Europe, became clones of Adolf Eichmann, despite the pressures to conform. The names of Oskar Schindler, Raoul Wallenberg, and Mies Giep are famous among those recognised as Righteous 'Among the Nations' in Yad Vashem, the Holocaust museum in Jerusalem. Thousands of other rescuers, not remembered, 'did what we had to do' as one said.[73] Among political communities under Nazi domination during the Second World War, Bulgaria was notable for its efforts to resist the deportation of its Jews. In June 1943 the German Ambassador to Sofia (Adolf-Heinz Beckerle) lamented that the Bulgarian people 'lacked the ideological enlightenment that we have', and that the Bulgarian man in the street 'does not see in the Jews any flaws justifying taking special measures against them'. When Beckerle was on trial in 1948 for wartime crimes, the defence lawyers noted that 'in Bulgaria there was no anti-Semitism in the conventional sense of the word'.[74] In pointing

[70] *Ibid.*, ch. 2, 'The Evolution of Eliminationist Antisemitism in Modern Germany', and ch. 3, 'Eliminationist Antisemitism: The "Common Sense" of German Society during the Nazi Period' (the quotation is at p. 79).
[71] This is the view of Christopher Browning, *The Origins of the Final Solution* (London: Heinemann, 2004), and Götz Aly and Susanne Heim, *Architects of Annihilation. Auschwitz and the Logic of Destruction*, trans. Allan Blunden (London: Phoenix, 2003).
[72] Primo Levi, *The Drowned and the Saved* (London: Abacus, 1998), pp. 71, 137–65, 169–70.
[73] Moving accounts are collected in Martin Gilbert, *The Righteous. The Unsung Heroes of the Holocaust* (London: Doubleday, 2002).
[74] *Ibid.*, p. 214.

out the historical specificity of the Bulgarian rescuers, these German jurists were inadvertently underlining the historical specificity of the Nazi perpetrators.

The intoxicating brew of Teutonic romanticism and racism in Nazi ideology as it developed in the interwar years sought to abolish the Enlightenment ideals of liberty, equality, and solidarity. The persecution and attempted destruction of the Jews (and other targets) represented a complete rejection of the Enlightenment's spirit of tolerance, rights, and democracy. The emancipation of Jews had been an important manifestation of enlightened politics in the nineteenth century, with anti-Semitism being what Bronner called 'the philosophy of those who choose to think with their gut'. Such bigotry always stood, he said, in 'inverse relation to the support for Enlightenment ideals'.[75] Nazi propaganda played on medieval (pre-Enlightenment) mythology, while from the beginning their politics and laws – contrary to Enlightenment sensibility – crushed tolerance and embedded racial discrimination. It is therefore difficult to understand why, in trying to explain the Holocaust, Enlightenment critics give such priority to the Nazi culture of bureaucratic efficiency (involving practices more or less shared with other industrialised states) as opposed to the Nazi negation of the Enlightenment's core values (which it shared only with other fascist regimes). The argument that the Holocaust was a 'legitimate resident' in the 'house of modernity', as Bauman claimed, is as flawed as it has been influential.[76] The most one can say in defence of Bauman's thesis is that if 'modernity' was doing any work at all as an explanatory factor, its impact was very uneven.

Given the universal horror (with the exception of those belonging to the disagreeable rump of Holocaust deniers) that greeted, and continues to greet, the emblematic image of Auschwitz, it is fanciful of sociologists such as Bauman to regard the Holocaust a 'legitimate resident' of the house of modernity. If it was so, how is its uniqueness to be explained? Why have other societies, fellow residents in the house of modernity, resisted engineering industrial-scale genocide against despised minorities? Why have they instead committed themselves to the promotion of human rights (if not always consistently their practice)? Historical specificity must be given its due. Compare, for example, the iconic lives of Adolf Eichmann and Eleanor Roosevelt. According to Arendt, Eichmann was lacking in values; in direct contrast, according

[75] Bronner, *Reclaiming*, pp. 81–94 (quotations at p. 94).
[76] Strong criticisms of Bauman include R. H. T. O'Kane, 'Modernity, the Holocaust and Politics', *Economy and Society*, vol. 26(1), 1997, pp. 43–61.

to Blanche Cook, values were integral to Eleanor Roosevelt's identity.[77] Before the Second World War she had opposed racism in the United States and fascism in Spain; she had supported Jewish refugees from Europe and after the war sought to discover the full horror of the Holocaust (with her own eyes and ears, as well as from the reports of others); she then worked tirelessly to get the United Nations to adopt the Universal Declaration of Human Rights, enshrining the ideals of liberty, equality, and solidarity across the world.[78] Here were two products of what is vaguely called modernity, but one was a true daughter of Enlightenment values, the other a cog in a power-mad racist machine. In 1948 Eleanor Roosevelt was prominent in attempting to restore globally the ideals and rational hopes of 1789, which the Nazis had explicitly attempted to abolish.

Two cheers for progress

For reason is the light of the mind and without her all things are dreams and phantoms.   Baruch Spinoza[79]

The idea of progress, as suggested earlier, was critical to Enlightenment projects. It was indeed 'the ultimate Enlightenment gospel' in the view of Roy Porter,[80] and its 'Lockean model', in his opinion, was its best exemplar. It consisted of an image of 'the mind maturing through experience from ignorance to knowledge', with this individual 'paradigm' being replicated universally: 'The individual could gain practical knowledge through the senses, could reason through words, and could find out his duties to God and his fellows. Being error-prone, man was imperfect; being educable, he was improvable. Mistakes could be expunged and advance would come by trial and error.'[81]

There was, of course, much hubris in the eighteenth and nineteenth centuries in some quarters about the direction and inevitability of

---

[77] Elisabeth Young-Bruehl, *Hannah Arendt. For Love of the World* (New Haven, Conn.: Yale University Press, 1982), p. 367 and ch. 8, 'Cura Posterior: Eichmann in Jerusalem'; see also her *Why Arendt Matters* (New Haven, Conn.: Yale University Press, 2006). Hannah Arendt, *Eichmann in Jerusalem. A Report on the Banality of Evil* (Harmondsworth: Penguin, 1985; 1st pub. 1963); Blanche Wiesen Cook, *Eleanor Roosevelt* (London: Bloomsbury, 1992), pp. 17–18.

[78] UNDHR was adopted on 10 December 1948; on Eleanor Roosevelt's role, see Cook, *Eleanor Roosevelt*, pp. 17–18.

[79] Quoted by Bronner, *Reclaiming*, p. vi.

[80] Porter, *Enlightenment*, p. 445; see Bronner, *Reclaiming*, pp. 17–40 ('In praise of progress').

[81] Porter, *Enlightenment*, p. 70.

progress, but the picture was never simple. Even in the Victorian age – where faith in progress was palpable – some thought that the combination of market ideology, technological development, and mass communication could lead to mass control rather than enlightened understanding.[82] Such dissenting voices represented the true spirit of enlightenment, not discipline and surveillance, as later claimed by Foucault.[83] Nietzsche better reflected the spirit of the Enlightenment when he called upon 'the man of tomorrow and the day after tomorrow' to stand 'in opposition to his today', to show the courage and imagination to 'create new values'; this was the stance necessary for modern men and women to steer their way through the dangerous future.[84] For Marshall Berman, all the 'great modernists' of the nineteenth century spoke in complex terms about the modern world – in voices resonating with 'self-discovery and self-mockery, with self-delight and self-doubt', denouncing modern life 'in the name of values that modernity itself has created'.[85] This view of progress is self-critical and sceptical. Berman wrote: 'All that is solid melts into air [Marx famously wrote] . . . and men at last are forced to face . . . the real conditions of their lives and their relations with their fellow men.' For Marx this not only referred to the melting of bourgeois forms, but also the possibility that the victory of communism would have to face the same threat of 'melting down in the modern air'. Marx had answers, but as Berman said: 'one of the distinctive virtues of modernism is that it leaves its questions echoing in the air long after the questioners themselves, and their answers, have left the scene'.[86] This is the spirit of progress in enlightened thinking: the belief that it is possible to create the conditions in which humans can dare to hope and dare to know in the interests of developing individual self-responsibility towards creating a world community of reciprocal responsibility.

In the light of these brief remarks about progress as a political idea, I offer five propositions for students of security:

1. Even if progress in the past has sometimes been associated with hubris, it does not follow that the concept is fundamentally flawed

As a central theme of Enlightenment thinking, progress became part of the metaphysics of the West and its view of history. Without doubt, the

---

[82] Gagnier, 'Wilde and the Victorians', p. 19.   [83] Porter, *Enlightenment*, p. 482.
[84] Marshall Berman, *All That Is Solid Melts into Air. The Experience of Modernity* (London: Verso, 1983), p. 23.
[85] *Ibid.*, p. 23.   [86] *Ibid.*, p. 21.

conception of progress that equated it with a law of nature was naïve and dogmatic.[87] As a result, it was no wonder that many became disillusioned about progress when it became apparent that scientific advance, technological development and knowledge accumulation did not guarantee happiness, perfectibility, and control over nature and ourselves. But if every major idea were consigned to the dustbin because some of its proponents went to extremes, adopted fundamentalist positions, or exhibited hubris, then human society would still simply be the product of the biological instincts of its members. The idea of love, for example, can drive people to extremes and it possesses a dark side, but it has become central to the invention of human being. Love could not exist without the potentiality of its opposite, nor could much of the world's literature and drama.

The rational response to the history of the idea of progress should be reflexivity, not rejection. *Reflexivity* is the idea that societies strategically monitor their own and others' behaviour to 'manage the rules that make the game of interaction possible, with the resources at their disposal, and regenerate them in so doing'.[88] Through reflexivity a more rational understanding of progress can be achieved. Many have learned the paradoxes and problems of progress: that control does not necessarily follow knowledge; that affluence does not buy happiness; that science does not necessarily promote peace; that the idea of progress can be appropriated for inhuman purposes; and that progress is rarely linear if it takes place at all. If the test of theory is practice, we must expect some failures, but failures in themselves do not mean that a trial was not worth doing in the first place. We learn through mistakes, as has been the case (to some degree) with the idea of 'development' in the Third World; there have been many disappointed hopes, but now there is better understanding.[89] Reflexivity is the essence of reason, and critical thinking above all must always be ready to turn in on itself, if it is to be true.[90] As a result of reflexivity, we know that the idea of progress

---

[87] Mary Midgley, *Wisdom, Information, and Wonder. What Is Knowledge For?* (London: Routledge, 1989), pp. 12–14.

[88] McSweeney is good on reflexivity: see *Security, Identity and Interests*, pp. 140–2, 206–19; for a postmodern reading of reflexivity – 'the burden we can neither carry nor throw off' – see Hilary Lawson, *Reflexivity. The Post-modern Predicament* (London: Hutchinson, 1985), quotation at p. 8.

[89] For a reassessment see Majid Rahnema with Victoria Bawtree (eds.) *The Post-Development Reader* (London: Zed Books, 1997).

[90] Ken Booth, 'Dare not to Know: International Relations Theory Versus the Future', in Ken Booth and Steve Smith (eds.), *International Relations Theory* (Cambridge: Polity, 1995), pp. 328–50.

is not what it was, but that in itself underlines the very progress of the idea.

2. *It is possible to talk of moral progress*

The idea of moral progress is always the most controversial of the dimensions of this controversial concept. Some assert that such progress is impossible because human nature always pulls us back. This was evident in Konrad Lorenz's 1960s theory of innate human aggression.[91] There are robust reasons for thinking such views are mistaken, and the roles of institutions in human culture are crucial in this regard.

We all learn (for good or ill) through the institutions of the societies in which we live, and this is one reason why we can at least consider the possibility of moral progress.[92] As generation follows generation, individual human beings are not born progressively more virtuous. Nor was there, from the start of the species, a gene coded 'Amnesty International'. There is only the biological possibility of learning different ways of behaviour through culture and institutions.[93] Some people have been lucky enough to have been born into societies whose institutions have taught them to behave in better ways than their forebears. None of my friends and acquaintances are slave owners or work in the slave trade. This might not have been the case in the past, especially had they lived in Liverpool or Bristol. This outcome is not because my friends were born with virtuous genes, unlike those of their ancestors who lived when slavery was big business in Britain. The key is that we live in a country that abolished slavery two centuries ago, and whose legal and political institutions promote social attitudes that reject slavery (a situation that is not the case, regrettably, in all contemporary societies[94]). Moral progress is not guaranteed by biology, but the potential for it is; and when it is invented, it has the potential to be sustained by benign institutions.

---

[91] Konrad Lorenz, *On Aggression*, trans. Marjorie Latzke (London: Methuen, 1966).

[92] Mary Midgley, *The Ethical Primate. Humans, Freedom and Morality* (London: Routledge, 1994).

[93] See Matt Ridley, *Nature Versus Nurture. Genes, Experience and What Makes us Human* (London: Fourth Estate, 2003).

[94] At the start of the millennium *The Index on Censorship* described slavery as 'alive and well as never before in history', involving over twenty-seven million victims: see its issue 192, 'The New Slavery', vol. 29(1), 2000, pp. 5–82. For background, Hugh Thomas, *The Slave Trade. The History of the Atlantic Slave Trade: 1440–1870* (London: Picador, 1997), is encyclopaedic.

The argument above implies that we know what we are talking about when we use the term 'moral progress'. I think we generally do, though there is plenty of room for discussion, especially across cultures. One helpful formulation in this regard is Peter Singer's idea of the 'transcultural judgement of history'. His examples of human betterment that have withstood the judgement of history include the struggle against slavery, the unionising of workers in the face of inhumane working conditions, the granting of the vote to women (and the right to be educated and hold property), the fight against Hitler, and the civil rights movement in the United States in the 1960s. Contemporary illustrations of being on the 'right side' include helping the poorest, promoting peaceful resolution, extending ethical concern beyond the human species, and protecting the environment. Quoting Henry Sidgwick, Singer refers to this as 'the point of view of the universe'.[95] To believe that moral progress is possible does not mean that specific instances of it can always be immediately or universally recognised, or that all political and social change in the name of progress is for the good of society.[96] But as earlier illustrations showed, it can happen, and we should recognise and celebrate it, not least because it nurtures the spirit of daring to hope.

There is, of course, plenty to regret in the history of the idea of progress. There have been countless victims in the *name* of progress, though really in the *cause* of someone's power-seeking. It has become standard to describe the twentieth century as being the world's most violent, though I have yet to see a persuasive comparative methodology of violence in all its dimensions and across many centuries. Having to opt to live in any century whatsoever, from behind a 'veil of ignorance', with no knowledge of one's class or gender or country or aptitudes, is not an enticing prospect. This is not said to minimise the violence of the twentieth century, but rather to suggest that its uniqueness may rest elsewhere than in its brutality. A different account of that bloody century might choose to show that the daily lives of many were lifted from traditional drudgery; there were significant developments in female emancipation (including some recognition of women's rights in international law); commitments were made to the idea of the development of poorer countries; racism and colonialism were delegitimised internationally; the goal of disarmament became a staple of

[95] Peter Singer, *How Are We to Live? Ethics in an Age of Self-Interest* (Oxford: Oxford University Press, 1997), p. 265.
[96] See Marshall Sahlins, 'The Original Affluent Society', in Rahnema and Bawtree, *Post-Development*, pp. 3–21.

international affairs; the need for a universal and multipurpose international organisation became accepted; a human rights culture was sponsored globally; and the legal scope for war was narrowed more than ever before in history. The fact that many people in some parts of the world began to live much longer was in itself a barometer of lives escaping their former biological destiny. It is not difficult to recall failed development projects, state hypocrisy on human rights, disappointed hopes about collective security, lack of progress in disarmament, world wars – and all the other instances of unfulfilled hopes and unrealised ideals. There were massive human wrongs in the twentieth century, but what was aspired to was often amazing, and what was achieved should not be lightly dismissed.

Although twentieth-century international politics witnessed terrible levels of political and other forms of violence, it was also a period of international standard-setting, and historians in future may well come to identify this as a key feature, rather than the violence. This standard-setting was the primary manifestation of moral progress internationally, and even if governments did not live up to their pledges, their commitments were a measure against which they could be called to account.[97] The Kremlin discovered this with the so-called 'Helsinki effect'. The general significance of the package of agreements at Helsinki in 1975 seemed to be the legitimisation of the status quo in Europe. Principle VII of the Helsinki Final Act dealt with 'human rights and fundamental freedoms', and this was considered by most leaders of the time to be 'diplomatic window dressing, a sop to domestic opinion'. In the event, this famous 'third basket' of Helsinki principles 'was to prove mortal' to the Soviet Union in the opinion of Tony Judt and other analysts of the period.[98] The Helsinki effect meant that by their standard-setting on 'human rights and fundamental freedoms' the signatories of the agreements created space for the growth of the Helsinki Rights movement, in which groups of citizens or individuals monitored their government's compliance with the commitments they had made, and even

---

[97] This argument has been well made in relation to the British Labour government's 'ethical foreign policy' by Nicholas J. Wheeler and Tim Dunne, 'Good International Citizenship: A Third Way for British Foreign Policy', *International Affairs*, vol. 74(4), 1998, and Tim Dunne and Nicholas J. Wheeler, 'Blair's Britain: A Force for Good in the World?' in Karen E. Smith and Margot Light (eds.), *Ethics and Foreign Policy* (Cambridge: Cambridge University Press, 2001), pp. 167–84.

[98] These quotations, and the one following, are from Tony Judt, *Postwar. A History of Europe Since 1945* (London: Heinemann, 2005), pp. 502–3.

the toughest governments found their legitimacy being eaten away from below.[99]

It is easy to be cynical about international standard-setting, but double standards are better than no standards, and hypocrisy, after all, is the tribute that vice pays to virtue. The twentieth century tested the idea of progress to the limit, but the idea survived: in some countries there were important civil and economic rights successes; in many there were improvements in people's daily lives; and in the international realm there was standard-setting of historical significance. As a result, tyrants came under more pressure, just as they flourished; war-loving leaders found it more difficult to justify aggressive wars; and governments faced new difficulties when attempting to disregard the rights and opinions of their own citizens and those of other states. This may not be much for the countless millions for whom the world has not worked, and is not working, but in wider historical perspective, it is a great deal.

3. Societies must have an idea of the ideal

In the final decades of the twentieth century, after the dreams of the 1960s had faded, the mood music of so many intellectuals in the West was played by the French philosopher Jean-François Lyotard, and his pronouncement that the postmodern was 'incredulity toward metanar-ratives'.[100] To such opinions, progress was passé, as were any ideals tra-ditionally associated with the Enlightenment. It did not seem to dawn on the purveyors of such views, especially those working in universities, that they would not have had a platform to express their views about Enlightenmnet values if brave people in the past had not been passion-ate about welfarist metanarratives, including ideals of public education and democracy. These values had to be fought for in order to get them implemented against the power structures of the day. The right to criti-cise had to be struggled over, so incredulity towards those who posture against the idea of progress embodied in such values, even while they exercise them, is always appropriate.

An ideal, according to Philip Allott, is 'when the mind conceives of the present in the light of a better future . . . The ideal is the better

---

[99] See Mary Kaldor, Gerard Holden, and Richard Falk (eds.), *The New Détente: Rethinking East–West Relations* (London: Verso, 1989), Margaret E. Keck and Kathryn Sikkink, *Activists Beyond Borders* (Ithaca, N.Y.: Cornell University Press, 1998), p. 24, Mary Kaldor, *Global Civil Society. An Answer to War* (Cambridge: Polity, 2003), ch. 3 ('The ideas of 1989'), and John Lewis Gaddis, *The Cold War* (London: Allen Lane, 2005), pp. 186–91.
[100] Jean-François Lyotard, *The Postmodern Condition* (Manchester: Manchester University Press, 1984; first published 1979), pp. xxiii–xxiv, 5.

potentiality of the actual, acting as a moral imperative in the present, with a view to making a better future.' It is the dialectic of the actual and the ideal, he argues, that has made human reality into a moral order.[101] Ideals here serve as standard-setting devices. Looking to the past, Allott considered that the gap between the really existing world and the ideal had served as a spur to creating a moral order in society; the gap allowed a judgement to be made about the state of the really existing world which in turn might inspire action, including self-sacrifice. Through these political struggles, human beings and societies are in a constant process of constitution and reconstitution, negotiating the idea of the possible and the idea of the desirable. As a result, Allott argued, 'a particular form' has been given to human reality – 'the world made by the human mind'. Consequently, looking to the present, 'We would not be as we are without the idea of the ideal'; and looking to the future, 'We will not be what we could be without the idea of the ideal.'[102]

Enlightenment is not imperialism. Many problems in world politics today can be placed at the door of the European imperialists of the nineteenth century and later, but, as the victims of the most powerful armies of the ancient world knew only too well, imperialism did not wait to be invented by the *philosophes*. Ideas of human betterment have existed across time and cultures; were it not so, human society would still be no more complex than that of our nearest primate relatives. 'A map of the world that does not include Utopia', Oscar Wilde famously pronounced, 'is not even worth glancing at.'[103] Such a view is neither culture-bound nor time-bound. Think of the teachings of the Buddha ('the enlightened one'), classical Greek notions of a 'golden age', Chinese enlightenments, religious traditions of providence and salvation, and all the 'enlightenments' through history and the long tradition of philosophising about common humanity.[104] Being human gives us the capacity to think up social and other ideals, and ideals help the invention of human beings.

[101] Such ideas inform the conceptualisation of emancipation developed by Pieterse: concern with autonomy, self-definition, the importance of a moral horizon etc.; see 'Emancipations', pp. 7–8.
[102] Philip Allott, 'Globalization from Above. Actualizing the Ideal through Law', in Ken Booth, Tim Dunne, and Michael Cox (eds.), *How Might We Live? Global Ethics in the New Century* (Cambridge: Cambridge University Press, 2001), p. 70; see also the version published in Philip Allott, *The Health of Nations. Society and Law beyond the State* (Cambridge: Cambridge University Press, 2002), pp. 7–96.
[103] Quoted in Ruth Levitas, *The Concept of Utopia* (New York: Philip Allan, 1990), p. 5.
[104] On the 'metaphor' of enlightenment see Allott, 'Globalization from Above', p. 67 (esp. n. 15). On cosmopolitan thinking see Derek Heater, *World Citizenship and Government. Cosmopolitan Ideas in the History of Western Political Thought* (Houndmills: Macmillan, 1996), and Jacques Baudot (ed.), *Building a World Community. Globalisation and the Common Good*

4. Progress is now a hard-wired political concept

While many continue to scoff at the very idea of progress – still imagining, against the facts, that poetry is impossible after Auschwitz – most people on earth think differently. They hope for a better world, and even think it may one day be possible. One cannot forget the universal spirit of liberty that was alive in 1989, which greeted the sight of 'ordinary people' taking hammers to the Berlin Wall, and the subsequent dismantling in the middle of Europe of a military confrontation that could have destroyed civilised life in the northern hemisphere; or the joy and admiration throughout the world at the pictures of Nelson Mandela leaving prison after twenty-seven years, and then speaking with dignified and magnificent tolerance and hope; or the physical and mental bravery of Chinese students in Tiananmen Square in the face of ruthless state violence, and especially the iconic image of the lone individual in front of of a line of tanks.[105] In 1989 the spirit of Enlightenment was transmitted in real time across the world.

The words of politicians, social workers, human rights activists, business leaders – not to mention the world's victims – tell us daily that an idea of progress informs their political, social and economic programmes, discourses and sources of legitimacy. While some of this might be window dressing, it is also a metaphysic. Despite the scepticism, the idea of progress remains a powerful discourse within many political cultures, and not only liberal democracy. People everywhere have hopes and fears; and whether it is advancing the former or escaping the latter, the idea of improved conditions of existence – in other words, progress – is hard-wired.

5. What is needed is more enlightenment, not its rejection

Daryl Glaser, a scholar from South Africa, and therefore somebody directly familiar with life in a state that was once committed to institutionalised racism, has offered an important counter to the Bauman thesis and the simplistic interlinking by postmodern writers of the Holocaust and modernity.[106] In a book written a decade after

(Seattle: University of Washington Press, in association with the Royal Danish Ministry of Foreign Affairs, 2001).

[105] The fascinating story of the still unknown 'Tank man' was told in a film by Antony Thomas, More4, 29 May 2006. The iconic photographs from 1989, familiar throughout the world, were not recognised by undergraduates at Beijing University in 2006.

[106] Daryl Glaser, *Politics and Society in South Africa* (London: Sage, 2000), p. 68.

Mandela's release, Glaser argued that it was not the surveillance, statistics, and regulation that were the aspects of Nazi behaviour demanding attention. Nor was it the 'lawfulness, planning, bureaucratic regulation or the professionalisation of knowledge' that fed into Nazi racial policies. That is, Glaser claimed that the features of modernity showcased by the Bauman thesis were not what demanded attention; rather, it was the 'institutionalisation of a racial hierarchy of wealth, status and power, enforced by repressive, often arbitrary state authority, assisted by bad laws'. What was wrong in Nazi Germany (and in apartheid South Africa) was not 'modernity', but laws and politics that served ideas of racial superiority – a prejudice that was directly contrary to 'modern ideals like social justice'. Modernity for Glaser delivered ideas of social justice to South Africa, while its modalities in the form of statistics and regulation, and so on constituted the very means by which illiteracy could be overcome, and the health of the disadvantaged improved.

Rejecting the logic and political implications of the Bauman thesis, Glaser advocated 'more and better law, effectively enforced, and more "scientific" information about the condition of the people, not less of these "modern" goods'. His view was that the people(s) of post-apartheid South Africa were in a better position than in the recent past, albeit still a perilous one, because the oppressed had identified with modernity's ideas of tolerance and equality, and had found solidarity in the global human rights supporters. Social development (improved literacy and better health), he stressed, requires planning, professionalised knowledge, and other modalities of modernity – not their rejection. What Glaser called the 'organisational machinery of "modernity"' to give effect to "modern" ideas like social justice'[107] does not guarantee the security and hence prospects for emancipation for South Africa's peoples, but it does give them hope.[108]

The idea of progress is not what it was, but is more useful as a result. It should never be considered as part of nature's plan for history, or pursued with hubris, but always with reflexivity. The ideals of emancipation that inform progressive politics are guides for judgement and action; without them societies will replicate structural and other oppressions, and humanity will never be what it might become.

---

[107] *Ibid.*
[108] See Ken Booth and Peter Vale, 'Security in Southern Africa', in Peter Vale, *Security and Politics in South Africa* (Boulder, Colo.: Lynne Rienner, 2003).

Community and identity

> Cas is Cas and Feath is Feath
>> Placards at rugby league games in Featherstone, circa 1994[109]

The first question of community, which is implicit in the pursuit of security and emancipation, is a simple one: where do *we* end and *they* begin? But the question of identity that underpins this question is more complex: *who or what* are 'we', and *who or what* are 'they'? To discuss community is to enter tricky conceptual and political waters. Despite this, and the manner in which 'community' is notorious for evading precise definition, I want to persist with the term as a way of expressing what it means to be a politically relevant *we*. If the term did not exist, it would have to be invented, and it would never be able to escape two difficulties of the original:

1. Community is a fuzzy word

Like 'motherhood' and 'apple-pie', community is the sort of word we are tempted to overuse because of its positive connotations (a sense of common identity, shared interests, mutual obligations, a sense of inter-dependence, common social understandings, cultural habits, etc.). The cultural critic Raymond Williams pointed out in a well-known discussion of the concept in the mid-1970s that community is a 'warmly persuasive word' to describe an existing or alternative set of relationships, and that unlike other terms of social organisation ('nation', for example) he said that it never seemed to be used unfavourably.[110] Ferdinand Tönnies in 1887 had influentially formalised the distinction between society and community (*Gemeinshaft* and *Gesellschaft*) and Williams followed this usage, describing community as always having referred both to actual groups of people and to a particular quality of relationship that implied a more immediate (more organic) relationship than implied by

---

[109] These placards appeared at demonstrations against the idea that Featherstone and Castleford, neighbouring mining towns in Yorkshire, should amalgamate their rugby league teams in order to compete more effectively, in the attempt to make the sport more of a globalised game and meet the demands of TV. A super-league was created, involving fewer but stronger teams, and with it players lost their organic relationship with the fans. In the Darwinian process, the fittest survived and the game became faster, more technically proficient, more professional, and the players (now mercenaries) became better paid. But something was lost. Star players no longer lived down the street, knew your dad, and said 'Ay up, cock, ow's tha doin?' The story is told by Ian Clayton, Ian Daley, and Robert Gale, *When Push Comes to Shove*, vol. II (Castleford: Yorkshire Arts Circus, 1995).

[110] Raymond Williams, *Keywords: A Vocabulary of Culture and Society* (Glasgow: Fontana, 1976), pp. 65–6.

society. He distinguished between 'the more direct, more total and therefore more significant relationships of community and the more formal, more abstract and more instrumental relationships of state, or of society in its modern sense'. Such distinctions are never as clear in daily life as in sociology, and in a world that is increasingly on the move, practice has ever more tended to outstrip theory.[111]

As with other fuzzy terms with ideological power ('imperialism' for example, at the other end of the hurray–boo spectrum) it is tempting to become exasperated, and to decide that it is probably best that they be eliminated from scholarly discussion. In this vein, one *Dictionary of Sociology* described community (in the late 1980s) as 'one of the most elusive and vague' terms, and announced that the word community was 'by now largely without specific meaning'.[112] The implication that the term had become redundant went nowhere; indeed, its use has grown and what it represents became even more popular. Any attempt to abandon the term 'community' would be futile: fuzzy concepts make the world go around.

It is a similar story with 'identity', another of sociology's fuzzy terms. We use it constantly and confidently, as if we know what we are talking about.[113] But do we stop to think about it? Under globalisation, nostalgia for the shared identity implied in the idea of community has grown,[114] but what exactly is involved in a shared identity? How many 'definite characteristics' have to be the same to add up to a common identity? Which shared characteristics should be sovereign in designations of identity? Can the test be objective, or only subjective? Can such a porous word as 'culture' be used to separate people in any meaningful way? Or 'religion'? Or 'ethnicity'? And on and on. Furthermore, even if these questions could be given answers to which all could subscribe – which they cannot be – the question still arises whether 'identity politics' is desirable when it is recognised (by all but tyrants of one sort or another) that individuals increasingly have multiple identities and for the most part attempt to live multifaceted lives? Tyrants, religious

[111] See Eric Hobsbawm, *The Age of Extremes* (London: Michael Joseph, 1994), p. 428.
[112] Nicholas Abercrombie, Stephen Hill, and Bryan S. Turner, *The Penguin Dictionary of Sociology* (Harmondsworth: Penguin, 1988), p. 44; William Davies suggested it might be better to 'relinquish' the word in 'Against Community', *Prospect*, no. 128, November 2006, pp. 15–16.
[113] On the idea of the reinvention of identity, see Zygmunt Bauman, *Community. Seeking Security in an Insecure World* (Cambridge: Polity, 2001), p. 15.
[114] This might explain the spurt of explanatory literature; see Gerard Delanty, *Community* (London: Routledge, 2003), for a thought-provoking critical introduction and an extensive bibliography.

fundamentalists, patriarchs, nationalists, and others seek to homogenise people by privileging and reifying one particular marker of identity – what Amartya Sen calls 'solitarism'.[115] This 'miniaturisation' of people, as he calls it, does a disservice to social reality, while at the same time helps to create potentially dangerous structural divides between people.

The idea of shared identity, the basis of the practice of community, is endowed with warm connotations, especially by those who want us all to celebrate 'difference'. This is a beguiling but dangerous path to follow. As will be seen later, when difference becomes privileged above all in politics, equality gets forgotten and indifference rules.[116]

2. Community is a politicised concept

Because of its positive connotations, the term community is often used to achieve political leverage. Nationalists promote the idea of a 'national community', while those anxious about the alienating features of contemporary life are drawn to the ideal of the 'neighbourhood community'. The most powerful states attempt to legitimise their (especially controversial) policies by claiming that they are acting for something they call 'the international community', surely one of the falsest terms ever spun. In these examples the term community is employed (in the local context) to appeal to the idea of a particular organic group of people,[117] or (in the international context) to attempt to improve the legitimacy of certain policies advocated by a coalition of willing governments. The term also appeals to new civil society groups seeking to garner solidarity behind progressive values. Transnational communities of environmentalists, for example, hope to promote commitment, identity, and mutual respect behind the shared goal of creating more space for people to take charge of their own lives and protect the natural world around them. On a grander scale, there is the idea of citizenship in a global 'human community', hoping to transcend the endless violence associated with a global tribal past.[118]

---

[115] Amartya Sen, *Identity and Violence. The Illusion of Destiny* (London: Allen Lane, 2006), defines 'solitarism' on p. xii; this will be taken up at length in chapter 8.
[116] This is a theme of Kenan Malik, *The Meaning of Race. Race, History and Culture in Western Society* (Houndmills: Macmillan, 1996).
[117] Bauman, *Community* is a critique of such nostalgia in the context of so much contemporary insecurity.
[118] A useful overview of the issues is Nigel Dower, *An Introduction to Global Citizenship* (Edinburgh: University of Edinburgh Press, 2003).

The fuzziness and politicisation of the term community adds to the worry that the concept has become lost in its own warm bath. Before attempting to show why it should be rescued, it is necessary to distinguish between two important senses of the word: *locality communities* and *value communities*.

A locality community is the more traditional conception of community, and refers to a geographically coherent, and usually somewhat small group of people. These are individuals linked by living in a local setting, be it a village, a neighbourhood in the suburbs, or a small town. It is generally thought that there is something natural or organic about such groups; they share contacts, a physical environment, attachment to some symbols and a history of association.[119] Communities here are bigger than families, but smaller than nations or regional identities. For Tönnies, the *Gemeinschaft* represented small pre-industrial entities based on kinship and neighbourhood, with close and complex interaction, whereas *Gesellschaft* implied the reciprocal, impersonal, contractual relations that were characteristic of the developing industrial Europe of his day.

Value communities embody both ancient and modern ways of thinking about relationships. In the conception of a religious community, embracing all followers of the same faith, it is an ancient idea. The contemporary version also includes those sharing (non-religious) ethical outlooks on life, whether resulting from politics (the 'peace movement'), profession (the 'academic community'), or sexual orientation (the 'gay community'). Here, geography is less important than a conscious commitment to identify with like-minded people, wherever they live. Such non-organic, trans-local conceptions of community are particularly significant for world security. Value communities share similar principles and standards, and want to live according to common precepts about 'the good life'.[120] Community here is rooted in ideas and ethics, not place. If the ideal of a local community is a notion of an organic, authentic (traditional) spirit, that of value communities is forward-looking solidarity around an ideal.

Human existence, according to Gandhi, was characterised by two necessary features, 'unity and disagreement'; consequently, he argued that 'every human association must fully acknowledge and find ways of

---

[119] On some of the ambiguities, see Charlotte Seymour-Smith, *Macmillan Dictionary of Anthropology* (London: Macmillan, 1986), p. 46.
[120] Of many places to start, a provocative one is Peter Singer, *Writings on an Ethical Life* (London: HarperCollins, 2001).

reconciling them'.[121] Along similar lines, Bhikhu Parekh saw this unity-in-diversity as necessary at all levels, from the local to the global.[122] The Gandhian challenge, in other words, is to reconcile the singular *I* with plural *we's*. This is not as impossible as it might seem, because the *I* is (potentially) impressively multiple. This necessitates the rejection from the outset of the idea that political community must be synonymous with homogeneity; instead, the ideal of political community in a critical theory of world security must express the idea that people(s) can 'be themselves' but in association with others. The southern African concept of *ubuntu* expresses this well. Barbara Nussbaum has explained that *ubuntu* refers to the interconnectedness of people, and the responsibility people have towards each other that results; it is about 'self-in-community' that gives rise to sayings such as the Zulu idea that 'It is through others that one attains selfhood.' While Nussbaum concentrated on relations at the face-to-face level, she believed that the ideas of interconnectedness associated with *ubuntu* – 'compassion, justice, reciprocity, dignity, harmony and humanity' – were essential for informing thinking at the global level.[123] This Zulu word expresses the idea I have more awkwardly characterised as 'the I-that-is-another'.[124]

The goal of a theory of world security is to help bring about, globally, Gandhi's vision of enabling people to be themselves but in association with a wider world. For this, the idea of overlapping *emancipatory communities* is an important building block.[125] As we have seen, communities in general are social organisations whose separateness caters for individual belonging and human variety. *An emancipatory community recognises that people have multiple identities, that a person's identity cannot be satisfactorily defined by any single attribution (religion, class, race, etc.), and that people must be allowed to live simultaneously in a variety of communities expressing their multifaceted lives. An emancipatory community is therefore a free association of individuals, recognising their solidarity in relation to common conceptions of what it is to live an ethical life, binding people together with a sense of belonging and a distinctive network of ideas*

[121] Bhikhu Parekh, *Gandhi's Political Philosophy. A Critical Examination* (Houndmills: Palgrave Macmillan, 1991), p. 215.
[122] *Ibid.*, p. 215; see also, for his own view of obligations, Bhikhu Parekh, 'Cosmopolitanism and Global Citizenship', *Review of International Studies*, vol. 29(1), 2003, pp. 3–17.
[123] Barbara Nussbaum, 'Ubuntu', *Resurgence*, no. 221, Nov./Dec. 2003, p. 13; see also the discussion of *ubuntu* and peacebuilding by Tim Murithi, 'African Approaches to Building Peace and Social Solidarity', *African Journal of Conflict Resolution*, vol. 6(2), 2006, pp. 18–23.
[124] Booth, 'Three Tyrannies', pp. 31, 56, 58–66.
[125] This is based on Ken Booth, 'Community', in Booth, *Critical Security Studies*, p. 109.

and support. Such a community, recognising the right of individuals to express themselves through multiple identifiers of difference, celebrates equality over identity; clearly, this conception is directly opposed to the ghettoised notion of community based on 'solitarism'.

The discussion so far has emphasised that while the concept of community is essential, it should not be romanticised. Neo-Nazis can come freely together with their own conception of the good life, including politics based on racial superiority. The 'gated communities' made up of recently enriched families is another community to be avoided. Not all communities are desirable. Communities are dependent variables; they are only as good as the values that animate them.

Whereas location is key to the organic conception of community, an emancipatory community does not require propinquity (though it does not exclude it). While local affinities have value in some contexts, such as cultural longing and loyalty ('Fy ing enfawr, fy ngwynfyd, -fy mhryder, / Fy mharadwys hyfryd')[126] or sport ('Feath is Feath'), world security requires the growth of trans-local networks of solidarity with respect to the values of world order discussed in the previous chapter. Communities expressing solidarity around such values as peace, human rights, and environmentalism already exist across the world, and while they sometimes have the power to influence the international agenda, they have not yet been able to change radically the games governments play.[127] Obviously, emancipatory communities working towards world security require local branches, and here national affiliation is often less of a barrier than class. Metropolitan-minded, middle-class progressive groups invariably find it more congenial to identify with distant strangers (which communications technology makes increasingly easy) than with neighbouring strangers experiencing poverty, domestic violence, disability, or mental health problems.[128] Our attention is always drawn to national boundaries, which are fenced or otherwise policed; other boundaries, often more divisive, are so powerful that they do not need policing.

---

[126] 'My great agony, my bliss – my anxiety, / My lovely paradise' could be feelings people express about many places; this happens to be Wales: Alan Llwyd, 'Cymru', 1978, quoted by Jan Morris, *Wales* (Oxford: Oxford University Press, 1982), p. 109.
[127] See the interesting arguments and illustrations in Margaret E. Keck and Kathryn Sikkink, *Activists Beyond Borders. Advocacy Networks in International Politics* (Ithaca, N.Y.: Cornell University Press, 1998), pp. 31–70.
[128] A welcome and important addition to this (still very limited) debate about international relations is Martha C. Nussbaum, *Frontiers of Justice. Disability, Nationality, Species Membership* (Cambridge, Mass.: Harvard University Press, 2006).

This discussion points to a fundamental proposition for a critical theory of security: equality must be prioritised above 'difference'. The prioritising of identity politics (especially if based on a single marker) is not calculated to promote co-existence in a world in which cultures, nations, and religions increasingly have to live in each other's pockets. Identity politics is problematic for world politics because it is committed to homogenising multiple identities according to the demands of patriarchy, religion, nationalism, or regime (sometimes all rolled up into one). Appealing to the 'ethos' of traditional culture as the cement for community is beguiling, but that ethos is invariably controlled and cultivated by elites who, whatever else they recommend, are above all concerned to maintain their traditional status.

The prospect of people living in a way that respects their multiple identities is maximised by universal values of tolerance rather than by leaving such matters in the hands of local power-brokers.[129] Those who are in the position of having others choose for them rarely live under the political, economic, or social conditions that make it possible to describe that choice as other than imposed.[130] If world security is to be advanced, mono-factoral labelling should be resisted as much as possible. Equally, the fashionable injunction to *celebrate* difference should be rejected. Why should we celebrate the 'difference' exhibited by cultures dominated by racist ideas or religious bigots, or by extreme nationalists, or by those with traditional practices that involve cruelty towards their weakest members? The call to celebrate difference is a potentially dangerous postmodernist metanarrative posing as tolerance. By all means let us enjoy differences between people(s) when they add to the richness of human experience – friends who are excellent story-tellers, people from other places exhibiting their interesting cultural arts and artefacts, women with red hair – but let us have a diversity of what we choose to celebrate. World security asks us to celebrate the possibility of human equality; this alone, if put into consistent and universal political practice, offers hope of eradicating universal human wrongs.

The homogenising potential of organic conceptions of community has been critically exposed by Alain Touraine.[131] In such communities, unity is more important than democracy, consensus than debate. His

[129] This is argued in Booth, 'Three Tyrannies', pp. 55–6.

[130] This is a theme of Malik, *The Meaning of Race*; these issues are discussed at more length in chapter 8 below.

[131] Alain Touraine, *Can We Live Together? Equal and Different* (Cambridge: Polity Press, 2000).

ideas do not rule out people having common goals, or unity when appropriate, but he warned against a world where community demands that diversity always bows the knee before unity. Democracy for Touraine is the way to promote the Gandhian reconciliation of *I* and *we*, and is a necessary guard against the narcissism of identity politics. He pointed particularly to the totalitarian tendencies of nationalism, where the fetishising of identity reifies human difference according to those who have the power to define what is different, what is 'the nation'.[132]

But can the *I* and *we* be reconciled through the structures of world politics? Can global governance become a community of emancipatory communities? The challenge for critical theory is not only to win ontological, epistemological, and praxeological debates about world politics, but to follow this through into global political practice. The test for each policy prescription therefore is whether they promote emancipatory global governance and what Ulrich Beck has called 'cosmopolitan states' (discussed below). Global governance refers to legitimised procedures for political activities (and not just those between governments) that are of global relevance. The precise character of those arrangements at this point is less important than the ideas that inform them, and in this respect enlightened world order values are central: if the global-we look after the processes, the structures will look after themselves.[133] But a few words about the prevailing structures are necessary.

Without doubt, the Westphalian settlement in 1648, closing the Thirty Years War, represented the prospect of a more stable international order in the wake of an era of ravaging wars of religion; but the price was heavy in terms of freedom of religious ideas. The principle that every territory was to retain 'in perpetuity' the religion it had in the *Normaljahr* (the reference year of 1 January 1624) created a *pax christiana*.[134] Most followers of minority religions emigrated from their homes, producing a form of territorial faith cleansing. This absolutism of the spirit, enshrined in the corrupting power of Westphalian sovereignty, helped to produce the statism that in turn helped to bring about the totalitarian and tyrannical horrors of the states system of the twentieth century. Despite the growth over time of some relatively decent sovereign states (such as the social democracies of Scandinavia – though they are not

---

[132] *Ibid.*, pp. 197–230.
[133] Ken Booth, 'Security Within Global Transformation', in Booth, *Statecraft and Security*, pp. 338–55.
[134] Benno Teschke, *The Myth of 1648. Class, Geopolitics, and the Making of Modern International Relations* (London: Verso, 2003), p. 241.

without their problems), the Westphalian system, in a normative sense, has had a very mixed record. Future world security requires a much less homogenising notion of community than the one bequeathed by the history of Westphalian 'nation-state' building. If enlightened world order values are to be operationalised, political community must be transformative, open, and reflexive; in other words, better able to reconcile the *I* and the *we* at all levels. This means a pattern of multilevel global governance made up of networks of emancipatory communities above and below the state, with the latter metamorphosing into Beck's *cosmopolitan states* which – in contrast to 'national states', which see any blurring of the border between the domestic/foreign realms as a threat to their existence – 'emphasise the necessity of solidarity with foreigners both inside and outside the national borders'.[135] Cosmopolitan states, unlike the Westphalian model, would be sensitive to their limits (see chapter 4).

A world community bound together by networks of emancipatory communities within and across cosmopolitan states, and infused by shared world order values will appear far-fetched to many schools of thought about international relations. The school of 'offensive realism', for example, rejects the very notion of world community, believing that the human condition remains one of 'kill or perish'.[136] Less fatalistic observers have somewhat more faith in the potentiality of sovereign states to behave in a civilised manner, but are equally sure that world community is not the future. Chris Brown has written: 'the ideal of a plurality of morally autonomous, just communities relating to one another in a framework of peace and law' is a more conceivable future than that of a world community 'with its own substantive ends'.[137] But

---

[135] See, for example, Ulrich Beck, *What is Globalization?* (Cambridge: Polity, 2000), pp. 87–113, and 'The Fight for a Cosmopolitan Future', *New Statesman*, 5 November 2001; David Held, *Democracy and the Global Order: From the Modern State to Global Governance* (Cambridge: Polity, 1995); and K. Hutchings and R. Dannreuther (eds.), *Cosmopolitan Citizenship* (London: Macmillan, 1999).

[136] In academic international politics, this phrase is associated with John Herz, and his original formulation of the 'security dilemma' in the early 1950s: see Booth and Wheeler, *Security Dilemma*, ch. 1. Though its antecedents lay in the distant past, the contemporary school of 'offensive realism' originated in the work of John J. Mearsheimer: his longest examination of it is *The Tragedy of Great Power Politics* (New York: W. W. Norton, 2001), esp. pp. 1–54, and 'Interview with John J. Mearsheimer', parts I and II, *International Relations*, vol. 20(1/2), 2006, pp. 105–23 and 231–43; for a different fatalistic perspective, shaped more by a Waltzian 'first image' interpretation rather than anarchy, see Colin S. Gray, *Another Bloody Century. Future War* (London: Phoenix, 2006), pp. 19–128, 333–97.

[137] Chris Brown, 'International Political Theory and the Idea of World Community', in Ken Booth and Steve Smith (eds.), *International Relations Theory Today* (Cambridge: Polity, 1995), p. 106; also Delanty, *Community*, pp. 153–7.

the moral autonomy of sovereign pluralities, as we know from such regimes as those of Pol Pot and Dr Voerwerd (and the worst dictators today),[138] is not a recipe for the growth of just communities. Furthermore, the framework of order and justice in which states operate is largely the gift of the greatest powers of their day, and there is (literally) all the difference in the world between the international orders of the era of Pax Britannica, when Britain was hegemon, and the 'Greater East Asia Co-Prosperity Sphere' briefly dominated by imperial Japan. Kant's peaceful federation offers a different (this time theoretical) model. Traditional international relations theory has considered Kant's to be a blueprint too far, and even middle-roaders of an English school persuasion think it neither possible nor desirable ('Beyond Hobbes but not as far as Kant' is their bumper-sticker).[139] But is the possibility of achieving a Kantian perpetual peace any more far-fetched today than the spread of the norm of democracy throughout the world must have seemed in the age of the divine right of kings? It is probably more conceivable, because (as will be discussed in chapter 10) there has been a continuous tradition of thinking about ethical universalism and global citizenship, and there has been an upsurge since the 1960s of civil society activity globally committed to progressive goals such as the elimination of nuclear weapons and the promotion of environmental sustainability. This led even the *New York Times* to begin to talk about there being 'two superpowers on the planet: the United States and world public opinion'.[140]

Under globalisation, governments understand the growing constraints on economic or moral autarky. Confronted by the challenge of the Great Reckoning, peoples may come to fear the dangers of a collapse into global turmoil. Chapter 9 gives a worst-case interpretation of what might happen, but the old axiom of 'the worse, the better' points to the incentive to build a peaceful federation globally. While there is much to fear in world politics, there are other possibilities immanent in the situation than global turmoil; and one resource for Kantian hope is a growing belief that the global status quo is not the answer.

The most extensive exploration of the issues discussed above from the perspective of critical international relations theory is Andrew

[138] For a snapshot, see the Special Report, 'The World's Top 10 Dictators', *New Statesman*, 4 September 2006.

[139] Robert Jackson, '"The Safety of the People Is the Supreme Law": Beyond Hobbes but not as far as Kant', in William Bain (ed.), *The Empire of Security and the Safety of the People* (London: Routledge, 2006), pp. 15–36.

[140] Quoted by Satish Kumar, 'The Other Superpower', *Resurgence*, no. 221, November/December 2003, p. 3.

Linklater's *The Transformation of Political Community.*[141] At the outset, he stated his aim as being to 'reaffirm the cosmopolitan critique of the sovereign states-system'.[142] Central to this was his criticism of the idea that sovereignty should be the basis of a principle of moral inclusion or exclusion. His normative goal was the 'enlargement of the sphere in which human beings treat one another as equals'.[143] Consequently, he looked towards the creation of political communities that (negatively) 'would not attach deep moral significance to differences of class, ethnicity, gender, race and alien status', while they (positively) would 'display sensitivity to the variations of culture, gender and ethnicity' and would 'reduce material inequalities' within and across their boundaries.[144] The statement of such goals and their advance in the real world of international politics was not utopian in Linklater's view; he believed it to be a historical-sociological possibility. Immanent critique suggested that there are 'the moral resources' within existing social arrangements which could be harnessed 'for radical purposes' – the latter being extending political community as the foundation for a post-Westphalian era. This is not the place to discuss the institutional dimensions of Linklater's argument (which in any case were not the main thrust of his work) save to say that they built on what we have now – a messy mixture of interstate relationships, including a core of supra-nationalism in Western Europe together with both 'solidarist' and 'pluralist' conceptions of international society elsewhere.[145] The idea of community as a dynamic form has been the theme of the writing of Habermas, whose ideas Linklater has done much to disseminate.[146] But Habermas has shared the ambivalence of other critical theorists towards community, viewing the totalising dangers of communitarian thinking with considerable disquiet. For Habermas, the image of the community created by hyper-nationalism and Nazi ideology was a recent and disturbing memory; nonetheless, he accepted, like the rest of us, that the concept of community is inescapable. With dialogue as the melody of his political theory, community is the context in which the public sphere and consensus can

---

[141] Andrew Linklater, *The Transformation of Political Community: Ethical Foundations of the Post-Westphalia Era* (Cambridge: Polity, 1998); see the Forum on the book in the *Review of International Studies*, vol. 25(1), 1999, pp. 139–75.
[142] Linklater, *Political Community*, p. 2.   [143] *Ibid.*, p. 4.   [144] *Ibid.*, p. 5.
[145] Nicholas J. Wheeler, 'Pluralist or Solidarist Conceptions of Humanitarian Intervention: Bull and Vincent on Humanitarian Intervention', *Millennium*, vol. 21(2), 1992, pp. 463–87.
[146] Jürgen Habermas, *Between Facts and Norms: Contributions to a Discourse Theory of Law and Democracy* (Cambridge: Polity, 1996), and *The Inclusion of the Other: Studies in Political Theory* (Cambridge, Mass.: MIT Press, 1998).

in principle develop best. Community is not therefore romanticised by Habermas; rather, like other critical theorists, he recognises that what matters is the type of community, and its communicative potential, not the existence of community as such. Again, communities are only as good as their values.

The concept of a 'security community' is one idea, arising out of the communicative essence in the very idea of community, that has had both empirical and theoretical purchase. The idea was first elaborated by Karl Deutsch and his co-workers in the 1950s, based on their work on communication theory.[147] A security community exists when institutions and practices develop among hitherto separate polities such that 'a sense of community' develops that is manifest in 'dependable expectations' of peaceful change through learning to harmonise interests, compromise differences, and reap mutual rewards. Politics between nations takes place independently of military rivalry. Deutsch elaborated his ideas based on the North Atlantic group of states. Later theorists of security communities have examined the potential for their development in other parts of the world.[148] The most mature model is that of Western Europe, but the idea has been explored even in relation to the hardest cases, notably the Middle East. Pinar Bilgin, for example, while recognising all the difficulties of developing a security community in the prevailing conditions of today's Middle East, has argued that the idea offers more promise for shaping a secure future for the region than other scenarios. Indeed, she saw the idea of a security community as 'realistic' in comparison with other approaches, given the region's 'potential for descent into chaos'.[149] Those tempted to dismiss this idea utterly should remember how implausible such an outcome once seemed in Europe, the site of centuries of interstate violence. It took two major wars within a generation to turn this cockpit of war into a zone of peace and integration, but within another generation the face of Western Europe had changed radically, and many believe permanently. The history of the European

[147] Karl Deutsch et al., *Political Community and the North Atlantic Area: International Organization in the Light of Historical Experience* (Princeton, N.J.: Princeton University Press, 1957).
[148] A significant attempt to revive the notion, with different perspectives and empirical referents, was Emanuel Adler and Michael Barnett (eds.), *Security Communities* (Cambridge: Cambridge University Press, 1998); also Alex J. Bellamy, *Security Communities and their Neighbours. Regional Fortresses or Global Integrators?* (Houndmills: Palgrave Macmillan, 2004), and Booth and Wheeler, *Security Dilemma*, ch. 7.
[149] Pinar Bilgin, 'Alternative Futures for the Middle East', *Futures*, vol. 33, 2001, pp. 423–36; also her *Regional Security in the Middle East. A Critical Perspective* (London: RoutledgeCurzon, 2005), pp. 163–94.

security community shows that the project of densifying cooperation and embedding trust is not always easy to keep on track, but disagreements in Brussels and nationalist frustrations among member states are primarily signs of the success of the project, when compared with the terrible headlines within living memory. It was put strongly in 2003 by Luc Ferry, a French MEP and philosopher, who declared that a war against Germany was absolutely inconceivable for the French, just as it was for the English against Italy or Spain against the Netherlands.[150] In international politics one should never say never, even in the Middle East, though we must all hope that the leaders and societies of the region find the resources to build a security community without first discovering the true costs of playing the game by the rules of the past.

Kant, from his base in Königsberg, believed that a global community of humans with common faculties and owing mutual obligations to each other was not only thinkable, but that its pursuit was an obligation. Such views are usually dismissed as utopian by orthodox realists who generally choose to overlook, or fail to see, that their founding fathers have also seen progress through political community. E. H. Carr ended what is considered one of the classic 'realist' texts,[151] *The Twenty Years' Crisis*, with a resounding call for the extension of community, seeing in it the solution to the apparently intractable problems of international relations. He wrote, 'social ends cannot be limited by a national frontier, and . . . [future] British policy may have to take into account the welfare of Lille or Düsseldorf or Lodz as well as the welfare of Oldham or Jarrow'. Whereas Kant thought he could offer a (conditional) guarantee of perpetual peace, Carr restricted himself to claiming that a broadening of 'our view of international policy; and . . . a direct appeal to the motive of sacrifice' were not bound always to fail. He believed that progress had to be made in broadening peoples' perspectives before progress could be made in global institutionalisation.[152] This was also the view of another iconic realist figure, Hans J. Morgenthau. In his classic text, *Politics among Nations*, he argued that a world state was the

---

[150] Quoted by Umberto Eco, 'May the Force Be with You', *Index on Censorship*, vol. 33(3), 2004, p. 131.

[151] The quotation marks are added because some of us see the book as more complex than its simple 'realist' label; Booth, 'Security in Anarchy: Utopian Realism in Theory and Practice', *International Affairs*, vol. 67(3), 1991, pp. 527–45. See also Michael Cox, 'A Guide to the Secondary Literature on E. H. Carr', in E. H. Carr, *The Twenty Years' Crisis, 1919–1939. An Introduction to the Study of International Relations* (Houndmills: Palgrave, 2001; reissued with a new introduction and additional material by Michael Cox), pp. lxiv–lxxi.

[152] E. H. Carr, *The Twenty Years' Crisis, 1919–1939: An Introduction to the Study of International Relations* (London: Macmillan, 1966; 1st pub. 1939), p. 239.

answer to the overwhelming nuclear danger facing human society, and that 'a world community must antedate a world state'.[153] Daring to be wise, Morgenthau endorsed the functionalist approach associated with David Mitrany, building community between people from the bottom up. All real realists eventually recognise the perils of statism, and conclude that the search for world community is a necessary condition in the construction of world security.[154]

The picture of global governance emerging above, with cosmopolitan states developing as part a world community of emancipatory communities, is not as streamlined an institutional blueprint as that which developed out of the Westphalian settlement. But if we are to escape the consequences of indefinite business-as-usual answers, world security requires different institutional arrangements. And less streamlined might be more appropriate. In any case, it is better not to try and micromanage the future, but rather establish broad principles. Susan Buck-Morss, in her study of 'mass utopia' – the industrial dreamworld of both capitalism and socialism in the twentieth century – ended with a message in a similar spirit. Following the twentieth century's abuse of 'the masses' (objects of manipulation by both 'revolutionary propaganda' and 'commodity advertising') she envisaged the prospect of their transformation into 'a variety of publics' – 'including a virtual global humanity, a potential "whole world" that watches, listens, and speaks, capable of evaluating critically both the culture of others and their own'.[155] That the 'new era' will be better is not guaranteed, she insisted; its development depended on 'the power structures in which people desire and dream, and of the cultural meanings they give to the changed situation'. But she did think there is some space for dreaming, though she emphasised that such imaginings 'will be dreamworlds, nothing more', if the old power structures remain intact. She suggested that the 'democratic, political promise' of new ways of thinking about politics 'would appear to be greatest when they do not presume the collectivity that will receive them'.

---

[153] Hans J. Morgenthau, *Politics Among Nations. The Struggle for Power and Peace* (New York: Alfred A. Knopf, 1960; 3rd edn), p. 520; see part 9, 'The Problem of Peace in the Mid-twentieth Century: Peace Through Transformation', pp. 499–536.
[154] For a discussion of this other 'Morgenthau' see Ken Booth, 'Morgenthau's Realisms and Transatlantic Truths', in Christian Hacke, Gottfried-Karl Kindermann, and Kai M. Schellhorn (eds.), *The Heritage, Challenge, and Future of Realism* (Bonn: Bonn University Press/V&R Unipress, 2005), pp. 99–128.
[155] Susan Buck-Morss, *Dreamworld and Catastrophe. The Passing of Mass Utopia in East and West* (Cambridge, Mass.: MIT Press, 2000), pp. 277–8.

Rather than consolidating traditional identities, Buck-Morss argued that human society needs to create new ones, 'responding directly to a reality that is first and foremost objective – the geographical mixing of people and things, global webs that disseminate meanings, electronic prostheses of the human body, new arrangements of the human sensorium'. These imaginings, she believed, 'freed from the constraints of bounded spaces and from the dictates of unilinear time, might dream of becoming, in Lenin's words, "as radical as reality itself"'. Reality has delivered many radical ideas in the course of human evolution, from the spread of the metanarrative of democracy in a species that once could not read or write, to global competitions in synchronised swimming. We should never underestimate Lenin's insight, for if one's timescale is long enough, there can be no doubt that human reality is indeed radical; occasionally, history moves in fast-forward, and one suspects that this century, for good or ill, will be one of those times.

The vision developed in this chapter requires a certain imagination. It looks to the building of world security on a platform of growing world community, organised through a pattern of global governance made up of a network of emancipatory communities, including cosmopolitan states. All these institutional nodal points will be bound by commitments to promoting equality, humanising power, and embedding human rights without presuming particular collective institutional forms; nonetheless, all will seek to fulfil 'democratic, political promise'. This image of world security requires imagination, but it is not another 'dreamworld'. It rests on immanent potential in the world today. Not the least significant of the resources for radical change is the growing sense of the terrible dangers that await if human society globally refuses to change.

4 Deepening, broadening, reconstructing

if I am not in favour of the abstract, with what am I to control the concrete? if I am not in possession of the concrete, with what am I to control the abstract?

Juan Gris, 1971 gallery catalogue[1]

This chapter is best considered as a long footnote to the conceptualisation of security developed in chapter 3, when important issues were left hanging in the air. The present discussion begins by focusing on 'deepening' and 'broadening' security, claiming that security in the political realm is above all a *derivative* concept, and suggesting what this means in relation to international agendas.[2] Deepening and broadening are often misunderstood, as will be explained. Of the two, the most basic move is deepening, because it is only through an understanding of the assumptions on which a conception of security rests that broadening, in its name can be appreciated. Deepening, in other words, reveals the political theory in which conceptions of security are anchored, and so the priorities that will shape the associated political agenda. By uniting security with political theory, the deepening move also provides a basis for a synthesis of critique and reconstruction – the process of creating a politics of emancipation.

---

[1] Quoted in Elisabeth Young-Bruehl, *Hannah Arendt. For Love of the World* (New Haven, Conn.: Yale University Press, 1982), p. 130.
[2] An earlier discussion was Ken Booth, 'Security and Self: Reflections of a Fallen Realist', in Keith Krause and Michael C. Williams (eds.), *Critical Security Studies. Concepts and Cases* (Minneapolis: University of Minnesota Press, 1997), pp. 110–12.

Security as a derivative concept

questions about security cannot be separated from the most basic questions of political theory.   R. B. J. Walker in 'The Subject of Security'[3]

Central to the task of exploring the theory and practice of security is what for many years I have called 'deepening': the idea that security in world politics is essentially a *derivative* concept. In short, different attitudes and behaviour associated with security are traceable to different political theories. It is a simple idea with enormous implications.

How one conceives security is constructed out of the assumptions (however explicitly or inexplicitly articulated) that make up one's theory of world politics (its units, structures, processes, and so on). Security policy, from this perspective, is an epiphenomenon of political theory. The core elements of security in the standard definition of the term discussed in the previous chapter (a referent, a danger, and the desire to avoid harm) are never conceived or operationalised in world politics from a neutral or self-standing foundation.[4] The labels 'strategic studies' and 'national security', for example, embrace particular discourses and practices with respect to security deriving from particular sets of political assumptions. They are not objective reactions to the world 'out there', the so-called real world, but rather are *from* somewhere, *for* someone, and *for* some purpose (to stretch the Coxian view of theory). Mainstream strategic studies derive from a particular social context, the interests of a particular referent group, and the world-view of a distinct political theory. The resultant discourse is constructed from these ideas. So, when orthodox realist voices within strategic studies announce the topic of 'European Security', the listener can expect pre-defined, traditionalist patterns of thought about referents, processes, and strategies (that is, states, the business of governments, and NATO policies). Even minor semantic shifts – 'Security in Europe' – stimulate different thoughts. What (and who) is 'Europe'? What do we mean by 'security'? Who or what is the referent, the threat, the possible solution? Rethinking security can begin with small tweaks in language.

The so-called real world inhabited by students of security is of course the same for everybody; what is different is not the 'out there' (what

---

[3] R. B. J. Walker, 'The Subject of Security', in Krause and Williams, *Critical Security Studies*, p. 63.
[4] Booth, 'Security and Self', pp. 110–12; and '75 Years on – Rewriting the Subject's Past, Reinventing its Future', in Steve Smith, Ken Booth, and Marysia Zalewski (eds.), *International Theory: Positivism and Beyond* (Cambridge: Cambridge University Press, 1996), p. 337.

some hypothetical omniscient being *knows* exists), but what is 'in here' (in the heads of observers). This is the meaning of John Searle's argument in *The Construction of Social Reality* that there is one world (as progressively revealed by the natural sciences) but many realities in the sense of 'facts by human agreement' in the social world.[5] The inseparable relationship between political theory and strategic action first became clear to me in the late 1960s after reading Anatol Rapoport's discussion of the derivative relationship between how nations fight and their underlying philosophy of war.[6] I will return to this in chapter 7; the important point for the moment is the force of his claim that how humans engage in war is not 'natural' in the sense of being determined by biology, but is a cultural phenomenon, the construction of different minds, times, and places. In other words, strategic policy is the outcome of 'facts by human agreement', not our genes; the latter constitute only the permissive factor.

The insight that the social world is 'constructed' rather than 'natural' led, from the late 1980s on, to an avalanche of academic literature looking at international relations through the lens of what became labelled 'social constructivism'. In its early days this approach consisted of a rather self-conscious body of theorists challenging the neorealist orthodoxy; there was a pioneer spirit among the 'constructivists' in different fields, though as Ian Hacking has pointed out, in their dwelling on the dichotomy between appearance and reality ('set up by Plato . . . given a definitive form by Kant') they were 'really very old-fashioned'.[7] Such was the momentum that gathered behind constructivism that he said that one could easily think that 'nothing can exist unless it is socially constructed'. Hacking offered numerous illustrations of constructivist momentum in various fields, from 'Authorship' to 'Zulu nationalism'.[8] Oddly, he did not acknowledge (or know about) the related outbreak

---

[5] 'Introduction' in John Searle, *The Construction of Social Reality* (London: Allen Lane, 1995).
[6] Anatol Rapoport, 'Introduction', in Karl von Clausewitz, *On War*, ed. with an introduction by Anatol Rapoport (Harmondsworth: Pelican Classics, 1968).
[7] Ian Hacking, *The Social Construction of What?* (Cambridge, Mass.: Harvard University Press, 2003), p. 49. Key early texts were Friedrich V. Kratochwil, *Rules, Norms, Decisions: On the Conditions of Practical and Legal Reasoning in International Relations and Domestic Affairs* (Cambridge: Cambridge University Press, 1989); Nicholas Onuf, *World of Our Making* (Columbia, S.C.: University of South Carolina Press, 1989); and Alexander Wendt, 'The Agent/Structure Problem in International Relations Theory', *International Organization*, vol. 41(2), 1987, pp. 335–70, and 'Anarchy Is What States Make of It: The Social Construction of Power Politics', *International Organization*, vol. 46(2), 1992, pp. 391–426.
[8] Hacking, *Social Construction*, pp. 1 and 25. He also argues (a view I have sympathy with) that there should be different names for different 'construct-isms', thereby overcoming the problems of the umbrella term; for what we are talking about, he prefers 'social constructionism' (see pp. 48–9).

of existence-through-social-constructionism in academic international relations stretching from anarchy to zero-sum thinking.

Given that so much is heard in the discipline about constructivism, and yet there will be so little in this book, I want to offer three points. First, contrary to many assumptions, social constructivism is not a *theory* of international relations. It tells us nothing about politics among nations in the way that realism, for example, does, with its categorical realities of states, power, anarchy, and strategy. Constructivism is a *method*, or meta-theory, about the way human society (including international relations) works. As such, it emphasises the role of ideas, the making of identities, the purchase of norms, the meanings of meaning, and the appearance/reality dichotomy.[9]

Second, as a method, constructivism is helpful, potentially leading us to ask some questions about reality and to understand particular attitudes and behaviour by eschewing the extremes of vulgar materialism and naïve idealism. In practice, we are all constructivists in some sense.[10] Within international theory, the tradition that owes most to some of the key ideas of constructivism (though predating it in practice) is the English school, with its emphasis on norms and rules within an 'international society' seeking to tame anarchy. The English school, remarkably, has had little to say about security,[11] however, a fact that is all the stranger given the central role played by Barry Buzan in the attempted

---

[9] Sympathetic short overviews are Christian Reus-Smit, 'Constructivism', in Scott Burchill *et al.*, *Theories of International Relations* (London: Macmillan, 1996), pp. 209–30, and Emmanuel Adler, 'Constructivism and International Relations', in Walter Carlsneas *et al.*, *Handbook of International Relations* (London: Sage, 2002), pp. 95–118; longer, and critical, is Maja Zehfuss, *Constructivism in International Relations. The Politics of Reality* (Cambridge: Cambridge University Press, 2002).

[10] One of the major and controversial contributions to constructivism is Alexander Wendt, *Social Theory of International Politics* (Cambridge: Cambridge University Press, 1999); see the 'Forum on Alexander Wendt's *Social Theory of International Politics*', *Review of International Studies*, vol. 26(1), 2000, pp. 123–80; explicitly in the field of security, the most interesting contributions are Emmanuel Adler and Michael Barnett (eds.), *Security Communities* (Cambridge: Cambridge University Press, 1998), and Michael C. Williams, 'Identity and the Politics of Security', *European Journal of International Relations*, vol. 4(2), 1998, pp. 204–25, and 'The Discipline of the Democratic Peace: Kant, Liberalism and the Social Construction of Security Communities', *European Journal of International Relations*, vol. 7(4), 2001, pp. 525–53.

[11] Evident, for example, in the literature extending from Hedley Bull's classic contribution, *The Anarchical Society. A Study of Order in World Politics* (London: Macmillan, 1977), to the set of essays in the Special Issue on the English school in *International Relations*, vol. 17(3), 2003; see also Andrew Linklater and Hidemi Suganami, *The English School of International Relations. A Contemporary Reassessment* (Cambridge: Cambridge University Press, 2006), and the 'Forum on the English School', *Review of International Studies*, vol. 27(4), 2001, pp. 465–513.

resurrection of the school as a research project since the late 1990s.[12] The traditional weaknesses of the English school, which its revival has not overcome, reflect in part the weaknesses of social constructivism as a whole, and this leads to the final point.

What constructivism offers is a challenge to those theories that claim international relations is *determined* by biology, human nature, anarchy, or production but, with only a few exceptions, 'constructivist security studies' is less than meets the eye.[13] This is because this ostensible school of security, deriving from a method rather than a political theory, reflects the political assumptions of the theorist rather than the political implications of a distinct theory. This makes 'constructivism' in international relations the broadest of broad churches, embracing the realist-inclined at one end of the spectrum (focused on states and traditional international behaviour) and the concerns of feminism and poststructuralism at the other (focused on meanings and language). This promiscuity is then compounded by the frustration one sometimes feels at 'social constructivist' explanations because they are 'both obscure and overused', to employ Hacking's general criticisms of the approach.[14] Without doubt, social constructivist approaches open up possibilities, including normative ones, in comparison with those associated with the realist family, but they also close them down. From within its own method, we do not know what is not socially constructed, or why. We do not know the deeper reality behind the reality of ideas. Maja Zehfuss has argued that constructivism 'limits the space for critical thinking' because it asserts 'a particular reality'; it does not allow us 'to think beyond what it asserts reality to be. Although reality may change in the future, through different practice, in the here and now it simply is.'[15]

Despite these worries about social constructivism, few will disagree with the proposition that the dynamics of the political world are importantly shaped by Searle's 'facts by human agreement'. It is seeking explanations for these, in security policy, that makes the deepening move so important; by drilling down, it is possible to discover how the referents, agents, and policies of different conceptions of security derive from the assumptions of different political theories. To illustrate this point in

[12] Barry Buzan, 'From International System to International Society: Structural Realism and Regime Theory Meet the English School', *International Organization*, vol. 47(2), 1993, pp. 327–52, and *From International to World Society: English School Theory and the Social Structure of Globalization* (Cambridge: Cambridge University Press, 2004).
[13] For a brief overview, see Steve Smith, 'The Contested Concept of Security', in Booth, *Critical Security Studies and World Politics* (Boulder Colo.: Lynne Rienner, 2005), pp. 38–40.
[14] Hacking, *Social Construction*, p. xii.   [15] Zehfuss, *Constructivism*, p. 262.

teaching contexts, I have long found the structure of a volcano to be a useful image. To begin, it is necessary to imagine a simple cross-section of a volcano, with three distinct elements:

- *Deep structure.* Basically, a volcano is the visible sign of a hole in the earth's surface. Below are the dynamics within the geological core whose changes create the surface activity, or determine a longer or shorter period of inactivity.
- *Fracture zone.* This is the volcanic cone itself, and the disturbed and changing landscape caused by the deeper turbulence. This does not mean that there is always violent activity in the fracture zone. The term refers to where visible action does take place.
- *Outputs.* Emerging from the depths, and out through the fracture zone, comes activity in the form of explosions, lava, or steam. Although this is what is immediately observable, it derives from dynamics taking place in the earth's deepest structures.

The analogy I want to make is between these three elements making up a volcano, and three (simplified) stages in which theories about the nature of world politics translate through struggle into strategic and tactical action in the name of security:

- *Deep structure (of politics).* These are basic ideas – political theories and philosophy – about what makes the world go around. What are the dynamics – materially and ideationally – that shape economic, social, and other forms of behaviour? What is it all about?
- *(Political) Fracture zone.* On the surface of politics we can see the fractured landscape produced by the interplay of the underlying ideas. These struggles might be violent or non-violent, but there is always struggle of some sort because politics is concerned with who gets what, when and how.[16]
- *(Policy) Outputs.* Finally there is practical reasoning about what delivers the strategic and tactical security outputs calculated to promote security. The latter include economic, military, human rights, and other dimensions. The choices are shaped by the deep structures of politics and the character of the struggles in the fracture zone.

[16] This was Harold Lasswell's formulation: *Politics. Who Gets What, When, How* (New York: Peter Smith, 1950).

Deepening, therefore, means understanding security as an epiphenomenon, and so accepting the task of drilling down to explore its origins in 'the most basic questions of political theory'.

Four theoretical approaches below, necessarily simplified, will illustrate the derivative character of security:

Realism

- *Deep structure.* The determining structure is the anarchical character of the international system, and the necessary search for power that this entails. Insecurity and conflict are unavoidable, as a result of flawed human nature (according to classical realism) or the dynamics of the states system (according to neorealists). When states are not facing direct strategic challenges, they are facing security dilemmas.[17]
- *Fracture zone.* Sovereign states are the referents in this system, and the conflict zone is characterised by interstate war, in actuality or predisposition. War is virtually inevitable in this Westphalian world.[18]
- *Outputs.* The strategic and tactical outputs that derive from the underlying political theory and experience of the anarchical system lead to the search for security through policies such as the balance of power and nuclear deterrence.

Marxism

- *Deep structure.* The engine of all politics, and indeed society, is historical materialism. This is the idea that the history of world politics is determined by economic forces, notably the conflict between different modes of production.
- *Fracture zone.* The consequence of the contradictions between vast socio-economic forces is the struggle between different classes – the main referents in this world view. Out of historical contradictions, feudalism gave way to capitalism, and Marx predicted that capitalism would in time give way to socialism and ultimately communism.

---

[17] This distinction is explored and illustrated throughout Ken Booth and Nicholas J. Wheeler, *The Security Dilemma. Fear, Cooperation, and Trust in World Politics* (Houndmills: Palgrave, 2008).
[18] The qualifier 'virtually' is there to cater for the 'defensive realist' view of Kenneth Waltz that nuclear weapons might suppress the logic of anarchy; see Kenneth N. Waltz, 'The Spread of Nuclear Weapons: More May Be Better', *Adelphi Papers*, no. 171 (London: International Institute of Strategic Studies, 1981).

- *Outputs*. The strategic outputs related to classical Marxism, seeking to bring about a communist world included the promotion of internal struggles (revolutionary moves against the dominant power structure) or external strategies (such as support for national liberation struggles). With worldwide communism would come global security.

Feminism

- *Deep structure*. Feminist thinkers have argued that what makes the political and social world go round, across history and across cultures, has been patriarchy: the domination of women by men. Patriarchy has shaped the organisation, culture, and theory of society.
- *Fracture zone*. The political struggle for feminists is constructed by the relationships between different genders under the condition of patriarchy: this, in some designations, is summed up in the idea of the 'sex war'.[19]
- *Outputs*. Theories and practices of security have been concerned with releasing women from traditional and discriminatory shackles. The type of strategy adopted depends upon whether the proponent is a liberal or a radical feminist; the former advocates emancipation-through-equality, the latter seeks the triumph of what are thought to be distinctively female values.

Racism

- *Deep structure*. A distinct body of thought propagated, among others, by Social Darwinians and Nazis has argued that race is what makes the world go around.[20] This viewpoint holds that there are fundamental differences in human behaviour attributable to 'racial characteristics'.
- *Fracture zone*. The zone of conflict here is the struggle between 'superior' races and the rest. Such theories are not as publicly legitimate today as they were in the age of empire, in Nazi Germany, or in South Africa in the era of apartheid for example,

---

[19] Powerfully argued in Marilyn French, *The War Against Women* (Harmondsworth: Penguin, 1993).
[20] See Kenan Malik, *The Meaning of Race. Race, History and Culture in Western Society* (London: Macmillan, 1996), p. 1.

but they have more purchase in many people's minds than public discourse might suggest. The racial fracture zone is evident today in attitudes towards immigrants, refugees, and asylum-seekers in many countries, debates over multiculturalism and integration, and in the overt hostility shown to minorities evident in outbreaks of anti-Semitism, anti-Roma behaviour, or Islamophobia.

- *Outputs*. When race is understood as a categorical structure of world politics, and race relations are conceived as a relationship between unequals, racist strategies have included direct violence (genocide and ethnic cleansing at the worst) or structural discrimination (internally, as in apartheid in South Africa, or externally, as in the old 'White Australia' policy). Security is synonymous with separation.

These illustrations show in a simplified manner how security agendas and strategic policies can be traced back to their political assumptions, thereby bringing security studies centrally into the study of politics.

The idea of *deepening* is frequently misconceived. One common mistake is to confuse it with a level-of-analysis move (security at the state level, the individual level, and so on). Roland Paris, writing in *International Security*, noted that the subject matter of security studies had undergone both broadening and deepening since the end of the Cold War, and then said: 'By deepening, I mean that the field is now more willing to consider the security of individuals and groups, rather than focusing narrowly on external threats to states.'[21] This sort of error is so extensive that one thinks there is almost a conspiracy to prevent the idea of security being unmasked as political theory, and instead left as a technical matter.

Without deepening in the sense of drilling down to uncover the political theory from which security attitudes and behaviour derive, security studies remains a largely technical matter, the military/strategic problem-solving dimension of realism. This latter perspective was explicit in Buzan's *Introduction to Strategic Studies: Military Technology and International Relations*.[22] Critical perspectives, in contrast, see security studies as a branch of political theory, not the hardware dimension

---

[21] This, despite a reference to the work of Richard Wyn Jones, which supports the interpretation of deepening being discussed here. See Roland Paris, 'Human Security: Paradigm Shift or Hot Air?', *International Security*, vol. 26(2), 2001, pp. 87–102 (reference at p. 97).
[22] Barry Buzan, *Introduction to Strategic Studies: Military Technology and International Relations* (London: Macmillan, 1987).

of realism. This does not imply that a critical theory of security has nothing to say about missile-targeting strategies or the deployment of frigates; what it does mean is that security studies must go beyond the technical and strategic, and open up fundamental questions about politics. While the *problem-solving* approach tends to turn all politics into practices of security (and a narrow view of security at that), the critical turn (through deepening) is concerned to interpret issues of security as questions of political theory.

This account of the derivative nature of security should clarify any uncertainties left over from chapter 1 regarding the relationship between realist political theory and the character of the security studies that dominated Western universities and research institutes during the Cold War. Military power, statism, and the status quo were the priorities that logically derived from the realist idea that international politics is an arena of conflict between sovereign states, an idea which in turn derived from essentialist understandings about selfish and fearful humans living in a state of nature or reductive structural theories about '*the* logic of anarchy'. At the same time, particular realist agendas and priorities reflected the historical and geographical parochialism, as well as the gender and other defining features, of those who professed them. Realism ('*for* someone and *for* some purpose') has been a theory *of* the powerful, *by* the powerful, *for* the powerful.[23]

A critical approach to world security seeks to uncover and challenge the orthodox approach that has been represented since the 1950s by Anglo-American university departments and research institutions, in which nationalistic ideas have masqueraded as truth. (Few had the forthrightness of Edward Luttwak, who asserted that the only purpose of academic inquiry in security studies is 'to strengthen one's own side in the contention of nations').[24] Such forthrightness, incidentally, explicitly ignores referents that theories other than realism consider categorical, notably gender, class, or race. These referents never therefore appear on the mainstream security studies agenda, despite the enormous levels of violence (structural and direct) against women everywhere, despite poverty being responsible for more premature deaths than war, and

[23] See my discussion in Ken Booth, 'Critical Explorations', in Booth, *Critical Security Studies*, pp. 4–10.
[24] Edward N. Luttwak, *Strategy and History: Collected Essays*, vol. II (New Brunswick, N.J.: Transaction Books, 1985), p. xiii; this is discussed in Ken Booth, 'Security and Emancipation', *Review of International Studies*, vol. 17(4), 1991, p. 318.

despite race doing more work than most in the West would admit.[25] When people(s) are being threatened, silences are particularly significant because of the political (and therefore material) mobilisation capacity of the word 'security'. It makes all the difference in the world to potential victims whether rape is defined as a security issue/war crime as opposed simply to a problem to be dealt with by 'women's studies' or 'sociology'. Equally, it matters whether global poverty is categorised as a security issue/global challenge rather than an item on the agenda of 'development studies'. Rape and poverty provoke more insecurity, day by day, for most people across the globe, than do the movements of a neighbour's army. While as students of security we should never ignore the agendas and pronouncements of military strategists, on what justifiable basis can we deny space on the security studies agenda to the violence and insecurity done by world politics to many women, the poor, and those oppressed because of race?

The critics of broadening must be directly challenged, though their concerns from a traditional perspective are understandable. Faced with so much evidence of human wrongs, resulting in so much insecurity across the world, one sympathises with the view expressed by Richard K. Betts that broadening makes security studies 'potentially boundless', or with Colin Gray's worry that security has become a 'notably unhelpful concept'.[26] To such critics I have two brief responses, one a comment, the other a question. The comment is that maintaining focus within the wide range of insecurity problems globally and locally is not difficult once one is clear about one's priorities and principles for world security; furthermore, coverage of different issue areas will be progressively helped by the growth of a division of labour among the community of scholars interested in pursuing critical approaches to security. At the level of government, sorting out priorities within a broadened security agenda is a matter for political decision, and one of the key aims of critical theorising is to bring politics more explicitly into the security field, where too much has become pre-defined. The question to be asked of critics who challenge either the broadening of, or the meaning of security, is this: when people(s) are seriously insecure, how (on what grounds) can one justify keeping any issue off the security

---

[25] Brought out by Sandra Whitworth in *Men, Militarism, and UN Peacekeeping: A Gendered Analysis* (Boulder, Colo.: Lynne Rienner, 2004).
[26] Richard K. Betts, 'Should Strategic Studies Survive?' *World Politics*, vol. 50(1), 1997, p. 9, and Colin S. Gray, *Another Bloody Century. Future Warfare* (London: Phoenix, 2006), pp. 60–1.

agenda? The only acceptable answer is a pragmatic one, based on priorities, not on principle. And finally, in relation to Gray's worry about the discussion of the usefulness of the concept of security, I would suggest a return to the discussion in chapter 3. Again I doubt whether the chronically or acutely insecure believe security to be a 'notably unhelpful concept'.

A particularly unjustifiable reason for giving in to the critics of broadening, including here the Copenhagen school, is the absence of a loud enough political voice on the part of the victims. Paraphrasing Cox once more: all silences are *'against* some body or *against* some thing'. None have been more silenced over the centuries than the victims of the slave trade, as its historians have discovered.[27] Such silences are not natural, they are political. Things do not just happen in politics, they are made to happen, whether it is globalisation or inequality. Grammar serves power.[28] Nature does not throw up 'silent majorities', 'poor people', or 'the powerless'. Politics does. The silent in world politics are not physically voiceless: they are politically silenced. The disenfranchised are not born without power: they are disempowered. There is no poverty gene to be discovered: people are made poor by political choices. In world politics, security (and insecurity) is made by political theories – what they say and also what they ignore and silence.

Security as society's agenda

Freedom of speech
Freedom of worship
Freedom from want
Freedom from fear.   Franklin Delano Roosevelt, 1 June 1941[29]

The broadening of the security agenda, if it takes place, is a function of deepening. When people speak about security, or carry out practices

---

[27] Commenting on the few direct testimonies of slaves over several centuries, Hugh Thomas said: 'the slave remains an unknown warrior'. In his *The Slave Trade. The History of the Atlantic Slave Trade: 1440–1870* (London: Picador, 1997), p. 799.
[28] I want to thank Cynthia Enloe for first getting me thinking along these lines, as a result of her presentation that led to 'Margins, Silences and Bottom Rungs: How to Overcome the Underestimation of Power in the Study of International Relations', in Smith *et al.*, *International Theory*, pp. 186–202.
[29] Roosevelt's Four Freedoms, from the Roosevelt Memorial in Washington, quoted by Hayward Alker, 'Emancipation in the Critical Security Studies Project', in Booth, *Critical Security Studies*, p. 194.

in the name of security, their words and actions are embedded in their deepest conceptions of the nature of world politics (even if they are not articulated). This means that security can be broadened only in the manner and to the extent allowed by the assumptions of its underlying political theory.

Much of the rethinking security debate has been about broadening. This was evident in the reference in chapter 3 to the resistance of the strategic studies orthodoxy to the prising apart of the concepts of strategy and security. The most familiar rhetorical defence of the orthodoxy in this regard has been the claim that broadening the concept of security is an invitation to disciplinary chaos. The most widely cited of the many defences of the disciplinary traditionalism has been Stephen M. Walt's article 'The Renaissance of Security Studies'.[30] One of its main themes was its attack on the idea of broadening the security agenda; it criticised the inclusion of non-military issues such as poverty and environmental decay. Walt argued that such expansion would destroy the field's 'intellectual coherence'. Despite this, he nevertheless proceeded to offer his own research agenda which proved to be extremely broad, and quite inconsistent with his basic argument: his attack on broadening was also an invitation to join in broadening. He listed for inclusion on his agenda 'the role of domestic politics, the causes of peace and cooperation, the power of ideas, the end of the Cold War, economics and security, refining existing theories, and protecting the database'. This was broadening without a theory, but such inconsistency among realists is not surprising, because of the clash between their desire to maintain their power credentials while responding to their experiences of a changing world. This tension reveals a critical problem at the heart of realism: the more realistic realism attempts to be, the more inconsistent it becomes, while the more theoretically consistent it remains, the more it departs from the real world.

It should now be clear that broadening itself is not a radical move in security policy; whether or not it is depends on the underlying political theory. The security agenda will be as broad or as narrow as the political theory that drives it. Since the late 1980s, broadening has generally been used to refer to the idea of including 'non-traditional' security issues on the security agenda (that is, non-military threats). Buzan categorised the

---

[30] Stephen M. Walt, 'The Renaissance of Security Studies', *International Studies Quarterly*, vol. 35(2), 1991, pp. 211–39; for a critique see Ken Booth and Eric Herring, *Strategic Studies. Keyguide to Information Sources* (London: Mansell, 1994), pp. 126–7.

issue areas for a broadened security agenda in relation to five 'sectors', each identifying 'specific types of interaction':[31]

- military sector ('relationships of forceful coercion')
- political sector ('relationships of authority, governing status, and recognition')
- economic sector ('relationships of trade, production, and finance')
- societal sector ('relationships of collective identity')
- environmental sector ('relationships between human activity and the planetary biosphere').

For Buzan, it was state interests that determine the character of these agendas. Buzan's key text, *People, States and Fear*, was not therefore a call for a radical rethink of security theory as much as a call to mainstream analysts to broaden the security agenda of states away from their overwhelming concern with military power.[32] This is why Wyn Jones argued that Buzan's book had been mis-titled, suggesting that its statist reference point (despite some attention being given to individual and supra-state levels) meant that *States and Fear* would have been more appropriate.[33]

Although *People, States and Fear* helped to raise awareness about the principle of a broadened security agenda, its own broadening did not escape the deep structure of its state-centric assumptions. In the second edition of the book, reflecting Buzan's involvement in developing the Copenhagen school, signs appeared of a serious commitment to broadening. Buzan wrote: 'If a multisectoral approach to security was to be fully meaningful, referent objects other than the state had to be allowed into the picture.' Subsequently, the Copenhagen school attempted to advance this argument.[34] One milestone was the multi-authored book

[31] Barry Buzan, Ole Wæver, and Jaap de Wilde, *Security: A New Framework for Analysis* (Boulder, Colo.: Lynne Rienner, 1998), pp. 7–8, and chs. 3–7.
[32] This was made explicit by Barry Buzan in a chapter entitled, 'Is international security possible?' where he argued that the military dimension had been paid 'disproportionate' attention: in Ken Booth (ed.), *New Thinking about Strategy and International Security* (London: HarperCollins, 1991), p. 36.
[33] Richard Wyn Jones, *Security, Strategy, and Critical Theory* (Boulder, Colo.: Lynne Rienner, 1999), p. 112; this book contains other telling comments on the work of Buzan and the Copenhagen school. See also Barry Buzan, 'The Timeless Wisdom of Realism?' in Smith *et al.*, *Positivism and Beyond*, pp. 47–65.
[34] Compare Barry Buzan, *People, States and Fear: An Agenda for International Security Studies in the Post-Cold War Era* (Brighton: Harvester-Wheatsheaf, 1991), pp. 9–20, Ole Wæver *et al.*, *Identity, Migration, and the New Security Agenda in Europe* (London: Pinter, 1993), pp. 24–7, and Buzan *et al.*, *Security*, pp. 7–8.

The European Security Order Recast: Scenarios for the Post-Cold War Era, in which attention shifted from the state as referent and sovereignty as the value to be secured, to society as the referent and identity as the value to be secured.[35] This move promised a major change in the Copenhagen school's approach, but this was not borne out in subsequent work. Why, in the school's multi-authored book *Security: A New Framework for Analysis*, was it claimed – almost begrudgingly – that referent objects other than the state *'had to be allowed* into the picture' (my emphasis)?[36] There is no answer from within the school's theory, except that referents other than the state have to be 'allowed' in because of the multisectoral ('broadening') approach. This logic gives causal power to the sectors; they determine the referents for security, not the other way round. This does not make sense. At this point, it would be helpful to make a longer digression, to engage with the Copenhagen school's take on security in general, because of its role in the debate about broadening.

One question opponents of critical approaches to security ask is whether the issues some want to place on a broader security agenda are really 'security' questions at all. These opponents ask 'whether it is actually appropriate to "securitize" such issues . . . [because] "securitization" induces highly inappropriate reactions' to some international problems.[37] My view is clear: there is no doubt that the agenda to be considered under the umbrella 'security' should be broadened, but equally I think that it is unhelpful to 'securitise' this agenda in the sense of that term identified with the Copenhagen school. Careful readers will have noted that I have not used the term 'securitise' up to this point; to do so, I think, would be to condone the infiltration into the security discourse of a concept (and way of thinking) that is seriously flawed.

'Securitisation studies' is the name sometimes given to the Copenhagen school's curious theoretical mixture of liberal, poststructural, and neorealist assumptions. The school has undoubtedly raised interesting questions, but its own answers are problematic.[38] At the heart of the matter is the concept of 'securitisation', which is best understood as having

---

[35] Barry Buzan, Morten Kelstrup, Pierre Lemaitre, Elzbieta Tromer, and Ole Wæver, *The European Security Order Recast: Scenarios for the Post-Cold War Era* (London: Pinter, 1990).

[36] Buzan *et al.*, *Security*, p. 8.

[37] See Chris Brown with Kirsten Ainley, *Understanding International Relations* (London: Palgrave Macmillan, 2005), p. 177.

[38] For a critical appraisal of the Copenhagen school, see Bill McSweeney, 'Identity and Security: Buzan and the Copenhagen School', *Review of International Studies*, vol. 22(1), 1996, pp. 85–97. I have learned much about the Copenhagen school (McSweeney coined the phrase) from Pinar Bilgin, Richard Wyn Jones (see also his *Security*, pp. 107–23), and Paul Williams – and not a few Danish graduate students, brought up in the school but

been a reaction against the perceived danger (arising from broadening the security agenda) that the traditional security mindset (characterised by militarised, conflictual, and zero-sum thinking) will be extended into what hitherto had been regarded as non-military areas by labelling them 'security'. The Copenhagen school further argues that threats to security do not exist outside discourse. Issues become security threats because state elites 'utter' security in reference to them: security is a 'speech act'.[39] In order to count as security issues, threats and vulnerabilities 'have to meet strictly defined criteria that distinguish them from the normal run of the merely political. They have to be staged as existential threats to a referent object by a securitizing actor who thereby generates endorsement of emergency measures beyond rules that would otherwise bind.'[40] Conceiving the securitisation of issues as synonymous with militarising them, Copenhagen-style security analysts seek to 'de-securitise' threats by bringing them into 'ordinary' politics.[41]

The general approach advocated by the Copenhagen school runs in parallel with several themes central to critical thinking about security: the stress on the political power and symbolism of the word 'security'; the appreciation of the resource and other implications of taking issues outside 'ordinary politics' and onto the security agenda; the understanding of security as an intersubjective concept; a commitment to the desirability of trying to avoid the militarising of issues by challenging the 'mind-set of security' that sees issues in zero-sum terms; and finally the search to resolve security issues without violence. All these views are compatible with those in this book. Henceforth, however, the paths diverge. Securitisation studies, for a start, rests on a confused conceptualisation of security, as discussed in chapter 3 (equating it with survival). In turn, security is essentialised, with a distinct political practice with its own logic (and this despite a claim that the concept is intersubjective). Note the following claim: 'We seek to find coherence not

who later studied in Wales. The core ideas of the Copenhagen school derive from the concept of securitisation as originally proposed by Ole Wæver: *Insecurity and Identity Unlimited* (Copenhagen: Centre for Peace and Conflict Research, 1994, Working Paper 14) and 'Securitization and Desecuritization', in Ronnie D. Lipzchutz (ed.), *On Security* (New York: Columbia University Press, 1995), pp. 46–86. Wæver's main themes were incorporated into the primary collective work of the Copenhagen school: Buzan *et al.*, *Security*. In the analysis below I attempt to assess the collective position, though there are sometimes contradictory emphases within it; the uncertainties have grown with the school's apparent incorporation into the 'CASE Collective'. See the latter's 'Critical Approaches to Security in Europe: A Networked Manifesto', *Security Dialogue*, vol. 37(4), 2006, pp. 443–87.
[39] Wæver, 'Securitization and Desecuritization', p. 55.
[40] Buzan *et al.*, *Security*, p. 5.   [41] *Ibid.*, pp. 4, 29, 209.

by confining security to the military sector but *by exploring the logic of security itself* to find out what differentiates security and the process of securitization from that which is *merely political'*(emphasis added).[42] The word 'itself' is a giveaway, implying a pre-defined view of what security is 'all about', while the two phrases – 'merely political' and 'security itself' – reveal a separation of security and politics which is astonishing from a critical theory perspective. What security is 'about' for the Copenhagen school is discourse. Consequently, attention is focused on who has said what to whom about security in particular contexts.[43] Such a discourse-centric approach misses chunks of reality, and is based on the fallacy that threats do not exist outside discourse. They clearly do so, empirically. The danger posed by global warming to low-lying island states was a physical process long before the discourse of environmental security was invented by its proponents and listened to by their audiences. And what about the security threats to those without a political voice? Left to securitisation analysts, more 'screams' would be left to 'fade away' (see p. 37).

Security in the Copenhagen school understanding is conceived as a negative value, a failure to deal with issues as normal politics:[44] security 'itself', as they see it, must be militarised, zero-sum, and confrontational. This view contrasts directly with the definition I offered in chapter 3, which argued that security is instrumental, and identified with emancipation. Whereas the latter conception seeks to open security up to political theory and the politics of progressive change, the language of 'securitisation' freezes security in a statist framework, forever militarised, zero-sum, and confrontational. Such a static view of the concept is all the odder because security as a speech act has historically also embraced positive, non-militarised, and non-statist connotations. This was the case in policies associated with 'social security'. The latter has looked to offer a safety net to the weakest in society (in relation to poverty and health not military threats). Securitisation studies, like mainstream strategic studies, remains somewhat stuck in Cold War mindsets.

Despite the welfare connotations of security just mentioned, the Copenhagen view insists that the notion of security 'carries with it a history and set of connotations that it cannot escape. At the heart of the concept we still find something to do with defense and the state.'[45]

[42] *Ibid.*, pp. 4–5.   [43] *Ibid.*, pp. 21–48.   [44] *Ibid.*, p. 29.
[45] Wæver, 'Securitization and Desecuritization', p. 47. The strong realist theme in the school is not surprising, given Buzan's robust neorealist credentials: see *People, States and Fear*, p. 373.

This static interpretation was accepted by Ole Wæver, the coiner of the term 'securitisation'; he wrote that 'a conservative approach to security is an intrinsic element in the logic of both our national and international political organizing principles'.[46] Any radical aspirations of the school are held back by such conservative assumptions of the theory, including the state-centric origins of the idea[47] (a point that has not been dented by a later attempt to soften the position by distinguishing between 'state-centric' and 'state-dominated' approaches).[48] This latter distinction is ritualistic, given the school's view of what is at the 'heart' of security,[49] and its assumptions about the centrality of the state.[50] Because securiti-sation is discourse-centric, and because states dominate the discourse, it follows that states will remain the dominating referent ('some actors are placed in positions of power by virtue of being generally accepted voices of security'[51]). The statist outlook is evident when Buzan and his co-writers argue that when an issue is securitised it becomes 'so important that it should not be exposed to the normal haggling of pol-itics but should be dealt with decisively by top leaders prior to other issues'.[52] In Wæver's words, 'The language game of security is . . . a *jus necessitatis* for threatened elites, and this it must remain.'[53] Phrases such as 'top leaders' and 'threatened elites' are state-centric giveaways, while 'must remain' is the language of conservatism. These issues are not helped by the failure to distinguish between an agent (which is a comment about relative power) and a referent (which is a normative label).[54]

Securitisation studies therefore suffer from being elitist. What mat-ters above all for the school is 'top leaders', 'states', 'threatened elites' and 'audiences' with agenda-making power. Those without discourse-making power are disenfranchised, unable to join the securitisation game. This top-down perspective is underlined by the limited attention given to human rights in the major work on securitisation,[55] although placing individual humans at the centre of international concern since

---

[46] Wæver, 'Securitization and Desecuritization', pp. 56–7.
[47] See the critique by Wyn Jones, *Security*, p. 109.   [48] Buzan *et al.*, *Security*, p. 37.
[49] On Buzan's state-centrism, see Wyn Jones, *Security*, pp. 112–13.
[50] See Steve Smith, 'Mature Anarchy, Strong States and Security', *Arms Control*, vol. 12 (2), 1991, pp. 325–39; and Wyn Jones, *Security*, p. 112.
[51] Buzan *et al.*, *Security*, p. 31.   [52] *Ibid.*, p. 29.
[53] Waever, 'Securitization and Desecuritization', p. 56.
[54] Pinar Bilgin was the first to make this point, in an early draft of her PhD thesis; see Pinar Bilgin, Ken Booth, and Richard Wyn Jones, 'Security Studies: The Next Stage?' *Nacao e Defesa*, vol. 84(2), 1998, p. 150, and n. 40 p. 195 below.
[55] Buzan *et al.*, *Security*, pp. 60–1, 149, 185.

the late 1940s – in the Universal Declaration of Human Rights – challenged the 350 or so years of sovereign state dominance. As a result of the relentlessly top-down perspective, what is supposed to be a radical move actually works in the interests of power, because with power goes discourse-making potential. Those outside the discourse are not only silent, but silenced. Lene Hansen has made this point very effectively in relation to the school's neglect of gender-related insecurity.[56]

Despite these criticisms, the Copenhagen school claims radical credentials, seeking 'to construct a more radical view of security studies by exploring threats to referent objects, and the securitization of those threats, that are nonmilitary as well as military'.[57] How this approach is 'more radical' is not clear, given the preoccupation with mainstream discourse and its audience, and the state-dominated/centric focus. Securitisation studies welds together glimpses of neorealism, poststructuralism, and English school constructivism, and consequently does not offer clear guidance about what to do next, politically speaking. Despite its intentions, it represents static theory, not least because of its fixed conception of a speech act.[58] Words can radically change their meaning, as is evident in the transformation of 'imperialism' from its nineteenth-century positive connotations to its negative connotations by the mid-twentieth century. Slavery, too, changed radically, from a word describing an economic process to one labelling a detested institution. By freezing 'security' in its Cold War conceptualisation, and so reifying it as military problem-solving, the Copenhagen school connives in making security studies a static and conservative project – the opposite of its intentions.

The conservative character of securitisation studies is further revealed by its emphasis on the 'audience' for a security speech act.[59] According to the theory, securitisation requires that a specific audience has to accept the claims of the securitising actor: 'Successful securitization is not decided by the securitizer but by the audience of the security speech act.'[60] In this book, in contrast, the existence and salience of a security issue does not depend on the political success of an actor reaching a particular audience; after all, we all know that in politics as in life in general, there are none so deaf as those who do not want to hear. Audiences with agenda-making power can choose not to be an 'audience',

---

[56] Lene Hansen, 'The Little Mermaid's Silent Security Dilemma and the Absence of Gender in the Copenhagen School', *Millennium*, vol. 29(2), 2000, pp. 285–306.
[57] Buzan *et al.*, *Security*, p. 4.
[58] For a Habermasian critique along these lines, see Wyn Jones, *Security*, pp. 111–12.
[59] The theory is outlined in Buzan *et al.*, *Security*, pp. 41–5.   [60] *Ibid.*, p. 31.

as happened with the UN Security Council (UNSC) during the Rwandan genocide in 1994.[61] The fact that a key audience did not accept the claims of those convinced that a genocide was taking place (thereby justifying a move beyond ordinary politics) did not make the mass murder in Rwanda any less of a 'security' issue for the silenced victims. Securitisation theory focuses on the accepting audience (a version of insider or problem-solving theory); critical theory reports also on the *problems* of such a perspective. Critical security studies must report upon and analyse both sorts of problems, and sometimes audiences need to be awakened or even created, and not simply interpreted. There are times when somebody has to speak for the victims.[62] If security is always a speech act, insecurity is frequently a zipped lip.

We would all presumably agree that the unnecessary securitisation (militarisation) of issues is to be deplored, but there are occasions when introducing a military dimension is sensible. Environmental protection, for example, sometimes requires preparation for the use of force. This is the case with warships or armed coastguard vessels patrolling exclusive economic zones. Massive human rights abuses – above all genocide – also legitimately raise the issue of forceful intervention. For the Copenhagen school, the answer to 'securitisation' is 'desecuritisation'. But the latter cannot be a general rule, if it means a lowering of the salience of some issues (given the political power of the label 'security'). Desecuritisation could indeed be a move by the powerful to lower the significance of real insecurities. Desecuritisation can disempower. Having issues settled by 'ordinary' politics is a nice idea: who would not prefer it to the threat of political violence? But 'ordinary' politics might not help in extraordinary circumstances; indeed, treating extraordinary issues as ordinary politics is a problem, not a solution. Great insecurity might be embedded in 'ordinary' politics, especially if the potential audience wants to hear no evil and victims are silenced. The ordinary politics of institutionalised racism can flourish if racism is 'desecuritised'. In such circumstances, desecuritisation is in the interests of power-holders; it can turn a victim's extraordinary situation into a power-holder's ordinary politics. The argument of this book is that some issues are too

---

[61] A key text – whose main title perfectly expresses the criticism being made here about securitisation – is Linda Melvern, *A People Betrayed. The Role of the West in Rwanda's Genocide* (London: Zed Books, 2000).

[62] These issues are discussed (with special reference to rural women in Bangladesh) in Brooke A. Ackerly, *Political Theory and Feminist Social Criticism* (Cambridge: Cambridge University Press, 2000), esp. 'Silent Voices and Everyday Critics: Problems in Political Theory, Solutions from Third World Feminist Criticism', pp. 1–31.

serious to be 'desecuritised'; and this may sometimes excuse the use of military force. Many security issues are better not dealt with as military issues (the EU, for example, has been a more promising instrument for extending security through eastern Europe than NATO), but at the same time it would be a mistake to desecuritise some issues, and so lower their salience. In the immediate aftermath of the terror attacks of 9/11 there was loud talk by some state leaders of reordering the world as part of rebuilding global security;[63] it did not take long for such ideas to be desecuritised and largely forgotten. Likewise, those who call for AIDS to be desecuritised are risking lowering the priority given to it. There is no reason in principle why AIDS should not, simultaneously, be high on the security agenda of certain countries and treated as a medical issue.[64]

Securitisation and desecuritisation are interesting but flawed ideas, and do not advance the cause of a more progressive security studies. The fundamental problem rests in the Copenhagen school's separation of the realms of politics and security, and its conservative view of the latter as an area destined for militarisation. A critical theory of security attempts to turn this way of thinking on its head by insisting that security is conceived as political theory, and understood in relation to emancipation.

While states remain the referent for realists and, for the most part, the Copenhagen school, critical theorising examines other referents of security; its first task is to reveal who and what different political theories privilege as categorical structures. The point here is not to attack Buzan's work – which was pivotal in promoting the theoretical turn in security studies – but rather to use it to illustrate that broadening security is not simply a matter of adding new ingredients to 'non-traditional' statist interests and mixing. Broadening can only be properly understood in relation to what Walker called 'the most basic questions of political theory', a move that exposes the assumptions from which the epiphenomenon of security derives – and the Copenhagen school has shied away from 'the most basic questions' because of its static concern with 'top leaders' and their traditional audiences.

The rich tradition of peace research is a much more fertile source for ideas about the problems and prospects of world security than the

[63] Notably by the British Prime Minister, Tony Blair. See the text of his speech to the Labour Party Conference in October 2001: http://politics.guardian.co.uk/labour2001/story/0,1414,5620006,00.html.
[64] Dennis Altman, 'AIDS and Security', *International Relations*, vol. 17(4), 2003, pp. 417–27, is a brief overview of why HIV/AIDS should be regarded as an international security issue.

intricacies of securitisation studies. Indeed, long before the critical turn in the academic study of international relations, the security agenda had been broadened by theoretical innovation undertaken by major peace researchers. Notable among these, as discussed in chapter 2, was Johan Galtung, whose concept of structural violence (the idea that violence is done to people as a result of the structure of relationships, and not simply as a result of the use of force) helped reconfigure the agenda of peace studies in the 1960s and beyond. Other innovations encouraged conceptual broadening. For example, as social science became more self-conscious, peace studies welcomed interdisciplinarity as essential to the study of war. This led to a growing trend to conceive interstate violence as a 'war system', demanding to be understood (in the words of Richard Falk and Samuel Kim) as a 'multidimensional reality possessing a firm hold on individuals and societies', linking war with 'the entire range of conflicts that occur in social processes at all levels of human interaction'.[65] At the same time, Third World security specialists were beginning to emphasise that internal problems rather than neighbouring armies were at the top of the security agenda of most developing states. In other words, the key to being more secure for 'new nations' was better governance in relation to such issues as intercommunal tensions rather than the threat of invasion. For most Third World specialists, therefore, security was always a broader concept than simply military strategy.[66] In the West, starting in the 1970s, what became called the 'alternative security' school sought to broaden the security agenda in a different way still, provoked by issues of immediate policy interest. The Euro-missile issue, together with intensifying superpower rivalry, focused this body of thinking to promote disarmament and (non-offensive) military restructuring to deal directly with the growing dangers of the Cold War. The promotion of human rights and democracy was advanced as a strategy to transcend the rivalries between the blocs, not least because threats were understood as multilevel, to people as well as states.[67]

---

[65] Richard A. Falk and Samuel S. Kim, 'General Introduction', in Richard A. Falk and Samuel S. Kim (eds.), *The War System: An Interdisciplinary Approach* (Boulder, Colo.: Westview, 1980), p. 5; this book is an excellent collection of relevant readings for this objective.
[66] For example, Abdul-Monem M. Al-Mashat, *National Security in the Third World* (Boulder, Colo.: Westview, 1985), and Caroline Thomas, *In Search of Security: The Third World in International Relations* (Brighton: Wheatsheaf, 1987).
[67] Mary Kaldor, 'Beyond the Blocs: Defending Europe the Political Way', *World Policy Journal*, vol. 1(1), 1983, pp. 1–23; and with Gerard Holden and Richard Falk (eds.), *The New Detente: Rethinking East–West Relations* (London: Verso, 1989).

Ideas about broadening have certainly not been confined to academic theorising; they have been familiar in the world of policymaking for many years. The so-called non-traditional agenda has been pursued with more or less enthusiasm depending on the particular government or branch of government concerned. The oil crises in the mid-1970s focused minds in a particularly acute fashion on the growing security stresses of an interdependent world, and on the need to think beyond military strategy.[68] Broadening has also been a priority for those (usually not among the leaders of the world's most powerful states) who early on became aware of the potential significance for global security of a variety of emerging threats, notably climate change.[69] What is more, broadening is not necessarily hostile to the interests of some military services. Navies were not slow to understand the importance for their budgets of new constabulary roles;[70] these functions have grown over the decades because of increased sensitivity to the importance of environmental protection, including fisheries. By the 1990s, broadening was accepted by political elites in many countries, though it was overwhelmingly conceived in statist terms (see the discussion of 'human security' in chapter 7). Another sign of change was the willingness of some governments to separate 'defence' and 'security' in official language, the former implying the military dimension, the latter referring to a broader range of threats. This change of usage was a signal that some officials appreciated better than disciplinary traditionalists that security and strategy were not synonymous, and that the military dimension of policy was best conceived as one facet of a broadened conception of security.

Even when state representatives adopt the language of a broadened conception of security, however, it is important to look behind their words, for governments co-opt persuasive language for their own purposes (see chapter 7). When this occurs, and governments talk the talk of broadening ('human security', for example), one should not expect any fundamental changes in their outlook. The test of any change from a traditional understanding of the 'national interest' is the seriousness with which a government is willing to promote world security ideas in their daily actions, and their willingness to bear associated costs. Without this,

[68] See Ken Booth, 'The Evolution of Strategic Thinking', in John Baylis, Ken Booth, John Garnett, and Phil Williams, *Contemporary Strategy. Theories and Policies* (London: Croom Helm, 1975), p. 43; for a longer account, see David Baldwin, 'The Concept of Security', *Review of International Studies*, vol. 23(1), 1997, pp. 5–26.

[69] Evident, for example, in *Our Global Neighbourhood. The Report of the Commission on Global Governance* (Oxford: Oxford University Press, 1995).

[70] K. Booth, *Navies and Foreign Policy* (London: Croom Helm, 1977), pp. 17–18, 265–8.

the discourse of broadening is merely tactical: statist feel-good rhetoric. The gulf of incomprehension on these matters between orthodox and critical viewpoints is the former's description of international society being increasingly willing to engage with a 'non-traditional' security agenda. To look at it this way is a total misconception. Many of these supposedly 'non-traditional security issues', newly discovered by governments and the disciplinary orthodoxy, are in fact *all too traditional* for those without a political voice, and who have suffered chronic human rights abuses, famine, poverty, or patriarchal violence.[71]

Security as political practice

Pessimists are cowards and optimists are fools.
Heinrich Blücher to American students[72]

The argument of the book so far points to two key moves in a critical theory of world security. The first is critique, which involves interpreting the world (the analytical process involved in deepening and broadening our conceptualisation of security); the second is reconstruction (which as used here is synonymous with politicising security: that is, attempting to rethink and revise the practices of security with emancipatory, reconstructive intent, as opposed merely to replicating business-as-usual).

Critique involves the sustained questioning of those ideologies, institutions, discourses, and ideas that have constructed and sustained particular structures in social, political, and economic life. This first move throws critical light on the knowledge-claims of the powerful (as well as the values represented by the oppressed – it must not be assumed that victimhood is synonymous with innocence). It includes interrogating the meaning of security and theories of human nature; and problematising the rationality and values of statism, nationalism, masculinism, capitalism, and other hegemonic ideas structuring human society. The second move is particularly important for Frankfurt school thinking, and represents the political practice arising out of 'immanent critique' (introduced in chapter 2, to be elaborated further in chapter 6). Reconstruction shifts attention to praxis, and relates critique to real people in real places – 'human choices situated in historic conditions' as McSweeney put it.[73] We have to begin where we are, and develop tactical and

---

[71] Ken Booth, 'Realities of Security', *International Relations*, vol. 18(1), 2004, pp. 5–8.
[72] Quoted in Young-Bruehl, *Arendt*, p. 136.
[73] Bill McSweeney, *Security, Identity and Interests. A Sociology of International Relations* (Cambridge: Cambridge University Press, 1999), pp. 198–219.

strategic action in the interests of security, community, and emancipation. This includes examining security at different levels for different
referents, from the individual to the global. The key questions are: security for whom? against which threats? and how is it to be achieved?
Attempting to answer these questions from a critical perspective can
result in a significantly different set of pictures to those projected by
power-wielders.[74] Understanding the operational dimensions of emancipatory politics, in relation to the parts and to the whole of human
society, is central to moving beyond critique to reconstruction. It is
always chastening when the conceptual saw finally rips into humanity's crooked timber.

What rips into the timber for global critical theorising of the sort
discussed in chapter 2 is the set of concepts about politics in action:
'praxis', 'emancipation', and 'political orientation'. These are integral
aspects of a critical theory of security, but they are frequently challenged
by realists for being preachy rather than 'academic', and by postmod-
ernists/poststructuralists for pushing flawed ideas of the Enlightenment. I will address each in turn.

The charge of bringing 'politics' into the study of 'Politics' is based
on the conviction that to do so undermines academic values such
as objectivity and science. This has been a familiar charge against
all social/economic/political projects challenging orthodoxy, common
sense, the status quo, business-as-usual, or a hegemonic discourse.
Chapter 2 recalled the attack on peace research in the Cold War. The
frame of mind behind ostensible defences of the purity of certain kinds
of scholarship was perfectly encapsulated in a story told to me by a
former colleague who, many years ago, in a different life, attended his
first meeting as a town councillor in the west of England. Just before
proceedings began, he was taken aside by one of the old-timers and
told: 'I hope you won't bring politics into the council chamber young
man – we are all good conservatives here.'

It has been the ideal of traditional social science to keep politics
and other value-laden matters out of academic enquiry. As was suggested in chapter 2 (and will be elaborated in chapter 6), critical theory
argues that value-freedom and objectivity are not possible (because all

---

[74] I tried to provide such a comprehensive picture, with a matrix constructed from Buzan's
'sectoral' approach, and multiple levels and agents, in Ken Booth, *A Security Regime in
Southern Africa: Theoretical Considerations* (Cape Town: University of the Western Cape,
Centre for Southern African Studies, 1994; Southern African Perspectives, Working Paper
Series, No. 30).

knowledge of the social world is contextual), nor is it desirable (in a world of injustice, knowledge should be emancipatory). Three further points are pertinent. First, against the charge that critical theory is 'political', the defence is not that it is not, but rather that traditional security scholarship is also political. During the Cold War, for example, strategic studies and national security studies were pumped up with definite political and social values (realism, nationalism, and masculinism for a start). Religion was not absent either, when one considers the Christian commitments of such prominent realist voices as Reinhold Niebuhr and George Kennan.[75] At the level of the subconscious, some of the mythology that has characterised the Judeao-Christian tradition may also have had an impact on how US society conceived its struggle with its global enemy.[76] The falseness of the orthodox outlook, with its pretension to be above the struggle, can best be illustrated not by the least sophisticated of its proponents, but through the words of one of its most sophisticated and philosophically literate exponents, Hedley Bull. At the end of his *Anarchical Society*, he wrote: 'The search for conclusions that can be presented as "solutions" or "practical advice" is a corrupting element in the contemporary study of world politics, which properly understood is an intellectual activity and not a practical one.'[77] Space does not permit the deconstructive efforts that might be invested in that one sentence; suffice it to say that his book up to that point had been drenched in his own value preferences about world politics (and much of his other work did not shy away from making it very clear what he thought should happen in the world). The very chapter preceding his haughty dismissal of searching for a 'solution', or of canvassing policies to represent 'the way ahead', begins with the question: 'how can [the states system] . . . best be reformed or reshaped so as to more effectively promote world order?'[78]

Second, all students of human society must ask: what is not *political* in some sense or other? This does not mean that academic work should be synonymous with party-political activism, but one should be explicit about the political values informing one's work. For critical theorists, as discussed in the previous chapters, this involves an alignment with

---

[75] A first-class introduction to the work of these and other leading realists is Michael Joseph Smith, *Realist Thought from Weber to Kissinger* (Baton Rouge: Louisiana State University Press, 1986).
[76] Note the discussion of Milton's *Paradise Lost* by Bernard Brodie, *Strategy in the Missile Age* (Princeton, N.J.: Princeton University Press, 1965), pp. 3–5.
[77] Bull, *Anarchical Society*, pp. 319–20.   [78] *Ibid.*, pp. 297 and 318.

certain goals (such as equality), processes (such as emancipation), and referents (such as common humanity). Politics can only be analysed politically – not neutrally – in historically situated conditions. Finally, it is necessary to return to the issue flagged in chapter 2 about the meaning of science. In North America in particular, many working within the discipline of international relations have come to believe their own propaganda about their work and 'normal science'.[79] The argument that critical (or what Robert Keohane called 'reflectivist') approaches cannot be considered real social science revolves around such matters as the employment of 'testable theories'.[80] But the challenge Keohane and others have thrown down before 'reflectivists' to meet the requirements of the dominant rationalist approach in effect represents a demand on them to stop being reflectivist.[81]

The charge that critical theorising is political should be turned back on those that make it. There is indeed a 'political orientation' in critical theory towards emancipation, but this has been made explicit. Is it not equally political – if not equally overt – to define reality and the discipline within the limits set by norms of the sovereign state system, by 'high' rather than 'low' politics as the stuff of security, by the identification of rationalists as the only true scholars, and by an implicit US-centrism as the Archimedean standpoint for judging? Behind a mask of science, supposedly describing 'the world as it is', are traditional security intellectuals describing their own reality through ethnocentric, class, and masculinist eyes, albeit tempered by academic values and methods. Theorists in glass houses should not throw stones.

The same warning could be addressed to scholars working in the postmodern/poststructuralist mode (though they defy easy categorisation by the nature of what they do, and also by design). This body of thought, which directs a different set of criticisms at the political orientation of critical theorising, is full of strictures against 'binary oppositions', the 'Western canon', 'emancipation', and 'metanarratives'. Despite this, the various strands of 'post'-theorising have been

---

[79] Richard Ned Lebow, *The Tragic Vision of Politics. Ethics, Interests and Orders* (Cambridge: Cambridge University Press, 2003), offers brief but trenchant comments on this fixation, including the 'physics envy' of some in the discipline: pp. 381–2.
[80] McSweeney argues (*Security, Identity and Interests*, p. 140) that Keohane confuses the terms 'reflexive' and 'reflective'; Keohane's pivotal role in the debate was 'International Institutions: Two Approaches', *International Studies Quarterly*, vol. 32(4), 1988, pp. 379–96.
[81] Chris Brown, 'Critical Theory and Postmodernism in International Relations', in A. J. R. Groom and Margot Light (eds.), *Contemporary International Relations: A Guide to Theory* (London: Pinter, 1994), p. 62.

characterised by binaries (most unhelpfully, the reification of the 'West' against the 'Rest'),[82] by their own dead white male canon (notably the cult of Foucault),[83] by hidden emancipatory/liberal ideas (including a teleology),[84] and by implicit metanarratives (such as the 'anti-metanarrative metanarrative' about embracing micro-narratives universally and 'celebrating difference').[85] The seduction of science is perhaps another similarity shared by rationalists and postmodernists, if the famous (or infamous) story of Alan Sokal's *Intellectual Impostures* is any

---

[82] This is not to say that the general criticism of 'binary oppositions' is invalid, for they frequently do imply settled identities and reified hierarchies. The West/Rest reification is particularly troublesome. See Kenan Malik's criticism of Edward Said in *The Meaning of Race: Race, History and Culture in Western Society* (London: Macmillan, 1996), pp. 217–59 (discussed further in chapter 8). Such reifications are standard among writers from a postcolonial perspective while they claim to be doing the opposite. Note the essentialising of the 'West'/'North'/'Europe' by Tarak Barkawi and Mark Laffey, 'The Postcolonial Moment in Security Studies', *Review of International Studies*, vol. 32(2), 2006, pp. 329–52, and of the 'West'/'Rest' by Stuart Hall, 'The West and the Rest: Discourse and Power', in Stuart Hall and Bram Gieben (eds.), *Formations of Modernity* (Cambridge: Polity in association with the Open University, 1992), pp. 275–320.

[83] Foucault's work on 'madness' is a standard reference for poststructuralist writers on international relations, yet I have not detected the plaudits being accompanied by an actual analysis of his ideas in historical and comparative context. To do so would reveal that Foucault was more a man of his time than his disciples appear to realise. His ideas must be understood in relation to those of others at the time, and earlier, who had begun to criticise prevailing thinking about 'mental illness' – notably the 'anti-psychiatry' school of Thomas S. Szasz, R. D. Laing, and David Cooper from the 1950s onwards. For a revealing set of personal and professional insights focusing on Laing, see Bob Mullan (ed.), *R. D. Laing: Creative Destroyer* (London: Cassell, 1997). While some of the understanding of mental illness certainly (and necessarily) has had cultural/social/historical dimensions, there is much more to say and be understood. Some mental health specialists (such as Martin Roth and Jerome Kroll) reject the thinking of those who categorise mental illness largely or wholly in relation to the prevailing systems of thought, insisting that the 'stability of psychiatric symptoms over time shows that mental illness is ... a real psychopathological entity, with an authentic organic basis.' See Roy Porter, *Madness. A Brief History* (Oxford: Oxford University Press, 2002), pp. 4–6, and Robert Boyers and Robert Orrill (eds.), *Laing and Anti-Psychiatry* (Harmondsworth: Penguin, 1972). The point here is not to dismiss the validity of the direction of some of Foucault's ideas on madness (though his foundations are certainly challengeable – see Andrew Scull, 'Scholarship of Fools: The Frail Foundations of Foucault's Monument', *Times Literary Supplement*, 23 March 2007), but rather to point out that his disciples in international relations owe it to him not to assume that everything he said about everything was original, brilliant, or even relevant.

[84] Eagleton has suggested that there is a notion of teleology implicit in the very use of the self-description 'post' in postmodern (Terry Eagleton, *The Illusions of Postmodernism* (Oxford: Blackwell, 1996), pp. 43–4), while Martha C. Nussbaum has pointed to the tendency in teaching situations of its proponents to give postmodernism 'the last word, as though it had eclipsed Enlightenment thinking'; see her *Cultivating Humanity: A Classical Defense of Reform in Liberal Education* (Cambridge, Mass.: Harvard University Press, 1997), p. 77.

[85] Ken Booth, 'Human Wrongs and International Relations', *International Affairs*, vol. 71(1), 1995, p. 116.

guide. Sokol, by an imposture of his own, exposed the abuse of, and naïvety towards, scientific concepts by iconic French postmodernists.[86]

Although a number of concerns are shared between largely French-inspired poststructuralism and critical theorising discussed in chapter 2 (such as a concern with language, the power/knowledge relationship, and the social context of knowledge), there are major differences. Above all, in the study of world politics the postmodern sensibility has set itself in opposition to the powerful ideas that grew in the wake of the Enlightenment: reason, emancipation, liberal humanism, progress, cosmopolitanism, and the rest. Such ideas have been seen by postmodernists to carry within them the seeds of imperialism, domination, false ideas about progress, oppression, patriarchy, the Holocaust, and so on. For postmodernism, the dark side of the twentieth century was the consequence of living under the shadow of Enlightenment ideas.

More important for present purposes than the inconsistencies, obscurantism, and faux radicalism of postmodernism/poststructuralism is the politics that derives from the associated ideas and assumptions. In the mid-1990s, while at the same time giving due regard to the 'rich body of work' inspired by postmodernism, Terry Eagleton argued nevertheless that its core features did not offer the strong ethical and anthropological resources necessary for a robust politics.[87] He pointed specifically to 'its cultural relativism, and moral conventionalism, its scepticism, pragmatism and localism, its distaste for ideas of solidarity and disciplined organization, its lack of any adequate theory of political agency: all these would tell heavily against it'. The site of the problem was the meeting of the postmodern mode with the politics of 'the real', to use the phrase of the French philosopher Clément Rosset, who feared in the

---

[86] Of all the attacks on postmodernism, none has been more controversial than that by Alan Sokal and Jean Bricmont, entitled *Intellectual Impostures. Postmodern Philosophers' Abuse of Science* (London: Profile Books, 1999). This book, written by a professor of physics at New York University and a professor of theoretical physics at the University of Louvain arose out of an 'infamous' article written by Sokal ('Transgressing the Boundaries: Toward a Transformative Hermeneutics of Quantum Gravity') which was a parody of the use of scientific concepts and language by postmodernists, and was published (as a serious contribution to the literature) in the US Cultural Studies journal *Social Text* in 1996. While praising 'moderate' postmodernism for providing a much-needed correction to 'naïve modernism' (p. 174), Sokal and Bricmont are highly critical of radical postmodernism for its obscurity, but notably its 'abuse of science' by the canon of French postmodernists (see p. ix).
[87] Eagleton, *Illusions*, pp. 134–5.

early 1990s that his own discipline was undergoing 'an escape from the real'.[88]

Worst of all for critics of postmodern politics was the way in which posturing against metanarratives threatened to marginalise the global downtrodden. Listen to the victims and note how often they have seen their futures as depending vitally on emancipatory grand narratives in favour of female and racial equality, for example. The political success of such projects, in turn, has depended on solidarity across cultures, nations, genders, races, and all the other mind-frontiers history has thrown up.[89] While relativism leads to the politics of the bystander, universal values and transnational solidarity provide hope to victims. Underlying some of the positions just discussed is the questioning by some poststructuralist thinkers about the very desirability of security in the first place. This is partly related to their sharing the misconception (see chapter 3) that 'security' is necessarily conservative and always must have negative consequences ('one man's security is another's insecurity'). Apart from these misconceptions it is an indulgence for the secure to think about celebrating insecurity.[90] It has been poststructuralism's failure to engage persuasively with politics (while sometimes pretentiously talking about its own engagement with 'the political') that has led it to have such a marginal impact on the study of security, whose final test is not philosophical stylishness, but political struggle.[91] Having said all that, if the postmodern/poststructuralist mode of thinking had not entered the academic study of international relations – which it did later than in most other fields, and has persisted for longer – we would have to have invented it: but as a provocation not as a politics, and as a mental irritant not a road-map towards security, emancipation and community.

Behind the commitment to critique and reconstruction discussed in this chapter is an assumption about hope in human potential. Fatalist

---

[88] Clément Rosset, *Joyful Cruelty: Toward a Philosophy of the Real*, ed. and trans. David F. Bell (New York: Oxford University Press, 1991), pp. vii, xiv, 8; see also Booth, 'Human Wrongs', esp. pp. 104–9.

[89] Paul Gilroy has been a notable champion of shared humanity and planetary humanism as responses to the persistence of racism: see, for example, *Between Camps. Race, Identity and Nationalism at the End of the Colour Line* (London: Allen Lane, 2000).

[90] See Michael Dillon, *The Politics of Security: Towards a Political Philosophy of Continental Thought* (London: Routledge, 1996), and James Der Derian, 'The Value of Security: Hobbes, Marx, and Baudrillard', in Lipschutz, *On Security*.

[91] For a different view, see Smith, 'Contested Concept', pp. 48–51; see also his 'Epistemology, Postmodernism and International Relations Theory: A Reply to Osterud', *Journal of Peace Research*, vol. 34(3), 1997, pp. 330–6.

critics of this book might say that even if the emancipatory goals of a critical theory of world security are desirable, they are not feasible because of the 'human condition'.[92] A brief diversion into discussing hope is therefore necessary at this point, including a clarification of the difference between hope and optimism.

Hope, it must be stressed, is categorically different from optimism: it involves a refusal to rule out the possibility of a better future, but – unlike optimism – does not assume it. The distinction is not always understood, even by international relations theorists. I *hope* that Featherstone Rovers, the rugby team of my boyhood, will win whenever they play, but I am never optimistic. Consequently, I look at the results but would never bet on them. I take one of the favourite sayings of Heinrich Blücher, Arendt's husband, quoted at the head of this section, to mean that it is cowardly to give way to fatalism, believing that nothing can be done to change things (pessimism), and foolish to believe that favourable outcomes are inevitable (optimism). Hope is the way to escape the trap. Hope energises political agency. In this regard, the hubris about progress that characterised some nineteenth-century thinking has been replaced in the West by decreasing faith in education, politics, and solidarity to bring about benign change. The phenomenon of low voter turnout is one symptom of the belief that nothing much can be done. Nonetheless, when people tell me that students are not interested in politics any more, I reply: 'It depends what you mean by *politics*.' It is true that many students in the West these days are not interested in the tweedledum and tweedledee party politics involved in the management of Galbraith's 'culture of complacency', but they are often concerned with the great issues of peace and war, famine, and poverty.

The late 1990s film *The Full Monty* was widely acclaimed and enjoyed for its humour, and the initiative shown by its leading characters. In terms of a politics of hope, the message it gave was profoundly depressing. In an earlier and more heroic age, workers who had been made unemployed would have banded together to try to change society, and at the same time sought self-improvement through education and progressivist solidarity. In the era of neoliberalism, the lesson of the film was for people to flash their assets (the unemployed steel-workers became male strippers) to those willing and able to pay. Take your chances while

---

[92] This concept is dissected and dismissed by Philip Allott, 'The Future of the Human Past', in Booth, *Statecraft and Security. The Cold War and Beyond* (Cambridge: Cambridge University Press, 1998), pp. 328–31.

you can seemed to be the warning. Society must challenge such messages, and restore a belief in collective political action. In this the old are not always a help. Major figures of the Frankfurt school, for example, became famously pessimistic, leading Madeleine Bunting to suggest that men of a certain age become gloomy about the world (she targeted Bauman and Adorno).[93] When one looks more widely, however, the old are frequently in the forefront of peace movements and other progressive groups.

Critics sometimes confuse pessimism with being realistic, just as they confuse hope with being optimistic. Although large sections of this book are a record of morbid symptoms about today's world, and forecasts of worse to come, it is not a pessimistic book; it seeks instead to be realistic in its analysis, while retaining a handle on hope in its assumptions. A better future is possible, and hope is always encouraged by the work of progressive social movements, caring NGOs, and skilful people who live global lives.[94]

The combination of attitudes just described is typical of the Enlightenment tradition. Stephen Eric Bronner has described the Enlightenment mindset as 'realists who understood the costs of progress' and pessimists concerning 'the ability of the powerful to exercise power prudently' (and hence the need for institutional accountability, popular sovereignty, the rule of law, etc.).[95] He went on:

> Their concern with furthering human happiness was informed by the difficulty, the intractability, of society with its vested interests. But this very insight enabled them to shift the cause of human misery from the classical notion of fate or the religious notion of original sin to society and the impact of ignorance, prejudice, authoritarianism, and inequality.

[93] Madeleine Bunting, 'Passion and Pessimism', *The Guardian*, 5 April 2003.
[94] Among the many possible references here, see Donella H. Meadows, *The Global Citizen* (Washington D.C.: Island Press, 1991); Jeremy Seabrook, *Pioneers of Change. Experiments in Creating a Humane Society* (Philadelphia, Pa.: New Society Publishers, 1993); Jeremy Brecher, John Brown Childs, and Jill Cutler (eds.), *Global Visions. Beyond the New World Order* (Boston, Mass.: South End Press, 1993); Michael Edwards, *Future Positive. International Cooperation in the 21st Century* (London: Earthscan, 2001); Peace Direct (ed.), *Unarmed Heroes: The Courage to Go Beyond Violence*, introduced by Anita Roddick (Forest Row, Sussex: Clairview, 2004); Tom Mertes (ed.), *A Movement of Movements. Is Another World Really Possible?* (London: Verso, 2004); Susan George, *Another World Is Possible If . . .* (London: Verso, 2004).
[95] Stephen Eric Bronner, *Reclaiming the Enlightenment. Toward a Politics of Radical Engagement* (New York: Columbia University Press, 2004), p. 39.

This mindset led the 'most sober' of Enlightenment thinkers to reject 'teleological sophistries' and insist on political actors offering a plausible connection between means and ends (in other words, immanent critique). Hope, and the idea of progress, were and are central to critique and reconstruction. Bronner is not the only writer who considers that such attitudes might be the Enlightenment's 'greatest legacy'.

Progress as rational hope, not utopian optimism, makes us think about both the potential openness of history and the need for standards by which to judge political attitudes and behaviour. In the actually existing world at the start of the twenty-first century, there is abundant evidence of human wrongs, as was made clear in chapter 1. But there is also evidence of happiness, dignity, peoples living in peace, old enemies being reconciled, wars having been stopped, and even ideas about the possibility of living in some balance with nature. Despite the manifold difficulties facing human society everywhere, there are rational grounds for hope. As Boulding liked to say, 'Whatever exists is possible.'[96]

---

[96] Quoted by Robert C. Johansen, 'Radical Islam and Nonviolence', in Fred Dallmayr (ed.), *Border Crossings. Towards a Comparative Political Theory* (Lanham, Md.: Lexington Books, 1999), p. 166.

181

5 Being, knowing, doing

There's philosophy and there's the rest of life.

A. J. Ayer[1]

The two previous chapters clarified key concepts relevant to a critical theory of world security. The present chapter begins to relate the discussion so far to the biggest questions of philosophy, before moving in chapter 6 to bring everything together into a comprehensive critical framework. All this takes place in the face of the verdict of Freddy Ayer, the doyen of English logical positivism, about the relationship of philosophy and life. This book, contra Ayer, does not accept the separation.

What is real?

Of all the terms that we employ in treating human affairs, those of *natural* and *unnatural* are the least determinate in their meaning.

Adam Ferguson, *An Essay on the History of Civil Society* (1767)[2]

Naked ghosts! One way I have tried over the years to introduce students to thinking about what is real has been to discuss the phenomenon of ghosts, and specifically their reality to some observers – but never a naked reality. Apparently, ghosts never appear in a naked condition. According to Ambrose Bierce in his wonderful *Devil's Dictionary*, this represents one insuperable obstacle to belief in the existence of ghosts. A ghost may be seen 'in a winding-sheet' or 'in his habit as he lived'.

---

[1] Attributed; quoted by Julian Baggini, *Making Sense. Philosophy Behind the Headlines* (Oxford: Oxford University Press, 2002), p. 265.

[2] Adam Ferguson, *An Essay on the History of Civil Society*, ed. Fania Oz-Salzberger (Cambridge: Cambridge University Press, 1995, 1st pub. 1767), quoted in Roy Porter, *Enlightenment. Britain and the Creation of the Modern World* (London: Allen Lane, 2000), p. 295.

But to believe in ghosts, Bierce contended, one has to believe not only in the power of the dead to make themselves visible 'after there is nothing left of them', but also to believe 'that the same power inheres in textile fabrics'. If that is the case, Bierce enquired, why do we never see 'a suit of clothes sometimes . . . [walking] abroad without a ghost in it?'[3] Whether we do or not, the point is that reality can be as radical as we make it.

Human life takes place in a material world in which things happen regardless of our thoughts; in its social dimensions it takes place, importantly, according to 'facts by human agreement', as was suggested in the previous chapter. A mountain has certain solid forms, whatever we think, and humans are born and die, whatever we think. But what Kant taught us is that nature and time are not features of reality – out there, waiting to be discovered by the human mind – but are inventions of the mind; they are ideas that humans use to comprehend the material world and to construct the social one. This includes 'international relations', just as much as other inventions of the mind.

History has repeatedly shown how the intelligent of one age have harboured ideas and beliefs about what is real that those of later times have considered mistaken. 'Truth is born of the times, not of authority. Our ignorance is limitless' are words Brecht gave to Galileo, whose discoveries about the solar system brought him to the attention of the Inquisition.[4] This insight echoes the Frankfurt school's view about the historical character of social knowledge. A fascinating illustration of this was the late appearance in biology (the academic subject not the behavioural reality!) of 'homosexual' animals. Ruling out same-sex relationships in non-human animals on social and theological grounds, successive generations of (Victorianised) scientists failed to see this sort of sexual activity when it was taking place directly in front of their eyes. They did not look closely enough or with enough care at what same-sex animals were actually doing to each other. The fact was that animal homosexuality had no place on their cognitive maps. Bruce Bagemihl's doorstep of a book, *Biological Exuberance*, makes it exuberantly clear that homosexual behaviour is common throughout the animal world.[5] So the sexual activity that zoologists so long described was not actually what animals did with each other, but was rather the consequence

[3] Ambrose Bierce, *The Devil's Dictionary* (Toronto: Coles, 1978), p. 48.
[4] Bertolt Brecht, *Life of Galileo*, ed. John Willett and Ralph Manheim (London: Methuen, 2001), p. 42.
[5] Bruce Bagemihl, *Biological Exuberance. Animal Homosexuality and Natural Diversity* (London: Profile Books, 1999).

of the observer's mindset regarding homosexuality.[6] Ancient Greeks and Egyptians apparently had no problem recognising the homosexual behaviour among (non-human) animals taking place in front of them, but this was not the case with Victorian British scientists. Scientific truths were, as Galileo recognised, 'born of the times'.

Politically speaking, the power to decide what is real (and what should be forgotten) is crucial. To be able to dominate the defining of reality is a step towards dominating politics (a proposition that will be elaborated in chapter 8). In the context of the politics of security, the question 'what is real?' must begin with ideas about the referent. It was one of Buzan's major contributions in *People, States and Fear* to identify the referent of security as the conceptual focus of security politics.[7] Implicit or explicit, pre-defined or argued-out, the question of what is real in relation to security depends upon the answer to the prior question, 'what is the referent?' (in other words, '*Whom or what is to be secured?*'). R. B. J. Walker put the issue neatly when he wrote, 'The subject of security is the *subject* of security.'[8]

Political realists have never had a problem about the 'subject of security'; the primary referent is the-definite-article-state. This book claims that other referents must be given space on the agenda, ranging from individuals to common humanity. The traditional counter from the realist perspective is that neither *individuals* nor *common humanity* represent categorical entities in world politics. Such arguments bring security practices and theory into the ambit of philosophical questions related to ontology, the 'nature of being'.

The study of ontology is central to metaphysics, the field dealing with questions about ultimate realities. In world politics, there continue to be contending theories about the nature of being; this nicely illustrates the Kantian view that what must be attended to is not international relations as a discoverable feature of reality, but 'international relations' as a feature of the mindsets that invent social reality. Different theories and belief systems have radically different ontologies: that is, views about the categorical structures or referent objects that comprise the entities that the theory or belief system considers to be actually existing, and so

---

[6] *Ibid.*, p. 84.
[7] Barry Buzan, *People, States and Fear: An Agenda for International Security Studies in the Post-Cold War Era* (London: Harvester Wheatsheaf, 1991; 1st edn 1983).
[8] R. B. J. Walker, 'The Subject of Security', in Keith Krause and Michael C. Williams (eds.), *Critical Security Studies. Concepts and Cases* (Minneapolis: University of Minnesota Press, 1997), p. 78.

constituting reality. Note, for example, the radically different categorical structures of world politics as seen by a political realist (sovereign states), a Marxist (socio-economic classes), or a feminist (gender categories). These distinct ontologies reflect wholly different ideas about what makes the world go round, politically speaking. In each case the categorical structure is pre-defined by the theory. Critics of each theory would claim that there is less reality observation taking place than the consequences of socialisation; it is not seeing is believing, but believing is seeing.[9] In this way, the proponents of different theories of international relations leave themselves open to the charge of being the social science equivalents of repressed Victorian zoologists.

Once power turns a theory into the common sense of a society, in Gramscian fashion, it changes a set of ideas into a thing. Mental concepts take on material forms, such as armies and diplomatic arrangements, and in so doing the radical reality of life itself tends to be forgotten under the hegemonial jackboot of common sense. This was behind Adorno's warning that 'all reification is a forgetting'.[10] In this sense, political realism and the-definite-article-state, the underpinnings of orthodox understandings of security studies, are exercises in forgetting as much as in analysis. And *all forgetting* – it should be added to the Coxian syllogism – is also *for* someone or *for* some purpose.

Orthodox theorising in security studies has tended to be static,[11] and no more so than in relation to thinking about the sovereign state. The latter is a topic which is of central concern to CSS, yet critical approaches are frequently attacked for not taking the reality of states sufficiently seriously. This is unfair. Critical approaches have attempted to get inside the state, historicise it, dissect it, see how it really works, and subject it to normative judgement. CSS actually takes states far more seriously than does realism, for which the-definite-article-state is *the* given ontological categorical structure. Students of critical theory tend to have the same sort of fascination with the state that atheists and agnostics have with God. That is, for critical theorists, the Westphalian state is a powerful entity they think about on a daily basis; it is not the pre-defined entity

---

[9] Robert Jervis showed how psychological complexities can interfere negatively with the way policymakers engage with the world outside in *Perception and Misperception in International Politics* (Princeton, N.J.: Princeton University Press, 1976); on strategy in particular, see Ken Booth, *Strategy and Ethnocentrism* (London: Croom Helm, 1979).

[10] Discussed in relation to security by Richard Wyn Jones in *Security, Strategy, and Critical Theory* (Boulder, Colo.: Lynne Rienner, 1999), p. 107.

[11] Joseph S. Nye, 'The Long-term Future of Nuclear Deterrence', in Roman Kolkowicz (ed.), *The Logic of Nuclear Terror* (Boston: Allen and Unwin, 1987).

of realist believers, for whom its existence is eternal and unproblematic, and so requires only a periodic ritualistic nod.

To problematise 'the state' should not be mistaken for a claim that sovereign states are dead, irrelevant, or cannot deliver: far from it. Nor should it be taken to imply a failure to recognise that some types of state are to be preferred over others, or that some states are more reliable producers of domestic and international security. From time to time some governments might indeed act as 'good international citizens', though even the best are inconsistent.[12] A critical approach to the study of the Westphalian state begins by guarding against the sort of pre-defined approach adopted by Victorian biologists towards their same-sex subject matter. Instead critical theorists should comprehend the phenomenon of sovereign states 'as if for the first time'. This entails examining the historical processes of state formation, dissecting claims about how they work today, and interrogating the ideology that places them at the pinnacle of decision-making power and loyalty. In these ways critical theories challenge the belief that sovereign states are and should be the categorical structures by which humans must indefinitely conceive their global lives. For realists, sovereign states have traditionally been the end of the story of world politics; for those seeking to develop a critical theory of world security they are but one of the starting-points.

States are therefore but one of the referents with which CSS engages. Students of security have to decide for themselves which 'elements of being' in human society interest them most. The categorical structures they might choose to study, in addition to states, include 'common humanity', 'nations', 'class', 'race', 'communities', 'genders', 'civilisations' and so on. I have put quotation marks around all these terms to emphasise that they are historically constructed entities (Searle's 'facts by human agreement'), not natural phenomena. In practice, the relevant referent will probably be chosen depending on the problem being investigated.[13] The quotation marks are also a reminder that ontological assumptions are political battlefields, as different theorists seek to

---

[12] For sympathetic discussions, see Andrew Linklater, 'What is a Good International Citizen?', in Paul Keal (ed.), *Ethics and Foreign Policy* (Canberra: Allen and Unwin, 1992), and Tim Dunne and Nicholas J. Wheeler, 'Blair's Britain: A Force for Good in the World?', in Karen E. Smith and Margot Light (eds.), *Ethics and Foreign Policy* (Cambridge: Cambridge University Press, 2001).

[13] In relation to a specific empirical study, see Ken Booth and Peter Vale, 'Critical Security Studies and Regional Insecurity: The Case of Southern Africa', in Krause and Williams, *Critical Security Studies*, pp. 334–5.

privilege their own referent in the struggle to win the prize of defining reality.

In his discussion of the work of Nathan Leites in the Cold War, attempting to reveal an 'operational code' of the Bolsheviks, Daniel Bell wrote that for 'Bolshevism' all politics was summed up in the formula *kto–kovo* literally 'who–whom', 'but in its most radical sense, "who kills whom"'. In such a world-view, Bell argued that political relations are between 'dominators and dominated, between users and used'. The politics of *kto–kovo* is 'guided by this fundamental rule: one pushes to the limit'. In this belief system, *who–whom* is an ontological question (politically-theoretically derived); and then it may be a death sentence.[14] This Bolshevik formulation predated the similar 'friends–foe' distinction made by the old Nazi, Carl Schmitt, which began to attract a rather surprising amount of attention from some international relations theorists at the turn of the millennium.[15] In her chilling account of the Stalinist Gulag, Anne Applebaum wrote: 'Totalitarian philosophies have had, and will continue to have, a profound appeal to many millions of people. Destruction of the "objective enemy", as Hannah Arendt once put it, remains a fundamental objective of many dictatorships.'[16] The most frightening phrase in this quotation is 'objective enemy': it implies death by definition, obliteration by ontology.

Ontology, as just revealed, is not therefore just a matter of abstract philosophising; it is what we take to be real, and so in security policy it is the basis of what we believe needs to be protected. This in turn impacts directly on such important issues as what we consider to be relevant knowledge, what the chief struggles are deemed to be, and how we might act. This is why the debate over understandings of 'security' is so important and why ontology must be turned into one of the battlefields in the study of international relations. This is also why defenders of mainstream theory have opposed opening up the debate, for what has been challenged has been their very control over defining what is real – and no-one welcomes that.

One of the weaknesses of the realist claim that sovereign states represent the categorical referent of world politics is their very

[14] Daniel Bell, 'Ten Theories in Search of Reality: The Prediction of Soviet Behaviour', in Vernon V. Aspaturian (ed.), *Process and Power in Soviet Foreign Policy* (Boston: Little, Brown and Co, 1971), pp. 300–1.
[15] Perhaps this is more understandable in books on realism: see Michael C. Williams, *The Realist Tradition and the Limits of International Relations* (Cambridge: Cambridge University Press, 2005), esp. pp. 84–93, 111–12, 118–19.
[16] Anne Applebaum, *Gulag. A History of the Soviet Camps* (London: BCA, 2003), p. 514.

conceptual uncertainty and variety. 'What is the state?' is not as easy a question to answer as one might think. For a start, there are different answers depending on whether one adopts a liberal, Marxist, realist, constructivist, postmodern feminist – or whatever – approach to interpreting the state.[17] The supposedly categorical structure of 'the state' includes everything from model Scandinavian social democracies to central African kleptocracies, and from a multi-capable superpower to a Pacific island micro-dot. Some sovereign states are powerful and long-lasting, but some are not, and the modern states system itself is a relatively recent invention in historical time. States as such are not 'natural', or surely by now there would be an agreed answer to the question: 'Why should I obey the state?' There is no such agreement. According to Brian Redhead, 'The answers . . . have ranged from the pragmatic: "Because if I don't they will cut off my head"; to the theological: "Because it is God's will"; to the contractual: "Because the State and I have done a deal"; to the metaphysical: "Because the State is the actuality of the ethical idea".'[18] The answers remain multiple because there are multiple theories of the state in the first place.

Westphalian states are contested and multifaceted historical phenomena, though there has been a tendency to see them as natural and inevitable. When colonialism was defeated, the leaders of the newly independent states took over the existing colonial boundaries. Many – postcolonial theorists and journalists (among others) – have criticised these boundaries as 'artificial', and have blamed them for some of the subsequent problems of Africa. It is asserted that the new states inherited the 'artificial' lines of the old colonial boundaries, as these were sometimes straight lines drawn by rulers, with rulers, for rulers in far-away European capitals. This much is true, but what is not the case is that one (colonial) set of boundaries was artificial, while those (tribal) boundaries existing previously were natural. All such political boundaries are 'artificial' in one important sense; they have all been drawn by the contingencies of power, whether immediate military power on the

---

[17] See John Hall (ed.), *States in History* (Oxford: Blackwell, 1986); John A. Hall and G. John Ikenberry, *The State* (Milton Keynes: Open University Press, 1989); Joseph A. Camilleri, Anthony Jarvis, and Albert J. Paolini (eds.), *The State in Transition. Reimagining Political Space* (Boulder, Colo.: Lynne Rienner, 1995); John M. Hobson, *The State and International Relations* (Cambridge: Cambridge University Press, 2000); Walter C. Opello and Stephen J. Rosow, *The Nation-State and Global Order. A Historical Introduction to Contemporary Politics* (Boulder, Colo.: Lynne Rienner, 2004).
[18] Brian Redhead, 'Introduction', in Janet Coleman, *Against the State. Studies in Sedition and Rebellion* (London: BBC Books, 1990), p. 1.

ground, or diplomatic power in faraway capitals. Political power draws boundaries, not nature. This is another area where we must beware peddlers of 'natural' products, whether in supermarkets or in postcolonial politics and theorising.

We must take seriously Ferguson's warning at the start of this section about the indeterminacy attaching to the words 'natural' and 'unnatural'. A river, for example, may be a barrier (if there is neither a bridge nor a boat to cross it) or a means of communication (being the most efficient way of travelling for a particular valley community). Rivers divide and unify in practice, but they have no natural (inherent) social significance; that is invested by history and technology – human appraisals. So to turn a particular river into a political boundary is not to conform with Nature's plan for borders, but rather to conform (contingently) with the human pattern of drawing political boundaries according to power arrangements. What is 'natural' is a human appraisal, and sometimes an excuse for human failings. At the end of 2005 Hurricane Katrina's destruction of large parts of New Orleans was consistently described as a 'natural disaster'. It was not. Nature did what nature does, but the blame for the disaster that befell many humans lay in earlier choices based on economic, social, and political appraisals and interests, including the hubris involved in building large parts of a major city below water level. Earlier choices had led to the creation of a distinct social and economic geography of race and class in New Orleans, while, in the aftermath of the disaster incompetent choices were made by the government and its agents. New Orleans in 2005 was a *human* disaster, not a natural one, though the idea of the latter will always be strong, because it is always easier to blame storms than the choices of one's own society – or oneself.[19]

Alongside the ahistorical assumption that 'the state' has always been around as a categorical – even natural – structure of human affairs, and will remain so, there has been an equally untenable view that the modern sovereign state arrived on the international scene (in 1648) by 'a sort of miraculous virgin birth'.[20] Sovereign states came from somewhere, as historical sociology has sought to reveal. If we take the Westphalian

[19] It remains to be seen whether the lessons have been learned; the comments of the senior Senator from Louisiana, Mary Landrieu, suggest not: 'An American Renaissance', *The World in 2006* (London: The Economist, 2005; 20th edn). Compare Gary Younge, 'Gone with the Wind', *The Guardian Weekend*, 29 July 2006.
[20] I have borrowed this from Michael Carrithers, *Why Humans Have Cultures. Explaining Anthropology and Social Diversity* (Oxford: Oxford University Press, 1992), p. 9; he made the point in relation to the emergence of cultures.

settlement as the symbolic starting-point of the modern state (and there are reasons why we might want to date it later[21]) it means that sovereign states have only been the dominant political organising form for about 350-plus years of a 'human' existence of one and a half million years (*Homo erectus*) or, perhaps even more relevantly, of the 40,000 years of *Homo sapiens*. This states system, which now seems as permanent and natural as the feudal system once did to our peasant ancestors, is approximately sixteen generations old. As this book is being completed, it is 115 years since my grandfather was born – almost exactly one-third of the way back to the meetings on the German plain that attempted to bring some sanity to European international politics after the Thirty Years War. Historically speaking, Westphalia was only yesterday.

During this brief span of history, transformation has been a characteristic feature of the sociology of states. Against the realist assumption of the fixity of *the* state, it is not uncommon to find historical sociologists arguing that 'both conceptually and empirically, the modern state is in transition and hence ripe for rethinking', that where the state has come from and where it is going is uncertain, and that this 'invites us to take care with any easy or generalized declarations'.[22] A theory of security must accommodate the conformability of states, as opposed to the ahistorical assumption of their primordial nature. Historically, empires have been more normal than sovereign states, but no more natural. In living memory, the advent of nuclear weapons and the growth of the human rights culture have dented traditional assumptions about state sovereignty, independence, and statist 'impermeability'.[23] Today globalisation and specifically changing relationships between states and markets are changing the textbook state model further;[24] the global triumph of capitalism has required states to downplay the historic ambition to be independent, and instead has required them to become local agents of the world capitalist good.[25] To reify 'the state' is to forget history and

[21] As argued by Benno Teschke, *The Myth of 1648. Class, Geopolitics and the Making of Modern International Relations* (London: Verso, 2003).
[22] Anthony P. Jarvis and Albert J. Paolini, 'Locating the State', in Joseph A. Camilleri, Anthony Jarvis, and Albert J. Paolini (eds.), *The State in Transition. Reimagining Political Space* (Boulder, Colo.: Lynne Rienner, 1995), p. 8.
[23] On the human rights dimension see Tim Dunne and Nicholas J. Wheeler (eds.), *Human Rights in Global Politics* (Cambridge: Cambridge University Press, 1999). On the nuclear revolution see John Herz, *International Politics in the Atomic Age* (New York: Columbia University Press, 1959).
[24] See David Held, Anthony McGrew, David Goldblatt, and Jonathan Perraton, *Global Transformations. Politics, Economics and Culture* (Cambridge: Polity, 1999).
[25] I first used this phrase in Ken Booth, 'Conclusion: Security Within Global Transformations?' in Ken Booth (ed.), *Statecraft and Security. The Cold War and Beyond*

to constrain the future. This is why world security depends on opening up ontological imaginations.

Statism cannot deliver world security in face of the prospect of the Great Reckoning signposted in chapter 1 and elaborated in chapter 9. A different set of organising principles is needed in today's smaller and globalised world. Beck's idea of 'cosmopolitan states' was introduced in chapter 3. The basis of his argument is that the 'nation-state' with its homogenising momentum, has become anachronistic. Today nation-states are challenged by the sheer volume of movement, which presents a threat, he argues, 'to the inner complexity, the multiple loyalties, the social flows and fluids that the age of globalisation has caused to slosh across their borders. And conversely, the national states can't help but see such blurring of borders as a threat to their existence.' These trends led Beck to advocate 'cosmopolitan states', committed to emphasising 'the necessity of solidarity with foreigners both inside and outside the national borders'.[26] For many, the idea of a cosmopolitan state might seem an oxymoron, but it is not so much a contradiction in terms as the idea that the good life, globally, can be delivered by sovereign statism. The idea of a cosmopolitan state is not simple idealism; it is based in practice. Seyla Benhabib has explained how the concept of 'foreign co-citizen' is a step in this direction. She writes: 'In a remarkable evolution of the norms of hospitality, within the European Union in particular, the rights of third-country nationals are increasingly protected by the European Convention on Fundamental Rights and Freedoms, with the consequence that citizenship, which was once the privileged status enti-tling one to rights, has now been disaggregated into its constituent ele ments.'[27] And to those who assert that the state is being undermined by cosmopolitanism, her response focuses on 'the privatization and corpo-ratization of sovereignty'; these, she persuasively argues, are the trends endangering democracy and popular sovereignty 'by converting pub-lic power into private commercial or administrative competence'. As a result, democracies are less able to regulate actions taken in their

(Cambridge: Cambridge University Press, 1998), p. 341; it was an adaptation of Hedley Bull's liberal hope that states might be vehicles for the 'world common good' in Hedley Bull, *Order and Justice in International Relations* (University of Waterloo, Ontario: The Hagey Lectures, 1983), pp. 11–12, 14.
[26] Ulrich Beck, 'The Fight for a Cosmopolitan Future', *New Statesman*, 5 November 2001; see also his *What is Globalization?* (Cambridge: Polity, 2000).
[27] Seyla Benhabib, *Another Cosmopolitanism* (Oxford: Oxford University Press, 2006), p. 37; the negotiation of the paradoxes involved is discussed on pp. 45–80.

name; there has been a 'flight of power from the control of popular jusrisdiction'.[28]

The-definite-article-state is pressed on all sides, but it has considerable resilience. One thing is certain, however: as human society globally faces up to the Great Reckoning, statism is normatively flawed and strategically irrational. More ontological space must be created for constructing cosmopolitan values. Any approach that degrades the identification with common humanity, whether it is in the name of religion, nationalism, or race, is calculated to promote turmoil in an increasingly over-populated, resource-challenged, and over-heated planet. This is why students of security must take ontology seriously: the 'imagined community' of common humanity, not sovereign states, is the first line of defence in the struggle for world security.[29]

What can we know?

> After scrutinizing closely the facts of the American Civil War, after seeing and listening to hundreds of the wounded, Walt Whitman declared: 'The real war will never get in the books'. Nor will the Second World War, and 'books' include this one.   Paul Fussell in *Wartime*[30]

Like ontology, epistemology is a site of contestation. When we start to take theorising about knowledge seriously, we begin to understand the force of the argument made by Steve Smith that 'much more than epistemology is at stake'.[31] What is at stake is political potentiality. In his famous essay inventing Frankfurt school critical theory, Max Horkheimer challenged the 'only one truth' posited by traditional theory, and the way this meant that the 'striving for peace, freedom, and happiness' from other theories and practices was set aside. 'There is no theory of society', he insisted, 'that does not contain political motivations.'[32] The political stakes involved in epistemology could not be higher.

---

[28] *Ibid.*, p. 177.
[29] The idea of 'imagined communities' is from Benedict Anderson, *Imagined Communities: Reflections on the Origin and Spread of Nationalism* (London: Verso, 1992; 2nd edn).
[30] Paul Fussell, *Wartime. Understanding and Behaviour in the Second World War* (Oxford: Oxford University Press, 1989), p. 290.
[31] Steve Smith, 'Positivism and Beyond', in Steve Smith, Ken Booth, and Marysia Zalewski (eds.), *International Theory: Positivism and Beyond* (Cambridge: Cambridge University Press, 1996), p. 38.
[32] Max Horkheimer, 'Postscript', in *Critical Theory. Selected Essays*, trans. Matthew J. O'Connell and others (New York: Continuum, 1992), pp. 222, 246.

Epistemology explores ways of knowing about the world: how justified are we in the framing of the beliefs we hold? How can we assert
the veracity of what we take to be knowledge? On what basis can we
claim to 'know' something (for example, that President Bush and Prime
Minister Blair were deceiving their publics in the way they sought to
legitimise their march to war on Iraq in March 2003)? What separates
'true' knowledge from mere beliefs or guesses (how sound, for example,
is the argument that democracy is a guarantee of peace between states)?
How might we adjudicate between the knowledge delivered by different theoretical positions (for example, between the generally benign
picture of the diplomatic system delivered by English school students
of diplomacy and the image of it as implicated in the exploitation of
women exposed by the findings of 'feminist curiosity')? How can we
judge questions of validity between different types of knowledge (for
example, between the arguments about human rights put forward by
relativists asserting the primacy of particularist knowledge and those
claiming the authority of universalism)? In short, how can we – whoever
we are – know we are right?

Theories of knowledge have changed throughout history, and not
least in the growth of the academic discipline of international relations
since it began in universities in 1919.[33] During this time, different types
of knowledge have constructed different political potentials. Chapter 2
discussed the contribution of feminist theorising in this regard, uncovering pictures of the world, both private and public, that had previously
been unseen. As a result, attitudes and behaviour thought to be natural (that word again) are now (much more) considered to be culturally,
socially, and politically produced, reproduced, and sanctioned. The consequences of such new understanding have led to a certain rethinking of
society and politics, and this has had some impact on legislation in many
countries with respect to 'domestic violence', and in the international
realm, in changed attitudes to rape in war.[34]

The critical approach to security advanced here is usually categorised
as part of the 'post-positivist turn' in international relations, beginning
in the 1980s. This will be discussed further in the next chapter, but my
key argument is to challenge the knowledge-claims of 'naturalism' as
opposed to 'positivism' as such. To reject naturalism is not to reject

[33] Smith, 'Positivism and Beyond', pp. 11–44.
[34] On the latter see Caroline Kennedy-Pipe and Penny Stanley, 'Rape in War: Lessons of
the Balkan Conflicts in the 1990s', in Ken Booth (ed.), *The Kosovo Tragedy. The Human Rights
Dimensions* (London: Frank Cass, 2001), pp. 67–84.

science, but to recognise limitations when science engages with the social world. Critical theory regards the study of human society to be radically different from that of the physical world, but this does not mean that the methods of positivism are always inappropriate. Used carefully, and in appropriate contexts, they can play a part in the development of human society in specific contexts.[35] There is no problem about a critical theorist adopting positivist procedures: it is a matter of choosing methodological horses for empirical courses. For example, employing positivist techniques to study voting patterns in the UN General Assembly is unproblematic (though it must be said that there is no relationship whatever between the effort and ingenuity that has been invested in 'quantitative IR' over the years, and its findings). Peace research has had a long association with positivism; there is no necessary relationship between positivism and realism or between post-positivism and idealism. The problem comes when positivism is seen as synonymous with a narrow definition of science, an issue (as I mentioned previously) that has figured in international relations almost from the start. Part of the difficulty is that the very term 'science' is disputed. Broadly, usage in North America insists on science being synonymous with rigorous hypothesis testing, while in Europe there is a more relaxed interpretation, with science being synonymous with systematic thought. The use of science in academic international relations in the latter sense is appropriate, but not the former. While the neutrality of the natural scientist with regard to the composition of matter or the laws of physics is not considered to be as neutral or objective as was once the case, it is of a completely different degree to that in the social sciences.[36] Science in the strong sense of the term cannot answer the basic questions of security. The challenge for students of security is to steer a pragmatic path between those who aspire to and claim too much for knowledge about human society and those who claim too little. In this uncertain terrain there are, however, secure anchorages for knowledge, as will be discussed in the next chapter.

[35] Michael Nicholson has argued that 'positivism' is more complex, philosophically and methodologically, than it has invariably been described by 'post-positivist' scholars, and also that being a positivist does not mean that one also has to be a realist. See Michael Nicholson, *Causes and Consequences in International Relations: A Conceptual Survey* (London: Pinter, 1996), and, more briefly, in *International Relations: A Concise Introduction* (Houndmills: Palgrave Macmillan, 2002, 2nd edn), pp. 123–5.
[36] These issues are succinctly discussed in Colin Wight, 'Philosophy of Social Science and International Relations', in Walter Carlsnaes, Thomas Risse, and Beth A. Simmons (eds.), *Handbook of International Relations* (London: Sage, 2002), pp. 23–51.

To say that theory in the study of world security cannot be scientific in the strong sense (neutral, objective, and positivist) is not a licence for 'anything goes'. The next chapter will discuss the need to defend an idea of truth, and subsequent chapters will criticise the idea that it is not possible to judge between values because the only standards that can be properly applied are those of the social group holding those values (relativism). These issues should encourage modesty in contemplating what might be reliable knowledge in world politics, but often the demands of theoretical 'elegance' (and hence the better prospects for having one's article accepted for publication by a 'leading' journal) encourage reductionism. The-definite-article-state has been one such simplification that cuts through complexity. From within the heart of the discipline, there is often the complaint that international relations lacks 'a theory of the state', but this assumes *a* theory is possible – at least one that can command a consensus. David Held is a notable proponent of the view that the very diversity of historical state forms puts into question whether a theory of *the state* is possible, or desirable.[37] Whether one regards this as a challenge to theorise or an encouragement to delve into history, the message for students of security is clear: we must internalise the diversity of stateness, not their definite-articleness.[38] Such a move would be a positive step in the search for answers to those questions, in R. B. J. Walker's words, 'about the character and location of political life to which the state and states system have seemed such a natural response for many for so long'.[39]

Because states are identified in realism as the primary actors in world affairs – they are said to have most agency – it is therefore assumed that they should be considered 'the primary referent' in thinking about security. This does not necessarily follow.[40] I have long used the analogy of a mother and baby: the mother is without doubt the primary agent (she has the greater capacity to act), but it does not follow that she is the primary referent in a normative sense. What is more, it would

[37] See, for example, David Held, 'Central Perspectives on the Modern State', in David Held *et al.* (eds.), *States and Societies* (Oxford: Martin Robertson, 1983), pp. 1–55.

[38] See chapter 2; Stephen Hobden and John M. Hobson (eds.), *Historical Sociology of International Relations* (Cambridge: Cambridge University Press, 2002), is a 'manifesto' for historical sociology.

[39] R. B. J. Walker, 'The Subject of Security', in Krause and Williams, *Critical Security Studies*, p. 63.

[40] Pinar Bilgin, 'Regional Security in the Middle East: A Critical Security Studies Perspective' (University of Wales, Aberystwyth, PhD thesis, 2002), pp. 38–51.

be a vulgar materialist conception of power that would assert that the physically stronger agent in the mother–baby relationship necessarily has more causal power to shape what happens; we all understand that a baby's needs generally rule over a mother's wants. There is a direct analogy here with citizens in the state–citizen relationship. Anti-statists regard states as a means, not an end, and believe it illogical to privilege the security of the means (the regime and the state machinery) as opposed to the security of the ends (the citizens).[41] All states to a greater or lesser extent will have agency, but it does not follow that they should therefore be regarded as the primary referent. Environmentalists conceive 'nature' or 'the global ecology' as their key referent, while recognising that primary agency on environmental matters lies with the United States (simultaneously both the world's hyper-power and hyper-polluter). From the start, environmental issues failed to raise the same attention within the White House of George W. Bush that they did among the growing numbers of ecologically sensitive people across the world (including in the United States itself); the primary referent for President Bush in this regard was not nature but the US economy. It would be a fascinating test of presidential power against corporate America, and the interest of electors in their own bottom line, were an individual to become president specifically on an environmentalist ticket, and committed to radical reform. In this respect, the eight years the environmental missionary Al Gore spent in the White House as Vice-President in the 1990s, next to the most powerful leader in the world, do not augur well.[42]

Ontological imagination, like theory and like forgetting, is '*for* someone or *for* some purpose'. Referents for students of security, other than states, might include, on a rising scale of inclusivity: individuals (described earlier as the litmus test for the health of any human grouping); families (nuclear and extended); ethnic and kinship groups (their condition is a measure of whether 'national security' is merely propaganda for the security of the regime, or whether it is a more deeply rooted conception); gender identity (this is but one important

[41] Ken Booth, 'Security and Emancipation', *Review of International Studies*, vol. 17(4), 1991, p. 320.
[42] Strangely, for a book written by a politician, Al Gore's *An Inconvenient Truth. The Planetary Emergency of Global Warming and What We Can Do About It* (London: Bloomsbury, 2006), is stronger on the science of climate change than on the politics – which brings to mind Einstein's quip about politics being harder than physics.

reminder that the security of humans cannot be located simply by territorial boundaries, because some referents never appear on political maps); class (in what is supposed to be a post-Marxist age this is a much-ignored referent, despite massive life-threatening and life-determining insecurity being the direct result of poverty); or the potential community of humankind (an emancipatory goal, with only limited institutionalised forms, but no less conceivable than other 'imagined communities' before they were made real); and on and on through the complex delineations of human society, and then the natural world, to the all-encompassing but controversial referent of Gaia.[43] Surely Gaia is a step too far, even for critical theorists interested in security? I think not, and the philosopher Mary Midgley has made a powerful case that the *global-we* desperately need to understand the problems we face as a whole, and has argued that James Lovelock's metaphor of Gaia (the Greek earth-goddess, mother of gods and of humans), while meeting some resistance as an idea, has achieved an important degree of scientific respectability. Such reconsideration of the paradigms represents progress in the invention of humanity. It is only a more holistic view of the earth, Midgley suggested – including conceiving the earth as functioning as an organic whole – that can give humans a more realistic view of ourselves.[44]

Talk of Gaia is far removed from what has generally been taught as international relations since the First World War, and especially that part of it understood as security studies. The old agenda of diplomacy and military strategy is still very much part of what has to be addressed, but it can only be a part, as the whole accelerates into a radical new world of multiple interactions under conditions of growing material stress. As the Great Reckoning rushes towards us, let us not be prissy Victorian realists, seeing only what we have been taught to see. Let the scales fall off our eyes, so we can better understand what human animals are *actually* doing to each other and their environment. And let us then describe the situation more accurately and sincerely, and do something about it in the common interest.

---

[43] A doughty defence of the Gaia hypothesis is offered by Mary Midgley, 'Individualism and the Concept of Gaia', in Ken Booth, Tim Dunne, and Michael Cox (eds.), *How Might We Live? Global Ethics in the New Century* (Cambridge: Cambridge University Press, 2001), pp. 29–44.
[44] *Ibid.*; also Patrick Curry, *Ecological Ethics. An Introduction* (Cambridge: Polity, 2006), esp. pp. 68–71.

How might we act?

> Philosophising is real as it pervades an individual life at a given
> moment.   Karl Jaspers in 'Philosophical Memoir'[45]

Thinking about thinking – a bumper-sticker definition of philosophy –
is important, but if human society is to be reinvented in an emancipatory
direction, then thinking about doing must be given its due. If Jaspers
(rather than Ayer) is correct, and philosophy is (and should be) real
in everyday life, two immediate issues are raised. The first involves
an acceptance of the idea of the essential unity of theory and practice,
and the second is the related view that (even) academic analysis and
generalisation are political tasks, if only in a weak sense of that term.

The relationship between theory and practice is one area where the
Marxist ancestry of the Frankfurt school is obvious.[46] For Marx the concept of 'praxis' (literally 'practice' or 'action' in the Greek original) was
given a distinctive meaning: 'the unity of theory and practice'. In other
words, there is mutual synergy: theory arises out of practice, practice
is shaped and modified as a result of theory, and theory develops in
the light of practice. Traditional thinking separates theory and practice,
but students of critical theory emphasise their mutuality. This dialectical relationship is also reflected in Robert Cox's argument regarding the
self-interested character of all theory, an approach which represents a
direct challenge to the professional self-image of the neutral social scientist giving impartial analyses and advice – the 'traditional' intellectual
in Gramsci's formulation. To say that theory is a form of practice and
practice is a form of theory is not of course to say that the two terms are
perfectly synonymous; there is a sensible distinction to be made between
words and action. To write a book about international relations is a form
of practice, but it is not the same sort of practice as donating money to a
charity, working for an NGO, or representing a government. Words can
lead to action, but generally actions speak louder.

Scholars who study security, whether they recognise it or not, have a
direct relationship with the real world conditions of relative insecurity
or security; their ideas can contribute to replicating or changing people's conditions of existence in specific situations. This is a scholarly

---

[45] Quoted in Elizabeth Young-Bruehl, *Hannah Arendt. For Love of the World* (New Haven,
Conn.: Yale University Press, 1982), p. 63.
[46] See Wyn Jones, *Security*, pp. 38, 68, 76, 118, 153–5.

responsibility to be considered with utmost seriousness because some-where, some people, as these very words are being read, are being starved, oppressed, threatened, or killed in the name of a certain theory of politics or economics – or security.[47] Several proponents of critical theory have argued, echoing Marx, that the aim is not just to under-stand the world: it is also to change it.[48] Feminists such as Nancy Fraser have been prominent in this regard.[49] But one has to be very careful as an academic about claiming too much. Governments are not primar-ily interested in truth – power comes first.[50] They will use knowledge gained from academic enquiry instrumentally, to strengthen their posi-tion, but their interest in knowledge is bureaucratic, not scholarly.[51] This raises the question of the appropriate audience for academic work. There is a long tradition assuming that those we seek to win over must be 'practitioners', by which is usually meant decision-makers and their officials. This is usually hoping too much. Such practitioners have a rational bureaucratic interest in knowledge, but they invariably believe that outsiders such as academics have little to contribute, because they lack the expertise and especially the privileged access to knowledge of the insider. Though the extent to which such views are held depends on the professional cultures of particular governments/bureaucracies, academics should be encouraged to think of practitioners much more broadly than 'governments' and 'officials', especially now that individ-uals as well as civil society groups are so much more skilled than in the past, and many are keen to be involved in international issues.[52] Society,

[47] Ken Booth, 'Security and Self: Reflections of a Fallen Realist', in Krause and Williams, *Critical Security Studies*, pp. 112–15; and 'Beyond Critical Security Studies', in Ken Booth (ed.), *Critical Security Studies and World Politics* (Boulder, Colo.: Lynne Rienner, 2005), pp. 272–6.
[48] See Mark Hoffman: 'Critical Theory and the Inter-Paradigm Debate', *Millennium*, vol. 16(2), 1987, pp. 232–49; also Wyn Jones, *Security*, esp. pp. 145–63.
[49] Nancy Fraser, *Unruly Practices: Power, Discourse and Gender in Contemporary Social Theory* (Cambridge: Polity, 1989).
[50] This is a theme of Noam Chomsky, *Failed States. The Abuse of Power and the Assault of Democracy* (New York: Metropolitan Books, 2006), and many other of his works.
[51] An old but interesting collection is Morton H. Halperin and Arnold Kanter (eds.), *Readings in American Foreign Policy* (Boston: Little, Brown, 1973).
[52] On increasingly skilled individuals, see James N. Rosenau, *Turbulence in World Politics. A Theory of Change and Continuity* (New York: Harvester Wheatsheaf, 1990), esp. pp. 13–16, 335–8; on the debate about 'practitioners', see William Wallace, 'Truth and Power, Monks and Technocrats: Theory and Practice in International Relations', *Review of International Studies*, vol. 22(3), 1996, pp. 301–21; Ken Booth, 'A Reply to Wallace', *Review of International Studies*, vol. 23(3), 1997, pp. 371–7; and Steve Smith, 'Power and Truth: A Reply to William Wallace', *Review of International Studies*, vol. 23(4), 1997, pp. 507–16.

local and global, and not the state is the key audience for academic enquiry in my opinion.

Critical approaches to international relations are frequently seen as 'too theoretical', not least by official practitioners. This misses the point, and is based on a misconception of the work theory does. The practical dimension of theorising has a long tradition. Enlightened thinkers of the eighteenth century 'shunned the scholastic', seeking both to understand and influence the world. David Hume's work, for example, was concerned with promoting practical morality.[53] But simplistic attacks on theory go on, though such critics, as Keynes famously implied, are usually the ventriloquist's dummy for long-dead theorists, but without recognising it. Simplistic attacks aside, it is always legitimate to ask of any theory purporting to have something to say about security in world politics what it means for real people in real places. Theories about gender, deconstruction, emancipation or whatever remain abstract and incomplete unless they engage with the real by suggesting policies, agents, and sites of change, to help humankind, in whole and in part, move away from existing structural wrongs. Such engagement is never easy, and may not result in clear answers, but the test of a body of scholarship in this field is whether it says anything meaningful about, or contributes however remotely or indirectly towards, the improvement of the security of individuals and groups in villages and cities, regions and states, and ultimately globally – and does this in ways that promote emancipatory aims.

The autonomy of academic enquiry is a long and significant tradition in liberal democracies, though not an unproblematic one. What has been achieved must be jealously guarded, as it is a mark of a tolerant and civilised society, but it is one that is fragile, especially in times of trouble. Even in liberal democracies academic freedom is threatened under conditions of Cold War or during a Global War on Terror. Elsewhere, the independently minded scholar is always under degrees of threat from state authorities. This was the case for those academics working in politics and international relations in South Africa during the apartheid years. Another compelling case was the challenge faced by

---

[53] Roy Porter, 'The Science of Politics', in *Enlightenment. Britain and the Making of the Modern World* (London: Allen Lane, 2000), pp. 184–204; see also Stephen Eric Bronner, *Reclaiming the Enlightenment. Toward a Radical Engagement* (New York: Columbia University Press, 2004), pp. 153–4, and Jonathan Israel, 'Locke, Hume, and the Making of Modernity', in *Radical Enlightenment. Philosophy, Modernity, and the Emancipation of Man 1670–1752* (Oxford: Oxford University Press, 2006), esp. pp. 53–9.

German intellectuals after the Nazi takeover in 1933. Arendt's experience was interesting.[54] She began by questioning the idea that 'thought is in the service of action', because it challenged philosophy's autonomy (the Ayer position); this shifted, and she found the concrete approach of Jaspers 'a revelation', later remembering: 'I perceived his Reason as praxis, so to speak', and the 'unity of her mind's life' emerged.[55] Other German intellectuals, notably Carl Schmitt and Heidegger, adjusted relatively comfortably to life under the Nazis, to their lasting discredit, while others still (Gerhard Ziegler, Konrad Meyer, and Fritz Arlt, for example) became the 'architects' of the annihilation of the Jews and others, providing academic analyses and writing reports as demographers, economists, and town planners. They ostensibly respected 'academic freedom' and would not join the Nazi party, but their work furthered and legitimised genocidal Nazi plans. They were cogs, able to deny to themselves what they were doing, while conniving in genocide. Experts, specialists, technicians, and intellectuals put their academic work in the service of the Nazis, and after the war many went back to their desks, apparently as if the Holocaust had not happened. Some got jobs in Britain and the United States.[56] If no argument so far has persuaded readers of the need for a permanently refreshed critical theory of society, always standing guard outside the existing situation and its institutions, challenging the status quo rather than being technicians to fix it, I hope this account of the roles played by intellectuals in building and legitimising Nazi power does the trick. The individuals identified were all very recognisable types, not monsters, but they played their part in the slide into monstrous times.

The experience of Germany's slide into barbarism in the 1930s is a warning about not only the monster a state can quickly become, but also the psychological and other dynamics that can co-opt ordinarily decent citizens into extremism in extraordinary times. Academics in liberal democratic states should not feel self-righteous about their own situations until they can demonstrate their own courage in threatening

[54] Among many discussions of this, see Young-Bruehl, *Hannah Arendt*, pp. 4, 44, 62–3, 84–5, 326–7.
[55] *Ibid.*, pp. 63–4 and 326–7 respectively.
[56] On the psychology of denial, see R. J. Lifton and E. Markusen, *The Genocidal Mentality. The Nazi Holocaust and the Nuclear Threat* (New York: Basic Books, 1990), esp. pp. 193–6, 203, 211, 235, 238. On the professionals of annihilation, see Götz Aly and Susanne Heim, *Architects of Annihilation. Auschwitz and the Logic of Destruction*, tras. Allan Blunden (London: Phoenix Books, 2002; 1st pub.1991). '"What we accomplished was tremendous!" A biographical postscript' is particularly chilling, pp. 112–14.

times. Once state power is mobilised for aggressive purposes abroad and brutal policies domestically, choices are closed down; this is why, in the most literal sense, security begins at home, to ensure that state power is kept away from the wrong hands. This means not only the maintenance of the institutions of democracy, but also the promotion of democracy imbued with cosmopolitan and non-violent values; it is all too easy to imagine, in periods of heightened tension, the election of ruthless regimes. Elections and other democratic institutions are not themselves guarantors of tolerance or peace.

Sovereign states exist, and in some form will continue indefinitely, but they should never be 'romanticised'.[57] Governments behave badly nearly all the time. It is almost impossible to use the word 'generosity' in the same sentence as 'government'. When did a government – not under electoral pressure, or facing an incensed citizenry – last surprise people by the absolute generosity of its financial and other rewards to war widows, old soldiers, coal miners suffering from work-related incapacities, people enduring mental health problems, uneducated single mothers, prisoners – among others?[58] The general failure of governments to distribute lavish financial rewards and medical facilities to those individuals (and their families) who have risked their lives for their country reveals the 'cold monster' of the state at its most ungenerous. To the machinery of the state the ordinary Joe is a means not an end, even in a liberal democracy. The testimony of Eugene B. Sledge is unforgettable. Born in 1923 in Alabama, and raised with all-American patriotism and optimism, he learned in the Pacific War what Paul Fussell claims 'all combat troops finally perceive'. Sledge wrote later: 'We come from a nation and a culture that values life and the individual. To find oneself in a situation where your life seems of little value is the ultimate in

---

[57] Discussed in Ken Booth, '75 Years On: Rewriting the Subject's Past – Reinventing its Future', in Smith *et al.*, *International Theory: Positivism and Beyond*, p. 336.

[58] The lack of generosity of governments towards their armed forces is particularly noteworthy, as the military accept as part of their duty a willingness to die on behalf of their country. Even in Britain, a nation with a long and proud military tradition, the record is poor. Kipling drew attention to it many years ago, in a famous poem, and it goes on to the present day, with complaints about housing and medical services for those who served in Iraq after 2003. Among civilians, the remaining survivors of the Arctic convoys were still seeking recognition for their bravery and sacrifices from the ungenerous British political elite sixty years after participating in one of the most dangerous and challenging campaigns of the Second World War: see Kamal Ahmed, 'Forgotten Heroes of the Arctic Convoy Frozen out of Honours', *The Observer*, 11 April 2004. When eventually recognition was given for the sacrifice and incredible devotion to duty, it was diminished by the need to have struggled for it, and in any case was too late for the many who had died over the previous sixty years.

loneliness.'[59] Fighting in the Pacific islands, with a brutal enemy to his front, and the cold monster of his own state to his rear, he discovered that 'We were expendable. It was difficult to accept.'

Power tends to corrupt, and sovereign power especially so. The old slogans are often the best 'It might be a good government, but it is still a bloody government.' Modern states in Western Europe grew out of the power struggle in feudal times in which one man's family sought to assert control over the families of everybody else. Few would go all the way with the anarchist position that states are an 'extraneous burden' on society,[60] and should be dispensed with, but more might accept Thomas Paine's view that society is 'a blessing' in a way the sovereign state is not.[61] At this stage of history sovereign states exist at best as necessary evils for human society. To those who believe in their civilising potential (in the manner of the English school tradition), a normative challenge is thrown up by the empirical fact that sovereign states are agents of insecurity within, as well as without. For many people on earth, life is 'solitary, poore, nasty, brutish, and short' within their state, as a result of government policy or incompetence; such insecurity is in the nature of some states, and not only, as Hobbes famously said, in the state of nature itself.[62]

---

[59] Quoted by Fussell, *Wartime*, p. 293. Such a sense of abandonment, following service for the nation, as well as during it, is not uncommon. This has been the case with both British and Argentine veterans from the Falklands War, for example. The case of Robert Lawrence, a British hero from that war, is poignant: see Mark Townsend, 'The Hardest Fight of All for a Falklands Hero', *The Observer*, 14 January 2007. Townsend recalls that, in the years following this very brief and self-contained war, more British veterans committed suicide than the 255 who died in the actual fighting. The ratio of suicide rates among US veterans of the Vietnam War has been comparable. A 1995 study in the United States said that 'no more than' 20,000 Vietnam vets had died of suicide from time of discharge to the end of 1993. However, a 1990 book written from within an organisation associated with the welfare of veterans claimed that over 150,000 had committed suicide, in addition to the over 58,000 who had died in the war. One doctor gave his view that there had been a massive under-reporting of suicides (e.g. of self-inflicted gunshot wounds) out of kindness to surviving relatives. See the 'Suicide Wall' website at www.suicidewall.com, dedicated to memorialising Vietnam veterans who have taken their own lives.
[60] The phrase is from Peter Marshall, *Demanding the Impossible. A History of Anarchism* (London: Fontana Press, 1993), p. 12.
[61] Paine is quoted by Marshall, and the phrase 'a state of society' is taken from William Godwin ('The most desirable condition of the human species, is a state of society'), *ibid.*, p. 12.
[62] Thomas Hobbes, *Leviathan*, ed. with an introduction by C. B. Macpherson (London: Penguin Books, 1988), p. 186. It is often forgotten that this influential book was much more concerned with *civil* war than interstate war, and that for Hobbes the 'state of nature' that existed between states was capable of more moderation than that in which individual humans find themselves.

Externally, states can wind up insecurity deliberately through aggressive policies or inadvertently through the workings of the security dilemma.[63] The image of sovereign states as 'guardian angels' is English school romanticism.[64] For the most part states fluctuate between the role of gangsters, prostitutes, fat cats, or bystanders. More people are threatened by the policies of their own governments than by neighbouring armies.[65] There is an analogy here with 'domestic violence'.[66] Just as women are more likely to suffer attacks from their husbands and partners than from hooded strangers, so people in general suffer more insecurity from their own government's aims, neglect, or incompetence than from the aggression of a neighbour's army. In South Africa, under the apartheid regime, the majority black population was kept brutally insecure. Any improvements in the security of the state actually signalled a proportionate decrease in the long-term security of the vast majority of the population. The goal of 'national security' was hostile to the security of the overwhelming number of people who lived in the state; at the same time, the norms of the society of states, such as the right of domestic jurisdiction, played directly into the hands of the elite presiding over the racist tyranny.[67] Sovereignty is often conceived as a protecting principle, but it is too often forgotten that what it often protects is the ability of brutal regimes to abuse their people.

In the 1990s, the concept of the 'failed state' became familiar: that is, states that were no longer able to maintain order and provide the basic services necessary for life. In many cases, civil war was endemic, with substantial power being in the hands of warlords, and civilian suffering being widespread.[68] But very successful states can also create problems for their citizens and their neighbours alike – and even those in distant parts of the world – through their domination of the winner/loser

[63] See Ken Booth and Nicholas J. Wheeler, *The Security Dilemma. Fear, Cooperation and Trust in World Politics*, (Houndmills: Palgrave, 2008) esp. part I.

[64] Nicholas J. Wheeler, 'Guardian Angel or Global Gangster? A Review of the Ethical Claims of International Society', *Political Studies*, vol. 44(1), 1996, pp. 123–35.

[65] R. J. Rummel has argued at great length that there is an inverse relationship between political rights and civil liberties and internal violence: see *Understanding Conflict and War*, vols. I–V (Beverly Hills, Ca.: Sage, 1975–81); see also his 'Roots of Faith II', in Joseph Kruzel and James N. Rosenau (eds.), *Journeys through World Politics* (Lexington, Mass.: Lexington Books, 1988), pp. 311–28.

[66] See, among many, Helena Kennedy, *Eve was Framed. Women and British Justice* (London: Vintage, 1993), pp. 82–139.

[67] Booth and Vale, 'Southern Africa'; see also, Robert Jackson and Carl G. Rosberg, 'Why Africa's Weak States Persist: The Empirical and the Juridical in Statehood', *World Politics*, vol. 35(1), 1985, pp. 1–24.

[68] William Zartman, *Collapsed States* (Boulder, Colo.: Lynne Rienner, 1995).

world of the capitalist order. Crocodile tears may be shed by leaders at press conferences and international gatherings, but when did any government seriously allow its economy to be hurt in order to help suffering humanity? It is one thing to announce an 'ethical foreign policy' as did the British government in 1997; it is another entirely to take risks with jobs by pursuing human rights policies vigorously. Scholars who have dug deep have revealed that there is little true humanitarianism at the heart of even states which both possess abundant resources and proclaim the idea of a responsible 'international community'. Evidence, for those who want it, can be found (among others) in Linda Melvern's work uncovering British and French duplicity during the Rwandan genocide, and Doug Stokes' work revealing US support for Colombian state terror.[69]

Sovereign states, as suggested earlier, will remain for the indefinite future, despite their failings and challenges such as privatisation and corporatisation. They will provide the frameworks for the public institutions necessary for health services, law and order, transport, efficient tax services, and so on. Locally and globally there is a need for mechanisms for producing redistribution and welfare. For several centuries this mechanism has been the 'nation-state' with its homogenising momentum, though today this is an anachronistic concept, as Beck argued earlier, in relation to his idea of 'cosmopolitan states'. An illustration was given earlier (that of 'foreign co-citizen') showing that such a development is not as radical as it first might appear. Reality is radical, if one allows it a long enough time span. Do not forget that peasants living under baronial power in medieval times could hardly have imagined their country not being run by kings and barons. Beyond their dreams was an institution called the universal franchise whereby they would be able to vote out their ruler by writing an X on a piece of paper. 'What, me learn to write? Change my ruler? What's an "X"?'

States are changing and will continue to do so, as necessary but flawed institutions. One of the key questions is the extent of their redemptive potential. In this regard, Benhabib has made the important point that if one sees the state and its institutions as 'agencies of repression' (as in Foucault's 'disciplinary subjection') then 'of course there can be no redemptive dialectic at work in the legal sphere and the institutions of politics'.[70] Redemption requires the erosion of statism, and checks

---

[69] Linda Melvern, *Conspiracy to Murder. The Rwandan Genocide* (London: Verso, 2004); Doug Stokes, *America's Other War. Terrorizing Colombia* (London: Zed Books, 2005).
[70] Benhabib, *Another Cosmopolitanism*, p. 163.

and balances are needed both without and within, for power tends to corrupt, and sovereignty above all. The answer, in principle, is not difficult. It lies in cosmopolitanising the decision-making power and power over loyalty that has been claimed by the nation-state for several centuries. If what passes for pluralist international society were to be replaced by cosmopolitan democracy externally, and if sovereign power domestically were replaced by democratic cosmopolitanism within, progress would have been made towards cosmopolitan statehood. In other words, instead of the Westphalian culture of statism, the organising culture of our global age should seek the replacement of the idea that there should be no higher decision-making body than the state by the institutions of cosmopolitan democracy, and no higher loyalty than the nation by the values of democratic cosmopolitanism.

Ordering reality

> Wilde concluded 'The Decay of Lying' with the argument that there are many kinds of lie . . . [but] in Wilde's mind the highest form of lying was art, 'the telling of beautiful untrue things'. To such a one realism offers only a lower form of truth. When a famous French painter who had just painted his back-garden was reprimanded by a critic for omitting to paint a tree in the centre of the lawn, his response was not to paint in the tree but instead to rush out into the garden, grab an axe and chop the tree down.   Declan Kiberd in 'Oscar Wilde'[71]

This chapter, like the French painter's lawn, has been the site of some conceptual clearing. In particular, I have discussed ideas of being, knowing, and doing in relation to realism's categorical structure in international politics, the sovereign state. The discussion can be briefly summarised. *Being:* what is real in world politics is a multitude of referents for security, with the sovereign state having a privileged position within the academic study of international relations. *Knowing:* what we can know, reliably, is that the Westphalian states system is a historical phenomenon, neither natural nor inevitable, and always subject to being in transition; the statism with which it has traditionally been infused is empirically and normatively flawed. *Doing:* how we might act depends on our political theory, but a critical perspective asks us to compare the reality of world politics constructed through statism with practices

---

[71] Declan Kiberd, 'Oscar Wilde: The Resurgence of Lying', in Peter Raby, *The Cambridge Companion to Oscar Wilde* (Cambridge: Cambridge University Press, 1997), p. 287.

shaped by the promotion of cosmopolitan democracy and democratic cosmopolitanism.

The next step is to give a complete picture of the theoretical framework that has grown out of the discussion so far and that will be developed in the rest of the book. It is my belief that theory, like philosophy, is not simply a pastime for the ivory tower.[72] A utilitarian approach to conceiving theory has been long advised by James N. Rosenau, who encouragingly taught us that when thinking theoretically we should not get hung up on the idea of developing a clear-cut definition of theory.[73]

With this in mind, I have found Philip Allott's conception of theory to be particularly helpful. Theory, he has written, is 'a mental ordering of the reality within which a particular society constitutes itself', offering explanatory and justificatory ideas for 'society's self-constituting'.[74] He distinguished between three different dimensions of theory: 'practical', 'pure', and 'transcendental' types. The critical theory of security developed in the rest of the book will speak to each.

Practical theory consists of the ideas 'that are present in actual social behaviour'. It is the operation of theory at the most immediate level: 'ideas as practice' in Allott's words.[75] As one part of the way a society forms its 'reality-for-itself',[76] these ideas 'express themselves in the course of social practice, the programme of actual willing and acting'; they are 'an integral and functional part of the day-to-day process' of society's real self-constituting, in general and in specific areas. *Pure theory* is 'the theory of practical theory (ideas about ideas)'. It is one level deeper than practical theory in relation to a society's forming of its reality-for-itself, and is a major element in a society's 'philosophy-for-itself'.[77] According to Allott's conceptualisation, pure theory is what society 'says to itself about what it is and why, and what it might choose to be'. It dominates society's self-constituting, as society debates within itself 'the nature and significance' of its make-up. Finally, *transcendental theory* is 'society's epistemology, its understanding of the source of

---

[72] See also Baggini, *Making Sense*, p. 265.

[73] Among the extensive literature on the aims, methods, and problems of theory, there is still no better starting place for students than James N. Rosenau's 'Thinking Theory Thoroughly', in which he lists nine mental qualities that best enable one to 'think theory': see his *The Scientific Study of Foreign Policy* (London: Frances Pinter, 1980), pp. 19–31.

[74] Philip Allott, *The Health of Nations* (Cambridge: Cambridge University Press, 2002), 3.20, 3.43(4), 4.43, 4.49, 12.6–7; and *Eunomia. New Order for a New World* (Oxford: Oxford University Press, 1990; pb edn with new preface, 2001), pp. 14–38.

[75] Allott, *Eunomia*, pp. 344–5. [76] Allott, *Health of Nations*, 3.20.

[77] Allott, *Eunomia*, pp. 344–5.

truth and value, its theory of theory'. It is theory at the deepest level, the grounding of a society's 'reality-for-itself' as Allot puts it.[78]

Allott contended that all three forms of theory 'are actualised as particular social phenomena in particular societies'.[79] This is the case in the realm of security, as it has been in the discipline of law, his own primary interest. All three forms will be actualised below: ideas that are present in how we carry out our security practices (doing), ideas from which those practices derive (knowing), and ideas that try to account for the truth claims behind the ideas about the ideas (being). To illustrate how a reality-for-itself is built up in the way behaviour becomes self-constituting, we can look at mainstream thinking about the security of states: *ideas-as-practice* include policies such as nuclear deterrence or the balance of power (which seek to promote stability according to the 'logic of anarchy'); *ideas-about-ideas* include the theory of political realism (which give shape to traditional security studies as well as diplomatic and strategic practices); and the *theory of theory* which for neorealists includes ideas about the structure of the states system, with politics organised around survival and security.

These three forms of theory provide the basis for the critical framework of world security to be elaborated in the next chapter. Its transcendental theory is human sociality, its pure theory is critical global theorising, and its practical theory is emancipatory realism.

[78] Allott, *Health of Nations*, 3.20.   [79] Allott, *Eunomia*, pp. 344 n. 2, 345 n. 3.

6   The world, the world

It's the pull of the world. I spent most of my childhood on my own, and some of it was in the mountains of Wales. I would go exploring with the idea in my head that the farther I was from home the better it would be . . . Now it's not just the Black Mountains of Dyfed, but the world.

Norman Lewis[1]

The title of this chapter has been purloined from Norman Lewis, regarded by some as the best travel writer of our age in the English language, and by Auberon Waugh as perhaps the best since Marco Polo. Lewis's book ends with the idea of 'the pull of the world', a phrase I use to end the chapter, which culminates in a framework of a critical theory of world security. (Some readers might like to move straight to p. 277 at this point, to see a map of where the chapter is going.) The framework is structured according to the three types of theory (transcendental, pure, and practical) introduced at the end of the previous chapter. Within each type, the key elements are built up from the earlier chapters in the book, and together they offer a theory of security that I believe to be realistic, comprehensive, coherent, useful, and emancipatory.

Transcendental theory

To say what *is* is to change human reality.

Philip Allott in *The Health of Nations*[2]

There must always be an 'is' when discussing world politics. The realist 'is-mantra' insists that the aim of academic international relations

[1] Norman Lewis, *The World, The World* (London: Jonathan Cape, 1996), p. 239.
[2] Philip Allott, *The Health of Nations. Society and Law Beyond the State* (Cambridge: Cambridge University Press, 2002), p. 4.

or security studies is to describe and explain the world, in the beguiling phrase, *as it is*. Philip Allott has brilliantly expressed the power of 'is' in such phrases, and has argued that the challenge facing us is not only to recognise that power, but also to understand its origin in the mind.[3] Every theory has to assume, as James Rosenau has put it, that 'human affairs are founded on an underlying order',[4] and so every theory needs its set of *is-foundations*. 'Is' is the sign in a theory that something real is being claimed, and all theories in international relations make such claims. To theorise is to assume something is real. The key question becomes, in the words of Heikki Patomäki and Colin Wight, 'not whether one should be a realist, but of what kind?' They add that 'for positivists, sense-experience is real; for postpositivists, discourses or intersubjectivity is real'.[5] Philosophical realism is explicitly accepted by all types of theorisers about world politics, even by those who reject those 'realists' who stole a march on the rest of the discipline by claiming for their own brand of theory the generic title for an activity in which everybody, in their different ways, is engaged. Realism achieved the brand-labelling status in international relations that Xerox achieved in copying.

The transcendental dimension of the overall theoretical framework proposed below is constructed out of eight main is-propositions. 'Human sociality' is the best overall label for them, implying as it does the radical possibilities immanent in the biology of being human. Out of this biological immanence, the conjunction through time, in concrete circumstances, of an evolving consciousness within bodies with genitals and stomachs as well as mind, resulted in *Homo erectus* becoming human beings: what we were, are, and will become.[6]

Biology is freedom

it is . . . our biology that makes us free.   Steven Rose in *Lifelines*[7]

The beginning of the transcendental theory of security is biology, the necessary condition. We are part of nature, though 'human nature' is

---

[3] Allott, 'Theory and Istopia', *ibid.*, pp. 3–8.
[4] This is one of the themes of James Rosenau, 'Thinking Theory Thoroughly', in *The Scientific Study of Foreign Policy* (London: Frances Pinter, 1980), pp. 19–31.
[5] Heikki Patomäki and Colin Wight, 'After Postpositivism: The Promise of Critical Realism', *International Studies Quarterly*, vol. 44(2), 2000, pp. 213–37, quotation at p. 218.
[6] The importance of understanding the human animal in its entirety, in a different field, is well made by Terry Eagleton, 'The Politics of Amnesia', in his *After Theory* (London: Penguin, 2004), pp. 1–22, esp. pp. 3–4.
[7] Steven Rose, *Lifelines. Biology, Freedom, Determinism* (London: Allen Lane, 1997), p. 309.

a term best avoided.[8] Its usage is invariably regressive, being mainly employed to try and trump arguments about what might or might not be possible in human society,[9] or to spread myths that contribute to human self-alienation through the internalising of fear, hate, shame, and conflict.[10]

A particularly dyspeptic understanding of the idea of human nature is John Gray's widely publicised book *Straw Dogs: Thoughts on Humans and Other Animals*.[11] Gray argued that political and scientific progress, and freedom, are fantasies, and projects to construct a better world are bound to fail. Whatever valid cautionary points are contained in such an argument are undermined by the nihilism and elitism displayed. If progress is an illusion, why do we not choose to return to the era when women were the playthings of the nearest aristocrat, when decaying teeth meant no respite from pain, or when most humans were simply too ignorant even to be bored? Theorists who criticise the idea of progress, as here, should feel embarrassed by their own empirical enjoyment of it. On one point, however, Gray is certainly correct, and that is his view that humans are not as far from the rest of the animal world as many habitually like to think.[12] Even so, Gray is not justified in arguing that we are as close to the rest of the animal world as *he* likes to think.

According to the philosopher Richard Norman, Gray presents his readers with the false antithesis of two 'equally absurd' ideas about humans: either that as a species we think we can be masters of our own destiny, or alternatively that we are no different from other animals.[13] Norman accepts that it would be 'absurdly pretentious' to think the former, but to claim that we are no different from other animals is at least as absurd. '*Which* other animals?' Norman asks, for all animals are different: 'An amoeba is different from an elephant, a woodlouse is different from a chimpanzee.' And humans are no exception in differing

---

[8] Beliefs about 'human nature', like international politics, are theory-derived. A good place to start is Leslie Stevenson, *Seven Theories of Human Nature* (Oxford: Oxford University Press, 1987); this constantly expanding field includes Kenan Malik, *Man, Beast and Zombie. What Science Can and Cannot Tell Us About Human Nature* (London: Weidenfeld and Nicolson, 2000), Jürgen Habermas, *The Future of Human Nature* (Cambridge: Polity, 2003), and Matt Ridley, *Nature via Nurture. Genes, Experience and What Makes Us Human* (London: Fourth Estate, 2003).
[9] Barbara Goodwin, *Using Political Ideas* (Chichester: John Wiley, 1992), p. 10.
[10] Philip Allott, 'The Future of the Human Past', in Ken Booth (ed.), *Statecraft and Security. The Cold War and Beyond* (Cambridge: Cambridge University Press, 1998), pp. 323–8.
[11] John Gray, *Straw Dogs: Thoughts On Humans and Other Animals* (London: Granta, 2002).
[12] *Ibid.*, pp. 3–6, 28–9.
[13] Richard Norman, *On Humanism* (London: Routledge, 2004), pp. 82–5.

from other species. Norman goes on, 'We do not differ by being "masters of our destiny", but we do differ by possessing the capacity to think about our situation, to assess what is good and bad about it, to weigh up different courses of action and to try to change things for the better.' In other words, while humans share many characteristics with other animals (like elephants and chimps, we need food and to reproduce) as far as I know no elephant or chimp has been able to write a book like *Straw Dogs*, reflecting on the nature of its own species.

Is there therefore no sense in which we can speak meaningfully of human nature, with its implication of shared characteristics across the whole species? I do not think we can, except for physical needs such as eating, sleeping, and sex. But these do not mark out any specific 'human nature'; they define *animal* and not specifically *human* characteristics. In trying to understand the human species it is necessary, much more so than is the case with other animals, to adopt a 'mutualist' conception of the interplay between nature and nurture – between biology and culture.[14] And it is nature (biology) that opens up the potential of nurture (culture). This position has been well put by the neuroscientist Steven Rose. In his book *Lifelines* he showed that complexity not reductionism is the key to understanding humans, and that the radical unpredictability of history, together with the choices humans have had and will have, underline the freedom immanent within human biology.[15]

What is is human sociality

We had thought that humans were just animals with cultures . . . intelligent, plastic, teachable animals, passive and comfortable to the weight of tradition. Now we see that humans are also active, they are also animals with history. They are inventive and profoundly social animals, living in and through their relations with each other and acting and reacting upon each other to make new relations and new forms of life.

Michael Carrithers in *Why Humans Have Cultures*[16]

If the beginning is in our existence in nature, the 'muddy bottom' of human reality, according to Gananath Obeyesekere, is 'sociality'.[17] Michael Carrithers has defined this concept as 'a capacity for complex social behaviour', and it is claimed that it is a reality that goes deeper than

---

[14] The 'mutualist' perspective is discussed in Michael Carrithers, *Why Humans Have Cultures. Explaining Anthropology and Social Diversity* (Oxford: Oxford University Press, 1992), p. 11, and is a central theme in Ridley, *Nature via Nurture*.
[15] Rose, *Lifelines*, pp. 73–96, 272–300.   [16] Carrithers, *Cultures*, pp. 32–3.
[17] Defined by Carrithers, *ibid.*, pp. 12–13.

the idea of 'culture', the level that bears a heavy (and often diffuse) load of explanation and political analysis. Biology creates sociality, which in turn creates culture. As explanations for human behaviour, biology and sociality go deep, but probably not deep enough for some readers, who will want to drill down further in order to find an answer to the ultimate *What is?* question. Is human reality the design of God? Or are we the products of cosmic chance? Big questions: but for present purposes they can be set aside. Indeed, in the final chapter I will argue that in the negotiating of tolerable and universal behavioural norms in support of world security it is usually not helpful to get entangled in debates about meta-explanations of Life. We need not drill down *all* the way to produce a critical theory of world security: sociality is far enough. This is inadvertently implied, as it happens, in the 'muddy bottom' metaphor, because there is always a deeper geological reality below any stream's 'muddy bottom'.

I take sociality to be the muddy bottom of human reality, but as a species humans have not been stick-in-the-muds. Over time the biological capacity to construct complex social behaviour has resulted in a multitude of weird and wonderful cultural anthropological forms.[18] With these in mind, who would question the verdict of the cultural anthropologist Carrithers that scholars studying human society should place 'change, not permanence, at the centre of our vision'?[19] Or question Lenin's view about the radical nature of reality? Without the freedom immanent within human biology, the early hominids 2.5 million years ago would not have been able to begin to produce the behavioural exuberance described by historians and cultural anthropologists – producing activities and artefacts beyond the wildest dreams (and indeed nightmares) of our distant ancestors. Not least of the radical realities made possible by sociality has been the contemporary global drama of international politics.

With regard to the promotion of world security in this drama, we have as a species to begin from where we are, even if, as the old saw has it, we would prefer not to be starting the journey from here. Chapter 1 showed that change is urgently needed in global-business-as-usual, and subsequent chapters will discuss some of the most serious challenges

[18] It is always eye-opening to pick up works of anthropology and gaze in wonder at what we were and are; two well-established ones are: Marvin Harris, *Culture, People, Nature. An Introduction to General Anthropology* (New York: HarperCollins, 1993; 6th edn), and William A. Haviland, *Anthropology* (Orlando, Fla.: Harcourt Brace, 1994; 8th edn).
[19] Carrithers, *Cultures*, esp. pp. 8, 10–11, 22.

we face. Of central significance in these changes is the developing of human consciousness at the species level, creating a global we-ness, out of the political micro-consciousnesses that history has bestowed upon us. This means, for example, fighting regressive notions such as 'the human condition' which hold us back from becoming what we might be.[20] The future will always be a horizon beyond our grasp, but humans seek to shape it, with some groups searching to bring about one thing, and others something else, in conditions in which all are pushed and pulled to varying degrees by the powerful structures that create the environment of the struggle. Marx put it best:

> Men make their own history, but they do not make it just as they please; they do not make it under circumstances chosen by themselves, but under circumstances directly encountered, given and transmitted from the past. The tradition of all the dead generations weighs like a nightmare on the brain of the living.[21]

Humans also make their own security (and insecurity) as an adaptable animal species in a natural environment.

Sociality, then, is part of what separates humans from other animals, though some of the latter do construct relatively complex relationships. But the difference in degree produces a difference in kind (though Gray would presumably not agree). Like other animals our lives are shaped by instinct and emotion, but our capacity for rational enquiry is quite distinct. Humans have the capacity for consciousness about their own mental states, and for making new choices in the light of re-evaluations – both individual and collective.[22] Freud showed us how radical such revisions might be.[23] The capacity for re-evaluation is probably more powerful today than ever in the past, given the acceleration of

---

[20] Allott, 'The Future of the Human Past', pp. 328–31. In the light of this view, it is interesting to recall perhaps the most famous book with the title *La Condition Humaine*, written by André Malraux, first published in 1933 in French, and later in English as *Man's Fate* (New York: Vintage Books, 1969). Although the book was set in China, one of Malraux's biographers said it told us more about his own complex character than about that country, and although Malraux described it as 'reportage', another of his biographers said he 'never wrote a book more based on imagination'. Such is the way we see and report *la condition humaine*. These matters are discussed in Ken Booth, 'British Diplomacy and Opinion during the Sino-Japanese Imbroglio 1933–1934' (University of Wales, PhD thesis, 1982), pp. 614–16.

[21] Karl Marx, 'The Eighteenth Brumaire of Louis Bonaparte', in Karl Marx and Frederick Engels, *Selected Works* (London: Lawrence and Wishart, 1991), p. 92.

[22] Norman, *On Humanism*, p. 85.

[23] A helpful introduction is Jerome Neu (ed.), *The Cambridge Companion to Freud* (Cambridge: Cambridge University Press, 1992).

knowledge production and new capacities to access it.[24] In this new and ever-changing context, biology and sociality continue to give us the freedom to create radical possibilities for human becoming. It yet remains to be told whether reason and desire can together produce the cosmopolitan sociality necessary to generate sufficient global we-ness to ensure sustainable world security on a planet on which divisions of tribe, nation, class, gender, religion, and race have so far prevailed.

Cognition is first

As we look back, it seems like wilful blindness. The abandonment of the radical economic foundations of the women's and civil-rights movements by the conflation of causes that came to be called political correctness successfully trained a generation of activists in the politics of image, not action . . . the political models in vogue at the time [the 1990s] . . . left many of us ill-equipped to deal with issues that were more about ownership than representation. We were too busy analyzing the pictures being projected on the wall to notice that the wall itself had been sold.   Naomi Klein in *No Logo*[25]

When a person makes a choice, a basic sociological question always arises: what is doing the work in shaping the action decided upon – emotion, political economy, discourse, genes, or any other of the multiple explanations of why humans do what they do? In engaging with this question social scientists make a basic distinction between *agents* and *structures*; it is an issue that has fascinated many international relations theorists when they have confronted their particular puzzles.[26]

An agent is defined as a person or group capable of making things happen. A structure is defined as something existing outside the agent – an independent conjunction of phenomena that shape an agent's actions. A familiar focus of discussion in academic international relations has been the role of the anarchical structure of the states system, and the extent to which it pushes state agents to behave according to a particular logic (prioritising security and pursuing it through policies such as balance of

[24] This is celebrated in James Martin, *The Meaning of the 21st Century. A Vital Blueprint for Ensuring our Future* (London: Eden Project Books, 2006).
[25] Naomi Klein, *No Logo. Taking Aim at the Brand Bullies* (London: Flamingo, 2000), p. 124.
[26] The literature on the agent–structure debate is enormous. My thoughts about its importance and (some of) its intricacies have been much affected by listening to Steve Smith and Colin Wight, and sometimes reading them: see Martin Hollis and Steve Smith, 'Beware Gurus: Structure and Action in International Relations', *Review of International Studies*, vol. 17(4), 1991, pp. 393–410, and Colin Wight, 'Philosophy of Social Science and International Relations', in Walter Carlsnaes, Thomas Risse, and Beth Simmons (eds.), *Handbook of International Relations* (London: Sage, 2002), p. 24, for a brief overview and references.

power). In a reference-point article Alexander Wendt argued that 'Anarchy is what states make of it',[27] thereby challenging realism's emphasis on the causal power of the structure. For many, the agent/structure relationship in international theory appears to be an insoluble chicken-and-egg reality. I do not think it is.

First, those who posit agents and structures as existing 'independently' confuse matters by their reductionism. There is an alternative to choosing one or other explanation, one that emphasises the formative power of the *interrelationship* between agents and structures. This position, primarily identified with the 'structuration theory' of Anthony Giddens, explains the manner in which agents (reflexive, and with the capability of acting) and structures (rules and resources) are mutually constitutive.[28]

Second, we must avoid getting too tied up in the internal logic of metaphors, such as that of chicken-and-egg. If we see it in these reproductive as well as reductive terms, the sociological question becomes: if structures are human inventions, and humans are the products of structures, which comes first? The escape is through realising that although it is sometimes helpful to think of agents and structures as analytically distinct, in life they can never be completely autonomous, and so can never constitute actually existing equivalents to chickens or eggs.[29] Agents, whether individuals or groups, are to some degree the products of their structures, but a *product* is not the same as a *prisoner*. The agent/structure dialectic is not a chicken/egg conundrum after all. Whereas it is always a chicken that emerges from a hen's egg, what grows out of one human society is not a copy in the same way. The thoughts of those involved play a role in what comes next that is denied to the hen. Using a different metaphor, we can consider human societies to be hand-thrown rather than factory-made pottery. The latter is an exact copy, the former never is, though it is made out of the same clay. The potter has some freedom to change things (for worse as well as better). It is this degree of freedom

[27] Alexander Wendt, 'Anarchy is what States Make of It: The Social Construction of Power Politics', *International Organization*, vol. 46(2), 1992, pp. 391–425.

[28] See, inter alia, Anthony Giddens, *Central Problems in Social Theory* (London: Macmillan, 1979), and *The Constitution of Society: Outline of the Theory of Structuration* (Cambridge: Polity, 1984). Assessments include Ira Cohen, *Structuration Theory: Anthony Giddens and the Constitution of Social Life* (London: Macmillan, 1989), Ian Craib, *Modern Social Theory: From Parsons to Habermas* (London: Harvester Wheatsheaf, 1992); David Held and John B. Thompson (eds.), *Social Theory of Modern Societies: Anthony Giddens and his Critics* (Cambridge: Cambridge University Press, 1989).

[29] Bill McSweeney, *Security, Identity and Interests. A Sociology of International Relations* (Cambridge: Cambridge University Press, 1999), pp. 138–9.

that ensures that human societies are hand-thrown, not factory-made products.

Third, we must give human cognition its due. The idea of freedom itself derives from having become human beings. Together, a sense of self, language, ideas, ideals, and learning have all played a part in creating the idea of freedom, and some structures nurture this idea more than others. Structures (social class, the states system, and so on) can be very powerful. The extreme end of the structuralist position argues that 'people do not speak but rather they are spoken (by the underlying structure of the language), that they do not read books but are "read" by books, and they do not create societies but are created by societies'.[30] If this is the case, how can change take place? This is where human cognition comes in, as the decisive intervention in the agent/structure dialectic. The sociologist/peace researcher Bill McSweeney has made this argument well in relation to security.[31] There always has to be a first mover, and this is cognition by a human agent (though not an agent completely autonomous of structural circumstances). Put simply, structures cannot conceive new structures, but human agents can, even if they cannot yet construct them. Cognition is the key. In McSweeney's words, human choices are 'situated in historic conditions, [they are] not the product of laws or structures external to the agent'. We can 'reconstruct' knowledge, and hence structures. This is the meaning of Wendt's argument about states constructing the character of anarchy, though his own viewpoint conceded too much to realism, and not enough to language. Other things can plausibly be said to 'make' anarchy, from globalisation to whatever makes the states that are supposed to have the most causal power (democracy and human rights, for example, might be the prime movers in creating a more benign anarchy).

Structures are indeed powerful, and so we should think of individuals as structured agents rather than as individuals exercising complete 'free will'. On 9 November 1989, individuals and families living in the eastern part of Berlin were confronted by a literally concrete historical challenge. Should they on that eventful day go to the events taking place near the Wall, or should they stay at home? Different choices were made by different people for different sets of reasons. While all lived under the domineering social and political structures imposed by the GDR regime, individuals faced specific structural conditions resulting from

---

[30] I. Craib, *Modern Social Theory: From Parsons to Habermas* (Brighton: Harvester Wheatsheaf, 1984), p. 109.
[31] McSweeney, *Security*, pp. 138–51, 198–219.

their marital status, age, and so on. So, whatever she was thinking and feeling on that historical day, a single mum with several small children, living on the outskirts of East Berlin could not easily leave home to join in the demonstrations. But she might have made that decision. She was under more structural pressure than a single man without children living towards the centre of the city, but she still had a choice. Women under similar structural pressures that day presumably made different choices. Structures obviously (always) affect people's decisions, but they do not determine them. They are a necessary part of an explanation of behaviour, but they are not sufficient, because nobody ever lives within a single structure. Consequently, it is for the historian to try to figure out the relative structural significance that led individuals to their decisions on 9 November 1989 – those associated with the East German state, those demanded by immediate responsibilities, or those promised by a different (post-Wall) life. Ordinary people living in East Berlin at that time operated under similar broad structural considerations, but how these were interpreted and balanced was in part the result of the individual's sense of freedom. In the event, of course, many decided not to stay at home on 9/11. They exercised the potter's freedom to change rather than replicate. The Wall did not fall; it was pushed.

Michel Foucault, like the rest of us, found these issues tantalisingly difficult. His early work argued that freedoms are illusory and that we 'construct ourselves in a way that is prescribed for us by the technologies of the self sanctioned by the modern regime of power', though later he did allow for agency.[32] Roxanne Doty, also from a poststructuralist perspective, attempted to transcend the structure/agency reductionisms by focusing on practices, but as Colin Wight has pointed out, this does not advance the argument because it does not reveal the conditions that make the practices possible.[33] Discourses construct their own objects, and in this sense can never be wrong, but those drawn to discourse explanations avoid the 'interesting and important question', which for Wight was: 'what constructed the discourses themselves?' This gets back to the question raised earlier by Naomi Klein: who owned the wall?

Finally, why is the agent/structure debate important for students of security? It must be admitted, despite all the brain power invested into thinking about it, that it is of limited predictive value. It will never tell

[32] A helpful discussion of this complex issue is in Mark Bevir, 'Foucault, Power, and Institutions', *Political Studies*, 47, 1999, pp. 345–59 (quotation at p. 354).
[33] Colin Wight, 'Interpretation All the Way Down? A Reply to Roxanne Lynn Doty', *European Journal of International Relations*, vol. 6(2), 2000, pp. 423–30.

us, for example, whether there will be nuclear war between India and Pakistan. What it will do, in the version that emphasises the interaction between human cognitions and dominant structures, is to keep alive the idea that change is possible (a door also kept open by the constructivist turn), while at the same time providing a reminder of the power of structures. Such an understanding – which involves rejecting fatalist logic about international relations – affects how one approaches the future. It might, for example, influence a student's choice of research. If it is believed that human agents are pivotal, research on the end of the Cold War would focus on Gorbachev and Reagan and the role of social movements in Europe, as opposed to the distribution of power between the two superpowers. One's choice does not have to be reductionist, of course, for arguing that changes in human cognitions are key does not eliminate the role of changing (structural) power factors. McSweeney has made the general point well: 'a reflexive theory of the social order can support the moral and emancipatory impulse of a critical theory of international relations which aims to expose the contingency of all social arrangements, and the human choice and interests which gave rise to them'.[34] This, he continued, advances the possibility of constructing alternatives to the international order and the organisation of international security.

History is made up as we go along

The past is never dead, it is not even past.   William Faulkner[35]

History is understood backwards though it is made forwards. Historians begin their work knowing how things ended, and this constrains their sense of the potential openness of human possibility. When understood through the prism of hindsight, history is made to make sense, and in a way that future history can never be to actual participants. So-called counter-factual history is no different, being equally written with (actually *against*) the knowledge of how the story ends. If Queen Victoria had been told that within fifty years of her death, Germany would not be ruled by her relatives but by a *totalitarian* political party, the Nazis, which set up *industrial death camps*, the first of which would be liberated by the *Red Army* (established to help secure *world revolution*) in the state of Poland (a country long abolished), and that the *Soviet Union*

[34] McSweeney, *Security*, p. 219.
[35] A favourite line of Hannah Arendt: see Elisabeth Young-Bruehl, *Hannah Arendt. For Love of the World* (New Haven, Conn.: Yale University Press, 1982), p. 385.

(a *workers' state*) would then join with the United States in dismembering and occupying Germany indefinitely, it is utterly certain that this long-serving head of state could not have joined the causal dots in advance. The future is a foreign land. Victoria would not have had the language to play the game; and only history could have taught it to her. As a result, the causal dots can only be joined with hindsight, and then only subjectively. The story can only be told backwards, and as such loses much in the telling.[36]

From its early days, Frankfurt school critical theory gave history a central role. Knowledge was seen as historically produced.[37] This meant that as the historical situatedness of an observer changes, so does our understanding of the past. This same general idea was developed later by Carr in his best-seller *What is History?* one of whose themes was that all history is contemporary history.[38] Anthropology also needed waking up to the idea that knowledge is produced through and by history. Carrithers, in the early 1990s, emphasised anthropology's inadequacies in that regard, with the tendency to see a timeless present rather than understanding 'the mutability' of human society – 'plasticity, change, temporality, metamorphosis, interactivity'.[39] We should think of ourselves, he insisted, as animals with a history. This, as was pointed out in chapters 2 and 5, is the view that animates historical sociologists in relation to the formation of states.

Since history is made forwards, what humans invent can be uninvented. Slavery was a social invention, not a necessity of nature, and it was abolished (legally if not everywhere practically) as a result of moral progress in the most powerful slave-owning states. The idea of hereditary monarchy, also once so powerful, is another example of an invented (and so uninventable) human institution, though it too strangely hangs on in some countries. One of the obstacles holding humans back from reinventing a more humane global order (more inclusive, equal, and cooperative) is the powerful grip of a generally gloomy view of the

---

[36] Don DeLillo's epic novel *Underworld* (London: Picador, 1998) reverses the chronology, so the reader knows what will happen in a way the characters cannot; even so, working out connections and causes is not easy or always possible; this gets at the uncertainty of history better than historians do, for they always provide a plot that moves to a denouement.

[37] Max Horkheimer, 'Traditional and Critical Theory', in *Critical Theory. Selected Essays*, trans. Matthew J. O'Connell and others (New York: Continuum, 1992), pp. 188–243.

[38] E. H. Carr, *What is History?* (Harmondsworth: Penguin, 1970; 1st pub. 1961); see esp. pp. 24–6.

[39] Carrithers, *Culture*, p. 33.

human past.[40] This has not been helped by the kernel of truth in Hardy's well-known line that war makes 'rattling good history' but peace is 'poor reading'.[41] The problem here is not that war stories are *naturally* more interesting than those that do not contain violence, but of a political economy that has enabled men to be the primary customers for books on war, and particularly so in Hardy's time. Together, over a long period, economy and society have helped to ensure the domination of masculinist definitions of what constitutes heroism and adventure, and therefore what makes 'a rattling good read'.

History is not what actually happened, but what the most influential historians have written about. Future history will be made by the interplay between biology, sociality, ideas, and structures. Marx's famous comment about history being made by men but not determined by them is pertinent. The challenge thrown before us in the first two decades of the twenty-first century is to make our own world history, but without succumbing to the pains of Churchill's equally famous comment that humans will always do the right thing in the end, but only when they have tried everything else.

Was does not equal is or will be[42]

Animal and vegetable organism does not change by large and few convulsions, but by small ones and many of them. So for the most part do states and men's opinions.

Samuel Butler in *Samuel Butler's Notebooks*[43]

A major task of critical theory is to confront essentialist thinking about human society. Essentialism is the idea that some phenomena have intrinsic properties, an eternal nature. It is a view contrary to the theme of Carrithers, introduced above, that we are animals with a history, in which 'new relations and new forms of life' are the norm.[44] The struggle against essentialism is a necessary one for a critical theory of security because essentialism is part of the mindset that reifies identities

---

[40] This argument is made with admirable brevity by Allott, 'The Future of the Human Past', pp. 332–5.
[41] Ken Booth, 'The Evolution of Strategic Thinking', in John Baylis, Ken Booth, John Garnett, and Phil Williams, *Contemporary Strategy*, vol. I: *Theories and Concepts* (New York: Holmes and Meier, 1987), p. 30.
[42] This is a reformulation of Yehezkel Dror's warning to strategic studies students, many years ago, against assuming 'Was Equals Is Equals Will Be', in *Crazy States. A Counter Conventional Strategic Problem* (Lexington, Mass: Heath-Lexington Books, 1971), pp. 4–5.
[43] Geoffrey Keynes and Brian Hall (eds.), *Samuel Butler's Notebooks* (London: Jonathan Cape, 1951), p. 127.
[44] Carrithers, *Culture*, pp. 32–3.

and constructs 'false necessities', and so inhibits progressive change. This involves, among other things, unpicking 'presentist' mindsets (that assume static and timeless social conditions),[45] and showing the potential for different sensibilities (including that of world citizenship).[46]

All feminist theorists (except the radical school) challenge assumptions about a fixed female nature. No matter how much the ideal of the mother is honoured in patriarchal society, it is nevertheless another way of keeping her tied to the kitchen and the cot. Those feminist approaches that emphasise material factors have no problems in using the term 'woman',[47] whereas poststructuralists can tie themselves in knots. Gayatri Chakravorty Spivak, for example, while attacking essentialism in general, has also spoken of the need for 'strategic essentialism' when talking of 'woman' or 'Asian', in order to confront the colonial 'Other'.[48] The problem with this approach is that if *you* can ascribe identity to others for 'strategic' reasons, you have no grounds for complaining when others do it to you.

Constructivism (discussed in chapter 4) is one school of thought which has offered a fundamental challenge to all essentialism, arguing in its strongest version that what is taken as reality is constructed by discourse and the ideas that support it: social reality is 'ideas all the way down'.[49] As was noted previously, Wendt's 1992 article ('Anarchy Is what States Make of It: The Social Construction of Power Politics') stands as the reference-point constructivist challenge to the reductive view of neorealists that there is only one logic to anarchy.[50] He later wrote: 'Anarchy as such is an empty vessel and has no intrinsic logic.'[51] In other words, add culture and stir. So, according to Wendt, if the prevailing global

---

[45] A point Carrithers made in the early 1990s with respect to students of anthropology, *ibid.*, pp. 4–11.

[46] Such ideas have been long-lasting in human history, though not prominent in mainstream international relations theorising. Accessible introductions are Derek Heater, *World Citizenship and Government: Cosmopolitan Ideas in the History of Western Political Thought* (Basingstoke: Macmillan, 1996), and *World Citizenship: Cosmopolitan Thinking and its Opponents* (London: Continuum, 2002), and Nigel Dower, *An Introduction to Global Citizenship* (Edinburgh: Edinburgh University Press, 2003); an important debate is Joshua Cohen (ed.), *For Love of Country: Debating the Limits of Patriotism* (Boston: Beacon Books, 1996).

[47] A strong defence of the concept of the female subject – 'woman' – against postmodernism is Alison Assiter, *Enlightened Women. Modernist Feminism in a Postmodern Age* (London: Routledge, 1996), esp. pp. 10–11 and 22.

[48] Gayatri Chakravorty Spivak, *In Other Worlds: Essays in Cultural Politics* (London: Methuen, 1987).

[49] Alexander Wendt, *Social Theory of International Politics* (Cambridge: Cambridge University Press, 1999), pp 92–138.

[50] Wendt, 'Anarchy Is what States Make of It'.   [51] Wendt, *Social Theory*, p. 249.

political culture is Hobbesian, then self-help is the logic; but a Lockean culture would produce a logic of restraint, while a Kantian one would produce a logic of friendship.[52] But the Wendtian approach concedes too much to realism and the agency of states. As was argued in the previous chapter, anarchy is 'made' by many things, not just states, and at several different levels. What about the work done by political economy and gender? And what makes states in the first place? Where do the ideas come from that fill the empty vessel? Are material interests the outcome of ideas, or their source? What would anarchy look like if world society was imbued with cosmopolitan values? Constructivism raises important questions, but does not always answer them, for it does not go all the way down.

To be human is to make meaning

> The construction of meaning aims to understand the past; and the wish to understand – to understand the past as well as the present – is a defining characteristic of humanity . . . Humans fulfil themselves as humans by developing their powers of interpretation. The more they try to understand the world, the more they understand themselves, and the more fully human they are.
>
> Tzvetan Todorov in *Hope and Memory*[53]

The idea that humans create meanings that give shape to their lives is a central theme in constructivism, as it is in anthropology. The anthropologist Conrad Phillip Kottak has written about the complexity of cultural learning, arguing that it depends on the human capacity to think symbolically, 'arbitrarily bestowing meaning on a thing or an event'.[54] Ian Hacking, on similar lines, has described the way ideas exist in a 'matrix' of institutions, other ideas, and complex material infrastructures.[55] In the beginning is biology, but biology alone cannot explain music, or even the amazing variety of manifestations and meanings given to the expression of human sexual needs and wants.[56]

Meaning is created and transmitted through culture, and people absorb their cultures consciously and unconsciously; and aspects

[52] *Ibid.*, pp. 246–312.
[53] Tzvetan Todorov, *Hope and Memory. Lessons from the Twentieth Century* (Princeton, N.J.: Princeton University Press, 2003), p. 123.
[54] Conrad Phillip Kottak, *Mirror for Humanity* (New York: Overture Books, 1996), p. 36.
[55] Ian Hacking, *The Social Construction of What?* (Cambridge, Mass.: Harvard University Press, 2003), pp. 10–11.
[56] Anthropology is a fascinating lens (see, for example, Kottak, *Humanity*, pp. 194–7), as is archaeology: see Timothy Taylor, *The Prehistory of Sex. Four Million Years of Human Sexual Culture* (London: Fourth Estate, 1996).

223

of what they absorb can be maladaptive as well as adaptive.[57] Anthropology does not support the idea that genetic differences explain cultural variation, but prefers explanations relying on a mix of biological, social, and psychological universals, as well as unique contingent and historically situated factors. Cultures tend to seek to replicate attitudes and behaviour, but they do not always succeed; there is scope for creativity, adaptation, diversity, and dissent. Mechanisms of change in human society include 'diffusion, acculturation, independent invention, cultural convergence, and globalisation'. Within security studies, the construction of meaning has been of particular concern for feminist theorists, and especially the way in which genderised meanings have developed and been replicated through tough language and sporting imagery.

Meaning is shaped and organised by language, as well as communicated by it, but language does not have enough explanatory purchase on its own for those who agree with the brain-specialist Susan Greenfield that consciousness exists well outside the text, indeed inside the womb.[58] Once we are born, and have been taught to talk, language both shapes and transmits meanings, but ideas transmitted by language do not go all the way down. There is biology. There would be no idea of 'darkness' if the human eye had been such that it could see equally clearly whatever the degree of 'light'. Similarly, if the average height of the human animal were only a few centimetres, it is doubtful whether the British would have come to regard dogs as 'man's best friend'. Body and mind cannot ultimately be separated.

Among the meanings humans make, those pertaining to morality are of particular relevance to the themes of this book. Mary Midgley has tapped here into Darwin and the idea of morality emerging as a response to natural conflicts of motive, but dependent on the distinctiveness of humans in terms of the capacity for reflection, reflexivity, and speech. By such processes, she has argued that the 'ethical primate' emerged, giving moral meaning to life.[59] The emergence in good shape of the globalised ethical primate following the Great Reckoning requires that more meaning be invested into building world community, while nonetheless seeking freedom (being able to some degree to 'act as a

---

[57] The rest of this paragraph is based on Kottak, *Humanity*, pp. 21–36 (quotation at p. 36).
[58] This is the view, for example, of some brain scientists such as Susan Greenfield; typical of her work is *The Human Brain. A Guided Tour* (London: Weidenfeld and Nicolson, 1997).
[59] Mary Midgley, *The Ethical Primate. Humans, Freedom and Morality* (London: Routledge, 1994).

whole in dealing with . . . conflicting desires'[60]). In the construction of a matrix of such ideas, the balancing of the local and the global will have to be negotiated; the interests of both must be satisfied, in part though not in whole, for the idea of inventing humanity to flourish.

Central to the project of a critical theory of security is the overthrowing of regressive discourses sustaining business-as-usual, and then inventing emancipatory alternatives. In this regard, the orthodox academic discourse of international relations has helped to create, sustain, and deepen the fractured political world of the human species. Its common sense has fixed in people's minds (and so has naturalised) such ideas as the inevitability of war and the impossibility of disarmament. Consequently, the behavioural logic of the states system has pointed to worst-casing the motives and intentions of other states, and acting accordingly.[61] Such a fatalistic mindset predicts an endless round – a timeless present – of strategic competition and collapsed hopes: *Another Bloody Century* as Colin Gray has put it, with characteristic bluntness. It will be so, he argues, because 'The popular fallacy that "war never solves anything", sadly invites the cynical corollary, "nor does peace".'[62] Critical theorists, as well as constructivists, argue to the contrary that if this turns out to be so it is because we keep replicating the ideas that have produced a world that does not work. There is no doubt that it will be *Another Bloody Century* if global society fails to give it a different meaning.

The individual is the ultimate referent

> Each person was originally one particle of Buddha's Light, Light which . . . scattered and came to have its own individuality, so it is important that each particle of light shines with its own unique brilliance.
>
> Ryuho Okawa in *The Essence of Buddha. The Path to Enlightenment*[63]

Politically speaking, individual human beings are primordial in a manner that groupings such as nations and sovereign states are not. I therefore consider individuals logically to be the 'ultimate' referent for thinking about security in a way contingent groups cannot be. Between

[60] *Ibid.*, p. 168.
[61] Ken Booth and Nicholas J. Wheeler, *The Security Dilemma. Fear, Cooperation, and Trust in World Politics* (Basingstoke: Palgrave, 2008), part II.
[62] Note the absence of a question mark in the title: Colin Gray, *Another Bloody Century. Future War* (London: Phoenix, 2006), p. 338.
[63] Ryuho Okawa, *The Essence of Buddha. The Path to Enlightenment* (London: Time Warner, 2002), p. 162.

the one person and the whole species are combinations thrown up by history; important, of course, but not transhistorical. But to recognise the unique light of each individual is not the same as embracing 'individualism' in one's political theory.

The idea of 'individualism' is not primordial. It is a contested theory about individuals. According to Gerard Delanty, contemporary usages of the term include the idea of 'moral individualism' (the individual as a pre-social responsible being), 'collective individualism' (stressing the social nature of the individual), 'autonomy of the self' (where autonomy is not compromised by socialisation), expressivist individualism (anti-political individualism), 'individuation' (the self-reflexive modern individual), and 'personalism' (the collective version of individuation).[64] The conclusion he came to is that social theory has correctly moved beyond a dichotomous view of the individual and community. Community is not something opposed to the individual, according to Delanty; he said (echoing the Zulu concept of *ubuntu*) that 'in collective action the self is enhanced in its identity'. This mutualist conception understands that individuals are generated collectively, and community is generated by multiple selves. In other words, there can be no 'atomistic' individuals, standing alone and apart from the matrix of the structural influences transmitted by relevant relationships. Even Margaret Thatcher, in her famous dismissal of 'society', still recognised that individuals live in the matrix of families. Individuals and groups, especially communities, exist in a mutualist relationship. Individuals do not simply live *in* a community, communities also live in *them*.

Not all those in the Frankfurt tradition would prioritise the individual referent, as I have for many years, but some have, including Horkheimer. Richard Wyn Jones has pointed to the latter's scorn at those who concern themselves with humankind as a whole rather than humans in particular, and to the need to keep in mind that the emancipation of the whole is the means to the emancipation of those who make up the whole.[65] Individual human beings should be regarded as the ultimate referent for a theory and practice of politics (including security) because, as the irreducible units of human society, they are both the start of agency and the litmus test of the health of a society.[66]

---

[64] Gerard Delanty, *Community* (London: Routledge, 2003), pp. 125–30.
[65] Richard Wyn Jones, *Security, Strategy, and Critical Theory* (Boulder, Colo.: Lynne Rienner, 1999), pp. 23–4.
[66] Ken Booth, 'Security and Emancipation', *Review of International Studies,* vol. 17(4), 1991, pp. 313–26.

The thrust of the argument here is not unique to critical theory, nor to Western thinking. Buddhism embraces the idea of the parts of humanity living life in relation to the whole, and that any ideology or theory that neglects the individual self 'will not bear fruit'.[67] In the beginning, individual souls were part of the life form of the Eternal Buddha, and then were split off, becoming one particle of Buddha's Light expected to develop its own character fully, and shine with its own unique light. The search for enlightenment, defined as true 'understanding' (a heightened awareness, knowledge, etc.) is what gives a 'great sense of happiness and strength'.[68] Another interesting non-Western perspective was Gandhi's emphasis on the individual in his reinterpretation of Hinduism.[69] In accordance with traditional Hindu philosophy, Gandhi distinguished between the self and the *ātman*. The self was a person's history, made up of life spans, a unique 'psychological and spiritual constitution', and dispositions inherited at birth. A person was also *ātman*, meaning the cosmic spirit manifested *through* every individual. The self was the basis of individuality for Gandhi: it defined a person's path and was the basis of freedom. Freedom was essential because each person was the 'sole architect of his self and uniquely responsible for his actions'; people saw and came to terms with the world in their own ways. In Gandhi's moral theory individual 'selves created the spiritual civil society and provided the principle of differentiation and freedom, whereas the *ātman* created the spiritual state and furnished the overarching framework of order'.[70] On the face of it, this is a radically individualistic view of human society, but Gandhi challenged the idea of individuality as the ultimate reality. The highest goal in his view was to attain *moksha*, 'to become one with or dissolve oneself into the cosmic spirit'. The key point in this discussion, however, is to underline a transcultural recognition of the uniqueness of the self in the context of its being part, along with every living being, of human collectivities.

While recognising that humans must live collective lives, McSweeney nevertheless endorsed, from a sociological perspective, the view that individuals, not states, must logically be the ultimate referent in the theory and practice of security. 'It would be absurd', he has written, 'to postulate a subject of security other than people.'[71] Security must 'make sense at the basic level of the individual human being for it to make

---

[67] These comments are based on Okawa, *Buddha*, pp. 162–3.   [68] *Ibid.*, p. 163.
[69] Bhikhu Parekh, *Gandhi's Political Philosophy. A Critical Examination* (Basingstoke: Palgrave Macmillan, 1989), pp. 85–109.
[70] *Ibid.*, p. 94.   [71] McSweeney, *Security*, p. 33.

sense at the international level'.[72] The phrase to 'make sense' here has several strands: it is related to the idea that the term 'security' derives its meaning from the need to protect human values, that these values give legitimacy and power to the mobilisation of resources in the name of security, and that states exist as the means not the end of security.

Reality is holistic

Another race is only an other, strolling
on the far side of our skin, badged with his weather.
> Carol Rumens, 'Outside Oswiecim'[73]

In everyday language, holism is the recognition that the whole is more than the sum of the parts. This was an important feature in Horkheimer's thinking when he helped invent critical theory.[74] He argued that we can only understand complex social systems in their entirety, and not simply in terms of their component elements.[75] Consequently, he logically advocated an interdisciplinary approach to knowledge. Such an approach has long been favoured by social scientists and philosophers interested in positive peace. In the 1970s, for example, Falk and Kim stressed the importance of a holistic approach to understanding the multifaceted phenomenon of the 'war system', and the philosopher Mary Midgley has long criticised the atomistic and reductive explanations in much modern science, and the negative impact this has had.[76] I support such approaches, and in this sense this book is at the opposite end of the spectrum to the 'parsimony' so valued by neorealists in their attempt to explain the interactions of states.[77] It is appropriate in the discussion of the transcendental dimension of the framework to emphasise the importance of embracing holistic approaches in understanding human society.

Reductionism is not always to be shunned, however. Visits to dentists are a reminder of what can be achieved by reductionist methods that focus on relieving a specific problem. But in other (most?) health-related areas, reductionism can be dysfunctional or counter-productive. Moving from a single tooth to a whole being, Western medicine has come to

---

[72] *Ibid.*, p. 16.
[73] Carol Rumens, *Thinking of Skins. New and Selected Poems* (Newcastle upon Tyne: Bloodaxe Books, 1993), pp. 87–90.
[74] Horkheimer, 'Critical Theory', p. 208.   [75] *Ibid.*
[76] Richard A. Falk and Samuel S. Kim, 'General Introduction', in *The War System. An Interdisciplinary Approach* (Boulder, Colo.: Westview, 1980), pp. 1–12; and Mary Midgley, *The Myths We Live By* (London: Routledge, 2003).
[77] The key reference is Kenneth N. Waltz, *Theory of International Politics* (New York: Random House, 1979), pp. 1–17.

accept (in theory if not regularly in practice) the desirability of understanding 'the whole person' and not simply focusing on specific pain in a specific location. Similarly, there is a growing acceptance that understanding the natural world requires more than focusing on its separate flora and fauna. The way in which formerly sceptical scientists now give much greater respect and recognition to James Lovelock's metaphor of Gaia is one such notable development.[78]

A critical theory of security must challenge parsimony and reductionism within the study of international relations, even at the risk of being criticised for presuming to offer a theory of everything. Within the mainstream, successive writers have attempted to find *the* answer to world politics, whether it is in anarchy, power, decision-making, language, human nature or whatever. In doing so, they leave much out in the name of parsimony and simplify through their reductive explanations. There have been many critics of such approaches. One, John Peterson, concluded that 'international politics is too important to leave so much of it unexplained in the name of theoretical elegance and artifice'.[79] Nonetheless, the *efficiency* of reductive explanations remains attractive to many scholars. A different take on the unhelpful character of reductive moves has been the flourishing of reductive binary oppositions. In chapter 4, I referred to the West/Rest problem, but no reductionism has been more regressive than *the idea of* the self/Other binary. This ultimate either/or separation of people reifies in a manner that is neither empirically justifiable, psychologically persuasive, nor politically constructive. It is the grammar that leads to the concentration camp. Carol Rumens, in contrast, in the lines of the poem quoted above, gave credit to human *anotherness* – what I call the I-that-is-another in all of us – in contrast to the fashionable reductive binary of separation. In the Rumens image there is no reifying of learned difference (self/Other) but rather the embedding of interconnectedness (I-that-is-another). The latter is the grammar of hyphenated commonality, not the imposed slash of necessary difference.

---

[78] Mary Midgley, 'Individualism and the Concept of Gaia', in Ken Booth, Tim Dunne, and Michael Cox (eds.), *How Might We Live? Global Ethics in a New Century* (Cambridge: Cambridge University Press, 2001), pp. 29–44.
[79] John Peterson, 'In Defence of Inelegance: IR Theory and Transatlantic Practice', *International Relations*, vol. 20(1), 2006, p. 20; see also Cynthia Enloe, 'Margins, Silences and Bottom Rungs: How to Overcome the Underestimation of Power in the Study of International Relations', in Steve Smith, Ken Booth, and Marysia Zalewski (eds.), *International Theory: Positivism and Beyond* (Cambridge: Cambridge University Press, 1996), pp. 186–202.

The organisation of key themes in this book (being/knowing/doing) is a small example of the general problem of reductionism. In the spirit of holism I should not have split the three areas, and instead should have emphasised their interrelationships, as in: one's doing shapes one's ideas about being ('The University of Life'); one's assumptions about being shapes what one considers to be knowledge ('believing is seeing'); what one knows shapes what one does ('there is nothing so practical as a good theory'); and so it goes, in a continuous feed-back loop.

A holistic perspective on human society is necessary for a theory of world security to develop effectively. Today, to a greater or lesser extent, we all live global lives. The global economy reshapes the conditions of existence, whether it is logging in the Amazon basin, growing a crop of mangetout in Kenya for European supermarkets, or learning English in order to work in an outsourced call-centre in India. Global political issues have local consequences, as the victims of terror and counter-terror have found since 9/11, whether in the United States, Indonesia, or Spain. And many people choose to live their local lives globally, through responsible environmentalism or expressions of solidarity to distant strangers.[80] In chapter 10 I will describe a direct action taken by four 'Ploughshares Women' in support of international law and all-human solidarity against statist norms. The efforts of these four ordinary (but extraordinary) women to change a government's policy and raise public consciousness, bring about disarmament, promote human rights, and encourage a sense of common humanity, represent a huge step away from the parsimony of traditional security studies and the reductionism of state-centrism. But their action is a symbol of why rethinking security should favour holism over reductionism, as well as representing what they called 'seeds of hope'.

Pure theory

> The fool doth think he is wise, but the wise man knows himself to be a fool. Touchstone (a clown), *As You Like It*, Act V, Scene I

Previous chapters have shown some of the problems of acquiring knowledge. Its accumulation and transmission is a priority for a critical theory of security, not for its own sake, but as Horkheimer argued in 1937 in

---

[80] On the difficulties of assuming global duties when the 'emotional distance' between people of different societies is 'so great', see Andrew Linklater, 'Distant Suffering and Cosmopolitan Obligations', *International Politics*, vol. 44(1), 2007, pp. 19–36.

order to advance emancipation. For this end, the following eight propositions, deriving from the pearl-beds of critical global theorising, provide a framework for an emancipatory approach to epistemology.

Truth is indispensable yet inaccessible

If God held all truth concealed in his right hand, and in his left hand the persistent striving for the truth . . . and should say, 'Choose!' I should humbly bow before his left hand and say, 'Father, give me striving. For pure truth is for thee alone.'   Gotthold Lessing[81]

As sixth-form grammar school boys many years ago, we were asked to consider Pilate's question: '*What is truth?*' Francis Bacon, the object of our study, guessed that Pilate was 'jesting', and famously recorded that he would not stay for an answer.[82] Academics, unlike Roman officials (but like 1950s grammar school boys) must always stay for an answer, even knowing that those available will be endlessly contested. Some answers reject the very idea of truth; others claim to have found it. The truth is that truth is both inaccessible and indispensable; it is as indispensable to liars as it is inaccessible for truth-seekers. Roger Scruton put it very well: 'The man who tells you truth does not exist is asking you not to believe him. So don't.'[83]

The difficulties just alluded to can be clarified by the familiar distinction between a conception of Truth that is objective and forever unknowable – though not to an omniscient being (should she, he, or it exist) – and a conception of truth that is intersubjective and historical, and in principle accessible. This separation of a transcendent Truth and daily truth was Gandhi's view, as it was Lessing's.[84] Like Lessing, students of CSS will take the left-hand path, putting to one side Truth with a capital T and instead striving for the best daily truths on offer about the understandings of reality of less-than-omniscient humans, the emancipatory validity of particular knowledge, and what might be meant by 'living in truth' politically (an issue to be discussed in chapter 10).

A well-established approach to thinking about truth is to identify its main theories. There are four in particular: the *correspondence* theory (the

---

[81] Felipe Fernández-Armesto, *Truth. A History and a Guide for the Perplexed* (London: Black Swan Books, 1998), p. vii.
[82] Francis Bacon, 'On Truth', in *The Essays*, ed. John Pitcher (London: Penguin, 1985), p. 61; the adjective *jesting* was added by Bacon.
[83] As quoted in Fernández-Armesto, *Truth*, p. 203.
[84] Glyn Richards, *The Philosophy of Gandhi* (Richmond, Surrey: Curzon Press, 1995), p. 2 and ch. 1.

idea that there is a correspondence between a proposition and the facts, such as 'the European Union contains twenty-five members'); the *coherence* theory (the idea that a proposition is made up of mutually verifying propositions, such as 'states pursue their national interests'); the *consensus* theory (the idea that what is true is what may be intersubjectively believed, such as 'war is an inevitable feature of international politics'); and the *pragmatic* theory (the idea that what is true is useful, such as the idea that 'liberal democratic states are a recipe for peace'). Only the first of these makes a real claim to reality, and all are contestable from different points of view.[85] These theories do not stop the jesting, but a theory of security must.

Among the many contributions to the debate about truth, one I find particularly useful was elaborated in the final book of the philosopher Bernard Williams. His *Truth and Truthfulness. An Essay in Genealogy* was conceived as a response to Nietzsche's criticism that a lack of 'historical sense is the hereditary defect of philosophers', together with a lack of the virtue of modesty.[86] Williams sought to intervene in the 'truth wars' that have torn the humanities and social sciences over recent decades, and to do so flying a flag seeking to affirm the importance of truth and truthfulness, but in a non-dogmatic manner. For him, truth is neither an ideological position, as claimed by those he called 'deniers of truth',[87] nor merely the obvious facts of those he called the 'commonsense party'.[88] Truth is neither divine nor relative; it is both difficult to define and out there. It has to be.

'Deniers of truth', the targets of Williams' book, are the purveyors of various forms of scepticism and relativism, together with postmodernism. Richard Rorty's 'liberal irony' was a particular object of attack. Williams strongly rejected Rorty's assertions about truth being what your contemporaries let you get away with, and that with God dead intellectuals needed to invent metaphysical fictions such as truth.[89] Williams believed the consequences of the intellectual uncertainty about truth to be profound – whether it arose from suspicion, being sceptical, the desire of not wanting to be fooled, or the wish not to be seen to be naïve. In Williams' view, the voguish denial of truth (which began long

---

[85] The following introductions are recommended: Paul Horwich, *Truth* (Oxford: Oxford University Press, 1990); Fernandez-Armesto, *Truth*, pp. 217–22; Bernard Williams, *Truth and Truthfulness: An Essay in Genealogy* (Princeton, N.J.: Princeton University Press, 2002); and Simon Blackburn, *Truth. A Guide for the Perplexed* (London: Penguin, 2006).
[86] Williams, *Truth and Truthfulness*.
[87] *Ibid.*, pp. 5–7.   [88] *Ibid.*, pp. 6–7.   [89] *Ibid.*, pp. 4, 147–8.

before the label 'postmodern' made such issues more public and fashionable) has been a threat to the humanities and social sciences, and to political life.[90] Of course, history shows that dictatorial passion for one true Truth has often been even more of a threat.

Williams offered his readers a genealogy of truthfulness, an approach that would have been applauded by both Nietzsche and Horkheimer for its attempt to situate theorising about truthfulness in a historical context. His main thesis, beginning 'in the State of Nature story',[91] focused on the two virtues of truthfulness, 'Sincerity' and 'Accuracy' (capitalised by Williams to show their special significance).[92] He claimed that these virtues have been essential throughout history for any group whose members had to communicate with each other, for without them effective communication would be impossible, and without that society would not work. Both virtues rely on a notion of truth, and therefore truth is an indispensable concept. Accuracy for Williams accords precisely with traditional academic virtues, such as seeking the best evidence, dealing with it impartially and logically, giving respect to alternative opinions and evidence, and so on. Sincerity means saying what one really believes as opposed to engaging in deception. Among other things, his truthfulness thesis is a challenge to the 'deniers of truth' because if they deny it they immediately undermine their own claims to sincerity and accuracy when, for example, claiming to be unmasking power. These virtues of truthfulness for Williams were not relative (indeed they are the conditions for human sociality) but his non dogmatic view of truth means that what different people understand to be true can be different. Two historians, for example, might both approach the evidence with Accuracy and Sincerity, but they might well conclude the truth of the matter to be different; indeed, inventing disagreement is almost their professional duty.

Truth, inaccessible as it is in an absolute form, is the indispensable condition of truthfulness, and without the latter's virtues society is impossible. In the late eighteenth century, in the face of prejudice, superstition, dogma, and arbitrary uses of power, the task facing the *philosophes*, as Bronner described it, 'was not the discovery of absolute truth but the establishment of conditions in which truth might be pursued'.[93] It has been those very anchorages of Enlightenment thinking – democracy, liberty, emancipation – which, among other things, have allowed

---

[90] *Ibid.*, pp. 1–19, 206–32. [91] *Ibid.*, pp. 41–62. [92] *Ibid.*, pp. 123–48, 172–205.
[93] Stephen Eric Bronner, *Reclaiming the Enlightenment. Towards a Radical Engagement* (New York: Columbia University Press, 2004) p. 29.

today's exemplars of those Francis Bacon called 'discoursing wits' to exercise their freedom to attack the very values that established the conditions that have allowed them to pursue their own criticisms.[94] The Enlightenment always has the last smile at its detracting discoursing wits.[95]

> ### An anchorage is the securest basis for knowledge
>
> That it is a bad thing to be tortured and starved, humiliated or hurt is not an opinion: it is a fact. That it is better for people to be loved and attended to, rather than hated or neglected, is again a plain fact, not a matter of opinion.
>
> Geoffrey Warnock in *Contemporary Moral Philosophy*[96]

Human society, as Allott argued earlier, exists within a matrix of is-sentences, and also through a maze of metaphors (there is another!). Sometimes metaphors are expressive, sometimes fanciful. Midgley is one philosopher who has exposed the problems metaphors can lead to, being particularly critical of the way science and philosophy have been pervaded by metaphors that owe more to gender and indeed misogyny than real thought.[97] Certain sciences are regarded as 'hard', she points out, and others as 'soft'. Why? For Midgley, the answer lies in gender. The philosopher of science Ian Hacking has criticised the overflow (another!) of metaphors, arguing that the metaphor of 'social construction', which once had 'shock value', is now tired.[98] One can say 'hear, hear!' to that in international relations. And critics of the project of international *development* have regularly attacked that beguiling metaphor. Gustavo Esteva has put the point forcefully: 'for two-thirds of the people on earth, the positive meaning of the word "development" . . . is a reminder of what they are not . . . [and] . . . To escape from it, they need to be enslaved to others' experiences and dreams.'[99]

A particularly persistent metaphor in theories of international relations since the 1980s comes from the world of builders and building: 'foundations'. At first sight, the debate between 'foundational' and 'antifoundational' positions is a simple issue. The foundational position is that our beliefs about the world can be tested against 'grounds' that may

[94] Bacon, *Essays*, p. 61.
[95] See, for example, John Gray, 'Beyond Good and Evil', *New Statesman*, 19 June 2006.
[96] Geoffrey Warnock, *Contemporary Moral Philosophy* (London: Macmillan, 1967), p. 60.
[97] Midgley, *Myths*, esp. pp. 88–95.
[98] Hacking, *Social Construction*, pp. 35–62 (quotation at p. 35).
[99] Gustavo Esteva, 'Development', in Wolfgang Sachs (ed.), *The Development Dictionary. A Guide to Knowledge as Power* (London: Zed Books, 1992), pp. 6–25 (quotation at p. 10).

be considered neutral, objective, incontrovertible, Archimedean, final, and so on. Such foundations might be the result of scientific discoveries ('laws'), or the revelations of God ('faith'). In these cases, then, truth claims (observations and beliefs) can be judged right or wrong, true or false because *foundations* exist on which all theories can be judged, regardless of time and place. The anti-foundational position regards knowledge about the human world (at least) as contextual, consonant with the words Brecht gave Galileo, quoted in chapter 5.

There are at least two good reasons why students of security should not get hung up on resolving this particular meta-theoretical argument. First, it can be side-stepped in the interests of living in society. It is not necessary for people to share beliefs at a meta-theory level in order to agree on how to behave towards each other. In other words, we do not have to harmonise about the origins of life or the purpose of the universe in order to believe in the desirability of the rules of diplomacy or the virtues of modest personal behaviour. This important argument will be elaborated in chapter 10. Second, it is possible (and helpful) to reject the either/or manner in which the problem is framed (foundational/anti-foundational) by incorporating elements of both and changing the metaphor – from foundations to *anchorages*.

An anchorage is a helpful metaphor for the knowledge that emerges from such a dialogue. An anchorage represents the best resting place in a dynamic environment, but one that is subject to change. Anchorages will shift in the course of a ship being at sea (a nicely ambiguous metaphor for the course of history), and they represent the most secure points contingently available to assess where we have come from and where we might head next. Anchorages for knowledge do not allow the settling of ultimate answers, but they do give the opportunity for asking the big questions (as far as possible at the time) about directions for thinking about what is real, what we can know, and what might we do. They provide the conditions for Accuracy and Sincerity discussed earlier [100] An anchorage in the sense used here echoes Karl Popper's 'falsifiability' thesis; that is, while I cannot prove that a particular set of social ideas (an anchorage) is universally valid – 'love' and 'hospitality' are in principle disprovable as guides to living – they hold until it can be definitively shown that there are better ones.[101]

---

[100] This is discussed further in Ken Booth, 'Dare Not to Know: International Relations Theory Versus the Future', in Ken Booth and Steve Smith (eds.), *International Relations Theory Today* (Cambridge: Polity, 1995), pp. 328–50.
[101] Karl R. Popper, *The Logic of Scientific Discovery* (London: Hutchinson, 1959).

While rejecting the idea of ultimate/objective/neutral foundations for knowledge, it does not follow that anything goes. Some ideas, historically invented and first nurtured in particular locations, have travelled well through space and time. This is why, to use W. B. Gallie's phrase, it is possible to have 'time-transcending dialogues' with great thinkers, and why some literature crosses cultures and centuries. This book is such a dialogue, with the body of ideas represented by critical global theorising; and its aim is to contribute to constructing an anchorage for a critical theory of security. One important anthropological anchorage on which this journey depends is Geoffrey Warnock's list of 'plain' facts listed in the quotation at the head of the section. Thinking about the earlier discussion about the distinction between emotions and feelings, I believe that the idea of love (a feeling) is not basic to being human (like the need for food or the emotion of fear). Love, rather, was an invention in the human story, somewhere and at some time on our evolutionary path, but one that has become so universally and deeply embedded in what it means to be a human being that it can be regarded as a fact not an opinion. Feelings like love, and needs like eating, have manifold cultural and historical manifestations, but taken together, Warnock's list represents an anchorage that is so secure that its items can be described as universal social facts. Consequently, at this point in history, it can be used to get our bearings for promoting and discussing human rights; what he identified are universal social facts beyond mere 'interpretations' or 'opinions' or 'perspectives' or 'stories' – the limp standpoints of Williams' deniers of truth. Warnock's social facts are the anthropological anchorage of my belief in the possibility and desirability of universal values.

Critical distance is truer than objectivity

> to think or reason comes to be, like every other employment, a particular business, which is carried on by a very few people.
>
> Adam Smith[102]

'Only a mindless person is objective' commented the nineteenth-century German historian Johann G. Droysen.[103] On the same theme, but marginally less confrontational to some colleagues, the Holocaust historian Yehuda Bauer commented: 'objectivism is basically uninteresting,

---

[102] Quoted by Roy Porter, *Enlightenment. Britain and the Creation of the Modern World* (London: Allen Lane, 2000), p. 87.
[103] Quoted by Yehuda Bauer, *Rethinking the Holocaust* (New Haven, Conn.: Yale University Press, 2002), p. 2.

because it reflects the chaos of an infinite chain of events, a chaos that in itself has no meaning'.[104] Yet despite such criticisms, the urge to believe in a notion of objectivity is strong.[105] Whether one is a juror or a scientist, the idea of being able to deliver a verdict that is detached/neutral/value-free is appealing; it is an opportunity to appear god-like: 'above it all' in the common phrase. An apparent *via media* between this aspiration and Droysen's put-down is to argue, like Thomas Nagel, that objectivity has degrees; we can all recognise that the standpoint of morality, as Nagel says, is less objective than the standpoint of physics.[106] But this is flawed reasoning, a categorical mistake. Objectivity is like pregnancy, not defined by degrees but by condition. Better than Nagel's suggestion is to drop the idea of 'objectivity' and replace it with the intellectually more honest idea of critical distance. This view is in line with the spirit of critical theory. In traditional theory (understood in the Horkheimerian sense) the observer/scientist/theorist seeks the goal of objectivity (being detached/neutral/value-free), but critical theory argues that this goal is impossible, and that theorists of the social world, seeking to describe and explain that world, cannot escape the contexts in which and from which they observe.

The idea of attempting to achieve a degree of critical distance (a phrase that nicely combines both the critical spirit and its operational practice) is to step back from one's context ('moments' in 'concrete historical circumstances' was Horkheimer's description), while realising that one is not stepping onto neutral ground, an Archimedean point, from which to describe and observe matters of interest. While the aim of critical distance shares the aims of objectivity (trying to free oneself from biases and so on) it recognises what is possible and what is not, and in that sense begins from a categorically different place.

Observers may attempt to put distance between their interested eye and interesting phenomena, but their gaze, however detached, and however much critical distance is achieved, does not transcend their lived lives. It would be 'mindless', to use Droysen's phrase, to imagine for example that humans are capable of writing objective history, for history must be re-written in the light of new knowledge, changing ideas, contemporary concerns, and the individual gaze of differently situated observers. Things change. One decade's heretical explanation might be

---

[104] *Ibid.*
[105] Blackburn, *Truth*, is an attempt to mediate between the 'relativist' and absolutist on such matters; see, for example, pp. xiii–xxi.
[106] This is discussed in Midgley, *Myths*, pp. 24–6, 39–41.

the consensus of the next. It is in such changeability that the ideas of anchorages and critical distance have purchase. They are the promising sites for thought between what Bauer calls 'the traps of mindless objectivism, a solipsistic subjectivism, and an endless relativization of facts'.[107]

'Traditional intellectuals' in Gramsci's conception seek objectivity, but in so doing pull the wool over their own eyes as well as everybody else's (albeit sometimes in good faith). Gramsci's 'organic' intellectuals are more self-conscious, though Bronner has rightly warned that their relationship to a party or a cause means that they risk losing their 'critical' edge; their role is therefore somewhat 'contradictory'.[108] Organic intellectuals face similar challenges to embedded journalists. To claim objectivity in the observation of the social world reveals a lack of self-understanding: therefore beware those claiming to be objective – they are likely to be the least so. Similarly, beware those who complain about people who bring 'emotion' into scholarship. Emotion is a problem if it interferes with academic virtues (respect for evidence, logic, etc.) but emotion should never be discounted in the sincere pursuit of accuracy. One thing we should have learned from the history of the past two centuries is that humans cannot live by reason alone; the emotions are not only unavoidable, they have functions.[109] To take pride in being unemotional in the face of global human wrongs is actually a form of emotion, and a strange one at that. Those who propound such views (claimants of objectivity and deniers of emotion) are not usually dissembling, but they do always lack critical distance in relation to themselves as theorists.

Knowledge has interests

Every fact is already a theory.   Goethe[110]

Richard Ashley first introduced the work of Habermas to students of international relations in the early 1980s (see chapter 2).[111] His particular concern was to explain the major contribution Habermas had made to critical thinking through his identification of three 'knowledge-constitutive interests'. For Habermas, humankind had three a priori

---

[107] Bauer, *Holocaust*, p. 2.   [108] Bronner, *Reclaiming*, p. 75.
[109] Antonio Damasio, *Descartes' Error. Emotion, Reason and the Human Brain* (London: Vintage Books, 2006), esp. pp. 191–6.
[110] Quoted by Bauer, *Holocaust*, p. 2.
[111] Richard K. Ashley, 'Political Realism and Human Interests', *International Studies Quarterly*, vol. 25(2), 1981, pp. 204–36.

interests in its organisation of knowledge: technical interests (empirical-analytical knowledge concerned with control and prediction in the material world – the domain of the natural sciences), practical interests (historical-hermeneutic knowledge concerned with meaning and understanding in the intersubjective world – the domain of history), and emancipatory interests (what is needed for self-conscious human development as opposed to simply existing – the domain of critical theory).[112]

Following quickly after Ashley, Robert Cox gave the idea of interests of knowledge a Gramscian twist (not to mention much greater accessibility) with his argument (chapter 2) that 'theory is always *for* someone and *for* some purpose'. For Cox there was 'no such thing as theory in itself, divorced from a standpoint in time and space. When any theory so represents itself, it is the more important to examine it as ideology, and to lay bare its concealed perspective.'[113] One's perspective does not have to be concealed, of course, as is evident in Enloe's explicit 'feminist curiosity' and Tickner's 'feminist knowledge' (see chapter 2).

If theories are 'always *for* someone' or '*for* some purpose', who or what is security theory *for*? To put it another way: if we know our historian by his facts, our feminist by her curiosity, do we know our security theorists by their referents? The practical and normative consequences of the choice of referent are critical. During the apartheid years in South Africa, for example, *state* or *national* security stood in direct contrast to the daily harm suffered by the overwhelming majority of the population. What was called 'national security' referred to the security only of one of South Africa's 'nations', that of the white minority, which had long been the most powerful.[114] While the white tribe dominated – as long as *its* national security was paramount – there was permanent insecurity for most of the rest the country's population. In such a situation, where the security of the (apartheid) state stood in direct opposition to the security of most people(s) who lived within it, which referent should be privileged? The choice was normative before it was practical.

To say that knowledge has interests and that theory is *for* someone or some purpose suggests that the relationship between facts and values is conceived differently to that presumed by traditional theory. Critical

---

[112] Jürgen Habermas, *Knowledge and Human Interests*, trans. J. Viertel (London: Heinemann, 1974).
[113] Robert Cox, 'Social Forces', *Millennium*, vol. 10(2), 1981, p. 128.
[114] Peter Vale, *Security and Politics in South Africa. The Regional Dimension* (Boulder, Colo.: Lynne Rienner, 2003), is a critical analysis of the situation during and after apartheid.

realists Patomäki and Wight have written: 'although facts are not merely values and vice-versa, they are mutually implicating. Facts are always value-laden . . . [and] if facts are always . . . value-laden, then values must in a sense be factually embedded.'[115] Thus the facts in chapter 1 giving evidence of a world that is not working are value-laden, while the values implied by Warnock's moral philosophy discussed earlier are factually embedded. The mutual implicating of facts and values results in different theories producing their own pictures of human society, and own versions of common sense. 'Power rolls out of the barrel of a gun' says the materialist, and 'The poor will always be with us' is the excuse of the conservative for being indifferent to poverty.

For Gramsci people have various 'conceptions of the world' which are imposed, absorbed passively, or are socialised from the past. Importantly, they are 'lived uncritically'.[116] This was his conceptualisation of 'common sense', and he argued that many elements in popular common sense contribute to people being willing to be subordinated in their lives, because such a mindset made situations of inequality and oppression appear to them to be natural and unchangeable. In everyday language common sense refers to what is considered to be a sound and practical approach to a problem, or a well-established understanding of an aspect of life. But for Gramsci common sense was Coxian, always '*for* someone and *for* some purpose', and not always negative. Common sense can contain elements of truth as well as misrepresentation, and it is on these contradictions that he argued that leverage might be obtained in a 'struggle for political hegemonies': his hope was that Marxist ideas would enter people's common sense, giving them a more critical understanding of their own situation. One does not have to agree with his politics to appreciate his insight into the political nature of common sense; or to accept the conclusion that, just like discourses and structures of power, some versions of common sense are more in the human interest than others.

Power and knowledge are related, though not simply

The only way of enjoying freedom of the press is to own one.

George Bernard Shaw (attrib.)[117]

---

[115] Patomäki and Wight, 'After Postpositivism', p. 234.
[116] Antonio Gramsci, *Selections from the Prison Notebooks*, ed. and trans. Quintin Hoare and Geoffrey Nowell Smith (London: Lawrence and Wishart, 1971), pp. 5–23, 323–77, esp. pp. 5–7, 9–10, 56, 97.
[117] Quoted in Brian Barry, *Why Social Justice Matters* (Cambridge: Polity, 2005), p. 235.

Although the idea of the relationship between power and knowledge is often seen to be a poststructuralist insight, different dimensions of it have been well understood for a long time. Plato asked us to think about the relationship between power and conceptions of justice, Gramsci's notion of common sense is all about power and knowledge, the intimate relationship between the two was central to Horkheimer's argument that knowledge derives from context, and E. H. Carr stressed the synergy between morality, law, and power.[118] Poststructuralists later delivered similar themes. For Foucault, notably, the production of truth was the result of political processes. Truth and power are therefore mutually dependent, though they are not the same; power/knowledge is in a 'circular relation'.[119] He wrote that the goal of his work had not been to analyse 'the phenomena of power, nor to elaborate the foundations of such an analysis',[120] so critics have argued that his analysis fails to explain how to enter the 'circular relations' of power/truth. Where does it all begin? Materialist analyses of power do give an answer, even if one disagrees with it; the circular relationship is broken into by the primacy of the material.

Power rolls out of the mouths of men, as well as the barrels of guns, and it is now better realised how language, concepts, and ideas are embedded in power, and help to perpetuate it (Gramsci's notions of hegemony and common sense). Some students of international relations in the 1980s, not necessarily neo-Gramscians, became increasingly familiar with the concept of 'discourse'. In everyday language, this refers to the verbal interaction between people, but in social science it took on a more complex meaning, referring to the framework of language (including definitions, images, rhetorical devices, metaphors, and so on) that makes, creates, and sustains a particular view that legitimises and rei-fies it – that makes it, in a sense, real. A discourse is revealed in a text, which again normally refers to something written, but in the technical sense was broadened to mean anything that could be 'read'. Television and film became text. As discourses are embedded, so is their power

---

[118] Ken Booth, Tim Dunne, and Michael Cox, 'Introduction', in Booth *et al.*, *How Might We Live?*, p. 4.
[119] The phrase is Foucault's: see Michel Foucault, *Power/Knowledge: Selected Interviews with Other Writings, 1972–1977*, ed. and trans. Colin Gordon *et al.* (Brighton: Harvester Press, 1980) pp. 131–3; also Paul Rainbow (ed.), *The Foucault Reader. An Introduction to Foucault's Thought* (London: Penguin, 1991), pp. 51–75, esp. pp. 74–5.
[120] Quoted in Rainbow, *The Foucault Reader*, p. 7. Foucault made this remark in 1982, referring to the previous twenty years, the period when he had been most productive and innovative.

to structure behaviour. They become 'regimes of truth' in Foucault's well-known phrase, upholding inequalities and oppressions.

These brief comments on power/knowledge have several important implications for students of security. First, not all 'regimes of truth' can be allowed to be equal; some are more emancipatory than others. One criticism of realism as a regime of truth is that it privileges certain interests over others, and the latter are then silenced or made invisible. Two, if knowledge becomes reduced to power in the international realm, power gets to explain everything. If that becomes the case, 'power' becomes a truism that explains everything and therefore nothing. Three, if we accept that there is a relationship between power and knowledge, a critical approach must seek to help give voice to the voiceless. This was a project gender theorists undertook on behalf of women, largely successfully (though there is a long way to go). Certain referents and issues are not only silent (or silenced) in most academic international relations texts. Race, for example, remains a largely under-explored dimension of the discipline (see chapter 8). Four, the knowledge/power relationship is one reason why we need a concept of truth, for without it power is the only arbiter. Finally, the challenge for a critical theory of security in these discussions, as everywhere, is to seek to uncover the sources of power in particular contexts, and what work it is doing, for without this, emancipatory realism will not advance in the realm of politics.

Problem-solving theory replicates, critical theory emancipates

theory never aims simply at an increase of knowledge as such. Its goal is man's emancipation from slavery.

Max Horkheimer in 'Traditional and Critical Theory'[121]

Robert Cox's important distinction between 'problem-solving' and 'critical theory' was signposted in Chapter 2.[122] What Cox did was bring together his own Gramscian-based insights with ideas from Horkheimer's seminal 1937 essay, although, as stated earlier, there is no evidence that Cox at that point was aware of Horkheimer's critical/traditional distinction.[123]

---

[121] Horkheimer, 'Traditional and Critical Theory', p. 246.
[122] Robert W. Cox, 'Social Forces, States and World Orders: Beyond International Relations Theory', *Millennium: Journal of International Studies*, vol. 10(2), 1981, pp. 126–55 (quotations at pp. 128–9).
[123] Note that it was pointed out in chapter 2 that Robert Cox did not cite the influence of the work of the Frankfurt school in his own important essays in the early 1980s: see Wyn Jones, *Security*, p. 3.

242

Problem-solving theory works inside a particular framework of ideas, accepting and replicating it, whereas critical theory stands outside (which gives the possibility of critical distance, never objectivity). According to Cox, problem-solving theories take 'prevailing social and power relationships and the institutions into which they are organised, as the given framework for action'. Critical theory, in contrast, calls those relationships and institutions into question 'by concerning itself with their origins and how and whether they might be in the process of changing'. It is directed towards 'an appraisal of the very framework for action, or problematic, which problem-solving theory accepts as its parameters'. Problem-solving theory, he said,

> takes the world as it finds it, with the prevailing social and power relationships and the institutions into which they are organized, as the given framework for action. The general aim of problem solving is to make these relationships and institutions work smoothly by dealing effectively with particular sources of trouble . . . the general pattern of institutions and relationships is not called into question.[124]

In short, problem-solving theory replicates, whereas critical theory in its analytical and political orientation is rooted in emancipatory possibilities.

By accepting and working inside existing parameters, problem-solving theory tends to perpetuate the status quo. Insider-theorising does not call existing practices or institutions into question; instead, it is calculated to make the institutions of the prevailing social order work more effectively. It legitimises as well as replicates the status quo, and over time makes patterns of social relations seem part of the natural order of things. In such ways, humans keep in power social orders that oppress. For Horkheimer, capitalism was a particularly oppressive order, one in which 'men by their own toil keep in existence a reality which enslaves them in ever greater degree'.[125]

It is a pity that Cox was not familiar with Horkheimer's work when he chose to contrast his conception of critical theory with what he called 'problem-solving' rather than what Horkheimer had called 'traditional' theory. Cox's labelling has played into the hands of those wanting to diminish critical theory by claiming it to be idealistic, not interested in solving problems. In reality, though, the very opposite is the case,

---

[124] Robert W. Cox and Timothy J. Sinclair, *Approaches to World Order* (Cambridge: Cambridge University Press, 1996), p. 88.
[125] Horkheimer, *Critical Theory*, p. 213.

with critical theory (both Horkheimerian and Coxian) being infused by the idea that struggling to make a better world should be what politics is all about. Although Cox chose a label that gave rhetorical advantage to his critics, his view was that critical theory has both technical and practical interests, and is a guide for strategic action to bring about a better world order; its knowledge-interest is solving problems, through tactical or strategic action for emancipatory purposes.[126]

In mainstream international relations realism defines the 'what' and the 'how', and does so in a way that reproduces particular global regimes of problems. By constituting identities, attitudes, and behaviour in particular ways, problem-solving realism actually reproduces the problems it seeks to solve. In contrast (see chapter 2) critical theory seeks to go beyond problem-solving *within* the status quo, and instead seeks to engage with the problem *of* the status quo. Meeting this challenge is the focus of parts III and IV of this book.

Positivism is problematic, empirical enquiry critical

> The 'facts which our senses present to us' are 'socially performed' in two ways: 'through the historical character of the object perceived and through the historical character of the perceiving organ. Both are not simply natural, they are shaped by human activity.'
>
> Max Horkheimer in 'Traditional and Critical Theory'[127]

Major cracks started appearing in the positivist hegemony in academic international relations in the 1980s, and interest grew in the so-called post-positivist turn. The CSS project has been seen as part of this turn, though for reasons discussed in chapter 2 it is the role of *naturalism* (the view that traditional science's methods of observation can yield objective knowledge in the study of human society) rather than *positivism* that is being questioned.

The methods of 'positivism' in accessing the social world, as has already been mentioned on several occasions, have been contentious. Following decades in which the scientific method had been introduced uncritically into many fields, Horkheimer's famous 1937 essay directly challenged the idea that just because the nature of the world was such that everything belonged to the world of nature, it did not therefore

---

[126] Cox, 'Social Forces', p. 130; see also Mark Hoffman, 'Critical Theory and the Inter-Paradigm Debate', *Millennium*, vol. 16(2), 1987, pp. 237–8.
[127] Horkheimer, 'Traditional and Critical Theory', pp. 200–1.

follow that everything could be studied in the same scientific way; in particular, he challenged the idea that the methods thought appropriate for studying the physical world were equally appropriate for studying the social.[128] Despite such challenges, positivism remained a dominant approach in the study of the social world, and it remains influential, especially in those schools of international thought straining for science.[129]

Although contested, the term positivism is being used in this book as generally synonymous with the attempt to employ the scientific method in the study of international relations. In Steve Smith's well-known (but not uncontroversial)[130] account of this issue, he identified four main assumptions of positivism: a belief in the unity of science ('naturalism' – the assumption that the natural world and the social world can be analysed by the same or similar methods); the belief that there is a clear distinction between facts and values ('objectivism' – the assumption that observers can escape their subjective positions and discover objective facts); the belief in regularities in the social world (and so the possibility of the discovery of laws in human social behaviour comparable with those discovered in nature); and the belief that the test of validation or falsification of any proposition is by appealing to the objective facts that have been discovered ('empiricism').[131] Whether or not this picture of positivism accords with that understood by those who call themselves positivists is not the main issue at this point. I am here concerned with the elements in the bottle rather than what is on the label.

In challenging naturalism, critical theory does not reject the idea of truth, deny all facts, refrain from trying to explain the real world, or reject empirical enquiry, or even, in their place, eschew positivist methods. To the contrary, critical theory engages with all these matters. For Horkheimer, practical activity entailed accumulating, analysing, and categorising knowledge. Modern societies need knowledge, he emphasised, and he accepted that established positivist methods – for all his criticisms – could sometimes yield it; he did not advocate throwing the (empirical) baby out with the (traditional theory) bath-water. After

---

[128] These issues are discussed in a sophisticated yet accessible way in Martin Hollis, *The Philosophy of Social Science. An Introduction* (Cambridge: Cambridge University Press, 1994).
[129] An invaluable though often indigestible overview of the relevant debates is Carlsnaes et al., *Handbook of International Relations*.
[130] See Wight, 'Philosophy', pp. 36–8.   [131] *Ibid.*, pp. 11–44 (esp. pp. 14–18).

all, critical theory was committed to understanding society in order to change it. A cautious and differentiated approach to the elements of positivism, evident in Horkheimer's seminal essay, is one with which Midgley has identified. In the course of writing numerous books, she has rejected the rampant version of positivism, with its claims to a universal criterion of science, and instead advocated a plurality of methods, each appropriate to its own task.[132]

Midgley's pragmatic approach to knowledge-gathering fits easily with John Searle's image of there being one world with many realities.[133] To access this world, critical theorists reject the 'incommensurability thesis',[134] which rules out the possibility of sensible conversations between different world-views or paradigms, because this undermines their ability to engage in critique. Instead, there is a constant rubbing together of abstract and concrete in the manner of Gris, in order to sharpen critique in the interests of better reconstruction. The assumptions and ideas of 'critical realism' are sympathetic with much of this discussion, including the view that there is something 'out there' independent of our perceptions (philosophical but not political realism), that reasons are causes, that the ideas and actions of actors are part of the constitution of reality, that agents and structures are mutually implicated, that theoretical accounts are part of reality until they are falsified (but that they do not exhaust what is real), and that epistemological relativism and rational judgement are compatible.[135] There is an 'out there' which can only be engaged through the theories 'in here', but what is in our minds is only part of reality, never its whole.

A critical theory of security is therefore empirical without being empiricist. It is interested in the reality of what is experienced, but does not believe that all knowledge is verifiable by experience. Accessing the real in the social world is not amenable to the same methods as those involved in accessing the natural world, but that is not a reason for not trying, as systematically and with as much critical distance as possible.

---

[132] Mary Midgley, *Myths*; and among earlier works, see especially *Wisdom, Information and Wonder: What is Knowledge For?* (London: Routledge, 1989).

[133] John Searle, *The Construction of Social Reality* (London: Allen Lane, 1995).

[134] Ole Wæver offers a postmodern solution to the problem in 'The Rise and Fall of the Inter-Paradigm Debate', in Smith *et al.*, *International Theory*, pp. 170–4.

[135] A case for critical realism is made by Colin Wight, 'Incommensurability and Cross Paradigm Communication in International Relations Theory: What's the Frequency Kenneth?', *Millennium*, vol. 25(2), 1996, pp. 291–319; Patomäki and Wight, 'After Postpositivism', pp. 231–7; and Heikki Patomäki, *After International Relations. Critical Realism and the (Re)Construction of World Politics* (London: Routledge, 2001).

Theory is constitutive

> 'But Gertrude doesn't look like that.'
> 'She will. She will.'   Picasso to a friend[136]

Powerful theories, like great art, shape how people see reality; and how one sees reality affects how one decides to act. At the start of the last century, Picasso painted an arresting (non-naturalistic) sculptural portrait of the writer Gertrude Stein, herself an experimentalist. One of her friends was horror-struck, and is supposed to have made the remark just quoted. But Picasso was right and her friend was wrong. Gertrude Stein is fixed in our minds as Picasso, not nature, made her. I used this story at the beginning of the 1980s to try to show how international society can reorder its images of reality as a result of the collective legitimisation of different practices. My argument was that the oceans were being 'territorialised' by the evolving network of legal rules, state interests, and maritime practices, and in particular the way in which the evolving law of the sea would constitute a different reality. Warships would increasingly become lawships, and the distinction between national control over land and sea would not be drawn so literally at the waterfront. In other words, a different conception of maritime space would, through different practices resulting from the changing legal regime, cause us to look at it in a new way.[137] The argument was a little premature, as maritime space does not yet look like that; but it will, it will.

In the mid-1990s, Steve Smith argued that the divide between those who believed that theories explained behaviour and those who believed they constituted behaviour represented 'the main meta-theoretical issue' facing international relations theory.[138] 'At base', he said, 'this boils down to a difference over what the social world is like; is it to be seen as scientists think of the "natural" world, that is to say as something outside of our theories, or is the social world what we make it?' The latter is obviously consonant with the idea that what we make of security is derivative of particular political theories. The Gramscian notion of common sense has already been discussed, and the way descriptions

---

[136] Ken Booth, *Law, Force and Diplomacy at Sea* (London: George Allen and Unwin, 1985), p. 37.
[137] *Ibid.*
[138] Steve Smith, 'The Self-Images of a Discipline: A Genealogy of International Relations Theory', in Booth and Smith, *International Relations Theory*, pp. 26–8; for a criticism of this perspective, see Wight, 'Philosophy', p. 37.

of the world merge into prescriptions through legitimising and naturalising certain ideas about human society: 'the poor will always be with us' and 'man is innately aggressive', for example. If societies are socialised to think it natural that some people are bound to be poor, and that men are itching to fight, then such behaviours will be endlessly replicated. If people act as if something is natural (or otherwise true), they will make it so. If, on the other hand, societies are organised in ways that regard such behaviours as unnatural and ethically abhorrent then what becomes politically desirable and feasible will change accordingly. The promise of emancipation will replace the replication of traditional problems.

These arguments are relevant to the role realist theory played during the Cold War: did it simply explain superpower behaviour, or did it help create the situation in the first place? The answer is complex. Typical Cold War strategies are explicable according to realist ideas, but those strategies in the first place had been thought through and implemented (*constituted*) by policymakers whose professional convictions and political world-view had been created by realist thinking (especially the idea of the balance of power). Realism as an explanatory theory claims that 'states act out of their interests'; realism understood as a constitutive theory argues that 'states are constructed as interest-maximising units'. What purport to be descriptions for the purpose of explanation merge into prescriptions for the purpose of policy relevance. The *is* becomes an *ought*. 'States are the main actors in world affairs' is both a factual statement within realism but also a prescriptivist statement suggesting that rational behaviour ought to be organised around the fact. This ambiguity is evident in the writing of the great philosopher of war, Carl von Clausewitz. When he gave his account of what he thought to be the 'true nature of war' (as rational, instrumental, and national)[139] there was a less than clear-cut distinction between what he thought he was describing (fact) and what he thought ought logically to be done (prescription).

Theories of world affairs can constitute and explain in a powerful partnership, and with a tradition as old as realism it is impossible to discern whether intuitive practices led to explanatory thinking (a posteriori) or whether prescription came a priori. At this point it is too late to matter, but theorists must try to be clear in their own minds whether

[139] This was Anatol Rapoport's characterisation; see Carl von Clausewitz, *On War*, ed. with an introduction by Anatol Rapoport (Harmondsworth: Pelican Books, 1968), esp. pp. 13–15. These issues are discussed at more length in chapter 7.

their *ought* is pushing the *is* in their descriptions; in other words, whether their explanations are really disguised prescriptions. This, in my view, is what has invariably happened in accounts of the world according to realism: it is prescriptivism veiled as positivism. Much international history, moreover, is a continuation of realism with an admixture of dates. Critical theory has no such difficulties, however, because of its breaking down of the fact/value distinction, the theory/practice nexus, the subject/object relationship, and the emancipatory purpose of knowledge. It is to the latter I finally turn.

Practical theory

Every new idea has something of the pain and peril of childbirth about it.

It seems to me that all tools resolve themselves into the hammer and the lever, and that the lever is only an inverted hammer or the hammer only an inverted lever whichever one wills. Samuel Butler[140]

The ideas that follow are emancipatory realism's functional equivalent of the 'logic of anarchy' in political realism; but no more than the latter can they comprise a recipe book for political projects. Actions not only speak louder than words, they are more difficult to bring about. In this respect emancipatory realism has both disadvantages and advantages over traditional realism. In important respects, operationalising emancipatory realism is more difficult, because it runs counter to the prevailing statist culture globally; but in other respects it is easier, because it represents an approach to world politics in which every one of us can engage. Those drawn to the idea of common humanity and world security do not have to wait for our political leaders to pronounce and strategise; in our different ways and contexts we can all practise cosmopolitan values or pursue egalitarian goals or promote sustainable lifestyles. Individually, we obviously do not have the agency of a government, and it is easy to be deterred by the enormity of the challenge; but we all have some space (talking to friends, choosing research topics, supporting particular charities, etc.), and we do not depend on our Foreign Ministers or political leaders in order to act as agents of common humanity. The challenge is to start to embody Gandhi's injunction to try to become the change we want to see in the world. I will take up this theme again in chapter 10.

[140] Butler, in *Samuel Butler's Notebooks*, pp. 230 and 123.

This is not the best of all possible worlds

man can change reality, and the necessary conditions for such change
already exist.

Max Horkheimer in 'Traditional and Critical Theory'[141]

A sound basis for philosophy-by-doing is the idea of immanent critique,
introduced in chapter 2. This, to recap, is the idea that situations have
within them possibilities of a better life; there is unfulfilled potential
in all situations. In this regard, Horkheimer's critique of the social and
economic order he faced was not based upon a blueprint of an ideal
model of society, but rather on the potential he identified within the
actually existing order.[142] Immanent critique involves identifying those
features within concrete situations (such as positive dynamics, agents,
key struggles) that have emancipatory possibilities, and then working
through the politics (tactics and strategies) to strengthen them. Emancipation is a politics of careful calculation as well as of hope.

It has been the idea of tragedy rather than hope, however, that has
attracted mainstream international relations theorists.[143] In the shadow
of two world wars, innumerable international crises, and a world-
threatening Cold War, this is hardly surprising. The influential and
regressive myth of tragedy will be discussed in chapter 10. It is rare
for students of international politics to come across (or be encouraged
to!) such scholars as Kenneth Boulding, who tried in his work to persuade us that there are resources for hope and that the global glass is
half full.[144] In *Stable Peace* (1978) he pointed out that more differences
of opinion in the world are settled daily by negotiation than by violence, yet the species' self-image as portrayed by specialists in international relations is doggedly conflictual. Boulding reminded us that
good things exist in society, and are therefore 'possible'; this was his
distinctive interpretation of the immanent potential in the world. *Really*
look around, he was saying, and think and hope; good things have been
achieved, so let us do it again. At different times and in different places
there has been predictable peace between states, reconciliation between

[141] Horkheimer, 'Traditional and Critical Theory', p. 227.   [142] *Ibid.*, p. 213.

[143] Note, for example, the importance given to the concept by John Mearsheimer, *The Tragedy of Great Power Politics* (New York: W. W. Norton, 2001), and Richard Ned Lebow, *The Tragic Vision of Politics. Ethics, Interests and Orders* (Cambridge: Cambridge University Press, 2003).

[144] Notably, Kenneth E. Boulding, *Stable Peace* (Austin: University of Texas Press, 1978); see also *Beyond Economics: Essays on Society, Religion and Ethics* (Ann Arbor: University of Michigan Press, 1965), and *Faces of Power* (Newbury Park, Calif.: Sage, 1989).

former enemies, harmonious co-existence between peoples of different religions and races, the pursuit and achievement of social justice, the development of security communities on a regional level with embedded trust, the pursuit of common security, successful conflict prevention and resolution, and many people have come to identify themselves as global citizens. A world that does not work for countless millions, with regressive and fatalistic views about our species, is not the best of all possible worlds. Tyranny, racism, hyper-nationalism, imperialism, and economic injustice are political choices made yesterday, manifest today. They do not have to be tomorrow's drumbeat.

A better world is a process not an end-point

I will issue a few revolutionary proclamations to the peoples of the world and then shut up shop.
Trotsky, first Commissar of Foreign Affairs, USSR[145]

The vision of Leon Trotsky in 1917 reflects a misbegotten view of history, though it is one to which some are prone in moments of triumphalism.[146] It was a similar mindset, but at a liberal-capitalist moment of triumph, that led Francis Fukuyama to announce 'the end of history' seven decades later.[147] History was another shop that did not shut. In this section, I want to emphasise world politics as *process*, not blueprint or end-point.

In a critique of the 'static' theory of nuclear deterrence, Joseph Nye made a useful distinction in the mid-1980s between what he called 'process' and 'end-point' utopian approaches.[148] This insight led to a rejection of the idea of pressing too strongly for particular long-term structures that might deliver security, and instead he advocated concentrating on those processes that seem to increase the chances that

[145] Quoted in Kurt London, *The Soviet Union; A Half-century of Communism: Papers* (Baltimore, Md.: Johns Hopkins University Press, 1968), pp. 335–6.
[146] What happened next in the Soviet Union was told with verve by Adam B. Ulam, *Expansion and Coexistence: The History of Soviet Foreign Policy, 1917–67* (London: Secker and Warburg, 1968), pp. 26–206.
[147] Francis Fukuyama, *The End of History and the Last Man* (London: Hamish Hamilton, 1992).
[148] Joseph S. Nye Jr, 'The Long-Term Future of Deterrence', in Roman Kolkowicz (ed.), *The Logic of Nuclear Terror* (Boston: Allen and Unwin, 1987), pp. 245–7. I used this as a central theme in relation to the security situation in Europe in the Cold War: see Ken Booth, *Steps Towards Stable Peace in Europe. A Theory and Practice of Co-existence* (Department of International Politics, University College of Wales, Aberystwyth: International Politics Research Papers, no. 4, 1988), pp. 9–10; later published in *International Affairs*, vol. 66(1), 1990, pp. 17–45.

we will reach nearer plateaux rather than the furthest mountain tops. Most utopian visions, according to Nye, point to distant horizons, and contain within them a sense that the particular journey will one day be completed. Illustrations of such thinking are the end-point utopian visions of general and comprehensive disarmament, world government, permanent peace, the final victory of communism, or the end of history. On the day these end-points are achieved, it is believed that politics as struggle stops, and is replaced by administration and management.

Instead of concentrating on such distant, controversial, and radical visions, the process-utopian approach focuses on progressive yet pragmatic processes that are not driven by a particular institutional blueprint, but rather by goals animated by progressive principles. Nye defined process utopias as benign or pacific trends, with the end-point being uncertain. The process utopian takes modest, reformist steps in order to make a better world somewhat more probable for future generations. What exactly that better world will look like must be settled by those future generations, when the concrete possibilities are clearer in the always changing context. We cannot now see far enough ahead to design institutions that will be appropriate for a century hence, but we can identify benign and peaceful principles to live by. It is especially futile to try to over-manage the long-term future in an era of rapid change. One generation must seek to establish progressive principles and benign conditions for the next, with the hope that if we look after the processes, the structures will look after themselves.

Politics is never an end-point, and to think it is courts disappointment, failure, and a reputation for foolishness. Such thinking also discourages planning for the day after the end of history. In other words, what should be done when the shop has to be reopened? We know very well the embattled history of the Soviet Union following the failure of world revolution after 1917. We also know the trouble caused by the neocon vision that developed in the United States following the end of the Cold War, which culminated in the disaster of the war against Iraq. Even in the latter the endism mindset of Trotsky and Fukuyama was evident in the planning of the White House for the war. Insufficient thought was given to what would happen after the military victory against Iraq's weak conventional forces. Teleology triumphed over strategy. The assumption was that military victory/regime change/democracy/peace and prosperity would follow in quick order. History did not end with military victory in Baghdad in 2003, no more than it did in Berlin in 1989 or in Moscow in 1917; it went into fast-forward.

No perfect society has yet been made, nor will ever be, but choices exist at all levels to construct the conditions for better possibilities. Together, a notion of the ideal and a calculation of immanent potentials are integral to political programmes for creating such conditions. At the same time, proponents of ideals and progress need to be able to defend themselves against all the usual charges levelled against 'utopian' thinking, ranging from naïveté to totalitarianism.[149] One piece of practical theory whose implementation will resist many of the usual charges is a commitment to the unity of progressive means and ends.

Means are ends

You're the good guys. You should act like it.

Laurie, elite Washington hooker[150]

Successful policymaking requires not just imagining a different world, but having the hands-on practical skills to turn hopes into agendas, effective policies, and institutions. Praxis has been emphasised throughout the book, and I want to deal with it here in relation to a historic debate in Western political philosophy (not to mention everyday life) about the relationship between ends and means. The themes in the arguments below are relevant to every one of us, whether we are members of the UN Security Council or leaders of transnational corporations, heads of state, or concerned citizens. If we share the political orientation of emancipatory realism, we must attempt to practise 'non-dualism' with respect to ends and means.[151]

A critical-theory perspective on means and ends must engage with the debate provoked by Theodor Adorno and Max Horkheimer about the contradictory tendencies of 'enlightenment'. Reason was supposed to free humans from what Kant had called our 'self-incurred immaturity', but in *Dialectic of Enlightenment* Adorno and Horkeimer argued that reason, when it degenerates into 'instrumental reason', can also imprison us. It does this by turning everything into an object to be subjugated. Ends justify means in a remorseless logic, which results in decision-makers operating independently of moral constraints. For Adorno and

---

[149] John Carey (ed.), *The Faber Book of Utopias* (London: Faber and Faber, 1999), is a rich anthology of utopias, with a generally sceptical 'Introduction' by the editor: 'What they build may . . . carry within it its own potential for crushing or limiting human life' (p. xi).
[150] Said to Sam and Josh: *The West Wing*, season 1, episode 10, 'In Excelsis Deo'.
[151] This draws heavily on an unpublished paper I presented at the Theological Consultation on Interrogating and Redefining Power, World Council of Churches, Crêt Bérard, Switzerland, December 2003, entitled 'Reasons of Power and Powers of Reason: Some Reflections from International Politics'.

Horkheimer, the goal of Enlightenment philosophy had been to liberate society, but it had instead created a totalitarianism marked by a tyranny of instrumental reason. They focused on the remorseless logic by which humans exerted their power over nature, with the result that nature came to be seen merely as a resource to be exploited. Such an attitude not only destroyed that which humans depended upon, but it also resulted in humans becoming alienated.[152] This form of instrumental reason did not promote the spirit of enlightenment, but created the conditions for its monster opposite.

The danger of such instrumental reason is familiar in international politics. 'Groupthink' has played a part in the failures and fiascos of decision-makers over the years, marked by the development of policies in which self-righteous ends were thought to justify the most terrible of means. Group dynamics can drown the voice of conscience, as well as banish wisdom.[153] The leaders of the superpowers in the Cold War believed they had the right to threaten nuclear catastrophe across the planet to promote their own national interests. At the same time, members of their military–industrial–academic complexes became so task-focused that they ignored the wider ethical contexts of what they were doing – replaying the roles of the blinkered bureaucrats constituting the 'Architects of Annihilation' in Nazi Germany. Lifton and Markusen described such individual and group psychological dynamics as part of a 'genocidal mentality'.[154] Instrumental reason turns people into cogs in genocidal machines and policies – Mutual Assured Destruction for example – without them fully appreciating what is happening. Thus eager engineers and striving social scientists transmute into 'Eichmanns of Armageddon'.[155]

---

[152] Theodor W. Adorno and Max Horkheimer, *Dialectic of Enlightenment*, trans. John Cumming (London: Verso, 1997; 1st pub. 1944); see also the lesser-known work by Max Horkheimer, *Eclipse of Reason* (New York: Continuum, 1974), in which he shows the ascendance of reason in Western philosophy, and its 'paradoxical nature'.

[153] Irving L. Janis, *Victims of Groupthink. A Psychological Study of Foreign Policy Decisions and Fiascos* (Boston: Houghton Mifflin, 1972); see also Ralph K. White, *Nobody Wanted War: Misperception in Vietnam and Other Wars* (Garden City, N.Y.: Doubleday, 1968).

[154] R. J. Lifton and E. Markusen, *The Genocidal Mentality: The Nazi Holocaust and the Nuclear Threat* (New York: Basic Books, 1990), esp. pp. 3, 16–50, 77–97, 192–279.

[155] I first used this phrase in 'Human Wrongs and International Relations', *International Affairs*, vol. 71(1), 1995, p. 109. Chilling support is given in Götz Aly and Susanne Heim, *Architects of Annihilation. Auschwitz and the Logic of Destruction*, trans. Allan Blunden (London: Phoenix, 2002), and Lifton and Markusen, *Genocidal Mentality*. There have been many honourable exceptions, of course, as can be seen regularly from the contributors to the invaluable *The Bulletin of the Atomic Scientists*.

The dualistic logic of instrumental reason draws attention to the dangers of separating means and ends. When instrumental reason rules, the 'means' become an instrumental tyranny that threatens to destroy the 'end' sought. Instead of there being an escape from self-incurred immaturity, a new prison is created – what might be called the irrationality of rationality. I am not using 'dualism' here in the sense philosophers use it, to refer to the theory that mind and matter are two distinct things, or in what I understand to be the theological sense, which refers to humans having two basic natures, the physical and the spiritual. By dualism I mean the tendency to interpret ends and means as separate or discrete entities, rather than mutually constitutive. Such a separation is deeply embedded in Western political theory, including the tradition of Machiavelli and Clausewitz. It has also been evident in the realist political thinking of non-Western traditions.[156] The common sense of such an approach is summed up in adages such as 'the ends justify the means' and 'don't will the ends without willing the means'.

Non-dualistic thinking requires that means/ends are true to each other. This is the only way by which fundamental change can be brought about and sustained. Dualism always threatens to replicate old ways. If, for example, those who want to create a radically new world attempt to do it through the employment of traditional strategic action (violence), then success will tend to confirm the lesson that violence is indispensable. Those who succeed by this logic will risk defeat by the same logic. As will be discussed in chapter 10, a better future can never be guaranteed, but it can be the object of rational hope if enough people live in the present in ways that are the equivalent of a better world. This means, on a daily basis and in whatever context one finds oneself, promoting the conditions for greater justice, increased cooperation, and less violence. In other words, a more harmonious world future is realistic if one commits to living in that future by what one does next, to the maximum extent possible in the circumstances. The aim of philosophy is not just to interpret the world, but to change it, but *how* it is changed is central to the meaning of change. Philosophy and politics must work in harmony if instrumental reason is not to exercise its infernal tyranny.

Albert Camus hinted at this general idea by suggesting that the means one uses today shapes the ends one might perhaps reach tomorrow.[157]

---

[156] See, for example, some of the selections in Evan Luard (ed.), *Basic Texts in International Relations* (Houndmills: Macmillan, 1992), ch. 1, 'The Ancient Chinese View'.
[157] Discussed by Stanley Hoffmann, *Duties Beyond Borders: On the Limits and Possibilities of Ethical International Politics* (Syracuse, N.Y.: Syracuse University Press, 1981), p. 197.

Many people know this instinctively in different contexts. For example, if one loves a child unconditionally one might hope that a well-adjusted adult will emerge. It is not guaranteed, but it is a rational hope. In chapter 3 I discussed Gandhi's conceptualisation of the relationship between *ahimsa* (non-violence) and 'Truth', with the former being conceived as the means and the latter as the end. In order to be a 'means', of course, something must be utilisable; but whatever it is, it should be true to the end being sought. Applying this to security and emancipation, the syllogism goes as follows: the practice of security (freeing people from the life-determining conditions of insecurity) seeks to promote emancipatory space (freedom from oppression, and so some opportunity to explore being human), while realising emancipation (becoming more fully human) is to practise security (not against other people, but with them). What this approach does is shift attention from ends at any price (potentially) to means as the goal; in other words, the focus is on the relationship between means and ends in relation to virtue. How should a virtuous person behave? This question is normative not empirical; it concerns the potentiality of human becoming, not fatalism about human nature. It changes the *problematique* into one of applied ethics, along the lines of Aristotle's view that by acting virtuously we become virtuous. Of course, it will always appear more difficult for a government to act virtuously in the ungoverned world of international politics than it is for an individual to pursue virtue ethics in a settled polity, but it is not impossible to move in that direction. The point is that some end might be very distant, but the means that are its equivalent are not; they can be employed at once. In this way, one lives in truth. Some of the practicalities of this approach are discussed at length in chapter 10.

Emancipation is the politics of inventing humanity

> The soft water's movement will conquer the strongest stone, in time.
> Bertholt Brecht, poem recounting the wisdom of the sage Laotse[158]

Students often ask me what I think 'humanity' and 'human' mean when I describe emancipation as the politics of inventing humanity, or as the goal of exploring what it might be to be human. I always answer – to their evident frustration – that it is too soon to say. This frustrating answer rises logically out of my evolutionary approach. What it means to be a human being today (with the exception of the remotest and most

---

[158] This poem was 'like a sacred talisman' for Arendt and those who thought like her, as they sought to survive through 'Dark Times'; Young-Bruehl, *Arendt*, pp. 150–1.

unchanged of indigenous peoples) is unimaginable from the perspective of a member of the species 5,000 years ago, let alone 5.8 million years ago (the latest dating of the earliest identifiable 'human' fossil). Being human is above all being historical, which means that I have no idea of what human beings might become over the coming hundreds never mind millions of years; this is increasingly the case in the context of developments in biotechnology and genetic research – 'playing God' as it is sometimes put, by intruding ever more into biological evolution.[159] The key to human being is consciousness, and human evolution is the evolution of human consciousness.[160] To be human 500 years ago did not involve thinking about putting money in a collection box for earthquake victims thousands of miles away, or writing a letter to a minister in a foreign government about the imprisonment of a poet, teacher, or other individual peacefully following their consciences. This is a way of saying that the answer to the question 'What does it mean to invent humanity?' is in the *exploring* and in the *becoming*; it is living what biology will set free. Consequently, emancipation (as the politics of inventing humanity) involves in the first instance creating the conditions to explore, and this requires the opening up of space through effective security policies to free people from life-determining threats. Security and emancipation are thereby conjoined, together with the idea of progress.

'Progress', Bronner has written, 'is an inherently rational idea.'[161] He then went on to argue, correctly, that if one holds this idea it does not then call for belief in the 'omnipotence of reason, the superfluous character of passion, or the existence of an objective solution to every problem'. He illustrated this from several Enlightenment thinkers, including Paul Friedrich Holbach, an atheist and technology enthusiast. Even this most 'rabid believer in progress' could write that 'it is not given man to know everything; it is not given him to know his origins; it is not given him to penetrate the essence of things or to go back to first principles'. The point, for the *philosophes* – and for Bronner – was not the discovery of 'absolute truth' but the establishment of conditions in which truth might be pursued. Likewise, emancipation is the project of creating conditions for the pursuit of what it might be to be a human being, as opposed to merely being human.

---

[159] Habermas, *Future of Human Nature*, examines the issue of genetic engineering and its ethical implications.
[160] This is a theme of Philip Allott, *Eunomia. New Order for a New World* (Oxford: Oxford University Press, 1990).
[161] Bronner, *Reclaiming*, p. 29.

Without an idea of progress (see chapter 3) there can be no politics of emancipation, and therefore the idea of humanity must remain static – a prisoner of old ideas, traditional practices, and inherited power structures (and their interests). Escaping history in the interests of world security demands the nurturing of cosmopolitan sensibilities, which, in a limited formulation, require no more than living by Kant's injunction regarding hospitality. Cosmopolitanism does not necessarily mean having to *like* everyone on earth.[162] It does, however, demand a commitment to moral cosmopolitanism, the idea of the equal moral concern of every individual, regardless of origins. In a well-known distinction, Charles Beitz separated such moral cosmopolitanism from institutional cosmopolitanism, by which he meant the reshaping of global institutions to allow world citizens to act accordingly; he emphasised that 'Cosmopolitanism about ethics does not necessarily imply cosmopolitanism about institutions.'[163] The essence of the ethics/institutions relationship was explained by Derek Heater. In his view ethical cosmopolitanism seeks to provide 'a moral basis for judging the aptness of particular kinds of institutions for ensuring that the cosmopolitan ethical principle of the equal worth of all human beings as world citizens is honoured in both political theory and practice'.[164]

Universalist ideas such as cosmopolitanism and emancipation have been attacked by communitarians, traditionalists, and others for being (more or less disguised) imperialism, elitism, homogenisation, and the imposing of Western values – and, at the same time, dangerous, impossible, and naïve.[165] Walter Truett Anderson described such attacks – approvingly – as one of the defining features of postmodernism. He wrote: 'the very concept of universality is ... "put into question" ... we're

---

[162] On the meaning of cosmopolitanism, see Chris Brown, *International Relations Theory: New Normative Approaches* (Hemel Hempstead: Harvester Wheatsheaf, 1992); Cohen, *For Love of Country*; Charles R. Beitz, 'International Liberalism and Distributive Justice: A Survey of Recent Thought', *World Politics,* vol. 51(2), 1999, pp. 269–96; Derek Heater, *World Citizenship and Government: Cosmopolitan Ideas in the History of Western Political Thought* (Basingstoke: Macmillan, 1996), and *World Citizenship. Cosmopolitan Thinking and its Opponents* (London: Continuum, 2002); Nigel Dower and John Williams (eds.), *Global Citizenship. A Critical Reader* (Edinburgh: Edinburgh University Press, 2002), and Nigel Dower, *An Introduction to Global Citizenship* (Edinburgh: Edinburgh University Press, 2003).
[163] Beitz, 'International Liberalism', p. 287; see also his *Political Theory and International Relations* (Princeton, N.J.: Princeton University Press, 1979).
[164] Heater, *World Citizenship*, p. 9.
[165] This defence is based on Ken Booth, 'Three Tyrannies', in Tim Dunne and Nicholas J. Wheeler (eds.), *Human Rights in Global Politics* (Cambridge: Cambridge University Press, 1999), pp. 51–64, unless stated otherwise.

all going to have to get used to a world of multiple realities'.[166] By positing 'universalism' and 'multiple realities' as opposites, however, Anderson revealed two familiar postmodern (and postcolonialist) fallacies. First, the assumption that 'universalism' and 'multiple realities' are necessarily in opposition is false; and second, the assumption that universalism is always nasty while the local realities are good flies in the face of the evidence.

Contrary to postmodernist assumptions, universality in practice is necessary to sustain real human diversity (though this is not to say that every idea claiming to be universalist is necessarily benign). One of the negative consequences of allowing anti-universalist attitudes to flourish, and 'difference' to triumph, is the space it leaves for authoritarian localism (of which there is a superabundance) to squash diversity. Universal standards about women's rights, for example, help to introduce and promote diversity into places where otherwise there is oppressive cultural homogeneity enforced by local patriarchal power-brokers.[167] Another illustration is the protection of the way of life of indigenous peoples against homogenising nation-statism. Diversity is better protected (to the extent political and economic power allows it) by the efforts and universal values of global civil society than by governments keen to develop national unity or exploit remote regions for tourism or mineral extraction. The survival of the Bushmen in Botswana, for example, is one such case.[168] Democracies do not have a good record in this regard, when one considers the sad plight of indigenous peoples in Canada and Australia. Against the multiple realities of local cultural and political power, many inhabitants of the planet have to look for solidarity from groups outside committed to universal solidarity. Nelson Mandela has recorded how important expressions of such support were in preventing his fellow prisoners from giving in to 'despair' and keeping hope alive in their 'Long Walk to Freedom' against apartheid.[169] He recorded his appreciation of the role of transnational solidarity against racism in opposing the apartheid regime, noting how 'ordinary folk throughout the world' had participated in protests and had helped shape

[166] Walter Truett Anderson (ed.), *The Fontana Post-modern Reader* (London: Fontana Press, 1995), p. 6.
[167] Julie Peters and Andrea Wolper (eds.), *Women's Rights, Human Rights. International Feminist Perspectives* (New York: Routledge: 1995), esp. 'The Persecuted, The Voiceless', pp. 317–55.
[168] The Survival International website is www.survival-international.org.
[169] Nelson Mandela, *Long Walk to Freedom. The Autobiography of Nelson Mandela* (London: Abacus, 1995), pp. 602–4.

historical facts.[170] It is difficult to avoid the conclusion that the 'nation-state' has been one of history's most effective devices in reducing human diversity; nation-statism homogenises in the name of promoting 'the national interest'.[171]

The problem of living in a world of multiple realities is not as bewildering as Anderson's flawed postmodern binary suggests, though this certainly does not mean that it is easy. Human rights, for all the familiar disputes over particularities, reveal how much actually existing universality there is in the world, including shared understandings of human wrongs and how much value commensurability exists across and within borders between religious, cultural, and other communities.[172] What matters in terms of the promotion of security, emancipation and community globally is not ultimately the psychological fact of multiple realities,[173] but of the potential and capability of agents to construct the political conditions for collective (legitimate) behaviour.[174] Chapter 10 will argue that it is possible for those with quite different meta-theoretical outlooks (an atheist and a believer, for example) to agree on what universally constitutes decent behaviour (such as attending to the poor and respecting the old). Human wrongs are universal, and people often find it easier to recognise these than they do the commensurate rights, but here again is another basis for thinking and acting universally, and reasoning together in the human interest. Agreement about wrongs does not guarantee they will be put right, but it is a step towards rightful action. Universality and multiple realities should not therefore be seen in opposition, but as necessary features of a possible diverse, egalitarian, and just human community of communities.

---

[170] Quoted in *The Guardian*, 13 July 1996: Editorial, 'Change the World'.
[171] Alain Touraine, *Can We Live Together? Equality and Difference*, trans. David Macey (Cambridge: Polity, 2000), sought to negotiate personal life projects for individuals between the pressures of cultural identity and individualist liberalism, in an era when communities increasingly asserted their identities against the power of globalisation. See also, for the external dimensions of nationalism's depredations, Philip Yale Nicholson, *Who Do We Think We Are? Race and Nation in the Modern World* (Armonk: M. E. Sharpe, 1999), and Mark Cocker, *Rivers of Blood, Rivers of Gold. Europe's Conflict with Tribal People* (London: Jonathan Cape, 1998).
[172] This is debated extensively and interestingly by the contributors in Cohen, *Love of Country*, and Dower and Williams, *Global Citizenship*.
[173] See Howard Kirschenbaum and Valerie Land Henderson (eds.), *The Carl Rogers Reader* (London: Constable, 2002), esp. pp. 401–501.
[174] The development of rightful membership and rightful conduct – the dimensions of legitimacy – has never been easy, even in relation to the more modest goal of constructing an international society; the key text here is Ian Clark, *Legitimacy in International Society* (Oxford: Oxford University Press, 2005).

Politics is the sphere of freedom

This purpose can be fulfilled only in a society which has not only the greatest freedom, and therefore a continual antagonism among its members, but also the most precise specification and preservation of the limits of this freedom in order that it can co-exist with the freedom of others.

Kant on 'the highest purpose of nature – i.e. the development of all natural capacities'[175]

Politics is the sphere of freedom, in the view of theorists such as Arendt, and it is achievable – balancing competing needs and wants – through a constitution of the sort envisaged by Kant. For Arendt freedom in the modern world consisted of the restoration of the political dimension to life; this had been eroded, she argued, by pressures of conformity, necessity, and simply coping with things. She thought freedom in the political realm could be restored in part by the way in which everyday life had been freed from the drudgery of the past.[176] In the decades since she wrote those things, there is even less drudgery in the rich world, but the problems of coping with life seem even greater. Freedom in the political realm is still awaiting achievement almost everywhere.

But what does it mean to give freedom to Arendt's *vita activa* and *vita contemplativa*? Nicholas Maxwell has defined freedom, pragmatically, as 'the capacity to achieve what is of value in a range of circumstances',[177] usefully leaving open the question of what is of value. The 'range of circumstances' must include the political structures and processes that allow the balancing of one's own motives and intentions with the condition of living alongside others with their own capacities and values. Because the key is balancing, Bronner has argued that 'freedom will never become fully manifest in reality' – something 'will always be missing'.[178] But the very exercise of restraint in relations with others is itself an exercise of freedom, when done out of duty rather than coercion.

At the base of the idea of politics as the sphere of freedom is freedom of speech. Without freedom of speech, no other freedom is possible: it is the condition of the freedom of religion and every other freedom. Freedom of speech has been much attacked by religious groups claiming that their

---

[175] Immanuel Kant, 'Idea for a Universal History with a Cosmopolitan Purpose', in Hans Reiss (ed.), *Kant's Political Writings* (Cambridge: Cambridge University Press, 1989), p. 45.
[176] Hannah Arendt, *The Human Condition*, Introduction by Margaret Canovan (Chicago: University of Chicago Press, 1998; 1st pub. 1958).
[177] Quoted in Daniel C. Dennett, *Freedom Evolves* (New York: Viking, 2003), p. 302.
[178] Bronner, *Reclaiming*, p. 21.

right not to be 'offended' (a very subjective idea) should always take precedence over the exercise of the freedom of speech of others (even ill-judged free speech). They are mistaken: freedom begins in offending people. Allowing the right to be offended to triumph over the right to offend is a recipe for the triumph of unreason. There is an ironical side to this, though it is lost on the vanguard of the offended. The latter, in the absence of freedom of speech, would not be able in the first place to criticise what they see as the misuse of freedom of speech. Likewise, such irony is lost on those right-on postmodernists who have berated the men of the Enlightenment (anachronistically, because they were of necessity 'men of their time') for ignoring gender. Without the conditions of possibility for a public realm, anchored in the freedom opened up by the Enlightenment, attackers of free speech (sometimes with violence) and critics of enlightenment would not have a platform for their views, or even the very concepts to engage effectively in sophisticated debate. What is more, it is through the public realm that reflexivity can be exercised, and errors rectified – including lapses of good taste (wilful offensiveness) and social blindness (patriarchal traditionalism). 'Where the Enlightenment valued liberty, discursive persuasion, and the critical exercise of reason', Bronner has written, 'the Counter-Enlightenment stood for obedience, coercive authority, and tradition.'[179] Enlightenment opens up the future, at the cost of making mistakes; unenlightenment closes it down, and makes bigger ones.

Global civil society plays a key role in the struggle for the defence of freedom of speech, the meta-freedom and the first line in the battle for all other freedoms. Among its champions for many years has been the *Index on Censorship*.[180] The aim of *Index*, when it was established in 1972, was 'to make public the circumstances of those who are silenced in their own countries, wherever that may be, and publish their work'.[181] Pursuing its goal of protecting freedom of speech responsibly involves many 'troubling questions'. Ursula Owen has identified the threats to free expression as 'religious extremism, relative values and cultural difference, the rise of nationalism, the rewriting of history, words that kill, pornography, violence on television, [and] freedom on the Internet'. Some of these issues include how freedom is used, and she argued that

---

[179] *Ibid.*, pp. 67–8.
[180] See *Index*, monthly, and the collection brought together by W. L. Webb and Rose Bell (eds.), *An Embarrassment of Tyrannies. Twenty-five Years of Index on Censorship* (New York: George Braziller Pub., 1998).
[181] Ursula Owen, 'Preface', *ibid.*, p. 15.

freedoms have been lost by the 'spoilt brats of civilisation' in the West 'when we allow ourselves to be dominated by the mediocrity of media moguls and the bottom line'.[182]

Clearly, errors can be made by proponents of freedom of speech, and offence can be caused unnecessarily, but these are errors of taste, and they never match the dangers threatened by those who claim that their right not to be offended should trump all other rights. Without doubt, one of the main fronts in the struggle for emancipatory world politics in the years to come will focus on free speech, against the cultural forces of relativism on the one hand and the economic power of corporations on the other. Bronner has argued that the 'right to criticism is the precondition for the exercise of autonomy and, if not the pursuit of absolute truth, then the rectification of error'.[183] Key writers of the Enlightenment, he went on, were committed to the idea that 'no age can commit the future to a condition in which it would be impossible to extend knowledge or correct errors'. Thomas Paine in his dedication to the *The Age of Reason* (1794 edition) surely gave the most succinct defence of freedom of speech possible. After saying that he had 'strenuously' supported the right of others to their opinion, 'however different that opinion might be to mine', he then offered the thought: 'He who denies to another this right, makes a slave of himself to his present opinion, because he precludes himself the right of changing it.'[184] In other words, to deny freedom of speech is to deny oneself the right to change one's mind. This, in turn, logically denies other individuals the right to grow and change their minds (demanding that they think what they have 'always' thought or believed); and it denies societies the possibility of progress (for they must reproduce themselves exactly according to the traditionalist and patriarchal mould). The case for freedom of speech does not need more justification. People should therefore be allowed to think and express themselves, freeing themselves of dogma and prejudice and the institutions that sustain them. The corollary of this is that society must develop legal and other institutions both to protect the possibility of freedom of speech, and to mediate between those in society who think differently.[185]

During the New Twenty Years' Crisis, as will be seen in chapter 9, fear has been and will be used politically by governments, and also by

---

[182] *Ibid.*, p. 16. [183] Bronner, *Reclaiming*, p. 67.
[184] Thomas Paine, *The Age of Reason. Being an Investigation of True and Fabulous Theology*, ed. Moncure Daniel Conway (Mineola, N.Y.: Dover, 2004; 1st pub. 1794), p. vii.
[185] See Hume's ideas, discussed in Bronner, *Reclaiming*, p. 140; see also Jonathan Israel, *Enlightenment Contested. Philosophy, Modernity and the Emancipation of Man 1670–1752* (Oxford: Oxford University Press, 2006), pp. 51–60.

religious and other fanatics, to attempt to constrain freedom of speech. Nadine Gordimer, who learned what it is like when freedom of speech is curtailed, working for much of her life under the oppressive conditions of apartheid South Africa, has endorsed the words of Rosa Luxemburg as a motto for all of us: 'Freedom means freedom to those who think differently.'[186] Protecting the right for freedom of speech – which must include the right to offend and be tactless – is the front line in the war on error.[187]

There is nothing so practical as a good theory

Let us drink to the success of our hopeless endeavour.
The toast of Soviet dissidents in the 1970s[188]

I first heard the rolled-up sleeves view that 'there is nothing so practical as a good theory' from a US Navy officer in the early 1970s. At that time, I shared the common (academic) view about the separation of theory and practice, but I soon began to understand the wisdom of his remark, whether the theory related to plumbing a house, planning foreign policy, or engaging in naval diplomacy.

I have already referred to Cox's somewhat unhelpful choice of words when he identified critical theory as something separate from 'problem-solving' theory. I hope I have already said enough to convince sceptics about the central concern of critical global theorising with the problem-solving necessary to construct a better world. The practice of theory in a broad sense converges with the issues discussed earlier in relation to the idea of theory being constitutive: that is, that theories contribute to creating the reality that they then go on to explain.[189] Explanatory theory, where it is influential, is not removed from the reality it describes because it becomes implicated in the replication of associated practices through the causal power of common sense. The fact that theorists and their supporters may not be aware of the work their ideas are doing is only an indicator of their power. In this way, theories are implicated in the practical world whether it is in the form of shaping the thinking of society (students, NGOs, etc.) or the agencies of the state (foreign and

[186] Quoted by Nadine Gordimer, *Living in Hope and History: Notes from Our Century* (London: Bloomsbury, 1999), p. 29.
[187] I first used this term in 'Windsor's World', *International Relations*, vol. 17(4), 2003, p. 508.
[188] Quoted by Owen, 'Preface', p. 15.
[189] Pinar Bilgin, 'Theory/Practice in Critical Approaches to Security: An Opening for Dialogue', *International Politics*, vol. 38(2), 2001, pp. 273–82.

defence ministries).[190] The direction of the Bush presidency in foreign affairs was from the start explained in terms of the neocon world-view (which both constituted and explained the attitudes of the Bush White House). The corollary of the naval officer's adage is that there is nothing so bad as an impractical theory, and the neocon project in foreign affairs has demonstrated this very clearly. While it was still possible for the project's supporters to be evangelical, an unnamed 'senior adviser' to the President told the journalist Ron Suskind that 'we're an empire now, and when we act, we create our own reality . . . We're history's actors, and you, all of you [journalists] will be left to just study what we do.'[191] Indeed.

Theory is implicated in practice through political argument as well as constitutive processes. This can be illustrated from the field of human rights, where the postmodern philosopher Richard Rorty has argued that 'long, sad, sentimental' stories are better foundations on which to base human rights than universalist ideas. This sort of basis for promoting rights has been strongly opposed by the anthropologist Richard A. Wilson. He considered 'emotion and courage' to be 'a very weak defence' of actions, as opposed to rational forms of argument. In his opinion, 'Rights without a metanarrative are like a car without seatbelts; on hitting the first moral bump with ontological implications, the passenger's safety is jeopardised.'[192] This issue will be taken up in chapter 8.

To date, students of security from critical perspectives have been more familiar with engaging with critics at the theoretical than the empirical level. As yet, engagement in the detailed policy analysis and advocacy that has always been at the forefront of the work of mainstream strategic studies has been limited. This is not surprising in the short run, because CSS is a relatively new approach.[193] Even so, there has been more than critics imagine,[194] not least because few critics are aware of the empirical

---

[190] See Jutta Weldes, Mark Laffey, Hugh Gusterson, and Raymond Duvall (eds.), *Cultures of Insecurity: States, Communities and the Production of Danger* (Minneapolis: University of Minnesota Press, 1999). The relationship between academic theorising and foreign policy is not a well-ploughed field; an exception is Alexander L. George, *Bridging the Gap: Theory and Practice in Foreign Policy* (Washington: US Institute of Peace, 1993).
[191] Quoted in Eliot Weinberger, *What Happened Here. Bush Chronicles* (London: Verso, 2006), p. 143.
[192] Richard A. Wilson (ed.), *Human Rights, Culture and Context. Anthropological Perspectives* (London: Pluto, 1987), p. 8.
[193] See the discussion in Wyn Jones, *Security*, pp. 151–3.
[194] Note the debate between William Wallace, 'Truth and Power, Monks and Technocrats: Theory and Practice in International Relations', *Review of International Studies*, vol. 22(3),

work.[195] Proponents of critical theorising about security (mostly) recognise that they must engage with the political agenda of the day if their work is to be taken seriously outside their own circle. The supposed general failure of poststructuralist writing in this regard, together with its general inaccessibility, is one reason why it has not made inroads; works purporting to be about international relations or world politics should not eschew engaging directly with states and weapons and the great issues of war and peace.[196] James E. King, an underappreciated US strategic theorist throughout the Cold War, used to say that if you are going to be academic about anything, you might as well be academic about something important. I share that view, and also what I call the 'Gray test'. I remember Colin Gray once arguing to the effect that the true test of any piece of strategic theorising was what it had to say about nuclear targeting on Moscow. The thrust of his remark did not mean that every piece of work had to be about the circular error probable, though he would have been pleased by even more attention devoted to that particular matter; rather, the thrust of his remark was that one's theorising should allow one to make a sensible contribution to discussions about security in concrete circumstances. I agree with this, and look forward to the engagement of critical scholars with an ever wider range of empirical issues (and especially the great issues of peace and war). I have no time for CSS that refuses to address the military dimensions of world politics.

The engagement of critical security theory with the specific issue of nuclear deterrence moves beyond the insider-theory approach, concerned with immediate policy-oriented issues relating to improving technology and effectiveness in the national interest of one state or another. Instead, it addresses the wider issues raised by prevailing policies in terms of security, emancipation, and community. An outsider-theory critique of the security dimensions of nuclear deterrence focuses, for example, on the balance of risks between nuclear and non-nuclear futures, and the alternatives available to the pursuit of politics by other

---

1996, pp. 301–21; Ken Booth, 'A Reply to Wallace', *Review of International Studies*, vol. 23(3), 1997, pp. 371–7; and Steve Smith, 'Power and Truth: A Reply to William Wallace', *Review of International Studies*, vol. 23(4), 1997, pp. 507–16.

[195] For a start, readers might look at the published work of the PhD students mentioned in the Acknowledgements.

[196] There is a parallel here with Terry Eagleton's disappointment about much contemporary cultural theory, following the path-breaking first generation: 'Those who can, think up feminism or structuralism . . . those who can't, apply such insights to *The Cat in the Hat.'* In Eagleton, *After Theory*, p. 2.

means than the ultimate terror weapon; the emancipatory dimension
focuses on the cultural aspects of reliance on 'nuclearism' and the moral
and psychological aspects relating to the genocidal mentality necessary
to make deterrence work; and the community dimension focuses on
the obstacles to extending we-feelings when there is a mutual threat of
annihilation, and on the contradictions between human rights commitments and nuclear possession. Moving beyond critique, the reconstruction move requires a discussion of the positive benefits to be gained in
terms of security, emancipation, and community through the building
of institutions and processes designed to eliminate the most destructive weaponry ever invented, and to promote law-governed behaviour.
'Nuclear weapons can never be disinvented, of course, but history shows
that military rivalries can be, and when this happens, weapons become
essentially irrelevant.'[197] The politics of reconstruction involves identifying ways of weakening the hold of supporters of the status quo,
strengthening the opposition, and promoting the adoption of sensible
transitional steps.

In contemplating the practice of a critical theory of security on issues
such as nuclear weapons, it is necessary to think in terms of a division
of labour. One individual cannot do everything, so workers on behalf
of critical security theorising must be mutually supportive. Some might
choose to be more theoretical, others more policy-oriented; some might
prefer to engage with policymakers, others with global civil society;
some will concentrate on the near term, others on more distant horizons.
All this work has value, and all add to the collective picture. Speaking
for myself, early on in my academic career I became disillusioned with
engaging with the world of politicians, officials, and military officers,
discovering that power is not interested in truth, only power.[198] Furthermore, it also became obvious that academics cannot compete on issues

---

[197] Ken Booth, 'Debating the Future of Trident: Who Are the Real Realists?' in Ken Booth
and Frank Barnaby (eds.), *The Future of Britain's Nuclear Weapons: Experts Reframe the Debate*
(Oxford: Oxford Research Group, *Current Decisions Report*, March 2006), p. 90. For my
views on the wider assessments of the military, political, cultural, and moral aspects
of nuclear weapons, see, inter alia: 'Nuclear Deterrence and "World War III": How Will
History Judge?' in Kolkowicz, *Logic of Nuclear Terror*, pp. 251–82, and 'Nuclearism, Human
Rights and Constructions of Security' (Parts One and Two), *International Journal of Human
Rights*, vol. 3(2), 1999, pp. 1–24, and vol. 3(3),1999, pp. 44–61.
[198] I wrote briefly about this in Ken Booth, 'Security and self: Reflections of a Fallen Realist',
in Keith Krause and Michael C.Williams (eds.), *Critical Security Studies. Concepts and Cases*
(Minneapolis: University of Minnesota Press, 1977), pp. 83–119, having sadly come to
see the force of Chomsky's verdict on the famous Quaker injunction: Noam Chomsky,
'Speaking Truth to Power?' (from 'Writers and Intellectual Responsibility') in *Peace News*,
May–August 1999, p. 25.

of everyday policy with governments and journalists because of the better access of the latter to the latest information. For most academics, too practical or immediate an involvement with current policy is probably not to be recommended; the relative advantage for the academic is being able to stand outside and take a longer view, to analyse ideas and circumstances in more depth, to invent and circulate ideas, and to disseminate different perspectives through students in the first place and then wider society. In short, by engaging in outsider rather than insider-theorising, by orienting debates to emancipatory rather than replicatory policies, and by serving society rather than the state, critical scholars can attempt to use their knowledge to move beyond helping today's *ancien régime* to dealing with the very problems it has created.

Community is the site of security

the search for community cannot be seen only as a backward-looking rejection of modernity, a hopelessly nostalgic plea for the recovery of something lost; it is an expression of very modern values and of a condition that is central to the experience of life today, which we may call the experience of communicative belonging in an insecure world.
Gerard Delanty in *Community*[199]

The significance of community for an emancipatory theory of security was discussed at length in chapter 3, and needs little further general elaboration. The key point concerns the desirability of the expansion of the moral boundaries of political community.[200] The historical phenomenon of the sovereign state is only one of the forms of political community conceivable, yet for many it has proved to be an oppressive institution internally, demarcating lines between 'citizens' and 'aliens', with all that may mean for rights and obligations, security and insecurity. At the end of the twentieth century there was a revival of older visions of political community and citizenship, with a mix of local communities below the state and ideas of world citizenship and value communities beyond it. Whatever its modality, community is central to the idea of security. Linklater has underlined this by pointing to the absence of safety, rights, and endowments in the case of the refugee: 'The plight of the refugees is a simple reminder that security is inextricably linked with membership of a political community in which all members respect one another and

---

[199] Delanty, *Community*, pp. 186–7.
[200] This is a key theme in all Linklater's work, but see especially *The Transformation of Political Community: Ethical Foundations of the Post-Westphalian Era* (Cambridge: Polity, 1998).

in which all of them have some say in shaping a form of life that they regard as their own.'[201]

Integral to the idea of community, as these words suggest, is respect. In this regard, a distinctive politico-ethical dimension of the Frankfurt tradition has been the notion of 'recognition' developed by Axel Honneth, involving the giving of positive status to an individual or group. He has identified three modes of recognition: emotional support (intimate social relationships such as love or friendship), cognitive respect (rights and legally based recognition as a member of society), and social esteem (accorded to an individual's traits and abilities).[202] Working at every level of recognition are issues relating to democracy and economics.

One of the lacunae in security studies has been economics, and this is especially significant in relation to the building of community. Roger Tooze has written how there have been parallels between orthodox economics and orthodox security studies, in the sense that both seek to take the politics out of their subject matter.[203] In this way, both orthodoxies are classic insider-theorising. They purport to be neutral and technical, objective even, when they are inherently political. Neither orthodoxy is friendly to human society. Within the academic literature of international relations, Thomas Pogge has powerfully underlined this point, showing how we (in the rich world) fail even according to our own principles by preserving the affluence of about one-sixth of the global population at the expense of everybody else.[204] For Tooze, positive movement towards 'real' security, community, and emancipation must be closely bound up with the re-theorisation of international political economics (IPE), which, like realism in politics, has provided a pre-defined notion of its subject matter, and hence what is regarded as legitimate knowledge. This particular conception of economics (resting on the assumptions of the underlying capitalist order) projects an image of being a rational activity (separate from politics), with any problems

[201] Andrew Linklater, 'Political Community and Human Security', in Ken Booth, *Critical Security Studies and World Politics* (Boulder, Colo.: Lynne Rienner, 2005), p. 113.
[202] Axel Honneth, *The Struggle for Recognition. The Moral Grammar of Social Conflicts* (Cambridge: Polity, 1995), ch. 5, 'Patterns of Intersubjective Recognition: Love, Rights, and Solidarity' (see chart at p. 129, and Translator's Note at p. viii); see also his 'The Intellectual Legacy of Critical Theory', in Fred Rush (ed.), *The Cambridge Companion to Critical Theory* (Cambridge: Cambridge University Press, 2004), pp. 336–60.
[203] Roger Tooze, 'The Missing Link: Security, Critical International Political Economy, and Community', in Booth, *Critical Security Studies*, pp. 133–58.
[204] Thomas Pogge, *World Poverty and Human Rights: Cosmopolitan Responsibilities and Reforms* (Cambridge: Polity, 2002).

that arise requiring technical solutions. But Tooze insists that this is not merely a technical matter, for 'economics' is within the 'realm of power', and so of politics. He writes: 'In other words, the claim that economics is non-political is a political claim.'[205] One of the consequences of this, as with orthodox international relations, is a narrow understanding of those who constitute *the* experts: insider-theorists only need apply. Public comment and analysis in most of the media on the economic issues of the day will be done by individuals working for a bank or financial organisation such as NatWest or Morgan Grenfell; these are economists who have been 'socialized'.[206] In the language of this book, they pass the Gray test of having something to say about an important issue of the day, but not the Cox test of exposing the real issues of their time. Without a differently constructed theory and practice of the global economy, it will not be possible to construct the sorts of communities that will serve as the site for security conceived as emancipation.

The relationship between the economic system and community is significant in ensuring not only that radical inequalities do not dangerously erode we-feelings, but also in order to ensure that people have the capability to participate effectively in community life in the first place.[207] An emancipatory community is not possible if individuals lack the ability to act as full members. In this regard, a significant stage in the development of critical theory was Habermas's 'communicative turn', looking to locate emancipatory potential in interaction/communication rather than production/work. By focusing on the spread of communication/community rather than uniting the revolutionary proletariat, Habermas took another important step in distancing the Frankfurt school from it origins in Marxism.[208] For Habermas 'communicative competence' could lead to a rational consensus in political debate (the idea of 'discourse ethics'). This is movement towards the 'dialogic cosmopolitanism' which Linklater has discussed as a means of enlarging the boundaries of community to engage 'non-nationals as equals in open dialogue'.[209] The fact of cultural difference for Linklater

---

[205] Tooze, 'Missing Link', p. 155.   [206] *Ibid.*, p. 144.
[207] This is discussed in chapter 7 in relation to human security and chapter 8 in relation to human capabilities.
[208] The key works were Jürgen Habermas, *The Theory of Communicative Action*, vols. I and II (London: Heinemann, 1984 and Cambridge: Polity, 1987). Two helpful entry points to this difficult writer are William Outhwaite, *Habermas: A Critical Introduction* (Stanford, Calif.: Stanford University Press, 1994), and William Outhwaite (ed.), *The Habermas Reader* (Cambridge: Polity, 1996).
[209] Linklater, *Political Community*, pp. 77–108 (quotation at p. 85).

is not a barrier to 'equal rights of participation within a dialogic community', for rights are universal, not culture-dependent.

The missing link between the idea of a dialogic community and the global realm is the idea of cosmopolitan democracy. The latter seeks to weld together, through dialogue, the global community of communities discussed in chapter 3. Communicative competence cannot be separated from economic and political capability. Constructing a global political reality which gives real expression to such ambitions faces major obstacles, and one of the biggest is the fatalistic assumption that it cannot be done. But then those same people who pour cold water on cosmopolitan democracy would have been the ones in the past who would have said that it was unrealistic to try to create democracies out of *anciens régimes*, or try to build welfare states out of fortresses of class privilege, or try to construct multipurpose and almost universal international organisations out of cockpits of Hobbesian conflict. There was nothing inevitable about such outcomes, but they emerged through struggle. There are no guarantees about cosmopolitan democracy's future. It, too, will be settled through struggle. There is nothing as radical as reality, as has been said several times, and advocates of the idea of cosmopolitan democracy are rising to an old radical challenge.[210]

The aim of cosmopolitan democracy is nothing less than an attempt to create a condition whereby international organisations, transnational corporations, and markets are steadily more accountable to the peoples of the world.[211] Ideas include transforming the present UN into a more democratic and accountable global parliament, establishing regional parliaments across the world, and extending the authority of successful bodies that presently exist such as the EU.[212] Human rights would be embedded in national legal systems and monitored by a new International Court of Human Rights. At the root of cosmopolitan democracy, as was seen in chapter 2, is the belief that if democracy is to succeed locally, it must be achieved globally, and hence must be embedded in

[210] See, for example, David Held, *Democracy and the Global Order: From the Modern State to Global Governance* (Cambridge: Polity, 1995).

[211] See chapter 2: a thought-provoking collection by leading theorists of cosmopolitan democracy is Daniele Archibugi, David Held, and Martin Köhler (eds.), *Re-imagining Political Community. Studies in Cosmopolitan Democracy* (Cambridge: Polity, 1998). See also Daniele Archibugi (ed.), *Debating Cosmopolitics* (London: Verso, 2003). This book contains a very useful survey of the relevant literature: Daniele Archibugi and Mathias Koenig-Archibugi, 'Globalization, Democracy and Cosmopolis: A Bibliographical Essay', pp. 273–91.

[212] See Daniele Archibugi, 'Principles of Cosmopolitan Democracy', in Archibugi *et al.*, *Political Community*, pp. 198–28.

the regimes and norms of global governance. Without a more democratic World Trade Organisation, for example, local democracy will be eroded. As it is, decisions about major aspects of national life, whether employment or health or the economy, are taken outside state boundaries and, as presently configured, the overwhelming proportion of states and people in the world have minuscule influence on key decisions. For global governance – legitimised procedures for political activities across the world – to be effective, there need to be overlapping structures of accountability, both horizontally and vertically; it is these that cosmopolitan democracy attempts to construct.[213] Without accountability at the global level, it will be difficult to sustain it locally.

The critics of cosmopolitan democracy are many. It is easy to attack the idea as utopian and naïve, for the vision is far ahead of the horizons of most of today's politicians and the conventional wisdom of political theorists. Specific criticisms include: the alleged impossibility of democracy above the level of the sovereign state; the unworkability of democracy on a global scale because of the vastness of the project; the absence of a proper 'demos'; and the tension between multiculturalism with its prioritising of group identity and cosmopolitanism with the high value it gives to equality and universality.[214] Such communitarian discontent is predictable, given this most fundamental challenge to its norms and ascendancy through the vision of building new forms of cosmopolitan political community.

There will be no emancipatory community without dialogue, no dialogue without democracy, and under conditions of globalisation democracy-in-one-country will not be sustainable. A critical theory of security requires cosmopolitan democracy to replace sovereign statism as the organising principle for world politics operating across a worldwide community of communities (including 'cosmopolitan states'), characterised by multilevel global governance. Some of the elements of such a world already exist, so it is not unthinkable; and the idea is more in tune with the demands of the times and the needs of world security than the fine words, crocodile tears, and nationalistic/elitist selfishness that characterise today's global business-as-usual. If it were argued that cosmopolitan democracy can 'never be achieved', I would probably agree, if the standard is perfection; I would quickly

---

[213] The key contribution was Held, *Democracy and the Global Order*.

[214] David Miller, 'Bounded Citizenship', in K. Hutchings and R. Dannreuther (eds.), *Cosmopolitan Citizenship* (Basingstoke: Macmillan, 1999). There is a helpful section on the critics in Archibugi and Koenig-Archibugi, 'Bibliographical Essay', pp. 280–2.

add, however, that the Westphalian alternative (against a background of 350 years of war and struggle) is presently characterised by failed states, rogue states, gangster states, the 'dictatorship of the rich', and the rest, while nowhere has democracy-in-one-county reached 'perfection'.

Equality is the condition for humanity

Every civilisation is born of a forgotten mixture, every race is a variety of mixtures that is ignored.   Henri Lopes in *Le Lys et le Flamboyant*[215]

In the Introduction I asserted the centrality of equality in a critical theory of world security. Just as freedom of speech is the bedrock of other freedoms, so equality is the bedrock of all other rights. It is inherent, for example, in emancipatory political processes such as democracy; but equality is complex in theory and difficult in practice. The task below is briefly to clarify the theoretical commitment to equality; chapter 8 will elaborate some of the implications of equality as a political orientation.

Several misunderstandings about the commitment to equality need to be overcome. *First, to pursue equality as a political value is not to oppose liberty*. There is no necessary contradiction between the two, though many ideologues of liberty would claim there is. This was the case with the US diplomat who, in an argument about foreign aid, asserted that the central value for Americans is liberty not the abolition of poverty.[216] In contrast to such views, Étienne Balibar has advocated what he calls *égaliberté* (a neologism possible in French but not in English) which recognises equality and liberty as mutually constitutive conditions for human emancipation. For Balibar this is a matter of concrete historical fact: 'There are no examples of restrictions or suppression of liberties without social inequalities, nor of inequalities without restriction or suppression of liberties.' Consequently, they must advance together.[217] There are difficulties in promoting equality, as Bernard Crick, an English champion of egalitarian principles has written, so it is necessary to be

---

[215] Quoted in Gordimer, *Hope and History*, p. 28; Lopes, a Congolese writer, was writing about mixed blood but also the exchange of ideas in Africa; his point is universal.
[216] Theodore Sumberg, *Foreign Aid as Moral Obligation?* (The Washington Papers, no. 10, 1973), discussed by Stanley Hoffmann, *Duties Beyond Borders. On the Limits and Possibilities of Ethical International Politics* (Syracuse, N.Y.: Syracuse University Press, 1981), p. 153.
[217] This is discussed in Alex Callinicos, *Theories and Narratives. Reflections on the Philosophy of History* (Cambridge: Polity, 1995), pp. 193–5, and *Equality* (Cambridge: Polity, 2000), pp. 22–4.

'thoughtful and careful'; but that is an invitation to try harder, not abandon the attempt.[218]

Second, equality is not synonymous with homogeneity. A common criticism of egalitarian policies is the argument that equality means 'sameness', and so its achievement will take out all the colour and interest in life. William Morris envisaged a utopia in which there was diversity and equality, and much splendid colour.[219] Sameness, in contrast, is a stock-in-trade of dystopias and sci-fi nightmares, with Orwell's *Nineteen Eighty-Four* standing at the apogee. Crick has criticised those opponents of equality who equate it with 'sameness' for demeaning human individuality: 'Can they really not imagine that everyone could have roughly the same standard of living, equal status and equal access to the processes of political power and yet still retain individuality?'[220] He quoted the great socialist, R. H. Tawney, who believed that inequalities 'repress not express natural, individual differences', and that the egalitarian socialist society would have more diversity, not less'. What is being proposed therefore is not some perfect 'equal society' (implying sameness) but societies committed to egalitarian principles (indicating justice and fairness) both within and across states; the distinction will become clearer in chapter 8 when I illustrate the politics of egalitarianism.

Third, an egalitarian society is not the same as one based on the idea of 'equality of opportunity'. The idea that equality of opportunity is the basis of an egalitarian society is a fundamental error. Crick has put it succinctly: 'Equality of opportunity, even if obtainable, could only be a one-off affair, a way of reshuffling or new-dealing the pack – unless everyone was childless and there was no inheritance of property, skills or even predispositions.'[221] Brian Barry has provided such a devastating contemporary critique of 'equality of opportunity', along similar lines, that nobody can seriously advocate it now without taking his warnings into account.[222] Parts of his argument are ancient, as he shows with an opening quotation from Martial in the first century BCE, which reminds us that any discussion of future opportunity must begin with an analysis of past advantages: 'If you're poor now, my friend, then you'll stay poor. These days only the rich get given more.'[223] There are sometimes

218 Bernard Crick, *Socialism* (Milton Keynes: Open University Press, 1987), p. 89.
219 Ruth Levitas, *The Concept of Utopia* (Hemel Hempstead: Philip Allan, 1990), pp. 106–30; see also Gillian Naylor (ed.), *William Morris by Himself. Designs and Writings* (Boston: Little, Brown and Co., 1996).
220 Crick, *Socialism*, pp. 91–2.   221 *Ibid.*, p. 89.   222 Barry, *Social Justice*, pp. 35–105.
223 Quoted *ibid*, p. 35.

274

exceptions to this at the individual level (lottery winners on the positive side, those who gamble away a fortune on the negative) but the inequalities of society stay the same. Equality of opportunity is not a means of promoting equality, but rather a competitive game to produce inequality. It proposes an equality of rules not of people, and in that way always produces winners and losers, and thereby legitimises economic inequality. According to C. Douglas Lummis this produces a 'remarkable paradox, a system which generates homogeneity and economic inequality, and pronounces the consequences just'.[224]

Clearly, there are big difficulties with the idea of equality, even with apparently inoffensive phrases such as 'equality of opportunity', and the amount of literature on the concept and the arguments about its practice are testimony to the difficulties. Even so, I agree with Crick that none are so insurmountable to justify abandoning it, and that 'an egalitarian society is both conceivable and desirable'.[225] He expressed his vision as follows:

> if by an egalitarian society is meant a classless society, one in which everybody would see each other as sister and brother, of equal worth and potential, then one can readily imagine a genuinely fraternal society with no conceit or constraint of class. It would not be a society in which everyone was exactly equal in power, status, wealth and acquired abilities, still less in end-products of happiness; but it would be a society in which none of these marginal differences were unacceptable and regarded as unjust by a public opinion – a public opinion which would itself become, as gross inequalities diminished, far more critical and active, far less inert and fatalistic than today. These margins would remain perpetually ambiguous, open, flexible, debatable, a moving horizon that is never quite reached, irreducible to either economic formula or legislative final solution; but less intense and less fraught with drastic consequences than today.

The 'drastic consequences' refer to the pragmatic arguments for an egalitarian society; these derive from the social, political, and psychological irrationalities of inequality.

The social epidemiologist Richard Wilkinson has drawn upon an extensive body of research showing how inequality negatively affects human relations and individual lives. Those who live in unequal

---

[224] C. Douglas Lummis, 'Equality', in Wolfgang Sachs (ed.), *The Development Dictionary. A Guide to Knowledge as Power* (London: Zed Books, 1992), p. 43.
[225] Crick, *Socialism*, p. 90.

societies have worse health and live shorter lives;[226] the levels of violence are higher;[227] and community life is weaker.[228] It is fascinating, for example, to understand how health is not simply a matter of material circumstances and access to health care; it is also a matter of relationships and social standing, and how one feels about it. Wilkinson's book *The Impact of Inequality* provides abundant empirical evidence explaining how the stresses of inequality translate into homicide rates and low levels of social capital. An affluent society can be a social failure.[229] Wilkinson offers ideas on how greater equality can be created, for example by reducing the effect of income differentials on access to essential services such as education, health, and public transport.[230] Such increased access is likely to increase an individual's sense of inclusion and citizenship. He accepts that developing a commitment to income redistribution may not be easy, but he does not consider progress towards his goals depends on 'some unrealistic perfect equality'.[231] His argument is informed by an egalitarian spirit, but his case is fundamentally pragmatic and empirical:

> rather than appearing to pursue greater equity because of some abstract commitment to a principle to be imposed on the population, we must make sure it is widely understood that the evidence shows that this is the road to a healthier, less stressful society, with higher levels of involvement in community life, increased social capital, and lower levels of violence. These links are far from mysterious; they are merely a restatement of what people recognized long ago, namely, that the important dimensions of the social environment for human well-being are liberty, equality, and fraternity.[232]

Were egalitarian societies of this sort to become global, or nearly so, it is difficult to imagine that interstate relations would be as conflictual as has been the case under anarchy constructed out of the timber of hierarchical rational egoism. Harmony might not be guaranteed, but force would be progressively marginalised between states whose societies were truly committed to making egalitarian principles work along the lines discussed above. Such states would surely be promoters of cosmopolitan democracy, and would seek to make it successful. Therein would be a means of providing for their own security: peace by peaceful means.

---

[226] Richard G. Wilkinson, *The Impact of Inequality. How to Make Sick Societies Better* (London: Routledge, 2006), pp. 101–43.
[227] *Ibid.*, pp. 145–67. [228] *Ibid.*, pp. 33–56. [229] *Ibid.*, pp. 1–31.
[230] *Ibid.*, p. 317. [231] *Ibid.*, p. 318. [232] *Ibid.*

The pull of the world

'Wake up!' Solzhenitzyn taunted the Kremlin's geriatrics after the inva
sion of Czechoslovakia in 1968: 'Your clocks are slow in relation to our
times!'   W. L. Webb in 'An Embarrassment of Tyrannies'[233]

The 'pull of the world' was Norman Lewis's phrase to describe how he
came to embrace not just the locality of his childhood 'but the world'.[234]
He learned to be part of the *global-we*, the I-that-is-another. A similar
shift in consciousness is collectively necessary if humans as political
animals are to achieve world security. In the academic realm this requires
reconceiving security studies away from its statist assumptions based
on rational egoism in favour of assumptions and norms that privilege
the potential human community as a whole. The ideas discussed in
this chapter offer a comprehensive approach to that goal, and they are
summarised below:

TRANSCENDENTAL THEORY = HUMAN SOCIALITY
Biology is freedom
What is is human sociality
Cognition is first
History is made up as we go along
Was does not equal is or will be
To be human is to make meaning
The individual is the ultimate referent
Reality is holistic

PURE THEORY = CRITICAL GLOBAL THEORISING
Truth is indispensable yet inaccessible
An anchorage is the securest basis for knowledge
Critical distance is truer than objectivity
Knowledge has interests
Power and knowledge are related, though not simply
Problem-solving theory replicates, critical theory emancipates
Positivism is problematic, empirical enquiry is critical
Theory is constitutive

---

[233] W. L. Webb, 'An Embarrassment of Tyrannies', in Webb and Bell, *Tyrannies*, p. 17.
[234] Lewis, *The World*, p. 1.

PRACTICAL THEORY = EMANCIPATORY REALISM
This is not the best of all possible worlds
A better world is a process not an end-point
Means are ends
Emancipation is the politics of inventing humanity
Politics is the sphere of freedom
There is nothing so practical as a good theory
Community is the site of security
Equality is the condition for humanity

This framework is a checklist for critical thinking about security. The two chapters that follow seek to put empirical meat on the theoretical bone by examining key areas of world politics. The aim is to deal with *being* more inclusively, with *knowledge* more critically, and with *doing* more progressively. The result, I hope, will help the struggle for a more cosmopolitan security studies against today's *ancien régime*. I do not claim that a shift towards a theory based on the potentials of human sociality, critical global theorising, and emancipatory realism on its own can bring about world security; my claim is rather that it can contribute to the conditions in which security, emancipation, and community might be pursued with more hope, and encourage through their implementation in concrete historical circumstances the harmonious convergence of means and ends. By responding positively to the pull of the world, according to the theory's checklist of propositions, we may collectively hope to live in better balance with each other and with the rest of nature. This requires a theoretical commitment to expose the dangers of continuing with global business-as-usual, and a political orientation warning the powers that be that their clocks are terribly slow in relation to our times.

Part III
Dimensions

7   Business-as-usual

His vision lay more in his brain than in his eye.
Émile Bernard, reputedly, about Cézanne[1]

Part II outlined a framework for a critical theory of world security. Part III is more empirical, attempting to show how aspects of such a theory might engage directly with major issues in world politics. The present chapter focuses on critique, going beyond problem-solving *within* the status quo, and instead engaging with several pressing problems *of* the status quo (the character of US global supremacy, the future of political violence, the politics of human security, and the state of nature). Critique takes on a more overtly political orientation in the chapter that follows, which develops the idea of emancipatory realism in relation to accessing knowledge, humanising globalisation, promoting equality, and nurturing human rights.

If we are to take seriously the injunction in chapter 1 to engage in 'ceaseless exploration', and to return to where we started and to 'know it for the first time', we must keep reminding ourselves that we need a differently thinking eye.[2] Parts I and II emphasised the insecurity-inducing power of pre-defined questions and answers, and inherited common sense. Attempting to overcome this is an old challenge. The Enlightenment promised its supporters – and in so doing threatened the *ancien régime* – an ideal of social justice, a model of citizenship, and a cosmopolitan sensibility. Together, new theoretical commitments and political orientations sought to attack prejudice and privilege, whether

---

[1] Semir Zeki, *Inner Vision. An Exploration of Art and the Brain* (Oxford: Oxford University Press, 1999), frontispiece.
[2] Zeki, *Inner Vision*; especially important is ch. 3, 'The Myth of the "Seeing Eye"'.

based on wealth, gender, race, or birth.[3] Today's *ancien régime* poses many similar problems. Against this, Brian Barry described the academic task for those looking to promote social justice as follows: 'It is not worth raising questions about progress until an articulate form is given to discontent with the status quo and the direction in which things are moving. People have to know that there is a rational, principled basis for dissatisfaction – outrage indeed – at what has been done and is being done to societies and our world.'[4] This chapter attempts to respond to this call by giving form to discontent about global business-as-usual.

The 'cracked looking-glass'

Life is the mirror . . . but art is the higher reality.
Oscar Wilde's rejection of Shakespeare's image of art[5]

In challenging the familiar view, derived from Shakespeare, that art is a mirror held up to life, Oscar Wilde said that the relationship between art and life ('representation' and 'reality' in other words) is more complex. He described the mirror itself not as a simple reflecting surface, but as 'a cracked looking-glass'. By this he meant something that did not depict a single image, but rather 'a multiplicity of broken images, much like a modernist painting'. In art – which Wilde considered 'the higher reality' than life – cubism had been invented to express the real form of things, and to avoid transitory matters such as light. A 'cracked looking-glass' reflects not one image of an onlooker, but multiple broken perspectives, and this image captures what we now understand to be true about humans, instead of the idea of a single, integrated, and unchanging subject – the reflection in a standard looking-glass. The idea of a cracked looking-glass therefore appeals because it reflects a multiplicity of images representing different facets of an observing self. Wilde's 'art' here aspires to a higher reality than the 'life' represented in traditional social science (the idea of reality being directly accessed by a subject looking at an object through a revealing lens); or by the media's image of providing a factual 'window' on the world (the traditional separation of 'news' and 'opinion'); or even by the traveller's

---

[3] Stephen Eric Bronner, *Reclaiming the Enlightenment. Towards a Politics of Radical Engagment* (New York: Columbia University Press, 2004), p. 35.
[4] Brian Barry, *Why Social Justice Matters* (Cambridge: Polity, 2005), p. 233.
[5] Declan Kiberd, 'Oscar Wilde: The Resurgence of Lying', in Peter Raby (ed.), *The Cambridge Companion to Oscar Wilde* (Cambridge: Cambridge University Press, 1997), p. 284.

conceit that 'I am a camera' (the famous opening words of Isherwood's *Goodbye to Berlin*).[6] The idea of real life as a set of fractured reflections in the cracked looking-glass of our hopes and fears, and dreams and nightmares, also fits well with Freudian thinking.[7] And behind the eye that looks in the mirror is a mind that thinks in a body subject to emotion. The human beings that engage with reality are, in Steven Rose's words, 'more than sophisticated computers, information processors, [and] cognition machines'.[8] Anaïs Nin expressed the point of the psychoanalyst and the brain scientist with perfect simplicity. 'We see things not as they are', she wrote, 'but as we are.'[9] What needs to be added, to finish her proposition, is a footnote reminding ourselves that what we see is via a cracked looking-glass, and that what 'we are' is complex indeed.

Opposing this view is the understanding of humans as essentially unchanging subjects; this is the image (among others) of patriarchs, religious fundamentalists, and nationalists. Art is one medium through which such essentialising has been revealed; here it has often literally been a mirror to life, reflecting, for example, the gendered character of society. This is evident in the stylised paintings of the Madonna, the militaristic and heroic statues of leaders, and symbolic expressions of a nation's *gloire*. It is evident that such paintings and statues have continuity, and this leads to the question: who *paid* to have such images made? The answer, to a man, is *men*. The (male) sponsors of art, historically, have seen things as *they are*, wanting their women to be women (patriarchs), people to respect the mighty (religious fundamentalists), and patriots to love their country 'right or wrong' (nationalists). Similar essentialising has been the way of political realism, in the manner in which states have been envisaged as static and uniform subjects. The very imagery employed (black-boxes and billiard-balls) conjures up hard edges and single colours. It has been one of the main aims of constructivist scholars to question the way realism has assumed that states have

[6] I pursued the problems of this metaphor in Ken Booth, 'Human Wrongs and International Relations', *International Affairs*, vol. 71(1), 1995, pp. 103–26.
[7] Jerome Neu (ed.), *The Cambridge Companion to Freud* (Cambridge: Cambridge University Press, 1992), is helpful.
[8] Steven Rose, *The 21st Century Brain. Explaining, Mending and Manipulating the Mind* (London: Jonathan Cape, 2005), p. 54; this interpretation is also consistent with John Searle's influential *The Construction of Social Reality* (London: Allen Lane, 1995), 'Introduction'.
[9] Ken Booth, 'Security and Self: Reflections of a Fallen Realist', in Keith Krause and Michael C. Williams (eds.), *Critical Security Studies. Concepts and Cases* (Minneapolis: University of Minnesota Press, 1997), pp. 88, 91, 113.

a fixed as opposed to a changing identity, performed through ideas and practices.[10]

The ideas and practices that shape theories that in turn constitute reality are part of the feedback loop linking political theories and political behaviour. Wilde knew about constitutive theory in this sense, even if he did not use the term. He claimed that people only started to feel oppressed by London fogs after it became fashionable for artists to paint fog – life imitating art. In similar vein I once heard it argued that nobody in England had felt bored until Elizabethan times, when 'boredom' was said to have been invented. There is no reason to suppose that grazing goats, presumably lacking a concept of boredom, have ever been in need of 'entertainment'; nor was this the case for young goatherds a thousand years ago, whose daily life was (almost) as routinised by their animals' daily round of grazing as the lives of the goats themselves. This is not the life of children today in the West, who are *taught* boredom almost from the moment they are born. The TV that provides babysitting services ensures this, for there is profit in overcoming boredom. In order to turn children into avid consumers, it is essential to make sure that they quickly learn boredom: boredom sells colourful educational toys and amazing electronic games. Overcoming boredom means profit. Capitalism thrives on people knowing that they do not like feeling bored; it is no coincidence that the two ideas of boredom and capitalism probably emerged at roughly the same time, about five centuries ago.

The idea of reality being a reflection in a cracked looking-glass of peoples' hopes and fears, their dreams and nightmares, and dispositions and experiences, is particularly poignant in the case of traumatic experiences. For Eva Hoffmann, born in Poland in 1945, 'in the beginning was the war, and the Holocaust was the ontological basis of my universe'.[11] Nonetheless, she recognised that '"Memory" in all its guises is the most slippery and Protean of human faculties'.[12] The Holocaust, and Jewish memories of it (real and imagined, and by different generations[13]), have played various roles in shaping Israeli attitudes and behaviour towards the security of the state and its people since the late 1940s, and so are crucial to understanding the politics of the Middle East. Hoffmann

---

[10] For example, Thomas Biersteker and Cynthia Weber (eds.), *State Sovereignty as Social Construct* (Cambridge: Cambridge University Press, 1996).
[11] Eva Hoffmann, *After Such Knowledge. A Meditation on the Aftermath of the Holocaust* (London: Vintage, 2005), p. 278.
[12] *Ibid.*, p. 165.
[13] These are different ways Hoffmann describes various forms of memory, *ibid.*

movingly described the responsibilities and difficulties of the 'second generation' – her own – who had not witnessed the Holocaust directly, but whose relatives had. Not least among the difficulties she envisaged was the danger of focusing on memory itself, as opposed to its object, that is, 'on the rituals of remembrance rather that their content'; the content was the historical object that fed the memory[14] *We see things as we are,* and Hoffmann described her own thoughts, feelings, and experiences, confessing that she chose not to live in Israel as a result of 'personal preferences rather than patriotic solidarity', yet still believed her feelings towards Israel were 'pre- rather than nonpolitical'. As a result, she felt 'an extra measure of identification when Israel's existence is threatened, and an extra dose of shame when it engages in what . . . [she considered] unjust aggression'.[15] And there has been a great deal of the latter. To many observers, including friends of Israel, tragedy is thought to be the only word to describe the way in which Israeli governments have acted in ways that have created a collective nightmare for Palestinians.[16] Hoffmann's is a moving and haunting story, with every page illustrating the power of the insight that we see things as *we are*, yet at the same time the difficulty of answering the question: 'What *are* we?'

The general point I am making is that there is no simple relationship between a subject and an object, a looking-glass and reality. Students of security must therefore challenge the 'cognitive, information-processing obsession' to which Rose and (some) other brain researchers have drawn attention, a perspective mostly blamed on Descartes.[17] The latter's famous dictum 'Cogito ergo sum', so powerful in philosophy (especially in the West), has been the basis of his influence, but also, according to neurologist Antonio Damasio, the basis of his 'error'.[18] Rose has revised Descartes: 'To understand the evolution of brains and behaviour, and the emergence of humanity, we need at the very least to insist on "Emotio ergo sum".'[19] Like Damasio, Rose insists on recognising that emotion is a fundamental aspect of existence and a driver of

---

[14] *Ibid.*, pp. 34–7, 165–6.   [15] *Ibid.*, pp. 248–9.
[16] But Norman Finkelstein argued that there was more to the history of what happened than tragedy: a 'Holocaust Industry' arose. He made the case that the Holocaust was exploited for Jewish/Israeli interests after their crushing defeat of the surrounding Arab states in the 1967 Six Day War. See his *The Holocaust Industry* (London: Verso, 2000).
[17] Rose, *21st Century Brain*, p. 54.
[18] Antonio Damasio, *Descartes' Error. Emotion, Reason and the Human Brain* (London: Vintage Books, 2006; 1st pub. 1994).
[19] Rose, *21st Century Brain*, p. 54.

evolution.[20] Complex forms of behaviour are part of what he has called 'expressing emotions'. But he does not rule out reason; he only seeks to give emotions (and feelings) their due. This view, according to Ronald de Sousa, is that humans are neither completely determinate machines, nor angels with pure and rational wills; they are somewhere in-between.[21] Emotions and feelings, it must be emphasised, can be rational (fear can lead to taking evasive action) as well as having irrational consequences (misplaced fear can be self-fulfilling). Emotions must be given space in our attempts to understand world politics, but they have often escaped attention.[22]

The tradition of focusing on the 'rational' in international politics and ignoring the 'emotional' has been particularly powerful in security studies. Note, for example, the hyper-rationality of the nuclear theorist Herman Kahn in the 1950s and 1960s in creating a particular image of 'strategic man', the basis for the satirical character of Dr Strangelove.[23] While Kahn exhibited intellectual virtuosity in the face of nuclear fear, there is increasing evidence that 'sophisticated computers' were not actually running policy during the Cold War; instead, the stage was directed by human beings who were less than omniscient, subject to emotions, and whose 'information processors' and 'cognition machines' were susceptible to glitches.[24] The Descartes-inspired image of 'sophisticated computers' guiding security policy was misleading; to a greater or lesser degree, Cold War policymakers were programmed by ethnocentric, ideological, and masculinist mindsets, as well as possessing normal human emotions stretched by abnormal levels of responsibility. One consequence of this was psychological 'denial' in relation to nuclear

[20] Antonio Damasio, *Looking for Spinoza. Joy, Sorrow and the Feeling Brain* (London: William Heinemann, 2003).
[21] See Keith Oatley, 'The Importance of Being Emotional', *New Scientist*, no. 1678, 19 August 1989, p. 33. See also Damasio, *Descartes' Error* and *Looking for Spinoza*; Rose, *21st Century Brain*, p. 54; and Stuart Walton, *Humanity. An Emotional History* (London: Atlantic Books, 2004).
[22] This is a key theme in Ken Booth and Nicholas J. Wheeler, *The Security Dilemma. Fear, Cooperation, and Trust in World Politics* (Basingstoke: Palgrave, 2008).
[23] The key works were Herman Kahn, *On Thermonuclear War* (Princeton, N.J.: Princeton University Press, 1960), *Thinking About the Unthinkable* (New York: Simon and Schuster, 1962), and *On Escalation: Metaphors and Scenarios* (London: Pall Mall Press, 1965); for contemporary critique, see Philip Green, *Deadly Logic: The Theory of Nuclear Deterrence* (Columbus: Ohio State University Press, 1966), and John C. Garnett, 'Herman Kahn', in John Baylis and John Garnett (eds.), *Makers of Nuclear Strategy* (London: Pinter, 1991), pp. 70–97.
[24] Robert Scheer, *With Enough Shovels: Reagan, Bush and Nuclear War* (New York: Random House, 1983), offers a set of fascinating insights.

weapons, and the potentially catastrophic consequences of their strategic prescriptions.[25]

One rare piece of self-knowledge on these matters was provided by Bernard Brodie, arguably the most interesting and wise of the first generation of US nuclear strategists.[26] In the late 1950s, at a time when his colleagues were constructing the hyper-rational world of nuclear strategising – what Philip Green called 'deadly logic'[27] – Brodie argued that 'the one great area' in US public affairs in which romanticism survived was national defence policy. By romanticism he meant departing from reality in favour of 'certain fantasies about ourselves and the world we live in'.[28] Romanticism, he said, 'exalts strong action over negotiation, boldness over caution, and feeling over reflection'; it also prompts us to imagine ourselves 'more courageous, alert, and idealistic than sober appraisals of our behavior would confirm'. Brodie, who for a period suffered writer's block and underwent psychotherapy, argued that war usually reflected 'the triumph of feeling over reflection', and expressed surprise at the lack of attention scholars gave to psychological explanations. His own life experience and his historical research gave him a feeling for the psychological complexities generally ignored by his colleagues. In the early 1960s Brodie did not get the call to Washington, to serve in the Kennedy administration, when other less outstanding scholars did.[29] Two years before Brodie died in 1978, Robert Jervis published a path-breaking book, *Perception and Misperception in International Politics*, which vindicated Brodie's recognition of the importance of perceptual complexities; unfortunately, the book has been honoured more through citation than engagement, given the dominance in the discipline of neorealism and rational choice theory.[30] The power of Descartes' error therefore rumbles on. Meanwhile, Brodie's warnings about romanticism remain ever fresh. When the Bush White House announced and began to prosecute its Global War on Terror, to 'smoke 'em out and hunt 'em down', impelled in part by the President's belief that 'this is what God

---

[25] R. J. Lifton and E. Markusen, *The Genocidal Mentality: The Nazi Holocaust and the Nuclear Threat* (New York: Basic Books, 1990), is revealing.
[26] This point is elaborated in Ken Booth, 'Bernard Brodie', in Baylis and Garnett, *Nuclear Strategy*, pp. 19–56.
[27] Green, *Deadly Logic*.
[28] Bernard Brodie, *Strategy in the Missile Age* (Princeton, N.J.: Princeton University Press, 1965), p. 266.
[29] Booth, 'Brodie', p. 38.
[30] Robert Jervis, *Perception and Misperception in International Politics* (Princeton, N.J.: Princeton University Press, 1976).

has asked him to do', romanticism (shaped by masculinism, Christianism, and fantasy) was tangible in Washington.[31] Militarised idealism and the triumph of feeling over reflection were etched on the faces of the cheer-leaders of the neocon project.[32]

Feminist theorising must always be given a voice in such discussions. The role of gender in relation to what may be going on 'in here' (in the heads of decision-makers) as opposed to what is happening 'out there' (in the real world) is one dimension of what it means to see things as we are. As was discussed in chapter 2, the first feminist theorists in security studies revealed not only the unrecognised insecurity of women, but also some of the specific roles played by gender in the construction of dominant thinking about security. This included the very language used to create, access, and communicate reality.[33] Myriam Miedzian has described how men as security specialists have conceived their problems and roles in terms of their sporting obsessions and other masculinist pursuits, while Tom Engelhardt (not a feminist writer) has interpreted the professional life of generations of US national security specialists as reflecting the culture of cowboy films – a traditionally very genderised genre.[34] In both these cases, life mirrored art, as Wilde told us it did. For radical feminism the relationship between sex and security is simpler and more linear than that proposed by more complex gender theory: for the former war, very directly, is the consequence of the aggressive (biological) nature of men. The title of Helen Caldicott's book, *Missile Envy*, insists that boys will be boys, whatever they compare.[35]

---

[31] The quotations, by Bush and by a 'close acquaintance' of the President, are in Eliot Weinberger, *What Happened Here. Bush Chronicles* (London: Verso, 2006), pp. 36 and 55 respectively.
[32] Irwin Stelzer (ed.), *The Neocon Reader* (New York: The Grove Press, 2004), gives a wide selection of such views, and draws a different conclusion. A critique of neoconservatism, bringing together classical realist warnings of its directions, and discussions of its resilience, is Michael C. Williams, 'What is the National Interest? The Neoconservative Challenge in IR Theory', *European Journal of International Relations*, vol. 11(3), 2005, pp. 307–37.
[33] Carol Cohn's work is revealing: see Carol Cohn, 'Sex and Death in the Rational World of Defense Intellectuals', *Signs: Journal of Women in Culture and Society*, vol. 12(4), 1987, pp. 687–718; and 'War, Wimps, and Women: Talking Gender and Thinking War', in M. Cooke and A. Wollacott (eds.), *Gendering War Talk* (Princeton, N.J.: Princeton University Press, 1993), pp. 227–46.
[34] Myriam Miedzian, 'Real Men, Wimps, and National Security', in Robert Elias and Jennifer Turpin, *Rethinking Peace* (Boulder, Colo.: Lynne Rienner, 1994), pp. 17–25; and Tom Engelhardt, 'Injun Country', *Le Monde diplomatique*, February 2006.
[35] Helen Caldicott, *Missile Envy. The Nuclear Arms Race and Nuclear War* (Toronto: Bantam Books, 1985), pp. 315–24.

Despite the supposed theoretical turn in academic international relations since the 1980s, the dominating professional self-image remains that of traditional social science. We explain the world as it is, by inspecting it through ever-stronger microscopes. As a result, much of the discipline remains trapped by a combination of a flawed ideal of science and a false image of objectivity. In reality, what we have is a cracked looking-glass, not a microscope, and ethnocentric and masculinist observers, not neutral observers. Of course, the torch-bearers of social science in the discipline will resist such a description, but many others know full well that even the most impressive mask constructed out of rational choice theory cannot hide the identity of its owner. Behind it, invariably, will be somebody who is more or less liberal, more or less nationalist, more or less masculinist, more or less middle-class, and more or less American. In this regard, the sociology of academic international relations is almost as interesting as the subject matter itself, though it is not what the supposedly leading journals rush to publish. Until they do, and reflexivity is given its head, the powerful mask will remain, and 'IR' will continue to be, as Stanley Hoffmann claimed in the late 1970s, 'An American Social Science'.[36] This is a looking-glass its owners are confident is not cracked.

Are we all Americans now?

> I never knew a man who had better motives for all the trouble he
> caused.   Thomas Fowler in (and about) *The Quiet American*[37]

In mid-2003 the then political correspondent of the BBC, Andrew Marr, announced in *Newsweek* that 'We Are All Americans'.[38] There was no doubt in his mind: no question mark. Marr described countries becoming bicultural (a local culture plus American), with the 4 per cent of the world's population living in the United States dominating the other 96 per cent. 'Compared with this', Marr gushed, 'Rome was just a village with attitude.' He reported that polling across a basket of countries indicated that Americans were regarded as 'friendly, united, religious and free', though 'arrogant', and that their government pursued a range of policies that were disliked. The latter included, above all, the US policies

---

[36] Stanley Hoffmann, 'An American Social Science: International Relations' (1st pub. in *Daedalus*, summer 1977) reprinted in his *Janus and Minerva. Essays on the Theory and Practice of International Politics* (Boulder, Colo.: Westview, 1986).
[37] Graham Greene, *The Quiet American* (Harmondsworth: Penguin, 1965), p. 59.
[38] Andrew Marr, 'We Are All Americans', *Newsweek*, 23 June 2003.

towards the Israel–Palestine conflict, world poverty, and global warming. President George W. Bush, to nobody's surprise at the time, had 'a terrible reputation'.[39] Whatever the blips though, Marr was confident US influence would grow:

> With half the world's R&D and a young population that will outstrip Europe's, America is likely to dominate more in the decades ahead, not less. Everyone has to come to terms with the fact – the 96 percent by becoming culturally bilingual, and Americans by realizing, as the British had to, that no superpower is an island. They cannot touch so far beyond their borders without being touched, and changed – perhaps more than they know.

Americans, Marr said, needed to think harder about how they wanted to be known in the rest of the world. He was right. And it is in the field of security, defined widely, where the results of such hard thinking could have most global consequence.

Although such confidence in a world future painted with the stars and stripes has been common since the early 1990s, it sometimes feels like only yesterday when serious writers were forecasting the 'overstretch' and 'decline' of US power.[40] Since the decline of declinism, however, the debate has shifted to the idea of the emergence of a US empire across swathes of the earth. This does not mean the resurrection of a formal empire on the old European model, but of a situation in which US power sets the key global agendas, gives the answers, and expects deference. But how is such political dominance to be named? 'Hegemony' is not exactly the word: a true hegemony requires acceptance and legitimacy, but this is not the situation in which the US hyper-power finds itself these days. Consequently, the disputed term 'empire' will suffice for many as the label for the complex world-leading role of the United States – until it draws in its horns, or until the rest of the world looks on it as benignly as the BBC's former political correspondent.[41] The folly and subsequent

---

[39] This criticism is by no means restricted to liberal and left-wing observers; note the stinging description of Bush by Max Hastings, 'a man of the political right', quoted in Irwin Stelzer, 'Neoconservatives and their Critics. An Introduction', in Stelzer, *Neocon Reader*, pp. 15–16.
[40] The most prominent declinist work was Paul Kennedy, *The Rise and Fall of the Great Powers* (London: Unwin, Hyman, 1988); compare Michael Cox, 'Whatever Happened to American Decline? International Relations and the New United States Hegemony', *New Political Economy*, vol. 6(3), 2002, pp. 311–40, and 'Empire, Imperialism and the Bush Doctrine', *Review of International Studies*, vol. 30(4), 2004, pp. 585–605.
[41] For a flavour of the debate, see Andrew J. Bacevich (ed.), *The Imperial Tense: Prospects and Problems of American Empire* (Chicago: Ivan R. Dee, 2000); Michael Hardt and Antonio Negri, *Empire* (Cambridge, Mass.: Harvard University Press, 2000), Tony Judt, 'Its Own

quagmire in Iraq following the US-led invasion of 2003 demands that searching questions be asked about the limits of US power, the extent of the imperial mindset in the US population, and the risks of a global backlash against even US 'soft power'. The answers to these questions will help to answer a much bigger one still: will this be an American (or, depending on one's historical perspective, another American) century?[42]

Students of US foreign policy frequently categorise their country's traditions of thought about international relations according to (interpretations of) the ideas of key figures in the nation's past: Alexander Hamilton, Thomas Jefferson, Andrew Jackson, and Woodrow Wilson.[43] Of these, the most prominent at the start of the twenty-first century has been 'Wilsonianism'. This tradition has been identified with the idea of the universal applicability of US values, notably democracy and the rule of law, and of the project of promoting these values vigorously, in more or less peaceful ways. Under the so-called neocons – hard-line Wilsonians rather than true 'conservatives' – this project has been renewed, seeking to remake the world in the US image as unilaterally as possible and as multilaterally as necessary.[44] As Ronald Steel rightly argued in 2003, Wilsonian neocons have honoured Wilson 'not as a failed idealist but as an imperial figure for a nation in the flush of an imperial age'.[45] What is more, he emphasised that Wilsonianism is not primarily a doctrine of democracy or of internationalism, but of US 'exceptionalism', the idea of the 'city on the hill'.

The imperial version of Wilsonianism (a complex mix of ideological ambition and power maximisation) has long been characterised and criticised by political realists in the United States as 'nationalistic universalism'. Founding fathers of realism, notably George Kennan and

---

Worst Enemy', *New York Review of Books*, 15 August, 2002 (a review of Joseph S. Nye, *The Paradox of American Power: Why The World's Only Superpower Can't Go It Alone*), Corey Robin, *Fear. The History of a Political Idea* (Oxford: Oxford University Press, 2004), Tony Judt, 'Dreams of Empire', *New York Review of Books*, 4 November 2004, Anne-Marie Slaughter, *A New World Order* (Princeton, N. J.: Princeton University Press, 2004), Emmanuel Todd, *After the Empire: The Breakdown of the American Order* (New York: Columbia University Press, 2004), Niall Ferguson, *Colossus. The Rise and Fall of the American Empire* (London: Penguin, 2005).

[42] On the problems and prospects, see Nicholas Guyatt, *Another American Century? The United States and the World Since 9/11* (London: Zed Books, 2003; updated edition).

[43] Walter Russell Mead, *Special Providence* (London: Routledge, 2002), for a positive view of Wilson, and on the desirability of realising Wilson's dreams in the twenty-first century, see Robert S. McNamara and James G. Blight, *Wilson's Ghost. Reducing the Risk of Conflict, Killing, and Catastrophe in the 21st Century* (New York: Public Affairs, 2001).

[44] See the collection in Stelzer, *Neocon Reader*.

[45] Ronald Steel, 'The Missionary', *New York Review of Books*, 2 November 2003.

Hans J. Morgenthau, were strongly opposed to this strain in US foreign policy because of its moralism and ambition,[46] but Wilsonian missionaries have generally been immune to such warnings, driven by their belief that the rest of the world is an American work-in-progress. This is dangerous and self-deluding idealism. During the Vietnam War the White House stayed committed to an increasingly unwinnable war out of the conviction that inside every little Vietnamese was an American waiting to burst out. Two generations later, the same conviction was evident in the Bush administration's ambitions for spreading democracy to the Middle East in the train of the invasion of Iraq.[47] The White House dreamed that in releasing Iraq from the tyrant Saddam Hussein (once, of course, *its* own tyrant) the Iraqi people would have the opportunity to get in touch with their inner American.

The powerful idealistic driver behind US grand strategy must never be overlooked,[48] though to many in the rest of the world US idealism looks indistinguishable from neo-imperialism (sometimes backed up by the hardest of hard power). In a speech at the opening of the World Social Forum in Mumbai in 2004 the Indian novelist Arundhati Roy spoke of the rage felt by much of the world at the ways in which US military and economic power were exercised. 'There isn't a country on God's earth', she said, 'that is not caught in the cross hairs of the American cruise missile and the International Monetary Fund chequebook.'[49] US administrations (and they are not alone in this) overlook how others *feel* at their peril. If overweening US state power tends to unite much opinion across the world, a commensurate sense of disappointment has increasingly been shared at the example set by US society. There was a

---

[46] Hans J. Morgenthau, *Politics Among Nations. The Struggle for Power and Peace* (New York: Alfred A. Knopf, 1965; 1st pub. 1948), pp. 233–59; George F. Kennan, *American Diplomacy, 1900–1950* (Chicago: University of Chicago Press, 1951), pp. 95–101.

[47] The preparation for the war is told in considerable detail in Michael Gordon and Bernard Trainor, *Cobra II. The Inside Story of the Invasion and Occupation of Iraq* (London: Atlantic Books, 2006).

[48] Conservative idealism is well described in John Micklethwait and Adrian Wooldridge, *The Right Nation. Why America Is Different* (London: Allen Lane, 2004).

[49] Arundhati Roy, 'The New Age of Empire', *WDM in Action*, Spring 2004, pp. 12–13. To some these words will sound extreme; the critical point is how US power *feels* to others. At an almost trivial level, I remember how it felt to be in US-occupied central London during the controversial visit of President Bush in November 2003. The manipulation of a peaceful demonstration against the Iraq War, in the capital city of the President's most loyal ally, was a relatively innocuous example of why Americans keep having to ask themselves why their government has become so hated. After the demonstration it was reported that Laura Bush had said that she had not been aware of the protest. Marie Antoinette lives! Longer expressions of Roy's views are *The Algebra of Infinite Justice* (London: Flamingo, 2002), and *The Ordinary Person's Guide to Empire* (London: Flamingo, 2004).

time when many people in many places dreamt the American Dream; in the first decade of the twenty-first century it has been badly tarnished, and it remains to be seen whether it is beyond repair. With it also disappeared the widespread sympathy proffered to the United States following the mass murder inflicted by terrorists on 11 September 2001. The headlines tracing the tarnishing of the decline of the reputation of the United States in the world included the sleaze and self-indulgence of the Clinton years;[50] the scandals in US business (the Enron affair);[51] the 'low-comedy, Keystone Cops-style coup d'état' that gave George W. Bush the presidency in 2000;[52] the intolerance exhibited by militant and self-righteous 'Christianism';[53] the shameful record and response of the Bush administration to Hurricane Katrina in 2005;[54] the violence and prevalence of guns throughout US society;[55] the fearful mix in 'the land of the free' of poverty, income disparities, and greed (nine out of thirty members of the Defense Policy Board of the US government were connected to companies awarded defence contracts for $40 billion between 2001 and 2002);[56] and the abuse of power revealed to the world at Guantánamo and Abu Ghraib.[57] There is more, much more, but that is enough. 'America can break your heart', W. H. Auden once wrote.[58]

Those many citizens of the United States concerned about the state of their country and its image abroad, and just as angry at the Bush White House as many non-citizens, sometimes console themselves with the thought that democracy ensures that every four years things change. How much better the reputation of the United States will be, some

---

[50] Christopher Hitchens, *No One Left to Lie to. The Triangulation of William Jefferson Clinton* (London: Verso, 1999), is an uncompromising analysis.

[51] Ken Lay's name has become the 'byword for boardroom deceit and corruption': Andrew Clark, 'Disgraced Boss Ken Lay Dies at Luxury Ski Chalet', *The Guardian*, 6 July 2006.

[52] This is the description of Kurt Vonnegut, whose righteous indignation was based in his experience of having 'fought a just war' for the Constitution against Nazism: see his *A Man without a Country* (London: Bloomsbury, 2006), esp. p. 99; Weinberger, *What Happened Here*, is a reminder, when the White House preaches democracy to others, of what happened in Florida 2000, and that if you did not laugh, you would have to cry: pp. 7–19.

[53] The term was coined by Andrew Sullivan, a dissenting Christian, in 'My Problem with Christianism', *Time*, 15 May 2006.

[54] Gary Yonge, 'Gone with the Wind', *The Guardian*, 6 July 2006.

[55] Memorably satirised by Michael Moore in his film *Bowling for Columbine* (Oscar Winner: Best Documentary Feature, 2003).

[56] Roy, 'The New Age', p. 12.

[57] Unbelievably, following the suicides of three inmates at Guantánamo, Coleen Graffy, the US Deputy Assistant Secretary of State for Public Diplomacy(!), told the BBC: 'Taking their own lives was not necessary, but it certainly is a good PR move': Suzanne Goldenberg and Hugh Muir, 'Guatánamo Suicides', *The Guardian*, 12 June 2006.

[58] A favourite quotation of Arendt's: Elisabeth Young-Bruehl, *Hannah Arendt. For Love of the World* (New Haven, Conn.: Yale University Press, 1982) p. 383.

domestic critics of Bush have argued, when, instead of neocon assertiveness and hard power, US external relations become based on the employment of Joseph Nye's idea of 'soft power', in the Jeffersonian tradition of seeking influence through commerce and culture, and with foreign affairs being conducted multilaterally rather than unilaterally.[59] With a new president, the hope always exists that there will be a change of direction. This was evident in the way the growing disapproval of the Bush–Cheney–Rumsfeld leadership was registered in the November 2006 US mid-term elections. This was a time when the parallels between the war in Iraq and that in Vietnam began seriously to deepen, with mounting casualties and domestic protests, and with official talk about drawing down US troop levels while boosting the role local forces could play ('Iraqisation' as the new 'Vietnamisation'). We had been here before. Policies that had failed when the men in the White House and Pentagon were young were being replayed at the expense of another generation of young soldiers and numerous foreign civilians.

The consolation that democrats in the United States (of whatever hue) find in the hope invested in a different president often appears to be an illusion when looked at from outside the country. In the opinion of those on the streets of Latin America and the Middle East, for example, changes in the occupancy of the White House do not seem to translate into different conceptions of US interests. And whether these are pursued through active interference or casual neglect, the outcome is business-as-usual. Doug Stokes has argued that US domination in Latin America rolls on, whatever the administration in Washington, or the prevailing ideological or pragmatic legitimation device; in the case of Colombia, this domination has involved complicity in state terror and widespread suffering.[60] A comparable picture in the more high-profile Middle East has been given in Stephen Zunes' account of the continuing failures, false ambitions, follies, and fallacies of US policy in that region.[61] On a wider canvas still, Ziauddin Sardar and Merryl Wyn Davies have argued that US corporations and popular culture attempt to colonise the lives of millions around the world, with their exports projecting the values of the United States, including definitions of what it means to be civilised, rational, developed, and democratic: in other

---

[59] Judt, 'Own Worst Enemy'.
[60] Doug Stokes, *America's Other War. Terrorizing Colombia* (London: Zed Books, 2005).
[61] Stephen Zunes, *Tinderbox: US Middle East Policy and the Roots of Terrorism* (London: Zed Books, 2003).

words, what it is to be human.[62] All this is not to say that elections in the United States have no effect on how Washington engages with the world, but the examples do underline that there are structural forces at play, and that to outsiders these seem to be more influential than any particular president. In short, what seems to be a meaningful choice between candidates to the political classes in the United States looks more like a revolving door of millionaires committed to advancing US interests to people in the streets of South America and elsewhere. Politicians in Washington come and go, but in the rest of the world US power rolls on, impressing and oppressing. At the end of 2006, the mid-term elections swung against the Republicans, and the report of the Iraq Study Group swung against the administration's strategy in the Middle East.[63] Commentators in and around the Washington political hot-house expected significant change. Marcin Zaborowski, however, knew better than to get carried away: 'A sea change in American foreign policy? Let's not hold our breath . . .'[64]

As the American Dream is as fragile as it is inescapable in many parts of the world, significant sections of US society seem utterly impervious to outside influences, and think and react only in terms of deeply ingrained stereotypes. Culturally, the oceans that separate the United States from the rest of the world are as difficult to navigate as they once were by sailing ship. To the south, the Mexican border might as well be another ocean. In a poignant comparison, Sardar and Davies note that the rest of the world watch US movies, but US movie-goers do not watch theirs. This same asymmetry exists with feelings. In the immediate aftermath of 9/11 a Palestinian journalist was asked what he would say if he could say only one thing to Americans. He replied simply: 'America, we feel your pain. Isn't it time you felt ours?'[65] Americans 'just don't get it', a senior Australian military officer told me in 2002. Consequently, a huge disjunction exists between the external image of the United States and the self-image of most (though certainly not all) US citizens. This has led many of them to scratch their heads: 'Why do people

---

[62] Ziauddin Sardar and Merryl Wyn Davies, *Why Do People Hate America?* (Cambridge: Icon Books, 2003), pp. 5–14.
[63] James A. Baker and Lee H. Hamilton, *The Iraq Study Group Report. The Way Forward – A New Approach* (New York: Vintage Books, 2006).
[64] Marcin Zaborowski, 'A Sea Change in American Foreign Policy? Let's Not Hold our Breath . . .', *Institute for Security Studies Newsletter*, no. 21, January 2007.
[65] Quoted in Ken Booth and Tim Dunne, 'Worlds in Collision', in Ken Booth and Tim Dunne (eds.), *Worlds in Collision. Terror and the Future of Global Order* (Houndmills: Palgrave Macmillan, 2002), p. 5.

hate America?' they ask, seeing themselves as a friendly and benevolent people. The answer is obvious to most outsiders.[66] Non-Americans who have increasingly fallen out with the United States now include many of those traditionally seen as friends and allies. The fissures between Europeans and Washington are wider than in the past, and their significance should not be underestimated. The ties that once bound (the memory of the Second World War and of the Cold War alliance against the Soviet threat above all) have become much weaker.[67]

Whether or not Washington engages with the rest of the world as its 'empire', in the formal sense of the term, many think the term appropriate, at least informally[68] and (in contrast to most of the opinions recorded above) the term is not necessarily used negatively. In the burgeoning literature on this topic, the term American empire 'is no longer a dirty word' according to the British (formerly left-wing) journalist John Lloyd.[69] Prominent among British advocates of the new imperialism, in addition to a clutch of opinion-formers formerly associated with the political left, has been Robert Cooper. In 2002, in what he meaninglessly insisted on calling the 'postmodern world', this one-time adviser on foreign affairs to Prime Minister Blair outlined a picture of 'a new kind of imperialism – one acceptable to a world of human rights and cosmopolitan values'. He subscribed to the view that the rest of the world wanted to live like Westerners, so that the new imperialism, resting on the 'voluntary principle', would bring order and organisation as well as human rights.[70] This outlook entailed an imperative to intervene, and Cooper described the campaign in Afghanistan following 9/11 as 'defensive imperialism'.[71] A sense of the right and duty to expand informs such thinking. Old phrases from the age of empire, such as *'mission*

---

[66] Discussions addressing this theme are: Strobe Talbott and Nayan Chanda (eds.), *The Age of Terror: America and the World After September 11* (New York: Basic Books, 2001); *What We Think of America* (London: Granta, 2002); Ziauddin Sardar and Merryl Wyn Davies, *Why Do People Hate America?* and *American Dream. Global Nightmare* (London: Icon Books, 2004).

[67] Key references are in Ken Booth, 'Morgenthau's Realisms and Transatlantic Truths', in Christian Hacke, Gottfried-Karl Kindermann, and Kai M. Schellhorn (eds.), *The Heritage, Challenge, and Future of Realism* (Göttingen: Bonn University Press, 2005), pp. 99–128.

[68] An excellent analytical overview is Jack Donnelly, 'Sovereign Inequalities and Hierarchy in Anarchy: American Power and International Society', *European Journal of International Relations*, vol. 12(2), 2006, pp. 139–70.

[69] John Lloyd, 'The Return of Imperialism' *New Statesman*, 15 April 2002.

[70] Robert Cooper, 'The Post-Modern State', in Mark Leonard (ed.), *Re-ordering the World: The Long-term Implications of 11 September* (London: Foreign Policy Centre, 2002), pp. 11–20 (quotation at pp. 17–18).

[71] *Ibid.*, p. 19.

civilisatrice' and 'white man's burden' resonate in today's 'the responsibility to protect' and 'international community'. Those who have failed to notice the idealism behind US dreams of power, and see only material interests, miss a great deal.

On the academic front, the case for the new imperialist enterprise has been put powerfully, if not always persuasively, by Niall Ferguson, notably in *Colossus*.[72] The case is made that, from the start of the US republic, imperial expansion has been as American as apple pie. Conquest took place across the continent, and a largely informal empire developed overseas. In words that recall the notion of the British empire being created 'in a fit of absent-mindedness', the renowned US journalist Walter Lippmann said in 1926, 'We continue to think of ourselves as a kind of great, peaceful Switzerland, whereas we are in fact a great, expanding world power . . . Our imperialism is more or less unconscious.'[73] And so, in a sense, it has remained. Ferguson, a supporter of the invasion of Iraq, doubted whether the people in the United States had the will or the means to emulate the British empire he so admires. Dangerously for any imperial power, the US political elite has tended to underestimate nationalism. So did Ferguson. Readers discover little about the targets of the power of the US in *Colossus*, but we should never be surprised when those targets fight back, as did other nationalists of a few generations ago, when they struggled to throw off their white colonial masters, and did so by showing they could bear much more pain. The writing is again on the wall in the asymmetrical conflicts of our time, between an external colossus and an occupied nation. The outcome will be settled by politics and feelings, not the weight of military hardware. Marwan Bishara posted this headline in 2006: 'THE US MOURNS ITS DEAD; RESISTANCE GROUPS CELEBRATE THEIRS.'[74]

The residual admiration that exists for US society in many parts of the world is drowned out by suspicion or even fear of US power. The balance is unlikely to change until US leaders accept that there are other than American ways of thinking.[75] By no means all US citizens are as deluded about their self-image as the neocons have been since the end of the Cold War. The delusion, based on a mix of ideology and nationalism, is fostered by mental isolationism. The latter runs through much

---

[72] Ferguson, *Colossus*.   [73] *Ibid.*, quoted p. 62.
[74] Marwan Bishara, 'US: World Empire of Chaos', *Le Monde diplomatique*, October 2006.
[75] It is possible to be a critic of the United States without being 'anti-American' or the proponent of a different economic order; see Will Hutton, *The World We're In* (London: Little, Brown, 2002).

US society, but has most causality when it affects those in power. In this regard, Fareed Zakaria has written forcefully about the dangers of the 'Imperial Presidency'.[76] In 2005 he described how, in President Bush's trips to Latin America and Asia, the President 'met few locals and saw little except palaces and conference rooms . . . Bush's travel schedule seems calculated to involve as little contact as possible with the country he is in . . . Most conversations are brief, scripted and perfunctory.' (Such criticism recalls the infamous brief visit made by President Clinton to Kigali, capital of Rwanda, in 1998, when he did not leave the airport and did not have the engines of Air Force One switched off; he used the word 'genocide' twelve times in a speech, though he had instructed his diplomats four years earlier not to use it when it mattered.[77]) The 'imperial style of diplomacy' that has been developed by the US government had become 'a one-way street', Zakaria said. Consultation simply meant being informed, and this was even the case with Tony Blair, the President's most faithful ally. Despite the price the British Prime Minister had to pay in terms of his reputation at home for his loyalty to Bush, Blair was a marginal figure in the priorities and decisions of the White House regarding the war in Iraq.[78]

Washington demands loyalty, but it does not listen. Zakaria reported one senior foreign official (who requested anonymity for fear of angering his US counterparts) as saying: 'When we meet with American officials, they talk and we listen – we rarely disagree or speak frankly because they simply can't take it in.' He then quoted the 'ardently pro-American' Chris Patten, who, recounting his experience as Europe's Commissioner for External Affairs, recalled: 'Even for a senior official dealing with the US administration, you are aware of your role as a tributary.' Patten went on to describe how foreign visits by US officials bring cities to a halt, and how 'innocent bystanders are barged into corners by thick-necked men with bits of plastic hanging out of their ears. It is not a spectacle that

---

[76] Fareed Zakaria, 'An Imperial Presidency', *Newsweek*, 19 December 2005; see also Evan Thomas and Richard Wolffe, 'Bush in the Bubble', *Newsweek*, 19 December 2005. An interpretation that emphasises the motive of fear behind US grand strategy is Benjamin R. Barber, *Fear's Empire: War, Terrorism and Democracy* (New York: W. W. Norton, 2003).

[77] Guy Arnold, *Africa. A Modern History* (London: Atlantic Books, 2005), pp. 856–7. Clinton apologised for his earlier misdeeds, but his words rank as hollow as any in the hypocritical history of diplomacy, given his well-practised skill in the art of apology.

[78] Compare the way the White House told Prince Bandar of Saudi Arabia about the US intention to attack Iraq just before it took place (the Israelis already knew), and the weasel words addressed to Blair the following morning: as reported from the inside by the investigative journalist Bob Woodward: *Plan of Attack* (London: Pocket Books, 2004), pp. 394–9.

wins hearts and minds.' Nor can the hearts and minds of Iraqis be won on the streets of their own country as soldiers, understandably terrified by the threat of suicide bombers, stop and search cars, with much gun-pointing, shouting, and rough-handling. Such behaviour takes place when the camera is pointing at them. What is it like when it is not?

Failing to take Jefferson's advice in the Preamble to the Declaration of Independence about giving a 'decent respect to the opinions of mankind', US officials were infamously hostile to what the UN weapons inspectors in Iraq had to say in the months before the war. This was because, in the words of Hans Blix, the inspectors could not see 'any other urgency [for war] than that being created by the US itself'.[79] Confronted by facts and interpretations they did not want to hear from the UN inspectors, though the latter's views were based on 'visits to sites, interviews and close examination of records from Iraq', the Bush–Cheney–Rumsfeld–Wolfowitz team 'misread them' to support preconceived convictions, paid them little attention when they could have saved them from errors, and 'distorted them' or subjected them to 'misrepresentation'.[80] The White House was equally impervious to extensive expressions of opinion across the world about the illegality and unwisdom of war against Iraq. To his own evident frustration, Zakaria reported that foreign officials increasingly regarded their US counterparts as clueless about the world they were supposed to be running. A former senior diplomat from Singapore told him in 2005 that two sets of conversations seemed to be going on at the time — 'one with Americans in the room and one without'. He said that Americans live in a cocoon, and feared that they did not understand the 'sea change in attitudes towards America throughout the world'. Small episodes sometimes speak volumes. And it would be an error on the part of hopeful US voters to believe that the only thing needing to be changed is the name of the President.

Observers of the United States have been here before. As it was in south-east Asia through the era leading up to and during the Vietnam War, and as it was throughout the Cold War, so once again incuriosity about how the rest of the world thinks and feels, and the lack of sensibility regarding the hopes and fears of others, is dangerous for all

---

[79] Hans Blix, *Disarming Iraq. The Search for Weapons of Mass Destruction* (London: Bloomsbury, 2004), pp. 146–7; Blix became Executive Chairman of the UN Monitoring, Verification and Inspection Commission in 2000.
[80] *Ibid.*, pp. 261–2.

around.[81] George W. Bush, who declared the War on Terror, ordered the attack on Afghanistan, and oversaw the invasion of Iraq – but who had himself avoided the call of duty when he could have fought for his country (earning himself the title 'chicken-hawk president'[82]) – came to preside over an administration whose ideological arrogance matched their mental isolationism, and whose nationalist universalism matched their lack of decent respect for the opinions of others. Such attitudes led the country into a war whose consequences are bound in the long-term to be even more far-reaching than the disastrous war in Vietnam. Between 2001 and 2003 the United States was transformed from being the object of sympathy across much of the world to being the target of hostility, and during a few months in 2003 the image of its troops in Iraq was transformed from liberators to brutal occupiers.[83] Were Shakespeare alive, he would not script President Bush as the figure of derision he became in much of the world,[84] but rather as the central figure in a national and family tragedy.

From the start, the presidency of G. W. Bush attracted hostility from friends as well as enemies of the United States, though some ardent loyalists such as the Prime Ministers of Australia and Great Britain stayed true. One result of the failures of US policy in the first decade of the twenty-first century was that even the previous Clinton administration came to be looked upon with nostalgia. The Clinton presidency was largely a wasted opportunity in foreign affairs; these years proved to be a precious moment when the end of the Cold War opened up space for positive institution-building for international cooperation. There was some scope for building the 'new world order' proclaimed by the first President Bush. But despite the declaration of 'assertive multilateralism' by Madeleine Albright, the Secretary of State, US policy in the Clinton years contributed to a gradual erosion of multilateral bodies such as NATO, the UN, and global economic institutions.[85] One benchmark of the character of Clintonian leadership was its ostensible attempt to reform

---

[81] This was a theme of Ken Booth, *Strategy and Ethnocentrism* (London: Croom Helm, 1979).
[82] Quoted in Stelzer, *Neocon Reader*, p. 16.
[83] On the mishandling of the war and afterwards, through the first-hand reporting of a US journalist, describing how US forces were transformed from liberators to brutal occupiers, see Aaron Glantz, *How America Lost Iraq* (New York: Jeremy P. Tarcher/Penguin, 2005).
[84] Steve Bell, *Apes of Wrath* (London: Methuen, 2004), was vicious, but reflective of much popular feeling against the Bush White House even within a friendly country.
[85] John Ikenberry has described the central US role in rebuilding the world after 1945 – the liberal economic order, the organisation of Western collective defence, and the UN system – in *After Victory* (Princeton, N.J.: Princeton University Press, 2001); sixty years later, what

multilateral peacekeeping operations in the aftermath of the genocide in Rwanda. These reforms ensured, in the words of Guy Arnold, an old Africa hand, that 'only the easiest, cheapest, and safest peacekeeping operations could be approved under them'. One headline of the time announced, 'THE US WASHES ITS HANDS OF THE WORLD.'[86]

The United States has many identities, and the one that chooses to reveal itself in the coming decades will be central to world security. There is the United States of true heroes, great music, wonderful writers, downhome virtues, democratic sensibility, commitment to due process, can-do enthusiasm, and pioneering spirit. And there is the United States that increasingly annoys the rest of the world – beyond the normal annoyance people always have with the most powerful. The White House began the twenty-first century badly, with the framing of its response to mass murder in terms of an imprudent Global War on Terror, which morphed into an unnecessary, illegal, and unwise invasion of Iraq in the face of much opinion across the world. Voices in the United States, including some senior military figures and political commentators, belatedly turned against that war, with even some neocon figures apologising for their earlier misjudgement. For the most part, the growing list of high-profile defectors from the administration's Iraq policy ('right-wing intellectuals', notably Kenneth Adelman, William Buckley Jr, Francis Fukuyama, Richard Perle, Andrew Sullivan, and George Will) did what former supporters normally do when things turn bad: they cover their own backs by claiming that the original aim was correct, but that its implementation was flawed.[87] To accept that it was the very idea that was mistaken from the start is a *mea culpa* few are brave enough to make, especially after such loss of life. And higher casualties are to come, as 2007 opened with air attacks on targets in Somalia, a commitment to increase US troop levels in Iraq, and sabre-rattling towards Iran.

Despite these critical observations above, there remains much to admire about US society, as was also suggested. In 2002 Zakaria noted that some sections of world opinion were willing to be led by the United States, 'but in a very different style'.[88] Anne-Marie Slaughter subsequently argued against the view that multilateral institutions were in

had been built had hit what he called a 'crisis of late middle age'. See 'A Weaker World', *Prospect*, no. 116, November 2005, pp. 30–3 (quotation at p. 30).

[86] Quoted in Arnold, *Africa*, p. 854.

[87] Rupert Cornwell, 'Are You Listening Mr President?' *The Independent*, 9 March 2006, and Oliver Burkeman, 'What's the Big Idea?' *The Observer*, 3 February 2007.

[88] Fareed Zakaria, 'They're Rooting For America, Too', *Newsweek*, 18 November 2002.

serious decline, claiming instead that they were sustained by a complex global web of disaggregated 'government networks'; at the same time, she portrayed the United States as a multilateral player in world affairs. She offered argument and evidence to support her claim that across the board, from trade to law to finance, the United States was integrated into global governance, and in ways that had impact on US behaviour just as it had on other parts of the world.[89] On the face of it, this argument is persuasive, but it fails to recognise the point Gramsci, Carr, or Galtung would have made, namely that the institutions of global governance will always primarily serve the interests of the most powerful member(s); the structures of trade, law, and finance will embed US power rather than constrain it. For the powerful, the appearances of multilateralism are not synonymous with the reality of 'democracy'; indeed, the democratic sensibility that is so identified with US political culture is widely regarded as stopping abruptly at the US waterfront. Whether the perspective is South American or European, African or Chinese, the White House only ever appears to be interested in getting its own way.

The picture of US power just given is not flattering, though flattery is what power loves. But whether one is a flatterer or a critic, US global power cannot be avoided. However Washington chooses to employ its power will be central to the ups and downs of future world security. One does not have to agree with President Bush when he told the rest of the world that the United States is 'the greatest force for good in history' to know that the United States has the potential to do much good.[90] But if future US policy is global business-as-usual, or only a matter of a superficial change with a superficially different president, world security faces a dangerous future.

There are some parallels between US dominance in the *global* balance of power these days with that of imperial/Nazi German dominance of the *European* balance of power in the past. For about a century, from the rise of Germany signalled by the victory over France in the Franco-Prussian War in 1870, to the utter devastation of Berlin in 1945, *the* outstanding problem in the international politics of Europe had been what to do about an over-powerful Germany.[91] During this period, expansionist conceptions of German security in the minds of its leaders in Berlin resulted in a chronic sense of insecurity among its

[89] Slaughter, *New World Order*.
[90] The quotation is from Judt, 'Dreams of Empire'.
[91] No British historian wrote about this more effectively than A. J. P. Taylor, *Struggle for the Mastery of Europe 1848–1914* (Oxford: Oxford University Press, 1954).

302

neighbours and far beyond. These years will for ever in European history be associated with international crises and world war. The solution to 'the German problem' in 1945 was to split up the over-powerful state, occupy it indefinitely, dismember parts of its existing territory and transfer them to neighbours, and try and embed the two new Germanys into superpower-dominated blocs. Following nearly half a century in which this solution was tried, and worked, it proved possible with the end of the Cold War to welcome the reunification of Germany as a democratic and non-militaristic polity, secure in powerful European institutions. In reality, however, the old problem of an over-powerful Germany had effectively been settled years before, when the German nation decided (in their hearts, their minds, economically, politically, and institutionally) to seek security within, not against, or over, Europe.[92]

The United States will remain the leading world power for years to come; some will measure it in decades, others will see it stretching much further ahead. But for the historical moment its leading role is assured, even though it cannot always get its way, and although there is a growing challenge represented by the impressive (but still uncertain) rise of China and India.[93] As long as the United States is motivated by 'nationalist universalism', it will be the hippo in the world's canoe, to adapt an African phrase. This was Germany's position in Europe through three tragic generations, until a solution was found – the construction of a canoe that could seat all. As in Germany's case, the excess of US power over those around it is no more in its own interests than it is in the interests of others. Various scenarios could cut US power down to size (some of which are more desirable than others) but cut down to size it will be, at some point in the future. Throughout history it has never been easy to be the world's leading power, and there are particular difficulties today. As things stand, the United States has neither the authority required to be a global hegemon nor the usable force to impose its will as a global imperial power. In their different ways, 9/11 and the disastrous war in Iraq are different symbols of the limits and vulnerabilities of the US Gulliver.[94] During the past two centuries, the heartlands of the great European empires were potentially vulnerable to other great

---

[92] Tony Judt, *Postwar. A History of Europe Since 1945* (London: William Heinemann, 2005), tells the story well.
[93] The case for continuing US military superiority and political pre-eminence was made by William C. Wohlforth, 'The Stability of a Unipolar World', *International Security*, vol. 24(1), 1999, pp. 5–41.
[94] This analogy was used long ago by Stanley Hoffmann, *Gulliver's Troubles, Or the Setting of U.S. Foreign Policy* (New York: McGraw-Hill, 1968), and was revived in Stanley Hoffmann

powers, but never to the peoples they had conquered or dominated. London was never threatened by its colonies, nor Brussels or Paris, even when their colonised subjects sought to be free.[95] In 2001 the symbolic heart of US power – military and economic – was attacked by terrorists, and more is threatened. Rome had 'attitude', Marr said, with the imperial stomach to place its troops, decade after decade, standing guard over its interests in very inhospitable places. This does not appear to be the American way, as even such a supporter of *Colossus* as Ferguson admits. Meanwhile, the hard power of the United States provokes a countervailing response at all levels, from suicide bombers against US interests[96] to the proliferation of nuclear weapons to deter US pressure.[97]

The United States might yet restore hegemonial authority in world politics, but it will not succeed as a global imperial power. Nor is old-fashioned isolationism an option in the global age. Democracy-in-one-country is unlikely to flourish in a sea of insecurity; it has to be working towards cosmopolitan democracy, or there will be no democracy at all over the long term.[98] For the United States to restore positive authority in world politics, Washington must follow the lead of its many citizens who do listen and engage with the world, and 'show decent respect'; policymakers must recognise that security these days is reciprocal or it is nothing; and its political and corporate elites must curb national greed and realise that US society must be a significant part of the change necessary if we are ever to see progress towards the justice that brings order, and the environmental sustainability that offers planetary hope. One thing is certain in all this. US global business-as-usual will not work. Exceptionalism is nothing more than a fancy term for radical ethnocentrism, and its pursuit will lead Washington to the fate of Rome. There will be no world security, or security for America, until the United States decides to come down from its hill and join the rest of the world.

with Frédéric Bozo, *Gulliver Unbound. America's Imperial Temptation and the War in Iraq* (Lanham, Md.: Rowman and Littlefield, 2004).
[95] The very special exception here is the case of the IRA attacks on London and elsewhere on the British mainland, in their campaign to loosen London's grip on Northern Ireland.
[96] The causes of suicide terrorism are discussed in Ami Pedahzur (ed.), *Root Causes of Suicide Terrorism. The Globalization of Martyrdom* (London: Routledge, 2006).
[97] Derek D. Smith, *Deterring America. Rogue States and the Proliferation of Weapons of Mass Destruction* (Cambridge: Cambridge University Press, 2006).
[98] This is the spirit, through the development of 'CivWorld', of Benjamin R. Barber, *Fear's Empire. War, Terrorism, and Democracy* (New York: W. W. Norton, 2003), pp. 200–14.

Is Clausewitz still relevant?

Enjoy the war while it lasts, because the peace shall be terrible.

Nazi propaganda, Second World War[99]

The war that began with the US-led invasion of Iraq will be running its course for many years beyond the day when President Bush flew his vainglorious banner, 'Mission Accomplished', on board USS *Abraham Lincoln*. Its course will also outrun the eventual US (and British) troop withdrawals. Within a short time of the declared victory, the experience had already heavily underlined some old lessons about war. Two immediately stand out. First, the conventional phase of the war confirmed that military giants are always likely, though never guaranteed, to win against technologically inferior forces by destroying their army (what Clausewitz generally regarded as the enemy's 'centre of gravity') in decisive battles.[100] Second, the conventional phase of the war was also a reminder that conducting military operations can sometimes be infinitely easier than fulfilling the political goals of peace. The war showed that peace, the supreme value, is less guaranteed than military encounters, even for the mighty.[101] War is a continuation of politics, as Clausewitz classically framed it, but many leaders have been fooled by the power of this simple adage to identify military victory with political success. But a war is only as good as the peace that follows it, and by this standard the US-led war into Iraq in 2003 has proved to be a disaster. President Bush, Prime Minister Blair, and those who supported their decision to invade Iraq were able to enjoy the brief war of 2003 while it lasted, but they quickly found the peace to be terrible.

The leaders of the United States and Great Britain would without doubt have wallowed in every spoonful of propaganda glory had the decisive military victory of their troops in Iraq been followed by stable peace, democracy, economic growth, and social justice. It is only right, therefore, that they be made to accept full responsibility for the actual outcome, namely the heavy costs of the invasion (to the Iraqi people

---

[99] This was a motto in the streets, created by the propaganda machine to try to encourage resistance to Allied war plans, especially the strategy of unconditional surrender. See www.codoh.com/germany/GERPERISH.HTML (accessed 7 August 2006).

[100] Clausewitz wrote, 'The real key to the enemy's country is usually his army': Carl von Clausewitz, *On War*, ed. and trans. Michael Howard and Peter Paret (Princeton, N. J.: Princeton University Press, 1976), p. 458. This is the standard edition in English; it contains introductory essays by the editors and Bernard Brodie, who also provided a Commentary.

[101] On the true objective of war, see Michael Howard, '*Temperamenta Belli*: Can War be Controlled?' in Michael Howard (ed.), *Restraints on War. Studies in the Limitation of Armed Conflict* (Oxford: Oxford University Press, 1979), pp. 1–16.

above all, to the fabric of international law, to trust in Western governments and so on), and its even bloodier aftermath (the insurgency, the civil war, the growth of terrorism, the resistance, the huge loss of civilian lives, the rising list of military casualties, and on and on). History *cannot* rescue the US President and the British Prime Minister from this folly, though Tony Blair has regularly invoked it as his final judge. For History to rescue the venture, it would be necessary to argue, in ten or twenty or fifty years' time, if and when peace and justice comes to Iraq (if indeed that state still exists), that the route chosen in 2003 was the only way by which democracy, peace, and justice could have come to Iraq, and that all the wrecked lives had been worth it. Such an argument will never be able to be made convincingly, because less costly and more hopeful alternative options were available (and who could now say they would have taken longer?). It is not exactly unknown for non-violent action by 'people power' to rein in or even overthrow tyrants; Islam sanctions refusal of cooperation with rulers who are unjust; and the eventual toppling of Saddam by the Iraqi people themselves certainly could not have been ruled out.[102] There were various ways by which the United States could have dealt with the military threat of Saddam Hussein, to the extent that his depleted forces posed one. Though alternatives existed, the Clausewitzian mindset, equating great military victories with greater political triumphs, is still powerful in the thinking of those with the military wherewithal to contemplate relatively easy success on the battlefield.

Clausewitz's unfinished and posthumous book, *On War* (*Vom Kriege*) is a classic, a reference point for all thinkers about war and politics. His influence in particular situations (as just suggested) might be problematic, but today (as will be argued later) the very relevance of his philosophy of war is under challenge. Even for those of us who seek to delegitimise political violence, his toppling is not necessarily to be welcomed. The philosophies of war that may consign Clausewitz's to the dustbin might even be worse for humanity.

Anatol Rapoport, analysing Clausewitz's work in the late 1960s, devised a three-fold categorisation of philosophies of war. He described *On War* as the epitome of the 'political philosophy' of war, the idea that war ought to be 'a rational instrument of national policy'.[103] He labelled

---

[102] This is well argued by Stephen Zunes, 'When the Hawk Kills the Dove', *New Internationalist*, no. 381, August 2005, pp. 16–17.
[103] Rapoport, *Clausewitz*, p. 13.

the two other approaches the 'eschatological' philosophy of war (the idea 'that history, or at least some portion of history, will culminate in a "final" war leading to the unfolding of some grand design – divine, natural, or human') and the 'cataclysmic' philosophy of war (conceiving war as 'a catastrophe that befalls some portion of humanity or the entire human race').[104] On the whole, war in the twentieth century coincided with the Clausewitzian paradigm. There were numerous wars that were rational, national, and instrumental, with the costs being thought bearable, at least by those who emerged victorious. Even the uniquely destructive Second World War could be counted as instrumental for the victors. The twentieth century also gave glimpses of Rapoport's other categories. He suggested that the eschatological philosophy was evident in the messianic Nazi doctrine of the Master Race, and the earlier belief of most Americans that their entry into the First World War was to convert a European squabble into a 'war to end war'.[105] The cataclysmic philosophy revealed itself in the voices of those who saw war as a scourge of God, or who believed the international system sometimes 'broke down' or 'exploded' because of intolerable stresses and strains. Some believed the collapse of the pre-1914 European order into the trenches of the Western Front to have been an accident waiting to happen. Expressed metaphorically, Rapoport likened the political philosophy of war to a game of strategy (chess), the eschatological to a mission (or the denouement of a drama), and the cataclysmic to a fire (or disease). The case I will make below is that the space for the exercise of the Clausewitzian philosophy of war is closing down, while that for the eschatological and cataclysmic philosophies is opening up.

The Clausewitzian paradigm promises to remain directly relevant to states in the context of self-defence (against an attack on their homeland) and resource wars (where the control of some raw material is considered a vital interest). These two rationales for war will no doubt steadily merge in future, as a result of the predictable scarcity of key materials, and the temptation to (or compulsion for) states to try and take by force that which they can not longer guarantee to control by other means. Welcome back to the nineteenth century! The growing demand (as populations and expectations rise) for non-renewable energy resources (short of a historic technological breakthrough), endangered resources (such as fish), and basic needs (above all water, but in some cases simply

[104] *Ibid.*, pp. 15–17.   [105] *Ibid.*, p. 16.

land if sea levels rise significantly) seems bound to lead to clashes of interest, and peaceful outcomes cannot be guaranteed.[106] Some weak states may become desperate, and Iraq's attack on Kuwait in 1990 was a harbinger of this. Saddam, financially broke after the long war with Iran in the 1980s, was keen to get his hands on the revenues of additional oil fields.[107] Other, stronger powers will also attempt to act in a preventive fashion, and the US-led invasion of oil-rich Iraq, to establish a dominating role in the region, seemed to be a harbinger of great-power acquisitiveness. Although the oil motive (securing access to a vital but declining resource) was consistently denied by the spokespeople of the invading governments, most commentators and political critics thought differently.[108]

Self-defence became one of only two legal justifications for resort to war according to the UN Charter; the other was with the endorsement of the Security Council. These limitations have not stopped governments going to war for other reasons, of course, but the new legal structure that was established following the twentieth century's two total wars has affected the way governments think about justifying their use of force, and perhaps the internal debates that precede action.[109] One of the ways governments have side-stepped the obstacle of Security Council endorsement has been to avoid calling war by its name; hence, in the British case, circumlocutions such as 'armed intervention' and 'conflict' attended the attack on Egypt in 1956 over the nationalisation of the Suez Canal, and the campaign to eject Argentinian forces from the Falklands Islands in 1982. Such manoeuvres might appear hypocritical, but they reveal how far international relations have come from the time when absolute monarchs could go to war because they loved fighting and were keen to enjoy the *gloire* that accompanied conquest. Again,

---

[106] For a selection of work on these themes, see Michael Klare, *Resource Wars: The New Landscape of Global Conflict* (New York: Henry Holt, 2001), Jan Selby, *Water, Power and Politics in the Middle East. The Other Israeli–Palestine Conflict* (London: I. B. Taurus, 2003), Toby Shelly, *Oil. Politics, Poverty and the Planet* (London: Zed Books, 2005). Barry, *Social Justice*, gives a salutary summary under the title 'Meltdown?' pp. 251–60, and Thomas J. Schoenbaum, *International Relations. The Path Not Taken* (Cambridge: Cambridge University Press, 2006), gives a useful list of the major flashpoints over water resources in each continent, pp. 244–7.
[107] On Saddam's motives see Andrew Cockburn and Patrick Cockburn, *Saddam Hussein. An American Obsession* (London: Verso, 2002), pp. 6–14, 84–5; and Con Coughlin, *Saddam. The Secret Life* (London: Macmillan, 2002), pp. 227–52.
[108] This case was made before the war, for example, by Milan Rai, *War Plan Iraq. Ten Reasons Against War on Iraq* (London: Verso, 2002), pp. 99–102.
[109] The legal dimensions of the use of force, and the position of the UN, are summarised by Schoenbaum, *International Relations*, pp. 96–147.

hypocrisy is famously part of the honour that (governmental) vice pays to (international legal) virtue. In other words, the legal delegitimisation of war threatens to embarrass those who want to use military force as a rational instrument of national politics in an aggressive Clausewitzian fashion. In the case of the US and British leaders in 2003, their failure to ensure Security Council endorsement for their planned invasion of Iraq was a huge blow to their reputations.[110]

When governments contemplate war, cost/benefit calculations change with circumstances, whether the reckoning is in lives or treasure or international reputation. Through the late twentieth century, the growing destructiveness of war contributed to the decline in the expectation of great-power war. The proliferation in the number and capabilities of nuclear weapons and intercontinental missiles, coming rapidly after the experience of total war, escalated the likely cost of a superpower conflict beyond belief, even beyond that of Clausewitz's imagined 'absolute war', which was in any case a logical idea rather than actual prescription.[111] Between nuclear weapons states, the Clausewitzian equation regarding the proper relationship between ends and means in war was turned on its head. These trends resulted in a growing consensus that great-power war has become obsolete, though not a possibility that could be disregarded completely.[112] It is not just the rising costs and declining legitimacy of war that have constrained its utility, but also the sheer difficulty confronting Clausewitzian instrumentality. Nothing is easily achieved at the interface of war and politics.[113] Some twentieth-century wars were positively instrumental for the victors, but they were still costly; sometimes, it was frustratingly extraordinarily difficult both on and off the battlefield to secure a clear-cut victory (as in the Korean War, 1950–3); and occasionally even impressive success on the battlefield could only be turned into an armistice (Israel's regular experience of war since 1948).

---

[110] A powerful critique is Philippe Sands, *Lawless World. America and the Making and Breaking of Global Rules* (London: Allen Lane, 2005).

[111] Clausewitz, *On War*, pp. 579–81.

[112] This debate has gone on over the decades: see Klaus Knorr, *On the Uses of Military Power in the Nuclear Age* (Princeton, N. J.: Princeton University Press, 1966); John Mueller, *Retreat from Doomsday: The Obsolescence of Major War* (New York: Basic Books, 1989), and Raimo Väyrynen (ed.), *The Waning of Major War. Theories and Debates* (London: Routledge, 2006).

[113] These issues were discussed at great length and subtlety by Bernard Brodie, *War and Politics*, part I.

Somewhat contradicting this argument was the arrival in the 1990s of 'spectator-sport war' on the part of the most powerful Western states.[114] These were wars that were geographically and otherwise remote from the society in whose name they were being fought. Civilians watched from afar the fighting of relatively small numbers of their own forces in places such as Kuwait, Bosnia, Kosovo, and Afghanistan. These wars were judged to be instrumental in the short-term. In the (air) war over Serbia in 1999, for example, no NATO lives were lost as a result of combat (as opposed to accident).[115] In the long-term, however, the instrumentality of these spectator-sport wars remains in doubt. Kuwait proved to be only the first round of what a decade and a half later appears to be a thirty-year Gulf War, long-term ethnic harmony in the Balkans remains problematic, Kosovo's status and inter-ethnic relations remain precarious, and the Coalition that moved into Afghanistan so successfully in the beginning, to bring about regime change, soon learned, like many invaders through history, that it is much easier to blaze into that inhospitable land with high hopes than to leave it with satisfaction about a job well done. After 11 September 2001, the leading Western military powers – specifically the United States – became willing to accept greater numbers of casualties than previously, as they engaged in conflicts that were part of the Global War on Terror. Their own homelands had become actual or potential targets, so the rationale for long-distance military intervention became self-defence, not 'humanitarian', though the adding of humanitarian rationales to wars fought for other purposes proved popular in Washington and London. With global issues having very local consequences (whether from international terrorism or the US global War on Terror), and with the number of civilian and military deaths in war inexorably rising, the space between the former spectators and contemporary violence began to get too close for comfort.

Higher costs can be contemplated when self-defence is the issue, and this will also be the case when key resources become scarce. In such situations, governments can usually mobilise their populations to make sacrifices, while at the same time blaming others for the need to do so. Whether democracies will have the staying power to see through the 'long war' envisaged by the White House in the aftermath of 9/11 is another matter; such staying power in democracies was something

---

[114] Colin McInnes, *Spectator-Sport War. The West and Contemporary Conflict* (Boulder, Colo.: Lynne Rienner, 2002).
[115] Described as 'unique in any war' by the Independent International Commission on Kosovo, *The Kosovo Report* (Oxford: Oxford University Press, 2000), p. 94.

General George C. Marshall doubted even in the context of the final stages of the Second World War: 'a democracy cannot fight a Seven Years War', he said.[116] The Iraq War will be a test of this, as Vietnam was over thirty years earlier. Following the premature triumphalism of the White House after the capture of Baghdad in April 2003, the realisation began to dawn that the mission that had been declared 'accomplished' had scarcely begun. Fundamental errors of strategic thinking came to light. What was revealed was the almost boyish naïveté of Western civilian leaders about the utility of military force; their limited understanding of the Clausewitzian corollary (that if war is a continuation of politics, peace is a continuation of the politics of war); their tendency to stereotype opponents at home and abroad; their failure to recognise the power of nationalism; and their strategic ethnocentrism. Like many of my generation, I had hoped that all these lessons had been well learned, though at a staggering cost in blood, from the wars of national independence in the 1950s and 1960s, and not least Vietnam. They had not been, at least by the key decision-making groups in Washington and London; nobody should ever underestimate the incuriosity of leaders about history and far away countries.[117]

In these different ways, the Clausewitzian paradigm is at a crossroads. Instead of war being rational, national, and instrumental, it is more than ever a breakdown of policy rather than a sensible choice. Between the most powerful states, technological innovation has abolished Clausewitzian war, turning such contests, if they were to occur, into exercises in Pyrrhic futility. And while technological innovation widens the gap between the rich and the poor (which sustains the hope of Clausewitzian instrumentality for the rich), it also encourages complacent strategic thinking. Technological advantage can be subverted by the human factor, and history provides ample evidence of the way in which various asymmetrical responses – including terrorism – enable the weak to employ 'unconventional' (though actually rather normal) strategies and tactics against the strong. Consequently, the future is likely to see a steady eclipse of Clausewitz and his 'direct' approach to war, and the

---

[116] Discussed in Ken Booth, 'American Strategy: The Myths Revisited', in Ken Booth and Moorhead Wright (eds.), *American Thinking About Peace and War* (Hassocks: Harvester Press, 1978), pp. 31–2.
[117] On Blair's incuriosity about foreign affairs up to becoming Prime Minister, see John Kampfner, *Blair's Wars* (London: The Free Press, 2003), pp. 3–14; on the 'Bush junta', see Weinberger, *What Happened Here*, where it is claimed that the President's 'ignorance of everything in the world borders on the pathological' (p. 58).

rising star of the ancient Chinese strategist, Sun Tzu, with his 'indirect' approach.[118]

The primacy of the Clausewitzian political philosophy of war for the past two centuries is not only being challenged on its own terms – in the shift from direct to indirect approaches – but also by the rise of eschatological and cataclysmic forms of political violence. Both represent growing threats to world security.

Messianic forms of political violence have been evident in the activities of al-Qaeda and 'international terrorism' in general. Even if al-Qaeda is no longer an easily identifiable 'it' – that is, a coherent hierarchical group as opposed to a supportive network – the aim of those associated with its brand name seems to be a radicalisation of the Muslim world rather than a specific set of political demands.[119] So Jihadists in the Islamic world clash with New Jerusalemists in the United States. Osama bin Laden's declarations are eschatological battle-cries on the field of faith rather than contributions to political philosophy,[120] while President Bush's declarations reveal the eschatological thinking of neocons and 'Christianists' in the absolutist language of fighting evil, the unsubtle politics of wanting the enemy 'dead or alive', and the anti-democratic belief that you are either with 'us' (US) or with the terrorists.[121] Such eschatological mirror-imaging is calculated to construct the very 'clash of civilisations' most people in the West once so roundly dismissed.[122] If the radicalisation of the Muslim world was one of bin Laden's aims in the 1990s, together with the construction of a clash of life-worlds between a radicalised Islam and the 'liberal West', then short-term strategic success has been his.

---

[118] On direct and indirect approaches, see B. H. Liddell Hart, an exponent of the latter: *Strategy: The Indirect Approach* (London: Faber, 1967; 1st pub. 1929). His extraordinary life is told by Alex Danchev, *Alchemist of War. The Life of Basil Liddell Hart* (London: Weidenfeld and Nicolson, 1998). See also Sun Tzu, the ancient Chinese exponent of the indirect approach: *The Art of War*, ed. S. B. Griffith, with a Foreword by Liddell Hart (Oxford: Oxford University Press, 1963); an imaginative leap into the unwritten diaries of Sun Tzu, this famous but little-known author of the book Liddell Hart described as 'the best short introduction to the study of warfare', is Foo Check Teck, *Reminiscences of an Ancient Strategist. The Mind of Sun Tzu* (Aldershot: Gower, 1997).

[119] The best account of al-Qaeda is Jason Burke, *Al-Qaeda. The True Story of Radical Islam* (London: Penguin Books, 2004); Peter Bergen offers a useful summary of motives: 'What Were the Causes of 9/11?' *Prospect*, September 2006, pp. 48–51.

[120] Bruce Lawrence, 'Introduction', in Bruce Lawrence (ed.), *Messages to the World. The Statements of Osama Bin Laden*, trans. James Howarth (London: Verso, 2005), pp. xx–xxii.

[121] A sympathetic overview of the neocon view of the world is Stelzer, *The Neocon Reader*. Weinberger, *What Happened Here* is a necessary antidote.

[122] On the original thesis, see Samuel Huntington, *The Clash of Civilizations and the Remaking of World Order* (New York: Simon and Schuster, 1996).

The cult of jihad in parts of the Islamic world has been paralleled by the revival in the West of the medieval idea of the 'just war'. Both are fed by eschatological thinking, and the more such thoughts are acted out, the more eschatological explanations of world affairs seem to make sense. Originally, just war thinking was devised as a way of restraining the violence in war, but the record suggests that it has served no such purpose.[123] For those wanting to delegitimise the use of force in world politics just war thinking serves a pernicious purpose by not only legitimising the very act of war, but also by implying that war may be a duty, because 'just' equals 'right'. A non-pacifist counter to the just war mindset was advocated by Kant, who saw war as something excusable or necessary in a violent world, but always wrong.[124]

In practice, the 'just war' doctrine has justified just about anything, according to Donald Wells.[125] If governments are convinced that right is on their side, their squeamishness about costs and casualties becomes more relaxed; military escalation can therefore follow, though always in the name of something called 'proportionality'. But what is not proportionate when Right is being pursued? Nobody has yet been able to supply a convincing calculus for proportionality; in practice, proportionality always proves to be a label that coincides with whatever technology and circumstance deem to be 'military necessity'. (Clausewitz himself would not have endorsed proportionality, for he did not like to hear of generals squeamish about shedding blood, and he favoured an escalatory edge over opponents.) It is not a coincidence that the self-righteousness that is fed by just war thinking revived alongside the

---

[123] The just war tradition (which is invariably written about by specialists in ethics rather than in strategy) is addressed in Frederick H. Russell, *The Just War in the Middle Ages* (Cambridge: Cambridge University Press, 1975), Michael Walzer, *Just and Unjust Wars. A Philosophical Argument with Historical Illustrations* (London: Allen Lane, 1978), Paul Ramsey, *The Just War: Force and Political Responsibility* (Lanham, Md.: Rowman and Littlefield, 1983), J. Johnson, *Can Modern War be Just?* (New Haven, Conn.: Yale University Press, 1984), Michael Howard, George J. Andreopoulos, and Mark R. Shulman (eds.), *The Laws of War: Constraints on Warfare in the Western World* (New Haven, Conn.: Yale University Press, 1994), Jean Bethke Elshtain, *Just War Against Terror: The Burdens of American Power in a Violent World* (New York: Basic Books, 2003), and Alex J. Bellamy, 'Is the War on Terror Just?', *International Relations*, vol. 19(3), 2005, pp. 275–96. A summary of my own unease at this tradition is Ken Booth, 'Ten Flaws of Just Wars', in Ken Booth (ed.), *The Kosovo Tragedy: The Human Rights Dimensions* (London: Frank Cass, 2001), pp. 314–24.
[124] Howard Williams and Ken Booth, 'Kant: Theorist Beyond Limits', in Ian Clark and Iver Neumann (eds.), *Classical Theories of International Relations* (Houndmills: Macmillan, 1996), pp. 78–81; for a misreading of Kant, see Brian Orend, *War and International Justice. A Kantian Perspective* (Waterloo, Ontario: Wilfrid Laurier University Press, 2000).
[125] Donald A. Wells, 'How Much Can the "Just War" Justify?', *Journal of Philosophy*, vol. 66(4), 1969, pp. 819–29.

doctrine of humanitarian intervention in the 1990s. Such interventions were the prerogative of the self-styled international community. This contingent grouping of (largely) Western powers sometimes metamorphosed into a 'coalition of the willing' (a euphemism used when the White House was unable to engineer a posse through formal channels of legitimacy). One feature of what many people have seen as identical to a new imperialism has been the re-writing of traditional understandings of sovereignty. Humanitarian coalitions of the willing have assumed they had the right, duty, and power – acting in the name of an international community its leaders had invented – to intervene when conflicts occurred involving extensive violations of human rights.[126]

When human rights are violated on a large scale, there is a commendable desire to 'do something', but this desire should prudently be calmed by the old injunction about not making things worse. As discussed earlier, humanitarian interventions have had a mixed record of success. Western leaders have too long believed they know best and that their troops can sort things out. As a result of their self-belief, it was not surprising that the sense of right, duty, and power evident in the re-conceptualisation of international law by Bush and Blair in 2003 and afterwards was transformed into the doctrine of 'regime change'.[127] They believed that something must and can be done when people in distant lands are facing great insecurity – it would be heartless to think otherwise – but whether the dispatch of foreign troops represents the most sensible way of responding to such feelings is another matter, except in cases of genocide. But genocide has been the very time when the major powers have never (at least so far) sent in their troops.[128] Strategic calculation is always present in humanitarian interventions, demonstrating that at best they can be said to be *in accordance with* humanitarian

---

[126] A sympathetic view of the doctrine, from an English school 'solidarist' perspective, is Nicholas J. Wheeler, *Saving Strangers* (Oxford: Oxford University Press, 2000). Tony Blair's speech in Chicago in 1999 represented the high-water mark of the doctrine of the international community; it is reprinted in Stelzer, *Neocon Reader*, pp. 105–16, and discussed in Kampfner, *Blair's Wars*, pp. 50–3, 61, 75.

[127] In Stelzer's collection of key neocon thinking, Blair's 'Doctrine of the International Community' is included in the same section as a William Kristol and Robert Kagan piece, 'National Interest and Global Responsibility', in which they argue that it cannot be assumed that bad regimes will change, and so the United States must assert its 'benevolent global hegemony': see Stelzer, *Neocon Reader*, pp. 53–139.

[128] Samantha Power, *'A Problem from Hell': America and the Age of Genocide* (London: Flamingo, 2003), concluded that the United States did 'so little to prevent, suppress, and punish genocide' through the twentieth century (p. 516); the United States was not alone in this, but it did (as Abraham Lincoln would have pointed out) have the power and therefore the responsibility.

objectives, whereas failure to act in the absence of strategic advantage shows that such interventions are not *out of respect* for humanitarian objectives.[129] If governments respected their obligations, as opposed to sometimes acting in accordance with them, they would have intervened with force in Rwanda in 1994.

The rise of humanitarian intervention represents a dent in the *national* dimension of the Clausewitzian philosophy of war, because it does not involve state against state, but rather a coalition of states acting against elements of 'failed' or 'rogue' states. As it happens, ever since the Second World War, political violence has frequently taken place between parties that were not states. The salience of intra-state conflict was already well in evidence by the 1960s;[130] such warfare is not therefore a phenomenon primarily related to the end of the Cold War, as is commonly claimed. Historical memories these days can be short. In principle, it is possible to conceive political violence within states as a continuation of politics in a Clausewitzian sense, but there are usually limits to such an understanding. The combatants in intra-state wars may be rather indeterminate political entities, such as the various paramilitaries, warlords, quasi-armies, and the rest in the Balkan wars in the first half of the 1990s.[131] Worse, the modalities of intra-state violence that took place in former Yugoslavia, Rwanda, and the DRC in the 1990s completely upturned the metaphor of a Clausewitzian game of chess, and replaced it with bloody images of extreme and often gratuitous brutality. It was often massacre, not war.[132]

By a strange symmetry, just as a nationalist incident in the Balkans sparked the era of total war in the twentieth century, it may be that the ethnic violence in the Balkans at the end of that century was the

---

[129] For a discussion of this important distinction, see Ken Booth, 'Military Intervention: Duty and Prudence', in Lawrence Freedman (ed.), *Military Intervention in European Conflicts* (Oxford: Blackwell, special issue of *Political Quarterly*, 1994), pp. 56–60.

[130] In 1966, for example, Robert S. McNamara, then US Secretary of Defense, reported that of 164 'internationally significant' outbreaks of violence, only 15 had been interstate: quoted by David Wood, 'Conflict in the Twentieth Century', *Adelphi Paper* 83 (London: International Institute for Strategic Studies, 1971), p. 1.

[131] The background and complex story is told well in Misha Glenny, *The Balkans 1804– 1999. Nationalism, War and the Great Powers* (London: Granta, 1999), and Susan L. Woodhead, *Balkan Tragedy. Chaos and Dissolution After the Cold War* (Washington D.C.: Brookings Institution, 1995).

[132] On this important distinction, see Thomas Nagel, 'War and Massacre', in Richard A. Falk and Samuel S. Kim, *War System. An Interdisciplinary Approach* (Boulder, Colo.: Westview, 1980), pp. 19–36, reprinted from *Philosophy and Public Affairs*, vol. 1(2), 1972; see also Michael Howard, '*Temperamenta Belli*: Can War be Controlled?' in Howard, *Restraints*, pp. 1–16.

harbinger of a type of warfare that will become all too common in the twenty-first: the ghetto wars of globalisation. Such intra-state struggles will be defined by state collapse, extreme ethnic brutality, elite manipulation, narcissistic identity politics, historical propaganda, naked fear, religious revival, neighbour versus neighbour violence, fluid political entities, and ethnic cleansing – all in the context of the unequal impact of the global economy and the lack of direct interest on the part of the major international players.[133] The shift from Clausewitzian political violence to inter-ethnic brutality is encapsulated in the title the journalist Janine di Giovanni gave to her eye-witness account of some of these conflicts: *Madness Visible*.[134]

This phenomenon, I fear, threatens to be part of the future of political violence in the global era unless there are radical changes in attitudes to violence. *Madness Visible* has been evident not only in the contagion of suicide bombings (including by grandmothers) and other types of civilian-on-civilian killings, but also in 'genocidal acts', and indeed genocide itself. Despite cries of 'Never again' after the Red Army came upon the death-camp at Auschwitz in 1945, the record shows that perpetrators of genocide can hope largely to get away with it. In Rwanda in 1994, with the simplest of weapons, mass murder took place that outstripped the death-rate even of the industrial slaughter of the Nazis.[135] Linda Melvern has meticulously detailed the complicity of leading Western states in this crime.[136] Here once again those the English school expect to behave with authority and in the pursuit of civilised values acted as 'great irresponsibles', to use Hedley Bull's label.[137] The Genocide Convention was not allowed to kick in, and the outcome was that up to a million Rwandans (mostly Tutsis) were massacred, and Rwandan society was traumatised. Where next? There were 'awful similarities', in Melvern's words, between the major powers' (lack of) response to genocide in Rwanda and their failure to act decisively to prevent extensive

---

[133] Some of these characteristics form part of what Mary Kaldor has called 'new wars': *New and Old Wars: Organized Violence in a Global Era* (Cambridge: Polity, 1999); for a critique, see Ken Booth, 'New Wars for Old', *Civil Wars*, vol. 4(2), 2001, pp. 163–70.

[134] Janine di Giovanni, *Madness Visible. A Memoir of War* (London: Bloomsbury, 2004); see also her *The Place at the End of the World. Essays from the Edge* (London: Bloomsbury, 2006).

[135] The US journalist Scott Peterson estimated that the daily kill rate in Rwanda was five times greater than that of the Nazi death-camps: Arnold, *Africa*, pp. 855–6.

[136] Linda Melvern, *A People Betrayed. The Role of the West in Rwanda's Genocide* (London: Zed Books, 2000), and *Conspiracy to Murder. The Rwandan Genocide* (London: Verso, 2004).

[137] Hedley Bull, 'The Great Irresponsibles? The United States, the Soviet Union, and World Order', *International Journal*, vol. 25 (Summer), 1980, pp. 437–47.

human rights abuses in the Darfur region of Sudan a decade later.[138] Once more, the 'G word' appears to have gone missing in diplomatic action. It therefore seems, despite Auschwitz, and despite Rwanda, the major military powers will not risk their soldiers' lives and treasure to intervene against genocide. Humanitarian intervention is one thing, but directly confronting the committing of what Melvern has called 'the greatest crime' is another. This record is not likely to have been lost on future *génocidaires*.

The absence of determined anti-genocide intervention on the part of international society, to use the dignified label of the English school, contributes to a situation in which there will be probably even more fertile conditions for genocide in the future than there were in the past.[139] The combination of ethnic narcissism, religious revivalism, intense population pressures, environmental deterioration, and system overload in some states will, under the roller-coaster conditions of globalisation, create circumstances in which particular elites, manipulated by ambitious leaders, will find rationales for victimising minorities and starting the momentum towards genocide. The future will not offer *Lebensraum* across borders for a pressured people, as the planet becomes more overcrowded; and as the planet becomes more overcrowded, traditional identities will everywhere be faced with the threat of outsiders/aliens/Others. In such circumstances, psychological and practical *Lebensraum* will only be available at home. The face of eschatological violence will then look inwards, and the messianic madness of racial, nationalist, religious, or ethnic superiority will slide into the logic of genocide.[140]

Genocidal massacre is not Clausewitzian, though it does involve instrumental violence. Eva Hoffmann described genocide as 'violence directed not to the ends of battle or of victory but purely to the identity and existence of the targeted group'. It is not political violence – rational, national, and instrumental war as Clausewitz would have

---

[138] Linda Melvern, 'Rwanda and Darfur: The Media and the Security Council', *International Relations*, vol. 20(1), 2007, pp. 100–3.

[139] Yehuda Bauer's view is that 'We live in an age when Holocaust-like events are possible', in *Rethinking the Holocaust* (New Haven, Conn.: Yale University Press, 2002), p. 16. The English school debates what 'the good international citizen' should do about genocide and gross violations of human rights: see Andrew Linklater and Hidemi Suganami, *The English School of International Relations* (Cambridge: Cambridge University Press, 2006), pp. 223–58 (esp. 250–1).

[140] On the sheer madness of what some Rwandans called 'genocidal logic', see the reportage of Philip Gourevitch, *We Wish to Inform you that Tomorrow We Will Be Killed with our Families. Stories from Rwanda* (New York: Farrar Straus and Giroux, 1998).

understood it – but rather 'the gratuitous and nihilistic desire to destroy the personhood as well as the lives of a community or tribe, to negate a group's ethos, tradition, cultural subjectivity'. This is why, Hoffmann argued, projects of genocide are accompanied not only by the violent extermination of the target group but also by 'seemingly extraneous and sometimes even costly practices of sadism and humiliation'.[141] Genocidal acts represent the violent rationality of visible collective madness, not the political rationality of Clausewitz.

If the era of Clausewitz is being overtaken by eschatological forms of violence, it may be completely usurped by the possibility of the third of Rapoport's categories, cataclysmic war. Here the idea of a pressure-cooker building up is relevant – accidents waiting to happen – in the 'long hot century' ahead (discussed more fully in chapter 9). It is inconceivable that a war involving the 'exchange' of nuclear devices could be considered Clausewitzian; the likely disparity between ends and means is too great. Carelessly and complacently, after the memories of the nuclear scares of the Cold War died down, the key players in international society have allowed international politics to drift into another potentially catastrophic era of nuclear risk. A sort of nuclear amnesia set in after 1989, which allowed a dangerous momentum of nuclear proliferation to build up, presaging an unstable new nuclear age.

By the first decade of the twenty-first century, the evidence for this was all around: several new nuclear powers had crossed or were about to cross the nuclear weapons threshold (India, Pakistan, and North Korea are in the first category, and Iran is feared to be in the lead in the second); the erosion was taking place of what passed as a nuclear 'taboo' in the strategic planning of some of the existing nuclear weapons states (Britain and France, as well as the United States); new and more 'usable' nuclear weaponry was being developed (mini-nukes and bunker-busters); some former elements of strategic nuclear stability were overturned (Russia abandoned the old Soviet commitment to 'no first nuclear use' and the United States abandoned the ABM Treaty); the weaponisation of space threatened to intensify security dilemmas in a number of capitals; the 'liberal interventionism' of the US–UK coalition provoked the search for

---

[141] Hoffmann, *After Such Knowledge*, p. 42. Martin Shaw has challenged the idea that war and genocide are 'categorically distinct' and instead described genocide 'as a particular form of modern warfare . . . an extension of . . . *degenerate war'*, in *War and Genocide. Organized Killing and Modern Society* (Cambridge: Polity, 2003), pp. 1–5, 34–53 (quotations at pp. 4–5); it is a powerful argument, and there are connections, but I think it is important to keep war and genocide conceptually separate.

independent deterrents on the part of future potential targets; the expectation of a new 'nuclear renaissance' for civilian purposes, encouraged by expectations of energy shortages, would increase the ease with which governments could weaponise should they desire; and, above all, there was a dangerous decline in the legitimacy of the regime associated with the Nuclear Non-Proliferation Treaty (NPT) which had effectively (if not entirely successfully) put a stopper on the genie of nuclear proliferation in the late 1960s. The decline of the non-proliferation regime in the new century seemed to be as steady as the rise of complacency on the part of those best able to do something about it.[142]

The collapse of the non-proliferation regime, and with it the disappearance of the ideal of an international commitment to nuclear abolition, will have many frightening implications for international security. The risks of accidental nuclear war will grow, because of crude fail-safe technology, the presence of systems vulnerable to first-strikes, and the increased prospect of technological failures because of more nuclear powers but less technologically sophisticated possessors. The risks of inadvertent nuclear war will also grow, because of the security dilemmas and strategic competition wound up during transition phases, the misunderstandings possible during periods when policymakers are facing steep nuclear learning curves, and the uncertainties provoked by the introduction of the most destructive technology in regions prone to hot wars. Moreover, the greater the number of nuclear weapons powers, the greater will the risk be of terrorists getting their hands on 'loose nukes' and, at the same time, the greater will the business opportunities be for nuclear weapons entrepreneurs in the style of A. Q. Khan.[143] The spread of nuclear weapons into regional imbroglios is highly dangerous, as Indian critics of their own country's acquisition have argued.[144] World security will be increasingly confronted over the decades ahead, short of a radical reversal of the pro-nuclear trends just described, with the

---

[142] I have argued this at greater length in Ken Booth, 'Conclusion', in Ken Booth and Frank Barnaby (eds.), *The Future of Britain's Nuclear Weapons: Experts Reframe the Debate* (Oxford: Oxford Research Group, March 2006), and in Booth and Wheeler, *Security Dilemma*, especially part II; see also Smith, *Deterring America*.

[143] See the Special Report, 'The Khan Network', *The Bulletin of the Atomic Scientists*, vol. 62(6), November/December 2006.

[144] See the comments of two prominent opponents of the Indian government's nuclearism: Arundhati Roy, 'The End of Imagination', in Roy, *Algebra of Infinite Justice*, pp. 3–37, and Amartya Sen, 'India and the Bomb', in Amartya Sen, *The Argumentative Indian. Writings on Indian History, Culture and Identity* (London: Penguin, 2006), pp. 251–69. See also George Perkovich, *India's Nuclear Bomb: The Impact on Global Proliferation* (Berkeley: University of California Press, 1999).

prospect of one or more cataclysmic wars involving nuclear weapons. The chances of this happening grow apace, as governments persuade each other that the 'ultimate insurance' for national security rests on being able to threaten others with nuclear genocide: MADness visible indeed.

It is still not too late to stop the nuclear drift, but time is running out. The NPT can yet be revived, but the prospects depend centrally on the Nuclear Weapons States (NWS) pursuing actions consistent with the Treaty, which means exercising restraint in any plans for the further development of their own nuclear weapons technology, taking a lead in nuclear disarmament, and above all pursuing a systematic programme of nuclear abolition through the creation of appropriate institutions.[145] But all the signs are that the NWS prefer business-as-usual, despite the provocation to proliferation it causes: the rest of the world is told (with more or less bullying) to exercise restraint, while the NWS show by their words and actions that they consider nuclear weapons to be absolutely essential for their own security. In addition to the overwhelming case for moving towards nuclear abolition universally on the grounds of the balance of risks (hostile pro-nuclear opinion always 'best cases' the nuclear future by marginalising the risks of nuclear strategy in a world of many nuclear powers), there are also cultural, ethical, and human rights grounds for resisting and rejecting the mindset of 'nuclearism'.[146] Business-as-usual has created a world on the cusp of having to face increased risks of 'cataclysmic' nuclear war.

In these different ways – the gathering momentum of eschatological and cataclysmic violence – the Clausewitzian political philosophy of war is becoming a fainter presence in the landscape of contemporary and future world politics. Already, in the *Madness Visible* in the Balkans in the 1990s, in the savagery of Rwanda, in terrorist 'spectaculars' after which no specified demands followed, in suicide bombings against random innocent targets, and in the free-for-all killing spree that became Iraq after the Coalition's Clausewitzian moment, murder and mutilation have been the medium, but what has been the message? Frighteningly, the message seems to be violence itself. Carl von Clausewitz: RIP.

[145] Two road-maps out of the war system are Robert Hinde and Joseph Rotblat, *War No More. Eliminating Conflict in the Nuclear Age* (London: Pluto, 2003), and Jonathan Schell, *The Unconquerable World. Power, Nonviolence, and the Will of the People* (London: Penguin, 2004).
[146] I have argued the former in Booth, 'Conclusion', and the latter in 'Nuclearism, Human Rights, and Constructions of Security' (parts 1 and 2) in *International Journal of Human Rights*, vol. 3(2/3), 1999, pp. 1–24 and 44–61.

Is human security possible?

In the final analysis, human security is a child who did not die, a disease that did not spread, a job that was not cut, an ethnic tension that did not explode in violence, a dissident who was not silenced. Human security is not a concern with weapons – it is a concern with human life and dignity. UNDP, *Human Development Report 1994*[147]

The concept of human security (possibly as far as one can get from the Clausewitzian paradigm while still staying within the Westphalian agenda) was developed at the end of the Cold War, when the United Nations Development Programme (UNDP) proposed a shift in the focus of security away from the threat of a superpower 'cataclysmic world event'. In 1994 UNDP identified four essential characteristics of human security (human security is a matter of universal concern, its issues are interdependent, it is better dealt with early than late, and it is people-centred); and seven categories of security challenge were listed (economic, food, health, environment, personal, community, political), together with six major threats (population growth, economic disparities, migration pressures, environmental degradation, drug trafficking, and international terrorism).[148] Human security, in this original formulation, was described as 'safety from chronic threats such as hunger, disease and repression' and 'protection from sudden and harmful disruptions in the patterns of daily life'. The UNDP Report underlined how the Clausewitzian paradigm dominated governmental agendas by pointing out that 'defence' (military spending) amounted to the combined income of 49 per cent of the world's population.[149]

In the subsequent decade, the concept of human security was developed at the political level. An important milestone was the 2003 report to the UN of the Commission on Human Security, chaired by Sadako Ogata and Amartya Sen, entitled *Human Security Now*.[150] On its second page it declared: 'The international community urgently needs a new paradigm of security . . . The state remains the fundamental purveyor of security. Yet it often fails to fulfil its security obligations – and at times has even become a source of threat to its own people.' Few could deny this, and though it was late in the day for the 'international community'

---

[147] UNDP, *Human Development Report 1994* (New York: Oxford University Press, 1994), p. 23.
[148] *Ibid.*, pp. 22–4. [149] *Ibid.*, p. 48.
[150] Sadako Ogata and Amartya Sen (co-chairs, and ten other Commissioners), *Human Security Now* (New York: United Nations, 2003).

321

to flag up this argument – which had been made elsewhere for many years – it was better done late than never. The words of the report that followed were potentially dynamite for the states that made up the UN. It said: 'That is why attention must now shift from the security of the state to the security of the people – to human security.' This was not a shift in priority governments were likely to embrace in practice, even as some of them proudly added the notion to their declaratory policies.

The Ogata–Sen report quickly came to occupy a prominent role in discussions of foreign policy in some countries, as well as at the UN. The governments of Canada, Norway, and Japan led the field in incorporating the concept into their foreign policies, though they did not always define it in the same way.[151] In the academic context, the concept of human security also attracted attention.[152] Like governments, academics redefined the concept. Caroline Thomas, for example, broadened it by moving beyond the more negative original conception of human security (protection *from*) to include a more positive dimension (participation *in*). Human security for Thomas became a condition in which 'basic human needs are met, and in which human dignity, including meaningful participation in the life of the community can be realised'.[153] Leaving aside questions relating to the meaning of 'dignity' and 'meaningful participation', and the uncertain identification of the referent community, the political orientation of this conceptualisation of human security is closely compatible with the critical theory of security being advocated in this book.

Although the label *human security* has a motherhood-and-apple-pie quality to it, the concept has attracted much criticism, as well as reinterpretation. Major criticisms include the following: the concept is unwieldly as a policy instrument, giving no sense of priority; it is vague

---

[151] Canada was particularly prominent; see (former Minister for Foreign Affairs) Lloyd Axworthy, 'Canada and Human Security: The Need for Leadership', *International Journal*, vol. 52(1), 1997, pp. 183–96, and *Navigating a New World. Canada's Global Future* (Alfred A. Knopf, 2003), esp. pp. 126–232.
[152] Extensive references are given at the end of each chapter of Ogata and Sen, *Human Security Now*; other sources include Caroline Thomas and Peter Wilkin (eds.), *Globalization, Human Security, and the African Experience* (Boulder, Colo.: Lynne Rienner, 1999), Caroline Thomas, *Global Governance, Development, and Human Security: The Challenge of Poverty and Inequality* (London: Pluto, 2000), Roland Paris, 'Human Security: Paradigm Shift or Hot Air?' *International Security*, vol. 26(2), 2001, pp. 87–102, Matt McDonald, 'Human Security and the Construction of Security', *Global Society*, vol. 16(3), 2002, pp. 277–95, Axworthy, *Navigating a New World*.
[153] Caroline Thomas, 'Introduction', in Thomas and Wilkin, *Globalization*, pp. 3, 6.

conceptually, with no analytical purchase; it is difficult if not impossible to measure; it is too expansive in its meaning; it does not provide a clear research agenda; it is only a reformulation of human rights; it is no more than a repackaging of well-established peace research ideas about human needs (the ideas of John Burton) and structural violence (the ideas of Johan Galtung); it promotes a false sense of priorities in the threats facing societies; it has been co-opted into statist agendas; and it contributes to stretching the concept of security to breaking point, while deflecting its attention away from the traditional concern with war.

On the positive side, supporters of the concept have claimed: it represents a new paradigm for thinking about security, focusing on the threats in 'daily life' that dominate most people's existence (food, crime, and so on); it shifts focus to 'human' rather than 'state' referents; it underlines the ways in which security and insecurity are interlinked across the world; it might help stimulate the minority (rich) world to feel a greater sense of responsibility for the immiseration of the majority (poor) world; it is a forward-looking concept which might help raise global consciousness in positive directions; it could encourage interdisciplinary research across areas that have traditionally gone their separate ways (security studies, development, peace research, conflict resolution); and it has the potential to energise support for particular projects (as it did with the convention against anti-personnel land mines).

If the concept of human security had resulted in a real shift in political focus from states as the primary security referent to states as local agents of universal human emancipation, and from using humans as a means of state policy to treating them as the ends of state policy, then its arrival would have represented something of historic political and psychological significance. Such a formulation would have represented a real triumph for the human rights project (to be discussed in the next chapter). So far, it has not had such an impact, nor is it likely to without radical changes in the way sovereign states behave. That said, we must be patient about the timescales for the influence of a new concept to grow. It is too soon to dismiss the possibility that human security commitments might have a standard-setting 'Helsinki effect', pushing states to carry out their commitments. But the grounds for optimism are limited. So far, human security has hardly dented business-as-usual. In practice, the concept has been co-opted by some governments, allowing them to tick the 'good international citizen' box of foreign policy, but without significantly changing their behaviour.[154] Two arguments about the politics of human security should suffice to justify this claim.

First, human security has taken on the image of the velvet glove on the iron hand of hard power. Governments have learned to talk the talk about human security without changing their priorities. Mark Duffield has argued that such 'soft power' techniques as human security are part of a wider 'technology of control' exercised by Western states on the developing world; indeed, he has described such moves as part of a reassertion of Western power in the world. In the case of human security, Western power is reasserted through the privatisation of international aid practice by leading states. This public–private instrument results in people in some other parts of the world being opened up to Western power at the level of the household.[155] Human security is seen (in Foucauldian language) as 'a contemporary expression of international biopower', in which a nation's natural life – health, employment, welfare – is placed at the centre of political calculation and state power. Because of its focus on domestic vulnerabilities, the implementation of human security initiatives would be impossible without the privatisation of aid (because of the particular knowledge of these agencies). Consequently, there has been a search for greater policy 'coherence' between private aid networks and relevant official bodies. In effect endorsing Duffield's argument about the public–private partnership in promoting Western state power in the world, Tony Blair's one-time foreign policy adviser, Robert Cooper, described the role of NGOs as 'indispensable' in what he considered the new and benign imperialism characterised by the 'voluntary principle' (or what in a different context has more tellingly been dubbed 'autocolonisation').[156] Not surprisingly, some human rights advocates have been disappointed by the cosier role played in governmental policies by aid agencies, interpreting

---

[154] The idea of the 'good international citizen' in English school thinking is discussed by Linklater and Suganami in *English School*, pp. 223–58.

[155] Mark Duffield, 'Social Reconstruction and the Radicalisation of Development: Aid as a Relation of Global Liberal Governance', *Development and Change*, vol. 33(5), 2002, pp. 1049–71 see also his *Global Governance and the New Wars: The Merger of Development and Security* (London: Zed Books, 2001).

[156] Cooper, 'Post-Modern State', pp. 17–19. On 'autocolonisation' see Karen Dawisha, 'Imperialism, Dependency and Autocolonialism in the Eurasian Space', in Ken Booth (ed.), *Statecraft and Security: The Cold War and Beyond* (Cambridge: Cambridge University Press, 1998), pp. 164–78; I believe the term was first used by Michael MccGwire to describe the relationship between certain parts of the 'near abroad' of (post-Soviet) Russia and Moscow.

the trend as threatening their moral authority and long-term practical potential.[157]

Second, human security has been co-opted and thereby diluted by state practices. Roland Paris, in a wide-ranging analysis of human security, has argued that the concept was 'slippery by design'.[158] Noting its multiple interpretations, he said: 'if human security is all these things, what is it not?'[159] At the same time, he expressed the view that some actors have 'appropriated' the term because the 'security' label conveys urgency, public attention, and resources.[160] Mark Neufeld has put empirical flesh on these comments in relation to the case of Canada, one of the leading proponents of the concept. Lloyd Axworthy, a former Minister of Foreign Affairs, described a human security orientation as contributing to 'a uniquely Canadian identity and a sense of Canada's place in the world'.[161] According to Neufeld, on the other hand, the concept of human security in the late 1990s and beyond played an ideological legitimising function in relation to Canada's domestic order.[162] He contended that Axworthy's attempts to initiate a renewal of Canada's own social programmes in line with human security discourse was 'blocked consistently' by the Department of Finance, whose priority was to eliminate the federal deficit. (Not surprisingly, and in parallel, the pursuit of 'global financial security' by the G8 at the international level did not promote human security.) So, although there had been a 'counter-consensus' in Canadian public life since the 1970s advocating a radically different conception of security (along the lines of what became labelled human security) from that of the traditional strategic (military) conception of the Ottawa elite, its views had been ignored by the government. However, in the 1990s the 'discursive terms of the counter-consensus' on security became the 'official lexicon' of the government through its endorsement of 'human security', though its rhetorical commitment did not shift security priorities from the state to the human level. Such accounts should give pause to human security enthusiasts. While not wishing to diminish the real sincerity with which some politicians and officials have pursued the goal of human security – in the spirit of the UNDP and the Ogata–Sen report – governmental attitudes and behaviour as

---

[157] See, for example, A. De Waal, *Famine Crimes* (London: James Carney, 1997).
[158] Paris, 'Human Security', p. 88.   [159] *Ibid.*, p. 92.   [160] *Ibid.*, p. 95.
[161] Axworthy, 'Canada and Human Security', p. 185.
[162] Mark Neufeld, 'Pitfalls of Emancipation and Discourses of Security: Reflections on Canada's "Security with a Human Face"', *International Relations*, vol. 18(1), 2004, pp. 109–23.

a whole underline two old and simple maxims 'words are cheap', and 'follow the money'.

The arguments above suggest that the practices associated so far with the concept of human security do much to keep in being the system that created the problem in the first place. Some households in poor countries will undoubtedly benefit materially from the human security work of the UN and specific governments, and that is to be welcomed at the human level; some oppressions will have been lifted off some backs, and some anxieties removed from some minds about how their families will get through the next day. But the manner in which human security politics seems to have been developing will not overcome systemic human insecurity. Such an outcome requires fundamental changes in the attitudes and behaviour of governments, as will be discussed in the next chapter. There are presently few signs of the shift to cosmopolitan democracy and democratic cosmopolitanism that such changes require. It is not surprising, therefore, to notice that academics writing from a realist perspective (when they can be bothered to notice 'human security') are more likely to agree with the way governments have endorsed the human security agenda than has been the case on the part of academics from the progressive 'counter-consensus', such as Neufeld and Duffield.[163] But the latter group of scholars have a much better idea about what has been going on. Paradoxically, given that realism is supposed to be *the* theory of power politics, scholars in the critical tradition have been more adept at exposing the work power does, in its many subtle and manifold manifestations.

Here then, in what appears to be a motherhood-and-apple-pie security concept, is another case where global business-as-usual finds a way of perpetuating inequality and insecurity by largely leaving things as they are. The critical tradition seeks to prioritise treating humans *out of respect* for their humanity, not just (occasionally) *in accordance* with it; individual humans are the ultimate referent for policy, and persons should be treated as ends and not means. This has not been the way of the powerful, constituted by Machiavellian ethics and Clausewitzian approaches to violence within the structures created by Westphalian norms. Business-as-usual, with an admixture of progressive rhetoric, will not deliver the improved human security the framers of the concept

---

[163] An example of a realist defence is Nicholas Thomas and William T. Tow, 'The Utility of Human Security: Sovereignty and Humanitarian Intervention', *Security Dialogue*, vol. 33(2), 2005, pp. 177–92.

first envisaged. The 'cold monster' of the sovereign state has appropriated human security in order to help further entrench its own.

Can nature survive?

High [oil] prices will lead to panic, panic leads to depression, and depression brings the chaos that breeds fascism. It has happened before, and seems to follow as night follows day. But it will be worse than before: there is far less room for manoeuvre in the present world than in the last great crash of 1929.   Colin Tudge[164]

This chapter has offered several critiques of different aspects of business-as-usual in world affairs. In so doing, it has attempted to reveal some of the complex ways in which power works. Nowhere is the issue of business-as-usual more significant, and questions of power more multi-faceted, than in the future of nature (more commonly referred to in this context as 'the environment'). Ironically, for students of politics, the state of nature is no longer simply a historical fiction, an imaginative concept to stimulate theorising, but the most pressing of future practical issues.

The state of nature is an issue in which everybody on earth plays a part: we all consume. Some individuals have made 'environmental sustainability' the centre-piece of their lives, campaigning, educating, recycling, and downsizing. Some world leaders have described threats to the environment as the most serious security problem of our time: others have looked the other way. And some societies consume vastly more than others (it is estimated that the resources of three planet earths would be needed if everybody consumed as much as the British, and five planet earths if everybody wanted to live like people in the United States[165]). Meanwhile, as environmental awareness grows apace in all developed countries, more people across the world are becoming consumers, especially with the middle classes of developing countries increasing their appetites. Many more people still, capitalism's forgotten, desperately *need* more. The threat to nature represented by the steady increase in consumption globally is being massively exacerbated by the continuing increase in the world's population. Lenin's famous adage that *quantity* has a *quality* all of its own was never more apposite. The world's population passed the six billion mark in 1999, and with a daily growth of

[164] Colin Tudge, 'Help Yourselves', *The Guardian*, 18 February 2006.
[165] Andrew Simms, *Ecological Debt. The Health of the Planet and the Wealth of Nations* (London: Pluto, 2005), provides a clear and comprehensive primer on the implications of this calculation.

about a quarter of a million babies, the figure by 2005 was already 6.5 billion; the median estimate by 2050 is 11 billion. There are lots of us now; there are almost as many of us *yet to come* by the time today's teenagers reach retirement age.[166] The potential size of the human population is a material reality about the future of world politics we have not begun to grasp: it is a perfect illustration of Marx's adage that humans only set themselves the problems they think they can solve.

The future state of nature confronts human society with what, with no hyperbole, is one of its greatest collective challenges ever. The only threat in the past that came near was the danger of 'nuclear winter' in the Cold War, following what Herman Kahn called a superpower nuclear 'wargasm'.[167] While doubts remain about *the precise accuracy* of the predictions, a growing consensus has developed among scientific communities about *the direction* of global warming and other environmental dangers. In 2006 Elizabeth Kolbert, a writer for the *New Yorker*, summarised the growing consensus by saying that 'truly terrible climatic disasters' are predictable, the 'tipping point' (beyond which processes are 'virtually impossible to stop') may be '20 years from now, or ten years from now, or, if truth be told, it could have already been reached ten years ago'. She said that the United States could 'go green' but was not sure it would acknowledge the scale of the problem before it was definitely too late.[168] She was correct to imply that what is predictable is that one day the White House *will* begin to acknowledge the scale of the problem, but more important (for words are often cheap – and cheapened) will be whether *it will take the actions* necessary to have positive effects before it is too late. The US government is by no means alone in this.

---

[166] Norman Myers, *The Gaia Atlas of Future Worlds* (London: Gaia Books, 1990), p. 38.

[167] Now largely forgotten, the idea of nuclear winter was a real and widespread fear in the 1980s, and a reminder of the potentiality of human agency to put an end to civilised life on earth. Although the modelling was contentious, the theory was that an all-out US–Soviet nuclear war would result in the sun being blocked out by debris in the atmosphere, resulting in mass extinction, such as that which might follow the impact of a huge asteroid. In this way, the victims of a superpower nuclear war would not only be the combatants, but everyone on earth. A good place to start is Carl Sagan, 'The Nuclear Winter' (1983) when he explored the 'unforeseen and devastating' effects of even a small-scale nuclear war on the earth's biosphere and life' (www.cooperativeindividualism.org/sagan_nuclearwinter.html). See also 'Does Anybody Remember the Nuclear Winter?', *SGR Newsletter*, no. 27, July 2003 (www.sgr.org.uk/climate/NuclearWinter_NL27.htm). The SGR is the organisation of Scientists for Global Responsibility.

[168] Elizabeth Kolbert, 'Can America Go Green?', *New Statesman*, 19 June 2006.

The threats to specific parts of nature are by now well known.[169] The headline problems include: 'climate chaos' and its implications for the rise of water levels (resulting in mass migration within and between countries); the dangers of pollution to health and food production ('mercury's global reach', for example); the 'massacre' (the word is Patrick Curry's) of biodiversity with its implications for many aspects of human life; the using up of non-renewable energy sources (with enormous geopolitical implications); the challenge of safeguarding freshwater ecosystems and providing enough water to satisfy the needs and wants of the increasing global population; the steady disappearance of topsoil from desertification and other threats – the thin skin on the earth's rocks which is vital for food production; the over-exploitation of the seas in every sense imaginable; and the destruction of the remote habitats ('wild places') and tropical rainforests which are important store houses of nature's resources. The list goes on, and the obstacles to achieving a sustainable world order are enormous. In addition to the appetites of the developed world, long stimulated and indulged daily in the cause of profit, there is the challenge of incorporating into the picture the growing economic giants of China and India, as well as striving but less powerful societies. Somehow – and nobody has a magic formula – trade and sustainable development have to be reconciled, by transforming corporations into organisations committed to sustainability, governments into decision-making bodies thinking globally and not just nationally, and consumers into defenders of nature. Until there is a radical shift along these lines, the threats to the state of nature will continue to grow. In 2004 Jared Diamond expressed the problem bluntly: 'There are about a dozen major environmental problems, all of them sufficiently serious that if we solved eleven of them and didn't solve the twelfth, whatever that twelfth is, any could potentially do us in.'[170] Such warnings add up to what the former US Vice-President Al Gore has dubbed, as he criss-crossed the world in the cause of consciousness-raising, 'an incon venient truth'.[171]

---

[169] To be recommended for their analysis as well as information: Simms, *Ecological Debt*; Jonathon Porritt, *Capitalism as if the World Matters* (London: Earthscan, 2005); Patrick Curry, *Ecological Ethics. An Introduction* (Cambridge: Polity, 2006); and the Worldwatch Institute, *State of the World. The Challenge of Global Sustainability* (London: Earthscan, 2006; 23rd annual edition). The latter is described as 'the environmentalist's bible'.

[170] Quoted by Curry, *Ecological Ethics*, p. 12.

[171] Al Gore, *An Inconvenient Truth. The Planetary Emergency of Global Warming and What We Can Do About It* (London: Bloomsbury, 2006); the excellent photographs and maps in this potentially inspiring popular book are spoiled by the shameless family self-promotion.

Green advocates like Gore and a growing body of literature (beginning with Rachel Carson's *Silent Spring* in 1962) have long warned of the coming dangers; a few were willing to listen at first, but now one has to be foolish to reject the warnings. We might yet be saved by fantastic technological breakthroughs, and some of the predictions might be wayward; but prudent policymakers should not stake their society's way of life on the unlikely happening rather than what now appears to be reasonably predictable. Despite this, turning conscious-raising into decisive action remains daunting. In contemplating the global environment in 1992 the UN Secretary-General Boutros Boutros-Ghali warned that 'one day we will have to do better' (not the most resounding clarion call) and ten years later his successor, Kofi Annan, expressed his fear that sustainability had become 'a pious invocation rather than the urgent call to concrete action that it should be'.[172] Some academic disciplines were no quicker than governments to respond to what was happening to nature; it is disappointing to record that texts on international relations began to reflect the growing sense of ecological crisis only in the late 1990s, though it quickly thereafter became a fixture on the agenda.[173] If international relations long marginalised the environment, the decisive *international* dimensions of ecological issues have largely been ignored by much of the green literature. Without effective action at the international level, there is no doubt that the tipping points will be reached in all of Diamond's dozen problems. Without international cooperation, the project of sustainability will fail. The fact is that the most *inconvenient truth* of all about the coming environmental crisis is not people's unwillingness to accept the arguments about the consequences of global warming (because people do, increasingly), but the challenge of getting governments to agree collectively (confronted by free rider temptations and prisoner's dilemma contexts) on radical changes to the behaviour of all their societies. Science is not the most inconvenient truth; inconvenient international politics is.

One of the scariest popular works on this topic, and also ostensibly one of the most authoritative (because it was written by Martin Rees, a distinguished British scientist) went under the title *Our Final Hour* in

---

[172] Quoted by Lorraine Elliott, *The Global Politics of the Environment* (Houndmills: Palgrave Macmillan, 2004), p. 238.

[173] But the extent and range of the discussion varies; see Karen Mingst, *Essentials of International Relations* (New York: W. W. Norton, 2004), pp. 280–95 and Joshua S. Goldstein, *International Relations* (New York: Pearson, 2005; 6th edn), pp. 416–55. An excellent general introduction is Elliott, *Global Politics of the Environment*.

330

the US edition, and *Our Final Century* in the British. If the titles did not agree on the timeframe, the shared subtitle of the first editions agreed on the odds: *The 50/50 Threat to Humanity's Survival*.[174] The theme of Rees's book, consonant with the argument here, was that humanity in the decades ahead will be more threatened than at any earlier phase in its history. This includes not only the threat of ecological disaster, but also of new technologies, as well as the possibility of destruction from outer space. Apart from the last point – a devastating meteor impact – Rees emphasised that what is particularly interesting about these threats is the degree to which they are human in origin.[175] He was confident that human society should be able to feed the world and save the planet, but instead he thought we were empowering more people with the potentiality to carry out ever more destruction, and at the same time producing an interconnected world that is increasingly fragile. As was mentioned in chapter 1, there are those who question the scientific consensus on global warming, and call people like Rees 'doomsayers'. Rees countered by describing the views of one of the most prominent, Bjørn Lomberg, as those of 'an anti-gloom . . . propagandist'.[176] Denial is a comfortable option, but even if there are genuine doubts about specific ecological predictions, there is surely enough evidence for communities to shift to operating on the precautionary principle: that is, acting in such a way as not to risk making things worse. Curry was justified in claiming that the complacent views of the deniers 'have received media attention out of all proportion to their merit'.[177]

The message is spreading, even if little of significance is done in practice, as people drive on their own to listen to lectures on the environmental crisis, take a boxful of bottles to the recycling bank in their SUVs, and fly around the world to international conferences to press restraint on those who have never even owned a moped. When it comes to the future of the state of nature, getting words and action sufficiently into sync, at all levels, will be a daily and daunting challenge. The size of the challenge to human society to create a better balance with the rest of nature, in the era of the global triumph of capitalism, cannot be overestimated.

---

[174] Martin Rees, *Our Final Century: The 50/50 Threat to Humanity's Survival* (London: Heinemann, 2003). The paperback British edition changed the subtitle to *Will Civilisation Survive the Twenty-First Century?* (London: Arrow Books, 2004).

[175] Note the social science 'risk theory' literature on 'manufactured risks', notably Ulrich Beck, *Risk Society. Towards a New Modernity* (London: Sage, 1992), and Ulrich Beck, *World Risk Society* (Cambridge: Polity, 1999); see also Barbara Adam, Ulrich Beck, and Joost Van Loon (eds.), *The Risk Society and Beyond* (London: Sage, 2002).

[176] Rees, *Final Century*, p. 109.   [177] Curry, *Ecological Ethics*, p. 9.

Nor, as was asserted earlier, can the difficulty of dealing effectively with the challenge. Politics will be critical, but the prognosis is not promising. The challenge of creating a sustainable world order is not a matter of negotiating a few difficult treaties, and then sticking by them, but of taking large steps towards the creation of a world community. To date, even far-reaching treaties have not been achieved. In 2006, for example, environmental measures were cited as potential barriers to trade in the WTO negotiations on non-agricultural market access by a range of countries, including Australia, India, Japan, Malaysia, Uruguay, and Venezuela.[178] Aaron Cosbey, a specialist on sustainable development, did not generally commend the WTO's Doha agenda highly in terms of its efforts in that direction, though he did identify a number of specific areas in which 'unprecedented' positive results were possible. But the usual sting was in the tail: 'it will take unusual political will to get there', he wrote.[179] There is little sign, even as political and corporate leaders use appropriate pro-environmental rhetoric, that any of them yet possess the 'unusual political will' to bring about radical change. But why should we expect better behaviour from our leaders than most of us exhibit ourselves? How many of us want less for ourselves, or for those who have few or no material comforts?

The challenge thrown up to human society by the destruction of nature needs to be understood as a whole – something the governments of the world find extremely difficult to do. Instead, it is being engaged with piece by piece. Part of the problem is that the threat to nature is not as immediately obvious and scary as was the nuclear threat to the whole of human society during the Cold War; what is more, in addition to the challenge of finding enlightened leaders is the need to make every individual aware of sustainability in relation to almost every choice they make, especially in the rich parts of the world. (Should I pop in the car to the library to find a footnote reference for that, or save some petrol?) The threat to nature is both the ultimate global issue, and at the same time profoundly local for everybody. Treaties between states are crucial in promoting the goal of sustainability, but there has also to be a global cultural change, encouraging those of us who have come to equate spending and consuming with comfort, status, and security to

---

[178] Table 8-1, in Aaron Cosbey, 'Reconciling Trade and Sustainable Development', in Worldwatch, *State of the World*, p. 142.
[179] *Ibid.*, p. 151; see also Anthony Payne, *The Politics of Unequal Development* (Houndmills: Palgrave Macmillan, 2005), pp. 179–88.

332

realise that we share a community of fate with everybody else on earth, and the rest of nature.

The goal just described requires leaders at every level of society to work as a matter of urgency to build up a community of hope, locally and globally. Such a community cannot be created if societies give in to identity narcissism, with either religion or ethnicity being a person's primary sense of self. If there is to be a sustainable planet with a much increased population – rather than a world politics characterised by the shortages and dangers of fascism forecast by Colin Tudge at the head of this section – then a world community must be nurtured involving nothing less than a changed relationship of state to state, government to people, region to region, minority world to majority world (and vice versa), people(s) to people(s), politics to economics, communitarian feelings to cosmopolitan responsibilities, and each of us to each other. Above all, the future must be grounded in a changed relationship between humans and nature. All this may sound grand, and a counsel of perfection, but these grand ideals should not be allowed to distract us from the significant progress that is possible, starting from where we are and acting on the basis of the precautionary principle.[180] One major danger, which I do not believe has been grasped, but which Tudge pointed towards, comes from the violent politics that might be provoked as a result of scarcities in food, the threat of energy shortages, climatic chaos resulting in the disruption of traditional agriculture, the stresses and strains of transition caused by changing material conditions, the wish to protect what one has in the face of desperate mass migrations as land disappears, and the instability in economic systems under radical uncertainty. The future of the real state of nature is forcing international politics back to its mystic state-of-nature origins.

The outlines of a coming struggle are becoming clear. On the one hand there is the prospect of revived hyper-nationalist, authoritarian, narcissistic, and violent politics in a world of threatened and actual

---

[180] Among the many approaches to the politics and economics of sustainability, two which deserve special attention are debt and justice. See, respectively, Simms, *Ecological Debt*, and Andrew Dobson, 'Globalisation, Cosmopolitanism and the Environment', *International Relations*, vol. 19(3), 2005, pp. 259–73. Another approach is the creation of 'a high order of democracy'; this, as Sunita Narian, Director of the Centre for Science and Environment in India has said, must be a democracy that 'is much more than words in a constitution'; see Sunita Narian, 'Foreword', *State of the World 2006*, p. xix. George Monbiot has written a widely publicised but much criticised work which provocatively offers a set of ideas (including a 'World Parliament') to bring about a revolution in the way the world is run: see *The Age of Consent. A Manifesto for a New World Order* (London: Flamingo, 2003), esp. pp. 67–137.

shortages of the things that keep modern societies going; and on the other hand there is the promise of the growth of world citizenship through the expansion of progressive global civil society, committed to environmental sustainability and emancipatory politics. The material dimension of nature's destruction has tended to attract attention – newsreel shots of polluted rivers, the edges of ice-caps crashing into the sea, polar bears dying with exhaustion – while the less photogenic politics of sustainability has been sidelined. Progress, if it is to succeed, will be grounded in a mixture of self-interest and ethics. 'Ecological ethics' is a subject area whose growth in the last decades of the twentieth century was a reflection of the steadily rising sense of global crisis. As in all other fields, adherents can be found for a variety of theoretical positions. Curry has categorised the range as 'Light Green or Shallow (Anthropocentric) Ethics' (such as 'lifeboat ethics'), 'Mid-Green or Intermediate Ethics' (such as 'animal liberation'), and 'Dark Green or Deep (Ecocentric) Ethics' (such as the 'Gaia theory' or 'Deep Ecology'). His own approach was to avoid advocating ethics by 'extension' from humans to other animals or other living things, but rather to start from the 'belief or perception, that nature – which certainly includes humanity – is the ultimate source of all value. And simply put, what is valued is what ultimately determines ethics.'[181]

At base, Curry described an ecological ethic as 'profound common sense'; and like other proponents, he insisted on the virtues of holism. The best-known version of this (and one in which Curry found much to criticise[182]) is James Lovelock's metaphor of 'Gaia'. As noted in chapter 6, the philosopher Mary Midgley has embraced the idea with enthusiasm, despite its New Age connotations, endorsing the way in which it asks us to conceive of the earth as an organic whole. She has also noted the growing scientific acceptability of this 'theory' (once only a 'hypothesis'), and has drawn attention to the tradition of great scientists who have seen no incompatibility between research, religion, and reverence (or between 'wisdom, information, and wonder' to use the title of one of her books).[183] Midgley, like others working in this field, has pointed to the many traditionalist ways of thinking that prevent a more sustainable approach to nature. These include creeds that claim

---

[181] Curry, *Ecological Ethics*, p. 2.   [182] *Ibid.*, pp. 68–71.
[183] Mary Midgley, 'Individualism and the Concept of Gaia', in Ken Booth, Tim Dunne, and Michael Cox (eds.), *How Might We Live? Global Ethics in a New Century* (Cambridge: Cambridge University Press, 2001), pp. 29–44; also see her *Wisdom, Information and Wonder. What Is Knowledge For?* (London: Routledge, 1989).

that only humans have value, the tradition of seeing duties as essentially contractual, and the habit of regarding nature as something to fight and control as opposed to something that is vulnerable and capable of severe injury. Her message – the only rational one – is the now familiar one from proponents of sustainability: time is running out, but much can be saved.

In the meantime, we fiddle on the biggest stage – international politics – while nature as humans have known it disappears. It is nonetheless possible at a different level to act every day like a world community, from recycling to supporting green causes politically. A small but important step, both cost-free and immediately possible for all, is to name things properly. In chapter 1 I endorsed the adoption of the WWF's advice about using the term 'climate chaos' (instead of the benign-sounding 'climate change'), and in chapter 5 I suggested that we should drop the term 'natural disasters' for certain occurrences, and instead understand them as the result of human choices in particular natural contexts. In these and other ways, environmental politics must be at the top of the world security agenda, for we are now at a stage in history when all other issues must be looked at, if only in part, in terms of their environmental impact. If human society continues with more or less business-as-usual – speaking about environmental responsibility without taking the necessary steps to implement change – then the shortages and disruptions forecast will come along, threatening to provoke the political extremism indicated by Tudge. Rising to the challenge and changing how we live globally – the old image of 'lifeboat earth', with people pulling together collectively as they have done in crises nationally – will to different degrees disturb the ways of life in which we (in the rich world) have become comfortable. In the past it has often taken war to bring about radical shifts. It took two world wars to persuade Europeans to give up the old game of nations that had torn them apart for centuries, and instead pursue the economics, sociology, human rights, and politics of community. Such a habit (confirmed by Winston Churchill, in his observation that humans will always do the right thing in the end, but only when they have tried everything else) gives little encouragement that we might engage with the environmental challenge through the politics of world community without first having had to suffer a nasty dose of extremist turmoil.

There is much ruin left in both nature and the human species. The more fragile of the two, during the six billion years of remaining sunlight, are humans. They are no more guaranteed to escape extinction than any other living species, when their habitat no longer works for them. Nature will survive, but in what form remains to be seen; its hospitality for the human species will depend importantly on the decisions made by humans themselves, and in the near future. But does the human future really matter in the long term? Are we not simply stardust in an infinite universe? The journalist Simon Hattenstone told Martin Rees the story of an astronomer who killed himself because he felt so small and insignificant when he stared at the stars. Rees disagreed. He did not share his fellow astronomer's despairing attitude. He said, 'it seems to me what makes things important is not how big they are, but how complex and intricate they are, and human beings are more complicated and intricate than either atoms or stars. So we needn't feel subordinate to the stars because we are smaller.' Size does not matter. Rees went on: 'If it's the only place where intelligent life exists, then tiny though it is on the cosmic scale, our earth is the most important place in the universe.'[184]

The power of this argument is underlined graphically when one looks at the spectacular images beamed back to earth by Magellan, Mariner, Voyager, and other spacecraft.[185] These amazing photographs show that the *global-we* (apparently) live alone in endless and inhospitable space. Until we know differently, we must therefore agree with Rees that the earth is the most important place in the universe. To gaze in wonder (reason demands no other) at the detailed images of the outer reaches of this universe, and to contemplate the earth's glorious minuteness, should persuade everybody of the urgency of working together as a nascent world community to ensure that nature flourishes in all its complexity, for its own sake, and also as the only refuge for the invention of humanity.

---

[184] Simon Hattenstone, 'The End of the World as We Know It (Maybe)', *The Guardian*, 24 April 2003.
[185] Michael Benson, *Beyond. Visions of the Interplanetary Probes* (New York: Harry N. Abrams, 2003). This is a book every child, everywhere, should be given.

8   Who will own the twenty-first century?

I. F. Stone said that if you expect an answer to your question during your lifetime, you're not asking a big enough question.

Kevin Danaher[1]

The previous chapter was a critique of some key issues affecting world security, which exposed the dangers of global business-as-usual. The present chapter shifts from critique to reconstruction, and brings to the foreground three political orientations that are basic to emancipatory realism (promoting equality, humanising globalisation, and inventing humanity). The theme is to pursue world security as if people really matter.[2] The chapter begins, however, by looking at the problem of representing the suffering that is at the heart of insecurity.

Regarding pain

Reality has abdicated. There are only representations: media.

Susan Sontag[3]

The journalist Janine di Giovanni in the late 1980s was inspired to change direction in her work by Felicia Langer, an Israeli lawyer who was devoting her life to defending Palestinians before Israeli military courts.

---

[1] Kevin Danaher, *10 Reasons to Abolish the IMF and World Bank* (New York: Seven Stories Press, 2001), p. 98.

[2] I make this point sensitive to the comment of the journalist Steven Poole – echoing a criticism I have heard numerous times from officials, politicians, and supporters of NGOs – about 'the slightly abstracted feel of much writing on international relations, as if the world were merely a particularly fascinating game of Risk'. It seems to be that much academic international relations fails to engage even those who are professionally or passionately engaged in the daily realities of the subject matter. See Steven Poole, 'Et cetera', *The Guardian*, 21 January 2006.

[3] Susan Sontag, *Regarding the Pain of Others* (London: Hamish Hamilton, 2003), p. 97.

Langer told her: 'Write about the small voices, the people who can't write about themselves.' She followed this vision, reporting the world 'from the edge'.[4] Di Giovanni's snapshots of life in the fracture zones of world politics, from Algeria in 1998 to Iraq in 2005, are required reading for students of world politics, showing something of the lives of real people in real places. This is not the case, students sometimes complain, in much that gets published in the academic literature of international relations. Journals in particular, they say, are frequently too abstract, too self-referential, too much for the profession rather than the world outside, and focused on theoretical point-scoring rather than on real people.

But what is real? I want now to return to the idea of the cracked looking-glass, and the complex relationship between observers and what (and how) they choose to observe. One important dimension of the argument is that the power to describe reality (whatever is said to be reality) is central to the reality of exercising power. A corollary of this is that the power to divert people from gazing at global suffering is central to the continuation of human wrongs. Those who set the agenda are ahead in shaping reality, whether in a parish council or the United Nations. That was the meaning of the remark made by the 'senior adviser' in the White House who said 'we create our own reality . . . We're history's actors.'

Such an attitude is one of political swagger, not untruth, though the two are often friends. Commentators have to watch out for both. As well as exhorting students of journalism to engage with big questions, I. F. Stone also warned them, 'Among all the things I'm going to tell you today about being a journalist, all you have to remember is two words: governments lie.'[5] Governments always did, and it was one of the laudable aims of the Enlightenment to try to hold governments accountable. In this task, the rise of print culture was crucial.[6] Some advances were made in checking power, even in relation to the notably unaccountable governments of the day, but their excesses of power and their capacity to twist the truth paled into insignificance in comparison with twentieth-century totalitarian leaders: Hitler with his Big Lies, Stalin with the

---

[4] Janine di Giovanni, *The Place at the End of the World: Essays from the Edge* (London: Bloomsbury, 2006), pp. 3–6; see also her *Madness Visible. A Memoir of War* (London: Bloomsbury, 2004).

[5] Quoted by Howard Zinn, *Terrorism and War*, ed. Anthony Arnove (New York: Seven Stories Press, 2002), p. 63.

[6] Roy Porter, *Enlightenment. Britain and the Creation of the Modern World* (London: Allen Lane, 2000), pp. 72–95.

Gulag, Mao with the Cultural Revolution, and Pol Pot with Year Zero. In 1767 – and it is as true today as then – Voltaire told the French people, 'Anyone who has the power to make you believe absurdities has the power to make you commit injustices.'[7]

Voltaire's words should be pinned near the computer screens of all students of security studies, as a reminder that what they read is *for* somebody and *for* some thing. Representations of the worlds of politics do not come unmediated, from nowhere, and simply for their own sake. Remember Winston Smith, the central figure in Orwell's *Nineteen Eighty-Four*, who was employed to falsify records in the 'Ministry of Truth', which of course was the organisation whose *raison d'être* was to administer lies. He knew the Party manufactured lies, which then 'passed into history and became truth'. A key slogan was: 'Who controls the past . . . controls the future: who controls the present controls the past.'[8] The slogan retains its purchase. Even if human society outside North Korea is not today faced by the totalitarian manipulation Orwell feared would come about, everybody on earth is targeted by the spin of some manufacturers of Truth seeking to control the present and future. In *Nineteen Eighty-Four* the Party called it 'Reality control'. This is what the Winston Smiths in Whitehall and Downing Street attempted in 2002–3 with their 'dodgy dossier' and other attempts at manipulation in the run-up to the invasion of Iraq.[9] They sought to persuade public opinion that Saddam Hussein represented a clear and present danger, and was a threat to the security of 'the world'. Many people in Britain (key opinion-formers like MPs as well as the general public) were predisposed to believe the government on such an important issue of national security. At the same time, in Washington, the White House also attempted reality control. A growing number of stories were suppressed in the US media in the name of 'national security'. After celebrating the conventional phase of the war, which went so well, the Bush administration desperately tried to cover up the reality on the ground during the unconventional phase, which went so badly.[10]

---

[7] Quoted by John Pilger, 'Columns', *New Statesman*, 7 July 2003.

[8] George Orwell, *Nineteen Eighty-Four* (London: Penguin, 1989), p. 37.

[9] Steven Kettell, *Dirty Politics. New Labour, British Democracy and the Invasion of Iraq* (London: Zed Books, 2006), pp. 81–109.

[10] As reported by Susan George, *Another World is Possible if...* (London: Verso, 2004), p. 139, drawing attention to Kristina Borjesson (ed.), *Into the Buzzsaw* (New York: Prometheus Books, 2002). See also the exposé of the Bush administration's 'desperate efforts to cover up [the] unfolding disaster in Iraq' in Bob Woodward's book *State of Denial: Bush at War Part III* (New York: Simon and Schuster, 2006), which led a *Guardian* editorial to comment

Reality control is not just for governments. Recall from chapter 6 Naomi Klein's warning that we must not become so distracted by the writing on the wall that we forget to ask who actually owns the wall. Big business knows that there is profit through descriptive power. In a discussion of corporate control of the media, Susan George has recorded that a reporter on Fox News was not allowed to tell a story that was likely to anger US agribusiness. The station manager said: 'We paid 3 billion dollars for these TV stations. We'll tell you what the news is. The news is what we say it is.'[11]

For governments and corporations, the way in which they choose to represent and disseminate reality is strategic business, a key aspect of exercising power. Susan Sontag has described photography, even poetry, as potentially having a strategic/instrumental role: 'If governments had their way', she has argued, 'war photography, like most war poetry, would drum up support for soldiers' sacrifice.'[12] An honest, intrusive, and open media is essential to expose and if possible disarm the 'weapons of mass deception' deployed by governments.[13] There is still plenty of scope for this in liberal societies, but in countries controlled by tyrannical regimes (the Zimbabwe of President Mugabe and the Burma of the generals, for example) brave individuals must take enormous personal risks in the interests of truth-seeking. This is one reason why the decline in foreign news coverage in the Western press is regrettable. Helping the spread of reliable knowledge is one means by which solidarity can be shown with those suffering under dictatorships.

The press has a vital role in trying to uncover deception by the powerful, and hold to account governments behaving badly. Sometimes – not always – the role is carried out with admirable skill and extreme courage. John Pilger collected several outstanding examples of the work of investigative journalists under the take-no-prisoners title (which would have earned the approval of I. F. Stone) *Tell Me No Lies*.[14] These first eye-witnesses to history included Martha Gellhorn at the concentration camp at Dachau, Seymour Hersh at the massacre at My Lai, Anna Politkovskaya in Chechnya, and Robert Fisk in the war in Iraq.

that this veteran reporter had 'not forgotten the duties of journalism': *The Guardian*, 4 October 2006, editorial, 'In Praise of . . . Bob Woodward'; in addition, Paul Harris, 'White House in Crisis over "Iraq Lies" Claims', *The Observer*, 1 October 2006.
[11] As told by George, *Another World*, p. 139.   [12] Sontag, *The Pain of Others*, p. 42.
[13] For example, Dilip Hiro, *Secrets and Lies. The True Story of the Iraq War* (London: Politico's, 2005).
[14] John Pilger, *Tell Me No Lies: Investigative Journalism and its Triumphs* (London: Jonathan Cape, 2004).

A piece by Seumas Milne (on Margaret Thatcher's 'Secret War against the Miners') is a healthy reminder that wrong-doing begins at home, and of the way governments sometimes seek to use 'security' as a discursive instrument of control. In the 1980s, coal miners in the UK were trying to defend their livelihoods and communities in the face of violent state power. They were labelled 'The Enemy Within' by Margaret Thatcher.[15] Milne revealed that while the miners were being accused of disloyalty, the election victories of Conservative governments between 1979–92 were 'underwritten' by millions of pounds donated by five foreign businessmen implicated in criminal tax evasion, insider dealing, and fraud. The largest single donor was 'an alleged Nazi collaborator and enthusiastic supporter of the Greek colonels' dictatorship'.[16] Milne's account revealed that while leaders screech, it is what they are silent about that sometimes speaks the most clearly. One of the heroes of *Tell Me No Lies*, Politkovskaya, alive when the book was published, was murdered in October 2006 in the increasingly illiberal Russia of President Putin. According to one fellow journalist, she had become an *izgoy* – somebody who becomes an outsider because of some flaw in their make-up. According to Anton Trofimov, 'in Putin's Russia, telling the truth is a flaw incompatible with the status of a journalist'.[17]

As governments give way to their instinct to exercise reality control, journalists should pursue their duty of providing 'many windows', to use Mary Midgley's phrase. In an old diary, I have a note that the banner of the *Huddersfield Advertiser*, a local newspaper in West Yorkshire, proudly declared, 'Let light ever shine on power lest power corrupts.' I do not know whether the paper survives, or whether it carried out its mission, but this is a perfect expression of the Kantian duty of 'publicity', and also a perfect Enlightenment metaphor (the idea of light and shining it on power). Such a banner remains a journalistic ideal, though some critics think that the ideal is suffering in our finest newspapers and TV because of the intrusion of corporate interests and political influence. Howard Friel and Richard Falk, following their analysis of the

[15] Seumas Milne, 'The Secret War against the Miners', in Pilger, *Tell Me No Lies*, pp. 284–331.

[16] *Ibid.*, p. 316.

[17] Quoted in James Meek, 'The Best Memorial', *The Guardian*, 14 October 2006. Anna Politkovskaya was murdered by a professional hit-squad as this book was being finished. She was the twelfth journalist killed during the six years of Putin's leadership. She had become the country's most prominent investigative journalist, both for her coverage of the Chechnya war and of high-level corruption: Yuri Zarakhovich, 'Nature Weeps as a Heroine is Buried', *Time*, 23 October 2006, and also Politkovskaya's 'A Condemned Woman', unpublished at the time of her death, in *The Guardian*, 14 October 2006.

Israel–Palestine conflict in the *New York Times*, concluded that it had seriously misrepresented the situation by ignoring negative dimensions of Israeli policy and behaviour, while marginalising the suffering and experience of the Palestinians. The result, they said, was that the readers of the *Times* in the United States were offered only a limited understanding of what many consider to be the crux of the whole Middle Eastern imbroglio.[18] Sometimes too much reality is hard to deal with, as was suggested in chapter 1, and may not be good for sales. In September 2006, in a small but revealing instance, *Newsweek* offered its international readers a cover declaring 'Losing Afghanistan', with the picture of a turbaned fighter with a grenade launcher at his shoulder. On the cover for the magazine's US readers was a photograph of the 'celebrity snapper' Annie Leibovitz with children, and the headline 'My Life in Pictures.'[19]

The deployment of mass deception on the part of liberal-democratic governments reached its apogee in modern times in the lead-up to the 2003 Iraq War. Much of the attempted deception was quickly exposed, though for the tens of thousands dead and seriously injured in the war (and still more to come in the even bloodier peace) it all came too late.[20] One consequence of the revelation of the false prospectus on which the invasion of Iraq was justified, however, will have been to make it much more difficult in future for governments in Washington and London to persuade their populations of the urgency of going to war on the basis of secret intelligence. The charge against the prime movers in the war, the Bush–Cheney–Rumsfeld team, was powerfully expressed by Ignacio Ramonet, director of *Le Monde diplomatique*: 'To justify a preventive war that the United Nations and global public opinion did not want, a machine for propaganda and mystification (organised by the doctrinaire sect around George Bush) produced state-sponsored lies with a determination characteristic of the worst regimes of the 20th century.'[21] The targets of these criticisms, we must remind ourselves, pride themselves on being beacons of democracy and free speech. Orwell called such

---

[18] Their work is discussed in Noam Chomsky, *Failed States. The Abuse of Power and the Assault on Democracy* (New York: Metropolitan Books, 2006), p. 85. An article entitled 'The Israeli Lobby' by John J. Mearsheimer and Stephen M. Walt was only able to find publication in a British journal, *The London Review of Books*, vol. 28(6), 23 March 2006; its authors, and the article, attracted considerable criticism from certain quarters, as well as applause from others.

[19] The motto of *Newsweek* is 'Our voices. Your voices. Every day'; see Dan Glaister, 'Newsweek Sugars Pill for US', *The Guardian*, 28 September 2006.

[20] Hiro, *Secrets and Lies*, and Kettell, *Dirty Politics*.

[21] Ignacio Ramonet, 'State-sponsored Lies', *Le Monde diplomatique*, July 2003.

corruption 'democratic totalitarianism', and Pilger has argued that it is endemic in the leading democracies. His evidence for this, in the British case, includes cover-ups in the sale of Hawk jets to Indonesia (when the latter was controlling East Timor through extreme terror), the 'culture of lying' in the Foreign and Commonwealth Office exposed by the Scott inquiry into arms-to-Iraq, and the deliberate and numerous lies in the run-up to the Iraq War (such as Blair's declaration that 'we do know of links between al-Qaeda and Iraq'). The BBC attracted vitriol from the cheerleaders of Blair's invasion of Iraq because of what the government complained was the Corporation's unprofessionalism (in other words, its perceived opposition to the government case); but Pilger produced figures showing a disappointing lack of coverage by the Corporation of dissenting views about the war.[22]

If the media's record is mixed in relation to the challenges of contemporary war, it is no less so in relation to the task of throwing light on egregious episodes of human rights abuses. In this regard, no case in recent times has been more telling than Rwanda. In her books and other writing on the genocide that took place in that country in 1994, Linda Melvern has exposed the complicity of the British (and other governments) in what happened, the widespread official hypocrisy and lying that took place, and the general irresponsibility of the press and other media.[23] The story is as bleak as it is unimaginably brutal. The British government claimed it did not know what was happening, and that it was going along with UN policies (although there were clear advance warnings for those who wanted to see, Whitehall had real-time information once the killing began, and the UK government played a leading role in the UNSC in devising its weak response). A Swiss national, the chief delegate of the International Committee of the Red Cross, first called the mass slaughter of Tutsis a 'genocide', and in Britain the first public statement that a genocide had begun was a press release by Oxfam. London tried to resist the term genocide becoming legitimised diplomatically, for that would mean the Genocide Convention and its obligations would kick in. For their part, the media were generally slow to respond to the horrific events on the ground, and tended to interpret

---

[22] John Pilger, 'Columns', *New Statesman*, 28 April 2003, 7 July 2003, and 4 August 2003.
[23] Linda Melvern, *A People Betrayed. The Role of the West in Rwanda's Genocide* (London: Zed Books, 2000), and *Conspiracy to Murder. The Rwandan Genocide* (London: Verso, 2004); the theme of this paragraph is based on Linda Melvern, 'Rwanda and Darfur: The Media and the Security Council', *International Relations*, vol. 20(1), 2006, pp. 93–104, and 'The UK Government and the 1994 Genocide in Rwanda', *Journal of Genocide Studies*, forthcoming.

what was happening as 'civil war', or 'tribalism', or 'tribal bloodletting' – characterisations that offered an excuse for Britain staying out. Challenged by Melvern to explain why the UK government had not acted decisively, a senior British 'insider' simply said: 'Of course we didn't . . . Neither the press nor the public was interested.' All this took place, Melvern reminds us, in the year 'in which we wept through Steven Spielberg's *Schindler's List'*, and during the time when Western leaders 'walked along the D-Day beaches to celebrate the defeat of fascism'.

A decade later, the media were again generally slow in bringing to general attention the extreme human rights violations taking place in Darfur; and, once more, there was only limited activity to report in the UNSC. World public opinion remained largely ignorant of the issues involved in this remote part of Africa. The media failed to raise public awareness, and to engage external sympathisers with the victors in active solidarity: was Darfur not worth a march? The UNSC again backed away from taking decisive steps to stop the violence.[24] One consequence of the prolonged lack of attention given to Darfur was that the perpetrators of a 'slow-motion genocide' were able to get away with it.[25] Lest it be thought that the media alone are to blame for failing to spread reliable knowledge and expose hypocritical governments, Mark Curtis has pointed to the general failure of the academic community (specifically in Britain) to shine a light on Whitehall's complicity in human rights abuses. His book *Web of Deceit* examined the role of successive British governments in a series of episodes where realpolitik was privileged over human rights. The worst cases he examined were British policy in relation to the massacres carried out by the Indonesian government in 1965, the depopulation of Diego Garcia starting in 1968, the overthrow of governments in Iran and British Guiana, and the repressive colonial policies in Kenya, Malaya, and Oman.[26] Such exposés reveal the startling gap that sometimes exists between the images governments seek to portray (in the case of Britain that of an ethical, lawful, and responsible member of the international community – a 'good international citizen' in the language of the English school) and the real images that are fixed in the minds of critics (in the case of Britain the image of an

[24] Melvern, 'Rwanda and Darfur', pp. 100–3.
[25] The phrase was first used about Bosnia by Diego Arria, the Venezuelan ambassador to the UN and leader of the UN non-aligned bloc; quoted by di Giovanni, *Madness Visible*, p. 203.
[26] Mark Curtis, *Web of Deceit. Britain's Real Role in the World* (London: Vintage, 2003).

infamously hypocritical and hard-nosed country when its government believes its interests are at risk).

When reality control is exercised so powerfully by governments, Langer's 'small voices' tend to be drowned out. This cannot be allowed to happen if trust is to become embedded between people(s) at multiple levels. This challenge is nowhere more intractable today than in the Israel–Palestine conflict. If that conflict is ever to be resolved through anything other than the complete military dominance of one side, many things are required, and not least diplomacy of the highest order.[27] At the societal level, the two nations/societies/religions must learn to enter into the counter-fear of those they presently fear themselves; they do not necessarily have to accept what they find in the minds of their enemies, but they do have to understand it.[28] Heightening the sensibility of persons towards each other's hopes and fears is one of the most useful roles journalists can perform. This has been written about with particular poignancy by the Israeli novelist David Grossman.[29] Starting from the position that the Israelis and Palestinians showed each other 'their darkest aspect', he argued in 2005 that this helped give them both 'excellent rationales' for their hostile actions; both 'turn their enemy into a clichéd version of humanity. A catalogue of stereotypes and prejudices.' The task he emphasised was that of bringing about a change of perspective through 'looking at reality from somebody else's eyes'; this, he believed, 'can free us from the tyranny of the one-and-only-story that a country . . . tells itself'. If only both sides could see themselves as others see them, Grossman hoped that they could then start reformulating their interactions in different ways, without 'the lexicon they use now', largely made up of 'words for violence, for borders, nationalism and extremism'. As an author, Grossman pursued his aims in his writing, and as a citizen of Israel he pursued them as a peace activist. Towards the end of the war in Lebanon in the summer of 2006 he called on his government to opt for diplomacy; three days later, on the day the UN-mandated truce was due to come into effect, his son, pursuing his duty as a soldier, was killed.

Despite the world becoming smaller in some senses – and few areas of geopolitical contestation are as compact as the site of the Israel–Palestine

---

[27] Ahron Bregman, *Elusive Peace. How the Holy Land Defeated America* (London: Penguin, 2005).

[28] This is explored at length in Ken Booth and Nicholas J. Wheeler, *The Security Dilemma. Fear, Cooperation, and Trust in World Politics* (Basingstoke: Palgrave, 2008) esp. ch. 9.

[29] David Grossman, 'To See Ourselves . . . ', *The Guardian*, 12 March 2005; Alex Kumi, 'Peace Activist's Son Killed', *The Guardian*, 14 August 2006.

conflict – it is not uncommon to hear people say that our understanding of each other has not grown. One interpretation of this suggests that reality has 'abdicated', leaving only representation in the form of the media – the so-called CNN effect. This view was flagged at the head of this section, in the quotation by Sontag; but she herself did not endorse it. She attacked what she regarded as this fashionable position, even while emphasising (in the context of photography) the complexities of representing reality. She said that several of the great iconic moments/images of the twentieth century had been staged, adding that we generally did not want to know this, preferring that the photographic images with which we had become familiar were the real thing, the actual moment. 'We want the photographer to be a spy in the house of love and death', she wrote, 'and those being photographed to be unaware of the camera, "off guard".' History in photographs can be as manipulated as written history. In this regard, great moments in history have been restaged almost as long as the invention of the camera, notably in the early days, in the work of Mathew Brady during the American Civil War. Some of the great images of the Second World War were also famously restaged, such as Yevgeny Khaldei's photograph of the Red Flag being hoisted above the Reichstag in 1945; and, of course, most iconic of all for Westerners, the raising of the US flag at Iwo Jima.[30]

While problematising the conventional opinion of the camera as 'the eye of history', Sontag was highly critical of the proposition (she called it 'radical' and 'cynical') that reality had 'abdicated' in favour of a 'society of spectacle'. The intellectual spearhead of this latter position in her opinion was Jean Baudrillard, who is famously or infamously associated with the idea that reality is synonymous with simulated images. 'Fancy rhetoric' is how Sontag dismissed this 'French speciality', though she recognised it as being persuasive to many.[31] In a key passage she wrote: 'To speak of reality becoming a spectacle is a breathtaking provincialism. It universalizes the viewing habits of a small, educated population living in the rich part of the world, where news has been converted into entertainment . . . It suggests, perversely, unseriously, that there is no real suffering in the world.' Against this, she insisted that there are many hundreds of millions of people who are 'far from inured to what they see on television. They do not have the luxury of patronizing reality.'[32]

Sontag's aim in *Regarding the Pain of Others* was to discuss how photography (like other forms of representation) is significantly concerned

[30] Sontag, *Regarding the Pain*, pp. 46–52.   [31] *Ibid.*, pp. 97–8.   [32] *Ibid.*, pp. 98–9.

with the way in which, in Elaine Scarry's words, 'other persons become visible to us, or cease to be visible to us'. Scarry explored this two decades before Sontag, in *The Body in Pain* (interestingly subtitled, for students of security, *The Making and Unmaking of the World*).[33] The two parts of Scarry's title fitted together, she argued, 'for what is quite literally at stake in the body in pain is the making of the world'. Her meditation on the vulnerability of the human body, seen in the infliction of pain for politics (primarily war and torture), is important for the study of world politics because it 'persistently brings one back to the reality of the body'.[34] The latter, as was argued in chapter 6, is the beginning of politics and the end of security.

Scarry's meditation also makes clear pain's 'inexpressibility', a view Sontag echoed with respect to photographs, for all they purport to show. Scarry influentially argued that pain in the end is the only thing that cannot be transmitted by words. Virginia Woolf, much earlier, had put the point very simply: 'English, which can express the thoughts of Hamlet and the thoughts of Lear', she wrote, 'has no words for the shiver or the headache.'[35] If one cannot describe one's own headache, how can we feel and express the deadly pain of unknown people in remote lands – the daily reality of world politics for so many? Here we have two profound problems at the heart of understanding world security: the impossibility of expressing bodies in pain, the very core of human insecurity, and the uncertainty these days about the reliability of knowledge, the very core of epistemology. The reality of world security is therefore rooted in the undescribable and the unknowable. But that does not mean there is no truth, for the reality that is undescribable and unknowable is at the same time undeniable. We all know this reality when it bites, when we ourselves are the victims of pain, and not merely spectators at the suffering of others.

Promoting equality

'The problem of the world's poor', defined more accurately, turns out to be 'the problem of the world's rich' . . . [massive change] does not call for a new value system forcing the world's majority to feel shame at

---

[33] Elaine Scarry, *The Body in Pain. The Making and Unmaking of the World* (New York: Oxford University Press, 1985), pp. 22–3.
[34] The quotation here is from the psychologist Anthony Storr's back-cover endorsement of Scarry's *Body in Pain*.
[35] Quoted *ibid.*, p. 4.

their traditionally moderate consumption habits, but for a new value system forcing the world's rich to see the shame and vulgarity of their overconsumption habits, and the double vulgarity of standing on other people's shoulders to achieve those consumption habits.

C. Douglas Lummis[36]

The centrality of equality for a theory of world politics has been emphasised in several parts of this book: in the felicitous phrase of Ronald Dworkin, it is the 'Sovereign Virtue'.[37] He has argued – a view that this book echoes – that no government is legitimate that does not show equal concern for the fate of all those citizens over whom it claims dominion. Other arguments about the *sovereign virtue* of equality also chime with the emancipatory political orientation of his book, notably his view that there is no genuine conflict between liberty and equality because liberty is conditional on equality. By implication, his belief in the significance of universal human rights as part of showing equal concern for each of us, means that what is true within borders is also true across them.

Dworkin's position, like Brian Barry's discussed in chapter 6, insists that equality be placed at the centre of politics. But what of international politics? Political theorists continue, generally, to ignore the international. For their part, mainstream international relations theorists have focused on the virtue of sovereignty rather than the 'sovereign virtue' of equality. This has been the case not only in realism, as one would expect, but also in most English school work, where one would have expected more interest, given the ostensible concern with civility and civilisation.[38] Some approaches generally seen as part of CSS, such as the Copenhagen school and postmodernism, have also ignored or marginalised the virtue of equality. In all these cases, one of the reasons for this is their narrow concept of politics, and so their lack of engagement with political economy (where issues of equality/inequality cannot easily be avoided). It is one of the main challenges facing a

---

[36] C. Douglas Lummis, 'Equality', in Wolfgang Sachs (ed.), *The Development Dictionary. A Guide to Knowledge as Power* (London: Zed Books, 1992) p. 50.

[37] K. Anthony Appiah, 'Equality of What?', *New York Review of Books*, 26 April 2001, is a critical discussion of Ronald Dworkin, *Sovereign Virtue: The Theory and Practice of Equality* (Cambridge, Mass.: Harvard University Press, 2000).

[38] A comprehensive and sophisticated reassessment of the English school, for example, finds occasion for only one passing reference to equality. The school's lack of engagement with the literature on the subject, not to mention political economy, is eloquent in its silence; see Andrew Linklater and Hidemi Suganami, *The English School of International Relations. A Contemporary Reassessment* (Cambridge: Cambridge University Press, 2006).

critical theory of security to ensure that equality, 'the sovereign virtue', be placed on top of the agenda of world security.[39]

One starting-point for my case is that inequality is bad for the security of all around. Evidence for this is abundant in political economy. In order to make a different case, President John F. Kennedy was apparently fond of saying that a rising tide lifts all boats.[40] This is a superficially attractive metaphor, but in fact serves only to obfuscate, and at the same time gratify the common sense of the powerful. A rising tide in nature does of course lift all boats in the same area to the same extent (*assuming they are all equally seaworthy!*), but a global capitalist tide (when it does rise) manages always to keeps boats at different levels, as well as sink a few. In other words, inequality is inherent in the capitalist system, even when absolute levels of poverty rise. It is not solely poverty that is iniquitous: inequality is. This was illustrated is chapter 6 by the discussion of the work of the social epidemiologist Richard Wilkinson, and the body of research on which he drew showing how inequality negatively affects human relations and individual lives.[41] And what is true domestically, he believed, is true internationally. He showed that egalitarian societies at home tend to be much more egalitarian as they look beyond their own boundaries.

Equality promotion of the sort being suggested here has been well represented in contemporary British political thought by Bernard Crick and Brian Barry; for both writers equality is a necessary and desirable political value, and one with a long (and international) history. Egalitarian principles have animated people in many lands at different times, and in the English tradition never more astutely than in the slogan of the 1381 Peasants' Rebellion: 'When Adam delved and Eve span / Who was then the gentleman?'[42] For supporters of an egalitarian society such as Crick and Barry, their commitment has been based on the belief that an egalitarian society would create the conditions for human achievement, and not oppress it into some dull sameness. As they have both argued, the various talents of people will be better developed without

---

[39] Dworkin, *Sovereign Virtue*, and Brian Barry, *Why Social Justice Matters* (Cambridge: Polity, 2005), esp. pp. 169–85 and (on international dimensions) pp. 261–73.
[40] Quoted by Alex Callinicos, *An Anti-Capitalist Manifesto* (Cambridge: Polity, 2003), p. 9.
[41] Richard G. Wilkinson, *The Impact of Inequality. How to Make Sick Societies Healthier* (London: Routledge, 2005); see also Callinicos, *Anti-Capitalist Manifesto*, pp. 4–14, and Richard Sennett, *Respect. The Formation of Character in a World of Inequality* (London: Allen Lane, 2003), esp. pp. 101–26, 247–63.
[42] Quoted by Lummis, 'Equality', p. 41.

the constraints of poverty, class, ill-health, and all those other deprivations that hold back the many and advantage the few.[43] This is as true globally as it is for the citizens of one's own village or city. An egalitarian society, as was argued in chapter 6, is not about sameness, but about the 'moral imperative' to respect all men and women equally; the latter, as W. G. Runciman noted, is not the same as 'to praise all equally'.[44] Talents that are particularly praiseworthy, Crick has argued, should not 'carry with them disproportionate rewards'. They often do, of course, especially in those celebrity-obsessed sections of contemporary society where consumerism, entertainment, and sport have replaced all other convictions.

The practical politics of an egalitarian vision for world security within and between states can be pursued along two parallel tracks.

1. The reduction of 'unjustifiable inequalities'[45]

In the real world (as opposed to a nightmare world of totalitarian genetic engineering and economic planning) there is no 'complete equality' to be 'finally . . . realized'. Perfect equality, even if desirable, is impossible; but the radical reduction of inequality is certainly not, and many inequalities cannot be justified. Poverty is obviously one, not least, as Crick has pointed out, because it limits freedom 'in nearly every possible way'. Crick's central argument in this regard is that if we believe in the moral equality of all humans, it follows that 'all inequalities of power, status and wealth need justifying'.[46]

The influential idea being followed here is John Rawls' 'difference principle', the idea, central to his theory of 'justice as fairness', that all have an equal right to the most extensive basic liberties. For Rawls, 'All social values – liberty and opportunity, income and wealth, and the bases of self-respect – are to be distributed equally unless an unequal distribution of any, or all, of these goods is to the advantage of the least favoured.'[47] In other words, in the pursuit of equality all inequalities require justification. This means that some inequalities might be excusable (additional pay for a member of a group of workers taking on more responsibility), but many are not, and all need to be justified in

---

[43] See, in particular, Bernard Crick, *Socialism* (Milton Keynes: Open University Press, 1987), pp. 88–98, and Barry, *Social Justice*, pp. 3–34.
[44] The quotation is in Crick's summary of Runciman in *Socialism*, p. 97.
[45] The phrase is Crick's, *ibid.*, p. 90.   [46] *Ibid.*
[47] John Rawls, *A Theory of Justice* (Oxford: Oxford University Press, 1972), pp. 62, 303.

terms of collective benefit.[48] The attempt by progressive civil society to promote 'fair trade', for example, is one way by which they seek to reduce some unjustifiable inequalities in wealth between farming communities in different parts of the world.

2. *The provision of egalitarian capabilities*

Theorists of equality, face-to-face with putting the principle into practice, frequently ask themselves: 'equality of what?' One influential answer to this question, and of direct relevance to world security, was given by the economist Amartya Sen in his exploration (sometimes with Martha Nussbaum) of the 'human capabilities' approach.[49] This idea focuses on capabilities to achieve 'functionings'. While sometimes criticised by relativists for its 'universalistic' conception of what it is to be 'human', the capabilities approach has sought in the minds of its creators to promote the freedoms by which people can 'actually enjoy to choose the lives they have reason to value'.[50] The outcomes will be different because of the diversity of human attitudes and experiences, but some things are shared, and these are the 'capabilities' to be promoted. The capabilities approach is grounded, in the view of its proponents, in ideas that transcend ethnocentric and other biases about the conditions people need to function as a human being. This means capabilities relating to lifespan (such as health), the ability to participate in political activities (such freedom of expression), the opportunity to act as a full member of society (having freedom of movement, for example), and the enjoyment of one's personal life (such as freedom of attachment). The egalitarian impulse here is what Lummis has called 'The Politics of Catching Up'. In the international realm, however, he has argued that policies that have been thought to promote human capabilities, notably those in the name of international development, have too often had the effect of producing 'devastating inequality'.[51]

[48] This is discussed, with admirable clarity, in the context of other approaches, by Callinicos in 'Equality and the Philosophers' in *Equality* (Cambridge: Polity, 2000), pp. 36–87.
[49] The evolution of his ideas on these matters can be traced through three major works: Amartya Sen, *Inequality Re-examined* (Oxford: Clarendon Press, 1992), *Development and Freedom* (Cambridge: Cambridge University Press, 2000), and *Rationality and Freedom* (Cambridge, Mass.: Harvard University Press, 2002); the latter has an extensive listing of his writings. See also, Martha C. Nussbaum and Amartya K. Sen (eds.), *The Quality of Life* (Oxford: Oxford University Press, 1993).
[50] Sen, *Inequality Re-examined*, pp. 39–40, 81.
[51] The quotations and argument are from Lummis, 'Equality', pp. 44–5. An excellent collection of relevant readings is Majid Rahnema with Victoria Bawtree (eds.), *The Post-Development Reader* (London: Zed Books, 2001).

Without the effective promotion of egalitarian capabilities to achieve the full range of human functionings, it 'is not too much to say', as the philosopher Ted Honderich has put it, 'that what we have before us are different kinds of lifetime'.[52] If this is true – and chapter 1 argued that a world that is not working for most of its inhabitants is very much a world of different lifetimes – then the global situation mocks what must be one of the most perfect definitions of equality ever conceived. Colonel Rainsborough, a Leveller, declared in the famous Putney Debates of 1647: 'I think that the poorest he in England hath a life to live as the greatest he.' Though a modernised version of this view would obviously both be conscious of gender equality and seek to give a wider geographical referent than one country, the strength of Rainsborough's words relies not on an appeal to religion or abstract principle, but on the fact that every person faces the existential challenge of having 'to live a life'.[53] Globalising the Leveller appeal is the greatest moral challenge facing human society in the twenty-first century, and a basic necessity in the search for stable world security.

So far, the discussion of equality and inequality has largely focused on a vertical conception of human society, relating to wealth and poverty. Equality has also been increasingly horizontally challenged. In the final decades of the last century, identity politics – 'the right to be different' – came to be proclaimed over 'the right to be the same'.[54] World security requires the reclaiming of equality. Unless it is reasserted as the 'sovereign virtue', greater levels of violence and oppression can be expected from beliefs about, and manipulations of, the narcissism of particular races and religions, cultures and communities. Identity 'roots' are important in the lives of most people to some degree; the problem is that they have become too important, resulting in the tyranny of difference over equality. When equality is pushed out of the door, racial and other claims tend to climb in through the window, and history warns us where this can end. In 1995, an Englishman with German grandparents went to explore his family's past on the fiftieth anniversary of the end of the Second World War. After visiting Dachau, he wrote, 'Humanity should be stateless. The alternative leads here . . . To hell with "roots".'[55]

[52] Quoted by Crick, *Socialism*, p. 95.
[53] Discussed and quoted by Lummis, 'Equality', p. 41.
[54] Kenan Malik's formulation: see his *The Meaning of Race. Race, History and Culture in Western Society* (Houndmills: Macmillan, 1996), p. 19.
[55] Roy Bainton, 'Hell Was Here', *New Statesman*, 28 April 1995.

Race has been one of those ideas that has made some humans kill. Ideas of racial superiority played a part in the growth in the distant past of the white empires, while today ostensible biological differences between people generate violence and shape policy in ways that are as obvious as they are invariably unspoken. Indeed, Philip Nicholson has argued that the 'destructive power of racial mythology' has been the most deadly human phenomenon in the modern age'. He illustrated this with reference to the view of John Dower that of the more than fifty-five million fatalities in the Second World War, 'most were civilians who perished after the outcome was certain, and whose loss was justified or deliberately carried out under officially sanctioned, national vilification policies built on racial, cultural or ethnic mythologies'. Subsequently, he added, every continent exhibited policies 'based on racial mythologies that have been condemned by biological and anthropological science as worthless and by most human rights advocates in and outside the United Nations as in defiance of all their basic codes'.[56] No sensible (as opposed to influential) categorisation of humans based on skin-colour is available. The human species overall is remarkably uniform genetically; there are more genetic variations within one 'race' than between them; and race has no scientific basis, though plenty have tried to give it one. Race is an idea that was invented in history, not a scientific category discovered in nature.[57] Gitta Sereny, historian of the extreme, has argued this in relation to 'inner racism', which she said comes to inhabit adolescents in much of humankind:

> Babies, we know, are not born with it; toddlers have no sense of it; children below the age of 8 or even 10 appear immune to it. Yet, as of that age, or just beyond it, playgrounds echo with the invectives expressing it; only a little later violent streetfights grow out of it; social and political life is permeated by it, and finally people, young and old, see their lives ruined and indeed some die by it.[58]

[56] Philip Yale Nicholson, *Who Do We Think We Are? Race and Nations in the Modern World* (New York: M. E. Sharpe, 1999), p. 3.
[57] Ken Booth, 'Three Tyrannies', in Tim Dunne and Nicholas J. Wheeler, *Human Rights in Global Politics* (Cambridge: Cambridge University Press, 1999), pp. 46–51. See also Paul Gilroy, *Between Camps. Nations, Cultures and the Allure of Race* (London: Allen Lane, Penguin Press, 2000); and, for an ostensibly scientific view, arguing that biology is destiny, see Richard J. Hernstein and Charles Murray, *Bell Curve: Intelligence and Class Structure in American Life* (London: Simon and Schuster, 1996).
[58] Gitta Sereny, 'Racism Within', in Nicholas Owen (ed.), *Human Rights, Human Wrongs. The Oxford Amnesty Lectures 2001* (Oxford: Oxford University Press, 2003) p. 244.

Still, despite the challenging theoretical themes involved in questions of race, and the significant political role it has played (and still plays) in world politics, it remains marginal or non-existent in mainstream scholarship in international relations, and even in critical and other alternative work.[59]

Kenan Malik, writing outside the academic discipline of international relations, has attempted to overcome such neglect. In a book on the 'meaning' of race, he criticised aspects of the work of prominent cultural, postcolonial, and poststructuralist theorists.[60] He argued that some leading authorities had contributed to an unhelpful 'discourse of race', while claiming to be doing the opposite. He wrote that while it was the standard practice of such theorists to reject binary oppositions, their own work reified and promoted such understandings in their emphasis on 'the West and its Others' and the 'West and the Rest'.[61] Malik was particularly critical of one of the icons of postcolonial theorising, Edward Said, for asserting a 'fundamental ontological distinction' between the West and the Rest. This led Malik to a wider critique of the 'confusions and contradictions' in Said's influential idea of 'Orientalism', a concept which he claimed was meaningless and unhelpful. He considered Said's characterisation of 'Western thought' to be ahistorical, unchanging, and essentialist; indeed, it reminded him of the myth of 'Western civilisation' propagated through the flawed reasoning of such extreme advocates of Western superiority as Gobineau and Goebbels. The growth and spread of such ahistorical notions of difference have been reified, in Malik's view, by the negative influence of Foucauldian ideas about

[59] Even an article criticising the 'Eurocentric' character of security studies, and seeking to replace it with the 'groundwork' for a postcolonial 'non-Eurocentric' approach, finds it possible to avoid talking deeply about race and racism; what is more, one of the rare explicit references is an assertion that the sort of CSS approach adopted in this book rests, 'as postcolonial thinkers take pains to point out . . . on profoundly Eurocentric and racist assumptions': see Tarak Barkawi and Mark Laffey, 'The Postcolonial Moment in Security Studies', *Review of International Studies*, vol. 32(2), 2006, p. 332. Readers will make up their own minds about this charge, but the soundness of such 'postcolonial' argumentation can be judged by the fact that the authors of the critique, who announced their intention as being to lay 'the groundwork for the development of a non-Eurocentric security studies', chose to label their own approach 'Melian security studies'; they thereby appropriated as the title for their 'non-Eurocentric' approach not only one of the most cited stories in Western international relations, but also one that derives from Thucydides' founding text in the Western historical canon about war.
[60] Malik, *The Meaning of Race*, esp. pp. 217–59.
[61] For example, Stuart Hall, 'The West and the Rest: Discourse and Power', in Stuart Hall and Bram Gieben (eds.), *Formations of Modernity* (Cambridge: Polity in association with the Open University, 1992), pp. 275–320.

power and truth. The result of all this, he said, was a terrible paradox, wherein 'theoreticians of difference' such as Levinas and Spivak had become mirror-images of those they ostensibly rejected. He then pointed to the danger that 'the advocates of racial thinking and the theorists of difference seemed to be equally indifferent to our common humanity'; in other words, both placed identity before equality. The 'framework' of ideas in postmodernism was the route, according to Malik, by which 'difference becomes resolved into *indifference*'. More generally, he went on, the pursuit of difference, and the valuing of difference over equality, 'provides no resources for the emancipation of the powerless or the oppressed'. Without a 'humanistic perspective', he believed, 'no emancipatory philosophy is possible'.[62]

Race, as was said, is not a scientific category, and in an ideal world would not be worth a second thought; but in the actual world we live in it is the perennial first thought of the racially socialised. Nor is culture a scientific category, but it is an equally powerful word these days; and, like race, it is proving to be politically and socially unhelpful. Culture is static, inherently contestable as a referent, and enormously influential in shaping political and social reality. Interestingly, in the sense in which the concept of culture is now so widely used, 'culture' did not become prominent until the twentieth century. It is only relatively recently, in the view of the anthropologist Bernard McGrane, that *culture* emerged as a 'decisive and almost inescapable part of our world'.[63] At that point, he argued, we started to divide peoples according to the vague notion of culture, a concept in which one could have much more confidence were there a greater consensus about a definition among those who study it.[64] In the nineteenth century, peoples were divided according to (Darwin-inspired) evolutionary development; before that, progressives in the Enlightenment had divided people on the basis of their knowledge/ignorance; and earlier still the key dividing principle had been to separate Christians from heathen. Writing before the end of the Cold War, McGrane could not have guessed how politically prominent the identity marker of culture would become, whether expressed by

---

[62] Malik, *The Meaning of Race*, p. 156.
[63] Bernard McGrane, *Beyond Anthropology: Society and the Other* (New York: Columbia University Press, 1989), p. 113; a powerful critique of the rise of 'culturalism' is Jean-François Bayart, *The Illusion of Cultural Identity* (London: Hurst, 2005).
[64] In a book I wrote in the 1970s I referred to over two hundred definitions of 'culture'; no doubt the number has increased greatly since then: Ken Booth, *Strategy and Ethnocentrism* (London: Croom Helm, 1979), p. 14.

Samuel Huntington or Osama bin Laden.[65] For many, like these two, culture is increasingly reduced to religion. As time passes, a large section of human society seems content to move back to the identity marker that helped characterise the Middle Ages.

Particularly since 9/11, difference based on religion has come to dominate other identity markers. It is, of course, an old story and was the cause of Amartya Sen's 'first exposure to murder'.[66] As a boy witnessing the Hindu–Muslim communal riots of 1944, Sen saw a man, then unknown, stumble into his parents' garden. The victim eventually died in hospital. Sen recalled: 'Kader Mia was a Muslim, and no other identity was relevant for the vicious Hindu thugs who had pounced on him.' In giving witness to the death of Kader Mia, and in giving the victim a name, Sen carried out the duty Felicia Langer described as speaking about 'the people who can't write about themselves'. There have been – and still are – countless such victims: people in the wrong place at the wrong time, labelled as being of the wrong race, religion, ethnic group, or culture, or whatever. One person's cherished roots can be an excuse for another person to become a murderer.

Sen's work on *Identity and Violence* is a powerful antidote to the 'theorists of difference' noted above, and it echoes some of Malik's earlier themes. In particular, Sen attacked the intellectual confusion that attends what he calls the 'miniaturization of human beings';[67] this is the mode of thought that consigns humans to 'one allegedly dominant system of classification', be that 'religion, or community, or culture, or nation, or civilisation (treating each as uniquely powerful)'.[68] The book goes on to criticise the stereotypes fashioned by difference theory that construct politically relevant ideas such as 'the monolithic Middle East' and 'the Western Mind'. Attacking the all too prevalent and powerful belief that people have one all-encompassing identity ('solitarist' is Sen's chosen term[69]) is the theme of his civilised and powerful book.

The solitarist perspective is bad for everyone, except, in the short-run, those whose power is legitimised by it, and fundamentalists who

---

[65] See Samuel Huntington's controversial, influential, and simplistic *The Clash of Civilisations and the Remaking of World Order* (New York: Simon and Schuster, 1996), and Osama bin Laden's polemical, influential, and simplistic pronouncements in Bruce Lawrence (ed. and intro.), *Messages to the World. The Statements of Osama Bin Laden*, trans. James Howarth (London: Verso, 2005).

[66] Amartya Sen, *Identity and Violence. The Illusion of Destiny* (London: Allen Lane, 2006), pp. 170–4.

[67] *Ibid.*, pp. xiii, xvi, 12, 20, 176–8, 185.   [68] Malik, *Race*, pp. xiii–xiv.

[69] Sen, *Identity and Violence*, esp. pp. xii, 178–82; he also used the term 'singular affiliation'.

refuse to recognise life's complexities. Sen rightly criticised those, like the British Prime Minister Tony Blair, who have mindlessly and wilfully insisted on putting all Muslims (except those who are said not to be 'true Muslims') into one 'community'. Such communitarian categorisation has many flaws. It does something to imprison individuals, by defining them in relation to one dominant identity marker, and it pushes all those in the identity community into a position whereby their views are expressed, mediated, and directed by unelected 'community leaders'.[70] Consequently, 'ordinary' Muslims are seen as having access to civil society only as 'Muslims', as opposed to the many other identity markers possible, such as liberals or feminists. The Christian PM, Tony Blair, who had been rather incurious about the world outside Britain before he took office, was nonetheless confident almost from the start in talking about the 'Muslim community' and the 'true voice of Islam'; one consequence of his approach was to impose a community solidarity and destiny on 'the Muslims' that is a mirror-image of that of the terrorists who have spoken in the name of Islam.[71] Solitarist perspectives are necessary for terrorism, but counter-productive on the part of those seeking to eradicate it.

To prioritise a religious marker of identity is both simplifying and simple-minded, flying in the face of what everybody who is awake should know, namely that Muslims are on different sides of many debates, just as Christians and non-believers are. In Sen's words: 'Muslims, like all other people in the world, have many different pursuits, and not all of their priorities and values need be placed within their singular identity of being Islamic.'[72] Such 'miniaturisation' is a dangerous fallacy in the politics of identity. I call it *theying*, and danger is around the corner whenever people start to say 'they are . . .', 'they believe . . .', 'they always . . .'. *They* is the giveaway word of solitarists and reifiers; it is a speech-act pointing to the fate of countless millions like Kader Mia, caught in the trap of identity's myths.

Sen's argument is not that 'identity', of itself, is negative; he starts with an expression of the positive aspects of identity, as a potential source of pride and joy, strength and confidence. But the argument quickly goes on to stress that 'identity can also kill – and kill with abandon' as a result of imposing a 'singular and belligerent' identity on people.[73] Humans have many identities, and these should be chosen, not discovered, Sen argues: we are 'diversely different' and should not be 'imprisoned'. Yet

[70] *Ibid.*, pp. 77, 164.   [71] *Ibid.*, p. 180.   [72] *Ibid.*, pp. 14 and 59–83.   [73] *Ibid.*, p. 1.

the 'Violence of Illusion' is powerful.[74] While identities for Sen are there to be chosen, he does not give sufficient attention to the various attractions as well as demands of adopting a solitarist identity. As Geraldine Bell has argued, 'until we understand the appeal of the belief of individuals that they have preordained roles in the working out of ancient, cosmic struggles, it will be difficult to replace them with reason'.[75] Such understanding is a priority, for when solitarist identities become violent, global threats become local, and foreign policymaking in multicultural societies becomes ever more difficult.[76] Once this is realised, the debate about the relationship between the invasion of Iraq and its aftermath, and 7/7 and other subsequent terrorist outrages, can be settled once and for all (and not in favour of the case made in the White House and Downing Street). The appeal of solitarist identities grew for many Muslims as the violence in Iraq intensified. This, plus images from Guantánamo and Abu Ghraib, served as triggers for a deepening and expansion of the appeal of solitarist identities; young Muslim men, in particular, wanted to see their lives as part of 'ancient, cosmic struggles'. 'Iraq' became a trigger to greater violence (or sympathy with violence) in the name of Islam for an unknown number of people across the world, just as surely as 'Bloody Sunday' had been a trigger for a further upsurge in solitarist Republican identity and violence in Northern Ireland in the 1970s.

The confrontation between difference and equality will be one of the main battlefields of world security for the foreseeable future. The tragedy is that difference and equality do not have to be opposites, for we are all singularly universal, in Sartre's famous phrase. This is not utopian dreaming, for equality has been a value propagated regularly by the institutions of international society. The problem is the limited amount that has been done to bring it about. The challenge is not the theory, but the practice. Religious fundamentalists can agree on the idea of the equality of all persons before God, but when it comes to the political, economic, and societal norms of people on earth, the inequality of nations, women, and classes becomes king. Governments have signed up for equality, but for the most part they are content with words, which help serve their self-delusion about the good they claim to be doing.

[74] *Ibid.*, esp. pp. 1–17 (quotation at p. xiv).
[75] Geraldine Bell, 'An Identity Crisis of our own Making', *The Observer*, 13 August 2006 (review of Sen's *Identity and Violence*).
[76] Christopher Hill compares the models of Britain, France, and the United States in this regard: 'Bringing War Home: Foreign Policy-Making in a Multicultural Society', *International Relations*, vol. 21(3), 2007, pp. 259–83.

Sen's thesis about identity and violence points in four main directions. First, it underlines the importance of greater mutual knowledge. This is not a panacea, but knowing makes *theying* more difficult. And part of 'knowing' is the old adage about 'learning by doing'. Here, some policies make things worse, such as 'faith schools', which legitimise social separatism rather than inclusion.[77] Second, it calls on us to resist practices that legitimise the 'miniaturisation' of religious and other identity groups. This entails treating individuals as the ultimate referent, reaching out for their multiple identities, and promoting the idea of equality. Three, the promotion of global democracy is an important step.[78] A key dimension here is what Sen calls 'intellectual fairness'. Democracy is not only a potential check on power, but Sen also believes that what he calls global democracy will be constitutive of world society. Finally, it is vital to practise equality and not only preach it. Sen advocates in this regard that the West overcome its 'false sense of comprehensive superiority that contributes to identity confrontation in an entirely gratuitous way'.[79] This is evident, for example, in Western pride in its inventiveness, without a proper understanding of the extent to which it has been deeply influenced by other parts of the world. All this is true, but the problem lies not only in the West. Many non-Western societies are not in a position to throw stones, given the way regimes and traditional societies treat their own people, and especially women.

The myths, dreams, narcissism, and power-plays of 'difference' dominate so much of contemporary world affairs, and usually for the worse. This led Malik to conclude: 'The question people ask themselves is not so much "what kind of society do I want to live in?" as "who are we?"'[80] As political ideals and ideologies have weakened, people now view themselves less as political animals and more in terms of other affiliations (cultural, ethnic, religious, etc.). This has led many to choose the solitarist option, which further magnifies difference and places yet higher obstacles before the search for world security. In the face of this, the need for a revival of egalitarian ideals is all the more urgent. The global political economy is a good place to start.

---

[77] Sen, *Identity and Violence*, pp. 160; he has persuasively argued the case for greater knowledge about the rest of the world in *The Argumentative Indian. Writings on Indian Culture, History and Identity* (London: Penguin, 2006).

[78] Sen, *Identity and Violence*, pp. 182–4.

[79] *Ibid.*, chs. 3–7; the argument is expanded in *The Argumentative Indian*.

[80] Kenan Malik, 'Illusions of Identity', *Prospect*, no. 25, August 2006, pp. 64–6.

Humanising globalisation

Money can change everything. Money can eat and dance. Money can make the dirty clean. Money can make the dwarf big.

Lucie Cabrol, in *The Three Lives of Lucie Cabrol*[81]

'When is equality not equality?' Anatole France gave one smart answer: 'The law, in its majestic equality, forbids the rich as well as the poor to sleep under bridges, to beg in the streets, and to steal bread.'[82] A similar riposte, favoured by early British socialists, was: 'Everybody of course is free to dine at the Ritz.' Behind both replies is the understanding that equality before the law, which gives recognition, is only one step, though an important one, in the search for equality; true equality requires the material expression of egalitarian principles if it is to be meaningful in peoples' daily lives.[83] For equality to be performed, and power humanised, money has to dance in the human interest.

Early in the twenty-first century, progressive global civil society identified strongly with the campaign to 'Make Poverty History' (MPH). This is an old and noble cause, for poverty forces people to live determined lives, deprived of the possibility of 'a life to live as the greatest he'. The history of the ambition to end poverty did not begin with MPH, nor will it end with it. During the 1790s, several major Enlightenment figures, notably Thomas Paine and Antoine-Nicolas Condorcet, ceased to regard poverty as a divine imposition on sinful humanity, and instead decided that it was remediable in principle because it was man-made in practice.[84] Needless to say, they failed to eradicate poverty, and indeed a harsh reaction to their ideas followed, resulting from the fear and hostility of the defenders (and beneficiaries) of the existing economic order. Out of this reaction came new forms of conservatism and political economy, and these consigned to oblivion the revolutionary hopes of Paine and Condorcet. As a result, Gareth Stedman Jones has argued that the welfare state that emerged in the early twentieth century owed 'little or

---

[81] *The Three Lives of Lucie Cabrol*, based on a story by John Berger, adapted by Simon McBurney and Mark Wheatley and devised by Theatre de Complicite (London: Methuen Drama, 1995), p. 33.

[82] The version quoted above is from www.wisdomquotes.com. I am grateful to Frances Nugent for bringing this fuller and spicier version to my notice. For a different translation and discussion, see Callinicos, *Equality*, pp. 26–7.

[83] This is a far more radical position than most supporters of 'equality of opportunity' ever realise: on the problems of the latter from an egalitarian viewpoint, see Barry, *Social Justice*, pp. 37–105.

[84] Gareth Stedman Jones, *An End to Poverty. A Historical Debate* (London: Profile Books, 2004); see also his 'A History of Ending Poverty', *The Guardian*, 2 July 2005.

nothing' to their ideas; instead, the significant development was the model of social legislation that came from Bismarckian Germany. This derived not from revolutionary ideals, but rather from the desire of big industrial enterprises to keep the workers efficient, and the hopes of governments to keep working-class movements at bay politically.[85]

The History of Making Poverty is a much older story than that of the campaigns to end it. Poverty remains prevalent within and between countries, despite the revolutionary challenge to age-old ideas at the end of the eighteenth century, the invention of the welfare state in the late nineteenth century, and the project of international development in the mid-twentieth century. The global economy continues to replicate inequality, though progress has been made in meeting basic needs and in legitimising egalitarian values. Nevertheless, under capitalism, the tide will always be as merciless to some as it is bountiful to others; it sinks and separates vessels, as well as raises and rewards. The iniquities of radical inequality remain, even as some absolute poverty is alleviated.

The discussion of inequality below focuses on globalisation and the national politics of uneven global development.[86] This is the focus because economic power is the basis for the exercise of most other forms of power (local dialects have become 'world languages', for example, as a result of the economic power that created the successful armies that advanced the power of those who spoke them). And if the economic order ('globalisation' for shorthand) is not humanised, then the equality of humankind to which the governments of the world rhetorically subscribe will be as meaningless as the formal equality (and actual inequality) that was made fun of by Anatole France and his British socialist contemporaries.

Before proceeding, we need a shared understanding of the contested concept of 'globalisation'; without this, we do not know what has to be humanised, and how. For a start, it is useful to think of globalisation as describing both a project and a process. *Globalisation as a politico-economic project* refers to the acceleration and triumph of the integrated global system under capitalism in the final quarter of the twentieth century. The term is synonymous with the spread of neo-liberalism and US power, and has been primarily a US project, though with many local agents of the global capitalist good. It is this dimension of globalisation that will be

---

[85] Stedman Jones, *End to Poverty*, pp. 199–223.
[86] An elaboration of this approach, which argues that this is the perspective in which a critical global political economy should be conceived, is Anthony Payne, *The Global Politics of Unequal Development* (London: Palgrave Macmillan, 2005).

the main focus of the discussion below. *Globalisation as a techno-cultural process* is synonymous with the shrinking of space and time through the communications revolution. The latter includes everything from the internet to jumbo jets, which have increasingly brought about multiple and complex interpenetrations of the local and the global, and the 'smaller' and '24/7' world. In practice, the project and process dimensions of globalisation interact in multiple and complex ways, but it is helpful to keep them distinct conceptually.

Short of a global catastrophe (general nuclear war or a devastating worldwide pandemic, for example) globalisation is here to stay. This does not mean it will necessarily maintain its same character. If China replaces the United States as the engine of the politico-economic project of globalisation, the techno-cultural processes would be much more dominated by whatever then passed for Chinese ways. If India, too, developed to the maximum of its geopolitical potential, globalisation would further take on an 'Asian' or at least non-Western character (different languages, different business norms, and so on – though the disciplines of capitalism do make some common behavioural demands). Globalisation is not destined to be painted for ever in the colours of the West, but as a project to promote a global economy under capitalism, and a process networking people everywhere, it is unlikely to be completely reversed short of Armageddon. Some who try to play down the significance of this secular historic trend point out that globalisation in one form or other has been around for centuries; this verdict is supposed to diminish globalisation, but it does the very opposite. The long historical trajectory embedding the idea of an integrated world economy and constructing a materially smaller world means that globalisation is here to stay.

The challenge for a critical theory of security is therefore to determine the form globalisation will take. The major debate is the one suggested by the development economist Susan George, which boils down to choosing the adjective to precede the word 'globalisation'.[87] The conventional choices are 'corporate-led', 'finance-driven', or 'neoliberal'.[88] All these were brought together in a breathtakingly direct definition by Percy Barnevick, several times European Businessman of the Year

---

[87] George, *Another World*, p. 6; this point is made in the (sensitive) context of defining 'the movement'. An engaging and empowering account, showing that 'there's more to the anti-globalisation movement than trashing Starbucks', is Paul Kingsworth, *One No, Many Yeses. A Journey to the Heart of the Global Resistance Movement* (London: Free Press, 2003).
[88] George, *Another World*, pp. 7–11.

until he was disgraced by greed and forced into early retirement. He is alleged to have said: 'I would define globalisation as the freedom for my group of companies to invest where it wants when it wants; to produce what it wants, to buy and sell where it wants and to support the fewest restrictions possible coming from labour laws or social conventions.'[89] Such a bravura attitude has been a key feature of actually existing globalisation, but it is not one likely to produce the adjective *humane* that I believe is necessary to accompany globalisation if world security is to be advanced. This view is also the direction in which George's analysis and advocacy have pointed for many years.[90] She put the point very clearly in 2001, at the World Social Forum at Porto Alegre, when she resisted the label 'anti-globalisation movement' by saying 'we are "pro-globalization" for we are in favour of sharing friendship, culture, cooking, solidarity, wealth and resources'.[91]

Such sentiments no doubt could be endorsed by Thomas L. Friedman, a *New York Times* journalist and one of the chief gurus of US-led, neoliberally dominated, technologically determined, corporately inspired globalisation: but his endorsement would be from the standpoint of a markedly different world-view. Friedman's *The World Is Flat* is ostensibly one of the most significant books on globalisation to appear in the first decade of the twenty-first century; it quickly attracted plaudits, winning the Financial Times/Goldman Sachs Business Book of the Year, and being advertised as 'The Bestselling Non-fiction Book in the World Today' in 2006.[92] The book's central theme is that the world is being 'flattened' (a relentlessly repeated metaphor), with barriers being broken down, production and efficiency being improved, neoliberal free-market policies setting human potential free, and people being able to live more fulfilling lives than ever before.[93] This is all related to the unparalleled development and expansion of technologies that connect knowledge and resources from all over the world, which in turn make possible the incredible speed and efficiency of transnationalised business.[94] It is a powerful book, of the powerful, for the powerful, and by a powerful individual, mixing ideas about the global economy with conspicuous name-dropping and tales of the author's globe-trotting.

---

[89] Quoted *ibid.*, p. 10.   [90] *Ibid.*, pp. 249–59, esp. 254.
[91] Quoted by Callinicos, *Anti-Capitalist Manifesto*, pp. 13–14.
[92] The advertising is on the book's jacket: Thomas L. Friedman, *The World Is Flat. The Globalized World in the Twenty-First Century* (London: Penguin, 2006; 1st pub. 2005).
[93] *Ibid.*: see 'The Ten Forces that Flattened the World', pp. 50–258.
[94] Note his Dell laptop story: *ibid.*, pp. 515–20.

Globalisation as praised by Friedman certainly makes the world smaller, and some parts richer, but as numerous critics have pointed out, it does not in its existing form make that world peaceful or liberal: 'Least of all does it make it flat' was John Gray's verdict.[95] Theoretically, the book is a curious mix when it comes to human agents. When it suits the argument, humans are central to economic success. They are 'the intangible things', constituting society's 'ability and willingness to pull together and sacrifice for the sake of economic development', and the presence of leaders 'with the vision to see what needs to be done . . . and the willingness to use power to push for change'.[96] But, as Gray has argued, when it comes to history Friedman's technological determinism leads him into giving 'misleadingly simple' interpretations. Friedman focused, for example, on the information revolution as a key factor ending the Cold War, while failing to recognise the role of older forces such as religion and nationalism (represented by the mujahidin in Afghanistan and the workers and churches in Poland).

Friedman's flat world is planet opportunity. He is confident of the road to success for a country able to get 'its act together', arguing that the 'basic formula' for economic success is 'reform wholesale, followed by reform retail, plus good governance, education, infrastructure, and the ability to glocalize'. This formula, plus 'the intangible things' (the human resources available) explains why 'one country's skyline change[s] overnight and another's doesn't change over half a century'.[97] For the powerful and the powerless alike, but for different reasons, this might not look to be too bad a world, but there are many reasons for holding back and not worshipping at the foot of the skyscrapers of Friedmanian globalisation. Not only are the geopolitical and environmental dimensions of the book underdeveloped, but only towards the end, in his discussion of 'The Unflat World', does he acknowledge that many people are living in poverty and deserve compassion.[98] Friedman's world is busy but lifeless. He claims that technology helps preserve if not increase global diversity,[99] but his anecdotes reveal a different story. It is a tale of outsourced call-centres, MBAs, CEOs, computer addicts, office-working consumers, and golf. In a

[95] John Gray, 'The World Is Round', *New York Review of Books*, 11 August 2005; this excellent review makes interesting comparisons between Friedman's and Marx's style of thinking. Callinicos had earlier noted the 'vulgar Marxist ring' in some of Friedman's writing: *Anti-Capitalist Manifesto*, pp. 51–2. Note also the critical comments of Robert J. Samuelson 'The World is Still Round', *Newsweek*, 25 July 2005.
[96] Friedman, *The World Is Flat*, pp. 416–17.   [97] *Ibid.*, p. 416.
[98] *Ibid.*, pp. 462–8, 476–8.   [99] *Ibid.*, pp. 506, 511–12.

life-world sense, this picture of the world is indeed flat, very flat indeed. His India is that of the Bangalore golf course,[100] while the war-ravaged, drug-infested, US-complicit, terror-infused, poverty-stricken country of Colombia is only briefly mentioned in a list of states that do not give creditors rights.[101] What is true of India and Colombia is true of Friedman's business outlook as a whole, sophisticated as it is. Overall, Friedman's world-view, and especially his book's bestseller status, simply underline the desire of people to believe what they want to believe. Flat-earthers, in the past and today, are unable to see beyond the horizon of their own beliefs.

The uni-direction of Friedman's globalisation does not give due significance to potential future uncertainty. The uneven impact of globalisation offers a complex picture as far as world security is concerned.[102] A few very brief snapshots follow:[103]

- *Military*. Positively, the integration of the world economy places extra incentives on conflict management, in order to keep business moving, though the differential concern of external actors in relation to instability in the Middle East as opposed to violence in the Great Lakes region of Africa is revealing. Negatively, globalisation gives space for the flourishing of certain modes of political violence. John Gray, for example, has seen in the organisation of al-Qaeda 'a perfect embodiment of globalisation'.[104]
- *Political*. Positively, some of the regulatory aspects of globalisation help economies work more profitably and can empower previously ignored workers. Negatively, the drive for profit by multinational companies can lead to the abuse of human rights. This occurred with some oil companies in South America and West Africa, when strong corporations and strong-arm

---

[100] *Ibid.*, pp. 3, 558–62; every sweeping statement by Friedman about India should be checked alongside those of Arundhati Roy, *Power Politics* (Cambridge: South End Press, 2001; 2nd edn) and *The Algebra of Infinite Justice* (London: Flamingo, 2002), and Sen, *The Argumentative Indian*.

[101] Compare Friedman on Colombia, *The World Is Flat*, p. 405, with Doug Stokes, *America's Other War. Terrorizing Colombia* (London: Zed Books, 2005).

[102] I have discussed these more fully in 'Two Terrors', in Ersel Aydinli and James N. Rosenau (eds.), *Globalization, Security, and the Nation State. Paradigms in Transition* (Albany, N.Y.: SUNY Press, 2005), pp. 32–7.

[103] The snapshots follow the 'sectors' of Barry Buzan, Ole Wæver, and Jaap de Wilde, *Security: A New Framework for Analysis* (Boulder, Colo.: Lynne Rienner, 1998), chs. 3–7; the illustrations are from Jan Aart Scholte, *Globalization: A Critical Introduction* (Basingstoke: Macmillan, 2000), and Booth, 'Two Terrors'.

[104] John Gray, *Al Qaeda and What it Means to be Modern* (London: Faber and Faber, 2003).

governments allied against workers and their supporters seeking improved life conditions.[105]

- *Societal*. Positively, the processes of globalisation have helped the growth of global consciousness and the densification of networks of global civil society.[106] These 'transworld solidarities' have helped indigenous peoples struggle against their governments and multinational corporations. Negatively, local identities and cultures have been threatened by the cultural power of 'McWorld',[107] and there is plenty of evidence from within the rich world that the pressures of competing in the global economy can erode local community and personal fulfilment.[108]

- *Environment*. Positively, globalisation may promote standards in places where previously there were none, but negatively globalisation has proved to be a net polluter, involving the carrying of produce huge distances, and encouraging the over-exploitation of resources such as fisheries, which then leads to insecurity about livelihoods and communities.[109]

- *Economic*. Supporters of neoliberal globalisation argue that it has had a very positive effect through global growth and increases in aggregate welfare.[110] Negatively, the key indicator affecting the security of real people in real places is not the global aggregate, or nationalised statistics, but how the figures play out in specific situations. Here, what can seem to be a significant improvement overall can hide real disparities in particular settings, especially for women.[111] Internal violence may be encouraged by the workings of the global system. The disintegration of Yugoslavia, and the associated ethnic conflict, were not only

[105] John Madeley, *Big Business: Poor Peoples. The Impact of Transnational Corporations on the World's Poor* (London: Zed Books, 1999), pp. 121–7.
[106] See, for example, Robin Cohen and Shirin M. Rai, *Global Social Movements* (London: Athlone Press, 2000).
[107] Benjamin R. Barber, *Jihad vs. McWorld* (New York: Ballantine Books, 1996).
[108] Robert Putnam, *Bowling Alone: The Collapse and Revival of American Community* (New York: Simon and Schuster, 1996).
[109] Worldwatch Institute, *State of the World 2006* (London: Earthscan, 2006).
[110] Charles Leadbeater, *Up the Down Escalator. Why the Global Pessimists Are Wrong* (London: Viking Penguin, 2002).
[111] The point has been made with respect to the uneven impact of the 'Asian miracle' within societies in the region: Jan Jindy Pettman, 'Questions of Identity: Australia and Asia', in Ken Booth (ed.), *Critical Security Studies and World Politics* (Boulder, Colo.: Lynne Rienner, 2005), pp. 171–4.

encouraged by the end of the Cold War, but also by the country's changing role in the global economy.[112]

These snapshots only begin to suggest the complex interrelationship between the project and processes of globalisation and their multifaceted and multilevel security implications. What are undeniable are the manifold negative impacts of globalisation on the security of both individuals and collectivities – the very opposite of humane globalisation. Students of security do not hear the countless millions of 'small voices' living in insecurity in the Panglossian descriptions of the 'flat world' from the cheerleaders of globalisation. India, by most accounts one of the coming powers of the decades ahead, is seen by Friedman in relation to fibre-optics, trade policy, and 'zippies'.[113] These things are part of the picture of course, but the India revealed by Amartya Sen and Arundhati Roy is much more complex, historical, and visceral. Sen and Roy tell us how Indians feel, and not, like Friedman, only how they adjust to the global economy. For Roy the view from the Bangalore golf course was yet more evidence of her country's 'cringing obeisance to Western corporate power'.[114]

Dams have been a potent symbol of countries adjusting to the global economy through industrial development, not least in India, and they have attracted considerable political and environmental controversy.[115] Ambitious dam-building has followed in the path of globalisation, as governments are pushed into the 'struggle or starve' mentality. The pressures are to compete internationally, create jobs, develop industrially, promote nationalism, and construct an efficient infrastructure. Governments not surprisingly have seen dam-building as a means of meeting these pressures and advancing state security under globalisation. Other voices have been raised to draw attention to the considerable insecurity that such projects may bring to poor people whose lives are affected. Roy has been the most prominent opponent internationally of her own government's pro-dam policies. She has claimed that there has been a direct, unnecessary, and negative correlation between the Indian government's high-profile economic-strategic projects for state security and the increased insecurity of many Indians. Against the background of India's nuclear tests and her belief that at least thirty-three million

[112] Susan Woodward, *Balkan Tragedy: Chaos and Dissolution after the Cold War* (Washington, D.C.: Brookings Institution, 1995).
[113] Friedman, *The World Is Flat*, pp. 126–9, 131–3, 214–24, 268–75.
[114] Arundhati Roy, *Power Politics* (Cambridge: South End Press, 2001), p. 107.
[115] Madeley, *Big Business*, pp. 115–20.

people had been displaced by dam-building over half a century, she said in 2001 that 'Bombs and dams are the corollary of India's slums: the bombs have diverted taxes, and the dams have deprived millions of their lands and their rivers.'[116] She has seen in the dam-building above all the story of modern India: 'its greed, its wanton violence and its centralisation of power'. The point to understand here is that globalisation can have very different impacts on security, depending on the referent. A related account of insecurity resulting from dam-building occurred in Namibia, when the Himba people were threatened. The Namibian government's plans involved moving the Himba from their traditional lands as part of their being assimilated into the project of national development. Paradoxically, the Himba discovered that their security (their collective identity) was more fundamentally challenged by their own state's dam-building policy following independence (in pursuit of Namibian nationalism and economic success) than it had been formerly by the brutal aggression of the armed forces of the apartheid regime in South Africa.[117]

Globalisation will continue to produce winners and losers in relation to feeling and being safe, even if the system can be tweaked here and there, as it was following the hyper-globalisation of the 1990s. The Asian financial crisis of 1997–8 was one among several developments leading to some reconsiderations of 'Washington Consensus' fundamentalism.[118] A group of former insiders broke ranks and began to criticise the workings of the deregulated world economy identified with the first version of the Washington Consensus. In particular, such major players in the running of the global capitalist order as Paul Krugman, Jeffrey Sachs, Joseph Stiglitz, and George Soros became prominent opponents of practices that had the power to cut a swathe of misery across whole regions in a short time, and their views played an important role in legitimising opposition not to the idea of globalisation itself, but the particular form

---

[116] Madeleine Bunting, 'Dam Buster', *The Guardian*, 28 July 2001. Among her own writings, see in particular, Arundhati Roy, 'The Greater Common Good' and 'The Ladies Have Feelings, so . . . Shall we Leave it to the Experts?' in *Algebra of Infinite Justice*, pp. 39–126, 165–91; and 'Power Politics: The Reincarnation of Rumpelstiltskin', in *Power Politics*, pp. 35–86.

[117] Peter Vale, *Security and Politics in South Africa. The Regional Dimension* (Boulder, Colo.: Lynne Rienner, 2003), pp. 156–7.

[118] Richard Higgott, 'Contested Globalization: The Changing Context and Normative Challenges', in Ken Booth, Tim Dunne, and Michael Cox (eds.), *How Might We Live? Global Ethics in the New Century* (Cambridge: Cambridge University Press, 2001), pp. 131–54, and Payne, *The Global Politics of Unequal Development*, pp. 73–102.

it had taken.[119] Dissatisfaction has grown with hyper-globalisation, but also the belief of those like Susan George has strengthened that because globalisation is here to stay, what matters is the adjective that goes with it. Reflecting this convergence has been the 'one-world' thinking of the philosopher Peter Singer. When he turned his attention to globalisation, he decided to treat it not primarily as an economic issue but as an ethical one.[120]

Singer examined, from a global rather than a nationalist-realist ethic, the major issues concerning 'One Atmosphere' (climate change), 'One Economy' (the WTO), 'One Law' (human rights), and 'One Community' (foreign aid). While his prescriptions were not unfamiliar to those interested in cosmopolitan thinking, his argumentation was stimulating, whether in discussing the obligation of the well-off to the poor through the lens of Bob and his Bugati,[121] or by bringing into the issues of globalisation the perspective of philosophers from Adam Smith to John Rawls. The challenge of our times, he stressed, is to develop 'the ethical foundations of the coming era of a single world community'.[122]

Singer's basic theme – consonant with this book – was that a growing number of issues 'demand global solutions', and that these solutions would come best through community.[123] He was nevertheless rightly concerned with the danger that global bodies might become 'either dangerous tyrannies or self-aggrandizing bureaucracies'. His chosen model for 'government beyond national boundaries' was the European Union and its principle of subsidiarity: 'if it works for Europe, it is not impossible that it might work for the world'.[124] Leaving aside the contested character of both these propositions, the idea running through his prescriptions was that of a 'community of reciprocity'.[125] In this regard, he saw the United States, more in sorrow than anger, as 'one great obstacle' to progress in international institution-building and in dealing with environmental damage; he thought the United States risked being seen 'universally   by everyone except its own self-satisfied citizens as the world's "rogue superpower"'.[126] He ended with a clarion-call to action to institutionalise the potential world community; developing a 'suitable' form of government for a single world, he accepted, is 'a daunting

---

[119] Callinicos, *Anti-Capitalist Manifesto*, pp. 8–9; see also Joseph Stiglitz, *Globalization and its Discontents* (New York: W. W. Norton, 2002), and George Soros, *George Soros on Globalization* (New York: Public Affairs, 2002).
[120] Peter Singer, *One World. The Ethics of Globalization* (New Haven, Conn.: Yale University Press, 2002).
[121] *Ibid.*, pp. 186–95.   [122] *Ibid.*, pp. 197–8.   [123] *Ibid.*, p. 199.
[124] *Ibid.*, pp. 200–1.   [125] *Ibid.*, pp. 168–75.   [126] *Ibid.*, pp. 198–9.

moral and intellectual challenge, but one we cannot refuse to take up. The future of the world depends on how well we meet it.'[127]

Many will dismiss Singer's arguments for being naïve and idealistic.[128] Nevertheless, his book offers a set of clear principles that are universally understandable. Such a 'one-world' perspective will have to be taken increasingly seriously – in face of all manner of communitarian nay-sayers – as global material conditions create a global community of fate. The ancient Chinese philosopher Mozi, contemplating the destructiveness of war (in the fifth century BCE) asked: 'What is the way of universal love and mutual benefit?' His reply was: 'It is to regard other people's countries as one's own.'[129] For much of history the powerful have indeed regarded other people's countries as (potentially) their own, through the lenses of imperialism. In this century, Mozi's injunction must be understood and respected (as he meant it) through the lens of ethics, as part of the commitment to equality (the-I-that-is-another) if global challenges are to be dealt with through cooperation rather than conflict.

Mozi's one-world injunction, like Singer's, points to the need for a theory of world security to be embedded in a theory of political economy. What follows begins in the problems and insecurities of the present dominant system. Transforming globalisation from a system characterised by the competitive accumulation of capital, crises of over-investment and profitability encouraged by financial speculation, the accelerated exploitation of the environment, and human winners and losers, requires increasingly radical political, economic, and cultural changes if the outcome is to result in the adjective 'humane' being married to globalisation. There have been many contributions to thinking about such a transformation, and some will be referred to below, but a good starting-point is the three-stage strategy proposed by Alex Callinicos to 'realize . . . [universal principles of justice] by bringing into being a different world'.[130]

Stage 1 involves recognising and analysing the problem. Callinicos labelled the essence of the problem 'Capitalism Against the Planet'.[131] Here there is obviously a basic debate between cheerleaders of neoliberal globalisation and their opponents. For the former, globalisation is

---

[127] *Ibid.*, p. 201.
[128] See, for example, Meghnad Desai, 'With the Best Will in the World', *The Times Higher Education Supplement*, 21 February 2003.
[129] Quoted by Singer, *One World*, pp. 196.
[130] Callinicos, *Anti-Capitalist Manifesto*, p. viii.   [131] *Ibid.*, pp. 21–66.

'flattening' the world in beneficial ways, and progress requires more of the same. For their opponents, the way globalisation has evolved since the 1980s in particular, perpetuates poverty and inequality (many would say it has made these things worse): it promotes irrational and inhumane outcomes; and its intensification of the competition between the multinational corporations that dominate the world only accelerates environmental destruction. Capitalist competition is not only between firms, but also between states, and their geopolitical conflicts (especially in the context of energy shortages) threaten a new era of major warfare. All the major challenges facing human society, according to Callinicos – poverty, social injustice, economic instability, environmental destruction, and war – have the same source: the global capitalist system.

Callincos's second stage involves moving beyond identifying the problem of the status quo to devising plans to move beyond it: 'Varieties and Strategies'.[132] Here, there is no homogeneous ideological position against capitalism, nor is there a shared set of ideas as to what should be done, where, and how. Callincos himself, in his *Anti-Capitalist Manifesto*, identifies a range of approaches, extending from what he calls bourgeois anti-capitalism (which accepts the benefits of capitalism but argues it should be more responsive to civil society) through to what he calls socialist anti-capitalism, looking towards a democratically controlled planned economy. As we have to begin where we are, the ground on which there might be movement in the near term is that of 'bourgeois anti-capitalism'. Two particularly significant reformist versions deserve more attention than space allows.

The first is by Joseph Stiglitz, whose *Making Globalisation Work* carries particular weight because of the author's background and authority. His CV includes being chair of Clinton's Council of Economic Advisers, chief economist at the World Bank, special adviser to the World Bank's president, and a Nobel Prize. Stiglitz was ousted from his post at the World Bank, ostensibly because of his attacks on the International Monetary Fund.[133] Given his background and authority, he became something of a hero of the anti-globalisation movement – not least because his critical perspective on making globalisation work goes beyond mere tweaking. It is conceived as part of *The Next Steps to Global Justice* (the book's subtitle). This bugle-call importantly reminds his readers that what is at stake in globalisation is not simply technical (when such issues

---

[132] *Ibid.*, pp. 67–105.
[133] Joseph Stiglitz, *Making Globalisation Work* (London: Allen Lane, 2006).

as the Doha Round or intellectual property rights are being discussed), but profoundly ethical, with practical consequences in terms of global justice.

The diagnosis offered by Stiglitz yields the verdict that the US-dominated globalisation project has failed (in a fundamental and long-term sense, as opposed to the profits of the successful), with dire consequences for most of the developing world and the former communist world. The partial exception is East Asia.[134] His prescriptions on trade and debt are radical. He advocated the opening up of the markets of rich countries to poorer ones without conditionality, while he approached the debt problem of poorer countries from the position that the blame lay not only with the foolishness and possible corruption of the borrower, but also with the lender for failing to have done proper risk analysis.[135] His prescriptions about roping in multinational corporations will not be welcomed by their CEOs, but they promise the way to fairer trade, while an important dimension of the latter is making global institutions – notably the IMF – more responsive to poorer countries.[136] Stiglitz's diagnosis will find much agreement in global civil society, but many governments and corporations will want to resist his interventionist prescriptions. While he criticised the free-market fundamentalism associated with the United States and the United Kingdom, he saw in the experiences of East Asia a more hopeful approach to globalisation, with government playing a more interventionist role, protecting infant industries and discouraging the precipitous liberalisation of financial and currency markets; these interventions involve promoting high levels of employment and limiting inequality (in earlier stages of the Chinese experiment with capitalism, for example, senior management typically received no more than three times the income of ordinary workers, whereas in the United States the difference is measured in hundreds of times).[137] Nor would beneficiaries from actually existing globalisation welcome the direction of his recommendations about fundamental reform of the relationship between the developed and developing world, and the primary role of the United States.[138]

A different reformist perspective is well captured in the title of Jonathon Porritt's book *Capitalism as if the World Matters*.[139] Part of this

---

[134] *Ibid.*, pp. 30–5, 45–8, 277.   [135] *Ibid.*, pp. 68–9.
[136] On the IMF, see *ibid.*, pp. xii, xiii, 56, 255, 266, 281–4.
[137] *Ibid.*, pp. 45–6.   [138] *Ibid.*, pp. 269–92.
[139] Jonathon Porritt, *Capitalism as if the World Matters* (London: Earthscan, 2006).

book is a familiar account from a leading and influential environmental campaigner of the world's biophysical limits, and how close we are to those limits as a result of population growth, climate change, resource depletion, and pollution (of water, air, and soil).[140] What gives Porritt's analysis a more radical edge is the way in which he identified the challenge to humanity not only as self-interest (in relation to individual and collective security) but also as a question of social injustice. In other words, he argued that the environment involves spiritual as well as economic and security issues, being tied up with the iniquities of inequality and the discovery that economic growth and happiness are not synonymous.[141] Nonetheless, basic to Porritt's position is the argument that the further development of capitalism, and the success of sustainability, are not necessarily incompatible. For this to happen, he stressed that capitalism must adapt to both the biophysical limits of the planet and the ethical demands of social justice; and he offered ideas about the ways in which it would be possible to work along these lines broadly within existing structures.[142] He identified the (human) obstacles to his reform programme as those people and groups who were the beneficiaries of today's status quo, those who lived in a state of denial about the planet's biophysical limits (much of public opinion and the corporate world, and a less-than-engaged media),[143] governments that were failing to face up to global problems, and those parts of the environmental movement itself that were unwilling to broaden their agenda from single-issue protests.[144] His cautious optimism lay in the values and hopes of global civil society, committed to and working towards a 'one-world' vision, and best practice in business.

One approach central to reformist ideas about 'best practice' is that of Corporate Social Responsibility (CSR). This was defined by the European Commission in 2001 as 'a concept whereby companies integrate social and environmental concerns in their business operations and in their interaction with their stakeholders on a voluntary basis'.[145]

---

[140] *Ibid.*; part I is an overview of 'Our unsustainable world'.
[141] *Ibid.*, pp. 50–6, 222–3, 228–30, 316–20.
[142] *Ibid.*; part II is 'A framework for sustainable capitalism'.
[143] One important exception to this generalisation about the media is *The Independent*, which published a long supplement: Jonathan Porritt, 'How Can Capitalism Save the World?', *The Independent*, 4 November 2005.
[144] Porritt, *Capitalism as if the World Matters*, pp. 216–17.
[145] Quoted by Marina Prieto-Carrón, Peter Lund-Thomsen, Anita Chan, Ana Muro, and Chandra Bushan, 'Critical Perspectives on CSR and Development: What we Know, What

Since the framing of that definition, CSR has been broadened to include corporate conduct on human rights and poverty reduction in the developing world. It is, like so much in this field, a complex and controversial concept, but one with security implications '*for* some body and *for* some thing'. The debate, not surprisingly, has been dominated by the rich world, though specialists from the developing world have begun, with their relevant empirical knowledge, to argue that the dominant management-oriented perspective on CSR and development is 'one-sided'. Instead, they have advocated focusing on the most vulnerable groups in the world, through adopting a 'people-centred' perspective as a counter to the dominant 'business case' perspective, which favours profit-making and ignores the 'actual impacts of CSR initiatives', as well as class and gender. CSR as conceived and practised, from this Third Worldist perspective, 'may do more harm than good'.[146] Business-as-usual, even when business is trying to do something unusual, is the problem.

Clearly, there is much to be argued over in the possible transitional strategies to lead today's global economy from where it is to a condition of humane globalisation; this is equivalent to Callincos's stage 3, 'Imagining Other Worlds'.[147] His own view has been that the values advanced by the anti-capitalist movement are justice, efficiency, democracy, and sustainability, and these are inconsistent with capitalist-led globalisation. His own preference was for neither market socialism nor a more regulated capitalism – the two most widely supported alternatives – because he did not think they were likely to work. Instead, he favoured a democratically planned socialist economy. His view is but one example of a growing body of literature challenging the logic of capitalism.[148] Callinicos recognised the reaction and resistance that such ideas provoke. The beneficiaries of the status quo would fight change; other powerful inhibitors he identified include what he called the 'strong sense' that despite the recognition of the problems of the system at present there is no realistic alternative. The Soviet Union did not offer

we Don't Know, and What we Need to Know', *International Affairs*, vol. 82(5), 2006, p. 978; see also the special issue of *International Affairs* on CSR, vol. 81(3), 2005, and Michael Blowfield, 'Corporate Social Responsibility – the Failing Discipline and Why it Matters for International Relations', *International Relations*, vol. 19(2), 2005, pp. 173–92.

[146] Prieto-Carrón *et al.*, 'CSR', pp. 986–7.

[147] Callinicos, *Anti-Capitalist Manifesto*, pp. 106–43.

[148] See, for example, David Schweickart, *Against Capitalism* (Cambridge: Cambridge University Press, 1993), and the more radical and programmatic Paul Feldman and Corinna Lotz, *A World to Win. A Rough Guide to a Future Without World Capitalism* (London: Lupus Books, 2004).

a promising model of 'socialism', for example. One of the potentially significant contributions of reformist voices such as Stiglitz and Porritt is the way they seek to recapture the idea that something quite significant can be done to bring about benevolent change in the interests of social justice globally, and the environment, but without revolution. Their efforts might help enough people to believe that there is nothing inevitable about neoliberal globalisation, and that change is possible as well as desirable. At that point, everything solid has the potential to melt into air, and globalisation might secure a different and benign adjective.

There can be no doubt that internationalised capitalism will have to change over the next half-century, because of the cumulating and potentially explosive problems it is stoking up. There can be no guarantee that what follows neoliberal globalisation will be more in the global human interest, especially if the decades ahead are marked by political and economic turmoil following from climate chaos and other problems. Change is necessary, but it is instructive to be reminded about the difficulty of bringing it about. Let us return to the starting-point of this discussion: the MPH campaign.

In the summer of 2005 MPH reached its maximum prominence (yet?) on the international stage. For many months the British Prime Minister, Tony Blair, and his Chancellor of the Exchequer, Gordon Brown, had drawn attention to their hopes and plans for changing the agenda of global development during the period of the UK's presidency of the G8. Following a summer of vigorous effort by NGOs to give the campaign publicity, not least by celebrity endorsements (and embarrassments), several important commitments were made at the summit held at Gleneagles in Scotland in July 2005; especially important were the commitments in trade, finance, and the environment.[149] As is often the case in international politics, when the leaders of powerful states come together (ostensibly) to advance ambitious common goals, the outcome proves to be disappointing once the details become clearer, and the rhythms of reality take over from the rhetoric of the state leaders.[150] This episode throws light on three dimensions of the previous discussion regarding the humanising of globalisation.

---

[149] The analysis below rests on Anthony Payne, 'Blair, Brown and the Gleneagles Agenda: Making Poverty History, or Confronting the Global Politics of Unequal Development?' *International Affairs*, vol. 82(5), 2006, pp. 917–35.

[150] *Ibid.*, pp. 919–23, 925–34.

1.   The intellectual challenge

Chapter 6 argued the case for a critical global economy to work synergistically with critical security theory. In this respect, the Gleneagles experience was a specific case that highlighted for Anthony Payne the general issue of the need to reconceive, from a critical perspective, the meanings and interplay of development, globalisation, and political economy.[151] Payne argued that orthodox models of development and international political economy – as celebrated by *The World Is Flat* proponents – continue to bring profits for the powerful, but do not work for the world. What Payne called 'the global politics of development' is not 'animated any longer – if indeed it ever was – by what the "North" is willing to do for the "South"'. The prevailing political condition is an altogether harsher one 'within which all the countries of the world . . . pursue as effectively as they can their chosen country strategies of development in the financial, trade and environmental policy arenas'. In essence, Payne argued, the challenge is to see development as a transnational issue, nationally pursued, within a global environment characterised by structural inequalities.[152] He said we should talk 'more properly' of the 'global politics of unequal development', and have a more nuanced approach. The 'North' is not a homogeneous bloc, for example. The members of the G8 dominate global financial politics, but on some issues they are major rivals (trade policy), and on others they have significant divisions (environmental controls). The significance of national perspectives is one that flat-earthers can easily overlook. Robert J. Samuelson, in a *Newsweek* critique of the Friedman take on globalisation ('The World Is Still Round'), argued that while 'everywhere we see the increasingly powerful effects of globalisation . . . the single most important reality of the economic well-being for most people is their nationality'.[153] But is it? What about class? What about gender? Elites in the developing world have a life to live that can only be dreamed of by the dirt-poor of the developed world. Nonetheless, Samuelson's warning about globalisation's vulnerability is important, and not least his view that 'The irony is that its fate rests heavily on the behaviour of that old fashioned creature – the nation-state.' The intellectual challenge, then, is to understand the national politics of global uneven development, for this remains one of the dynamos of globalisation as a project.

---

[151] Payne, *ibid.*, discusses the moves required in the rethinking, pp. 923–5.
[152] *Ibid.*, pp. 934–5.   [153] Samuelson, 'The World Is Still Round'.

2. The political challenge

Payne was correct in arguing that the Gleneagles agenda could not have made poverty history, regardless of the decisions taken by the partici- pants. Such a goal was not 'within the compass of the G8 to deliver'.[154] Nonetheless, at the level of rhetoric – in terms of legitimising a normative goal for the self-defining international community – it was undoubtedly in the right direction, and Blair and Brown were to be congratulated for that, and the skill with which they put the agenda together. Equally, long-term global civil society pressure to get the issues on the agenda in the first place was decisive. As was the case with the UN conference on the global environment at Rio in 1993, however, while global civil society can sometimes get issues on the global agenda, state and corpo- rate power then takes over. Success requires all major stakeholders to be acting together, and according to the right 'conceptual framework'. But for Payne the conceptual framework within which the major players operated in 2006 was 'long since . . . outdated', with outworn categories of 'both action and analysis', serving the interests of an entrenched pro- fessional 'development community'.[155] Even when the spirit seems to be willing, with politicians and campaigners appearing to share a com- mitment for change, and comprehending the dynamics of the 'global politics of unequal development', the obstacles to progress remain substantial.

3. The spiritual challenge

The fundamental question still on the table is a subset of the title of this chapter: *whom* will globalisation be *for*? At one level, this points to an empirical prediction, but the real meaning of the question is ethical, and for some spiritual; it is not merely technical or 'economic'. Adam Smith, for one, would not have found this way of ending the discussion inappropriate. He wrote in *The Theory of Moral Sentiments*: 'For to what purpose is all the toil and bustle of this world?' In *The Wealth of Nations*, the answer he gave, in the words of Robert Heilbroner, was that 'all the grubby scrabble for wealth and glory has its ultimate justification in the welfare of the common man'.[156] The latter has not been the referent for the business of nations to date, nor the language of mainstream aca- demic international relations and security studies. But the message is

---

[154] Payne, 'Gleneagles', p. 934.   [155] *Ibid.*, p. 923.
[156] Robert L. Heilbroner, *The Worldly Philosophers. The Lives, Times and Ideas of the Great Economic Thinkers* (Harmondsworth: Penguin, 1991), p. 74.

beginning to get through, and some are quicker to grasp it than others. The idea of conceiving globalisation and security as ultimately an ethical/spiritual challenge as opposed to a set of technical questions was understood at once by a group of young Peruvian diplomats I addressed in Lima, in 2000. They knew well enough that the world is not working when over half its inhabitants survive on two dollars a day or less, and they knew that before one could answer the technical question – how can globalisation be made to work better? – it is first necessary to answer the fundamental ethical question: who *should* own the twenty-first century?

Inventing humanity

> Sooner or later . . . one has to take sides. If one is to remain human.
> Mr Heng to Thomas Fowler in *The Quiet American*[157]

Despite the casuistry and hypocrisy surrounding the practice of universal human rights on the part of some governments all of the time, and all governments some of the time, the continuation and prominence of human rights issues on the global agenda represents a huge advance in the prospects for world security in the blink of a historical eye. Confronted by human rights critics and sceptics, the appropriate perspective to adopt for proponents is one that encompasses the almost 4,000 years since the Babylonian king Hammurabi first issued a set of laws requiring charges to be proved in a trial.[158] In the period since then, societies have self-created (or 'received from God') any number of statements of rights seeking to set standards relating to the obligations individuals should have towards each other, or that states should have towards their citizens. The arrival of new and more humane standards, in their day, all represented incremental advances (and important anchorages) in the emancipatory struggle against human wrongs. For the most part, however, these historic standards applied only to a given group of people. And even when such ideas pointed in a universal direction, as in the French Revolution,[159] they were not universally adopted. This is why

---

[157] Graham Greene, *The Quiet American* (Harmondsworth: Penguin, 1965), p. 172.
[158] William F. Shulz, *In Our Own Best Interest. How Defending Human Rights Benefits Us All* (Boston: Beacon Press, 2002), pp. 4–5.
[159] The darkening of the bright hopes is well told in Simon Schama, *Citizens. A Chronicle of the French Revolution* (London: Viking, 1989).

the signing of the Universal Declaration of Human Rights (UDHR) in 1948 was a profound historical achievement.[160]

One-time director of Amnesty International USA, William F. Shulz, has commented on the historical novelty of the UDHR as follows: 'Remarkable as it seems, it took almost four thousand years from the days of Hammurabi for the world to agree on a statement of rights that nearly everybody active on the international scene acknowledged applied to everybody else – even to one's enemies! – simply because everybody is a human being.'[161] It is easy to be jaded and sceptical about what was said and done in 1948 when one surveys the history of human wrongs since that time. Nonetheless, to refuse to be other than thrilled about this advance in human consciousness and regulatory potential suggests a lack of historical imagination, not to mention insensitivity regarding the pain of others. The UDHR became a key anchorage for promoting future world security by placing human rights to the fore (though often not the forefront) of politics among nations. Human rights, like great art, bad prisons, and struggling mental health provision, tell us about ourselves, and what and where and who we are as a species. They are integral at this stage of history in the invention of humanity.

An age of universal rights in general presupposes an embryonic world society, in which its members in principle recognise (in the words of the UDHR) the 'inherent dignity and . . . the equal and inalienable rights' of all other persons, regardless of 'race, colour, sex, language, religion, political or other opinion, national or social origin, property, birth or other status'.[162] The towering historical significance of this document is all too often overlooked by those sceptics more concerned to expose human hypocrisy, political disagreement, and conceptual niceties than to recognise the promise of emancipation the document represented to the countless victims of power and neglect across the world.

The theory and practice of human rights since 1948 has faced considerable criticism from politicians and academics.[163] From 'ordinary people'

---

[160] Micheline R. Ishay (ed.), *The Human Rights Reader* (New York: Routledge, 1997), is a useful anthology, with passages from classical and contemporary documents.
[161] Shulz, *Best Interest*, p. 5.
[162] The Universal Declaration is in Ishay, *Human Rights*, pp. 407–12.
[163] Positive yet questioning overviews of the issues are Geoffrey Robertson, *Crimes Against Humanity. The Struggle for Global Justice* (Harmondsworth: Penguin, 2002; 2nd edn) and Jack Donnelly, *Universal Human Rights in Theory and Practice* (Ithaca, N.Y.: Cornell University Press, 2003; 2nd edn). Critical yet engaged overviews are Chris Brown, 'Universal Human Rights: A Critique', in Dunne and Wheeler, *Human Rights*, pp. 103–27, and David Chandler (ed.), *Rethinking Human Rights. Critical Approaches to International Politics* (Houndmills: Palgrave Macmillan, 2002).

the criticism is often down-to-earth. Many, in different countries, have asked their local version of the question William Shulz was once asked in Knoxville, following a talk about human rights abuses of unknown people in distant and unknown places: 'But what does all of this have to do with a person in East Tennessee?'[164] This 'East Tennessee' question must be answered by human rights supporters at various levels and in different ways. One powerful response is to try and engage people's sympathies by trying to make immediate the pain and oppression some suffer. In Cambodia, Loung Ung's father was taken away by the Khmer Rouge when she was small, and he was murdered, presumably after torture. Ung needed to know that her beloved 'Pa' was killed quickly: 'I need to believe that they did not make him suffer', she said, probably more in hope than expectation.[165] Shulz himself, who related this story, was not convinced about the effectiveness of such an approach, though personalising human rights abuses has always been important in his organisation's campaigns.[166] His own approach was to try and engage the unconvinced of East Tennessee and elsewhere in the United States by arguing about pragmatics, showing that the even-handed enforcement of human rights norms was not only consistent with the highest US values, but was also in the interests of the United States. He believed that if ethical and legal issues were to hold people's attention, then 'they must be framed, to the extent possible, in the language of realpolitik'. His belief was that 'If large numbers of Americans are ever to care about human rights violations around the world, they must be able to see the implications of those violations for their own lives here at home.'

Finding a persuasive answer to Shulz's question – 'what does all of this have to do with ... [me]?' – is just one obstacle that has had to be faced by proponents of universal human rights. In an influential series of interventions in the debate, Michael Ignatieff began to describe human rights at the end of the twentieth century as undergoing a 'Midlife Crisis'.[167] In 1999 he argued that through the next half-century 'we can expect to see the moral consensus which sustained the Universal Declaration [of Human Rights] in 1948 splintering still further'. He thought the splintering was bound to grow, not just between 'the West and the Rest' but

---

[164] Shulz, *Best Interest*, p. 1.   [165] Related by Shulz, *ibid.*, p. 197.
[166] An outstanding contribution to this debate is Norman Geras, *The Contract of Mutual Indifference. Political Philosophy after the Holocaust* (London: Verso, 1999); see also Linklater's discussion of the difficulties of engaging sympathetically with 'distant strangers': 'Distant Suffering and Cosmopolitan Obligations', *International Politics*, vol. 44(1), 2007, pp. 19–36.
[167] Michael Ignatieff, 'Human Rights: The Midlife Crisis', *New York Review of Books*, 20 May 1999.

also between the United States and Europe: 'the ground we share may actually be quite limited', he added. This did not mean 'the end of the human rights movement' in his opinion, but rather the recognition that 'we live in a plural world of cultures which have a right to equal consideration in the argument about what we can and cannot, should and should not do to other human beings'. In future, he suggested, rights will not be 'the universal credo of a global society, not a secular religion, but something much more limited and yet just as valuable: the common ground on which our arguments can begin'. I agree with the latter, but, contra Ignatieff, believe that this is possible only because human rights are to a greater or lesser extent an actually existing universal credo.

Human rights are 'about' what it means to be human at this point in history. They are part of what is involved in exploring that idea and, as was argued in chapter 6, inventing humanity is synonymous with emancipation, though there is no blueprint or end-point as to its form. Human rights have become an integral element in the evolution of human consciousness, telling us something about what we now are as a species, just as slavery or religious totalitarianism did in different societies in the past. Even those who attack the human rights project are drawn into this argument on the project's own conceptual territory. Humans will not necessarily survive for another 5.8 million years, and it is not even guaranteed that those who follow in the next few generations will behave in more civilised ways towards each other. Be that as it may, the conception of security advanced in this book, with its emancipatory purpose, assumes that it is possible. The hope is to create the space for people to respond to 'the pull of the world' in empathetic and non-violent ways, with the search for emancipation replacing the will to power, and common humanity trumping imperialism and tyranny. The way humans conceive of their humanity is critical to the future of world security. Whether humans survive over the long term, and if so how, rests significantly on the direction taken by the evolution of human consciousness; and at this stage of history the idea of human rights helps shape that consciousness.

But will human rights survive their 'midlife crisis'? Human rights have been under challenge from a regiment of political realists, post-structuralists, communitarians, relativists, elitists, sceptics, and the world's tyrants and their supporters. The starting-point for a critical theory counter-attack (what I will call the emancipatory-constitutive approach) is a rejection of the idea of basing human rights on an essentialist view of human nature. Such a standpoint immediately diverges from most human rights thinking, namely the simple and powerful view that we have human rights because we are human. Rhoda Howard, for one, began her important book on the social character of human rights with this standard formulation: 'Human rights are rights that one holds merely by virtue of being human.'[168] In a formal sense, one cannot quibble with this, because it is the basis of the Universal Declaration, which speaks to 'all members of the human family'. Nonetheless, there are advantages in standing the standard formulation on its head, and instead proposing that *Homo sapiens* should promote human rights *not because* we are human, *but to make us* human.[169] This re-formulation sees human rights as constitutive of humanity and not some static idea, be it theologically ordained or an assumption about the character of human nature. From my perspective human rights are not only rules concerned with regulating behaviour, but they also represent an emancipatory ideal concerned with inventing humanity by constituting persons as rights-bearing, equal, free individuals with the potential to 'live a life'. The re-formulation of the standard formula about human rights is an expression of the sociological-evolutionary approach central to Frankfurt school explanations of social phenomena. Conceiving human rights as constitutive (*to make us human*) rather than understanding them as an inalienable/essentialist entitlement (*because we are human*) offers significant theoretical advantages.

Above all, what I call the emancipatory-constitutive approach represents a dynamic as opposed to a static theory of human rights. Jack Donnelly, a social constructivist before the discipline knew it, discussed such an approach in the mid-1980s, insisting that human rights have not been 'given' to humans 'by God, nature or the physical facts of life'. For Donnelly, 'human rights arise from human action [and] represent the choice of a particular moral vision of human potentiality and the institutions for realising that vision'. In other words, human rights are invented through politics and society, not discovered through revelation. This is an evolutionary perspective, with particular conceptions or lists of human rights being seen as the 'result of the reciprocal

---

[168] Rhoda E. Howard, *Human Rights and the Search for Community* (Boulder, Colo.: Westview, 1995), p. 1.

[169] I first argued this in 'Three Tyrannies'; the present version was presented in a preliminary form at an ISA panel in Hong Kong in 2002, and I want to record the helpful conversations I had with Jack Donnelly. See his *The Concept of Human Rights* (London: Croom Helm, 1985), esp. pp. 31–43, 'The Social Construction of Human Rights' in Dunne and Wheeler, *Human Rights*, pp. 71–102, and *Universal Human Rights in Theory and Practice* (Ithaca, N.Y.: Cornell University Press, 2003), esp. p. 16.

interaction of moral conceptions and material conditions of life, mediated through social institutions'.[170] Such an intersubjective understanding was expressed by Howard as follows: 'Human rights are human rights because humankind has decided they are. Human beings create their own sense of a morally worthwhile life.'[171] From this perspective, the attacks of the critics of human rights can be countered from an emancipatory-constitutive approach on three particular fronts: ethics, epistemology, and politics.

1.   Ethics

Critics of human rights draw attention to two ethical problems in particular. First, they see the whole human rights project as part of a contemporary preoccupation with rights (which they believe is unhealthy). The view that human rights are part of a widespread and obsessive concern with rights involves the claim that such a perspective is at the expense of an older tradition of ethics, which emphasises ideas such as dignity, duty, self-knowledge and the rest.[172] The philosopher Simon Blackburn reflected such a viewpoint when he said: 'one peculiarity of our present [ethical] climate is that we care much more about our rights than about our "good"'.[173]

A second criticism is that the human rights discourse requires an essentialising of the human (as in the syllogism that rights are due 'merely by virtue of being human'). It implies we have a shared understanding of 'human' or 'human nature'. This is a line of attack that has been led by the US philosopher Richard Rorty. Writing at the time of the Balkan conflicts in the early 1990s, he argued that some people did not define certain other groups to be human, and not therefore subjects for human rights. Such a view, which made it possible to support human rights while killing and mutilating people was 'wholly human' in Rorty's opinion. He wrote:

> The Serbs, the moralists, Jefferson, and the Black Muslims all use the term 'men' to mean 'people like us'. They think the line between humans and animals is not simply the line between featherless bipeds and all others . . . There are animals walking about in humanoid form.

---

170 Donnelly, *Concept of Human Rights*, pp. 31, 35.
171 Howard, *Human Rights*, pp. 10–15 (quotation at p. 15).
172 Michael Freeman, *Human Rights. An Interdisciplinary Approach* (Cambridge: Polity, 2002), pp. 14–31.
173 Simon Blackburn, *Being Good. A Short Introduction to Ethics* (Oxford: Oxford University Press, 2000), p. 3.

> We and those like us are paradigm cases of humanity, but those too different from us in behavior or custom are, at best, borderline cases.[174]

The distinction being made is between what Rorty called 'true humans and pseudohumans', and those acting on such a distinction did not believe they were themselves violating specifically *human* rights when they killed or mutilated 'pseudohumans'. Such a refusal to extend the concept of *human* to all members of the species in one's *universe of obligation* (to use Helen Fein's phrase) was of course a particular feature of the racial policy of the Nazis, with what Bauman called their 'social production of moral indifference' and 'social production of moral invisibility'.[175]

The emancipatory-constitutive approach to human rights counters these two sets of criticisms by bringing *virtue ethics* to the debate; such a move roots the rights project in duties as well as rights. By uniting virtue ethics ('being good and living well') with rights, the human rights project is relieved of the complaint about its obsessive (and implicitly selfish) concern with a 'rights-culture'. Instead of the standard logic ('*They* should be accorded human rights because *they* are human'), the emancipatory-constitutive logic goes: '*I* (or *we*) should respect human rights because *I* am (or *we* are) human.' There is no racist or other casuistry (on the lines described by Rorty) by which people can escape from this formulation; it engages a person's duty and dignity, and only sociopaths might deny their own human-ness.

Critics of the 'rights obsession' argue that other things are more important than rights. Julian Glover, for one, has argued: 'In ordinary life kindness counts for more than belief in human rights. In thinking about how to live, small is beautiful.'[176] Freeman has countered such a view with a simple but powerful observation of daily life in some parts of the world: 'Ordinary people . . . are sometimes not permitted an everyday life.' They may face everything from terror to 'ethnic cleansing'. He then offered an important reminder to those of us living in the relatively comfortable world:

---

[174] Richard Rorty, 'Human Rights, Rationality, and Sentimentality', in Stephen Shute and Susan Hurley (eds.), *On Human Rights. The Oxford Amnesty Lectures 1993* (New York: Basic Books), p. 112.

[175] Zygmunt Bauman, *Modernity and the Holocaust* (Cambridge: Polity, 2002), pp. 12–27 (Fein is quoted at p. 26); see also Geras, *Mutual Indifference*, esp. pp. 1–82.

[176] Jonathan Glover, *Humanity. A Moral History of the Twentieth Century* (London: Jonathan Cape, 1999), p. 41.

> The concept of human rights becomes relevant to ordinary people when the relative security of everyday life is absent or snatched away. It has often been said that human rights are most needed when they are most violated. Where they are generally well respected, we tend to take them for granted, and may consequently underestimate their importance.[177]

In short, human rights are an essential security issue, though this seems to be lost on those universal human rights sceptics whose own everyday lives are not troubled by life-determining insecurity.

2. Epistemology

The emancipatory-constitutive formulation shifts the discussion away from debates about political doctrines and their authority (as in whether human rights 'exist' through 'natural rights', 'natural law', and so on) to the plane of social idealism, in which humans can make their futures, but not determine them. Human rights from this perspective are part of human self-constituting.

Powerful theories construct and explain, as was discussed in chapter 6. The constitutive point I am making about human rights was seen in Shakespeare's work by Harold Bloom, in a book he appropriately called *Shakespeare: The Invention of the Human*.[178] Bloom's central claim was that 'Shakespeare will go on explaining us, in part because he invented us.'[179] He argued that because of Shakespeare, new modes of consciousness came into being through the changing relationships between the characters, and within them, as they developed, as they reconceived themselves, and as they overheard themselves talking. Central to Shakespearean 'invention' is the idea of 'reflexivity' discussed in earlier chapters. Shakespeare became a writer with global influence because enough people believed his characters spoke to them; we are in the characters, and they are in us. As a result, Shakespeare's plays have informed the language people speak; and his principal characters have become part of the mythology of educated groups. The great playwright's continued prominence throughout the world[180] is certainly not because his work is easily accessible; nor can his prominence be explained simply as a consequence of the preferences of an imperial power (if so, why has his

---

[177] Freeman, *Human Rights*, p. 3.
[178] Harold Bloom, *Shakespeare: The Invention of the Human* (London: Fourth Estate, 1999).
[179] *Ibid.*, p. xvii.   [180] *Ibid.*, pp. 1–17.

work been so admired in Russia).[181] The answer lies in the argument that Shakespeare helps constitute and explain us; he helped to invent us and reveal us; and he is simultaneously in our heads and 'our psychologist'.[182]

Similar claims can be made about human rights and the invention of the human. The language of human rights informs our discourse (the UDHR preamble talked of 'a world in which human beings shall enjoy freedom of speech and belief and freedom from fear and want . . . as the highest aspiration of the common people'); they give us our mythology (real heroes such as Martin Luther King, Nelson Mandela, and Aung San Suu Kyi – and real villains such as Stalin, Pinochet, and Mugabe); and they help tell us what sort of people we are or might aspire to be (we were once slave-owners, but now we try to treat everybody equally and fairly, even if we fail to achieve our best hopes). Human rights open up the human future freer of self-constructed 'essentialisms', 'false necessities', and statist absolutisms/certainties. Just like the script of a play, human rights are regulative, steering the behaviour of the actors, while at the same time encouraging the audience to identify with one or more of the characters while reacting against others. Human society is self-constituting through the canon of its great literature and the anchorages of its great political ideas and moments.

3.   Politics

In the politics of human rights the emancipatory-constitutive approach has several advantages over the standard formulation (we have human rights 'because we are human'). This is because it stresses the future rather than the past, dynamic possibilities rather than hegemonic common sense, and new identities rather than cultural essentialism. Such an approach challenges the powerful but problematic idea of cultural relativism, which serves the interests of the traditionally powerful and legitimises the idea of an ever more splintered world. The politics of human rights are turned by the emancipatory-constitutive approach into a globally inclusive political project, concerned with inventing humanity, and not merely asserting rights.

The relativist position has been defined by Diane Orentlicher as follows: 'Moral claims derive their meaning and legitimacy from the

---

[181] The corollary of this is the deep respect in which great Russian literature is held in the English-speaking world – places never under the political control of Moscow.
[182] Bloom, *Shakespeare*, pp. xvii, xix, xx, 4, 17.

(particular) cultural tradition in which they are embedded.'[183] Cultural relativism is a powerful political idea, not least because it has been loved by traditional power-holders. It is a highly problematic notion.[184] First, 'culture', a contested term and a relatively recent invention, is never a clear referent for politics. Who speaks for a culture? Who or what are its authentic voices? Where are its boundaries? Second, those living within designated 'cultures' are frequently divided over key issues. What is doing the causal work in particular instances: is it gender or class or some other explanation, or is it the vague concept of culture (which for many these days is synonymous with religious heritage)? Culture is a vague explanatory tool, and when it comes to politics, the championing of cultural relativism is the promoting of *theying* on a fabulous scale. For relativists, culture is the trump card; but it is an unsafe concept, offers a reductive view of people, and is an unreliable political referent.

The issues just discussed were much in evidence in the so-called Asian values debate in the 1990s. 'Asian values' were explicitly advanced as a challenge to what were asserted to be 'Western values' by leaders of China, Malaysia, and Singapore; the growing economic power of these countries gave their leaders confidence to make claims internationally about having distinct cultures (and also gave them hope that the move would legitimise and strengthen their own power at home). Most outsiders could see that the Asian values discourse was manipulated to serve the interests of particular regimes, but there were genuine differences of opinion about the degree to which fundamentally different conceptions of rights were engaged in the debate.[185] Scepticism about the emphasis being placed on Asian values proved to be well justified. It was easier to answer the question 'Whose interests did the idea of Asian values serve?' than it was to answer such questions as 'What and where is Asia?' and 'Who is its authentic voice when it comes to values?'

---

[183] Diane F. Orentlicher, 'Relativism and Religion', in Amy Gutman (ed.), *Human Rights as Politics and Idolatry* (Princeton, N.J.: Princeton University Press, 2001), p. 141.
[184] Jack Donnelly, *International Human Rights* (Boulder, Colo.: Westview, 1993), pp. 34–8; Booth, 'Three Tyrannies', pp. 46–51; Chris Brown, 'Universal Human Rights: A Critique', in Dunne and Wheeler, *Human Rights*, pp. 103–27; Bhikhu Parekh, 'Non-ethnocentric Universalism', in Dunne and Wheeler, *Human Rights*, pp. 128–59; Freeman, *Human Rights*, pp. 108–14; Gutman, *Human Rights*, pp. 72–7, 141–6.
[185] Among many discussions of the 'Asian values' issue, see Donnelly, *Universal Human Rights*, pp. 107–23, Andrew Hurrell, 'Power, Principles and Prudence: Protecting Human Rights in a Deeply Divided World', in Dunne and Wheeler, *Human Rights*, pp. 277–302, and Linda S. Bell, Andrew J. Nathan, and Ilan Peleg (eds.), *Negotiating Culture and Human Rights* (New York: Columbia University Press, 2003).

Attitudes and behaviour deriving from the culture of one's community or communities are obviously deeply implicated in the notion of identity, but the vague concept of culture can easily become a powerful and hard-edged symbol playing into the hands of those Sen called 'solitarists' – those who, for whatever reason, have an interest in human 'miniaturisation' rather than complexity. In this regard it is interesting that the study of anthropology, which promoted the idea of culture as a referent in the nineteenth century, and subsequently revelled in exposing exotic differences between peoples, has swung around, and now tends to emphasise greater transcultural similarities than had formerly generally been the case.[186] In politics, however, as was discussed earlier, the end of the twentieth century saw the right to be different asserted over the right to be equal. In the former colonial world, the radical demand for previously subjected peoples to have equal rights during their struggles for independence from their imperial rulers has steadily shifted in the contemporary era to an emphasis on difference.

The arguments here should not be taken to mean that 'cultural' differences should not be taken seriously. They should, because for many they represent important realities in relation to how they believe they should live their lives. The Vienna Declaration of 1993 put it sensibly, when it affirmed the principle of the universality of human rights while insisting that 'the significance of national and regional particularities and various historical, cultural and religious backgrounds must be borne in mind'.[187] There is therefore room for dialogue, but only if participants accept (against postmodernists, cultural relativists, and others) that 'universal' and 'Western' are not synonymous, while 'universal' and 'local' are not opposites.[188] What the discussion points to in security terms is the need to be sensitive to cultural particularity analytically, and to universalist potentialities politically. The latter, it should be remembered, is not inconsistent with the idea that some rights apply only to special categories of people, such as women and children; this was recognised by both the UDHR and the Vienna Declaration.[189] Rather than getting tied up in futile debates that reify local/universal, Rest/West, communitarian/cosmopolitan binaries, and sterile debates about transhistorical 'foundations' for human rights claims, Andrew Hurrell has usefully

[186] McGrane, *Beyond Anthropology*, pp. 11–12.
[187] Quoted by Freeman, *Human Rights*, pp. 101–2.
[188] In a different context, see the same discussion in Terry Eagleton, *The Idea of Culture* (Oxford: Blackwell, 2000), pp. 92–3.
[189] Freeman, *Human Rights*, pp. 101–2.

argued (though through too statist a framework) the pragmatic case that there is scope to discuss and develop the human rights culture from the basis of what 'has evolved in practice'.[190]

When cultural values and norms oppress, universal human rights offer people some protection. Even so, in a well-known statement of opposition to human rights, Alisdair MacIntyre argued that human rights did not exist; they were superstitions, he said, like the belief in witches and unicorns.[191] MacIntyre's mistake, as Michael Freeman has pointed out, was to see human rights as 'things' that people can 'have', like mobile phones, whereas they are *'just claims* or *entitlements* that derive from moral and/or legal rules'. Freeman's way of thinking 'defeats' the idea that human rights are superstitions, 'for there is nothing superstitious in thinking about what human beings may be entitled to'.[192] This is exactly the approach being advocated in this chapter, with the emancipatory-constitutive approach rejecting the rigidities of either/or thinking about local/universal in human rights. World security strategies and tactics seek to find multilevel space for both/and (*both* individual *and* community, *both* community *and* universal).[193] These are the spaces we can open up to explore what it might mean to be human. The more constrained the space, the more miniaturised the human that will emerge.

When confronted by some casuistry or other about the concept of human rights, it is always helpful in breaking a log-jam to follow Michael Freeman's lead and focus the discussion on some 'realities' (though William Shulz, earlier, was not so keen on such an approach). Freeman began one of his books by relating the story of Lal Jamilla Mandokhel, a sixteen-year-old Pakistani girl who had been repeatedly raped. Her attacker was detained by the police, and she was handed over to her tribe. The council of elders decided she had brought shame on the tribe, and so should be put to death. Such 'honour killings' are relatively commonplace in Pakistan.[194] Relativists and others might claim that 'outsiders' like Amnesty International have 'no right' to interfere, because they do not belong to the culture of the community, and are not inside its customs and values. This is a standpoint I utterly reject (though in

---

[190] Hurrell, 'Power, Principles and Prudence', esp. pp. 291–300.
[191] Alisdair MacIntyre, *After Virtue* (Notre Dame, Ind.: University of Notre Dame Press, 1981), p. 67.
[192] Freeman, *Human Rights*, pp. 5–6.
[193] Peter Jones, 'Individuals, Communities, and Human Rights', in Booth *et al.*, *How Might We Live?* pp. 22–3.
[194] Freeman, *Human Rights*, p. 1.

making such a claim, I am not saying that the customs and values of other people should not be treated with appropriate respect, and individuals should be treated with appropriate standards of decency – but the understanding of what is 'appropriate' will change with circumstances, for it is not appropriate to be respectful and decent in face of cruelty).

There is always a case for being involved; whether it is sensible to engage directly, and how, is a different matter. In the case of Lal Jamilla, we may not have lived in the same tribe, but there are other bonds by which we could claim to be relative to her. We may know what it is to be a mother or father, or a brother or a sister; we have all been somebody's daughter or son; and we understand deep relationships with people as friends, partners, and all manner of supportive contacts. 'Relativism' cannot be allowed to be monopolised by the domineering concept of culture. We are all *relative* to Lal Jamilla in some sense, depending on our own situation, and on the details of her own cruelly shortened life. We can claim a network of connections with her that gives us the right (as potential friends/allies/supporters/kindred spirits/comrades/friends at court/witnesses, and so on) to say, as a writer in an Amnesty International publication once did in a different case, that certain behaviour is 'torture not culture'.[195] Actual cases of human rights abuses bring home what is involved if we fall into the trap of being guided by the flawed reasoning of relativists who are able to enjoy security in their own ordinary lives. Human rights begin in human wrongs. 'That', said Michael Ignatieff, 'I take to be the elemental priority in all human rights activism: to stop torture, beatings, killings, rape, and assault and to improve, as best we can, the security of ordinary people.'[196] This means we must sometimes push aside the traditional barricades that serve to separate us, and insist on taking sides.

Cultural relativism, as a determinant of political decisions, suffers from the basic conceptual flaw just indicated: to whom or to what is relativism relative? There are no sensible lines we can draw around people like Kader Mia and Lal Jamilla unless we are prepared to succumb to a totalitarian spirit of solitarism. To do so would be to concede power to the structures of a past that does not work. Others claim the opposite, of course, and at the extreme are willing to kill (or commit suicide) to try to preserve the past; it might succeed for a while, perhaps a long time, but

---

[195] A. Robson, 'Torture not Culture', *AIBS Journal*, September/October 1993, pp. 8–9.
[196] Michael Ignatieff, 'Dignity and Agency', in Gutman, *Human Rights*, p. 174.

in the end it will fail. The implausibility of cultural relativism was brilliantly (and amusingly) illustrated in the play (and film) by the Iranian director Ayub Khan-Din, *East is East*. Set in the north of England in 1971, the elusive goal of relativism was revealed by the film in all its illogicalities, humour, and pathos – and sometimes violence – by focusing on the issue of arranged marriages for the offspring of a Pakistani father and his (second) wife, who was English. The plot of the film revolved around the dilemmas of the children regarding the culture or belief structures they should follow in their own lives. Should they follow their father (looking back to the country he had left), their mother (representing the country in which they lived), the mosque (which sought to impose religious authority on an increasingly secular community), the street (where the children learned about life), wider British society (which was increasingly liberal), or their own reasoning and consciences? The children thought about their predicament in different ways, while their hormones raged and their relations with their parents, friends, and each other were under strain. Whose cultural values should be embraced by the elder son, who was gay? Should the mother be on the side of her husband or rebellious son? Such questions proliferated throughout the film, revealing the instability of sure foundations in a cultural melting pot – increasingly everybody's home in the ever more liquid world of globalisation. By revealing the implausibility of cultural relativism, but its influence over those committed to traditional power structures, the film identified major battle-lines in contemporary and future world politics. The characters in the film struggled to make sense of their lives, and came to different conclusions about the ways they wanted to live. Only tyrants of one sort or another would want it any other way, determined as they are to 'miniaturise' the lives of people by insisting on traditionalist notions of identity, shackled to the unicorn of cultural relativism.

To be true to their nature, human rights must be promoted through means that reflect human rights values. This, above all, means dialogue. In this regard, following the spirit of the Vienna Declaration quoted earlier, proponents of human rights must recognise the influence of relativism, but not give way to it. Peter Baehr has argued that to give way would in any case reflect a 'rather paternalistic way of thinking' towards developing countries.[197] It would be patronising, he said, to assume that others are not ready for political freedom, or would not appreciate

---

[197] Peter R. Baehr, 'The Universality of Human Rights', paper presented at the ISA Annual Convention, Chicago, 21–25 February 1995.

it. It would also play into the hands of repressive regimes, ignore the victims of oppression, and be socially and economically dysfunctional. As time passes, it will by no means be certain that such liberal values will continue to be so persuasive. In the mid-1990s I wrote: 'it may be that under the pressure of population growth, environmental decay and Asian power that the idea of individual freedom, so central now, will seem irresponsible. Human rights as now conceived in the West are by no means set to head the agenda through the rest of history.'[198] This is still the case today. The answers to the questions raised in this discussion cannot be found exclusively in the West. If human rights are to play their role in the invention of humanity along the lines suggested earlier, the answers have to be sought through multilevel transcultural dialogue. In this respect, the domination of the past by the West is not as discouraging for the future as critics sometimes maintain. Human rights have not been a crude imposition of Western imperialism,[199] it is too simple to assert that the UDHR is merely a Western document,[200] and Western states do not necessarily defend all its provisions.[201] 'The West' is neither the sole problem nor the sole solution, but is part of both. What is more, emancipation is needed in the West, as it is elsewhere.

Despite the multiple criticisms of human rights, as concept and project, there is no sounder anchorage at this stage of history for discussing how human society should interact, locally and globally, in ways that have some promise of carrying forward the emancipatory goals discussed in this book. Human rights are an anchorage for a universal discourse about the self-constitution of a world community that seeks to place at the centre of the global agenda the duties and rights of individuals as opposed to the power-plays of states. The idea that we should give rights to others, universally and regardless of their status, is one of the greatest inventions in species social evolution. It promises to make us better human beings by instilling ideas of respect and dignity universally, and in so doing it offers a glimpse of world security based on common humanity, in contrast to centuries of unachievable national security based on the competitive will to power.

---

[198] Booth, 'Three Tyrannies', p. 54.   [199] *Ibid.*
[200] Donnelly, *Universal Human Rights*, p. 22.
[201] Howard, *Human Rights*, p. 45; Booth, 'Three Tyrannies', p. 55; Freeman, *Human Rights*, p. 114.

Part IV
Futures

9 The New Twenty Years' Crisis

Crisis? What Crisis?
> *The Sun*, 19 January 1979, criticising 'Sunny Jim' Callaghan[1]

'Have you ever felt you were in two moments at once?' Tom Engelhardt (co-founder of the American Empire Project) asked himself this question in October 2005 as he was driving south to New York City 'on a day when New Orleans had just gone under water and the president was stumbling to address the nation'.[2] There he was, he recounted, 'watching a world I knew well go by, no different than ever, and I felt as if I were slipping effortlessly through some future Pompeii'. He continued,

> All the obvious phrases were wandering through my brain – 'fiddling while Rome burns', 'apres nous le deluge' – and what I was thinking as well was that, if we don't begin to prepare soon for what we know is coming, if we don't do something to mitigate it, we or our children or their children are going to end up abandoning lives as precipitously, and in at least as much chaos, as the inhabitants of New Orleans.

The sense Engelhardt had of living in two moments at once is one many of us feel about the global situation as a whole in the first decade of the twenty-first century. It is a Gramscian time, as was suggested in chapter 1, with the old dying and the new not able to be born. This is the theme of the two final chapters of the book, with the present chapter

---

[1] This famous headline was criticising the attitude of the then UK Prime Minister, 'Sunny Jim' Callaghan, for apparently failing to recognise the 'mounting chaos' around him. Discussed in Francis Wheen, *How Mumbo-Jumbo Conquered The World. A Short History of Modern Delusions* (London: Fourth Estate, 2004), pp. x–xiii.
[2] See http://www.tomdispatch.com and published as 'The Last Days of New Pompeii', *Le Monde diplomatique*, October 2005. The American Empire Project publishes work questioning the character of the US which has 'increasingly embraced imperial ambitions' and its relationship with the rest of the world.

looking at the world we thought we knew slipping 'effortlessly', to use Engelhardt's term, towards global turmoil by mid-century. Whether this extrapolation becomes historical fact, or will contribute to the warnings that might reverse things, will depend on decisions made (or not made) during the remaining years of the New Twenty Years' Crisis. This decisive period began with the terror attacks on the United States on 11 September 2001.

The Great Reckoning

> Is any man afraid of change? Why, what can take place without change? What then is more pleasing or more suitable to the universal nature? . . . canst thou be nourished unless the food undergoes change? And can anything else that is useful be accomplished without change? Dost thou not see thyself also to change is just the same, and equally necessary for the universal nature?
>
> Marcus Aurelius, *Meditations*[3]

The idea of a New Twenty Years' Crisis has been trailed from the beginning of this book. The term refers to a unique world-historical challenge resulting from a particular concatenation of global-level threats. The crisis is defined by the need to make a set of crucial political decisions in six issue areas. If the decisions are avoided, or made badly, the Great Reckoning by mid-century threatens to be an era of terrible global turmoil. As ever, however, a crisis is a relatively brief span of opportunity as well as danger. From the perspective of the first years of the twenty-first century, the dangers appear to be gaining the upper hand, not least because of the widespread sense of the poor quality of contemporary world leadership. The most newsworthy of the unwise decisions of this period, of course, was that of the Bush administration's determination to declare a 'war on terror' in response to the attacks on 9/11.[4] In taking this decision, the White House chose to deal with the terror challenge as military business-as-usual; it then announced an unachievable goal; and as a result of what followed (the march into the disaster of Iraq) distracted the world's most powerful state from the world's most fundamental problems.

---

[3] Marcus Aurelius, *Mediations*, trans. George Long (London: The Softback Preview, 1996), p. 53.
[4] Argued persuasively by Louise Richardson, *What Terrorists Want* (London: John Murray, 2006), pp. 209–42.

World history has obviously been rent by many crisis periods in the past, but only one has previously had the potential to do as much harm to so many people as the Great Reckoning of the first half of this century. As was mentioned in chapter 7, this was the Cold War threat of up to 50,000 nuclear weapons being available for discharge across the northern hemisphere, with the danger of a 'nuclear winter' piling a global environmental catastrophe on top of a civilisational holocaust. The Great Reckoning confronts us with a different and more complex set of global threats; its particular character derives from the converging at the same period of history of many interacting global challenges. In this sense it represents a more demanding test even than the Cold War, which, for all its dangers and difficulties, did have bipolar clarity. The Great Reckoning is potentially the stuff of nightmares, and there is little time to turn things round.

The events that marked the beginning of the New Twenty Years' Crisis have sometimes been said to have shattered the complacency of the rich world. At the time, 9/11 was frequently described as a 'wake-up call' to the United States. If it was, the alarm was only faintly heard. In one sense, that infamous day changed everything (because the world's one super-power reshaped its agenda) but it really changed nothing (because the agenda that emerged from the Bush–Cheney–Rumsfeld mindset simply reasserted crude bipolar, Manichean ways of thinking that echoed the ethnocentrism and ideological fundamentalism of the past). Consequently, the agenda that universal reason required to meet today's multilevel global threats became marginalised. Even if wiser leadership prevails in Washington and elsewhere, world security will by no means be guaranteed, but there would be cause for hope that humanity might emerge from the Great Reckoning if not unscathed, at least with the mindsets and institutional structures for rebuilding a better future. But first we must understand the dangers with which opportunity must wrestle; the rest of this chapter discusses the concatenation of threats gathering in world politics. It is a forecast and an extrapolation, not a prediction. It is chastening, if only half valid.

Many – the Sunny Jims of academia and public life – will deny that there is a mounting crisis, conceding only that, as ever, there are some tough issues out there. Others, more wary, will champion specific global threats, such as the environment, terrorism, or nuclear proliferation. What has been largely missing in the debate has been recognition of the synergy between the converging dangers, and the negative political dynamics that could be provoked. In the world's chief centres of

397

power and political opinion-forming, there is a Panglossian reluctance (see chapter 1) to accept that today's world order could tumble as completely as other apparently permanent world orders did in the past.[5] Unless we are lucky, or wiser, the inhabitants of 'the culture of contentment' will have to learn to expect surprises – disasters – just like the majority of other people on earth. Ordinary life will cease to be ordinary. We cannot continue to assume that tomorrow will be like today.

The New Twenty Years' Crisis results from the convergence of three different sets of crises that are synergistically connected but moving to different temporal pulses. The three crises nest within each other, and throw up in different forms the three fundamental questions that dominated the earlier chapters of the book. The broadest dimension of the problem is an *epochal crisis* (the situation resulting from the disjunction in world history between global human intelligence and the state of the world – what is the reality of the world?). Nesting within that there is a *structural crisis* (the tensions caused by what was called in chapter 1 'the ideas that made us' reaching the limits of their viability – do we know what we have become?). Finally, nesting within that, there is the most immediate set of challenges, the *decisional crisis* (the urgent need for human society in the first two decades of this century to settle its priorities in six flashpoint areas whose outcome will largely determine how well or how badly human society engages with the Great Reckoning – what must be done?). The synergy of these three crisis pulses defines the New Twenty Years' Crisis, and shows that world security today is not simply facing a set of tough problems. It is a time of world-historical challenge, when the global status quo must be critically analysed and progressively changed. If mishandled, the converging threats will have terrible global impacts.

Epochal crisis

Something very new is happening in the world.   Anthony Giddens[6]

---

[5] While accepting that we are living in a time of historical crisis, James Martin is confident about the future, ultimately because of his faith in 'technologies that are infinite in all directions': see his *The Meaning of the 21st Century. A Vital Blueprint for Ensuring our Future* (London: Transworld Publishers, 2006), p. 403.
[6] 'Anthony Giddens and Will Hutton in Conversation', in Will Hutton and Anthony Giddens (eds.), *On the Edge. Living with Global Capitalism* (London: Vintage, 2001), p. 1.

The central question of the epochal crisis is: where does human society, globally, stand in the broadest sweep of history?[7] There is 'no view from nowhere' answer to such a question of course (see chapter 6), but I invite you, as a thought experiment, to place yourself in the role of a caring but critical God, contemplating the human experiment over millions of years of evolution. Hold out an orange at arm's length, and think of it as representing the earth. How would you assess what humans had done during their time on earth? What are the broadest generalisations you could make about human society on this small planet at this moment of geological time? What is real?

I suggest that an omniscient God might proffer four broad propositions about the human experiment as it appears in this epoch. First, humans have not achieved as much progress as many of them think. While technological development has been fantastic, especially since the Industrial Revolution, and some social development has been remarkable, there is so much humans do not know, and they continue to commit dreadful mistakes. They forget that for most of history the cleverest people regarded the world as flat, and they think that they are not susceptible to similar category errors. Can there be any doubt that people in a thousand years' time (if there still are any) will regard us as comparably limited in our understanding of the world as people today regard their eleventh-century ancestors? Yet, typical of human hubris, the futurologist James Martin has claimed that 'during the 21st century, knowledge capability will increase by two to the power of 100 – an unimaginably large number – a thousand billion billion billion'.[8] Is anybody convinced that wisdom capability will grow alongside knowledge? Hubris will be measured by the gap between knowledge claims and wisdom shortfalls.

The second proposition of an omniscient God might be that the self-images held by the most powerful groups today – seeing themselves as advanced, peaceful, and decent – must be treated with caution. There are indeed impressive expressions of humanitarian sympathy across political and other borders, but seen with godly critical distance, global sociology looks like a 'dictatorship of the rich', with a minority presiding over an oppressed majority. The complacent 'haves' do not blatantly tell the poor of the world to 'eat cake', but Marie Antoinette has now gone (almost) global. She shops till she drops, but is only able to consume

---

[7] A earlier but lengthier examination of some of these themes is in Ken Booth, 'Two Terrors, One Problem', in Ersel Aydinli and James N. Rosenau (eds.), *Globalization, Security, and the Nation-State* (Albany, N.Y.: SUNY Press, 2005), pp. 27–30.

[8] Martin, *21st Century*, pp. 402–3.

on the scale she does because of a global economy running on the hard work and poverty of the majority.

Proposition 3 is that human society now lives in the early stages of the world's first true Global Age.[9] Time and space are being reinvented, with humans having to reconceive how to live globally. Economics, politics, identities, and boundaries have to be reassessed in a smaller world. The impacts of globalisation are uneven, but for growing numbers the intrusion of the global into the local is an ever more distinctive feature of daily life. The mobility of so many people, for work and play, marks out the Global Age. As never before in history, as the saying goes, the world is now many people's village (though none should forget the many for whom their village is still the world).

The final proposition that might be offered in this thought experiment is that this Global Age is characterised by a pandemic of 'morbid symptoms' – some of which were discussed in chapter 1. Accompanying these morbid symptoms is a sense that nobody is in control. Even the most powerful state in the world cannot get its way on many issues. But there is a more fundamental social-psychological problem running through the new global sociology: the sense of 'turbulence':[10] a belief that we are in a 'runaway world',[11] where so much is 'on the edge';[12] the fear that we are in a 'risk society';[13] and the fear of fear.[14] The apparently uncontrolled and dysfunctional dynamism of important aspects of this Global Age is the outcome of the networks of ideas that shaped today's global sociology; these structures themselves are under strain, and it is to these I now turn.

---

[9] Martin Albrow, *The Global Age* (Cambridge: Polity, 1997); see Ken Booth, 'Security and Transformation', in Ken Booth (ed.), *Statecraft and Security: The Cold War and Beyond* (Cambridge: Cambridge University Press, 1998), pp. 338–55.

[10] James N. Rosenau, *Turbulence in World Politics: A Theory of Change and Continuity* (Princeton, N.J.: Princeton University Press, 1990).

[11] Anthony Giddens, 'Affluence, Poverty and the Idea of a Post-Scarcity Society' in Booth, *Statecraft and Security*, p. 309.

[12] Hutton and Giddens, *On the Edge*.

[13] Ulrich Beck, *Risk Society. Towards a New Modernity* (London: Sage, 1992); see also Barbara Adam, Ulrich Beck, and Joost Van Loon (eds.), *The Risk Society and Beyond* (London: Sage, 2002).

[14] The structural crisis has been accompanied by a growing literature on fear – enough, I believe, to inaugurate a new interdisciplinary field of Fear Studies; see, for example, Frank Furedi, *Culture of Fear. Risk-taking and the Morality of Low Expectation* (London: Continuum, 2005; 1st pub. 1997), Corey Robin, *Fear. The History of a Political Idea* (Oxford: Oxford University Press, 2004), Joanna Bourke, *Fear. A Cultural History* (London: Virago, 2005).

Structural crisis

> There were two 'Reigns of Terror' [at the time of the French Revolution] . . . the one wrought murder in hot passion, the other in heartless cold blood; the one lasted mere months, the other had lasted a thousand years; the one inflicted death upon ten thousand persons, the other upon a hundred millions; but our shudders are all for the 'horrors' of the minor Terror, the momentary Terror.
>
> Mark Twain in *A Connecticut Yankee in King Arthur's Court* (1889)[15]

The central question of the structural crisis is: have 'the ideas that made us' – the phrase used in chapter 1 – reached their end of their viability?[16] Continuing the earlier thought experiment, our sociologically inclined God, surveying the human experiment, might sum up the structural crisis by adopting today's bureaucratic jargon, and declare that the most powerful ideas that shaped human society globally are no longer 'fit for purpose'. This section can be brief, because of discussions earlier in the book.

The major theories identified in chapter 1 as having made and replicated human society globally are alive and well, though having morbid effects. In the light of the discussions in the previous chapters, a snapshot of each will suffice:

- *Patriarchy.* In approximately 60 per cent of the 1,600 mosques in liberal Britain in 2006, the males who ran them turned away those women who also wanted to pray in 'houses of God'.[17]
- *Proselytising religion.* In September 2005 the president of Iran, Mahmoud Ahmadinejad, celebrated the return of religion in world politics, saying 'Humanity is once again joined in celebrating monotheism. Faith will prove to be the solution of many of today's problems.'[18]

---

[15] Mark Twain, *A Connecticut Yankee in King Arthur's Court*, Introduction by Roy Blount (New York: The Modern Library, 2001; 1st pub. 1899), p. 114. Twain's brilliant insight was drawn to a wider audience by an editorial in the *New Statesman*, 'Never Forget the other Terror' (editorial), 5 November 2001, and 'Twin Terrors', *New Internationalist*, no. 340, November 2001.

[16] Booth, 'Two Terrors', p. 30.

[17] 'Dispatches: Women Only Jihad', investigation by Tazeeen Ahmad, UK Channel 4, 30 October 2006.

[18] Quoted by John Gray, 'Apocalypse Soon', *The Guardian*, 28 October 2006.

- *Capitalism.* Paul Volker, former chair of the US Federal Reserve Board, described the Asian economic crisis of the late 1990s as *'the ordinary workings of global financial capitalism'*.[19]
- *Statism.* Before he became US ambassador at the UN, John Bolton asserted that 'There is no United Nations. There is an international community that occasionally can be led by the only real power left in the world – that's the United States – when it suits our interests and when we can get others to go along.'[20]
- *Race.* A Eurobarometer poll at the end of the 1990s found that one-third of those interviewed described themselves as 'not at all racist', a third as 'a little racist', and a third as 'quite or very racist'.[21]
- *Consumer democracy.* The veteran British socialist Tony Benn, on retiring after fifty-one years in the House of Commons, and so released from the constraints of party and parliament, declared that he had finally become 'free to devote more time to politics'. By this he meant he could support the causes to which he was committed without the distractions and limitations of a parliamentary system that he believed no longer sought to struggle over the big questions in life, but existed to manage an economy and conduct elections between Tweedledum and Tweedledee.[22]

Each of the big ideas identified above once seemed to be an answer to the great questions of life, but arguably they have conspired together to create a distinctive global sociology which does not work for the majority of people in the world, or for nature as a whole.

Although the powerful and long-lasting structures of patriarchy, proselytising religion, statism, capitalism, race, and consumerist democracy have been pushed to, or beyond, the limits of their viability, resistance to change is predictable. Many, and by definition the contingently powerful, have an interest in maintaining the contemporary

[19] Quoted by Roger Tooze, 'The Missing Link: Security, Critical International Political Economy, and Community', in Ken Booth (ed.), *Critical Security Studies in World Politics* (Boulder, Colo.: Lynne Rienner, 2005), p. 142.
[20] Quoted by Noam Chomsky, *Failed States. The Abuse of Power and the Assault on Democracy* (New York: Metropolitan Books, 2006), p. 86.
[21] Gitta Sereny, 'Racism Within', in Nicholas Owen (ed.), *Human Rights, Human Wrongs. The Oxford Amnesty Lectures 2001* (Oxford: Oxford University Press, 2003), p. 237.
[22] Tony Benn, *Free at Last! Diaries 1991–2001*, ed. Ruth Winstone (London: Hutchinson, 2002), p. xiii.

ancien régime against any revolution in the global mind; the threat they fear is from the embedding of cosmopolitan enlightenment, a sensibility that would dare us to use reason, universal hospitality, and empathetic knowledge to advance the cause of the 'point of view of the universe'.

Decisional crisis

what is the horror of swift death by the axe, compared with life-long death from hunger, cold, insult, cruelty and heartbreak? . . . A city cemetery could contain the coffins filled by that brief Terror which we have all been so diligently taught to shiver at and mourn over; but all France could hardly contain the coffins filled by that older and real Terror – that unspeakably bitter and awful Terror which none of us has been taught to see in its vastness or pity as it deserves.

Mark Twain on the two Terrors of the French Revolution[23]

In addition to the epochal/structural strains, tensions, and crises in global history and sociology just outlined, there is a set of immediate challenges requiring urgent and radical decision. These are manifestations of the 'morbid symptoms' discussed particularly in chapter 1. The historical challenge is daunting: can human societies, individually and collectively, exercise the necessary judgement, and institute appropriate action, in six major issue areas quickly enough to prevent a collapse into an era of global turmoil? The issue areas have been discussed implicitly or explicitly throughout the book; each, separately, is serious enough, but their potential synergy is explosive. The challenge of the New Twenty Years' Crisis for human society, in whole and in part, is to take a set of fundamental decisions, before the second decade of this century is finished, about future directions, priorities, and policies with respect to *universal vital interests*. Avoiding decisions, or taking false ones, will accelerate the momentum and depth of the Great Reckoning, and ensure there is nothing but turmoil. The fundamental decisions facing human society concern flashpoints in the following six issue areas: security dilemmas and strategic challenges, globalisation threats, population stress, environmental chaos, governance overload, and the rise of unreason. Each deserves a book; what follows is a snapshot.

[23] Twain, *A Connecticut Yankee*, p. 114.

1.   Security dilemmas and strategic challenges[24]

The 'security dilemma' is the idea that unresolvable uncertainties arising out of the 'other minds problem', and the ambiguous symbolism of
weaponry, tends to produce strategic competition between states (and
also ethnic groups under conditions of emerging anarchy). This in turn
creates an interacting spiral of danger (through arms racing, for example) even if the parties involved have no hostile motives or intentions
in the first place. Security competition of this kind, spurred on by mistrust and fear, should be distinguished from 'strategic challenges', which
refer to confrontations and possibly conflict arising from the ambition
of one or more state actors to achieve political leverage or the control
of land; in these cases it is not a question of a lack of understanding
about motives and intentions, for these are well enough understood.
Surprises will be 'technical' rather than 'behavioural'.[25] Security dilemmas and strategic challenges represent the traditional insecurities of the
states system, of course, but there is good reason to think that they will
not disappear under the manifold pressures of 'a world on the edge'.
Colin Gray has prophesied *Another Bloody Century*, with the future of
great power rivalry being very reminiscent of the past. After describing
history as 'the only guide' available to thinking about the future, and
then referring to one historian's views about the 'ambitions, vanities,
and quirks' complicit in strategic history, he gave his judgement: this is
'the way things are and the way they will remain'.[26] With fear rampant,
and insecurities globalised (from uncertainty about what is in the ruck-
sack of a fellow train or bus passenger, to the uncertainties of life in a
world of diffusing nuclear weaponry), the security dilemma is an idea
whose time has come.[27]

Among the most threatening security dilemmas and strategic challenges in coming decades, the following stand out: the provocation that
will be caused by the deployment of US Ballistic Missile Defense and
the weaponisation of space, and the likelihood that other governments
will respond on the basis of fatalistic assumptions; the possibility of a

---

[24] This distinction is made in Ken Booth and Nicholas J. Wheeler, *The Security Dilemma.
Fear, Cooperation, and Trust in World Politics* (Houndmills: Palgrave, 2008), 'Introduction'.
[25] The distinction is Klaus Knorr's; see his 'Failures in National Intelligence Estimates:
The Case of the Cuban Missiles', *World Politics*, vol. 16(3), 1964, pp. 455–67.
[26] Colin S. Gray, *Another Bloody Century. Future War* (London: Phoenix Books, 2005),
pp. 396–7.
[27] The theme of Booth and Wheeler, *Security Dilemma*, ch. 10.

Cold War between China and the United States (as the power of the former increases, and both react in ethnocentric incomprehension); the rise of India (as its economic potential pushes it to the superpower status its nationalists crave); the revival of a more assertive Russia (too easily written off, too humbled, yet a potential energy superpower); the proliferation of nuclear weapons to regional adversaries, thereby ratcheting up the dangers in long-running confrontations (notably over Kashmir, in the Korean peninsula, and the Middle East); the spread of international terrorism to yet more groups and situations, as political hopes and ambitions are stymied, and spectacular destructive potential increases; a profusion of failed states resulting in ethnic conflict, genocide, and mass migration; and local crises and conflicts over ever more precious territory, as competition grows over access to non-renewable energy supplies and scarce water. The list of threats is longer, but those are the most urgent. Although war between the major powers now appears a remote possibility, because of its destructiveness, power-balancing can be expected against the United States, and this will lead to strange bedfellows, with the dangers of proxy wars, accidental nuclear wars, and inadvertent wars in their wake. If worst-case forecasting everywhere prevails, and states begin to position themselves fatalistically in the expectation of harder times ahead, then insecurity will intensify to potentially intolerable levels.

The most urgent set of decisions about these most traditional of international political concerns relates to nuclear weapons.[28] The relatively successful NPT regime began to look very sickly in the aftermath of the disappointing 2005 Review Conference, shortly followed by growing anxiety about the nuclear weapons ambitions of Iran and then the declared explosion in 2006 of a nuclear device by North Korea. At that time, according to Mohamed ElBaradei, director of the International Atomic Energy Agency (IAEA), there were roughly three dozen countries 'with civil nuclear power, who have the technologies and understanding to develop nuclear weapons in a short period of time'.[29] Who realistically can believe that world security will increase in direct proportion to the number of new nuclear weapons states?[30] And who can realistically argue that nuclear non-proliferation will prosper while existing

[28] Discussed at length *ibid.*, chs. 6 and 10.
[29] 'Faith in an Old Nuclear Order Will Compound the Dangers' (editorial), *New Statesman*, 16 October 2006.
[30] Many years ago, Kenneth Waltz gave 'defensive realist' credence to this view; see his *The Spread of Nuclear Weapons: More May Be Better*, Adelphi Paper no. 171 (London: International Institute for Strategic Studies, 1981).

nuclear weapons states (NWS) justify their own possession as the 'ultimate insurance' for their national security.

It is my clear view that the balance of risks favours moving away from the accelerating threats of a proliferating world towards global nuclear abolition (the explicit goal of the NPT), and the parallel step of moving away from the notion of nuclear weapons as the ultimate insurers of national security towards the unequivocal support for their illegality.[31] Pro-nuclear opinion in different countries claims that because we live in an uncertain world, it is rational that their own states develop or keep nuclear weapons (seemingly ignoring the point that what is rational for one country in this regard is the recipe for rational nuclear possession universally). There is no doubt that we live in an uncertain world, but the point is that the *predictable uncertainties* of nuclear proliferation (the increased dangers of accidental or inadvertent nuclear war, the increased risk of nuclear material being acquired by terrorists, etc.) are more threatening than the *unpredictable uncertainties* of abolition (treaty 'break-out', cheating, etc.). If the trends to nuclear proliferation are not stopped almost immediately, then we face the prospect of a new nuclear age, this time with many more nuclear powers, complex security dilemmas, and the problems resulting from confrontations between states whose nuclear weapons systems and command and control arrangements are less technologically sophisticated than those of the long-established nuclear powers. The world was lucky to escape the first (largely bipolar) nuclear age without a catastrophe; it will be luckier still to survive a multipolar age characterised by nuclear contagion.[32]

---

[31] In relation to the British government's thinking in 2006 about replacing Trident see, inter alia, Lee Butler, 'At the End of the Journey: The Risks of Cold War Thinking in a New Era' (pp. 763–9) and Michael MccGwire, 'Nuclear Deterrence' (pp. 771–84) in 'Britain's Nuclear Weapons Debate', Special Issue of *International Affairs*, vol. 82(4), 2006; and Ken Booth and Frank Barnaby (eds.), *The Future of Britain's Nuclear Weapons: Experts Reframe the Debate*, Current Decisions Report (Oxford: Oxford Research Group, March 2006). See also Ken Booth, 'The Certainty of Uncertainty' (December 2006) on the David Davies Memorial Institute website (www.aber.ac.uk), and the legal opinion of Philippe Sands, 'The United Kingdom's Nuclear Deterrent: Current and Future Issues of Legality' (www.greenpeace.org.uk).

[32] Nuclear dangers and risks in the Cold War and beyond are discussed, inter alia, in Bruce G. Blair, *The Logic of Accidental War* (Washington D.C.: Brookings Institution, 1993), Scott D. Sagan, *The Limits of Safety: Organisations, Accidents, and Nuclear Weapons* (Princeton, N.J.: Princeton University Press, 1993), Aleksandr Fursenko and Timothy Naftali, *"One Hell of a Gamble": Khrushchev, Castro and Kennedy, 1958–1964 – The Secret History of the Cuban Missile Crisis* (New York: W. W. Norton, 1997), Robert S. McNamara and James G. Blight, *Wilson's Ghost. Reducing the Risk of Conflict, Killing, and Catastrophe in the 21st Century* (New York: Public Affairs, 2001), esp. pp. 188–91, Joseph Cirincione, 'Lessons Lost', *Bulletin of the*

2. Globalisation threats

The two dimensions of globalisation discussed in chapter 8 – the capitalist global economy (project) and the smaller world (process) – constitute a secular trend, though it need not take the particular forms it has since the final decades of the last century. Short of a global catastrophe, it was argued that the reversal of globalisation – the spread of autarky or cultural isolationism – is highly remote. Interdependence will ensure that sovereign states will remain generally open (and to a degree vulnerable) to each other,[33] but state borders will remain powerful shapers of human behaviour; they are changing their meaning in some ways, but they are certainly not disappearing. Where one's passport or identity card was issued remains a significant indicator of every individual's potential security (or the opposite).

Even were governments and corporations to pursue the path of humanising globalisation with vigour (a goal discussed in chapter 8), uneven impacts would remain for a prolonged period in the military, political, societal, environmental, and economic 'sectors' of security, to use Buzan's categorisation. Globalisation's uneven impacts, it will be recalled, are manifest in the form of winners/losers and relative haves/have-nots, as they are between states and regions, classes, the educated and the uneducated, the young and old, and men and women. Specific security threats to these referents include: the erosion of local cultures and economies, the spread of pandemics, the growth of radicalisation and terrorism, human rights abuses, political disempowerment, environmental degradation, and economic downturns or collapses interacting with ethnic and other insecurities. While there is no direct relationship between terrorism and poverty, the latter is a potentially powerful lever to be manipulated by rabble-rousers.

The decisional challenges in the issue area of globalisation relate to humanising key structures and processes: strong and visionary decisions are necessary. With regard to globalisation as a project, decisions must be made about the ways in which the global economy is run (and for whom). Its humanising measure will be in the degree of progress achieved towards fair trade, debt cancellation, the eradication of poverty, and the promotion of equality. With regard to globalisation as a process, decisions must be made to better manage the tensions of

Atomic Scientists, vol. 61(6), 2005, pp. 42–53, Bruce G. Blair, 'Primed and Ready', *Bulletin of the Atomic Scientists*, vol. 63(1), 2007, pp. 33–7.
[33] The original and classic text on interdependence is Robert Keohane and Joseph J. Nye, *Power and Interdependence: World Politics in Transition* (Boston: Little, Brown, 1977).

a smaller world (and with a more inclusive understanding of interests) and this must be manifest in the growth of mutual respect between peoples, the devolution of recognition, the protection of local languages, and so on. Such decisions will be made more complicated and more difficult to implement because of the traditional dynamics in interstate relations, which tend to encourage governments to look outwards with mistrust and inwards with amity.

3.   Population stress

The growth of the global population is a dynamic specialists in international relations have simply not begun to address. As the insecurities generated by Global Age pressures cross-fertilise with the traditional insecurities of the Westphalian world, continued population growth adds yet new layers of danger; it is a potentially highly destabilising factor in the global mix. Consider the scale of the change. Someone born in the mid-1930s entered a world in which there were about two billion people on earth; by the time they retired from work (aged sixty-five) there were about six billion, a three-fold increase in one lifetime. By the time their grandchildren (born about 1990) might retire (2050s) that population will have almost doubled again.

Some states and regions will cope with the population surge better than others, but challenging questions are thrown up for all. How will economies cope with the extra people? Will they find employment? What about the environmental consequences – the greater demands for food and water for a start? Where and how will they all be housed? What are the sociological impacts of so many more people being born, looking for marriage partners, having (or being prevented from having) children of their own? What will the nutrition of these extra billions look like? How will order be maintained, as well as essential services, in teeming cities that threaten urban sprawl over whole regions? What are the implications for transnational crime, for political extremism, and for international terrorism of the availability of so many potentially restive young men? Will the 100-mile cities of the future be the sites of rootlessness, rage, and revolution? How will these mega-cities fit into the story of a world in which economic crises cannot be ruled out, resource wars are predictable, and clashing civilisations may be the path to the promised land according to particular ideological/religious radicals? Where will the armies of the unemployed be deployed? Will overpopulation in some regions lead to mass migration and international crises? The list of questions thrown up by the growth of the global population is endless. And some of the answers will have to take account of the fact that 'the street' in most parts of the world will be more streetwise; that is, the have-nots will have increasing access to knowledge about the haves. Perhaps the scenarios of this future world might be better sketched by novelists and film-makers than international relations specialists. Be that as it may, a world of more than twelve billion people is a material reality with which international relations scholars must engage; for the time being it is largely being ignored, part of the discipline's 'escape from the real'.[34]

While there has been a flattening out of the upward trend in global population trends, the direction has continued upwards. As a result, the threat of humans overwhelming the rest of nature grows, and with it a further decline in the prospects of those in poor countries ever being able to 'live a life'. Controlling the birth rate, globally, is as much a matter of world security for the twenty-first century as the control of the nuclear arms race was for the second half of the twentieth. Brian Barry is a rare political theorist who has taken this issue seriously, reminding his readers of the warning of John Stuart Mill that 'causing the existence of a human being' is one of the most significant of actions, and therefore does 'not exceed the legitimate powers of the state'.[35] A theorist who was not of the same view was E. H. Carr, who in 1936 declared jokingly that advice on birth control was not a matter for a professor of international politics.[36] Such advice was hardly sensible even in the period when he gave it. One of the ostensible 'founding fathers' of realism should have better understood that population size and growth rates were key variables in national security policies in the age of conscription. Today, for different reasons, no professor of international relations should ignore the critical materiality of birth rates for the future of both national and world security.

4. The destroying of nature

The world is getting used up before our very eyes. Recalling her youth (she was born in 1919) the novelist Doris Lessing said, 'The world had

---

[34] The phrase is Clément Rosset's, in his *Joyful Cruelty: Toward a Philosophy of the Real*, ed. and trans. David F. Bell (New York: Oxford University Press, 1993). It is discussed, together with population issues, in Ken Booth, 'Human Wrongs and International Relations', *International Affairs*, vol. 71(1), 1995, pp. 103–26.

[35] Brian Barry, *Why Social Justice Matters* (Cambridge: Polity, 2005), pp. 255–7, 308, n. 24.

[36] E. H. Carr, 'Public Opinion as a Safeguard of Peace', *International Affairs*, vol. 15(6), 1936, pp. 846–62. I questioned the validity of such coyness in my own inaugural lecture, in the same hall, and also questioned the conventional interpretation of Carr simply as a realist; see Ken Booth, 'Security in Anarchy: Utopian Realism in Theory and Practice', *International Affairs*, vol. 67(3), 1991, pp. 527–45, esp. p. 544.

unused places then. We don't now. Even wild places are used for adventure holidays, and the remotest for men to try boys' own adventures ... it is all used.'[37] (The exploration of space, it might be remembered, has been used as an opportunity for men to practise golf-swings.[38]) And while there have been some triumphs in helping nature recover – a cleaner river that allows fish to return, the revival of a declining species of bird – they do not seem to keep pace with what has been lost. Rivers helped give birth to civilisations, but in too many places today they are being destroyed by those they helped create. Rivers have always had particular symbolism in India, and this makes all the more poignant Arundhati Roy's image of a river that had become 'just a slow, sludging green ribbon lawn that ferried fetid garbage to the sea ... On warm days the smell of shit lifted off ... [it] and hovered ... like a hat.'[39] Nature is being overwhelmed by the growth, spread, demands, and carelessness of human society.

The threat to the global environment is one issue area that has attracted vastly more public attention since the 1980s, as was discussed in chapter 7. While some governments, notably that of the United States, have stood aside from embracing the growing consensus about what needs to be done and who is to blame, the eco-deniers who feed the complacent have themselves become increasingly marginalised and attacked. In June 2004, forty-eight Nobel Prize-winning scientists accused President Bush and his administration of distorting science.[40] Across the United States, there are plenty of signs that many citizens are much more far-sighted than their President, but as the superpower polluter, the lifestyle obstacles to change are enormous. The mood of researchers and writers about the environment has steadily darkened, with a growing acceptance of the possibility (and for some the probability) of the destruction and collapse of human social systems as a result of the climate chaos and related predictions.[41] In February 2007 was published what was claimed to be the most authoritative, independent, scientific advice on the issue, the report of the Intergovernmental Panel on Climate Change. It sought

[37] Emma Brookes, 'Doris Lessing. A Singular Survivor', in Annalena McAfee (ed.), *Lives and Works* (London: Atlantic Books, 2002), p. 98.
[38] Marina Hyde, 'Is this What the Final Frontier Has Become? A Golf Course?' *The Guardian*, 25 November 2006.
[39] Arundhati Roy, The *God of Small Things* (London: Harper Perennial, 1997), pp. 124–5.
[40] Al Gore, *An Inconvenient Truth* (London: Bloomsbury, 2006), p. 268.
[41] The term 'climate chaos' was advocated by the World Wildlife Fund in preference to what Johann Hari called the 'strangely smoothing' label of 'global warming': Johann Hari, 'Don't Call it Climate Change – it's Chaos', *The Independent*, 15 November 2005.

to make projections more accurate on the basis of broader evidence and the involvement of more scientists. Its verdict was to establish the link between human activities and global warming more directly than previously, such that it would thereafter be difficult for sceptics to hold their position. If the worst projections turn out to be accurate, the future will be one of reduced food production, increased flooding, more disease, animal extinction, water shortages, and extreme weather.[42] Some governments have already begun planning for the 'tensions and conflicts – both within and between states'.[43]

At the heart of the deteriorating state of nature is the role of human behaviour in the rising global temperature, which in turn threatens to bring about a series of interconnected epochal events, from the melting of the ice-caps to changing the direction of the oceans' currents. As a result of the environmental chaos, widespread food shortages can be expected globally, some communities will become unsustainable, jobs will be lost or threatened, droughts and floods and other extreme events will challenge long-established patterns of life, and massive economic disruption will occur which will make it all the more difficult to divert energy and resources from responding to immediate insecurities to building world society and spreading aid. Out of such possibilities, societies may disappear, as some have in the past. In *Collapse. How Societies Choose to Fail or Survive*, Jared Diamond has illustrated this from a range of historical cases.[44] His cases show that collapsing societies sometimes create the conditions for the rise of what the historian Herbert Butterfield called 'Hobbesian fear', with much resultant brutal behaviour; but Diamond also saw the potential for the best of humanity.[45] In a particularly haunting and thought-provoking metaphor for our time, he asked us to wonder what the man thought as he cut down the last palm tree on Easter Island, a civilisation that now exists only in its dumb statues.[46] Unlike Easter Island's last man, global society is not yet at the end of the road. Diamond concluded his book with 'cautious optimism'. We face 'big risks', he thought, but our problems are not insoluble, there has been a positive spread of environmental thinking, there is scope to engage in long-term planning and to reconsider

[42] David Adam, 'Worse than we Thought', *The Guardian*, 3 February 2007.
[43] These are words from the 2003 UK Defence White Paper, quoted by Josh Arnold-Foster, 'A Matter of Security', *New Statesman*, 29 January 2007.
[44] Jared Diamond, *Collapse. How Societies Choose to Fail or Survive* (London: Penguin, 2006).
[45] *Ibid.*, 'Part Four: Practical Lessons'; on Butterfield, see Booth and Wheeler, *Security Dilemma*, ch. 1.
[46] Diamond, *Collapse*, pp. 79–119, esp. pp. 114 and 119.

our 'core values' (in a 'low-impact' direction), and unlike those societies that have collapsed in the past we have a much better chance to learn from the mistakes of others, and quickly.[47] But it yet remains to be seen whether we will be able to resist the temptation to cut down the last tree, and whether we can sufficiently internalise a more enlightened sense of intergenerational duty and cosmopolitan care. Far-reaching decisions must be made now.

But is there time? Some believe the 'tipping point' for environmental collapse has already been passed. The consensus, reassuringly, is that there still might be time, and that even if the bleakest predictions do not come about (if the energy crisis is mitigated or even avoided by a technological revolution) that it is nevertheless sensible to operate on the basis of the precautionary principle. Confronting all those of us who are not fatalists (believing it is too late anyway) and eco-deniers (what crisis?) is a set of very tough decisions in order to promote sustainability. What needs to be done is clearer than how international agreements might come about, and then be followed by resolute action. There is already a high level of agreement at the global civil society level about the desirable environmental road-map: making sustainable development the organising principle of democratic societies, valuing nature, ensuring fair shares, requiring that the polluter pays, constructing good governance, and adopting a precautionary approach (these were the 2001 'UK Sustainable Development Commission's Principles for Sustainable Development').[48] Differences occur between those environmentalists who believe that societies can make progress relatively painlessly in a capitalist global economy (Al Gore), to those who argue that emerging solutions can be found within 'the embrace of capitalism' but that much needs to be done (Jonathan Porritt), to those who believe that much more radical measures are necessary – so radical, in fact, that governments will have to enforce what are likely to be very unpopular restrictions on well-established lifestyles in the rich world (George Monbiot).[49] All agree, however, that action has to be taken soon at the levels of individuals, corporations, and states.

Perhaps the greatest challenge is not at the national level, but to get agreement internationally. Unless the rogue states that constitute the

---

[47] *Ibid.*, 'Reasons for Hope', pp. 521–5.

[48] These are printed in Jonathon Porritt, *Capitalism as if the World Matters* (London: Earthscan, 2006), pp. 290–1; see also pp. 284–303.

[49] For a full range of views, see Patrick Curry, *Ecological Ethics. An Introduction* (Cambridge: Polity, 2006); also, Gore, *An inconvenient Truth*, Porritt, *Capitalism as if the World Matters*, and George Monbiot, *Heat: How to Stop the Planet Burning* (London: Allen Lane, 2006).

axis of pollution agree collectively, and quickly, then the tipping point will surely have arrived by mid-century if the environmental scientists are correct in their calculations. The outcome for world security would then be highly unpredictable. Working towards relevant and radical international agreements is one of the biggest challenges of all the decisional crises in the New Twenty Years' Crisis. It is another 'inconvenient truth' raised by Al Gore's consciousness-raising book and film about the environment, but for which the former Vice-President and globe-trotting 'Get around on less' campaigner was not able to offer a persuasive international road-map to his readers. Not surprisingly, he saw his immediate challenge being to win his own country round to his way of thinking, and he rightly identified the Bush administration as a major obstacle. The US President was seen as having a key role in shaping politics and public opinion,[50] and Gore's criticism of the Bush administration was justified. But there is a failure that is more telling still than the lack of environmentalist credentials of a President long dubbed the 'toxic Texan'. Readers (and viewers of Gore's related film) would have understood more about the difficulty of negotiating the road-map to a more sustainable planet had this champion of environmental issues explained why, as Vice-President of his country, with special access to the President of the world's most powerful state for eight years, he had so signally failed to ensure that the White House became green.

5. Governance overload

The somewhat grandiose concept of 'global governance' refers to those theories and practices that seek to provide legitimised procedures for political activities (and not just those of governments) which are of global relevance. A network of global governance has developed since the 1980s, but it remains poorly equipped to handle the most long-term and significant issues between states that relate to security conceived broadly.[51] The priority issues to be addressed through the appropriate institutions of global governance, based on the discussion so far in this chapter, are listed below; how they are resolved (or whether they

---

[50] Gore, *Inconvenient Truth*, pp. 286, 312.
[51] Out of the extensive literature on this, the following collections are recommended: Raimo Väyrynen (ed.), *Globalization and Global Governance* (Lanham, Md.: Rowman and Littlefield, 1999); Joseph S. Nye and John D. Donahue (eds.), *Governance in a Globalizing World* (Washington D.C.: Brookings Institution Press, 2000); David Held and Mathias Koenig-Archibugi (eds.), *Taming Globalization. Frontiers of Governance* (Cambridge: Polity, 2003); Rorden Wilkinson, *The Global Governance Reader* (London: Routledge, 2005).

are) will determine whether world society emerges from the first two decades of the century in good shape.

Key governance issues are: preventing the War on Terror being both a distraction and source of expanding danger as a result of radicalising relations between the Islamic world and the rest; avoiding the drift to a Sino-US Cold War as a result of the determination of US administrations to weaponise space and seek superiority in missile defence; reversing the rush to a world of many nuclear powers; slowing and reversing global warming; promoting sustainable development as the organising principle of policy for all states; checking population growth globally and in key pressure-points; creating the rules for fair trade; and taking steps to eradicate poverty globally through debt relief and good governance. In order to pursue such ambitious objectives effectively, there is the prior need to improve the capacity and change the culture of international society, or what Robbie Robertson has described as the need for 'globalized humanity' to develop a 'new consciousness of itself' if it is to avoid the destabilising and violent effects of earlier (though not as thoroughgoing) waves of globalisation.[52] Such a development would be eased by the promotion of cosmopolitan democracy – a democracy that is not an instrument for rampant localism but for a more effective transmission of cosmopolitan values. UN reform is one obvious need, but the organisation's inability to make progress, after many years of discussion, is a symptom of the problem it seeks to address, as is the label 'international community', a smoke-screen behind which the great powers pursue their own interests as the 'Great Irresponsibles' in Hedley Bull's well-known phrase.[53]

Winston Churchill, as mentioned in chapter 6, is credited with saying words to the effect that humans will always do the right thing in the end, but not before they have tried everything else. The limited capabilities of global governance so far offers little comfort when we contemplate the concatenation of predictable crises outlined above. Keeping Churchill's adage in mind, it is depressing to recall that it took two world wars within a generation to provoke the 'Great Irresponsibles' of the traditional European states system to make rapid and far-reaching steps towards multilevel integration. The challenge to global governance in anticipation of today's Great Reckoning is to prove Churchill wrong by

---

[52] Robbie Robertson, *The Three Waves of Globalization. A History of a Developing Global Consciousness* (London: Zed Books, 2003).
[53] Hedley Bull, 'The Great Irresponsibles? The United States, the Soviet Union, and World Order', *International Journal*, vol. 25, Summer 1980, pp. 437–47.

taking decisive, rapid, and far-reaching steps in constructing networks of global governance that will bring about the degree of organisational and cultural integration that will encourage progressive decisions to be taken in the collective interest.

The political task facing global civil society in the years ahead is to keep up the pressure on the most powerful states about the coming dangers, and to encourage them to act in the collective interest before it is too late. A particular duty is to try and encourage governments to behave in ways that blend ends and means (as was discussed in chapter 6, and will be elaborated in chapter 10). It is obviously impossible to eradicate all the insecurities resulting from globalisation immediately, but it is possible immediately to pursue policies that humanise globalisation. Adopting such a posture will be easier if progress has been made along the lines of civilising the states system discussed in chapter 5, with the growth of 'cosmopolitan states'. The potential transcultural sensibility Beck envisaged belongs within his theory of a 'world risk society'. Out of the latter's unintended consequences, and notably the ecological crisis, is the possibility that new thinking might emerge from 'the fact that the threat knows no frontiers'. In the past, national consciousness and national histories delivered national enemy images. This may be so in future, but Beck wondered whether 'for the first time people will experience the common character of a destiny'. The growth of a sense of a community of fate would help the growth of cosmopolitan states: 'Paradoxical as it may seem, it is arousing a cosmopolitan everyday consciousness which transcends even the borders between man, animal, and plant. Threats create society, and global threats create global society.'[54] The idea of a 'cosmopolitan state' to Westphalian mindsets is an oxymoron, of course, and for many impossible to imagine; but so would have been the idea of a 'nation-state' to a medieval mindset, imprisoned by ideas of kings, popes, feudalism, and God, long before what Charles Manning used to call 'the notion of the nation' had first been invented. The cosmopolitan state, in the Global Age, as the transmission belt between networks of global governance above it, and devolved responsibilities below it, is a challenging and inspired new notion, though not one that will appeal to either statists or nationalists.

Time is short for global governance to be in a position to respond effectively to the multiple challenges of the decisional crisis, but the end

[54] Ulrich Beck, *What is Globalization?* (Cambridge: Polity, 2000), pp. 26, 38–42 (quotation at p. 38); also see Beck, *Risk Society*, and *World Risk Society* (Cambridge: Polity, 1995), and Adam *et al.*, *Risk Society and Beyond*.

of the Cold War should remind us 'never to say never'. The rapid melting into the air of the all too solid ideational and material realities of the Soviet–US Cold War tells us that systemic transformation cannot be dismissed as utopian dreaming. In the 1980s the Cold War had become ideologically barren and the threat of nuclear war dangerously close. Today, we are faced by a Great Reckoning in which major ideas have reached the limits of their viability, and insecurity is rising dangerously. The challenge could not be clearer: will this generation of political leaders use the foresight and reason available to them to think globally and construct a framework for global governance for common humanity, or will they, like the man who cut down the last tree on Easter Island, continue into a shrinking future carrying on with business-as-usual?

6. A season of unreason

Despite the predictions of 'end of history' triumphalism in the final decade of the twentieth century, the great questions of politics, economics, and life have not been settled. Religion, for example, has made a comeback on the world stage, as well as continuing its feuding between its proselytising sects and its struggles with secularism. And it is surely predictable, furthermore, as material conditions change over coming decades, that we will witness the appearance of economic ideologies questioning the liberal-capitalist model. Of all the predictions made at the end of the Cold War, therefore, surely the most flawed was the belief that ideological struggles had been cast into the dustbin of history. It is no part of the present argument to assume that 'ideology = unreason'; rather, my case is that the great battle of ideas did not end when 'history' supposedly did, and that, in this new age of ideas, what have flourished have been unreason and reaction, rather than the seed-beds of universal emancipation.

Francis Wheen dated the symbolic end of the twentieth century as 1979, not at the more conventional turning-points of 1989 or 2001. In that year Margaret Thatcher came to power reasserting 'Victorian values' and quoting St Francis of Assisi. Meanwhile, Ayatollah Ruhollah Khomeini returned to Iran intending to restore a system that had existed 1,300 years previously, and was accompanied by people quoting poems reflecting 'chiliastic optimism'.[55] For Wheen, thus began an era 'colonised' by cults and quackery, gurus and irrational panics, premodernists and postmodernists, medieval theocrats and New Age mystics,

---

[55] Wheen, *How Mumbo-Jumbo Conquered the World*, pp. vii–xiv.

and moral confusion and mumbo-jumbo.[56] The ground for a new age of wars of ideas was being well fertilised even before the old age of ideology had been declared to have come to an end. Typical of the creeping unreason that has emerged, Wheen pointed to a British Prime Minister (Blair) who claimed to be a 'progressive moderniser' and an advocate of 'education, education, education', but who nevertheless defended 'creationism' in school science classes (as opposed to restricting it to religious education). Wheen also criticised intellectuals ostensibly committed to Enlightenment values who appear reluctant to defend them for fear of being labelled liberal imperialists.[57] 'The sleep of reason brings forth monsters', he reminded his readers in 2004, and pointed to the 'monsters galore' that had emerged during the previous two decades.

This season of unreason is one of the morbid symptoms of our time, with the most unpredictable consequences.[58] The 'monsters galore' are all around: religious fanaticism and militancy, political extremism, genocidal tendencies, terrorism, brutality, and hatred. Specific instances of these since the start of the 1990s include the 'madness visible' in the Balkans, genocidal slaughter in Rwanda, the Taliban's medieval modalities, radicalisation in the Islamic world, brutal Hindu nationalism, the political rise of the religious right in the United States, seeping anti-Semitism and anti-Roma attitudes in eastern Europe, the revival of populist right-wing movements in western Europe, and state-sponsored Holocaust-denial in Iran. In such a brew, the emergence of a 'clash of civilisations' might no longer be simply a crude and contested academic theory but a dangerous self-fulfilling prophecy.

The manner in which religion has once more taken centre stage in politics has already been noted. In Europe, for example, secular polities are faced with an increasingly religious world order (that is, communities of faith, wherever they live, wherever they come from, who see themselves as primarily religious). A key dynamic here is the potential reason/faith security dilemma, with Arab opinion seeing the West as a threat to Islam, and Western opinion seeing Islam as a threat to its values.[59] As with other types of security dilemma, the dangers in this particular potential conflict will increase in direct proportion to the lack of 'security dilemma sensibility' shown on all sides; this requires people to learn to empathise with each other's fears, and understand the role that one's own attitudes and behaviour may play in stoking up

---

[56] *Ibid.*, esp. pp. 1–39, 262–312.   [57] *Ibid.*, p. 7.
[58] Discussed in Booth, 'Two Terrors', pp. 38–9.
[59] Richard Gott, 'Reason Blinks in the Light of Faith', *The Guardian*, 20 April 1996.

those fears.[60] Without doubt, a clash of civilisations (Huntington's 'thoroughly unsound' theory)[61] could be an outcome if unreason is allowed to rule the day. The clash with which we are faced is better conceived, as Edward Said put it, not as one between 'Civilisations', but as a 'Clash of Ignorance':[62] the result of flawed interpretations and crude responses to the faith/religion security dilemma. History suggests that once fundamental spiritual beliefs become implicated in politics – the public sphere where ideally reasonable discussion, compromise, and consensus takes place – trouble can be expected. When faith asserts itself, there is a tendency for people to allocate themselves roles (or have them allocated) in traditional and comforting narratives rather than embed themselves in the uncertainties of reason. It is common to hear people introducing a sentence with the words 'As a . . .' ('Muslim' or 'Christian' or whatever). Such discursive practices reveal a preference for conversational role-playing (Sen's 'solitarism') rather than dialogue through rational discussion; it involves listening but not hearing, and speaking to a script that cannot be rewritten without destroying the narrative that gives it meaning. For solitarists, however, their role in their traditional narrative is all.

When unreason is in season, trouble can begin in what at first might seem the unlikeliest of places, and with what appear to be innocent manifestations. Take the proliferation of St George's flags throughout England in 2006, a year when such displays might have been expected, for it was the time of another festival of World Cup football. J. D. Ballard, however, a bleak writer for our times, saw in this badging of national identity – certainly not the most virulent site of what he was describing – a process in which 'the white middle class retribalizes itself'. He added, 'It's not racist, yet', but he was not confident where it might end: 'the whites are now saying, "Remember us?"' He gave another chilling comment on the ties that bind British (and possibly the whole of Western) society: 'Holding things together is consumerism. It imposes the only values we have.' Ballard might have drawn a comparison with eastern Europe in the 1970s and 1980s, when modest consumerism was the only tie that bound those societies to the bankrupt ideology of Soviet-defined socialism. Consumerism did not prove enough, especially as economies faltered, to prevent the all too solid Iron Curtain from melting into air

---

[60] Booth and Wheeler, *Security Dilemma*, 'Introduction'.
[61] The term is Gray's, *Another Bloody Century*, p. 93.
[62] Edward Said, 'The Clash of Ignorance', *The Nation*, 22 October 2001.

when there was no longer an ideology with a repressive army to maintain it. Ballard's is a warning about the potential fragility of democracy, liberalism, and even reason in the face of their many opponents and under conditions of intense global stress. Ballard is best known for his book *Empire of the Sun*, an account of his time as a boy spent in a Japanese camp in the Second World War. The memory of such experiences confront our 'culture of contentment' with unwelcome visions of future catastrophes. Ballard recalled: 'After Pearl Harbor, my secure and settled life was just swept away. It taught me that conventional reality can't be trusted, that human beings are not always governed by reason. They can be very cruel.'[63]

Remember us?

Blood is stronger than syllogisms.   Anonymous fascist[64]

The final 'morbid symptom' to be added to the mix, and one that finds echoes from the interwar years, is the idea that our times are primed for 'fascism'. Fascism is a controversial term, and some readers who may have accepted the argument of this chapter so far will bridle at its use. I will attempt to justify it shortly, but for the moment want only to make the less contentious claim that when a concatenation of threats overloads policymakers and societies, the wisest decision-making cannot be guaranteed.[65] My argument below is that a revival of fascist values might be the chief political consequence of the synergy between the epochal, structural, and decisional pulses that mark out the early twenty-first century.

Fascism needs a trigger, and the earlier discussion pointed to many possibilities in the mix we face of converging political, social, economic, technological, and environmental challenges. There have been abundant warnings of the coming dangers to human society, globally and locally, but the richest and most powerful in the world for the most part do not want radical change, in any case do not know how to do it, and many of them do not think they must. It is therefore safe to

---

[63] Donald Morrison, 'His Dark Material', *Time*, 30 October 2006.
[64] Quoted by John Hoffman and Paul Graham, *Introduction to Political Ideologies* (Harlow: Pearson Longman, 2006), p. 140.
[65] Among the key texts on group dynamics negatively impacting on decision-making, Irving L. Janis, *Victims of Groupthink. A Psychological Study of Foreign Policy Decisions and Fiascos* (Boston: Houghton Mifflin, 1972), is a classic.

assume that things will have to get much worse before they can get better, and in this gap there is space for political extremism to grow. Out of the morbid symptoms outlined above and in chapter 1, it is possible to identify a range of specific issues that might combine in concrete situations to create the opportunity for extremism. In particular, it includes the possible consequences of environmental chaos (such as mass migration and famine) and social stress (arising out of the pressures attendant on living in multicultural societies, and social rootlessness following the erosion of established social and religious beliefs) – all exacerbated by the growth of the global population. When environmental chaos and social stress simultaneously converge, the press of events might well inflame a host population into feelings of rage and fear, fed by growing anxieties about the influx of disease and alien ways of behaving, and of being swamped by racially and ethnically different people. Stunned by a sense of helplessness, and increasingly insecure about the future, a traditional population that feels itself so embattled may come to believe that their leaders are not standing up for them, and quickly lose faith in the legitimacy of established institutions. If, in such circumstances, economic collapse were to follow, there would be a powerful trigger for an upsurge of fascist values, as growing numbers came to fear the loss of their jobs and security, and as their sense increased that ordinary politics was not working for them.

In conditions such as those just sketched, it is not difficult to understand the appeal to fearful and confused people of a charismatic leader. In crises, the promise of answers, safety, and hope is beguiling. Such conditions therefore offer great opportunities for rabble-rousers to exploit; they supply people who are ready, willing, and able to be manipulated. And let us not forget that a gear-shift to extremism can be very quick. The rapid rise of Hitler in 1932–3, following the apparent collapse of his movement a decade earlier, is a salutary reminder of how quickly situations can change, and how what one year seemed unlikely can in the next become probable.[66] In Europe in the 1930s the complacency of good and moderate citizens unwittingly assisted in the rise of extremism, and may do so again – and not only in Europe. And the extremists

[66] The story has been told many times, and in great depth, but not more persuasively than by Laurence Rees, *The Nazis. A Warning from History* (London: BBC Books, 1997), pp. 13–85. Alois Pfaller, a young man who turned his back on the Storm Troopers because of their anti-Semitism, joined the Communist Party instead because he was looking for a radical solution to Germany's problems; he later recalled: 'The danger is always here, when crises are happening, that people come who say they have the wisdom and the answer, and they can bring salvation to everybody' (pp. 33 and 47).

know it. In 2005 Nick Griffin, the leader of an extreme right-wing party in the UK (the British National Party) told US white supremacists and European far-right party activists in New Orleans to prepare for 'an age of scarcity that will be a once-in-200 years opportunity'. He went on: 'When the revolution comes . . . it is going to come in Europe, and it's going to come very suddenly.' 'Bang', he said; 'One month they don't support you, the next month – if you've done your home-work and the circumstances are right – they are prepared to support you.'[67]

Fascism, I believe, is primed for revival if the predictable insecurities of the coming decades are not effectively dealt with. This does not imply the rise of clones of Mussolini and Hitler; indeed, the force of their sym-bolic legacy is one of the difficulties facing the serious use of the term 'fascist' today. Because of the total discrediting of fascism after 1945, and the fact that many people use the label in loose and accusatory fashion in daily language, as a multi-purpose 'boo word' to be directed against the authoritarian-inclined, from fellow office-workers to football referees, political groups no longer rush to self-identify as fascists. Before 1945, however, fascism had a more precise meaning, though its actual mani-festation in different countries took on local forms. If we take 'fascism' to be generally synonymous with 'right-wing authoritarian extremism', it is possible to identify a range of features that capture its essence as a set of political ideas.[68]

Fascism can be defined under the following generic headings: *leader-ship* (the appeal and authority of a charismatic leader is a central fea-ture of all fascist movements); *the nation and the state* (the power of the state is paramount, matched only by the mystique of the nation; individuals live for the state, not vice versa; fascists are drawn to a communitarian – invariably mythical – past; there is an almost reli-gious longing for the unity of the people – the latter being defined by 'blood and belonging'; extreme nationalism expresses itself in a xeno-phobic hatred of foreigners); *political modalities* (fascist movements see

[67] Ian Cobain, 'Inside the BNP: Papers Reveal Election Strategy', and 'Racism, Recruitment and how the BNP Believes it is just "One Crisis Away from Power"', *The Guardian*, 22 December 2006.
[68] What follows is based on a range of old and new interpretations of fascism, notably Carl J. Friedrich and Zbigniew Brzezinski, *Totalitarian Dictatorship and Autocracy* (New York: Praeger, 1966; 2nd edn), Paul Wilkinson, *The New Fascists* (London: Pan Books, 1983), Roger Griffin, *The Nature of Fascism* (London: Routledge, 1995), Robert O. Paxton, *The Anatomy of Fascism* (London: Penguin, 2005), Hoffman and Graham, *Political Ideologies*, pp. 134–62 (with weblinks). Paxton has a thorough bibliographical essay, pp. 221–49.

themselves as revolutionary, seeking to rejuvenate their societies; they are flexible ideologically and in practice; in outlook they are conservative in important ways – recognising the authority of the church and propertied classes – but they are modernist towards technology and have totalitarian impulses in relation to imposing their values on all society; in organisation fascists are anti-democratic and authoritarian, and in behaviour intolerant and action-oriented); *social values* (a fascistic society is characterised by the power of patriarchy; racist attitudes and policies; the valuing of loyalty, order, sacrifice; the honouring of physical prowess over intellectual pursuits; a fascination with flags, uniforms, and the trappings of identity; and a view of the redemptive power of violence); *foreign policy* (fascist external behaviour is aggressive, imperialist, militaristic, and expansionist – if possible; power and force are the message, if not the means); *economic policy* (while fascist movements classically had some 'socialist' credentials, being anti-capitalist in rhetoric, in practice they were deeply implicated in big business, merging state, industrial enterprises, and the professional classes); and *general worldview* (fascism is attracted to romantic micro-narratives while opposing metanarratives promoting universalist ideas such as 'common humanity' or liberal ideas such as individualism; reason is rejected in favour of thinking with the blood).

Is world politics primed for the triumph of such attitudes? Is this picture a bad dream, or just bad analysis? Some readers will want to think it both bad dream and bad analysis, because they want to enjoy the state of denial discussed in chapter 1. Other critics will focus on the use of the term 'fascist', and will argue that it is difficult to map contemporary movements onto classical fascism. I agree, up to a point, with this latter view, but do not think it undermines my general case that the predictable insecurities of coming decades will provoke attitudes associated with fascism, and increase the chances that it will take hold in some societies. There can be little doubt that fascism is immanent in contemporary politics, and we cannot be sure where the story will end.

The astute observer of European history, Neal Ascherson, argued that the rightist 'populist' swing in Europe at the start of the twenty-first century did not threaten a 'neo-Nazi upsurge', but he was drawn to ask whether it was a 'formless embryo' of a new fascism. These parties 'may not be fascists or neo-fascists. But could they be pre-fascists?', he asked. Ascherson did not see them as having the unity of traditional fascist parties, but he reminded his readers that fascism had deep roots in

European conservatism.[69] A darker reading of the trends in Europe was given in 2002 by Martin Jacques. He drew attention to the racist parties of the extreme right which had achieved power in Austria, Denmark, and Italy; were 'resurgent' in France, the Netherlands, Switzerland, Norway, and Belgium; and had achieved some political salience in parts of Britain. After describing symptoms such as the declining status of politics and politicians (echoes of Weimar!) and declining voter turnout, Jacques concluded there was not so much a 'frontal assault from fascism', but rather 'a corrosion from within'. He saw a racist element in the rise of populism, with migration as a focus. In the background was the War on Terror, which, despite protestations to the contrary, he believed had a West versus Muslim complexion and a 'distinctly racist colouration'. Europe was on a slippery slide, while the 'unashamedly' imperial policy of the United States 'spoke of a new sense of Caucasian superiority' which was bound to fuel a reaction. He feared extreme right-wing views 'could become increasingly respectable within'.[70] History never repeats itself exactly, but one cannot therefore reject the possibility that it might repeat itself substantially. Stephen Smith put it this way: 'History mutates. It comes back in different forms . . . the nationalism now rife in Europe is a more timid mutant of fascism. It comes with a suit and a smile. But beware. Its parentage is the same, and who knows what a monster it might grow into.'[71]

While Europe attracts most attention – it was the home of classical fascism after all – it is not the only source of potential mutants.[72] Two possibilities in particular deserve comment. First, what are the chances of fascism developing in the United States, whose normal politics in any case begins to the right of Europe? Here, Richard Rorty is one philosopher (and Edward Luttwak is one political scientist) who has expressed the fear that fascism may have a future in the United States. Writing in the late 1990s – and the argument would be stronger today – Rorty warned of the 'immiseration' of American workers, the spread of a world economy run by a ruling class with no sense of community with its workers in any country, and a US divided into hereditary social castes. Faced with such a deteriorating situation, he envisaged a populist reaction against

---

[69] Neal Ascherson, 'The Warning Shot', *The Observer*, 12 May 2002.
[70] Martin Jacques, 'The New Barbarism', *The Guardian*, 9 May 2002.
[71] Stephen Smith, 'Copenhagen Flirts with Fascism', *The Guardian*, 5 June 2002; on the general phenomenon, see Angus Roxburgh, *Preachers of Hate: The Rise of the Far Right* (London: Gibson Square Books, 2002).
[72] Paxton, *Anatomy of Fascism*, pp. 172–205.

governmental failure to protect jobs and wages, the possible rise of a strongman, the consequent loss of civil rights by racial and gay groups, and the revival of contempt for women. Once these things have occurred – a 'disaster for the country and the world' – Rorty said people would start to wonder why they did not resist. He drew parallels between this possible future for the United States and the end of Weimar and the rise of Hitler.[73]

The second area outside Europe where the idea of fascism has been discussed focuses on the Islamic world. In particular, as the War on Terror expanded and extended, and after the war against Iraq in 2003 led to an upsurge of violence and terrorism, the charge of fascism became directed at extremist tendencies within the global Islamic community. The charge attracted worldwide attention because it was made (or rather repeated) by the President of the United States.[74] According to Stefan Durand, the use of the term 'Islamic fascism' by President Bush and various US officials after August 2006 was strategic; by implying that a wide range of movements in the Islamic world were the successors of the totalitarian movements of the twentieth century, he said it was hoped to legitimise 'warlike policies based on crude analogies and the politics of fear'. Durand rejected the idea that the groups Bush referred to conformed with a strict definition of fascism; he did agree, however, that Muslim fundamentalist movements exhibited 'certain traditional features of fascism'; he identified these as 'a paramilitary dimension, a feeling of humiliation and a cult of the charismatic leader'. He thought that other defining characteristics were lacking ('expansionist nationalism, corporatism, bureaucracy and the cult of the body'), and especially a 'partisan state'. Classical European fascism, he said, was embedded in an 'integral nationalism'; the Islamic movements being singled out, however, had important transnational dimensions. Durand also emphasised that extremism in the Islamic world appealed only to a 'narrow fringe'; they were not like the mass movements of interwar European fascism/Nazism.

[73] Richard Rorty, 'The American Road to Freedom', *New Statesman*, 8 May 1998.
[74] Stefan Durand, 'The Lie that is "Islamofascism"', *Le Monde diplomatique*, November 2006. Durand claimed that the term dates from 1990 and was coined by the British historian Malise Ruthven. For an interpretation that is more supportive of the President's position, see Francis Fukuyama, 'History and September 11', in Ken Booth and Tim Dunne (eds.), *Worlds in Collision. Terror and the Future of Global Order* (Houndmills: Palgrave Macmillan, 2002), esp. pp. 32–4; for a more complex interpretation of the 'terror war' see Paul Berman, *Terror and Liberalism* (New York: Norton, 2004).

While 'Islamofascism' as a generic term is incongruous, according to Durand, he was quick to point out that fascist influence was 'not entirely absent in the Islamic context'. He pointed to authoritarian regimes 'that could be termed fascistic', and then twisted the knife by adding that 'most of them are faithful allies of the US in its war against terrorism'. As a result of their role in supporting US foreign policy, he claimed that the Uzbek, Kazakh, and Turkmen dictators had been spared US criticism, 'although the semi-fascistic nature of their regimes is obvious'. Other regimes had been let off lightly, notably the Saudi monarchy and Gaddafi's dictatorship. The term 'fascist' could have been applied to Iraq under Saddam, Durand noted, a regime that had been supported by the West until Saddam's invasion of Kuwait. Before that, Saddam's regime had been 'ultra-nationalistic, based on an unbounded cult of the leader, made no distinction between the public and private realms, and was expansionist'. The United States had also supported the Afghan guerrillas in the 1980s. The latter, then lauded as the 'moral equivalents' of the US founding fathers, twenty years later were attacked as Islamofascists. And once upon a time US, British, and Israeli intelligence services had backed the Muslim Brotherhood. The diplomatic, ideological, and geopolitical picture is therefore much more complex than it was made to appear through the White House's use of the label 'Islamofascism'. For Durand, those movements in the Muslim world that resorted to terrorism, and which displayed fascist tendencies, should be 'criticised, and loudly', but he thought that the use of the 'Islamofascism' label served only to 'stigmatise whole populations and establish a direct connection between religion and extremist parties'. He did not believe the US neocons were interested in nuance, only in the 'emotive charge' of a term whose purpose was to prepare public opinion to accept 'preventive' war: a 'fascist threat', after all, requires a massive response.[75] While the term 'Islamofascist' is therefore one to be used with considerable caution, there is one dimension of radical Islamism which does raise the worst nightmares of interwar fascism, and that is the anti-Semitism exhibited by some individuals and groups.

Whatever gains have been made by universal reason since the time of the Enlightenment, human society today is once again confronted

[75] Lest it be thought that Islamophobia is a US phenomenon, see Stryker McGuire, 'The Fear Factor', *Time*, 6 May 2002, which emphasised what he saw as the growing politics of hate in Europe, and in which he compared ethnic relations in Europe unfavourably with the United States, with its long tradition of ethnic assimilation. A scholarly comparison is given by Christopher Hill, 'Bringing War Home: Foreign Policy-Making in a Multicultural Society', *International Relations*, vol. 21(3), 2007, pp. 259–83.

by reaction and unreason. This is particularly troubling on the very foothills of the twenty-first century, given the predictably dangerous times that lie ahead. This chapter has warned that massive shocks cannot be ruled out, threatening the very bases of existing world order, and when multiple insecurities converge there is always the possibility that people will turn in hope and despair to charismatic leaders of extremist parties, movements, and groups. World security interests would not be furthered if the concatenation of morbid symptoms characterising the Great Reckoning gave the opportunity for the coming to power of far-right authoritarian governments, whose remedy for global problems would be the absolute privileging of their own people, the rejection of reason, and the triumph of the extremist attitudes listed earlier. The warning signs are clear. Of course, the third decade of the twenty-first century will not be an exact copy of the third decade of the twentieth century, but unless the warnings are heeded, it may be closer than most of us now suppose.

10 A long hot century

We Have Worlds Inside Us
Edvard Munch, title of painting[1]

Whatever decisions and patterns of behaviour emerge from the New Twenty Years' Crisis, human society, globally, will face a *long hot century*.[2] It is the extent of the turmoil that remains to be seen. As presaged by the advent of superpower nuclear plenty in the 1950s,[3] and then the densification of globalisation over the next four decades, global interaction and issues have increasingly turned human society into a community of fate. The concatenation of threats resulting from the interplay between the epochal, structural, and decisional crises takes this to a new level. In these circumstances, the rational goal for human society is to create a world security community of communities, where war is practically unthinkable, and in which global issues can be pursued as collectively as possible. We have worlds inside us, but also one outside to lose.

Some critics of this book's empirical thesis might say that were the dangers that have been highlighted (especially in chapters 1 and 9) to

[1] Painting of 1894: see Iris Müller-Westermann, *Munch by Himself* (London: Royal Academy of Arts, 2005), pp. 132, 134. Munch took the idea from a poem by Paul Erik Tøjner, 'The Tree of Knowledge': 'Nothing is small, nothing is large / We carry worlds inside us' (from the exhibition, 'Edvard Munch by Himself', Royal Academy of Arts, October–December 2005).
[2] I chose this as the title of a lecture I gave at the Australian Defence Force Academy in 2002. I thought I had coined the phrase, but a search led to the discovery that it had been used by a Governor of Michigan, George Romney, who in 1968 said, against the background of the Vietnam War and riots in US cities, that the United States faced not only long hot summers at home, but 'the equally forbidding prospect of a long, hot century' throughout the world; quoted by William Safire, *Safire's Political Dictionary* (New York: Random House, 1978), p. 387.
[3] A major and insufficiently recognised theoretical contribution to understanding the impact of nuclear weapons on the traditional role of the territorial state was John H. Herz, *International Politics in the Atomic Age* (New York: Columbia University Press, 1959).

427

come about, they would swamp any suggestions that have been made (and will be offered in the present chapter) about dealing with them effectively. Such a criticism may well prove to be correct, but if it is, so much the worse for all of us. Other critics will complain that the extrapolation of morbid symptoms throughout the book has been too pessimistic, while the references to cosmopolitan possibilities have been too optimistic. These critics, too, may well turn out to be correct about what actually happens in future, but they will have misunderstood my claim. For reasons explained in chapter 3, optimism and pessimism have played no part in my analysis, yet it seems to be impossible to avoid being accused of one or other; the 'frequent vulgarity' of their use is also something that has attracted John Berger's ire.[4] The theoretical commitment that has informed the analysis has been realistic not pessimistic, and the political orientation has been infused by hope not optimism. Uniting this realism of the intellect and hope of the will, to rephrase Gramsci, it is my belief, apparent throughout the book, that the Great Reckoning is not a time for sliding away from the spirit of the Enlightenment. Kant's famous injunction, 'Dare to be wise', was never more urgently needed.[5] Reflexive reason, animated by emancipatory politics and a cosmopolitan sensibility, building on the immanent potentials of world community, offers rational hope for advancing equality, humanising globalisation, and promoting human rights. These are at the heart of the Enlightenment's unfinished project of inventing a very uncommon humanity.

Means /ends

> As soon as these politicians are elected, that's the end of it . . . They have nothing to do with the people who put them in power.
> Joshiah Masiamphoka, subsistence farmer, Malawi[6]

The cosmopolitan project will remain incomplete unless the relationship in political life between means and ends is reconceived. The danger here, introduced in earlier chapters, is that of instrumental reason: the powerful tradition of dualism in political theory and practice. The

[4] John Berger, 'An Angel's Rage', *Le Monde diplomatique*, November 2006.
[5] Stephen Eric Bronner, *Reclaiming the Enlightenment. Towards a Politics of Radical Engagement* (New York: Columbia University Press, 2004), pp. 151–67; Jonathan I. Israel, *Enlightenment Contested. Philosophy, Modernity, and the Emancipation of Man 1670–1752* (Oxford: Oxford University Press, 2006), pp. 863–71.
[6] Quoted by Joshua Hammer, 'Freedom Is Not Enough', *Time*, 14 November 2005.

challenge therefore facing emancipatory realism is that of embedding non-dualistic politics (that is, attempting to change the world by means that are equivalent to the changes we wish to bring about). Emancipation, after all, is a process not an end-point; it is being through becoming. Conceiving means/ends in a non-dualistic manner is not 'rocket science', as they say, but politically speaking it might as well be for those politicians and their supporters who seem unable to understand how the pursuit of an aim by its opposite prejudices the very objective being sought. I could illustrate this from numerous historical and contemporary cases, but I have chosen to discuss four means/ends themes in relation to US policy during the presidency of G. W. Bush. This is not because the Bush White House is an easy target, but because it is typical in everything but its prominence; furthermore, the failings of the world's most causal government are always the most consequential. The section will close with a discussion of the same four themes in relation to Africa, because of the rather different significance that continent has in world affairs.

1. Political violence

If we hope to reduce the scope of political violence, and ultimately eliminate war, one test of every aspect of a state's external policy must be whether it contributes to the delegitimation of violence as an instrument of politics. Ridding the world of war has been a long-held objective in international relations, collectively agreed in the International Treaty for the Renunciation of War as an Instrument of National Policy (the 'Kellogg–Briand pact') of 1928, in which eventually sixty-eight states renounced war as an instrument of national policy and committed themselves to settling disputes peacefully. Practically speaking, it proved, as was said at the time, to be a momentary 'international kiss' and a 'pious declaration against sin'. Despite such put-downs, violations of it were integral to the Nuremberg and Tokyo war crimes trials.[7]

Standard-setting is important in all social learning. Role models are also significant. The Bouldingesque aphorism 'If it exists it is possible' is relevant here. Western and central Europe, the historical cockpit of nationalist realism, and of political violence extending from terrorism to world wars, appears to have transcended international conflict by evolving into a Deutschian security community. Is such a development

---

[7] The contemporary quotations are in Zara Steiner, *The Lights that Failed. European International History 1919–1933* (Oxford: Oxford University Press, 2005), p. 573.

the result of unique historical factors? Must Europe remain the only multistate mature security community? If war can be transcended there, why not more generally?[8] There are of course many obstacles in the path of the construction of a world security community, where war becomes 'unthinkable' globally. These include: the realist fatalist assumption that there is no alternative; the Clausewitzian calculation of governments that specific objectives can only be secured by force; continued masculinist honouring of the military ethos; the religious legitimation of political violence in the militant traditions of Just War and Jihad; and the Waltzian view that wars occur when states cannot get their way on vital interests because there is nothing to stop them. Despite such obstacles, the empirical reality of security communities ensures that the end of war remains a rational hope.

The argument here is not a pacifist one; it accepts that political violence is sometimes excusable (in self-defence, for example). What must be overcome is the readiness with which certain governments use violence as a continuation of politics, as well as their employment of discursive practices that legitimise violence. The result of such behaviour is to replicate the idea that states are the ultimate war machines, which thereby constitutes and reconstitutes the states system as a war system. Eradicating the *potential* for violence in world politics is, of course, impossible. 'What is not a weapon in the wrong hands?' – the question disarmers grappled with in the run-up to the World Disarmament Conference in 1932 – is as pertinent as ever. The goal in relation to world security is, instead, to seek to marginalise and delegitimise the use of force as an instrument of politics. If states consistently pursued such a goal, the Clausewitzian rationale for using force would atrophy over time, with states maintaining armed forces solely as badges of independence and for vital disaster services, but no longer as instruments of external relations. Weapons cannot be 'disinvented', as is often said, and so the security dilemmas they provoke cannot ultimately be escaped; but security dilemmas can be transcended by creating the political conditions of trust (notably in the form of security communities).[9] In this

---

[8] Ken Booth and Nicholas J. Wheeler, *The Security Dilemma: Fear, Cooperation, and Trust* (Houndmills: Palgrave, 2008), ch. 7; the most thorough analysis of this important concept is Adler and Barnett, *Security Communities* (Cambridge: Cambridge University Press, 1998); see also Alex J. Bellamy, *Security Communities and their Neighbours. Regional Fortresses or Global Integrators?* (Houndmills: Palgrave Macmillan, 2004). The original conception was Karl Deutsch *et al.*, *Political Community and the North Atlantic Area: International Organization in the Light of Historical Experience* (Princeton, N.J.: Princeton University Press, 1957).

[9] Booth and Wheeler, *Security Dilemma*, chs. 7 and 10.

sense war, though not the potential for violence, can be consigned to the dustbin of history.

By the test of contributing to the delegitimising of political violence, the Bush presidency has been a massive failure. The US-led decision to initiate a preventive war against Saddam Hussein's Iraq in 2003 not only failed this test, but it also proved to be a calamity in its own terms. For critics of the war (no supporters of Saddam Hussein, unlike the major intervening governments in the past) it was more important that the regime in Baghdad be changed *rightfully* than be deposed by *whatever means possible*, and that policy toward Iraq was conceived in relation to the wider Middle East. This meant, above all, that the United States and its Coalition partners give priority to conflict resolution in the Israel–Palestine imbroglio.[10] The war against Iraq failed every test in relation to the goal of delegitimising violence. It was unnecessary (there were alternatives), unrequired (Iraqi military power was eroding and contained), unneeded (the UN inspection system had largely been a success), illegal (it was not sanctioned by the UNSC), and unwise (because of its predictable negative consequences). The proponents of the invasion later pressed critics – following the deposing of Saddam – to agree with them that the world was a 'better place' without the Iraqi dictator. 'Of course' was the invariable answer, but the main point is that the world would be a 'better place' without many things (poverty, North Korea's nuclear weapons, nasty dictators, etc.) but that is not necessarily a justification for initiating preventive wars to bring about the regime changes that might have the desired result. Saddam was deposed but did the world or region become 'a better place' with the UN flouted, with duplicity and self-delusion displayed on a grand scale by the US and UK governments, with European governments deeply split, with new levels of mistrust in institutions and intelligence, with (uncounted) thousands of civilian dead in Iraq, with a growing death-toll in US, UK, and other military personnel, with the creation of the conditions for civil war in Iraq, with the turning of that country into a hothouse for local terrorists and a 'recruiting sergeant' for international terrorism, with the distraction of attention and resources from other more pressing dangers, and with unknown twists yet to come? Political violence cannot be delegitimised through preventive war.

[10] An impressive historical overview of the conflict, focusing on Israel, is Avi Shlaim, *The Iron Wall. Israel and the Arab World* (London: Penguin, 2001); a fascinating insight into the problems of negotiation is Ahron Bregman, *Elusive Peace. How the Holy Land Defeated America* (London: Penguin, 2005).

2. Democracy

Leaders who claim to be the standard-bearers of democracy must behave democratically. This test has particular urgency when such leaders attempt to persuade their citizens to go to war. There were mass protests across the world against the coming war in Iraq in the months leading to the invasion in 2003;[11] these were enough to encourage some governments, potential allies, to reject the Anglo-American regime-change project. The extent and depth of the protests were not of themselves proof that the protesters' arguments were valid, but such a degree of opposition in democracies *demands* that leaders listen more, and consult, and consider whether it is wise to go into a war when their citizenry is seriously divided. It is interesting to speculate, in this respect, whether Bush and Blair would have risked sending conscript armies on such a contested mission. One suspects not.

Protest against the coming war was ignored and belittled by the White House, as the leading policymaking group replayed the ideological certitudes, ethnocentric miscalculations, and arrogance of power that had led to the long and lost war in Vietnam.[12] Not surprisingly, if democratic impulses could be ignored at home, this was even more the case internationally. As a result of Tony Blair's influence, Washington did seek to use the UN to endorse the war, but the global body was cynically employed as an instrumental means, not as a consultative end, and it was ultimately ignored.[13] If a powerful state believes in democracy, even if it is the world's only superpower, it must sometimes accept that it might not get its way. As it was, the White House attempted through arm-twisting to bring the UNSC to endorse the war, and so make it legal. It failed, but even if this move had worked, and formal legality had been achieved, going to war would still have been unwise.

Behaving democratically on the international stage, has never been the way of US governments; like other states in the past, they have confused great power with great wisdom. US administrations since the Second World War, while urging the virtues of democracy, and ostensibly actively promoting it, have often found it impossible to bring about

---

[11] A colourful celebration of those protests, showing that peace is not only better than war, but more fun, is Barbara Sauerman (ed.) *2/15 – The Day the World Said No to War* (New York: Hello, 2003).

[12] A set of interesting essays interrogating Vietnam–Iraq analogies is John Dumbrell and David Ryan (eds.), *Vietnam in Iraq. Tactics, Lessons, Legacies and Ghosts* (London: Routledge, 2007).

[13] Philippe Sands, *Lawless World. America and the Making and Breaking of Global Rules* (London: Allen Lane, 2005), pp. 174–203.

a marriage of means and ends.[14] Whether in the UN (where the appointment of the blusteringly anti-UN figure of John Bolton as ambassador in 2005 could not be seen as other than a deliberate provocation to the global body), or in reacting against the inconvenient verdicts of foreign electorates (such as the victories of Allende in Chile in 1973 or Hamas in Palestine in 2006), the Washington way with democracy beyond its own waterfront has been to endorse it only as long as it is seen as serving the interests of the United States. This has been the case whether Washington has been in a 'multilateral' or 'unilateral' mood. When it comes to international relations, hubristic exceptionalism always overcomes the US commitment to democracy.

If the United States is serious about promoting democracy it should support it. Consistency is the test of whether US administrations *respect* democracy, or only sometimes act *in accordance* with it. The latter is the general verdict on US attitudes in the world outside the United States. Its record in promoting rogue states in the name of geopolitical interests, for example, greatly undermines its democratic credentials in the eyes of people in the street everywhere. Under the influence of maxims such as 'the enemy of my enemy is my friend', US governments have supplied local strongmen with weapons and diplomatic backing; meanwhile, they appear to have been relaxed about the way various tyrants have treated their own people. Agencies of the US government, when it has been thought necessary, have actually conspired in helping such strongmen maintain domestic 'order'. Saddam Hussein began as a regional strongman, and he lasted so long because his Western backers placed their own geopolitical interests before the well-being of the Iraqi people.[15] In the recent past, it was 'anti-communism' that provided the rationalisation for building up local tyrants in pursuit of geopolitical ambitions; today it is 'anti-terrorism'. Whatever the rationalisation, realism replicates rogues; and it is in the character of local strongmen to bite the hand that feeds them, if one day they come to believe it to be advantageous.

---

[14] This is relentlessly argued by Noam Chomsky, *Failed States. The Abuse of Power and the Assault on Democracy* (New York: Metropolitan Books, 2006).
[15] During the Iran–Iraq War (1980–8) the US allowed Kuwaiti tankers to sail under the US flag, which meant that 'the United States effectively joined, on the Iraqi side, in the so-called "tanker war"'. The Iranian President, Akbar Hashemi Rafsanjani, came to believe that the United States was even more comprehensively on the Iraqi side following the US attack on Iranian oil facilities, the elimination of the Iranian navy, and the shooting down of an Iranian civilian airliner. See Andrew Cockburn and Patrick Cockburn, *Saddam Hussein. An American Obsession* (London: Verso, 2002), p. 81.

3. Law

Those who wish to live in a law-governed world should judge their own external policy according to the test of lawfulness. This will mean that powerful governments will sometimes be prevented from doing what they would otherwise choose to do, or what their power might enable them to do. If the rule of law is to prevail between as well as within states, the mightiest must consent, at times, to behave lawfully, even when that means they do not get what they want.

The vast majority of international law specialists have argued that the 2003 Iraq War was contrary to international law.[16] This was also the authoritative view of Kofi Annan, UN Secretary-General at the time. Furthermore, the evidence is overwhelming that the legal case for the war 'was assembled after the decision to invade had been taken'.[17] The Bush–Blair leadership groups argued, before, during, and after the war, that their actions were both legal and legitimate. To most of world opinion, to the contrary, their actions revealed an ultimate contempt of international law, unless it was *their* international law. By adopting the position they did, they subsequently lost the right to criticise other states if and when the latter chose to place their own interests and interpretations beyond the constraints of international law. And their hypocrisy has not won friends or influence. Governments do not like to be lectured to by those who show only rhetorical respect for the law themselves. In the US case, what is particularly galling to many is the way it has allowed its friends (notably Israel) to disregard UN resolutions, while it has stressed compliance on those states it deems guilty until proved innocent. The imprudence of double standards, which goes hand-in-hand with treating other states with a lack of respect, is a lesson the White House may learn once again in the years to come as it seeks the assistance of Syria and Iran to help it extricate its diminishing 'coalition of the willing' from Iraq.[18] Superpowers should consider how others feel, as well as think.

After the ultimate disregard of the UN by the White House in relation the legality of the invasion of Iraq, the international lawyer Thomas Schoenbaum argued that the 'supreme irony' was the way in which the

---

[16] Thomas J. Schoenbaum, *International Relations. The Path Not Taken* (Cambridge: Cambridge University Press, 2006), pp. 8–9.
[17] *Ibid.*, p. 8; see also Sands, *Lawless World*, pp. 175, 193, 200–1.
[18] As recommended, for example, by the bipartisan Iraq Study Group: James A. Baker and Lee H. Hamilton, *The Iraq Study Group Report* (New York: Vintage Books, 2006), pp. 50–4.

administration then 'found the United Nations indispensable to realizing the goal of peace and democracy in Iraq'.[19] Because picking up the pieces smashed by the ill-named international community is in part what the UN exists for, Kofi Annan had no choice but to swallow his pride and try and do the honourable thing, whatever he thought of the original invasion.

Respect for the law should also have been central to the US response to the 9/11 attacks. Though the decision to declare a War on Terror was 'understandable' according to Louise Richardson, it was also 'very unwise'. It created the impossible goals (as stated by Bush) of attempting to 'rid the world of the evildoers' and to 'root out terrorism in the world', instead of the 'more modest and more achievable goal' (as identified by Richardson) of 'containing the threat from terrorism'.[20] One of the unacknowledged (because subconscious) drivers of the administration's reaction to international terrorism was the masculinist mindset of the neocons dominating policymaking; this played a part both in way the sense of outrage was expressed by the administration, and particularly in the way the 'bad guys' had to be dealt with. Grandiose goals were claimed (including bringing democracy to the Middle East) and just cause endlessly repeated; but the conduct of the war and its aftermath showed yet again that it is possible to justify anything if the cause is considered to be right (from enormously high Iraqi civilian casualties to the 'rendition' of prisoners).[21]

By choosing to react to the terror attacks according to a 'warfighting rather than crimefighting' logic, US policy risked reproducing the attitudes of the terrorists.[22] When people persuade themselves that war is the only way of pursuing right (like Jihadists on the other side) self-righteousness sets in, and law gets sidelined. The distinction between combatants and non-combatants (not at all a concern to al-Qaeda) is not decisive when one chooses to conduct operations in which 'collateral damage' is unavoidable: 'military necessity' rules As a result,

[19] Schoenbaum, *The Path Not Taken*, p. 121.
[20] Louise Richardson, *What Terrorists Want. Understanding the Terrorist Threat* (London: John Murray, 2006), p. 242; also, Patricia J. Williams, 'Peace, Poetry and Pentagonese', in Ken Booth and Tim Dunne (eds.), *Worlds in Collision. Terror and the Future of Global Order* (Houndmills: Palgrave Macmillan, 2002), pp. 336–47.
[21] See Donald A. Wells, 'How Much Can the "Just War" Justify?', *Journal of Philosophy*, vol. 66(4), 1969, pp. 819–29.
[22] Ken Booth and Tim Dunne, 'Worlds in Collision', in Booth and Dunne, *Worlds in Collision*, p. 13; see also, in the same volume, Williams, 'Peace, Poetry and Pentagonese'.

the civilian death-toll in the War on Terror inexorably rises. Meanwhile, unacceptable practices in the treatment of prisoners have been revealed. The Pentagon felt justified in conducting 'renditions', which involve turning over prisoners to compliant associate states where torture can be inflicted, more or less out of sight and mind.[23] The immediate US reaction to 9/11 was understandably (and rightly) clothed in the sense of injustice that comes from suffering mass murder out of a clear blue sky; but as the 'war' has proceeded, the reaction has increasingly failed the conventional test of 'proportionality'. The death and injury of hundreds of thousands of civilians have already been caused in excess of the numbers who suffered in the United States on 9/11; and many more will suffer in this 'long war', which is threatened to continue for perhaps a generation (even if a new president quietly drops the rhetoric associated with the Bush War on Terror). Law, not war, should have been the heart of the response to 9/11 from the beginning. In the struggle against terrorism, aspects of which undoubtedly must involve violence, long-term political success requires that prisoners are treated according to the highest standards, that the temptation is resisted of allowing 'anti-terrorism' to overrule humanity, and that the lives of innocents in all lands are measured equally. Terrorists begin to lose when whatever support they have ebbs away; they therefore begin to win when their victims increase that support by dismantling their own commitment to justice, democracy, liberty, law, and virtue.

A law-governed world is one of the conditions for world security. Among those whose interests it serves are states and groups of states that are presently dominant but may not be in future.[24] Self-interest and collective interest point here in the same direction, adding yet further weight to the criticism of those who do not show international law appropriate respect. The challenge has been summed up by Philip Allott as follows: 'International Society . . . chose to be an unsocial society creating itself separately from the development of its subordinate societies, ignoring the ideal of democracy, depriving itself of the possibility of using social power, especially legal relations to bring about the survival and prospering of the whole human race'. To meet the challenge, international society must reconceive itself, 'using social power, and especially legal relations'.[25]

---

[23] Schoenbaum, *The Path Not Taken*, p. 255.
[24] Note the principles advanced by Schoenbaum, *ibid.*, pp. 302–5.
[25] Philip Allott, *Eunomia: A New Order for a New World* (Oxford: Oxford University Press, 1990), p. 417.

4. Human rights

Those who wish for a world of human rights must not connive in human wrongs. In the conduct of its War on Terror, the Bush administration after 2001 committed 'systemic violations of domestic and international human rights laws'.[26] Torture was practised, though it is a technique a civilised society must reject whatever the provocation or temptation.[27] When considering any potential instrument of policy, whether torture or nuclear strategy, it is critical to consider not only what one's actions *might* do to the enemy, but also what they *are* doing to oneself. In this regard, the photographs of Pfc. Lynndie England and the hooded, naked Iraqi prisoners in Abu Ghraib made public in 2004 spoke volumes. In Guantánamo, during the same period, a 'variety of forms of physical and mental torture' were employed against 'enemy combatants'.[28] The list of 'techniques' carried out against prisoners at that infamous location should be appended as a footnote to all the fine-sounding rhetoric of the Bush administration about human rights. In his Second Inaugural Address in 2005, President Bush said that justice starts with legitimacy, which, as summarised by Schoenbaum, 'means democracy, liberty, and an end to tyranny everywhere in the world'.[29] Tyranny will not be eradicated from human society through the methods of tyrants.

To ask for consistency on human rights is not a counsel of perfection. It is good politics. As it is, the exposure of abuses by agents of the US government has eroded the legitimacy of its case in its struggle against terrorism, because the appalling behaviour that has been exposed appears to justify the accusations of its enemies, and so swell their support, if only passively in many cases. Nor is my argument a counsel of perfection in the sense that I am asking for behaviour that is impossible. There are indeed models for consistent and noble behaviour in US history; they existed, and so are possible. One notable case was an episode in the country's very foundation, when more Americans died in British prison ships than in all the battles of the Revolutionary War.[30] The British tried to excuse their callous treatment of prisoners on the grounds that they were 'merely rebels'. General George Washington, though outraged at the treatment his men were receiving, did not respond in kind

---

[26] Schoenbaum, *The Path Not Taken*, p. 255.
[27] Rosemary Foot, 'Torture: The Struggle over a Peremptory Norm in a Counter-Terrorist Era', *International Relations*, vol. 20(2), 2006, pp. 131–51; see also Michael Ignatieff, 'If Torture Works . . .', *Prospect*, no. 121, November 2006, pp. 34–7.
[28] Schoenbaum, *The Path Not Taken*, p. 255.   [29] *Ibid.*, p. 302.
[30] The account below, including the quotations, is taken from Richardson, *What Terrorists Want*, pp. 250–1.

when his own forces captured 221 British prisoners at Princeton. He instructed the officer in charge: 'Treat them with humanity, and let them have no reason to complain of our copying the brutal example of the British army in their treatment of our unfortunate brethren.' Washington taught his men that the principles (ends) for which they were fighting had to be respected in every action (means). For George Washington, ends/means were related non-dualistically. For that Washington there would have been no Abu Ghraib or Bagram or Guantánamo or rendition. The disrespect shown to prisoners in the Bush presidency has, in Richardson's words, 'seriously undermined America's legitimacy in the eyes of its allies and the non-committed and confirmed its perfidy in the eyes of everyone else'. The failure of the White House to repudiate aspects of its policies conclusively, 'by holding the most senior people responsible', has increased the number of recruits to terrorism, discouraged others from 'lifting a finger' to help the United States, and made more difficult the task of 'driving a wedge between the terrorists and the communities that produce them'. George Washington/George W. Bush? The Princeton 221/Abu Ghraib? The Revolutionary War/the War on Terror? Ends and means? QED.

5. Out of/into Africa

The discussion so far has focused on the divorce between means and ends in the context of political and legal issues. I want to finish by returning to the economic dimension, and illustrate it from sub-Saharan Africa, a huge area that is witness to daily brutality, distress, and abject leadership. It also contains amazing promise, great variety, and infinite humanity. Indeed, the invention of humanity began in Africa, and if globalisation is to be humanised, Africa is its biggest and most poignant test.

The leaders of the world try to talk movingly about Africa.[31] In practice, however, words and actions, and ends and means are frequently strangers.[32] In 2005 Anthony Payne drew attention to the fact that Africa after 2002 had been accorded 'a measure of priority in the politics of

---

[31] Tony Blair was central to promoting Africa's importance in the UK's foreign policy priorities (and also played a leading role internationally); see Paul D. Williams, *British Foreign Policy under New Labour, 1997–2005* (Houndmills: Palgrave Macmillan, 2005), 'Healing a Scar on the World's Conscience?', pp. 75–96.

[32] See Royal African Society, *A Message to World Leaders: What About the Damage We Do to Africa?* (London: Royal African Society, June 2005): 'It's not just about thinking up good things we should do to Africa – it's about the bad things we should stop doing'. See also the 'Royal African Society's Response to the Consultation Paper' (issued by the

aid', but then correctly predicted that the upcoming Gleneagles summit would 'provide one further moment when Africa will, albeit briefly,
be the focus of global concern'. In face of a history of such fleeting
moments, it is tempting to give way to 'Afro-pessimism'. The problems
of Africa have not only been the result of the ambitions of outsiders; post-
independence Africa has often had to suffer leaders who were either too
weak or too strong for their country's own good. The result has been that
this continent, characterised by so much variety in so many things, has
shared a depressingly similar history. This was put with heart-rending
simplicity by the Biafran novelist Chimamanda Ngozi Adichie: 'how
similar the histories of many African countries are, how passionately
people believed in ideas that would disappoint them, in people that
would betray them, in futures that would elude them'.[33]

As long as business-as-usual continues, the 'African renaissance', long
talked about, will remain a dream. Globalisation has not produced the
positive results promised. Starting in the 1980s 'structural adjustment
programmes' were tried and failed.[34] Then, neoliberal fundamentalism was reformed into 'adjustment with a human face', but to little
better effect.[35] In 2000–1 the New Partnership for Africa's Development (NEPAD) became the next 'big idea', seeking to halve poverty
in Africa by 2015, based on a mixture of conventional neoliberal ideas
mixed with a political strategy aimed at getting the euphemistically
labelled 'development partners' to 'put their money in the same place as
their mouths'.[36] In the event, corruption, unaccountable governments,
human rights abuses, and war have continued across the continent. In
2002 President Bush signed a pledge to 'make concrete efforts' to provide 0.7 per cent of US national income to assist the world's poor. Three
years later, the figure was 0.15 per cent.[37] Ends and means? Follow the
money, not the words.

Another test of the world turning its back on Africa has been the
lack of attention generally given to 'Africa's Great War' in the Democratic Republic of Congo, marked by so many intervening neighbours,

Commission for Africa), November 2004: www.royalafricansociety.org (I thank Paul
Williams for drawing these documents to my attention).
[33] Chimamanda Ngozi Adichie, 'Truth and Lies', *The Guardian*, 16 September 2006.
[34] See the verdict of a senior UNICEF officer: Ian Hopwood, 'Africa: Crisis and Challenge',
in Ken Booth (ed.), *Statecraft and Security: The Cold War and Beyond* (Cambridge: Cambridge
University Press, 1998), pp. 247–69.
[35] Anthony Payne, *The Global Politics of Unequal Development* (Houndmills: Palgrave
Macmillan, 2005), p. 38.
[36] *Ibid.*, pp. 163–4.
[37] Jeffrey D. Sachs, 'The Class System of Catastrophe', *Time*, 10 January 2005.

so much plunder, so much violence, so many victims, and so much external neglect.[38] It is unimaginable that such a Great War could have taken place on any other continent and be met by so much indifference on the part of the so-called international community. Together, the failings of governments within the continent, and the interests pursued by those outside, have conspired to commit swathes of Africa to a brutal fate. Occasionally, some outsiders (other than the NGOs struggling to give development a human face) have sat up and listened when global celebrities have tried to sing Africa into their lives, or when they have used it as an exotic background. Yet, as the acute reader of world affairs Mary Riddell has lamented: 'God help Africa if death, poverty and starvation are only visible to the West if refracted through a prism of borrowed celebrity'.[39]

For Africa, as with some other parts of the developing world, 'freedom' from colonisation did not prove to be enough.[40] Africa echoes with the warnings of 1960s 'dependency theorists' who (focusing originally on South America) pointed to the way in which the former colonial world had achieved the trappings of political independence, but actually continued to exist in a condition of economic dependence. Africa is not all gloom, however. At times, some states were declared to be relatively successful – Tanzania, Botswana, and Uganda, for example – but rarely have achievements been sustained. Malawi maintained free elections and a free press for a decade, then food crises got worse, testing Sen's influential claim about the relationship between dictatorship and famine. The assumption that grew in the 1980s that more democracy might be the solution to famine did not necessarily work twenty years later, when the chronic problem of food shortages became exacerbated by climate change, with parts of Africa drying out. Climate change, of course, is largely the result of the excesses of the rich world: once again, Africa is not primarily the cause of its problems, but the victim of the behaviour of others. And Jeffrey D. Sachs, director of the Earth Institute, Columbia University, reminds us that even catastrophes have unequal impact: 'What the rich world suffers as hardships the poor world often suffers as mass death.'[41]

The absence of strong and embedded institutions in many African states contributes to the continent's immiseration. Whereas countries

---

[38] Guy Arnold, *Africa. A Modern History* (London: Atlantic Books, 2006), pp. 885–902.
[39] Mary Riddell, 'The Politics of Bob', *The Observer*, 1 January 2006.
[40] Joshua Hammer, 'Freedom Is Not Enough', *Time*, 14 November 2005.
[41] Sachs, 'Class System of Catastrophe'.

in the West have some hope of coping with bad leaders, because the institutions are bigger than personalities, this is not the case in much of Africa.[42] Prime Minister Zenawi of Ethiopia, for example, a member of Tony Blair's 2004 Commission for Africa – another big idea for Africa, modelled on the Brandt Commission – pledged to run free and fair elections, but according to one report, when the time came he 'did not appear to have thought about the possibility of losing'. He did indeed hold elections, but they were marred by rigging and intimidation, and he charged opposition leaders with treason.[43] Western leaders are certainly not alone in divorcing words and deeds, and ends and means.

The immiseration of much of Africa is obviously not a condition that can be eradicated overnight, but actions equivalent to a more humane globalisation can begin at once, bringing ends/means into harmony. The challenge for individuals, societies, and governments outside the continent is not simply to pile charity into Africa, though it has a role, but to help where possible develop an ethics of autonomy along the lines suggested by Richard Sennett (chapter 1), involving non-demeaning assistance and the strengthening of *their* autonomy rather than the exercising of *our* sense of pity. The aim is for institutions to help individuals achieve self-affirming respect.[44] It is then up to Africa.[45] The challenge is enormous, requiring revolutions in the mind, as well as material redistribution. If it is not done, if means and ends stay divorced, then Africa will remain, as Chimamanda Ngozi Adichie has said, a story of 'what happens when the shiny things we once believed in begin to rust before our eyes'.[46]

Beliefs and norms

I will humanise even the enemy. I don't see Jews as devils or angels but as human beings.   Mahmoud Darwish[47]

The marriage of means/ends is a key to trust-building, which in turn is a key to successful emancipatory politics; yet trust is a concept that has been almost entirely ignored in international relations theorising.[48] But

[42] Simon Robinson, 'Africa's Game of Follow the Leader', *Time*, 5 December 2005.
[43] Katy Guest, 'March of Democracy Falters in Africa', *The Independent*, 15 November 2005.
[44] Richard Sennett, *Respect. The Formation of Character in a World of Inequality* (London: Allen Lane, 2003), pp. 101–26, 247–63.
[45] A fair account of the obstacle of corruption is given by Arnold, *Africa*, pp. 921–39.
[46] Adichie, 'Truth and Lies'.
[47] Maya Jaggi, 'Mahmoud Darwish. Poet of the Arab World', *The Guardian*, 8 June 2002.
[48] Booth and Wheeler, *Security Dilemma*, ch. 9.

there is a more fundamental problem still facing world security in the opinion of many observers, and that is what they see as the insurmountable obstacle to global human harmony resulting from the incommensurability between different belief systems. This is an influential view, but it is flawed.

An important distinction exists between what Philip Windsor called 'values' and 'norms' (but for clarity I will substitute *beliefs* or *meta-theories* for what he called 'values').[49] Norms refer to the appropriate standards of social and other forms of behaviour, whereas beliefs/meta-theories are the underlying ideas (spiritual faith, for example) that support one's attitudes and behaviour. For several decades at the end of the twentieth century, Windsor expressed worries about the future of human society globally, not least because of what he saw as the failure of 'sustained dialogue' between cultures. He advocated intercultural sensitivity while avoiding cultural relativism. In practice this meant endorsing the universal human rights project but insisting that brute Westernisation be avoided, by leaving the promotion of human rights for citizens of each culture 'to achieve their rights in their own way'. He thought the beliefs/norms distinction offered some promise (though never a guarantee) of allowing groups to co-exist more effectively. The distinction was aimed at enabling groups to respect the diversity of beliefs people may have (their underlying world-views) while criticising particular acts (norms of behaviour) which might be considered oppressive or cruel. In other words, one does not have to attack somebody's fundamental beliefs in order to question a norm of behaviour they may support; there are always other grounds for the latter. By keeping beliefs and norms separate, Windsor hoped it would be possible, for example, to criticise the cruelty of female genital mutilation from a universal and humane perspective, while carefully trying to disentangle this norm from the traditional religious and cultural beliefs with which it had become identified historically.[50]

[49] Mats Berdal (ed.), *Studies in International Relations. Essays by Philip Windsor* (Brighton: Sussex Academic Press, 2002), 'Cultural Dialogue in Human Rights' and pp. 7–12; see also Ken Booth, 'Windsor's Wisdom', *International Relations*, vol. 17(4), 2003, pp. 504–8.
[50] An authoritative discussion of female genital mutilation as a violation of the integrity of women, and a rejection of women as 'equal and responsible members of society' has been given by the first woman surgeon in Sudan: Nahid Toubia, 'Female Genital Mutilation', in Julie Peters and Andrea Wolper (eds.), *Women's Rights, Human Rights. International Feminist Perspectives* (New York: Routledge, 1995), pp. 224–37. For an illustration of an attempt at negotiating between the universal and the traditionalist/patriarchal in a particular setting, see Bhikhu Parekh, *Rethinking Multiculturalism. Cultural Diversity and Political Theory* (Basingstoke: Palgrave, 2000), pp. 264, 275–6, 278–9, 280–1, 293–4.

Emancipatory politics involve negotiation in the space between beliefs and norms; a key to success in practice lies in showing solidarity with sites of resistance against cruel practices that exist within particular identity groups. Windsor discussed the complex relationships between foundational beliefs and behavioural norms, as they have existed through time, and believed the political challenge in cross-cultural debates was to try and ensure that a criticism of a norm was not meant or interpreted as an attack on people's beliefs, the meta-theory of their traditional attitudes. Such an approach, he hoped, would improve the prospects for cultural groups to respect each other. Were this achieved, it would be a major step towards what he called 'a common history rooted in cultural diversity . . . one defined by its engagement in becoming, not by its origin in being'.

Windsor's wisdom calls on people(s) to reason together about family values, humanitarian intervention, pornography, crime, freedom of speech, and so on at the level of human dignity, social harmony, or international stability – without calling each other's underlying beliefs into fundamental question. One can oppose (or not) such norms as capital punishment or humanitarian intervention regardless of whether one believes life on earth is the result of a wondrous accident or the creation of a loving god. This Habermasian appeal to reason and dialogue does not eradicate differences, because some people will claim that certain norms are utterly implicated in faith-based markers of identity; but attempting to reason together, separating beliefs and norms, offers a radically different prospect for political community than the fatalism implied in Huntington's highly influential and deeply problematic thesis of the 'clash of civilisations'.[51] Nonetheless, as was argued in chapter 7, such a clash is an outcome the US neocon project under Bush and the radical Islamist project under Osama bin Laden seem calculated to bring about; there does not have to be a clash between the multifaceted worlds of the 'West' and 'Islam' at the level of norms, but the confusion of stereotypes, misunderstanding, and ignorance at the level of beliefs risks bringing it on.[52]

The idea that different belief systems can reason together is not a utopian project, for there is considerable agreement about norms of

[51] Samuel P. Huntington, 'The Clash of Civilisations', *Foreign Affairs*, vol. 72(3), 1993, pp. 22–49; see also his *The Clash of Civilisations and the Remaking of World Order* (London: Simon and Schuster, 1996).
[52] Edward W. Said, 'The Clash of Ignorance', *The Nation*, 22 October 2001.

behaviour across cultures,[53] just as there are radical differences of opinion about norms within so-called faith or cultural (or 'civilisational') communities. Against Huntingtonian fatalism, it is important to give more recognition to those who argue, with a surer touch of the empirical evidence, about the space that exists for constructive dialogue. Hayward Alker, for example, has written about the potential for 'culturally sensitive concepts of emancipation' being linked in a 'posthegemonic way to similarly culturally sensitive, concretely researchable conceptions of existential security'.[54] Bhikhu Parekh, seeking to negotiate universal concepts of rights into the reality of cultural diversity, has offered sensible principles about the ways ahead in the real world of cultural interpenetration.[55] And Amartya Sen, in an article deftly called 'The Reach of Reason', has described how the Mughal Emperor Akbar at the end of the sixteenth century, and in the context of the multi-denominational character of India at the time (Hindus, Muslims, Christians, Jains, Sikhs, Parsees, Jews, etc.) thought that 'the pursuit of reason' rather than 'reliance on tradition' was the way ahead. He established the foundations of state secularism and religious neutrality, insisting that 'no man should be interfered with on account of religion, and anyone is to be allowed to go over to a religion that pleases him'. Sen commented that such sense 'has become all the more important for the world today'.[56]

Nobody should – or could – pretend that negotiating in the space between beliefs and norms will be easy. Sometimes it may be, but occasionally great courage, as well as great sensitivity will be necessary in order to advance peace and sense in the face of inflamed beliefs, especially if what is being threatened is patriarchy-sustaining. People have

---

[53] See Fred Dallmayr, *Dialogue Among Civilisations* (Basingstoke: Palgrave Macmillan, 2002); Martha C. Nussbaum, *Cultivating Humanity. A Classical Defense of Reform in Liberal Education* (Cambridge, Mass.: Harvard University Press, 1997), is a distinguished contribution to the debate about what is needed in Western universities in order to study other cultures, gender, and race from a viewpoint that is both critical and universal.

[54] Hayward Alker, 'Emancipation in the Critical Security Studies Project', in Ken Booth (ed.), *Critical Security Studies and World Politics* (Boulder, Colo.: Lynne Rienner, 2005), pp. 189–213.

[55] Bhikhu Parekh, 'Non-Ethnocentric Universalism', in Tim Dunne and Nicholas J. Wheeler (eds.), *Human Rights in Global Politics* (Cambridge: Cambridge University Press, 1999), pp. 128–59 (in which he argued that it is possible and necessary to develop non-ethnocentric universal values), and 'Cosmopolitanism and Global Citizenship', *Review of International Studies*, vol. 29(1), 2003, pp. 3–17 (in which he rejected the notion of global citizenship but argued for a globally oriented national citizenship).

[56] Amartya Sen, *The Argumentative Indian. Writings on Indian Culture, History and Identity* (London: Penguin, 2006), p. 274.

traditionally shown a great capacity to rationalise their determination to keep hold of power as a commitment to protect principles (and for the most part have done it unconsciously). And when men get mad, some individuals and groups are willing to kill to resist reason. Gandhi, infamously, was assassinated while attempting to redefine philosophical Hinduism in 'activist, social, and worldly terms'.[57]

Much opinion across the world seems to have limited confidence in the prospects for intercultural dialogue, as they witness violent street demonstrations and terrorism 'in the name of God'. Pictures on the TV news appear to legitimise academic reifications of incommensurability between clashing 'civilisations'. The crude and archaic thinking which sustains such fatalism has been evident in the revival of the discourse of 'evil' in public life – not least in international relations.[58] In introducing a set of essays on the concept, Catherine Lu identified the main questions on evil as follows: 'Can the rhetoric of evil capture the moral reality and complexity of human relations, especially in world politics? Does it help or hinder rational and moral decision-making? If we find the concept or rhetoric of evil problematic, can we actually do without it?'[59] The best answers so far have been given by Phillip Cole. In his applied-philosophy approach to the concept, he argued that there are moral, political, and psychological reasons for rejecting the very idea of 'evil'; it is, he said, 'a highly dangerous and inhumane discourse and we are better off without it'.[60] The reason for this was the role he claimed it had played as a 'mythological concept' in the 'grand narratives of world history'. In a key sentence, he wrote: 'To describe someone as evil is not to say anything about *them*, but is to place them as victims of a narrative force, as characters in a story in which they play a specific and prescribed role.'[61] The myth of evil has flourished in the era of the Global War on Terror (a label that lives on as the term is tactically dropped). Fighting 'the Monster of Terrorism' has involved engaging with a 'demonic enemy' ('defined by hate' and with a 'mad intent' according to Bush) which draws on a conception of 'monstrous evil'.[62]

---

[57] Bhikhu Parekh, *Gandhi's Political Philosophy. A Critical Examination* (London: Palgrave Macmillan, 1991), pp. 104–9.

[58] A revival matched by new scholarly interest: see 'Evil and International Affairs', Special Issue of *International Relations*, vol. 18(4), 2004, edited by Catherine Lu; and Phillip Cole, *The Myth of Evil* (Edinburgh: Edinburgh University Press, 2006).

[59] Lu, 'Editor's Introduction', in 'Evil and International Affairs', p. 403.

[60] Cole, *Myth of Evil*, p. 21.   [61] *Ibid.*, p. 23.   [62] *Ibid.*, pp. 230–1.

Cole's attack on the myth of evil had three prongs.[63] First, he advocated that the concept of evil *should* be eliminated from political and other discourse, though he recognised that whether it *can* be eliminated is another matter. The latter in part is the result of our being confronted by situations so extreme that we struggle for a word to describe them, and for many people 'evil' alone seems to fill the gap. Nonetheless, he dismissed its explanatory and descriptive purchase. The idea of 'evil agency', he argued, is neither a valid explanation nor an indispensable description of the world, and it does not help understanding; yet it is common in politics, the law, the media, and popular culture. Cole had no doubts that the myth of evil 'obstructs our understanding'. He described it as 'a black-hole concept which gives the illusion of explanation, when what it actually represents is a failure to understand'. The myth also brings along a baggage of feelings: 'the complete condemnation of those described as evil, their rejection as not *really* human, and the impossibility of communication and negotiation, reform and redemption'.

Second, Cole maintained that the idea of evil is neither a philosophical nor a religious idea, but a mythological concept, with a 'specific role in certain narratives'. This means that when someone is described as evil they are not being *explained* but rather *situated* 'in a story in which they play a specific and prescribed role'. Their 'history, motives and psychology' are ascribed by the narrative plot. Consequently, we 'do away with any need to understand' them; we do not look beyond 'the narrative of evil'. If we did so 'we may discover people very different to those we have imagined'. We look at an 'evil terrorist', but rarely at the human behind the label.

Finally, Cole stressed the importance of fear, a factor whose explicit causality has been traditionally ignored in academic international relations.[64] He pointed to the role fear has played in global terrorism, the run-up to the Iraq War, and issues such as mass migration, commenting that 'we are most scared of what we cannot see, and this terror undermines the foundations of our world'. The first challenge facing us, therefore, is 'to actually study these phenomena in their detail'[65] and 'look beyond imaginary monsters fabricated by our political leaders

---

[63] What follows is a summary of Cole, *ibid.*, pp. 235–41.
[64] Booth and Wheeler, *Security Dilemma*, ch. 3.
[65] Booth, 'Windsor's Wisdom'. In line with this, I welcome the development of the subfield of critical terrorism studies, marked by the inauguration of a new journal, *Critical Studies on Terrorism*.

and the media'. The second and 'far more difficult challenge' is to 'stop being scared'. Cole contended that it is in the gap between 'what we know and what we fear' that the *'real* black hole' exists, 'where the discourse of evil, the *myth* of evil, takes root and grows'.

Peddlers of the myth of evil will object strenuously to these arguments. 'What about the Holocaust?' is a predictable reaction. 'How can such an episode be explained or described as other than *evil*?' they will ask. Again, such questions are based on false reasoning. Yehuda Bauer, a distinguished historian of the Holocaust, has insisted – arguing on similar lines to Cole – that we should look for an explanation that does not take refuge in an inexplicable agent – something 'beyond human comprehension'.[66] Bauer has written:

> If some God or some Devil, or a combination of both, or some mysterious force that is neither, were drawn in to explain the inexplicable, or if the event were simply left unexplained, then again we would be removing the Holocaust to an ahistoric sphere where it could not be reached by rational thinking, not even by rational explanations of the irrational.[67]

Bauer himself did not totally rule out use of the word 'evil' (as I would) because he needed a radical word to describe something he considered unprecedented in history. This was the motive of the Nazi murderers, which he identified as the messianic aim of delivering humankind from the global threat of the 'Jewish problem'.[68] The motive might be unprecedented, but he did not consider the behaviour of the Nazis was 'inhuman': indeed, he thought it 'only too human'.[69]

People are drawn to the concept of evil when they are confronted by acts that are so cruel that they cannot find persuasive explanations for them; in such situations 'evil' is the cause that fills the understanding gap. This is not satisfactory. The existence of the gap should be a challenge to try harder, not give way to mythology. Bauer has put it well: 'That something is in principle explicable does not mean that it has been explained or that it can readily be explained.'[70] Bauer's position here is directly contrary to that of those conservative historians and other critics who disapproved of the film *Downfall*, on the last days of Hitler, on the grounds that it turned the German leader into a human being.[71] Bauer, in

---

[66] Yehuda Bauer, *Rethinking the Holocaust* (New Haven, Conn.: Yale University Press, 2001), p. 15 (see pp. 14–38 for the general argument).
[67] *Ibid.*, p. 16.　[68] *Ibid.*, p. 22.　[69] *Ibid.*, p. 21.　[70] *Ibid.*, p. 22.
[71] *Downfall*, written and produced by Bernd Eichinger (2004).

contrast, insists that we must recognise the human in the horror. What is 'totally unsatisfactory', he emphasised, is 'an attempt to escape historical responsibility by arguing that this tragedy [the Holocaust] is something mysterious that cannot be explained. If this were true, then the criminals would become tragic victims of forces beyond human control. To say that the Holocaust is inexplicable, in the last resort, is to justify it.'[72]

This is a profound verdict, and should cause the peddlers of the myth of evil to stop in their tracks. In similar vein, Phillip Cole has written that we should not forget that one of the major factors bringing about the Holocaust in the first place was 'a particular discourse of evil, the anti-Semitism that drove Hitler and his followers, the belief that the Jews represented a cosmic evil enemy bent on the destruction of the German people and civilisation in general'.[73] The message of these arguments is that the myth of evil should be abolished from political and social discourse, even when confronted by what appears to be radically inhuman and inexplicable, such as the Holocaust. Part of the challenge of inventing humanity must be to resist the ideational structures that sustain and are sustained by regressive mythologies, such as that of 'evil'.

The mythology of evil flourishes when the political sphere is seeded by religiosity, as it has increasingly been, globally, since the final decades of the last century.[74] Governments throughout the world, in some cases for the first time in many years, have been under pressure from organised religions to allow them a greater say in the public sphere, occasionally with the risk of violence in the background; yet the complex interplays between security and religion remain a curiously under-researched area.[75] When politics becomes less an arena for reason and rational dialogue, with a view to progressive social change, and more a marketplace or battlefield in which religions project their proselytising narratives, the greater is the likelihood of Manichean thinking (with narratives of good and evil) and actual violence. Stephen Eric Bronner has warned that 'the larger mainstream religious organizations have – historically – opposed virtually every scientific advance, every new philosophical movement, and every progressive political development'.[76] And Sam Harris has given us at least one good reason why it is important to heed

---

[72] Bauer, *Rethinking the Holocaust*, p. 38.   [73] Cole, *Myth of Evil*, p. 236.

[74] On the distinction between religion and religiosity and its importance to Enlightenment and Marxist thinking, see Bronner, *Reclaiming*, pp. 165–7.

[75] One not entirely satisfactory attempt to bring the concepts together is Robert A. Seiple and Dennis R. Hoorer (eds.), *Religion and Security. The New Nexus in International Relations* (Lanham, Md.: Rowman and Littlefield, 2004).

[76] Bronner, *Reclaiming*, p. 165.

Windsor's advice about keeping basic beliefs from the public sphere, pointedly reminding us that religion is the only area of knowledge in which it is honoured to hold beliefs based on ancient books preaching 'the truth of propositions for which no evidence is even *conceivable*'.[77] In other words, there is no arguing against faith.

The religious revival in world politics towards the end of the twentieth century was one of the major factors behind the rise of identity politics. Difference based on faith is now everywhere. Some governments have felt susceptible to pressure from religious interests (though by exercising ostensible 'tolerance' towards minorities claiming to be offended or unfairly treated they risk inciting the growth of intolerance, by appeasing the minority and alienating the majority); and some societies have become less confident in their secularism (backing away from a confrontation, for example, about the spread of 'faith schools' – who is to decide which is a respectable 'faith' suitable to teach the young, and which an unacceptable cult? And if 'faith' schools are acceptable for children, based on parental fiat, why not 'ideological' schools, based on the deeply held political beliefs of parents?). In the West, Christianism has ridden on the back of Islamism, resulting in growing challenges to freedom of speech, and the gradual entrenching of discourses of difference. When these supplant discourses of equality, watch out: in some conditions celebrating being different can lead politics to become the site of the deepest pit of identity narcissism: racism.

Michael Ignatieff, for one, has criticised the regressive character of much of what passes as identity politics in relation to race, and has suggested that what is needed for intercommunal life is a dose of 'liberal realism'.[78] Borrowing from Isaiah Berlin, he has argued that it is necessary to distinguish between 'positive' and 'negative' tolerance, the latter being the minimum required in a liberal sense (meaning the protection of minorities, equal treatment of people in public agencies, level playing fields in employment, and so on); this is enough, he speculated, for tolerable community life. He claimed that it is not necessary for groups to love each other, reach out to each other, or even to particularly value each other's culture in order to live together. We have to behave appropriately in our social lives, while living in 'unfathomably different universes'

[77] Sam Harris, *The End of Faith. Religion, Terror, and the Future of Reason* (London: The Free Press, 2004), pp. 11–79 (quotation at p. 23).
[78] Michael Ignatieff, 'Less Race, Please', *Prospect*, April 1999; Ignatieff has written an admiring biography of his remarkable friend, *Isaiah Berlin. A Life* (London: Chatto and Windus, 1998).

449

according to Ignatieff. (Note the argument earlier that unfathomability at the metaphysical level need not be a bar to shared norms at the social and political level, though part of the difficulty of living together in harmony is that too many people believe it is a bar.) What is 'desperately needed', Ignatieff argued in 1999, is a 'happy indifference' towards collective identities, and a 'genuine conviction' that the differences that matter are between individuals. He thought such a situation 'still a generation away'. There is no doubt things have got worse since he wrote those words.

One illustration of the growing clash of incivility was the issue of the Danish newspaper cartoons at the beginning of 2006. Here, the gulf was exposed between the ideals of Western liberalism and the temper of militant Islam. It was an episode in which both cartoonists and protesters used the opportunity to cause offence to those they did not 'particularly value' (to use Ignatieff's phrase). However, this is not to assign moral equivalence between the two sides of the confrontation. Whereas the publishers of the cartoons might be accused of a lapse of taste, or of unnecessarily stirring up trouble, the protesters who committed violence on the grounds of being offended by some cartoons threatened the freedom of speech which was argued in chapter 6 to be the very foundation of all freedoms. The deep irony in the confrontation was utterly lost on even the peaceful protesters against the cartoons, who sought to use their own right of freedom of speech to try to close down the freedom of speech of others. Having sometimes to be offended is part of enjoying the right of freedom of speech. This is not to say, of course, that deliberate offensiveness is to be recommended, but freedom of speech is too vital a foundation for civilised life to be sacrificed because some section of society claims to be offended. Who is not offended by something or other, every day? Being offended is not a cause for closing down freedom of speech, and less still for threatening a violent response. To publish material likely to cause offence is clearly provocative, and may be ill-advised; but to kill because one feels offended is murder. There is a profound threat to society once anything is placed out of the bounds of free speech. When a society starts placing certain things out of bounds, where might it end? This is especially worrying when governments everywhere appear keen to tighten up their control of their societies. In some countries there is the crime of blasphemy, but this is a crime against reason, for who or what should define (apart from tradition) what constitutes a 'religion' deserving of exclusion from the ambit of freedom of speech? The very idea of blasphemy is a step backwards to premodern times. And if the right to offend is taken away with respect to religious beliefs, why not other basic beliefs? In the totalitarian states of the twentieth century, giving offence to the authorised version of the party's ideology was the secular equivalent of blasphemy, and was punished with great brutality.[79]

It is striking that the people who want to close down freedom of speech, and who tend to insist dogmatically that we live in 'unfathomably different universes', never appear to be the most culturally aware and knowledgeable members of their societies. In contrast to cultural solitarists, those who are writers, artists, and musicians tend to be bridge-builders across the chasms that history and power have constructed. The Nobel Prize winner Nadine Gordimer has praised many African writers in this regard. Recalling how Léopold Senghor, at the first Congress of African Writers and Artists in 1956, had used the phrase 'We are all cultural half-castes', Gordimer countered by declaring that his life had 'refuted' this view because the phrase 'half-caste' implies a diminution of one identity by another. This was not the case, she wrote, insisting that the life of Senghor 'proves that it is possible to keep your own culture and identity intact while fully appropriating another; while participating widely, pinning yourself to thought-systems, ideas, mores, of other peoples . . . He is perhaps the most successful example of cultural wholeness achieved in Africa in a single individual.'[80] Such wholeness can only be accessed across those bridges solitarists refuse to build.

Solitarism prefers islands without bridges, on which traditional networks of power can flourish unchallenged. Ideas are part of that power, and the incommensurability thesis one of its props. Harris has argued in this vein that even 'moderate' religion is not benign, for it nurtures the potential for extremism on the part of religious identity groups by perpetuating the importance of believing ancient revelations.[81] In this

[79] One of many stories is Irina Ratushinskaya, *Grey is the Colour of Hope*, trans. Alonya Kojevnikov (London: Hodder and Stoughton, 1988).
[80] Nadine Gordimer, *Living in Hope and History. Notes from our Century* (London: Bloomsbury, 1999), pp. 53–4. The collection in Ian Jack, *The View from Africa* (London: Granta 92, Winter 2005) is a testimony to Gordimer's view, and the idea of 'cultural wholeness' is reflected in the view of a musicologist about the 'series of marriages' between African and European musical languages (pp. 14–15). In India, Rabindranath Tagore is a shining example of the same cultural wholeness: see 'Tagore and his India', in Sen, *Argumentative Indian*, pp. 89–120.
[81] Harris, *End of Faith*, pp. 22–3.

way, moderation is a reservoir that keeps alive the possibility of violence 'in God's name', one of the all-too-familiar but terrible headlines of our time. It became commonplace at the start of the new millennium to read reports such as the following (from 2006): 'Religious tension arises in holy city after bomb blasts'. Following the deaths of over twenty people at a Hindu temple at Varanasi, a witness was quoted as saying: 'Always the Muslims kill Hindus. It's time we Hindus did the same to them'.[82] Against the bloody background of centuries of religious violence and discrimination, and with reports of faith-inspired or faith-legitimised violence in the foreground, Harris made the plea, 'We must finally recognize the price we are paying to maintain the iconography of our ignorance'.[83] This was another way of endorsing Windsor's wisdom, where this section of the book began; it is another injunction to take fundamental belief out of the public realm. The aim should therefore be to reserve religion for private spaces, fostering politics as the sphere for the use of reason in the service of constructing norms whereby people in a multistate, multinational, multicultural, multireligious, multiclass, and multigendered world can live with mutual hospitality.

The message of the discussion so far is that we must resist allowing our global lives to be fatalistically determined by the identity narratives that contingent power and history have constructed around us. Inspiration can be taken from Mahmoud Darwish, whose 1988 book, *A Bed for the Stranger*, was his first entirely devoted to love. Reflecting on it, he described even the ability to love as a 'form of resistance'. He went on: 'we Palestinians are supposed to be dedicated to one subject – liberating Palestine. This is a prison. We're human, we love, we fear death, we enjoy the first flowers of spring. So to express this is resistance against having our subject dictated to us. If I write love poems, I resist the conditions that don't allow me to write love poems.'[84] Equally, students of international politics should write with *amor mundi* ('love of the world', as Arendt called it)[85] about security, emancipation, and community, and thereby resist the conditions that discourage them from so doing. In this way, every essay can be turned into an act of resistance to history, and a message of hope.

[82] Justin Huggler, 'Religious Tension Rises in Holy City after Bomb Blasts', *The Independent*, 9 March 2006.
[83] Harris, *End of Faith*, p. 23.   [84] Jaggi, 'Mahmoud Darwish'.
[85] Elisabeth Young-Bruehl, *Hannah Arendt. For Love of the World* (New Haven, Conn.: Yale University Press, 1982), p. xvii.

'The odd thing about assassins'

Everything exists for some end, a horse, a vine. Why dost thou wonder?
Even the sun will say, I am for some purpose, and the rest of the gods
will say the same. For what purpose then art thou?

Marcus Aurelius, *Meditations*[86]

When she came across a mug inscribed with Margaret Mead's well-known line – 'Never doubt that a small group of thoughtful, committed citizens can change the world; indeed, it's the only thing that ever does' – the philosopher Mary Midgely got to thinking about 'what changes the world?'[87] It struck her that the words on the mug were badly at odds with current thinking, which associates change with something on a much larger scale – 'perhaps economic causes, perhaps a shift in the gene pool, perhaps cultural evolution'. Structural conditions, without doubt, are enormously powerful and the pulling and pushing of the states system, capitalism, and patriarchy have been emphasised throughout this book. Every person on earth, to a greater or lesser extent, is a product of the structures they inhabit, and that inhabit them; but that is not the same as being a prisoner, though the room for choice in some circumstances may be small. Even though that may be the case, a sociological understanding of the power of structures should not be allowed to lead to a fatalist approach to life, or human society will simply replicate regressive global mindsets in infinitely more dangerous material conditions.

Fatalist logic has been powerful in both classical and contemporary thinking about world politics.[88] It sustains theories such as 'offensive realism', whose leading proponent's main work is appropriately entitled *The Tragedy of Great Power Politics*.[89] Albeit with different conceptualisations of the idea of 'tragedy', many authors since the beginning of the discipline have wanted to interpret world politics through the prism of tragedy.[90] A critical theory challenge to the idea of tragedy focuses on the *functions* the idea has performed. What emerges is that the *idea of*

---

[86] Marcus Aurelius, *Mediations*, trans. George Long (London: The Softback Preview, 1996), p. 64.

[87] Mary Midgley, *The Myths We Live By* (London: Routledge, 2004), pp. 75–81.

[88] Booth and Wheeler, *Security Dilemma*, part I.

[89] John J. Mearsheimer, *The Tragedy of Great Power Politics* (New York: W. W. Norton, 2001); this is the definitive account of offensive realism, and though the approach has relatively few true (academic) believers, it is a logic of world politics with which all must engage.

[90] For a notable contemporary example, see Richard Ned Lebow, *The Tragic Vision of Politics. Ethics, Interests and Orders* (Cambridge: Cambridge University Press, 2003). A prolonged discussion of tragedy and international relations has been conducted in the journal *International Relations* by a group of scholars who come to a different conclusion

tragedy has been tragically constitutive of thought, imprisoning human self-constitution as negatively as such ideas as 'human nature' and 'the human condition'. The idea of tragedy threatens to complicate decision-making by inflicting guilt about doing 'wrong', regardless of the path one chooses, instead of keeping focus on the prospect of doing right, and it serves to reconcile people to sub-optimal outcomes. As a result of mindsets constructed in part by the idea of tragedy, it is not surprising that behaviour constituting tragedy is not uncommon. The idea of tragedy arose in drama, and that is where it should remain.

The end of the Cold War, followed by the indecisive 1990s (a decade so lacking in direction that nobody could find a more inspired label for it than 'post-Cold War') was rounded off by the denouement of the ill-inspired War on Terror. The story of Clinton, Bush, Cheney, and Rumsfeld could not have been better conceived by Shakespeare: *The Tragedy of the Princes of Washington*. 'To be or not to be' is the perennial existential dilemma, but deciding to repeat the old flaws does not have to be the perennial answer. Hamlet had to make the choices he did because Shakespeare programmed him that way, but worldly princes could give different answers. Some have chosen not to repeat the old flaws. In their different ways, by behaving as they did and placing themselves in the shoes of their ostensible enemies, Sadat, Gorbachev, and Mandela showed that fatal flaws are the result of allowing oneself to be programmed as a prisoner of fate, as opposed to choosing to become an autonomous actor.[91] There are other examples. After the Second World War, western European societies, led by visionary politicians, took the 'leap in the dark' of European integration; it transformed the warring states of Europe into a security community characterised by predictable peace. After 1985, Gorbachev and Reagan began to make choices that transformed the then almost hysterical superpower Cold War into a situation of common security.[92] Powerful theories constitute behaviour, and in world politics there has been nothing as fatal as the idea of fatalism, or as tragic as the idea of tragedy. These ideas have imprisoned imaginations about human possibility, and forced us to forget that everything

from the one I offer below: see the articles by Mervyn Frost, James Mayall, Nicholas Rengger, Richard Ned Lebow, Chris Brown, and J. Peter Euben in vols. 17(4), 2003; 19(3), 2005; and 21(1), 2007.
[91] This is a central theme in Booth and Wheeler, *Security Dilemma*; the importance of courage in leaders, involving a willingness to take great leaps in the dark in order to foster trust, is discussed in Peter Mangold, *National Security and International Relations* (London: Routledge, 1990), pp. 63–4.
[92] See Booth and Wheeler, *Security Dilemma*, chs. 8 and 6, respectively.

solid, including sometimes the worst of international times, can be made to *melt into air*.

It is not difficult to understand the pull of fatalism. The majority of people on earth probably believe that life is *against* them, for it has been made to be such, and they feel quite helpless to do anything about it. Such is the power of insecurity. The rest, a minority globally, feel that life is good, and many seem to assume that people on the whole get what they deserve, and that if the rest of the world worked harder and had better governments they also would be better off. Too easily, luck is mistaken for virtue. Complacency is another thing that is '*for* someone and *for* some purpose'. Being able to find the resources for hoping for benevolent change against fatalism and complacency is an achievement in itself, but putting it into political practice requires powerful and skilful agency. This is not lacking across the world; it exists in abundance in the individuals and groups who attempt to live their lives according to Gandhi's injunction that 'We must be the change we wish to see in the world.'[93] It is given to few of us to be UN Secretary-General or President of the United States, but in this globalised age it is more possible than ever before for people to inhabit their own foreign policies.[94]

Progressive global civil society informed by world security principles represents critical theory's organised political orientation at this period of history. But the idea of 'global civil society' is much contested in terms of its potential agency and normative characteristics.[95] Here, I want to focus only on those groups that share the general emancipatory aims discussed in this book.

As generally understood, civil society exists in the spaces between state institutions and the extended family; global civil society, a more

[93] Elaborated in Ken Booth, 'Security and Self: Reflections of a Fallen Realist', in Keith Krause and Michael C. Williams (eds.), *Critical Security Studies. Concepts and Cases* (Minneapolis: University of Minnesota Press, 1999), pp. 83–119.
[94] I first made this argument in 'Security and Emancipation', *Review of International Studies*, vol. 17(4), 1991, pp. 313–26. On skilled individuals, see James N. Rosenau, *Turbulence in World Politics: A Theory of Change and Continuity* (London: Harvester 1990), Margaret E. Keck and Kathryn Sikkink, *Activists Beyond Borders. Advocacy Networks in International Politics* (Ithaca, N.Y.: Cornell University Press, 1998), and Robin Cohen and Shirin M. Rai (eds.), *Global Social Movements* (London: Athlone Press, 2000).
[95] Positive interpretations are Mary Kaldor, *Global Civil Society: An Answer to War* (Cambridge: Polity, 2003), and Michael Edwards, *Civil Society* (Cambridge: Polity, 2004). Although the latter book is not explicitly about the global dimension, it identifies strongly with the work of writers such as Richard Falk and Mary Kaldor: see p. 39. Less positive are Michael Walzer (ed.), *Toward a Global Civil Society* (New York: Berghahn, 1997), and Chris Brown, 'Cosmopolitanism, World Citizenship and Global Civil Society', in Peter Jones and Simon Caney (eds.), *Human Rights and Global Diversity* (London: Cass, 2000).

recent and difficult term, refers here to that subset of transnational organisations and movements that operate in that space, seeking to use and expand the global public sphere in the interests of promoting emancipatory aims such as peace, democracy, environmental sustainability, and economic justice.[96] In this global public sphere, ideally, something approximating what Mary Kaldor, herself a prominent theorist and activist in global civil society, has called a 'civilised' conversation will take place: Muslim fundamentalists, for example, will recognise that 'Jews' and 'Crusaders' are also 'human beings', and Americans will accept that 'Afghan and Iraqi lives are equal to American lives'.[97] Although Kaldor was not sanguine about such prospects when she wrote those words in 2003, given the direction being taken by the War on Terror, her hopes for equality, globally, were an echo of the inspiring words of the Leveller Colonel discussed in chapter 8, whose own vision could only hope at that time for equality in one country.

Michael Edwards, director of the Ford Foundation's Civil Society Program, and a self-declared 'civil society revivalist', has described the importance of civil society agency with candour and passion:

> At its best, civil society is the story of ordinary people living extraordinary lives through their relationships with each other, driven forward by a vision of the world that is ruled by love and compassion, nonviolence and solidarity. At its worst, it is little more than a slogan, and a confusing one at that, but there is no need to focus on the worst of things and leave the best behind. Warts and all, the idea of civil society remains compelling, not because it provides the tidiest of explanations but because it speaks to the best in us, and calls on the best in us to respond in kind.[98]

A phrase such as 'love and compassion' is alien to mainstream international relations, though it animates the spirit of emancipatory global civil society.

As agents of progressive change, global civil society confronts five main sets of criticisms. First, its organisations are not seen as particularly democratic (as if governments are even liberal democracies!). Second, NGOs are often thought to be non-accountable (though their members can easily and without cost stop giving financial support – an opting-out that only the bravest can contemplate in relation to their own state). Three, much of the networking associated with global civil society

---

[96] Kaldor, *Global Civil Society*, pp. 1–14 discusses five different usages of the term.
[97] *Ibid.*, p. 159.   [98] Edwards, *Civil Society*, p. 112.

is criticised for beginning in the West and being dominated by people from the West (this is true, but it is only a basic problem if organisations fail to be open to influences from other parts of the world, and do not seek to empower people from elsewhere as part of their programmes – all organisations have to begin somewhere). Four, some organisations are attacked for intervening in local politics, and so being vulnerable to the charge of quasi-imperialism (this is a charge most organisations are now well aware of, and generally attempt to respond to appropriately, recognising that in some circumstances non-intervention is a form of intervention). Finally, non-state actors are criticised as bit-players on a stage where states remain all-powerful (some states are, of course, uniquely powerful, but the biggest NGOs have more cash than the smallest states, and being confronted by great power is not logically a reason to leave the stage, but rather to try and civilise the scripts of the powerful). The root-and-branch criticisms of global civil society cannot therefore be allowed to win the argument, but they nonetheless remain as a healthy warning against any drift towards hubris.

When supporters of progressive civil society groups are not being charged with excessive optimism and elitism, they are sometimes tempted themselves to give way to helplessness. Peter Singer has emphasised that people should resist such feelings; they can do this by giving something of themselves to the world, and in so doing achieving personal fulfilment.[99] The first step for any individual is to engage in their own critical reflection on the world.[100] Singer then offers further words of encouragement: 'Anyone can become part of the critical mass that offers us a chance of improving the world before it is too late . . . You will take up new causes . . . [and] the world will look different . . . you will find plenty of worthwhile things to do. You will not be bored, or lack fulfilment in your life. Most important of all, you will know that you have not lived and died for nothing.'[101] What this entails in practice will depend on each individual, but the approach to ends and means discussed earlier opens up the possibility for each person to inhabit their own world security policy, behaving according a global ethical position – Henry Sidgwick's 'the point of view of the universe'.[102] There is plenty of scope to do *something*, and even if many of these actions seem to be small

---

[99] Peter Singer, *How Are We to Live? Ethics in an Age of Self-Interest* (Oxford: Oxford University Press, 1997), pp. 279–80.
[100] There is no shortage of ideas: for example, Yorick Blumenfeld (ed.), *Scanning the Future. 20 Eminent Thinkers on the World of Tomorrow* (London: Thames and Hudson, 1999).
[101] Singer, *How Are We to Live?* pp. 279–80.   [102] Quoted by Singer, *ibid.*, p. 236.

fry in relation to the grandest world stage, the chances are that they will not be in relation to one's life and sense of being, and at least one other person on earth. An individual's world security policy might involve questioning the global state of affairs with friends and colleagues, volunteering to help a civil society group, protesting, letter-writing, giving financial support to appropriate organisations, and stopping *theying*. And just because one cannot immediately do something good about *X*, one can respond to a sense of outrage or pity by doing more about *Y*. By trying to live in truth, mending the split between means/ends in pursuit of world security principles, each of us has some capacity to use the power of reason to nudge global human society away from its addiction to solitarism and the reasons of power. If enough people live globally – taking strength from each other – the structures that divide might yet melt into the air, as did those of feudalism, the divine right of kings, the colonial empires in living memory, and – only yesterday – the structures of Soviet-style communism.

The phrase 'ordinary people living extraordinary lives' was quoted earlier. For countless millions in the developing world, the immediate life/death security threat is (literal) self-defence against predictable and preventable disease. Global health is one of today's battlegrounds, and one of tomorrow's subject areas in security studies.[103] Health is a major area where ordinary people do extraordinary things, and it is the necessary condition for the security of the self. After looking at the lives of '18 Heroes' *Time* magazine in its 'Global Health 2005' section challenged its readers: 'Think the problems of the developing world are unsolvable? Meet the people who are out there solving them. Then imagine what they might do with more bed nets, better drugs and a few more helping hands'.[104] Nowhere is the description of 'ordinary people living extraordinary lives' better illustrated than by people who have attempted to build bridges across what for a long time has been seen as the world's most intractable political divide – that between Israel and Palestine. 'We refuse to be enemies' has been the determination of the brave political bridge-builders, echoing Mahmoud Darwish earlier. Resisting the discipline of academic international relations,

---

[103] 'HIV/AIDS Special Issue', *International Affairs*, vol. 82(2), 2006, and 'Special Issue: Global Health', *International Relations*, vol. 19(4), 2005.
[104] '18 Heroes', *Time*, 7 November, 2005; the message of the article was somewhat undermined towards the end, as it could not resist honouring the philanthropy of mega-rich Western celebrities.

where only leaders and diplomats are known, I want to name some extraordinary 'ordinary people' recognised by the *New Internationalist* in 2002 for their work: Cedar Duaylis (citizen); Jeff Halper (the Israeli Committee against Housing Demolitions); Jeremy Milgram (a member of Rabbis for Human Rights); Fatín Mukarker (writer); Basem Ra'ad (editor); and Mohammed Abraham Sad (nurse).[105] Civil society groups and individuals have made contributions to building peace with more success elsewhere, sometimes by forging effective partnerships with governments and international organisations. Examples include the Athwaas Initiative in Kashmir, the Boroma process in Somalia, the Children's Movement of Peace and Return to Happiness in Colombia, the Dhammayietra Peace Walk in Cambodia, the Dartmouth Conference Regional Conflicts Task Force in Tajikistan, and Peace Brigades International in Colombia.[106] Elise Boulding has written that such accounts of conflict transformation offer 'concrete evidence of what is possible', while Adam Curle said they educate 'those who haven't fully realised what is happening'.[107]

Individuals and groups such as those just mentioned live their lives as world citizens every bit as fully as individuals and groups who live as national patriots. In so doing, they resist the jibes of communitarian scholars such as Michael Walzer who, when debating with Martha Nussbaum about such matters in the mid-1990s, insisted: 'I am not even aware that there is a world such that one could be a citizen of it.' He went on to say that nobody had offered him world citizenship, or described its naturalisation process, or its institutions or decision-making procedures, or its benefits or obligations, or the 'world's calendar and the common celebrations'.[108] Nussbaum rightly responded by pointing out the 'very long tradition in concrete political thinking' of this alternative way of being, echoing norms dating from the Stoics, including the renunciation of wars of aggression, embracing duties of hospitality, denouncing colonial conquest, and giving money to promote the good of distant strangers[109]

[105] Jeremy Milgram, 'We Refuse to be Enemies', *New Internationalist*, no. 348, August 2002, p. 13.
[106] These examples are among the many in Dylan Mathews, *War Prevention Works. 50 Stories of People Resolving Conflict* (Oxford: Oxford Research Group, 2002), and Paul van Tongeren, Malin Brenk, Marte Hellema, and Juliette Verhoeven, *Peace Building II: Successful Stories of Civil Society* (Boulder, Colo.: Lynne Rienner, 2005).
[107] See their forewords to Mathews, *War Prevention*, pp. 6–7.
[108] Michael Walzer, 'Spheres of Affection', in Joshua Cohen (ed.), *For Love of Country. Debating the Limits of Patriotism* (Boston: Beacon Press, 1996), p. 125.
[109] Martha C. Nussbaum, 'Reply', *ibid.*, pp. 133–4.

What is more, Nussbaum argued that there are now numerous 'practical opportunities for world citizenship', never before available in history.[110] Despite these arguments, and the empirical evidence of people living as world citizens, Walzer was not persuaded.[111] Without doubt, a 'cosmopolitan sensibility' requires what Bronner described as 'a leap in perspective' beyond inherited communitarian boundaries; such a leap is certainly possible, and represents 'more than the sum of national cultures'.[112] It is this *leap* that Walzer could not make or even conceive while his perspective remained that of a 'cosmopolitan American' as opposed to an American cosmopolitan.

For some, the leap will be intellectually difficult, if not impossible. Others have already made it, seeking to inspire the rest of us to follow; and some leaps require physical courage as well as empathetic imagination. Sometimes, deciding to live as a global citizen can place people in very direct opposition to their own government. In 1996, for example, four 'Ploughshares Women' were tried by the Crown court in Liverpool for having damaged a Hawk aircraft being sold by Britain to the government of Indonesia.[113] They faced up to ten years in prison for their direct and public action (they had already spent six months in prison awaiting trial). A major part of their defence was that they regarded the British government and British Aerospace (BAe) as complicit in the crimes of the government of Indonesia in the course of its illegal and brutal occupation of East Timor. One of the defendants, Angie Zelter, later wrote that their 'action against the arms trade to Indonesia was an example of a small citizens' group attempting to further global security because the constituted authorities were unwilling or unable to act in a globally responsible manner'. Another, Lotta Kronlid, told the court: 'We don't have to obey a government that makes immoral and unjust decisions'. Andrea Needham said: 'I believe that above all else in life, we are called to love and to be human.' Then, Joanne Wilson: 'I have decided to take personal responsibility for the disarmament of Hawk aircraft destined for Indonesia by hammering on parts of the plane essential to their ground attack role.' And Zelter again: 'I am not willing for innocent civilians to be killed in my name and for this to be "justified" as

---

[110] See, for example, *Global Civil Society Yearbook* (Oxford: Oxford University Press, annual), and Cohen and Rai, *Global Social Movements*.
[111] Compare Walzer, 'Spheres of Affection', p. 126.   [112] Bronner, *Reclaiming*, p. 147.
[113] The quotations from the case are all from Angie Zelter, 'Civil Society and Global Responsibility: The Arms Trade and East Timor', *International Relations*, vol. 18(1), 2004, pp. 125–40.

providing jobs for British people. I wish to act as a responsible member of the world community.' Reflecting later, Zelter stressed: 'We must all not only live locally but also take our global responsibilities seriously and humanely.' With such words, global citizens like these rip apart the conservative and unimaginative metaphor of 'concentric circles' of allegiance, with the outer one necessarily being weakest. The jury in the Crown court, to the delight of the women's many supporters, tore up the arguments of the prosecution and declared them to be 'Not guilty. Not guilty on all counts!'[114]

The image of relationships globally as concentric circles works for many, but certainly not all. For world citizens, the 'imagined community' extends everywhere beyond the family; boundaries of race and nation are utterly without moral purchase. Walzer asked Nussbaum (their debate was taking place at around the same time as the Ploughshares action and trial) why being a 'cosmopolitan American' was not good enough. He said he accepted Nussbaum's arguments for a 'cosmopolitan education', but was baffled by the idea of this vague 'world' to which Nussbaum said he should be loyal:' I am wholly ignorant', he admitted.[115] When people (like the Ploughshares group) are living their lives as world citizens as far as possible within the constraints of statist structures, this bafflement seems to me to be of the same order as the person who is supposed to have asked Louis Armstrong, 'What is jazz?', earning the reply: 'If you have to ask, you'll never know.'[116]

An imagined world community of communities, comprising multiple and overlapping identities is an ontological reality for many people. Nussbaum has described such a world-view (echoing the Stoics) as follows:

> We should regard our deliberations as, first and foremost, deliberations about human problems of people in particular concrete situations, not problems growing out of a national identity that is altogether unlike that of others . . . the invitation to think as a world citizen . . . [is], in a sense, an invitation to be an exile from the comfort of patriotism and its easy sentiments, to see our own ways of life from the point of view of justice and the good. The accident of where one is born is just that, an accident; any human being might have been born in any nation . . . we should not allow differences of nationality or class or ethnic membership or even gender to erect barriers between us and our fellow

[114] *Ibid.*, p. 125.   [115] Walzer, 'Spheres of Affection', p. 125.
[116] I want to thank Chris Brown for the authentic version of this quotation, as well as this one.

461

human beings. We should recognize humanity wherever it occurs, and give its fundamental ingredients, reason and moral capacity, our first allegiance and respect.[117]

It does not follow from this, as Charles Beitz has influentially argued, that 'moral' and 'institutional' cosmopolitanism should be synonymous.[118] Even a Kantian world republic might not be the most desirable project for moral cosmopolitans in their search to promote universal moral equality. Pragmatic considerations might lead them to reject the centralising of decision-making globally, on the grounds of the remoteness of the central organs of a world state from its worldwide citizenry. Having noted that, one might ask whether moral cosmopolitanism has any meaning without at least some institutionalisation: values need organisations to carry them.

When a 'cosmopolitan American' such as Walzer is baffled by the idea of world citizenship, it would seem that such a goal is a considerable distance from achieving the support of a global critical mass. Against such a conclusion is the sense of a growing community of fate identified by Ulrich Beck and others, discussed in the previous chapter; they suggest that radical change could come about much more quickly than now seems possible. If, for the purpose of building world security, we must be the change we want to see in the world as individuals – as Gandhi maintained – the same is also the case for security studies. This has been one of the rationales for the book: actually theorised security studies must also be the change we want to see. But to argue for the primacy of a critical theory of security is not to argue for disciplinary totalitarianism. Such would be contrary to the nature of the critical project. Furthermore, intellectual pluralism is desirable in order to keep everybody honest.[119] Tomorrow's security studies should be pluralistic, and informed by accessibility, relevance, and engagement. Chris Brown put it this way, speaking for the discipline as a whole: 'If scholars of "International Relations" can manage to develop the right mind-set they can be at the forefront of the study of global society and politics in the new

[117] Martha C. Nussbaum, 'Patriotism and Cosmopolitanism', in Cohen, *Love of Country*, p. 7.
[118] Charles R. Beitz, *Political Theory and International Relations* (Princeton, N.J.: Princeton University Press, 1979), and 'Cosmopolitan Liberalism and the States System', in Chris Brown (ed.), *Political Restructuring in Europe: Ethical Perspectives* (London: Routledge, 1994). I have benefited greatly from listening to Chris Brown on Beitz's work, and reading papers on it, some unpublished.
[119] A point of agreement between John Mearsheimer and his critics: 'Roundtable: The Battle Rages On', *International Relations*, vol. 19(3), 2005, pp. 337–60.

century; if not, the discipline will be one more casualty of the "runaway world".'[120] Much depends, of course, on the meaning one attaches to the phrase 'right mind-set', but I hope this book leaves no reader in doubt as to what I think it should contain. There is much to be done, even for those who accept this point, and students of security studies and international relations are not the only or even the main obstacle to reconstructing world security. We should not beat our breasts too strongly, for much of mainstream political science is even more mired in self-absorption, having little to say about the global context of national politics, with its theorising being very much domesticated. At this point, the social sciences in general have ignored 'the international' much more than specialists in the international have ignored them. The spectre of the Great Reckoning, however, offers a real incentive for the social sciences to come together to do what John Herz identified as 'survival research',[121] under the intellectual roof of international/world/global specialists; the goal is to explore alternative ways of conceiving and practising security to those advocated by the proponents of scholarly business-as-usual.

Since the late 1970s, the agenda of academic theorising in international relations has broadly been established by the neorealism inspired by Kenneth Waltz's *Theory of International Politics*.[122] His book was an exercise in 'parsimonious' theorising, and it remains the discipline's apogee in that regard. There is a role for parsimonious theory, but only a limited one, in saying a few big things about a big issue. Such theory has only limited purchase in relation to the multilevel approach to world (rather than statist) security issues discussed in this book. A theory of world security must give due weight to the many worlds that make up world politics, and not just relations between governments, based on assumptions about a relatively autonomous 'international' realm. In contemplating security comprehensively, account must be given, at one level, to the fact that humans are animals, with natural needs, and at another, that they have a highly developed consciousness which includes a sense of existing on a lonely and increasingly fragile

[120] Chris Brown, *Understanding International Relations* (Houndmills: Palgrave Macmillan, 2001; 2nd edn), p. 262.
[121] See John H. Herz, 'An Internationalist's Journey Through the Century', in Joseph Kruzel and James N. Rosenau (eds.), *Journeys Through World Politics* (Lexington: Lexington Books, 1979), pp. 247–61, and 'The Security Dilemma in International Relations: Background and Present Problems', *International Relations*, vol. 17(4), 2003, pp. 411–16; for reflections on the relevance of 'survival research', see Booth and Wheeler, *Security Dilemma*, ch. 10.
[122] Kenneth N. Waltz, *Theory of International Politics* (New York: Random House, 1979).

planet in the midst of inhospitable space. It is from these very different perspectives – the most personal and the most immense – that we need to consider security in the twenty-first century. The old levels-of-analysis approach to international relations has become stretched beyond breaking-point, not least because the levels are increasingly difficult to separate. Where are the 'levels' (or indeed territorial boundaries) in the global politics of the environment when nature is being destroyed because humans have stomachs and genitals? States obviously remain key political entities, but state-centrism is more than ever blinkered; consequently, only approaches that are multidimensional will help us think with more sophistication about what is real, what we can know, and how we might act. And only answers that deliver cosmopolitan answers will offer hope of human society surviving the Great Reckoning without catastrophic turmoil. We need to reconceive 'we' in theory, and then implement it in practice, and for this leadership is required in all walks of life, in civil society as much as in government, but good followers are also essential. World citizens will make Bronner's 'leap in perspective' in relation to four key commitments: to think that all humanity is the potential community for political ideas; to believe in the moral equality of all humans; to embrace and promote universal emancipatory values; and to act in ways that exhibit solidarity beyond borders (in the light of personal capabilities and statist constraints).

A cosmopolitan outlook, such as the one just described, was well understood by the Stoics, a fact that shows that some powerful ideas travel and survive, even when they lack states and kings and guns to back them. Such ideas travel and survive, in part because of the time-transcending lives of some of those who have supported them. It is occasionally said that great writers have two lives: an earthly one when they do their work, and a historical one after they are dead but when their words still live on. The same is true for great political, philosophical, and spiritual figures. They live beyond death because their voices continue to speak, and people converse with their thoughts. In this way, great lives transcend time and materiality, and even the brutal ways in which their earthly lives ended. Who now remembers the names of the killers of Socrates, the fascist Public Prosecutor at Gramsci's trial, the man who shot Gandhi, or the killer of Martin Luther King? But who thinks that these universal figures who were their victims are dead? In 1968 the *Chicago Sun-Times* published a cartoon showing Gandhi, assassinated in 1948, smiling at the recently assassinated Dr King. Gandhi said to him: 'The odd thing about assassins, Dr. King, is that they think they've killed you.'[123]

Daylight?

> The story is told of a rabbi whose disciples were debating the question of when precisely 'daylight' commenced. The one ventured the proposal: 'It is when one can see the difference between a sheep and a goat at a distance'. Another suggested: 'It is when you can see the difference between a fig tree and an olive tree at a distance'. And so it went on. When they eventually asked the rabbi for his view, he said: 'When one human being looks into the face of another and says: "This is my sister" or "this is my brother" then the night is over and the day has begun'.   Klippies Kritzinger in *Believers in the Future*[124]

'Light has always been a potent symbol', wrote Roy Porter in one of his brilliant studies of the Enlightenment; that was a time, he said, when there was more light in the world, both literally (in street lighting) and metaphorically (in epistemology).[125] This metaphor retains its power, as Kritzinger's story shows. The rabbi speaking above exactly captures the normative spirit of this book. Put more prosaically than in the epigraph, the theory of world security offered here has sought to encourage the creation of a politics in which the instrumental value of security allows the development of the political conditions for reasoned dialogue and the embedding of trust so that we – *the global-we* – can see the I-that-is-another, and the another-that-is-oneself in the same light. Such an outcome requires the imperatives of nationalist realism to be replaced by the imperative of promoting security, emancipation, and community for the universe of individual referents. The rational egoism of nationalist-realist thinking, and its propensity to promote business-as-usual, is a major part of the problem in the Great Reckoning, while the world-historical crisis we face demands that the centuries of speculating, dreaming, and theorising about world community be part of the solution. But theorising and dreaming are not enough. For such a community to become politically meaningful, and so make decisions in the interests of the collective, there has to be hard bargaining, tight

---

[123] Cartoon by Maudlin, *Chicago Sun-Times*, 1968, reprinted in Bhikhu Parekh, *Gandhi: A Very Short Introduction* (Oxford: Oxford University Press, 1997), p. 113.
[124] Quoted by Farid Esack, *On Being a Muslim. Finding a Religious Path in the World Today* (Oxford: Oneworld Publications, 1999), p. 137.
[125] Roy Porter, *Enlightenment. Britain and the Creation of the Modern World* (London: Allen Lane, 2000), pp. 44–6.

commitments, and many forms of action infused by radical trust. World security requires first-class leaders in every field, and people skilled in diplomacy. In the beginning, however, lights have to be switched on and turned up in the universal mind. If nature is to be saved, and human security achieved, a 'one world' sensibility is a necessary building-block.

Chapter 9 began by discussing the feeling of being in two moments at the same time. It was also mentioned that early last century a similar feeling was famously described by one of the most brilliant of the contributors to critical global theorising, Antonio Gramsci, when he identified his own times as an 'interregnum'. Today, once more, old and new are colliding, and morbid symptoms are proliferating; for shorthand, I have described this throughout the book as human society's Great Reckoning. So far, in most people's mind, it is one distant black cloud on the horizon. In the 'culture of contentment' we in the West have become complacent about the risks of calamitous shocks to normality, as happened in 1914 or the 1930s. We have experienced several generations of remarkable political stability and economic growth, and are generally complacent about the concatenation of global threats presently gathering momentum in the guise of that black cloud. If human society is not to avoid the consequences of a global 'clash of ignorance' in an overcrowded, over-heated, overexploited planet, then far-reaching decisions are required in the six key issue areas of world security discussed in chapter 9. Regrettably, the primary responsibility for making the decisions to bring about benign changes rests on those who are most content and who gain most from business-as-usual. These include the governments of the strongest states, the directors of the biggest corporations, and the consumers and voters in the richest societies. It is for this reason that the bulk of the criticism throughout the book has been directed at the rich world. They are the people and societies with the power to do most, and so demand most critical attention; as I also belong to that sector of human society, it is right that it is the first and main focus of my analysis and advocacy. But, critical as I have been of Western leaders and societies, no part of this book is the result of ethno-guilt. Everywhere there are human wrongs a-plenty – countries with corrupt leaders and cultures excusing cruelty by citing tradition. These wrongs are egregious (and perhaps the focus of another book), but they are not presently the most pressing or the most causal in relation to reconstituting world security.

Under the shadow of a dangerous future, this book has discussed a number of progressive ideas and resources immanent within human society. Whether these prove to be puny in relation to the worst extrapolations of the Great Reckoning remains to be seen, but as individuals we can only do what we can do; it may not be enough, but we can say that we have tried. Collectively, new worlds *can* be built, and quickly. I offer three encouragements about hope, action, and change. From Nadine Gordimer's reflections on the century in which she lived most of her life, I take some lines she liked from Seamus Heaney, who called on us to believe that sometimes 'The longed-for tidal wave / Of justice can rise up, / And hope and history rhyme'.[126] From a booklet on nuclear disarmament by Janet Bloomfield and Pamela Meidell, I take some lines from Shelly Douglass, who called on us to think we can make a difference, whatever the challenge: 'We must act as if we have all the time in the world / We must act as if this is the only moment we have'.[127] And finally, from Marx, I take his own insight on change (referred to several times already in the book), namely that 'all that is solid melts into air'. In short, never say never about history, for reality can be truly radical.

Hope, action, and change in the disciplinary context of this book must be focused on how security studies will be conceived and practised, seeking to engage ever more effectively with life's three most fundamental questions: what is real? what can we know? how might we act? The answers given in this book do not promise utopia. Emancipation is a process, not an end-point, and new challenges and new inequalities will always be thrown up, as changes take place in the political and material environment. Critical theory can never rest. Existential uncertainty in human society means that security dilemmas cannot be escaped, though their negative dynamics can be transcended if approached with appropriate skill (and attended by luck).[128] If a critical theory of world security were to become mainstream security studies, and even political practice, there would still be the necessity of constant efforts to problematise the status quo. Reflexivity is critical theory's heartbeat. Critical theory, to be true to itself, must always be critical. Herbert Marcuse put it well, back in the 1960s: 'Critical theory preserves obstinacy as a genuine

---

[126] Gordimer, *Hope and History*, p. ix.
[127] Quoted by Janet Bloomfield and Pamela Meidell, *As Time Goes By* (Port Heuneme, Calif.: The Atomic Mirror, 2004, www.atomicmirror.org), p. 8. In the period between these words being written and the copy-editing stage of the book Janet Bloomfield unexpectedly and tragically died. She had lived her life by the words quoted, in the cause of peace generally and the elimination of nuclear weapons in particular.
[128] The distinction between 'escape' and 'transcend' is discussed in Booth and Wheeler, *Security Dilemma*, part III.

quality of philosophical thought.'[129] This is not an idle comment: remember that Marx disavowed Marxism, Horkheimer and Adorno revised their views of the Enlightenment, and Gandhi said 'Down with Gandhism'.

Obstinacy is badly needed on the part of those who believe in the power (though not the omnipotence) of reason, and the immanence (though not the guarantee) of world community. Such Enlightenment values are confronted by a melange of intellectual nay-sayers and political reactionaries. Academic critics snipe, but their own theories do not seem to offer a hopeful way ahead for the global collective. It may happen that human society will escape the worst of the outcomes discussed in chapter 9, but if that proves to be the case, it will be by luck more than political judgement at this stage. There are some utopian dreams these days about technological fixes for humanity's biggest challenges; it is certainly not unthinkable that there could be the invention or discovery of new, clean, and plentiful energy sources, for example, that would mitigate the severest dangers ahead about resource crises. But technology is not ultimately the answer; the long-term future rests on reinventing our collective minds, not in accumulating gadgets.[130] That the latter might be the way ahead is a version of *problem-solving* in the narrow sense, characteristic of classical realism, and realism (whose past has finally caught up with it) cannot promise world security in the long term. Other approaches within security studies are no better than realism, and some are worse. Some contain interesting ideas, but not strategies to live by: the approach of securitisation studies, for example, is so conservative in its assumptions that the radical hopes of its proponents prove to have boots of concrete; postmodernist approaches (as they generally do not like to be known) are invariably obscurantist and marginal, providing no basis for politics; constructivism is a method and not a theory of international relations, and so is no more use politically than the political assumptions that underlie it; and the English school is so limited in scope and elitist in conception that it addresses few of the real issues.

In comparison with these other approaches, a critical theory of security has much to offer. It shows, above all, that the values for which

---

[129] Herbert Marcuse, *Negations: Essays in Critical Theory* (1968), pp. 142–3, quoted by Norman Geras, 'Minimum Utopia: Ten Theses', in Leo Panitch and Colin Leys (eds.), *Socialist Register* (London: Merlin Press, 2000), p. 51.

[130] An example of an approach that places too much faith in 'scientific breakthroughs' is James Martin, *The Meaning of the 21st Century. A Vital Blueprint for Ensuring our Future* (London: Eden Project Books, 2006).

the great figures of the Enlightenment stood in the eighteenth century are no less relevant today than was the case then. Translated into the language of this book, this means an agenda characterised by the pursuit of security as emancipation, of emancipation as equality, and of equality through universal community. Animating this syllogism is cosmopolitan solidarity, checked and rechecked by obstinate reflexivity. The agenda sketched in chapter 8, and the critical global theorising that underpinned it, leaves its advocates nowhere to hide, for its comprehensive framework engages our multiple interests and identities – as students, citizens, and individuals. It asks us to reassess our inherited attitudes about the security dimensions of world politics, and to look at them 'as if for the first time'. It asks us to face what is really real, and demands an ontologically inclusive answer – rejecting both the reifications of realists and the negativism of postmodernists. It asks us what we can know, and challenges us to provide an epistemologically sophisticated and self-reflexive response. And it asks how we might act, and makes us uncomfortable if we are inclined to leave our answers in the seminar room.

Leaving nowhere to hide includes what Martha Nussbaum has called 'the comfort of local truths . . . the warm, nestling feeling of patriotism . . . the absorbing drama of pride in oneself and one's own'.[131] Becoming a 'citizen of the world' or embracing 'cosmopolitanism' does not mean rejecting one's own roots she insists, though I would insist that having *pride* in one's roots (the ticket one draws in the lottery of birth) is as foolish as having pride in other accidents of birth, such as being born with blonde hair. One can legitimately feel lucky about such things (or not) but pride is a different thing. As it happens, choosing to be a 'world citizen' as one of one's identities, and then doing something about it, is easier than in the past, because of communications technology. Nonetheless, the power of 'local truths' remains, and very powerful people have a vested interest in ensuring that remains so. Consequently, Nussbaum says that to choose to be a citizen of the world is 'often a lonely business'. It is 'a kind of exile', said the Stoic Diogenes.[132] But it is a kind of exile many people across the world *want to embrace*, because it actually involves escaping from the greatest loneliness, and this comes from our *being exiled* by what history has thrown up in terms of imposed borders and divisive global common sense.

---

[131] Nussbaum, 'Patriotism and Cosmopolitanism', p. 15. [132] *Ibid.*

In this era – perhaps tragically, perhaps heroically – human society is face-to-face with the Great Reckoning between traditional global common sense and the growing recognition that it is unsustainable materially and regressive morally. The promise of more security/emancipation exists for human society globally if we accept the existential uncertainty of 'exile' in uncommon humanity rather than continue to give way to the false certainties that have made us – what Nussbaum called those 'props of habit and local boundaries' that comprise 'an idealized image of a nation, a surrogate parent who will do one's thinking for one'. But nations are not the only invisible iron curtains in our minds: gender, class, religion, and race also do too much of our thinking. Unlike these traditional props, Nussbaum believed that cosmopolitanism 'offers no such refuge; it only offers reason and the love of humanity'.[133] If world security is to mean anything at this historic crossroads, we must extend reason and love across the boundaries constructed around being human by the contingencies of history and power. We got this way, but we did not have to. But why did we not do better? Why can we not live together in more harmony? Why do we fight so often? Is religious tolerance too much to ask? Must power corrupt? As ever, in the words of the Polish Nobel Laureate Wisława Szymborska, 'the most pressing questions / are naïve ones'.[134] If, in response to them, human society continues with global business-as-usual, the future will be bleak. The alternative outlined in this book – a radical reorientation of the idea of world politics based on the potentiality of human sociality, the promise of critical global theorising, and the struggle of emancipatory realism – does not guarantee success – nothing ever can – but it does offer signposts to a more hopeful global being, knowing, and doing. Holding us back are the false certainties inherited from the past. Our historic challenge has been expressed with characteristic simplicity and acute witness by Szymborska: 'We know how to divide ourselves', she has written, 'but to put ourselves together?'[135]

---

[133] *Ibid.*
[134] These are lines from Wisława Szymborska, 'The Century's Decline' (dating from the mid-1980s), in *View with a Grain of Sand. Selected Poems,* trans. Stanislaw Barańczak and Clare Cavanagh (London: Faber and Faber, 1996), pp. 147–8.
[135] Quoted in Gordimer, *Hope and History*, p. 178.

Index

CAMBRIDGE STUDIES IN INTERNATIONAL RELATIONS